Atlas of the World

Reprinted October 2007

1st edition July 2007 for the Automobile Association

Publisher's notes:
Published by Automobile Association Developments Limited
whose registered office is Fanum House, Basing View,
Basingstoke RG21 4EA, UK. Registered number 1878835.

Copyright © Hema Maps Pty Ltd
Brisbane, Australia
www.hemamaps.com
Based on original data © Research Machines PLC

Hardback edition with slipcase
ISBN-13: 978 0 7495 5306 7
ISBN-10: 0 7495 5306 5

Hardback edition (without slipcase)
ISBN-13: 978 0 7495 5095 0
ISBN-10: 0 7495 5095 3

Paperback edition with slipcase
ISBN-13: 978 0 7495 5628 0
ISBN-10: 0 7495 5628 5

A CIP catalogue record of this atlas is available
from The British Library.

Disclaimer:
The contents of this atlas are believed to be correct at the
time of latest revision. However, the publishers cannot be
held responsible for any loss or damage occasioned to any
person acting or refraining from action as a result of any use
or reliance on material in this atlas, nor for any errors,
omissions or changes in such material. This does not affect
your statutory rights.

Cover design:
© Automobile Association Developments Limited.

Printer:
Printed in U.A.E. by Oriental Press, Dubai.

Front cover photographs:
AA World Travel Library:
tl C Sawyer; tc A Kouprianoff; tr K Paterson; cl N Sumner;
c C Sawyer; cr B Davies; bl D Corrance; bc G Marks; br P Kenward.

Photographs:
p11 L Cook/Science Photo Library,
p13 R Royer/Science Photo Library,
p15 R Edmaier/Science Photo Library,
p17 K Svenson/Science Photo Library,

Atlas of the World

Contents

Europe

Asia

Africa

Oceania

North America

South America

Key Map

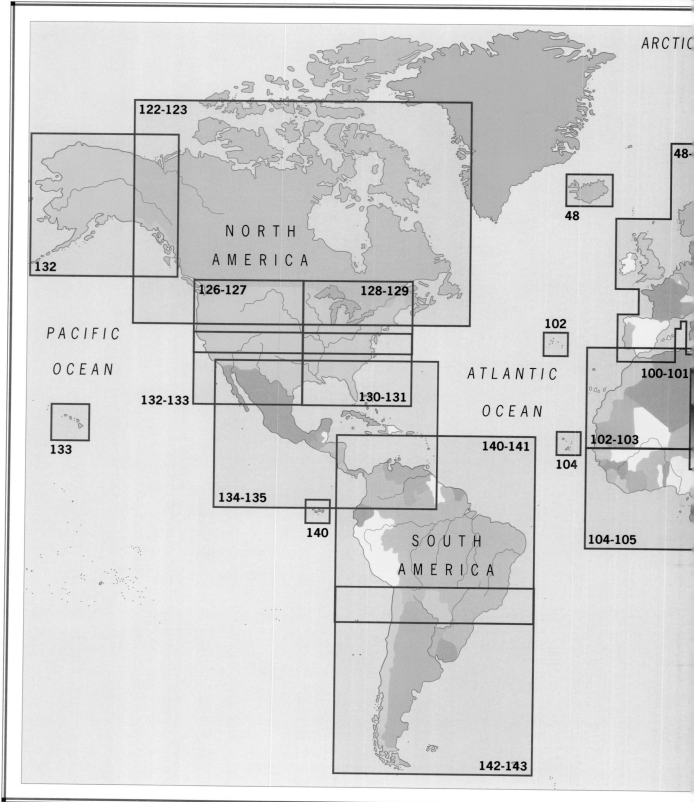

ARCTIC

122-123

132

NORTH
AMERICA

48-

48

PACIFIC

OCEAN

126-127

128-129

102

ATLANTIC

133

132-133

OCEAN

100-101

134-135

130-131

140-141

102-103

104

140

104-105

SOUTH
AMERICA

142-143

KEY TO CONTINENTAL RECORD SYMBOLS

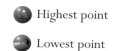 Highest point

Lowest point

 Lowest average annual rainfall

Highest average annual rainfall

 Longest river

Largest lake

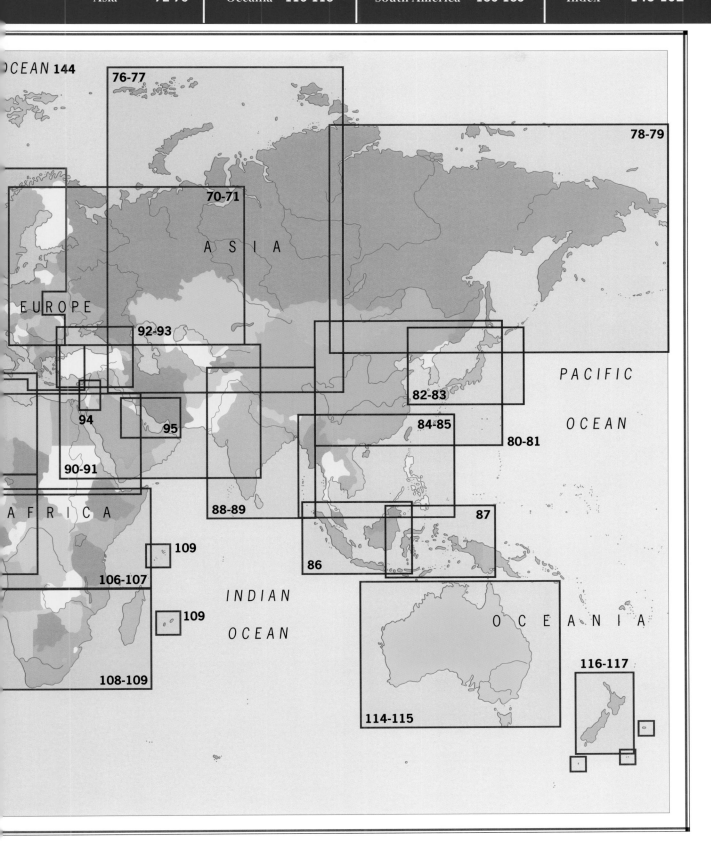

OCEAN **144**

76-77

78-79

70-71

ASIA

EUROPE

92-93

PACIFIC

OCEAN

82-83

94

95

84-85

80-81

90-91

AFRICA

88-89

87

109

106-107

86

INDIAN

109

OCEAN

O C E A N I A

108-109

116-117

114-115

The first eight symbols show the most extreme value of the feature described, as well as its location.
*If that description is in **bold**, it is not only the continental record, but also the World record.*

- Coldest place
- Hottest place
- Estimated population
- Population density
- Land area
- Number of countries (including dependencies)

World

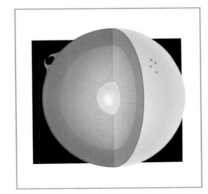

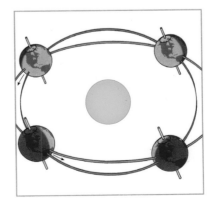

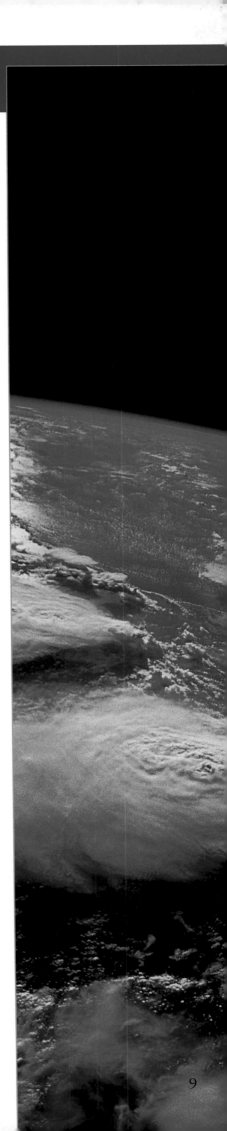

The Earth is one member of a Solar System of nine planets orbiting our local star – the Sun. All these bodies formed from a single cloud of gas and dust around 4.5 billion years ago as it was compressed, possibly by shockwaves from a giant supernova explosion. The centre of the cloud collapsed most rapidly, becoming denser and attracting more material until eventually it reached a point so hot and dense that nuclear reactions began inside it. These reactions continue today and are the source of the sunlight that heats our planet and sustains life. The Sun is critical to the regulation of our climate and environment – fine alterations in Earth's orbit are thought to cause periodic ice ages, so we are fortunate that the Sun is not likely to change drastically for another 5 billion years.

On a shorter scale, the Sun's output does have slight fluctuations. A cycle of sunspot formation (comparatively cool regions of the Sun's surface caused by magnetic activity), reaches a maximum every 11 years. From 1645–1705 almost no sunspots were seen, a dip in solar activity which coincided with a 'mini-Ice Age' of unusually low temperatures on Earth.

Once the Sun had formed, a disk of material would have been left outside the newly-formed star, which condensed to form the planets. Particles in the gas and dust cloud collided and stuck together, becoming increasingly larger bodies. Eventually these 'proto-planets' were pulled into a spherical shape by their increasing gravity.

The Solar System we see today reflects the composition of that gas and dust cloud, and divides into two regions. The inner portion contains the four terrestrial (Earth-like) planets – from Mercury orbiting close to the Sun, through Venus and Earth, to Mars. Beyond the orbit of Mars lies the asteroid belt, a ring of rocky debris, outside which are the gas giants, enormous planets created where the cloud bulged with huge quantities of gas.

The inner rocky worlds

The terrestrial planets are all very different. Mercury is a small, baking world, quite similar to our own Moon, and covered in craters. Venus is shrouded in a thick atmosphere of carbon dioxide and toxic molecules, with a surface pressure 95 times that of Earth's atmosphere, and temperatures of 470°C.

▶ **THE SUN**

The Sun is a massive ball of hydrogen gas **[B]**, *1.39 million km across. Energy is generated at its heart, where temperatures exceed 15 million°C, by nuclear fusion – the joining together through a chain reaction of two hydrogen atoms to form one helium. In the process, a large amount of excess energy is released, carried to the surface of the Sun in giant convection cells, and then radiated across the Solar System from the top of the 'photosphere' – the visible disk of the Sun, with a temperature of 5500°C.*

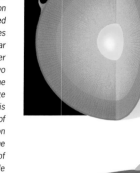

B

4

3

2

1

A

◀ **THE SOLAR SYSTEM**

The solar system consists of 9 planets **[A]**: *Pluto [1], the smallest, is the furthest away from the Sun, though once in every 248.6 years its orbit crosses inside Neptune's path. Neptune [2], the outermost of the gas giants, has a diameter of 49,400km, and orbits every 164.8 years.*

Uranus [3] is similar in size to Neptune and orbits every 84 years. All the gas giants have ring systems, but Uranus's are second only to Saturn's. The planet is tilted at over 98° to the plane of the Solar System, so it seems to roll around its orbit.

Beyond the Earth's orbit, Mars is famous as the Red Planet – a colour given by rust in its surface dust. Although smaller than Earth, there is evidence that Mars once had a thick atmosphere, and that water ran on its surface – although now it is frozen into polar ice-caps.

The gas giants

The outer Solar System contains worlds quite different from those nearer the Sun – the gas giants. Largest of these is Jupiter, more massive than all the other planets in the Solar System put together, with churning weather systems that include the Great Red Spot, a storm large enough to engulf Earth. Beyond Jupiter lies Saturn, with its spectacular ring system of icy particles, and then the smaller giants Uranus and Neptune. Space probes have shown that Jupiter, Uranus and Neptune also have thin ring systems, although these are nothing to match Saturn's spectacle.

All four of these worlds have large families of moons orbiting round them. Jupiter has a vast family of moons, including Io, the most volcanic body in the Solar System, whose eruptions launch yellow plumes of sulphur into space, scarring its surface with streaks. The most interesting member of Uranus's satellite system is Miranda – a small, deeply-cratered world which displays so many variations in terrain that it must have suffered some great cataclysm in the past. Neptune's giant satellite Triton has active geysers shooting water, ammonia and methane 8km above its surface.

Saturn [4] is noted for its spectacular ring system – the planet has a diameter of 105,000km, while the rings stretch out to 300,000km. It orbits the Sun every 29.5 years, and has a huge family of satellites.

Jupiter [5] orbits the Sun every 11.9 years. With a diameter of 137,400km it is the largest planet in the Solar System. It has complex weather systems, including the Great Red Spot, a storm with a diameter larger than the Earth's.

Between Jupiter and Mars is the asteroid belt [6], rocky debris left over from the Solar System's formation. Inside it lie the terrestrial planets. Mars [7], the red planet, circles the Sun in 1.9 years, and has a diameter of 6790km. Its surface is scoured by massive dust storms, and it shows evidence of running water on the surface in its past. Next in towards the Sun is our own blue planet, the Earth [8], with a diameter of 12,700km. Within the orbit of the Earth lies its near twin Venus [9], circling the Sun in 225 days, and with a diameter of 12,100km. The atmosphere of Venus, however, is a poisonous mixture of carbon dioxide and other gases, with clouds of sulphuric acid. Mercury [10] is the second smallest planet with a diameter of only 4,880km, and a solar orbit that lasts 88 days. Its proximity to the Sun (58 million km) makes it a scorched world with no atmosphere, and a cratered surface similar to that of the Moon. It orbits the Sun once every 88 days.

◀ *The Sun is just one of over 200 billion stars in the vast spiral of the Milky Way galaxy, like every other star that we see with the naked eye in the night sky. It lies roughly two-thirds of the way towards the edge of the galactic disc, orbiting the centre at a speed of 250 kilometres per second, taking 200 million years to complete each revolution. This view is what the galaxy would look like to an observer outside. But because of our position in the plane, we see the dense star clouds as a pale band across the sky.*

The Earth's satellite, the Moon, is so large by comparison with our own world (at 3746km, it is over one-quarter the Earth's diameter) that astronomers consider the two together as a 'double planet'. This massive size and proximity means that the Moon has a great influence on the Earth itself, for example through the tides.

The origins of the Moon are open to debate – some believe that the Moon is a chunk of debris flung off when the still-molten Earth collided with another body the size of Mars, in the early days of the Solar System. Since then, the two bodies have had very different histories. The Moon's small size meant that it cooled more quickly and its low gravity made it unable to hold onto an atmosphere – the factor which has been crucial in shaping our own planet's terrain. In fact, the Moon has altered so little that it provides valuable information about the history of the early Solar System. The lack of an atmosphere also means that, unlike Earth, the Moon is not shielded from the extremes of heat from the Sun. Temperatures at noon climb to 150°C, while at night they can plummet to -200°C. These acute differences can even cause moon-quakes as the surface stretches and contracts.

A familiar face

The Moon's surface divides into two distinct types of terrain, which can be easily distinguished with the naked eye from Earth. The bright highlands are highly cratered areas created more than 4 billion years ago during an era of bombardment by rock particles from space. The numbers of these particles dwindled until only a few massive chunks were left, which created enormous impact basins as they crashed into the Moon's surface. The gnarled highlands contrast sharply with the smoother, darker Maria (from the Latin for seas).

After the cratering had died away, the Moon seems to have undergone a brief period of intense volcanic activity. Red-hot fissures opened up across its surface, out of which huge volumes of lava poured, flooding low-lying areas. These lava lakes solidified to form the Maria, marked by only a few, very small craters.

Lunar attraction

The changing direction of the Sun and Moon from Earth cause our monthly cycle of tides. Twice a month, at full and new moon, the high Spring Tides occur, with Moon and Sun lined up, or directly opposed, so the tidal effect is at its strongest. Such tidal effects have influenced the Earth-Moon system as a whole. Over millions of years, the friction of the oceans' movement has slowed the lunar 'day', so it now lasts exactly as long as the time the Moon takes to orbit Earth, with the result that it always keeps the same face turned towards us.

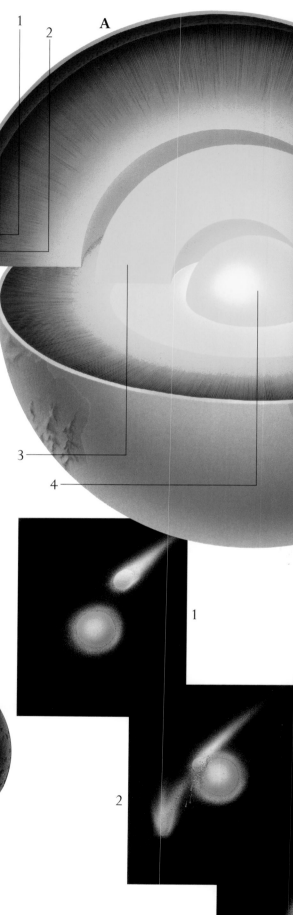

▶ **STRUCTURE OF THE MOON**
The Earth's satellite, the Moon [B], has a structure that reflects its different size, and possibly origin. Because it is a much smaller body – around one-twentieth the volume of the Earth – it has a higher surface area to volume ratio. It cooled down more rapidly early in the history of the Solar System, and is now inactive. The lunar crust [1] is actually thicker than Earth's – an average of 70km, though it is thinner on the Earth-facing side, possibly due to the tidal effects of the Earth's gravity. This could be a possible explanation of why the smooth 'seas' are found far more on this side, formed from eruptions of lava through the thin crust. Beneath this lie layers of solidified, cold rock, which decrease in rigidity. At the centre there may be a cold core [2], although its existence is still debated.

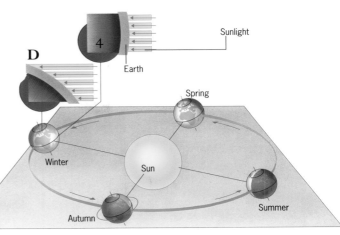

Sunlight

Earth

THE STRUCTURE OF THE EARTH

The Earth has the shape of a squashed ball or a spheroid **[A]**. *It has a diameter at the poles of 12,703km, but is wider at the Equator, thrown outward by the rapid daily spin which causes a 'bulge'. The crust [1], on which lie the continents and oceans, is a thin layer of rock varying in depth between 10 and 20km. Below this lies a mantle [2], divided into two regions. The upper mantle extends down to 3000km, and divides into the mainly solid lithosphere and the mostly molten aesthenosphere. Beyond this, the molten rock of the upper and lower mantle extends down towards the molten outer [3] and solid inner [4] cores of iron and nickel, around 7000km across, at the centre of the Earth. It is the rotation of this core that is believed to generate the Earth's magnetic field, in an effect similar to that of a dynamo.*

THE EARTH'S SEASONS

The Poles of the Earth are tilted at 23.5° **[D]**. *As it orbits the Sun, different parts of the globe receive a varying amount of sunlight through the year-long cycle of the seasons [3]. For six months of the year, the Northern Hemisphere is tilted towards the Sun, which therefore appears higher in the sky, giving warmer temperatures and longer days [1]. Six months later, when the Northern Hemisphere is tilted in the other direction, the days are shorter and the Sun stays* *closer to the horizon [2]. The situation is reversed in the Southern Hemisphere. The Tropics of Cancer and Capricorn are lines around the* *globe at the lines of latitude +/- 23.5°. They mark the northernmost and southernmost points where the Sun appears directly overhead.*

Spring

Winter

Sun

Autumn

Summer

Fossil records show that there were once 400 days in each Earth year, so the same effect must also be slowing its rotation as well. Hence in the distant future, the spin of the Earth could be so slow that its day and year are equal, so that one scorched side of the planet will permanently face the Sun.

Complete coverage

Very occasionally, as the Moon orbits around the Earth and it in turn moves around the Sun, all three bodies – Sun, Earth and Moon – line up exactly and an eclipse is seen. If the Earth blocks out the Sun shining onto the full Moon, a rather unspectacular lunar eclipse happens. Far more spectacular are solar eclipses, when the new Moon passes right across the face of the Sun. By chance the Moon and Sun have discs in the sky that are almost the same size. This means that total solar eclipses can only be seen for short periods of time from tiny regions of the Earth. The effect is breathtaking as the Moon covers the bright central disk of the Sun, and reveals the wispy white corona of gas streaming out from the Sun's surface.

E

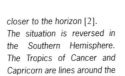

HOW THE MOON BEGAN

The Moon orbits too far from the Earth to be a captured asteroid. Instead, it is thought to have been formed when a body the size of Mars collided with the still-molten Earth during the formation of the Solar System, some 5 billion years ago [1]. The collision resulted in a stream of debris being thrown off into orbit round the Earth [2], and this eventually condensed to form the Moon [3]. The iron-rich cores of the two original bodies combined and remained within the Earth, becoming its very dense central region, whilst the Moon formed from the two lighter outer sections. This may explain why the Earth is thought to have a more complicated structure than the Moon, and also the lack of iron in Moon rock.

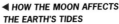

HOW THE MOON AFFECTS THE EARTH'S TIDES

The proximity of the Moon to the Earth, coupled with its size, causes strong gravitational forces between the two worlds, which is shown in the tides [E].
As the Moon exerts a gravitational pull on the Earth, it draws the seas towards it, and creates a bulge in the seawater on one side of the planet. At the same time, the Earth itself is attracted towards the Moon, pulling it away from the sea on the opposite side of the globe *and creating a smaller tidal bulge on the opposite side. Because the Moon is relatively slow-moving, the tidal bulges in the sea remain in almost the same place, while the Earth rotates under them [1,2,3,4]. As each bulge passes a point on the Earth roughly once each day, seashores experience two high and two low tides each day (although the shape of an inlet can alter their spacing). As the Moon circles the Earth once a month, the tides occur at different times each day.*

▼ *During the brief minutes of the eclipse, the corona of the Sun can be seen.*
Normally this is an invisible halo, made up of two distinct regions of gas which overlap, the K-corona and the F-corona. The latter reaches out many millions of kilometres from the Suns surface while the K-corona extends for a mere 75,000km.

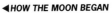

We think of the ground as being steady and immovable: in fact the surface of the Earth is in a constant state of movement, propelled by the intense heat of the interior. Although our planet is 12,700km wide, the crust on which the continents and oceans lie is only a few tens of kilometres thick at its deepest. This thin crust is broken into slabs or plates, which float on top of an inner molten layer, the mantle. Where these plates collide with each other or slowly draw apart are areas of violent activity, subject to earthquakes and studded with volcanoes. This drama is not restricted to dry land: satellite photography has shown that the two-thirds of Earth's surface under the ocean is just as fascinating, with features such as chains of volcanic mountains that stretch for 60,000km around the globe.

The idea that the continents are slowly moving was first put forward to explain how the coastlines of different continents appear to fit together like pieces of a jigsaw puzzle. For example, the eastern coast of South America nestles snugly into the western coast of Africa. Such continental drifts can be traced back to a point around 250 million years ago, when all the land masses on Earth were joined into a supercontinent called Pangaea (from the Greek for all earth), surrounded by a single vast sea, the Tethys Ocean. This supercontinent slowly disintegrated into the major land masses we know today.

Geologists call their model for the movements of the Earth's crust plate tectonics. This describes the surface, both continents and ocean floor, as being split into plates whose movements are driven by the churning of the molten rock in the inner mantle. The largest plates are as wide as the Pacific Ocean, while others are much smaller. Their thickness varies from around 10km beneath the oceans, to 30km under major land masses, and up to 60km where a plate has to support the weight of a mountain range. In general, ocean floor plates are made of dense basaltic rocks, while the continents are formed from less dense granite.

Earthquakes

Most of the areas where plates are separating are hidden beneath the ocean. At the fault between the plates molten rock wells up through a fissure and solidifies, creating new ocean floor. Only in a few places can this process be seen on dry land, notably in the volcanoes of Iceland, which sits on a fault called the Mid-Atlantic Ridge.

Plates can meet in a number of ways. At earthquake zones they grind past each other in opposite directions, being compressed so that they store huge amounts of energy. This is released in calamitous movements of the ground – earthquakes. The most famous earthquake zone of all, the San Andreas Fault in California, is a region where the North American and Pacific Plates are moving past each other. Earthquake prediction hinges on the theory that major quakes are preceded by 'quiet' periods during which the plates lock together, and store up the energy. Not all the plate boundaries are earthquake or volcano zones — the Himalayas are the result of a head-on collision between the relatively fast-moving Indo-Australian Plate, and the Eurasian Plate. These two continental plates buckled upwards, forming the mountain range, and halting the Indo-Australian plate's movement. Conversely, not all volcanoes are at plate boundaries. The volcanic Hawaiian Islands, for instance, lie in the middle of the Pacific Plate.

▼ **PANGAEA**

The continents of the world have not always looked as they do today **[A]**. The process of plate tectonics means that that they have migrated across the surface of the Earth. 200 million years ago, in the Jurassic era, all the land masses were joined in a single supercontinent, Pangaea [1]. Eventually, 120 million years ago, Pangaea split in two, the northern Laurasia made up of present-day North America and Eurasia, and the southern Gondwana, comprising South America, Africa, Australia and India [2].

By 40 million years ago the world had taken on a familiar look, although India had yet to collide with Eurasia (and create the Himalayas in the process) and Australia was still located very close to Antarctica [3].

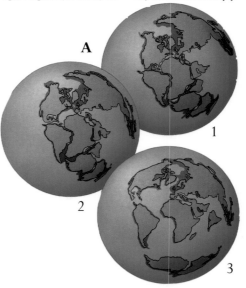

A

1

2

3

▼ **PLATE TECTONICS**

The processes of plate tectonics can be seen most clearly on a section of ocean floor **[B]**. At a subduction zone [1], an oceanic plate meets a much thicker continental plate and is forced down into the Earth's upper mantle. The heat in this zone melts the upper basalt layer of the oceanic plate, forming liquid magma which then rises to the surface and is vented through volcanoes.

At a mid-oceanic ridge [2] new crust is constantly being generated where two plates are separating. Magma rises up from the Earth's mantle, forcing its way through cracks in the crust, and solidifying. As the cracks expand, a striated ocean floor is formed. When the new crust solidifies, traces of iron in it align with the Earth's magnetic field and so preserve a record of the various reversals in the field over millions of years.

A hot spot volcano [3] forms where the crust thins above a hot plume rising from the inner mantle. It is only the latest in a string of volcanoes that form as the oceanic plate moves over the stationary plume. The earlier volcanoes become extinct, subsiding to volcanic islands with coral fringes, and eventually become atolls, where only the ring of coral remains above the surface of the ocean.

B

1

2

3

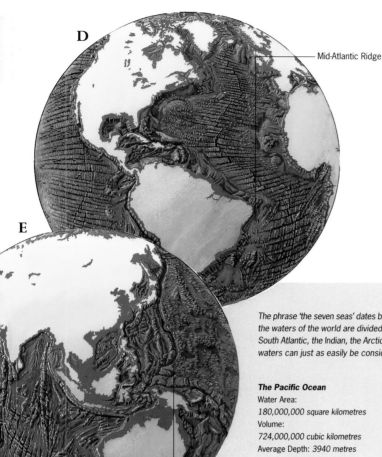

D — Mid-Atlantic Ridge

E

Marianas Trench

◀ **THE ATLANTIC AND THE PACIFIC**

The floors of the two largest oceans reveal important differences in their structures.

The Atlantic Ocean [D] is divided by the Mid-Atlantic Ridge that runs for its entire length, from Greenland down to the Antarctic Plate. This is a region where the Earth's crust is stretching, new floor being pumped out so that the Atlantic is gradually widening. As the rock is pulled apart, large slabs sink, creating the series of rifts that run parallel to the ridge along its length. Only in a few places does the ridge emerge above the sea, most spectacularly in Iceland, the shape of which is constantly being redefined by volcanic activity.

In contrast, the floor of the Pacific Ocean [E] shows signs of many different seismic activities. It is surrounded by the so-called 'ring of fire' – volcanic zones where the oceanic plates dive below continental ones and create volcanoes. At other places, oceanic plates converge, creating trenches where one plate dives below the other, such as the Marianas Trench, the deepest place on Earth.

THE SEVEN SEAS

The phrase 'the seven seas' dates back to the seas known to Muslim voyagers before the fifteenth century. Nowadays, the waters of the world are divided into seven oceans – the North Pacific, the South Pacific, the North Atlantic, the South Atlantic, the Indian, the Arctic and the Antarctic. But divisions such as these are in reality arbitrary, as all these waters can just as easily be considered as parts of one continuous global ocean.

The Pacific Ocean
Water Area:
180,000,000 square kilometres
Volume:
724,000,000 cubic kilometres
Average Depth: 3940 metres

The Atlantic Ocean
Water Area:
106,000,000 square kilometres
Volume:
355,000,000 cubic kilometres
Average Depth: 3310 metres

The Indian Ocean
Water Area:
75,000,000 square kilometres
Volume:
292,000,000 cubic kilometres
Average Depth: 3840 metres

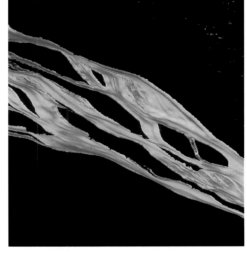

◀ *Lava which erupts from the earth's surface can take on a number of forms Aa, or block lava, is runny, and quickly forms a hard pastry-like crust when it cools. Pahoehoe lava has a sheen to it like satin and often consolidates in rope-like forms. When this kind of lava comes into contact with the sea it takes on the form of a jumbled heap of pillows, hence its name pillow lava.*

▼**SEA CHANGE**

A coastal region [C] is shaped by the forces of longshore drift. Sand is pushed along the shore by ocean currents to build up spits [1], bars [2] and sometimes enclosing bays to form lagoons.

A river carries vast amounts of sediment out to sea, which is deposited to form a delta [3]. Under the sea, the accumulation of sediment forms the continental shelf [4], a region that slopes gently out from the coastline for about 75km, to depths of 100-200m. In places it is cut through by submarine gorges, formed either by rivers when the sea level was lower or by the undercutting effect of river currents flowing out to sea. The shelf gives way to the steep continental slope, which dives to depths of several kilometres. From the base of the slope, the continental rise extends up to 1000km from the coast into the ocean.

C

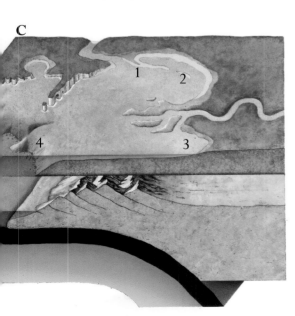

This chain of volcanic mountains is caused by a semi-permanent 'hot spot' where molten magma rises from the depths of the mantle through the crust, and spews out of a volcano. Although the hot spot in the mantle is stationary, the Pacific Plate, and with it the volcano, is continually moving. Hawaii itself is only the most recent in a chain of 107 volcanic vents formed by the plume. As the plate moves on, each volcano becomes extinct, and a new one forms further along the chain. Many thousands of these 'hot spot' volcanoes are known – mostly beneath the ocean surface – so there must be hundreds of hot plumes in the mantle to have created them all.

While plates are being destroyed in the subduction zones where they collide, new plate material is being produced all the time deep beneath the ocean surface. The sea floor is just as geologically fascinating as the continental land surface, and is still awaiting full exploration.

Occasionally, the volcanic activity of the mid-oceanic ridges reaches the surface, and forms islands. At other places, hot gases venting from the depths of the Earth create pools of warmth on the ocean floor, where life can flourish.

Over billions of years, the harsh landscape created by geological activity such as plate tectonics and volcanism has been softened and sculpted by the eroding forces of ice, water and air. Glaciers have ground out valleys, and rivers have carved huge gorges, including America's Grand Canyon. At the same time the steady pounding of the seas and oceans eats away and remodels coastlines.

Studies of the changing climate in the past show that the Earth has gone through periodic 'ice ages' when the ice-caps pushed into temperate regions closer to the Equator. These periods were critical in shaping the landscape that we see today – during the last Ice Age, which ended 10,000 years ago, an ice sheet covered most of Northern Europe, Asia and North America. The ice ages can be dated by drilling out an ice core from a polar cap. Each year a layer of new ice is laid down, which in colder years – during ice ages – is thicker. These records surprisingly reveal that over the last 4 million years, successive ice ages have gripped Earth for longer than the warmer periods in between.

Variations in the Earth's climate are thought to be the result of cyclical changes in its orbit, which becomes more, then less, elongated. According to these models the Earth's average temperature should currently be on the increase – which means that the measured increases in temperature cited as evidence of global warming and the greenhouse effect may have a natural cause.

Getting in shape

During the ice ages, massive glaciers formed across the globe. As these vast, slow-moving rivers of ice rolled forward, the sheer weight of ice ground down rocks in their paths, leaving a softened, altered landscape once they had retreated. These forces are still at work today: on Greenland and in Antarctica there are many glaciers which eventually find their way to the sea, where they break up into icebergs.

Although glaciers are the most dramatic form of erosion, there are others: over longer periods, rivers and seas can cut through rock and carve out valleys. Even rain has a profound cumulative effect on rock. Raindrops dissolve gases from the atmosphere and become dilute acid, chemically attacking igneous rocks formed from volcanic lava. In time, the particles broken off build up to great depths and are converted by pressure and heat into sedimentary rocks such as limestone. When these are subjected to the intense heat of the Earth's crust they become metamorphic rocks, such as marble and slate.

▼ A WOBBLING WORLD
The climate of the Earth is not constant but gradually varies over time in cycles of thousands of years [B]. The shape of the Earth's orbit around the Sun can vary between an almost perfect circle [1] and a pronounced ellipse [2] over a cycle of around 100,000 years. When the orbit is more elliptical, the climate of the Earth is more extreme. At the same time, another cycle changes the angle of tilt of the planet between a minimum 21.8° and a maximum 24.4° [C]. At the maximum inclination, every 22,000 years, the climate is most extreme, and the seasons are especially marked, with the Poles pointing further away from the Sun during winter. When the effects of these cycles are combined, they lead to ice ages of varying severity, the last of which ended around 10,000 years ago.

▶ EARTH SCRAPER
Glaciers [A] are dramatic rivers of ice slowly creeping down valleys and carving mountain ranges into a series of sharp peaks. They usually originate where ice or hard-packed snow builds up in a cirque [1], a basin near a mountain top. After a sufficient mass has built up, it will start to move under its own gravity, wearing down rocks by pressure, scraping and frost action, to form glacial spoil called 'moraines'. The boulders of moraine underneath the glacier act as abrasives, scouring the landscape.
Lateral moraines [2] are rocks cut away and pulled along at the sides of the glacier. Where two ice-rivers meet, the lateral moraines can join to form a medial moraine [3] – a stripe of rubble down the centre of the glacier. As the glacier grinds along over rocks and boulders, the stresses induced can open up deep and jagged splits called crevasses [4]. A glacier terminates at a snout [5] which may empty into the sea, or a great lake. On dry land the shape of the snout depends on the climatic conditions, and especially the rate at which the snout melts compared with the rate at which the glacier advances. If the the two rates are exactly balanced, the snout remains in the same place, but

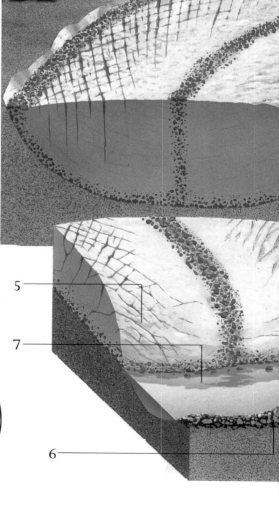

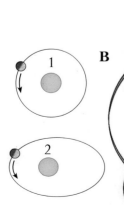

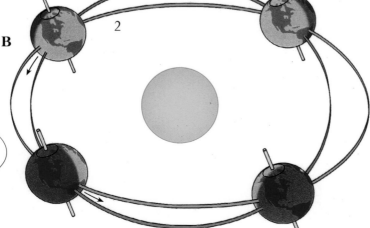

1

2

B

1

2

5

7

6

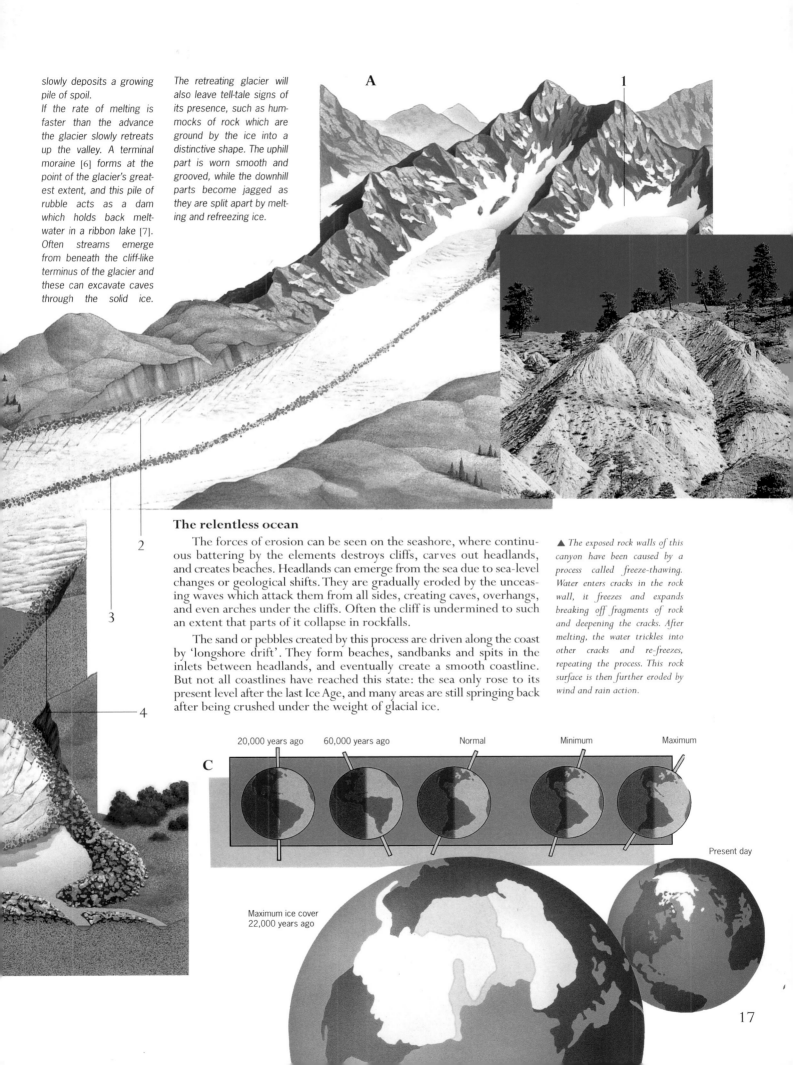

slowly deposits a growing pile of spoil.

If the rate of melting is faster than the advance the glacier slowly retreats up the valley. A terminal moraine [6] forms at the point of the glacier's greatest extent, and this pile of rubble acts as a dam which holds back meltwater in a ribbon lake [7]. Often streams emerge from beneath the cliff-like terminus of the glacier and these can excavate caves through the solid ice.

The retreating glacier will also leave tell-tale signs of its presence, such as hummocks of rock which are ground by the ice into a distinctive shape. The uphill part is worn smooth and grooved, while the downhill parts become jagged as they are split apart by melting and refreezing ice.

The relentless ocean

The forces of erosion can be seen on the seashore, where continuous battering by the elements destroys cliffs, carves out headlands, and creates beaches. Headlands can emerge from the sea due to sea-level changes or geological shifts. They are gradually eroded by the unceasing waves which attack them from all sides, creating caves, overhangs, and even arches under the cliffs. Often the cliff is undermined to such an extent that parts of it collapse in rockfalls.

The sand or pebbles created by this process are driven along the coast by 'longshore drift'. They form beaches, sandbanks and spits in the inlets between headlands, and eventually create a smooth coastline. But not all coastlines have reached this state: the sea only rose to its present level after the last Ice Age, and many areas are still springing back after being crushed under the weight of glacial ice.

▲ The exposed rock walls of this canyon have been caused by a process called freeze-thawing. Water enters cracks in the rock wall, it freezes and expands breaking off fragments of rock and deepening the cracks. After melting, the water trickles into other cracks and re-freezes, repeating the process. This rock surface is then further eroded by wind and rain action.

20,000 years ago   60,000 years ago   Normal   Minimum   Maximum

Present day

Maximum ice cover 22,000 years ago

17

Contrasting conditions

We talk so much about the weather because of its infinite changeability. As the Sun's radiation heats up the Equatorial zones of the planet much more than the Polar regions, it creates wide temperature contrasts. The hottest places on Earth can be a blistering 50°C in the shade, while in the depths of an Antarctic winter, levels as low as -70°C have been recorded. This variable heat produces hot air at the Equator, which rises, while cooler air further north and south sinks under it, producing wind patterns that stretch across the globe. These in turn create swirling eddies of air that can absorb water vapour over the sea, forming clouds, and deposit it as rain over land. Such air currents couple with the variable heat of the Sun to produce the wide variety of climates found on Earth, ranging from hot, rainless deserts to cool, wet, temperate coastal regions.

The atmosphere of the Earth just after it formed was an unbreatheable mixture of hydrogen and helium. In time this was replaced by an equally unbreatheable mixture belched out from volcanoes, which in turn has been modified by lifeforms to the air we breathe today. This is made up of 78 per cent nitrogen, 21 per cent oxygen, and a small proportion of carbon dioxide, which plants then recycle into oxygen. The remainder of the atmosphere is water vapour and small traces of other gases. The balance is a delicate one, perfectly suited to life as it has evolved, and the entire planet – both living things and minerals – is needed to maintain it.

The outer limits of the atmosphere stretch 2400 km above the surface, but the lower 15km, the troposphere, is the densest, holding nearly all the atmosphere's water vapour – which condenses under different conditions to create clouds. Beyond this region, up to 40 km high, lies the stratosphere, which contains a thin ozone layer that blocks out harmful ultra-violet radiation.

Climate types

Land near the Equator has weather patterns typified by those of southern Asia. For six months of the year cold dry winds blow from the land out to sea, giving arid conditions and little rain. In the summer the wind reverses direction and starts to blow warm air off the ocean. This air is heavy with water vapour and triggers torrential rainstorms over land.

Weather in the temperate latitudes of northern Europe is dominated by the jet stream, a band of high winds at altitudes of about 12km. It forms where warm air from the tropics meets cold Polar air, creating a jet of air travelling at speeds around 200kmh in summer, 400kmh in winter. The jet stream's direction develops in a similar way to a slowly flowing river, meandering and forming eddies. These are seen as high-pressure anticyclones, wind systems that create clear, dry weather, or low pressure depressions with associated clouds and weather fronts.

The circulation patterns of the oceans are just as important in regulating climate. In general, the oceans circulate in large eddies, clockwise in the Northern Hemisphere, anticlockwise in the Southern.

— Hadley cell

A

▲ **CREATING WINDS**

The amount of heat absorbed at the Equator is much greater than at the Poles. The temperature difference creates giant circulation cells which transfer heat from the Equator to the Poles [A]. The Hadley cell is driven by hot air rising from the Equator which cools and returns to the surface at 30° latitude. Some of this returning air is drawn back towards the Equator, creating the trade winds. The Ferrel cell guides warm air towards the Poles, creating winds which the Earth's rotation skews to become the Westerlies. Where these winds meet cold air blowing directly from the Pole, frontal depressions form giving unsettled weather. At the cell boundaries jet streams form – channels of high winds which encircle the planet. This circulation from the Equator to the Poles is complicated by the Earth's rotation, creating the Coriolis force which bends winds to the right in the Northern Hemisphere, and to the left in the Southern Hemisphere.

▶ *Deserts can be created in many ways, and they may be hot or cold. The Antarctic, being one of the driest places in the world, is classed as a cold desert. The Sahara and the Arabian Deserts are classic examples of hot deserts. The photograph shows a sand dune in the Simpson Desert in Australia.*
Winds blowing over the land constantly shift dunes in ever changing patterns.

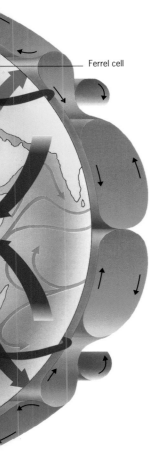

Ferrel cell

▶ A tornado can form during a very severe thunderstorm [C]. Hot air evaporating off land or sea rises rapidly through the atmosphere, condensing to form clouds. As surface air rushes inward the low pressure at the centre of the storm, the spin of the Earth makes the whole complex spin, producing a typhoon or hurricane (right). Tornadoes occur when the fast-rising thermals, which create a storm, begin to spin even more quickly, perhaps in response to the local geography. As the thermal winds up on itself, it draws a funnel of cloud down from the bottom of the storm towards the ground, where the winds often exceed 200kmh. The extreme low pressure sucks up material from the ground, flinging it out at the top of the tornado, sometimes to land several kilometres away. Waterspouts are similar vortices that form over water.

C

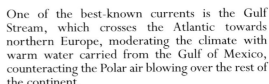

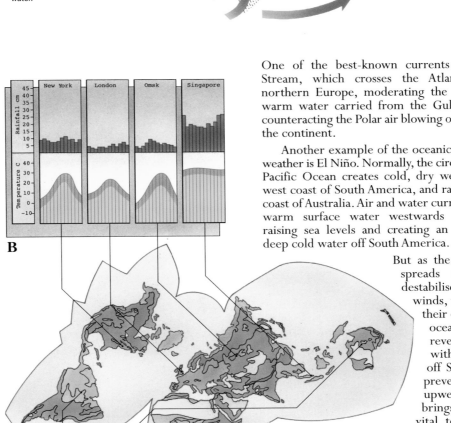

B

▶ VARIETY OF CLIMATE
The patterns of rainfall and temperature around the world divide the Earth into different regions of vegetation [B]. Seven cities around the world illustrate the wide variety of weather these produce.

New York has an east coast continental climate, with cold winters, hot summers and steady rainfall all year round. London's climate is marine west coast, similarly wet to New York's but with less variation between summer and winter temperatures. Omsk has typical steppe climate, with low rainfall and very cold winters followed by hot summers. Singapore's tropical climate gives almost constant hot and very wet weather. Manaus in Brazil's region of tropical savanna has constant high temperatures, with very dry summer months. A desert climate like that of Alice Springs has very high average temperatures (with a slight dip during the southern winter months), but almost no rain throughout the year.
The Nigerian capital, Lagos, has a constantly hot tropical rainforest climate, characterised by its extremely wet summer months.

- ⬤ Deciduous forest
- ⬤ Steppe
- ⬤ Evergreen forest
- ⬤ Tropical rainforest
- ◯ Tropical savanna
- ◯ Desert
- ◯ Tundra

One of the best-known currents is the Gulf Stream, which crosses the Atlantic towards northern Europe, moderating the climate with warm water carried from the Gulf of Mexico, counteracting the Polar air blowing over the rest of the continent.

Another example of the oceanic effect on the weather is El Niño. Normally, the circulation of the Pacific Ocean creates cold, dry weather on the west coast of South America, and rain on the east coast of Australia. Air and water currents circulate warm surface water westwards to Australia, raising sea levels and creating an upwelling of deep cold water off South America.

But as the warm water spreads eastwards it destabilises the trade winds, which reverse their direction. The ocean circulation reverses as well, with warm water off South America preventing the cold upwelling which brings up nutrients vital to fish stocks. On land, Australia experiences drought, and South America suffers torrential rain. Such drastic climatic changes show how delicate the balance is between climate and the environment.

Major volcanic eruptions can also affect the climate, throwing dust particles high into the upper atmosphere, where they block out sunlight. Sudden climate changes are believed to have caused mass extinction of life on Earth in the past, and as yet there is little humanity can do to counter, or even predict, these changes.

Peopling the Globe

The origins of humankind are very hard to determine. The fossil record of our ancestors is very patchy, and thus the story involves large amounts of guesswork. Archaeologists believe that between 7 and 10 million years ago, a human ancestor, called Ramapithecus, developed from the same stock as chimpanzees and gorillas. The route from these creatures to modern man can be traced in terms of changing skeletons. Bipedal motion required a sturdy pelvis, while the increasing intelligence of these progenitors can be followed through increasing brain capacities. Ramapithecus was succeeded by Australopithecus, whose later form is named Homo habilis, the handy man, because fossil evidence shows that it used simple tools.

Homo erectus appeared in Africa 1.7 million years ago and spread to the rest of the world roughly 1 million years ago. They were almost as tall as modern humans, with skull capacities twice as large as Homo habilis. This species lived longer in Asia than in Africa – it includes Peking Man, who lived 250,000 years ago. It was gradually succeeded by our species, Homo sapiens, which appeared in Africa more than 500,000 years ago. The expansion was a slow drift as bands of hunter-gatherers followed prey animals. There can have been no population pressure: 10,000 years ago the world population was between 5 and 10 million, about the population of New York City today. As people settled in various places, climate and food sources led them to evolve differently. For example, those in very hot Equatorial countries kept a dark skin to protect them from ultraviolet sunlight; those in colder climates developed lighter skins to maximise the effect of a weaker sun – vitamin D, essential to bone growth, is gained from sunlight.

At first only Africa, Asia and the warmer parts of Europe were colonised: America and Australia remained empty for thousands of years. Movement between continental land masses was made possible by climate changes. During the last Ice Age, much of the world's water was locked into the ice caps. Sea levels dropped dramatically, what is now the Bering Strait became a land passage, and vast stretches of ocean became navigable by small boats.

Hunters to farmers

For two million years, human ancestors lived as hunter-gatherers, following a nomadic pattern of life, with a diet of animals and seasonal fruits.

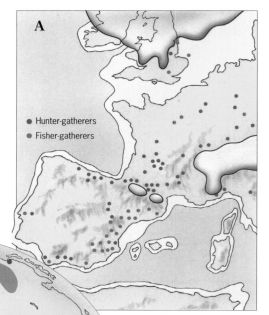

A

- ● Hunter-gatherers
- ● Fisher-gatherers

◄ **HOMO SAPIENS**
From central and southern Africa Homo sapiens spread out to populate the whole world **[B]**. The first migration spread from Africa eastwards across to Asia. Routes branched off to northern Africa and southern Europe. A second wave occurred 15,000 years ago, when glaciation provided a land bridge across the Bering Strait, allowing movement from northern Asia to the Americas.

B

- ● Evidence of Homo sapiens
- ▲ Prehistoric Americans

C

○ Early settlements

◄ **THE FIRST FARMERS**
The first farming settlements, which developed into the first cities, were probably founded around 10,000 years ago in the 'Fertile Crescent' **[C]**, a band of land stretching from the Mediterranean to the rivers Tigris and Euphrates, in modern Jordan, Lebanon, Syria, Turkey and Iraq. Civilisation also flowered along the banks of the river Nile, similarly suited to agriculture. From simple farmsteads grew villages, towns, cities and eventually whole civilisations.

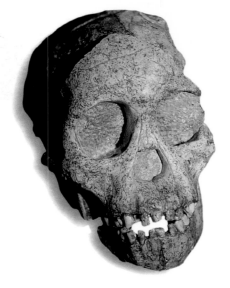

This changed between 20,000 and 10,000 years ago with the development of agriculture. About 15,000 years ago, as temperatures rose, primitive farming practices began to appear wherever the climate allowed it. The most important of these were Mesopotamia, the crescent between the rivers Tigris and Euphrates in modern Iraq, south-eastern Turkey and eastern Syria, the Nile valley, Central America and north-east China. Once wandering groups settled down the population soared, increasing from 5 to 300 million in 8000 years.

Small farming settlements developed into villages, then towns, then cities. Social and political organisations developed to control large groups of people. Gradually, the great civilisations grew, in the fertile fields of these first settlements. Along the Nile Valley, the Egyptians started to build a sophisticated culture around 3000BC, at the same time as the Sumerians were developing a system of city states in Mesopotamia. Similar civilisations appeared in China and Central America. Influences from these civilisations rippled outwards, laying down the pattern for the shape of the modern world.

▲ *This skull of* Australopithicus africanus *is over 2 million years old.* Africanus *was the first hominid to leave the forest for the open plain.*

▶ **OUT OF AFRICA**

It is now considered that the ancestors of humankind first appeared in Africa [D]. As well as indications of early Homo sapiens, the evidence for Africa's claims to be the cradle of humanity comes from fossils of Australopithecus and Homo erectus found in South Africa, Olduvai Gorge in Kenya, and Ethiopia. These are older than any others so far discovered in the world and so it seems likely that the human beings who evolved in Africa gradually spread out to other parts of the world. This is corroborated by fossils of a later date found in India, Java and China which indicate the direction of migration out of Africa. Early Homo sapiens fossils have also been found in China, southern Europe, North and South America and the Middle East. In Europe, the fossils found so far are confined to early forms of Homo sapiens and Neanderthal man, whose traces have been found in Germany, Hungary, France, Belgium, Greece, Czechoslovakia, Russia and the Middle East.

D

▲ Homo erectus
▲ Homo habilis
● Australopithecus
■ Early paleolithic

E

Caucasian
Mongol
Negroid
Indian/Caucasian
Aboriginal
Caucasian/Mongol
Negroid/Caucasian

▲ **FIRST MIGRATIONS**

Human beings it seems could not stay long in one place [E].
At first, migrations were slow and took place over thousands of years. From their African prototype, people adapted physically, in response to extremes of climate, gradually evolving into the various races that populate the world today. These races developed in certain areas, as shown on the map above, however, the forces of the modern world from the age of discovery onwards created later movements that have spread people around the world. These modern migrations, some voluntary, others enforced as in the slave trade, are also shown.

There are more than 6 billion people in the world today. This figure is rising at a rate of 140 million each year, an increase of more than the population of Japan. But until comparatively recently, the rate of increase of the world population was low. Two thousand years ago, there were an estimated 300 million people on Earth; by 1650 this had increased to a mere 500 million. Then in only 200 years this number had doubled, and in the 150 years since then it has increased five-fold. In spite of recurrent famine and war, the world population seems set on an inexorable upward curve, doubling every 39 years.

This population explosion is a result of social developments since the Industrial Revolution. Proportionally there are the same number of births each year – or perhaps fewer. But the advances of improved sanitation and nutrition made possible by the industrial and scientific advances of the 18th and 19th centuries meant that fewer babies died at birth and that people lived longer.

At first these changes were confined to the countries of the developed world, in Europe and America, but as they have spread around the world, the population has ballooned. Now in most European countries the population remains stable, mainly because of the availability of reliable contraception. Indeed, in some countries the birth rate has fallen below the number needed to maintain stability; this will result in a top-heavy 'age pyramid', with too many grandparents and not enough grandchildren to support them. Some countries, such as France and Sweden, have tried to encourage people to have more babies through maternity payments and tax discounts for large families.

In the developing world the situation is different. There are many cultural and religious objections to the use of contraception. In a traditional agricultural community, too, a large family was desirable. As well as ensuring that the parents would have surviving children to look after them, many children provided a workforce to farm the land. But fewer people now live on the land, as farming becomes mechanised; and a large family in an urban industrialised setting just creates more mouths to feed. China, the most populated country in the world, has solved the problem, rationing families to one child each.

The rush to the cities

All over the world, more people live in cities than in the country, because it is no longer possible to make a living working on the land.

B

>100 ⬤ No of people
11-100 ◯ per sq.km
8-10 ◔
<2 ◑

A

73
79
+0.9%
+33.4%
70
60
50
40
30
20
10
United States
US $ 28,020

59
69
1+24%
+8%
70
60
50
40
30
20
10
Brazil
US $ 4,400

▲ GLOBAL POPULATION
The global population is distributed in clumps and clusters around the world. In hotter countries, most people live on a narrow ribbon along the coast, leaving vast arid inner tracts of land under-populated. In cooler countries, the population is able to spread itself more evenly about the landmass. The map makes clear the huge numbers of people living all across China and India, in contrast with the comparatively sparse population of much of the United States. The graphics around illustration [A] show for each continent the rate of population growth, the average longevity of men and women, the gross national product per capita (a measure of wealth), and the calorific intake per head as a percentage of an adult's average daily requirement. These illustrate the gap in health and wealth between the developed world and the developing nations.

1750
1900
2000

D

◀ GROWTH 1750–2000
The growth of the human population can be shown [D] by demonstrating the number of people that would occupy each 2km² of land of the Earth's surface at various eras: 1750, 1900 and 2000.

▶ POPULATION GROWTH
The Earth's population has swollen from a mere 250 million 1000 years ago (roughly the present-day population of the United States) to 6 billion today.

For most of the intervening period growth was very slow, and there were even slight declines caused by plagues such as the Black Death. However, from about the time of the Industrial Revolution the rate of growth increased, accelerating further with each improvement in hygiene and healthcare.

A graph of world population growth over the past 300 years [C] can be split to show how the relative increases in each continent have been staggered. Throughout recorded history, the population of Asia has been greater than that of all the other continents combined. However, during the 19th century the population of Europe grew at twice the rate of Asia's, thanks mainly to the improvements in living conditions brought about by scientific advances and the Industrial Revolution. This rate of growth has slowed in Europe this century, whereas that of Asia has accelerated spectacularly – its population seems likely to have tripled in the fifty years from 1950. Over the last two centuries the populations of North and South America have been increasing just as fast. In the 19th century this was due to immigration, whereas this century's gains can be attributed to better health and hygiene, improvements which have gradually spread to the developing world.

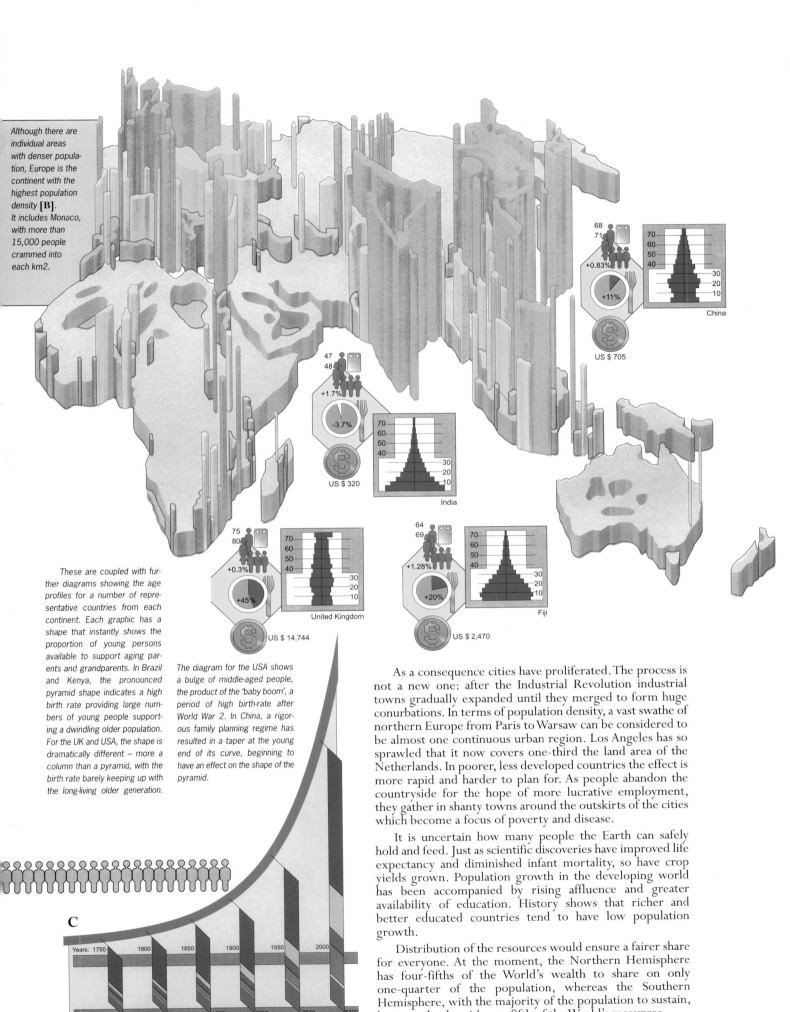

Although there are individual areas with denser population, Europe is the continent with the highest population density [B]. It includes Monaco, with more than 15,000 people crammed into each km2.

These are coupled with further diagrams showing the age profiles for a number of representative countries from each continent. Each graphic has a shape that instantly shows the proportion of young persons available to support aging parents and grandparents. In Brazil and Kenya, the pronounced pyramid shape indicates a high birth rate providing large numbers of young people supporting a dwindling older population. For the UK and USA, the shape is dramatically different – more a column than a pyramid, with the birth rate barely keeping up with the long-living older generation.

The diagram for the USA shows a bulge of middle-aged people, the product of the 'baby boom', a period of high birth-rate after World War 2. In China, a rigorous family planning regime has resulted in a taper at the young end of its curve, beginning to have an effect on the shape of the pyramid.

As a consequence cities have proliferated. The process is not a new one: after the Industrial Revolution industrial towns gradually expanded until they merged to form huge conurbations. In terms of population density, a vast swathe of northern Europe from Paris to Warsaw can be considered to be almost one continuous urban region. Los Angeles has so sprawled that it now covers one-third the land area of the Netherlands. In poorer, less developed countries the effect is more rapid and harder to plan for. As people abandon the countryside for the hope of more lucrative employment, they gather in shanty towns around the outskirts of the cities which become a focus of poverty and disease.

It is uncertain how many people the Earth can safely hold and feed. Just as scientific discoveries have improved life expectancy and diminished infant mortality, so have crop yields grown. Population growth in the developing world has been accompanied by rising affluence and greater availability of education. History shows that richer and better educated countries tend to have low population growth.

Distribution of the resources would ensure a fairer share for everyone. At the moment, the Northern Hemisphere has four-fifths of the World's wealth to share on only one-quarter of the population, whereas the Southern Hemisphere, with the majority of the population to sustain, has to make do with one-fifth of the World's resources.

China
68
71
+0.83%
+11%
US $ 705

India
47
48
+1.7%
-3.7%
US $ 320

United Kingdom
75
80
+0.3%
+45%
US $ 14,744

Fiji
64
69
+1.28%
+20%
US $ 2,470

C
Years: 1750 1800 1850 1900 1950 2000
World population 790 million 980 1260 1650 2500 6200

AFGHANISTAN

Capital:	Kabul
Area:	647,500 km²
Population:	31,056,997
Currency:	Afghani (AFA)
Main Religions:	Sunni Muslim 80%, Shi'a Muslim 19%, other 1%
Main Languages:	Pashtu 35%, Afghan Persian (Dari) 50%, Turkic languages 11%, 30 minor languages 4%
Int Dial Code:	93
Map Page:	91

ALBANIA

Capital:	Tirana
Area:	28,748 km²
Population:	3,581,655
Currency:	Lek (ALL)
Main Religions:	Muslim 70%, Albanian Orthodox 20%, Roman Catholic 10%
Main Languages:	Albanian (Tosk is the official dialect), Greek
Int Dial Code:	355
Map Page:	68

ALGERIA

Capital:	Algiers
Area:	2,381,740 km²
Population:	32,930,091
Currency:	Algerian dinar (DZD)
Main Religions:	Sunni Muslim 99%, Christian and Jewish 1%
Languages:	Arabic (official), French, Berber dialects
Int Dial Code:	213
Map Page:	103

ANDORRA

Capital:	Andorra la Vella
Area:	468 km²
Population:	71,201
Currency:	Euro (EUR)
Main Religions:	Roman Catholic
Main Languages:	Catalan (official), French, Castilian
Int Dial Code:	376
Map Page:	61

ANGOLA

Capital:	Luanda
Area:	1,246,700 km²
Population:	12,127,071
Currency:	Kwanza (AOA)
Main Religions:	Indigenous beliefs 47%, Roman Catholic 38%, Protestant 15%
Main Languages:	Portuguese (official), Bantu and other African languages
Int Dial Code:	244
Map Page:	98

ANTIGUA AND BARBUDA

Capital:	Saint John's
Area:	442.6 km² (Antigua 281 km²; Barbuda 161 km²)
Population:	67,000
Currency:	East Caribbean dollar (XCD)
Main Religions:	Anglican (predominant), Protestant, Roman Catholic
Main Languages:	English (official), local dialects
Int Dial Code:	1 + 268
Map Page:	135

ARGENTINA

Capital:	Buenos Aires
Area:	2,766,890 km²
Population:	39,921,833
Currency:	Argentine Peso (ARS)
Main Religions:	Roman Catholic 92%, Protestant 2%, Jewish 2%, other 4%
Main Languages:	Spanish (official), English, Italian, German, French
Int Dial Code:	54
Map Page:	142

ARMENIA

Capital:	Yerevan
Area:	29,800 km²
Population:	2,976,372
Currency:	Dram (AMD)
Main Religions:	Armenian Orthodox 94%
Main Languages:	Armenian 96%, Russian 2%, other 2%
Int Dial Code:	374
Map Page:	93

AUSTRALIA

Capital:	Canberra
Area:	7,686,850 km²
Population:	20,264,082
Currency:	Australian dollar (AUD)
Main Religions:	Anglican 26.1%, Roman Catholic 26%, other Christian 24.3%, non-Christian 11%
Main Languages:	English, native languages
Int Dial Code:	61
Map Page:	114

AUSTRIA

Capital:	Vienna
Area:	83,870 km²
Population:	8,192,880
Currency:	Euro (EUR)
Main Religions:	Roman Catholic 74%, Protestant 5%, Muslim and other 21%
Main Languages:	German
Int Dial Code:	43
Map Page:	63

AZERBAIJAN

Capital:	Baku
Area:	86,600 km²
Population:	7,961,619
Currency:	Azerbaijani manat (AZM)
Main Religions:	Muslim 93.4%, Russian Orthodox 2.5%, Armenian Orthodox 2.3%, other 1.8%
Main Languages:	Azerbaijani (Azeri) 89%, Russian 3%, Armenian 2%
Int Dial Code:	994
Map Page:	93

BAHAMAS, THE

Capital:	Nassau
Area:	13,940 km²
Population:	303,770
Currency:	Bahamian dollar (BSD)
Main Religions:	Baptist 35%, Anglican 15%, Roman Catholic 13%, Pentecostal 8%, Methodist 4%, Church of God 5%
Main Languages:	English, Creole
Int Dial Code:	1 + 242
Map Page:	135

BAHRAIN

Capital:	Manama
Area:	665 km²
Population:	698,585
Currency:	Bahraini dinar (BHD)
Main Religions:	Muslim 81% (Shi'a & Sunni), Christian 9%
Main Languages:	Arabic, English, Farsi, Urdu
Int Dial Code:	973
Map Page:	95

BANGLADESH

Capital:	Dhaka
Area:	144,000 km²
Population:	147,365,352
Currency:	Taka (BDT)
Main Religions:	Muslim 83%, Hindu 16%, other 1%
Main Languages:	Bangla (official, also known as Bengali), English
Int Dial Code:	880
Map Page:	88

BARBADOS

Capital:	Bridgetown
Area:	431 km²
Population:	279,912
Currency:	Barbadian dollar (BBD)
Main Religions:	Protestant 67% (Anglican 40%, Pentecostal 8%, Methodist 7%, other 12%), Roman Catholic 4%
Main Languages:	English
Int Dial Code:	1 + 246
Map Page:	135

BELARUS

Capital:	Minsk
Area:	207,600 km²
Population:	10,293,011
Currency:	Belarusian ruble (BYB/BYR)
Main Religions:	Eastern Orthodox 80%, other (including Roman Catholic, Protestant, Jewish, and Muslim) 20%
Main Languages:	Belarusian, Russian
Int Dial Code:	375
Map Page:	70

BELGIUM

Capital:	Brussels
Area:	30,528 km²
Population:	10,379,067
Currency:	Euro (EUR)
Main Religions:	Roman Catholic 75%, Protestant or other 25%
Main Languages:	Dutch 60%, French 40% legally bilingual (Dutch and French)
Int Dial Code:	32
Map Page:	55

BELIZE

Capital:	Belmopan
Area:	22,966 km²
Population:	287,730
Currency:	Belizean dollar (BZD)
Main Religions:	Roman Catholic 50%, Protestant 27%
Main Languages:	English (official), Spanish, Mayan, Garifuna , Creole
Int Dial Code:	501
Map Page:	134

BENIN

Capital:	Porto-Novo
Area:	112,620 km²
Population:	7,862,944
Currency:	Communaute Financiere Africaine franc (XOF)
Main Religions:	Indigenous beliefs 50%, Christian 30%, Muslim 20%
Main Languages:	French (official), Fon and Yoruba, tribal languages
Int Dial Code:	229
Map Page:	105

BHUTAN

Capital:	Thimphu
Area:	47,000 km²
Population:	2,279,723
Currency:	Ngultrum (BTN); Indian rupee (INR)
Main Religions:	Lamaistic Buddhist 75%, Hinduism 25%
Main Languages:	Dzongkha (official), Bhotes speak various Tibetan dialects, Nepalese dialects
Int Dial Code:	975
Map Page:	88

BOLIVIA

Capital:	La Paz (seat of government); Sucre (legal capital and seat of judiciary)
Area:	1,098,580 km²
Population:	8,989,046
Currency:	Boliviano (BOB)
Main Religions:	Roman Catholic 95%, Protestant 5%
Main Languages:	Spanish (official), Quechua (official), Aymara
Int Dial Code:	591
Map Page:	140

BOSNIA AND HERZEGOVINA

Capital:	Sarajevo
Area:	51,129 km²
Population:	4,498,976
Currency:	Marka (BAM)
Main Religions:	Muslim 40%, Orthodox 31%, Roman Catholic 15%, Protestant 4%, other 14%
Main Languages:	Croatian, Serbian, Bosnian
Int Dial Code:	387
Map Page:	66

BOTSWANA

Capital:	Gaborone
Area:	600,370 km²
Population:	1,639,833
Currency:	Pula (BWP)
Main Religions:	Christian 72%, Badimo 6%
Main Languages:	Setswana, Kalanga, Sekgalagadi, English
Int Dial Code:	267
Map Page:	108

BRAZIL

Capital:	Brasilia
Area:	8,511,965 km²
Population:	188,078,227
Currency:	Real (BRL)
Main Religions:	Roman Catholic (nominal) 74%, Protestant 15%
Main Languages:	Portuguese (official), Spanish, English, French
Int Dial Code:	55
Map Page:	141

BRUNEI

Capital:	Bandar Seri Begawan
Area:	5,770 km²
Population:	379,444
Currency:	Bruneian dollar (BND)
Main Religions:	Muslim (official) 67%, Buddhist 13%, Christian 10%, indigenous beliefs and other 10%
Main Languages:	Malay (official), English, Chinese
Int Dial Code:	673
Map Page:	86

BULGARIA

Capital:	Sofia
Area:	110,910 km²
Population:	7,385,367
Currency:	Lev (BGL)
Main Religions:	Bulgarian Orthodox 82.6%, Muslim 13%, Roman Catholic 1.5%, Uniate Catholic 0.2%, Jewish 0.8%
Main Languages:	Bulgarian, Turkish
Int Dial Code:	359
Map Page:	67

BURKINA

Capital:	Ouagadougou
Area:	274,200 km²
Population:	13,902,972
Currency:	Communaute Financiere Africaine franc (XOF)
Main Religions:	Indigenous beliefs 40%, Muslim 50%, Christian 10%
Main Languages:	French (official), native African languages belonging to Sudanic family spoken by 90% of the population
Int Dial Code:	226
Map Page:	104

BURUNDI

Capital:	Bujumbura
Area:	27,830 km²
Population:	8,090,068
Currency:	Burundi franc (BIF)
Main Religions:	Christian 67% (Roman Catholic 62%, Protestant 5%), indigenous beliefs 23%, Muslim 10%
Main Languages:	Kirundi (official), French (official), Swahili
Int Dial Code:	257
Map Page:	106

CAMBODIA

Capital:	Phnom Penh
Area:	181,040 km²
Population:	13,881,427
Currency:	Riel (KHR)
Main Religions:	Theravada Buddhist 95%, other 5%
Main Languages:	Khmer (official) 95%, French, English
Int Dial Code:	855
Map Page:	84

CAMEROON

Capital:	Yaounde
Area:	475,440 km²
Population:	17,340,702
Currency:	Communaute Financiere Africaine franc (XAF)
Main Religions:	Indigenous beliefs 40%, Christian 40%, Muslim 20%
Main Languages:	24 major African language groups, English (official), French (official)
Int Dial Code:	237
Map Page:	105

CANADA

Capital:	Ottawa
Area:	9,984,670 km²
Population:	33,098,932
Currency:	Canadian dollar (CAD)
Main Religions:	Roman Catholic 42%, Protestant 23%, other 18%
Main Languages:	English 59.3% (official), French 23.2% (official), other 17.5%
Int Dial Code:	1
Map Page:	122

CAPE VERDE

Capital:	Praia
Area:	4,033 km²
Population:	420,979
Currency:	Cape Verdean escudo (CVE)
Main Religions:	Roman Catholic, Protestant
Main Languages:	Portuguese, Crioulo
Int Dial Code:	238
Map Page:	104

CENTRAL AFRICAN REPUBLIC

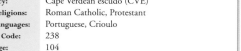

Capital:	Bangui
Area:	622,984 km²
Population:	4,303,356
Currency:	Communaute Financiere Africaine franc (XAF)
Main Religions:	Indigenous beliefs 35%, Protestant 25%, Roman Catholic 25%, Muslim 15%
Main Languages:	French (official), Sangho , Arabic, Hunsa, Swahili
Int Dial Code:	236
Map Page:	106

CHAD

Capital:	N'Djamena
Area:	1.284 million km²
Population:	9,944,201
Currency:	Communaute Financiere Africaine franc (XAF)
Main Religions:	Muslim 50%, Christian 35%
Main Languages:	French (official), Arabic (official), Sara and Sango, over 100 different languages and dialects
Int Dial Code:	235
Map Page:	100

CHILE

Capital:	Santiago
Area:	756,950 km²
Population:	16,134,219
Currency:	Chilean peso (CLP)
Main Religions:	Roman Catholic 89%, Protestant 11%
Main Languages:	Spanish
Int Dial Code:	56
Map Page:	142

CHINA

Capital:	Beijing
Area:	9,596,960 km²
Population:	1,313,973,713
Currency:	Yuan (CNY)
Main Religions:	Daoist (Taoist), Buddhist, Christian 3-4%, Muslim 1-2%
Main Languages:	Standard Chinese or Mandarin (Putonghua), Yue (Cantonese), Wu (Shanghaiese), Minbei (Fuzhou), Minnan (Hokkien-Taiwanese), Xiang, Gan, Hakka
Int Dial Code:	86
Map Page:	80

COLOMBIA

Capital:	Bogota
Area:	1,138,910 km²
Population:	43,593,035
Currency:	Colombian peso (COP)
Main Religions:	Roman Catholic 90%
Main Languages:	Spanish
Int Dial Code:	57
Map Page:	140

COMOROS

Capital:	Moroni
Area:	2,170 km²
Population:	690,948
Currency:	Comoran franc (KMF)
Main Religions:	Sunni Muslim 98%, Roman Catholic 2%
Main Languages:	Arabic (official), French (official), Comoran
Int Dial Code:	269
Map Page:	109

CONGO

Capital:	Brazzaville
Area:	342,000 km²
Population:	3,702,314
Currency:	Communaute Financiere Africaine franc (XAF)
Main Religions:	Christian 50%, Animist 48%, Muslim 2%
Main Languages:	French (official), Lingala and Monokutuba
Int Dial Code:	242
Map Page:	105

CONGO, DEM. REP. OF THE

Capital:	Kinshasa
Area:	2,345,410 km²
Population:	62,660,551
Currency:	Congolese franc (CDF)
Main Religions:	Roman Catholic 50%, Protestant 20%, Kimbanguist 10%, Muslim 10%, other 10%
Main Languages:	French (official), Lingala, Kingwana, Kikongo, Tshiluba
Int Dial Code:	243
Map Page:	106

COSTA RICA

Capital:	San José
Area:	51,100 km²
Population:	4,075,261
Currency:	Costa Rican colon (CRC)
Main Religions:	Roman Catholic 76.3%, Evangelical 13.7%, other Protestant 0.7%, Jehovah's Witnesses 1.3%,
Main Languages:	Spanish (official), English spoken around Puerto Limon
Int Dial Code:	506
Map Page:	135

COTE D'IVOIRE

Capital:	Yamoussoukro - capital since 1983, Abidjan is the administrative center
Area:	322,460 km²
Population:	17,654,843
Currency:	Communaute Financiere Africaine franc (XOF)
Main Religions:	Muslim 35%, Indigenous 25%, Christian 20%
Main Languages:	French (official), 60 native dialects
Int Dial Code:	225
Map Page:	104

CROATIA

Capital:	Zagreb
Area:	56,542 km²
Population:	4,494,749
Currency:	Kuna (HRK)
Main Religions:	Roman Catholic 87.8%, Orthodox 4.4%,
Main Languages:	Croatian 96%, other 4% (Italian, Hungarian, Czech)
Int Dial Code:	385
Map Page:	66

CUBA

Capital:	Havana
Area:	110,860 km²
Population:	11,382,820
Currency:	Cuban peso (CUP) and convertible Peso (CUC)
Main Religions:	Roman Catholic 85% , Protestants, Jehovah's Witnesses, Jews
Main Languages:	Spanish
Int Dial Code:	53
Map Page:	135

CYPRUS

Capital:	Nicosia
Area:	9,250 km² (3,355 km² in the Turkish Cypriot area)
Population:	784,301
Currency:	Cypriot pound (CYP); Turkish new lira (YTL)
Main Religions:	Greek Orthodox 78%, Muslim 18%,
Main Languages:	Greek, Turkish, English
Int Dial Code:	357
Map Page:	92

CZECH REPUBLIC

Capital:	Prague
Area:	78,866 km²
Population:	10,235,455
Currency:	Czech koruna (CZK)
Main Religions:	Roman Catholic 26.8%, Protestant 2.1%, Orthodox 3%
Main Languages:	Czech
Int Dial Code:	420
Map Page:	51

DENMARK

Capital:	Copenhagen
Area:	43,094 km²
Population:	5,450,661
Currency:	Danish krone (DKK)
Main Religions:	Evangelical Lutheran 95%, other Protestant and Roman Catholic 3%, Muslims 2%
Main Languages:	Danish, Faroese, Greenlandic, German, English
Int Dial Code:	45
Map Page:	49

DJIBOUTI

Capital:	Djibouti
Area:	23,000 km²
Population:	486,530
Currency:	Djiboutian franc (DJF)
Main Religions:	Muslim 94%, Christian 6%
Main Languages:	French (official), Arabic (official), Somali, Afar
Int Dial Code:	253
Map Page:	101

DOMINICA

Capital:	Roseau
Area:	754 km²
Population:	68,910
Currency:	East Caribbean dollar (XCD)
Main Religions:	Roman Catholic 77%, Protestant 15% (Methodist 5%, Pentecostal 3%, Seventh-Day Adventist 3%, Baptist 2%, other 2%), none 2%, other 6%
Main Languages:	English (official), French patois
Int Dial Code:	1 + 767
Map Page:	135

DOMINICAN REPUBLIC

Capital:	Santo Domingo
Area:	48,730 km²
Population:	9,183,984
Currency:	Dominican peso (DOP)
Main Religions:	Roman Catholic 95%
Main Languages:	Spanish
Int Dial Code:	1 + 809
Map Page:	135

EAST TIMOR

Capital:	Dili
Area:	15,007 km²
Population:	1,062,777
Currency:	US dollar
Main Religions:	Roman Catholic, Muslim
Main Languages:	Tetum, Portugese, Indonesian, English
Int Dial Code:	670
Map Page:	87

ECUADOR

Capital:	Quito
Area:	283,560 km²
Population:	13,547,510
Currency:	US dollar (USD)
Main Religions:	Roman Catholic 95%
Main Languages:	Spanish (official), Amerindian languages (especially Quechua)
Int Dial Code:	593
Map Page:	140

EGYPT

Capital:	Cairo
Area:	1,001,450 km²
Population:	78,887,007
Currency:	Egyptian pound (EGP)
Main Religions:	Muslim (mostly Sunni) 90%, Coptic Christian and other 6%
Main Languages:	Arabic (official), English and French
Int Dial Code:	20
Map Page:	100

EL SALVADOR

Capital:	San Salvador
Area:	21,040 km²
Population:	6,822,378
Currency:	Salvadoran colon (SVC); US dollar (USD)
Main Religions:	Roman Catholic 83%
Main Languages:	Spanish, Nahua
Int Dial Code:	503
Map Page:	134

EQUATORIAL GUINEA

Capital:	Malabo
Area:	28,051 km²
Population:	540,109
Currency:	Communaute Financiere Africaine franc (XAF)
Main Religions:	Christian (predominantly Roman Catholic)
Main Languages:	Spanish (official), French (official), Pidgin English, Fang, Bubi, Ibo
Int Dial Code:	240
Map Page:	105

ERITREA

Capital:	Asmara
Area:	121,320 km²
Population:	4,786,994
Currency:	Nakfa (ERN)
Main Religions:	Muslim, Coptic Christian, Roman Catholic, Protestant
Main Languages:	Afar, Amharic, Arabic, Tigre and Kunama, Tigrinya, other Cushitic languages
Int Dial Code:	291
Map Page:	101

ESTONIA

Capital:	Tallinn
Area:	45,226 km²
Population:	1,324,333
Currency:	Estonian kroon (EEK)
Main Religions:	Evangelical Lutheran, Russian Orthodox, Estonian Orthodox, Baptist, Methodist, Seventh-Day Adventist
Main Languages:	Estonian (official), Russian, Ukrainian, English, Finnish
Int Dial Code:	372
Map Page:	49

ETHIOPIA

Capital:	Addis Ababa
Area:	1,127,127 km2
Population:	74,777,981
Currency:	Birr (ETB)
Main Religions:	Muslim 45%-50%, Ethiopian Orthodox 35%-40%, animist 12%, other 3%-8%
Main Languages:	Amharic, Tigrinya, Oromigna, Guaragigna, Somali, Arabic, English
Int Dial Code:	251
Map Page:	107

FIJI

Capital:	Suva
Area:	18,270 km²
Population:	905,949
Currency:	Fijian dollar (FJD)
Main Religions:	Christian 52% (Methodist 37%, Roman Catholic 9%), Hindu 38%, Muslim 8%, other 2%
Main Languages:	English (official), Fijian, Hindustani
Int Dial Code:	679
Map Page:	112

FINLAND

Capital:	Helsinki
Area:	338,145 km²
Population:	5,231,372
Currency:	Euro (EUR)
Main Religions:	Evangelical Lutheran 89%, Greek Orthodox 1%, none 9%, other 1%
Main Languages:	Finnish 93.4% (official), Swedish 5.9% (official), small Lapp- and Russian-speaking minorities
Int Dial Code:	358
Map Page:	48

FRANCE

Capital:	Paris
Area:	547,030 km²
Population:	60,876,136
Currency:	Euro (EUR)
Main Religions:	Roman Catholic 90%, Protestant 2%, Jewish 1%, Muslim 3%, unaffiliated 4%
Main Languages:	French 100%, Provencal, Breton, Alsatian, Corsican, Catalan, Basque, Flemish
Int Dial Code:	33
Map Page:	58

GABON

Capital:	Libreville
Area:	267,667 km²
Population:	1,424,906
Currency:	Communaute Financiere Africaine franc (XAF)
Main Religions:	Christian 55%-75%, Animist, Muslim less than 1%
Main Languages:	French (official), Fang, Myene, Bapounou/Eschira, Bandjabi
Int Dial Code:	241
Map Page:	105

GAMBIA, THE

Capital:	Banjul
Area:	11,300 km²
Population:	1,641,564
Currency:	Dalasi (GMD)
Main Religions:	Muslim 90%, Christian 9%, Indigenous beliefs 1%
Main Languages:	English (official), Mandinka, Wolof, Fula
Int Dial Code:	220
Map Page:	104

GEORGIA

Capital:	T'bilisi
Area:	69,700 km²
Population:	4,661,473
Currency:	Lari (GEL)
Main Religions:	Georgian Orthodox 65%, Muslim 11%, Russian Orthodox 10%, Armenian Apostolic 8%
Main Languages:	Georgian 71% (official), Russian 9%, Armenian 7%,
Int Dial Code:	995
Map Page:	93

GERMANY

Capital:	Berlin
Area:	357,021 km²
Population:	82,422,299
Currency:	Euro (EUR)
Main Religions:	Protestant 34%, Roman Catholic 34%, Muslim 3.7%, unaffiliated or other 28.3%
Main Languages:	German
Int Dial Code:	49
Map Page:	52

GHANA

Capital:	Accra
Area:	239,460 km²
Population:	22,409,572
Currency:	Cedi (GHC)
Main Religions:	Indigenous beliefs 38%, Muslim 30%, Christian 24%, other 8%
Main Languages:	English (official), African languages (Akan, Moshi-Dagomba, Ewe, and Ga)
Int Dial Code:	233
Map Page:	104

GREECE

Capital:	Athens
Area:	131,940 km²
Population:	10,688,058
Currency:	Euro (EUR)
Main Religions:	Greek Orthodox 98%, Muslim 1.3%, other 0.7%
Main Languages:	Greek 99% (official), English, French
Int Dial Code:	30
Map Page:	68

GRENADA

Capital:	Saint George's
Area:	344 km²
Population:	89,703
Currency:	East Caribbean dollar (XCD)
Main Religions:	Roman Catholic 53%, Anglican 13.8%, other Protestant 33.2%
Main Languages:	English (official), French patois
Int Dial Code:	1 + 473
Map Page:	135

GUATEMALA

Capital:	Guatemala
Area:	108,890 km²
Population:	12,293,545
Currency:	Quetzal (GTQ), US dollar (USD), others allowed
Main Religions:	Roman Catholic, Protestant, Indigenous Mayan beliefs
Main Languages:	Spanish 60%, Amerindian languages 40%
Int Dial Code:	502
Map Page:	134

GUINEA

Capital:	Conakry
Area:	245,857 km²
Population:	9,690,222
Currency:	Guinean franc (GNF)
Main Religions:	Muslim 85%, Christian 8%, Indigenous beliefs 7%
Main Languages:	French (official), each ethnic group has its own language
Int Dial Code:	224
Map Page:	104

GUINEA-BISSAU

Capital:	Bissau
Area:	36,120 km²
Population:	1,442,029
Currency:	Communaute Financiere Africaine franc (XOF)
Main Religions:	Indigenous beliefs 50%, Muslim 45%, Christian 5%
Main Languages:	Portuguese (official), Crioulo, African languages
Int Dial Code:	245
Map Page:	104

GUYANA

Capital:	Georgetown
Area:	214,970 km²
Population:	767,245
Currency:	Guyanese dollar (GYD)
Main Religions:	Christian 50%, Hindu 35%, Muslim 10%, other 5%
Main Languages:	English, Amerindian dialects, Creole, Hindi, Urdu
Int Dial Code:	592
Map Page:	141

HAITI

Capital:	Port-au-Prince
Area:	27,750 km²
Population:	8,308,504
Currency:	Gourde (HTG)
Main Religions:	Roman Catholic 80%, Protestant 16% (Baptist 10%, Pentecostal 4%, Adventist 1%, other 1%)
Main Languages:	French (official), Creole (official)
Int Dial Code:	509
Map Page:	135

HONDURAS

Capital:	Tegucigalpa
Area:	112,090 km²
Population:	7,326,496
Currency:	Lempira (HNL)
Main Religions:	Roman Catholic 97%, Protestant
Main Languages:	Spanish, Amerindian dialects
Int Dial Code:	504
Map Page:	134

HUNGARY

Capital:	Budapest
Area:	93,030 km²
Population:	9,981,334
Currency:	Forint (HUF)
Main Languages:	Hungarian 98.2%, other 1.8%
Int Dial Code:	36
Map Page:	66

ICELAND

Capital:	Reykjavik
Area:	103,000 km²
Population:	299,388
Currency:	Icelandic krona (ISK)
Main Languages:	Icelandic
Int Dial Code:	354
Map Page:	48

INDIA

Capital:	New Delhi
Area:	3,287,590 km²
Population:	1,095,351,995
Currency:	Indian rupee (INR)
Main Religions:	Hindu 80.5%, Muslim 13.4%, Christian 2.3%, Sikh 1.9%,Buddhist, Jain, Parsi 2.5%
Main Languages:	English, Hindi 30%, Bengali, Telugu, Marathi, Tamil, Urdu, Gujarati, Malayalam, Kannada, Oriya, Punjabi
Int Dial Code:	91
Map Page:	88

INDONESIA

Capital:	Jakarta
Area:	1,919,440 km²
Population:	245,452,739
Currency:	Indonesian rupiah (IDR)
Main Religions:	Muslim 88%, Protestant 5%, Roman Catholic 3%, Hindu 2%, Buddhist 1%, other 1%
Main Languages:	Bahasa Indonesia (official), English, Dutch, local dialects
Int Dial Code:	62
Map Page:	86

IRAN

Capital:	Tehran
Area:	1.648 million km²
Population:	68,688,433
Currency:	Iranian rial (IRR)
Main Religions:	Shi'a Muslim 89%, Sunni Muslim 10%, Zoroastrian, Jewish, Christian, Baha'i 1%
Main Languages:	Persian and Persian dialects 58%, Turkic and Turkic dialects 26%, Kurdish 9%, Luri 2%, Balochi 1%
Int Dial Code:	98
Map Page:	90

IRAQ

Capital:	Baghdad
Area:	437,072 km²
Population:	26,783,383
Currency:	New Iraqi dinar (NID)
Main Religions:	Muslim 97% (Shi'a 60%-65%, Sunni 32%-37%), Christian or other 3%
Main Languages:	Arabic, Kurdish, Assyrian, Armenian
Int Dial Code:	964
Map Page:	90

IRELAND

Capital:	Dublin
Area:	70,280 km²
Population:	4,062,235
Currency:	Euro (EUR)
Main Religions:	Roman Catholic 88.4%, Church of Ireland 3%
Main Languages:	English, Irish (Gaelic)
Int Dial Code:	353
Map Page:	57

ISRAEL

Capital:	Jerusalem
Area:	20,770 km²
Population:	6,352,117
Currency:	New Israeli shekel (ILS or NIS)
Main Religions:	Jewish 76.5%, Muslim 15.9%, Arab Christian 1.7%
Main Languages:	Hebrew (official), Arabic, English
Int Dial Code:	972
Map Page:	94

ITALY

Capital:	Rome
Area:	301,230 km²
Population:	58,133,509
Currency:	Euro (EUR)
Main Religions:	predominately Roman Catholic, Protestant, Jewish and Muslim
Main Languages:	Italian (official), German, French, Slovene
Int Dial Code:	39
Map Page:	64

JAMAICA

Capital:	Kingston
Area:	10,990 km²
Population:	2,758,124
Currency:	Jamaican dollar (JMD)
Main Religions:	Protestant 61.3%, Roman Catholic 4%, other 34.7%
Main Languages:	English, Creole
Int Dial Code:	1 + 876
Map Page:	135

JAPAN

Capital:	Tokyo
Area:	377,835 km²
Population:	127,463,611
Currency:	Yen (JPY)
Main Religions:	Shinto and Buddhist 84%, other 16% (including Christian 0.7%)
Main Languages:	Japanese
Int Dial Code:	81
Map Page:	83

JORDAN

Capital:	Amman
Area:	92,300 km²
Population:	5,906,760
Currency:	Jordanian dinar (JOD)
Main Religions:	Sunni Muslim 92%, Christian 6% (majority Greek Orthodox), other 2%
Main Languages:	Arabic (official), English
Int Dial Code:	962
Map Page:	94

KAZAKHSTAN

Capital:	Astana
Area:	2,717,300 km²
Population:	15,233,244
Currency:	Tenge (KZT)
Main Religions:	Muslim 47%, Russian Orthodox 44%, Protestant 2%, other 7%
Main Languages:	Kazakh (Qazaq, state language), Russian (official)
Int Dial Code:	7
Map Page:	77

KENYA

Capital:	Nairobi
Area:	582,650 km²
Population:	34,707,817
Currency:	Kenyan shilling (KES)
Main Religions:	Protestant 45%, Roman Catholic 33%, indigenous beliefs 10%, Muslim 10%
Main Languages:	English (official), Kiswahili (official)
Int Dial Code:	254
Map Page:	107

KIRIBATI

Capital:	Tarawa
Area:	811 km²
Population:	105,432
Currency:	Australian dollar (AUD)
Main Religions:	Roman Catholic 54%, Protestant (Congregational) 30%, Seventh-Day Adventist, Baha'i, Latter-day Saints and Church of God
Main Languages:	English (official), I-Kiribati
Int Dial Code:	686
Map Page:	113

KUWAIT

Capital:	Kuwait
Area:	17,820 km²
Population:	2,418,393
Currency:	Kuwaiti dinar (KD)
Main Religions:	Muslim 85% (Sunni 70%, Shi'a 30%), Christian, Hindu, Parsi, and other 15%
Main Languages:	Arabic (official), English
Int Dial Code:	965
Map Page:	95

KYRGYZSTAN

Capital:	Bishkek
Area:	198,500 km²
Population:	5,213,898
Currency:	Kyrgyzstani som (KGS)
Main Religions:	Muslim 75%, Russian Orthodox 20%, other 5%
Main Languages:	Kirghiz (Kyrgyz) - official, Russian (official)
Int Dial Code:	996
Map Page:	77

LAOS

Capital:	Vientiane
Area:	236,800 km²
Population:	6,368,481
Currency:	Kip (LAK)
Main Religions:	Buddhist 60%, Animist and other 40%
Main Languages:	Lao (official), French, English
Int Dial Code:	856
Map Page:	84

LATVIA

Capital:	Riga
Area:	64,589 km²
Population:	2,274,735
Currency:	Latvian lat (LVL)
Main Religions:	Lutheran, Roman Catholic, Russian Orthodox
Main Languages:	Latvian or Lettish (official), Lithuanian, Russian
Int Dial Code:	371
Map Page:	49

LEBANON

Capital:	Beirut
Area:	10,400 km²
Population:	3,874,050
Currency:	Lebanese pound (LBP)
Main Religions:	Muslim 59.7% (including Shi'a, Sunni, Druze, Isma'ilite, Alawite or Nusayri), Christian 39% (including Orthodox Christian, Catholic, Protestant)
Main Languages:	Arabic (official), French, English, Armenian
Int Dial Code:	961
Map Page:	94

LESOTHO

Capital:	Maseru
Area:	30,355 km²
Population:	2,022,331
Currency:	Loti (LSL); South African Rand (ZAR)
Main Religions:	Christian 80%, Indigenous beliefs 20%
Main Languages:	Sesotho (southern Sotho), English (official), Zulu, Xhosa
Int Dial Code:	266
Map Page:	108

LIBERIA

Capital:	Monrovia
Area:	111,370 km²
Population:	3,042,004
Currency:	Liberian dollar (LRD)
Main Religions:	Indigenous beliefs 40%, Christian 40%, Muslim 20%
Main Languages:	English 20% (official), ethnic group languages
Int Dial Code:	231
Map Page:	104

LIBYA

Capital:	Tripoli
Area:	1,759,540 km²
Population:	5,900,754
Currency:	Libyan dinar (LYD)
Main Religions:	Sunni Muslim 97%
Main Languages:	Arabic, Italian, English
Int Dial Code:	218
Map Page:	100

LIECHTENSTEIN

Capital:	Vaduz
Area:	160 km²
Population:	33,987
Currency:	Swiss franc (CHF)
Main Religions:	Roman Catholic 80%, Protestant 7.4%, unknown 7.7%, other 4.9%
Main Languages:	German (official), Alemannic dialect
Int Dial Code:	423
Map Page:	62

LITHUANIA

Capital:	Vilnius
Area:	65,200 km²
Population:	3,585,906
Currency:	Litas (LTL)
Main Religions:	Roman Catholic (primarily), Lutheran, Russian Orthodox, Protestant, Evangelical Christian Baptist, Muslim, Jewish
Main Languages:	Lithuanian (official), Polish, Russian
Int Dial Code:	370
Map Page:	49

LUXEMBOURG

Capital:	Luxembourg
Area:	2,586 km²
Population:	474,413
Currency:	Euro (EUR)
Main Religions:	Roman Catholic with Protestants, Jews, and Muslims
Main Languages:	Luxembourgish (national language), German (administrative language), French
Int Dial Code:	352
Map Page:	55

MACEDONIA

Capital:	Skopje
Area:	25,333 km²
Population:	2,050,554
Currency:	Macedonian denar (MKD)
Main Religions:	Macedonian Orthodox 67%, Muslim 30%, other 3%
Main Languages:	Macedonian 70%, Albanian 21%, Turkish 3%, Serbo-Croatian 3%, other 3%
Int Dial Code:	389
Map Page:	68

MADAGASCAR

Capital:	Antananarivo
Area:	587,040 km²
Population:	18,595,469
Currency:	Madagascar Ariary (MGA)
Main Religions:	Indigenous beliefs 52%, Christian 41%, Muslim 7%
Main Languages:	French (official), Malagasy (official)
Int Dial Code:	261
Map Page:	109

MALAWI

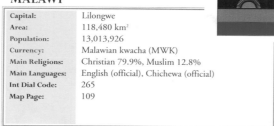

Capital:	Lilongwe
Area:	118,480 km²
Population:	13,013,926
Currency:	Malawian kwacha (MWK)
Main Religions:	Christian 79.9%, Muslim 12.8%
Main Languages:	English (official), Chichewa (official)
Int Dial Code:	265
Map Page:	109

MALAYSIA

Capital:	Kuala Lumpur; Putrajaya is the federal government administration centre
Area:	329,750 km²
Population:	24,385,858
Currency:	Ringgit (MYR)
Main Religions:	Muslim, Budhist, Duoist, Hindu, Christian, Sikh, Shamanism
Main Languages:	Bahasa Melayu (official), English, Chinese dialects (Cantonese, Mandarin, Hokkien, Hakka, Hainan, Foochow), Tamil, Telugu, Malayalam, Panjabi, Thai
Int Dial Code:	60
Map Page:	86

MALDIVES

Capital:	Male
Area:	300 km²
Population:	359,008
Currency:	Rufiyaa (MVR)
Main Religions:	Sunni Muslim
Main Languages:	Maldivian Dhivehi (dialect of Sinhala, script derived from Arabic), English
Int Dial Code:	960
Map Page:	89

MALI

Capital:	Bamako
Area:	1.24 million km²
Population:	11,716,829
Currency:	Communaute Financiere Africaine franc (XOF)
Main Religions:	Muslim 90%, Indigenous beliefs 9%, Christian 1%
Main Languages:	French (official), Bambara 80%, numerous African languages
Int Dial Code:	223
Map Page:	102

MALTA

Capital:	Valletta
Area:	316 km²
Population:	400,214
Currency:	Maltese lira (MTL)
Main Religions:	Roman Catholic 98%
Main Languages:	Maltese (official), English (official)
Int Dial Code:	356
Map Page:	65

MARSHALL ISLANDS

Capital:	Majuro
Area:	181 km²
Population:	60,422
Currency:	US dollar (USD)
Main Religions:	Christian (mostly Protestant)
Main Languages:	English (official), two major Marshallese dialects from the Malayo-Polynesian family, Japanese
Int Dial Code:	692
Map Page:	112

MAURITANIA

Capital:	Nouakchott
Area:	1,030,700 km²
Population:	3,177,388
Currency:	Ouguiya (MRO)
Main Religions:	Muslim 100%
Main Languages:	Hasaniya Arabic (official), Pulaar, Soninke, Wolof, French
Int Dial Code:	222
Map Page:	102

MAURITIUS

Capital:	Port Louis
Area:	2,040 km²
Population:	1,240,827
Currency:	Mauritian rupee (MUR)
Main Religions:	Hindu 48%, Roman Catholic 23.6%, Muslim 16.6%, other christian 8.6%
Main Languages:	English (official), Creole, French, Hindi, Urdu, Hakka, Bojpoori
Int Dial Code:	230
Map Page:	109

MONTENEGRO

Capital:	Podgorica
Area:	14,026 km²
Population:	630,548
Currency:	Euro (EUR)
Main Religions:	Orthodox, Muslim, Roman Catholic
Main Languages:	Serbian, Montenegrin
Int Dial Code:	381 (shared with Serbia - new code expected)
Map Page:	66

MEXICO

Capital:	Mexico
Area:	1,972,550 km²
Population:	107,449,525
Currency:	Mexican peso (MXN):
Main Religions:	Nominally Roman Catholic 89%, Protestant 6%, other 5%
Main Languages:	Spanish, Mayan, Nahuatl
Int Dial Code:	52
Map Page:	134

MOROCCO

Capital:	Rabat
Area:	446,550 km²
Population:	33,241,259
Currency:	Moroccan dirham (MAD)
Main Religions:	Muslim 98.7%, Christian 1.1%, Jewish 0.2%
Main Languages:	Arabic (official), Berber dialects, French
Int Dial Code:	212
Map Page:	102

MICRONESIA, FED. STATES OF

Capital:	Palikir
Area:	702 km²
Population:	108,004
Currency:	US dollar (USD)
Main Religions:	Roman Catholic 50%, Protestant 47%, other 3%
Main Languages:	English (official), Trukese, Pohnpeian, Yapese, Kosrean
Int Dial Code:	691
Map Page:	112

MOZAMBIQUE

Capital:	Maputo
Area:	801,590 km²
Population:	19,686,505
Currency:	Metical (MZM)
Main Religions:	Catholic 23.8%, Muslim 17.8%, Zionist Christian 17.5%
Main Languages:	Portuguese (official), indigenous dialects
Int Dial Code:	258
Map Page:	109

MOLDOVA

Capital:	Chisinau
Area:	33,843 km²
Population:	4,466,706
Currency:	Moldovan leu (MDL)
Main Religions:	Eastern Orthodox 98.5%, Jewish 1.5%, Baptist
Main Languages:	Moldovan (official), Russian, Gagauz (a Turkish dialect)
Int Dial Code:	373
Map Page:	67

MYANMAR (BURMA)

Capital:	Naypyidaw
Area:	678,500 km²
Population:	47,382,633
Currency:	Kyat (MMK)
Main Religions:	Buddhist 89%, Christian 4% (Baptist 3%, Roman Catholic 1%), Muslim 4%, Animist 1%, other 2%
Main Languages:	Burmese
Int Dial Code:	95
Map Page:	84

MONACO

Capital:	Monaco
Area:	1.95 km²
Population:	32,543
Currency:	Euro (EUR)
Main Religions:	Roman Catholic 90%
Main Languages:	French (official), English, Italian, Monegasque
Int Dial Code:	377
Map Page:	62

NAMIBIA

Capital:	Windhoek
Area:	825,418 km²
Population:	2,044,147
Currency:	Namibian dollar (NAD); South African rand (ZAR)
Main Religions:	Christian 80% - 90% (Lutheran 50%), Indigenous beliefs 10%-20%
Main Languages:	English 7% (official), Afrikaans, German 32%, indigenous languages: Oshivambo, Herero, Nama
Int Dial Code:	264
Map Page:	108

MONGOLIA

Capital:	Ulaanbaatar
Area:	1.565 million km²
Population:	2,832,224
Currency:	Togrog/tugrik (MNT)
Main Religions:	Buddhist Lamaism 50%, Muslim, Shamanism, and Christian
Main Languages:	Khalkha Mongol 90%, Turkic, Russian
Int Dial Code:	976
Map Page:	75

NAURU

Capital:	no official capital; government offices in Yaren District
Area:	21 km²
Population:	13,287
Currency:	Australian dollar (AUD)
Main Religions:	Christian (66% Protestant, 33% Roman Catholic)
Main Languages:	Nauruan (official), English
Int Dial Code:	674
Map Page:	112

NEPAL

Capital:	Kathmandu
Area:	147,181 km²
Population:	28,287,147
Currency:	Nepalese rupee (NPR)
Main Religions:	Hinduism 80.6%, Buddhism 10.7%, Muslim 4.2%
Main Languages:	Nepali (official; spoken by 90% of the population), 30 major dialects, English
Int Dial Code:	977
Map Page:	88

NETHERLANDS

Capital:	Amsterdam; The Hague is the seat of government
Area:	41,526 km²
Population:	16,491,461
Currency:	Euro (EUR)
Main Religions:	Roman Catholic 31%, Protestant 21%, Muslim 4.4%, other 3.6%, unaffiliated 40%
Main Languages:	Dutch
Int Dial Code:	31
Map Page:	55

NEW ZEALAND

Capital:	Wellington
Area:	268,680 km²
Population:	4,076,140
Currency:	New Zealand dollar (NZD)
Main Religions:	Anglican 14.9%, Roman Catholic 12.4%, Presbyterian 10.9%, Methodist 2.9%,
Main Languages:	English (official), Maori (official)
Int Dial Code:	64
Map Page:	116

NICARAGUA

Capital:	Managua
Area:	129,494 km²
Population:	5,570,129
Currency:	Gold cordoba (NIO)
Main Religions:	Roman Catholic 72.9%, Evangelical 15.1%
Main Languages:	Spanish (official)
Int Dial Code:	505
Map Page:	135

NIGER

Capital:	Niamey
Area:	1.267 million km²
Population:	12,525,094
Currency:	Communaute Financiere Africaine franc (XOF)
Main Religions:	Muslim 80%, Indigenous beliefs and Christians
Main Languages:	French (official), Hausa, Djerma
Int Dial Code:	227
Map Page:	103

NIGERIA

Capital:	Abuja
Area:	923,768 km²
Population:	131,859,731
Currency:	Naira (NGN)
Main Religions:	Muslim 50%, Christian 40%, Indigenous beliefs 10%
Main Languages:	English (official), Hausa, Yoruba, Igbo (Ibo), Fulani
Int Dial Code:	234
Map Page:	105

NORTH KOREA

Capital:	P'yongyang
Area:	120,540 km²
Population:	23,113,019
Currency:	North Korean won (KPW)
Main Religions:	Buddhist and Confucianist, some Christian and syncretic Chondogyo (Religion of the Heavenly Way)
Main Languages:	Korean
Int Dial Code:	850
Map Page:	82

NORWAY

Capital:	Oslo
Area:	324,220 km²
Population:	4,610,820
Currency:	Norwegian krone (NOK)
Main Religions:	Church of Norway 85.7%, Roman Catholic 2.4%, Muslim 1.8%, Pentecostal 1%, other christian 2.4%
Main Languages:	Norwegian (official)
Int Dial Code:	47
Map Page:	48

OMAN

Capital:	Muscat
Area:	212,460 km²
Population:	3,102,229
Currency:	Omani rial (OMR)
Main Religions:	Ibadhi Muslim 75%, Sunni Muslim, Shi'a Muslim, Hindu
Main Languages:	Arabic (official), English, Baluchi, Urdu, Indian dialects
Int Dial Code:	968
Map Page:	91

PAKISTAN

Capital:	Islamabad
Area:	803,940 km²
Population:	165,803,560
Currency:	Pakistani rupee (PKR)
Main Religions:	Muslim 97% (Sunni 77%, Shi'a 20%)
Main Languages:	Punjabi 48%, Sindhi 12%, Siraiki 10%, Pashtu 8%, Urdu 8%, Balochi 3%, Hindko 2%, Brahui 1%
Int Dial Code:	92
Map Page:	91

PALAU

Capital:	Koror
Area:	458 km²
Population:	20,579
Currency:	US dollar (USD)
Main Religions:	Christian (Catholics, Seventh-Day Adventists, Jehovah's Witnesses, Assembly of God, the Liebenzell Mission, and Latter-Day Saints), Modekngei 33%
Main Languages:	English and Palauan, Tobi and Angaur
Int Dial Code:	680
Map Page:	112

PANAMA

Capital:	Panama
Area:	78,200 km²
Population:	3,191,319
Currency:	Balboa (PAB); US dollar (USD)
Main Religions:	Roman Catholic 85%, Protestant 15%
Main Languages:	Spanish (official), English 14%
Int Dial Code:	507
Map Page:	135

PAPUA NEW GUINEA

Capital:	Port Moresby
Area:	462,840 km²
Population:	5,670,544
Currency:	Kina (PGK)
Main Religions:	Roman Catholic 22%, Lutheran 16%, Presbyterian/Methodist/London Missionary Society 8%, Anglican 5%, Protestant 10%, Indigenous beliefs 34%
Main Languages:	English, Pidgin English, Motu
Int Dial Code:	675
Map Page:	112

PARAGUAY

Capital:	Asuncion
Area:	406,750 km²
Population:	6,506,464
Currency:	Guarani (PYG)
Main Religions:	Roman Catholic 90%, Mennonite, and other Protestant
Main Languages:	Spanish (official), Guarani (official)
Int Dial Code:	595
Map Page:	142

PERU

Capital:	Lima
Area:	1,285,220 km²
Population:	28,302,603
Currency:	Nuevo sol (PEN)
Main Religions:	Roman Catholic 90%
Main Languages:	Spanish (official), Quechua (official), Aymara
Int Dial Code:	51
Map Page:	140

PHILIPPINES

Capital:	Manila
Area:	300,000 km²
Population:	89,468,677
Currency:	Philippine peso (PHP)
Main Religions:	Roman Catholic 83%, Protestant 9%, Muslim 5%
Main Languages:	Filipino, English, eight major dialects including Tagalog, Cebuano, Ilocan, Hiligaynon or Ilonggo and Bicol
Int Dial Code:	63
Map Page:	85

POLAND

Capital:	Warsaw
Area:	312,685 km²
Population:	38,536,869
Currency:	Zloty (PLN)
Main Religions:	Roman Catholic 95%, Eastern Orthodox, Protestant, and other 5%
Main Languages:	Polish
Int Dial Code:	48
Map Page:	50

PORTUGAL

Capital:	Lisbon
Area:	92,391 km²
Population:	10,605,870
Currency:	Euro (EUR)
Main Religions:	Roman Catholic 94%, Protestant
Main Languages:	Portuguese, Mirandese
Int Dial Code:	351
Map Page:	60

QATAR

Capital:	Doha
Area:	11,437 km²
Population:	885,359
Currency:	Qatari rial (QAR)
Main Religions:	Muslim 95%
Main Languages:	Arabic (official), English
Int Dial Code:	974
Map Page:	95

ROMANIA

Capital:	Bucharest
Area:	237,500 km²
Population:	22,303,552
Currency:	Leu (RON)
Main Religions:	Eastern Orthodox 86.8%, Protestant 7.5%, Roman Catholic 4.7%
Main Languages:	Romanian, Hungarian, German
Int Dial Code:	40
Map Page:	67

RUSSIAN FEDERATION

Capital:	Moscow
Area:	17,075,200 km²
Population:	142,893,540
Currency:	Russian ruble (RUR)
Main Religions:	Russian Orthodox, Muslim
Main Languages:	Russian
Int Dial Code:	7
Map Page:	74

RWANDA

Capital:	Kigali
Area:	26,338 km²
Population:	8,648,248
Currency:	Rwandan franc (RWF):
Main Religions:	Roman Catholic 52.7%, Protestant 24%, Adventist 10.4%, Muslim 1.9%, Indigenous beliefs 6.5%
Main Languages:	Kinyarwanda, Bantu vernacular, French, English
Int Dial Code:	250
Map Page:	106

SAINT KITTS AND NEVIS

Capital:	Basseterre
Area:	261 km² (Saint Kitts 168 km²; Nevis 93 km²)
Population:	39,129
Currency:	East Caribbean dollar (XCD)
Main Religions:	Anglican, other Protestant, Roman Catholic
Main Languages:	English
Int Dial Code:	1 + 869
Map Page:	135

SAINT LUCIA

Capital:	Castries
Area:	616 km²
Population:	168,458
Currency:	East Caribbean dollar (XCD)
Main Religions:	Roman Catholic 67.5%, Seventh Day Adventist 8.5%, Pentecostal 5.7%, Anglican 2%, Evangelical 2%
Main Languages:	English (official), French patois
Int Dial Code:	1 + 758
Map Page:	135

SAINT VINCENT & THE GRENADINES

Capital:	Kingstown
Area:	389 km² (Saint Vincent 344 km²)
Population:	117,848
Currency:	East Caribbean dollar (XCD)
Main Religions:	Anglican 47%, Methodist 28%, Roman Catholic 13%, Seventh-Day Adventist, Hindu, other Protestant
Main Languages:	English, French patois
Int Dial Code:	1 + 784
Map Page:	135

SAMOA

Capital:	Apia
Area:	2,944 km²
Population:	176,908
Currency:	Tala (SAT)
Main Religions:	Christian 99.7% (London Missionary Society; includes Congregational, Roman Catholic, Methodist, Latter-Day Saints, Seventh-Day Adventist)
Main Languages:	Samoan (Polynesian), English
Int Dial Code:	685
Map Page:	113

SAN MARINO

Capital:	San Marino
Area:	61.2 km²
Population:	29,251
Currency:	Euro (EUR)
Main Religions:	Roman Catholic
Main Languages:	Italian
Int Dial Code:	378
Map Page:	63

SÃO TOMÉ AND PRÍNCIPE

Capital:	São Tomé
Area:	1,001 km²
Population:	193,413
Currency:	Dobra (STD)
Main Religions:	Christian 80% (Roman Catholic, Evangelical Protestant, Seventh-Day Adventist)
Main Languages:	Portuguese (official)
Int Dial Code:	239
Map Page:	105

SAUDI ARABIA

Capital:	Riyadh
Area:	1,960,582 km²
Population:	27,019,731
Currency:	Saudi riyal (SAR)
Main Religions:	Muslim 100%
Main Languages:	Arabic
Int Dial Code:	966
Map Page:	90

SENEGAL

Capital:	Dakar
Area:	196,190 km²
Population:	11,987,121
Currency:	Communaute Financiere Africaine franc (XOF)
Main Religions:	Muslim 92%, Indigenous beliefs 6%, Christian 2% (mostly Roman Catholic)
Main Languages:	French (official), Wolof, Pulaar, Jola, Mandinka
Int Dial Code:	221
Map Page:	104

SERBIA

Capital:	Belgrade
Area:	88,361 km²
Population:	9,396,411
Currency:	New Yugoslav dinar (YUM)
Main Religions:	Serbian Orthodox, Muslim, Roman Catholic, Protestant
Main Languages:	Serbian (official), Romanian, Hungarian, Slovak, Croatian, Albania
Int Dial Code:	381
Map Page:	66

SEYCHELLES

Capital	Victoria
Area:	455 km²
Population:	81,541
Currency:	Seychelles rupee (SCR)
Main Religions:	Roman Catholic 90%, Anglican 8%, other 2%
Main Languages:	English (official), French (official), Creole
Int Dial Code:	248
Map Page:	109

SIERRA LEONE

Capital:	Freetown
Area:	71,740 km²
Population:	6,005,250
Currency:	Leone (SLL)
Main Religions:	Muslim 60%, indigenous beliefs 30%, Christian 10%
Main Languages:	English (official), Mende, Temne, Krio (English-based Creole)
Int Dial Code:	232
Map Page:	104

SINGAPORE

Capital:	Singapore
Area:	692.7 km²
Population:	4,492,150
Currency:	Singapore dollar (SGD)
Main Religions:	Buddhist (Chinese), Muslim (Malays), Christian, Hindu, Sikh, Taoist, Confucianist
Main Languages:	Chinese (official), Malay (official and national), Tamil (official), English (official)
Int Dial Code:	65
Map Page:	86

SLOVAKIA

Capital:	Bratislava
Area:	48,845 km²
Population:	5,439,448
Currency:	Slovak koruna (SKK)
Main Religions:	Roman Catholic 60.3%, Atheist 9.7%, Protestant 8.4%, Orthodox 4.1%, other 17.5%
Main Languages:	Slovak (official), Hungarian
Int Dial Code:	421
Map Page:	51

SLOVENIA

Capital:	Ljubljana
Area:	20,273 km²
Population:	2,010,347
Currency:	Tolar (SIT)
Main Religions:	Catholic 57.8%, Muslim 2.4%, Orthodox 2.3%, other christian 0.9%
Main Languages:	Slovenian 91%, Serbo-Croatian 6%, other 3%
Int Dial Code:	386
Map Page:	63

SOLOMON ISLANDS

Capital:	Honiara
Area:	28,450 km²
Population:	552,438
Currency:	Solomon Islands dollar (SBD)
Main Religions:	Church of Melanesia 32.8%, Roman Catholic 19%, South Sea Evangelical 17%, Seventh Day Adventist 11.2%, United Church 10.3%, Christian Fellowship Church 2.4%, other christian 4.4%
Int Dial Code:	677
Map Page:	112

SOMALIA

Capital:	Mogadishu
Area:	637,657 km²
Population:	8,863,338
Currency:	Somali shilling (SOS)
Main Religions:	Sunni Muslim
Main Languages:	Somali (official), Arabic, Italian, English
Int Dial Code:	252
Map Page:	107

SURINAME

Capital:	Paramaribo
Area:	163,270 km²
Population:	439,117
Currency:	Surinamese guilder (SRG)
Main Religions:	Hindu 27.4%, Muslim 19.6%, Roman Catholic 22.8%, Protestant 25.2%, Indigenous beliefs 5%
Main Languages:	Dutch (official), English, Sranang Tongo, Hindustani, Javanese
Int Dial Code:	597
Map Page:	141

SOUTH AFRICA, REPUBLIC OF

Capital:	Pretoria (executive); Bloemfontein (judicial); Cape Town (legislative)
Area:	1,219,912 km²
Population:	44,187,637
Currency:	Rand (ZAR)
Main Religions:	Christian 68%, Muslim 2%, Hindu 1.5%, Indigenous beliefs and Animist 28.5%
Main Languages:	IsiZulu, IsiXhosa, Afrikaans, Sepedi, English, Setswana, Sesotho, Xitsonga
Int Dial Code:	27
Map Page:	108

SWAZILAND

Capital:	Mbabane; Lobamba is the royal and legislative capital
Area:	17,363 km²
Population:	1,136,334
Currency:	Lilangeni (SZL)
Main Religions:	Zionist 40%, Roman Catholic 20%, Muslim 10%, Anglican, Bahai, Methodist, Mormon, Jewish
Main Languages:	English (official), Swati (official)
Int Dial Code:	268
Map Page:	109

SOUTH KOREA

Capital:	Seoul
Area:	98,480 km²
Population:	48,846,823
Currency:	South Korean Won (KRW)
Main Religions:	Christian 26%, Buddhist 26%, Confucianist 1%
Main Languages:	Korean, English
Int Dial Code:	82
Map Page:	82

SWEDEN

Capital:	Stockholm
Area:	449,964 km²
Population:	9,016,596
Currency:	Swedish krona (SEK)
Main Religions:	Lutheran 87%, Roman Catholic, Orthodox, Baptist, Muslim, Jewish, Buddhist
Main Languages:	Swedish
Int Dial Code:	46
Map Page:	48

SPAIN

Capital:	Madrid
Area:	504,782 km²
Population:	40,397,842
Currency:	Euro (EUR)
Main Religions:	Roman Catholic 94%, other 6%
Main Languages:	Castilian Spanish (official) 74%, Catalan 17%, Galician 7%, Basque 2%
Int Dial Code:	34
Map Page:	60

SWITZERLAND

Capital:	Bern
Area:	41,290 km²
Population:	7,523,934
Currency:	Swiss franc (CHF)
Main Religions:	Roman Catholic 41.8%, Protestant 35.3%
Main Languages:	German (official) 63.7%, French (official) 19.2%, Italian (official) 7.6%, Romansch (official) 0.6%, other 8.9%
Int Dial Code:	41
Map Page:	62

SRI LANKA

Capital:	Sri Jayewardenepura Kotte
Area:	65,610 km²
Population:	20,222,240
Currency:	Sri Lankan rupee (LKR)
Main Religions:	Buddhist 70%, Hindu 15%, Christian 8%, Muslim 7%
Main Languages:	Sinhala 74%, Tamil 18%, other 8%
Int Dial Code:	94
Map Page:	89

SYRIA

Capital:	Damascus
Area:	185,180 km²
Population:	18,881,361
Currency:	Syrian pound (SYP)
Main Religions:	Sunni Muslim 74%, Alawite, Druze, and other Muslim sects 16%, Christian 10%, Jewish
Main Languages:	Arabic (official); Kurdish, Armenian, Aramaic, Circassian, French, English
Int Dial Code:	963
Map Page:	90

SUDAN

Capital:	Khartoum
Area:	2,505,810 km²
Population:	41,236,378
Currency:	Sudanese dinar (SDD)
Main Religions:	Sunni Muslim 70%, indigenous beliefs 25%, Christian 5%
Main Languages:	Arabic, Nubian, Ta Bedawie, diverse dialects of Nilotic, Nilo-Hamitic, Sudanic languages, English
Int Dial Code:	249
Map Page:	100

TAIWAN

Capital:	Taipei
Area:	35,980 km²
Population:	23,036,087
Currency:	Taiwan dollar (TWD)
Main Religions:	Buddhist, Confucian, and Taoist 93%, Christian 4.5%, other 2.5%
Main Languages:	Mandarin Chinese (official), Taiwanese (Min), Hakka dialects
Int Dial Code:	886
Map Page:	85

TAJIKISTAN

Capital:	Dushanbe
Area:	143,100 km²
Population:	7,320,815
Currency:	Somoni (SM)
Main Religions:	Sunni Muslim 85%, Shi'a Muslim 5%
Main Languages:	Tajik (official), Russian
Int Dial Code:	992
Map Page:	91

TANZANIA

Capital:	Dodoma
Area:	945,087 km²
Population:	37,445,392
Currency:	Tanzanian shilling (TZS)
Main Religions:	Christian 45%, Muslim 35%, indigenous beliefs 20%; Zanzibar - more than 99% Muslim
Main Languages:	Kiswahili or Swahili, Kiunguju, English, Arabic
Int Dial Code:	255
Map Page:	107

THAILAND

Capital:	Bangkok
Area:	514,000 km²
Population:	64,631,595
Currency:	Baht (THB)
Main Religions:	Buddhism 95%, Muslim 3.8%, Christianity 0.5%, Hinduism 0.1%, other 0.6%
Main Languages:	Thai, English, ethnic and regional dialects
Int Dial Code:	66
Map Page:	84

TOGO

Capital:	Lome
Area:	56,785 km²
Population:	5,548,702
Currency:	Communaute Financiere Africaine franc (XOF)
Main Religions:	Indigenous beliefs 59%, Christian 29%, Muslim 12%
Main Languages:	French (official), Ewe and Mina, Kabye and Dagomba
Int Dial Code:	228
Map Page:	104

TONGA

Capital:	Nuku'alofa
Area:	748 km²
Population:	114,689
Currency:	Pa'anga (TOP)
Main Religions:	Christian (Free Wesleyan Church claims over 30,000 adherents)
Main Languages:	Tongan, English
Int Dial Code:	676
Map Page:	113

TRINIDAD AND TOBAGO

Capital:	Port-of-Spain
Area:	5,128 km²
Population:	1,065,842
Currency:	Trinidad and Tobago dollar (TTD)
Main Religions:	Roman Catholic 29.4%, Hindu 23.8%, Anglican 10.9%, Muslim 5.8%, Presbyterian 3.4%, other 26.7%
Main Languages:	English (official), Hindi, French, Spanish, Chinese
Int Dial Code:	1 + 868
Map Page:	135

TUNISIA

Capital:	Tunis
Area:	163,610 km²
Population:	10,175,014
Currency:	Tunisian dinar (TND)
Main Religions:	Muslim 98%, Christian 1%, Jewish and other 1%
Main Languages:	Arabic (official), French (commerce)
Int Dial Code:	216
Map Page:	103

TURKEY

Capital:	Ankara
Area:	780,580 km²
Population:	70,413,958
Currency:	Turkish lira (YTL)
Main Religions:	Muslim 99.8% (mostly Sunni), other 0.2% (Christian and Jews)
Main Languages:	Turkish (official), Kurdish, Arabic, Armenian, Greek
Int Dial Code:	90
Map Page:	92

TURKMENISTAN

Capital:	Ashgabat
Area:	488,100 km²
Population:	5,042,920
Currency:	Turkmen manat (TMM)
Main Religions:	Muslim 89%, Eastern Orthodox 9%, unknown 2%
Main Languages:	Turkmen 72%, Russian 12%, Uzbek 9%, other 7%
Int Dial Code:	993
Map Page:	91

TUVALU

Capital:	Funafuti
Area:	26 km²
Population:	11,810
Currency:	Australian dollar (AUD); also a Tuvaluan dollar
Main Religions:	Church of Tuvalu (Congregationalist) 97%, Seventh-Day Adventist 1.4%, Baha'i 1%, other 0.6%
Main Languages:	Tuvaluan, English
Int Dial Code:	688
Map Page:	112

UGANDA

Capital:	Kampala
Area:	236,040 km²
Population:	28,195,754
Currency:	Ugandan shilling (UGX)
Main Religions:	Roman Catholic 33%, Protestant 33%, Muslim 16%, Indigenous beliefs 18%
Main Languages:	English, Ganda or Luganda, other Niger-Congo languages, Nilo-Saharan languages, Swahili, Arabic
Int Dial Code:	256
Map Page:	106

UKRAINE

Capital:	Kiev (Kyiv)
Area:	603,700 km²
Population:	46,710,816
Currency:	Hryvnia (UAH)
Main Religions:	Ukrainian Orthodox - Moscow Patriarchate, Ukrainian Orthodox - Kiev Patriarchate
Main Languages:	Ukrainian, Russian, Romanian, Polish, Hungarian
Int Dial Code:	380
Map Page:	70

UNITED ARAB EMIRATES

Capital:	Abu Dhabi
Area:	82,880 km²
Population:	2,602,713
Currency:	Emirati dirham (AED)
Main Religions:	Muslim 96% (Shi'a 16%), Christian, Hindu, and other 4%
Main Languages:	Arabic (official), Persian, English, Hindi, Urdu
Int Dial Code:	971
Map Page:	90

VATICAN CITY

Capital:	Vatican City
Area:	0.44 km²
Population:	932
Currency:	Euro (EUR)
Main Religions:	Roman Catholic
Main Languages:	Italian, Latin, French
Int Dial Code:	39
Map Page:	64

UNITED KINGDOM

Capital:	London
Area:	244,820 km²
Population:	60,609,153
Currency:	British pound (GBP)
Main Religions:	Christian 71.6%, Muslim 2.7%, Hindu 1%
Main Languages:	English, Welsh, Scottish form of Gaelic
Int Dial Code:	44
Map Page:	56

VENEZUELA

Capital:	Caracas
Area:	912,050 km²
Population:	25,730,435
Currency:	Bolivar (VEB)
Main Religions:	Roman Catholic 96%, Protestant 2%, other 2%
Main Languages:	Spanish (official), numerous indigenous dialects
Int Dial Code:	58
Map Page:	140

UNITED STATES

Capital:	Washington, D.C.
Area:	9,631,420 km²
Population:	298,444,215
Currency:	US dollar (USD)
Main Religions:	Protestant 52%, Roman Catholic 24%, Jewish 1%, Muslim 1%
Main Languages:	English, Spanish
Int Dial Code:	1
Map Page:	124

VIETNAM

Capital:	Hanoi
Area:	329,560 km²
Population:	84,402,966
Currency:	Dong (VND)
Main Religions:	Buddhist, Hoa Hao, Cao Dai, Christian (Roman Catholic, some Protestant), Indigenous beliefs, Muslim
Main Languages:	Vietnamese, English, French, Chinese, and Khmer
Int Dial Code:	84
Map Page:	84

URUGUAY

Capital:	Montevideo
Area:	176,220 km²
Population:	3,431,932
Currency:	Uruguayan peso (UYU)
Main Religions:	Roman Catholic 66%, Protestant 2%, Jewish 1%, nonprofessing or other 31%
Main Languages:	Spanish, Portunol, or Brazilero
Int Dial Code:	598
Map Page:	143

YEMEN

Capital:	Sanaa
Area:	527,970 km²
Population:	21,456,188
Currency:	Yemeni rial (YER)
Main Religions:	Muslim including Shaf'i (Sunni) and Zaydi (Shi'a), Jewish, Christian, and Hindu
Main Languages:	Arabic
Int Dial Code:	967
Map Page:	90

UZBEKISTAN

Capital:	Toshkent (Tashkent)
Area:	447,400 km²
Population:	27,307,134
Currency:	Uzbekistani sum (UZS)
Main Religions:	Muslim 88% (mostly Sunnis), Eastern Orthodox 9%, other 3%
Main Languages:	Uzbek 74.3%, Russian 14.2%, Tajik 4.4%, other 7.1%
Int Dial Code:	998
Map Page:	77

ZAMBIA

Capital:	Lusaka
Area:	752,614 km²
Population:	11,502,010
Currency:	Zambian kwacha (ZMK)
Main Religions:	Christian 50%-75%, Muslim and Hindu 24%-49%, Indigenous beliefs 1%
Main Languages:	English (official), Bemba, Kaonda, Lozi, Lunda, Luvale, Nyanja, Tonga, 70 other indigenous languages
Int Dial Code:	260
Map Page:	108

VANUATU

Capital:	Port-Vila
Area:	12,200 km²
Population:	208,869
Currency:	Vatu (VUV)
Main Religions:	Presbyterian 31.4%, Anglican 13.4%, Roman Catholic 13.1%, indigenous beliefs 5.6%
Main Languages:	English, French, Pidgin
Int Dial Code:	678
Map Page:	112

ZIMBABWE

Capital:	Harare
Area:	390,580 km²
Population:	12,236,805
Currency:	Zimbabwean dollar (ZWD)
Main Religions:	Syncretic (part Christian, part indigenous beliefs) 50%, Christian 25%, indigenous beliefs 24%, Muslim and other 1%
Main Languages:	English (official), Shona, Sindebele, tribal dialects
Int Dial Code:	263
Map Page:	108

KEY TO MAP SYMBOLS

Political Regions

CANADA   country

ONTARIO   state or province

————————   international boundary

————————   state or province boundary

—·—·—·—·   undefined/disputed boundary or ceasefire/demarcation line

Communications

————————   motorway

————————   main road

– – – – – –   other road or track

————————   railway

✈   international airport

Hydrographic Features

river, canal

seasonal river

 waterfall, dam

lake, seasonal lake

salt lake, seasonal salt lake

ice cap or glacier

Cities, Towns & Capitals

■ **CHICAGO**   over 3 million

■ **HAMBURG**   1 – 3 million

● **Bulawayo**   250 000 – 1 million

● Antofogasta   100 000 – 250 000

◉ Ajaccio   25 000 – 100 000

. Indian Springs   under 25 000

LONDON   country capital

Columbia   state or province capital

urban area

Cultural Features

.. Persepolis   ancient site or ruin

▪▪▪▪▪▪▪▪▪▪   ancient wall

Topographic Features

▲ Mount Ziel 1510   elevation above sea level (in metres)

▾ 133   elevation of land below sea level (in metres)

⊃⊂ Khyber Pass 1080   mountain pass (height in metres)

Each page also features a guide to relief colours

The World in

Maps

Political

Physical

41

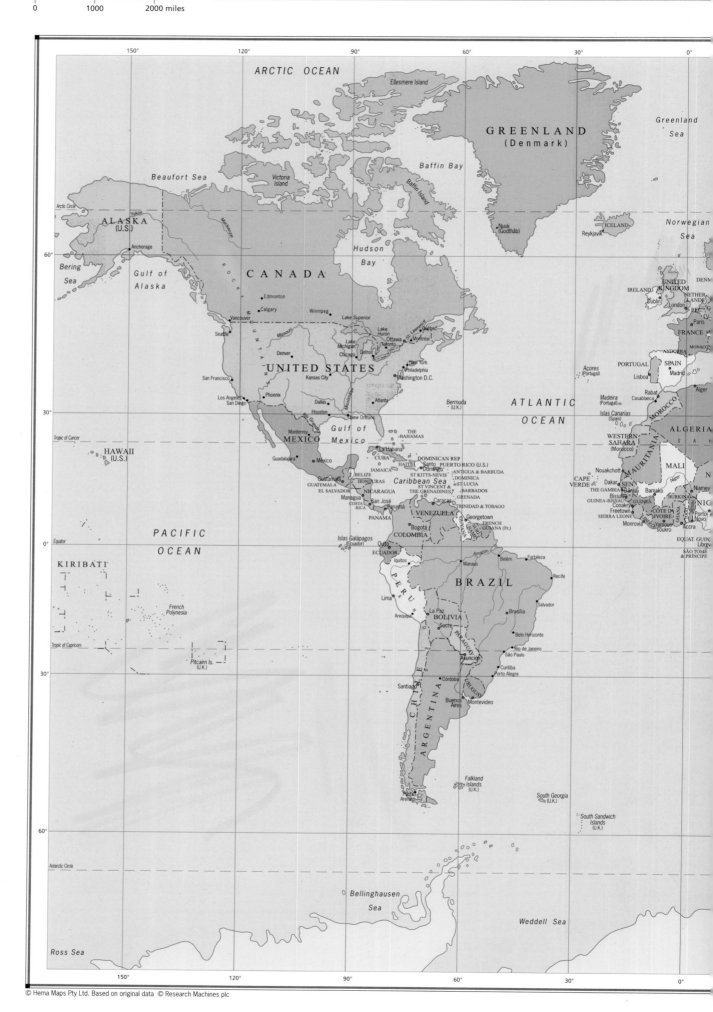

0	1000	2000	3000	4000 km

0	1000	2000 miles

ARCTIC OCEAN

Ellesmere Island

GREENLAND
(Denmark)

Greenland
Sea

Beaufort Sea

Victoria
Island

Baffin Bay

Baffin Island

Nuuk
(Godthåb)

ICELAND

Norwegian
Sea

Arctic Circle

ALASKA
(U.S.)

Yukon

Mackenzie

Hudson
Bay

Reykjavik

UNITED
KINGDOM
DENM

Bering
Sea

Anchorage

Gulf of
Alaska

60°

CANADA

Bay

IRELAND

Dublin

London

NETHER-
LANDS

BEL

ROCKY

Edmonton

Calgary

Winnipeg

Lake Superior

Paris

FRANCE S

Vancouver

Lake
Huron

St Lawrence

Québec

MONACO

Seattle

MOUNTAINS

Missouri

Lake
Michigan

Ottawa

Toronto

Montréal

Açores
(Portugal)

PORTUGAL

ANDORRA

SPAIN

Denver

Chicago

Detroit

New York

Lisboa

Madrid

San Francisco

UNITED STATES

Kansas City

Philadelphia

Washington D.C.

Madeira
(Portugal)

Rabat

Casablanca

Alger

MOROCCO

Los Angeles
San Diego

Phoenix

Dallas

Mississippi

Atlanta

Bermuda
(U.K.)

ATLANTIC

Islas Canarias
(Spain)

WESTERN
SAHARA
(Morocco)

ALGERIA

S A

30°

HAWAII
(U.S.)

Rio Grande

Houston

New Orleans

OCEAN

Tropic of Cancer

MEXICO

Gulf of
Mexico

THE
BAHAMAS

Nouakchott

MAURITANIA

MALI

Guadalajara

Monterrey

La Habana

CUBA

Dakar

Niger

SEN

Mexico

DOMINICAN REP

PUERTO RICO (U.S.)

CAPE
VERDE

THE GAMBIA

Banjul

Bamako

BURKINA

Niamey

N

JAMAICA

HAITI

Santo
Domingo

ANTIGUA & BARBUDA

GUINEA-BISSAU

Bissau

BELIZE

ST KITTS-NEVIS

DOMINICA

GUINEA

Conakry

GHANA

NIG

Guatemala

HONDURAS

Caribbean Sea

ST LUCIA

SIERRA LEONE

Freetown

CÔTE D'
IVOIRE

Accra

Porto-
Novo

GUATEMALA
EL SALVADOR

Managua

NICARAGUA

ST VINCENT &
THE GRENADINES

BARBADOS

GRENADA

Monrovia

LIBERIA

Yamous-
soukro

BENIN

TOGO

San José

COSTA
RICA

Panama

Caracas

TRINIDAD & TOBAGO

EQUAT. GUIN.

SÃO TOMÉ
& PRÍNCIPE

Equator

PACIFIC

OCEAN

PANAMA

Islas Galápagos
(Ecuador)

Bogotá

COLOMBIA

VENEZUELA

Georgetown

FRENCH
GUIANA (Fr.)

GUYANA

SURINAME

Libre

Quito

ECUADOR

Amazon

Belém

Fortaleza

0°

KIRIBATI

Iquitos

PERU

Manaus

BRAZIL

Recife

Lima

French
Polynesia

La Paz

BOLIVIA

Arequipa

Sucre

PARAGUAY

Brasília

Belo Horizonte

Salvador

Tropic of Capricorn

Pitcairn Is.
(U.K.)

Asunción

Rio de Janeiro

São Paulo

Curitiba

Porto Alegre

URUGUAY

30°

CHILE

Santiago

Córdoba

ARGENTINA

Buenos
Aires

Montevideo

Falkland
Islands
(U.K.)

South Georgia
(U.K.)

South Sandwich
Islands
(U.K.)

60°

Punta
Arenas

Antarctic Circle

Bellinghausen
Sea

Weddell Sea

Ross Sea

Mt. Everest, China/Nepal : 8,848 m or 29,029 ft	Arica, Chile : 0.08 cm or 0.03 in	Nile, Egypt : 6,690 km or 4,160 mi
Dead Sea, Israel/Jordan : 400 m or 1312 ft	Mawsynram, India : 1187.2 cm or 467.4 in	Caspian Sea : 371,000 km² or 143,240 sq mi

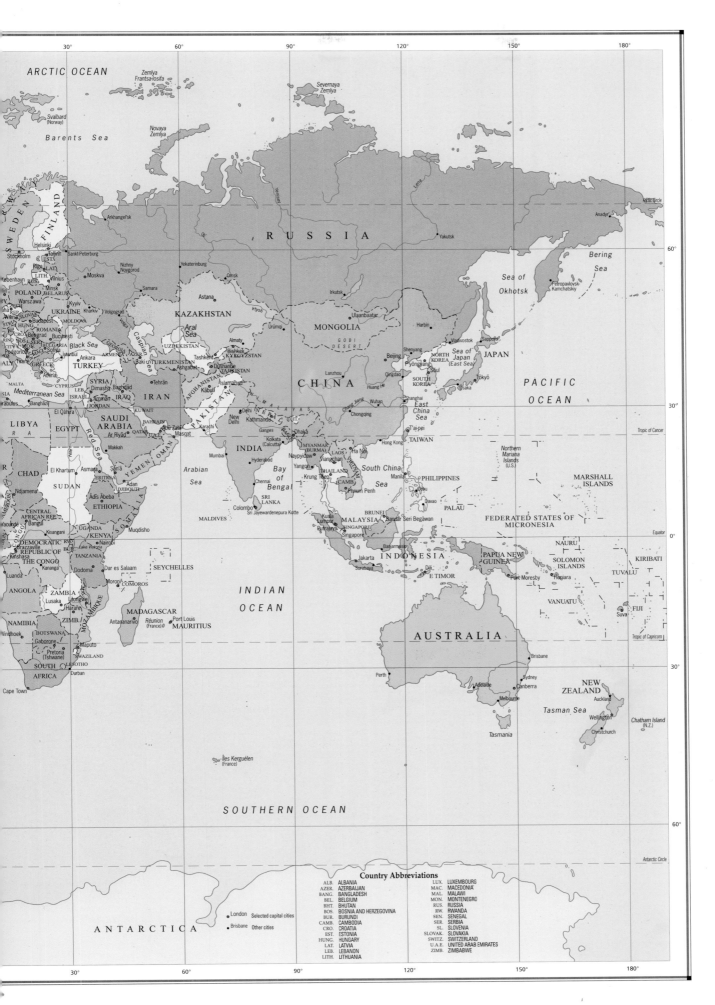

Country Abbreviations

ALB.	ALBANIA	LUX.	LUXEMBOURG
AZER.	AZERBAIJAN	MAC.	MACEDONIA
BANG.	BANGLADESH	MAL.	MALAWI
BEL.	BELGIUM	MON.	MONTENEGRO
BHT.	BHUTAN	RUS.	RUSSIA
BOS.	BOSNIA AND HERZEGOVINA	RW.	RWANDA
BUR.	BURUNDI	SEN.	SENEGAL
CAMB.	CAMBODIA	SER.	SERBIA
CRO.	CROATIA	SL.	SLOVENIA
EST.	ESTONIA	SLOVAK.	SLOVAKIA
HUNG.	HUNGARY	SWITZ.	SWITZERLAND
LAT.	LATVIA	U.A.E.	UNITED ARAB EMIRATES
LEB.	LEBANON	ZIMB.	ZIMBABWE
LITH.	LITHUANIA		

• London Selected capital cities

• Brisbane Other cities

Verkhoyansk & Oymyakon, Russia : -68°C or -90°F

Al Aziziyah, Libya : 58°C or 136°F

5,900,825,000

43 per km² or 112 per sq mi

136,268,000 km² or 52,614,000 sq mi

192

```
0    250      500      750     1000 km
0  100  200   300   400   500 miles
```

ATLANTIC

OCEAN

ICELAND
Reykjavik

Norwegian
Sea

Faeroes
(Denmark)

Rockall

Shetland Is.
(U.K.)

NORWAY

SWEDEN

FIN

Trondheim

Bergen

Stavanger

Oslo

Stockholm

Gulf of Bothnia

Sundsvall

Tampere

Kiruna

Tromsø

Baltic Sea

Göteborg

Gotland

Vänern

Outer
Hebrides

Orkney Is.

SCOTLAND

Glasgow

Edinburgh

NORTHERN
IRELAND

Belfast

IRELAND

DUBLIN
(BAILE ÁTHA CLIATH)

UNITED

KINGDOM

WALES

Cardiff

ENGLAND

BIRMINGHAM

Plymouth

LONDON

North
Sea

DENMARK

Århus

København
(Copenhagen)

Bornholm

Gdańsk

RUSSIA

Kaliningrad

Hrodna

Tallinn

ES

LAT

Riga

LITHU

Kaunas

English Channel

's-Gravenhage
(The Hague)

Amsterdam

NETHER-
LANDS

Hannover

HAMBURG

Elbe

BERLIN

Ems

Channel
Islands

Bruxelles
(Brussels)

BELGIUM

Bonn

Frankfurt

GERMANY

Rhine

WARSZAWA
(WARSAW)

Wisła

POLAND

Luxembourg

LUXEMBOURG

Seine

PARIS

Loire

FRANCE

Strasbourg

MÜNCHEN
(MUNICH)

Odra (Oder)

PRAHA
(PRAGUE)

CZECH REP.

L'viv

Elbe

Danube

WIEN
(VIENNA)

SLOVAKIA

Bratislava

ROM

Carpa

Cabo Fisterra

Bay
of
Biscay

Bordeaux

Lyon

Massif
Central

Bern
4808
Mt.
Blanc

Vaduz
LIECHTENSTEIN

SWITZERLAND

Alps

Rhône

Genova
(Genoa)

MILANO
(MILAN)

Ljubljana

SLOVENIA

AUSTRIA

Zagreb

CROATIA

BUDAPEST

HUNGARY

Cluj-
Napoca

Andorra
la Vella

ANDORRA

Marseille

MONACO

SAN
MARINO

Appennines

BOSNIA &
HERZEGOVINA

Sarajevo

MONTENEGRO

Podgorica

SERBIA

BEOGRAD
(BELGRADE)

PORTUGAL

LISBOA
(LISBON)

Tajo

MADRID

SPAIN

Ebro

Pyrenees

BARCELONA

Corse
(Corsica)
(France)

Ajaccio

VATICAN
CITY

ROMA
(ROME)

ITALY

Adriatic
Sea

Sea

SOFIYA
(SOFIA)

BUL

Skopje

MACEDONIA

Cabo de
São Vicente

Valencia

Islas Baleares
(Balearic Islands)

Eivissa

Menorca

Mallorca

Sardegna
(Sardinia)
(Italy)

NAPOLI
(NAPLES)

Taranto

TIranë
(Tirana)

ALBANIA

Strait of Gibraltar

Gibraltar (U.K.)

Ceuta
(Spain)

Mediterranean

Cagliari

Tyrrhenian
Sea

Kerkyra
(Corfu)

GREECE

RABAT

Melilla
(Spain)

Sea

Palermo

Mte. Etna
3340

Sicilia
(Sicily)

Ionian
Sea

Athina
(Athens)

ALGER
(ALGIERS)

Valletta

MALTA

Ae

Tunis

AFRICA

Tarābulus
(Tripoli)

Kriti
(Crete)

Banghāzī

metres feet
8000   26250
6000   19690
4000   13120
2000   6560
1000   3280
500   1640
200   656
0   0
656   200
3280   1000
6560   2000
13120 4000
19690 6000
26250 8000
feet   metres

Elbrus, Russia : 5,642 m or 18,510 ft

Astrakhan, Russia : 16.3 cm or 6.4 in

Volga, Russia : 3,531 km or 2,194 mi

Caspian Sea : 29 m or 84 ft

Crkvica, Bosnia-Herzegovina : 465 cm or 183 in

Caspian Sea : 371,000 km² or 143,240 sq mi

Ust'-Shchugor, Russia : -55 °C or -67 °F

Seville, Spain : 50 °C or 122 °F

699,644,000

68 per km² or 177 per sq mi

10,245,000 km² or 3,956,000 sq mi

43

ATLANTIC
OCEAN

Norwegian
Sea

Reykjavik ● **ICELAND**

Arctic Circle

Faeroes
(Denmark)

Rockall

Shetland Is.
(U.K.)

Outer
Hebrides

Orkney Is.

SCOTLAND

● **Glasgow**

Edinburgh

NORTHERN
IRELAND

Belfast

North
Sea

IRELAND

DUBLIN
(BAILE ATHA CLIATH)

UNITED

WALES

KINGDOM

● **BIRMINGHAM**

Cardiff

ENGLAND

Plymouth

LONDON

English Channel

Channel
Islands

NORWAY

Bergen

Oslo

Stavanger

Trondheim

SWEDEN

Sundsvall

Gulf of Bothnia

Tromsø

Lapp

Kiruna

FIN

Tampere

DENMARK

Århus

København
(Copenhagen)

Göteborg

Vänern

Stockholm

Gotland

Bornholm

Baltic Sea

Tallinn

EST

LAT

Rīga

LITHUA

Kaunus

RUSSIA

Kaliningrad

Hrodna

Amsterdam

s-Gravenhage
(The Hague)

NETHER-
LANDS

Bruxelles
(Brussels)

BELGIUM

Luxembourg

LUXEMBOURG

PARIS

Strasbourg

Bonn

HAMBURG

Hannover

GERMANY

BERLIN

Frankfurt

Ems

Elbe

Rhine

Odra (Oder)

Gdańsk

Wisła

WARSZAWA
(WARSAW)

POLAND

Vistula

L'viv

FRANCE

Loire

Seine

PRAHA
(PRAGUE)

CZECH REP.

Elbe

WIEN
(VIENNA)

SLOVAKIA

Bratislava

BUDAPEST

Carpat

Bay
of
Biscay

Cabo Fisterra

Bordeaux

Lyon

Massif

Central

Rhône

Danube

MÜNCHEN
(MUNICH)

Bern **Vaduz**

SWITZERLAND **LIECHTENSTEIN**

4808
Mt.
Blanc

A l p s

AUSTRIA

Ljubljana

SLOVENIA

Zagreb

CROATIA

HUNGARY

Cluj-
Napoca

ROM

PORTUGAL

LISBOA
(LISBON)

Tajo

MADRID

SPAIN

Cabo de
São Vicente

Ebro

Pyrenees

Andorra
la Vella

ANDORRA

Marseille

Genova
(Genoa)

MILANO
(MILAN)

Apennines

SAN
MARINO

MONACO

Adriatic Sea

BOSNIA &
HERZEGOVINA

Sarajevo

BEOGRAD
(BELGRADE)

SERBIA

MONTENEGRO

Podgorica

SOFIYA
(SOFIA)

BUL

BARCELONA

Valencia

Islas Baleares
(Balearic Islands)

Corse
(Corsica)
(France)

Ajaccio

VATICAN
CITY

ROMA
(ROME)

ITALY

NAPOLI
(NAPLES)

Tirane
(Tirana)

ALBANIA

MACEDONIA

Skopje

Strait of Gibraltar

Gibraltar (U.K.)

Ceuta
(Spain)

Melilla
(Spain)

Sardegna
(Sardinia)
(Italy)

Eivissa

Mallorca

Menorca

Mediterranean

Cagliari

Tyrrhenian
Sea

Taranto

Kerkyra
(Corfu)

GREECE

RABAT

ALGER
(ALGIERS)

Palermo

Sicilia
(Sicily)

Mte. Etna
3340

Sea

Ionian
Sea

Athina
(Athens)

Tunis

Valletta

MALTA

A F R I C A

Tarābulus
(Tripoli)

Kriti
(Crete)

Banghāzī

Elbrus, Russia : 5,642 m or 18,510 ft

Caspian Sea : 29 m or 84 ft

Astrakhan, Russia : 16.3 cm or 6.4 in

Crkvica, Bosnia-Herzegovina : 465 cm or 183 in

Volga, Russia : 3,531 km or 2,194 mi

Caspian Sea : 371,000 km² or 143,240 sq mi

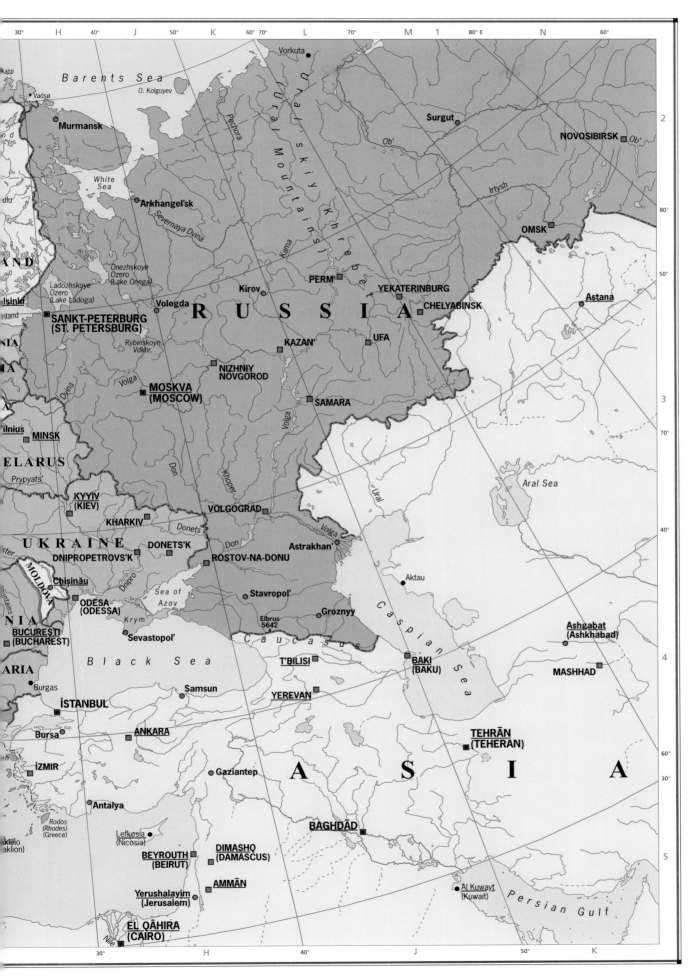

30°   H   40°   J   50°   K   60° 70°   L   70°   M   1   80° E   N   60°

Vorkuta

Barents Sea

O. Kolguyev

Kapp

Vadsø

Murmansk

White Sea

Pechora

Ural'skiy Khrebet (Ural Mountains)

Ob'

Surgut

2

NOVOSIBIRSK

Ob'

Arkhangel'sk

Severnaya Dvina

Irtysh

80°

OMSK

50°

Onezhskoye Ozero (Lake Onega)

Ladozhskoye Ozero (Lake Ladoga)

Kirov

PERM'

YEKATERINBURG

Astana

Vologda

R U S S I A

CHELYABINSK

lsinki

SANKT-PETERBURG (ST. PETERSBURG)

Rybinskoye Vdkhr.

KAZAN'

UFA

nland

Dvina

NIZHNIY NOVGOROD

Kama

lu

NIA

A

Volga

MOSKVA (MOSCOW)

Volga

SAMARA

3

ilnius

MINSK

Don

70°

ELARUS

Prypyats'

KYYIV (KIEV)

Khoper

Ural

VOLGOGRAD

Aral Sea

40°

KHARKIV

Donets

U K R A I N E

Don

DONETS'K

Astrakhan'

ster

DNIPROPETROVS'K

ROSTOV-NA-DONU

Volga

MOLDOVA

Dnipro

Aktau

Chişinău

Sea of Azov

Stavropol'

NIA

ODESA (ODESSA)

Krym

Elbrus 5642

Groznyy

Caspian Sea

Ashgabat (Ashkhabad)

BUCUREŞTI (BUCHAREST)

Sevastopol'

C a u c a s u s

ntains

4

ARIA

B l a c k   S e a

T'BILISI

BAKI (BAKU)

MASHHAD

Burgas

Samsun

YEREVAN

İSTANBUL

Bursa

ANKARA

TEHRĀN (TEHERAN)

60°

İZMIR

Gaziantep

A S I A

30°

Antalya

Rodos (Rhodes) (Greece)

BAGHDĀD

kleio aklion)

Lefkosia (Nicosia)

5

BEYROUTH (BEIRUT)

DIMASHQ (DAMASCUS)

Al Kuwayt (Kuwait)

P e r s i a n   G u l f

AMMĀN

Yerushalayim (Jerusalem)

EL QÂHIRA (CAIRO)

Nile

30°   H   40°   J   50°   K

Ust'-Shchugor, Russia : -55 °C or -67 °F

Seville, Spain : 50 °C or 122 °F

699,644,000

68 per km² or 177 per sq mi

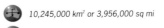

10,245,000 km² or 3,956,000 sq mi

43

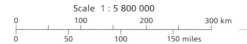

Scale 1 : 5 800 000

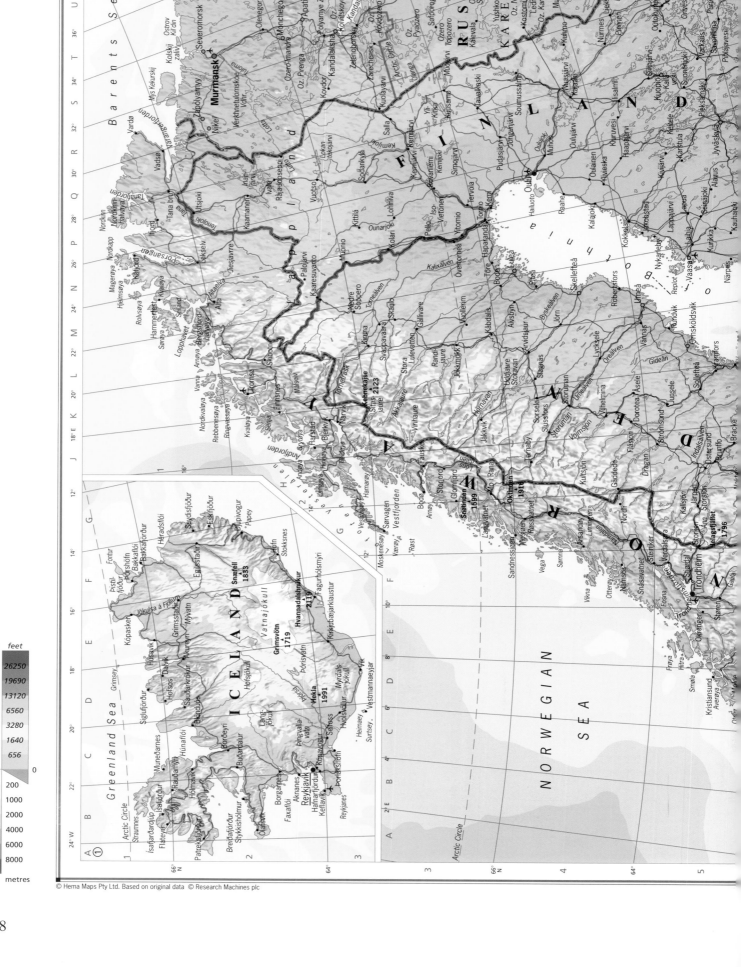

metres	feet
8000	26250
6000	19690
4000	13120
2000	6560
1000	3280
500	1640
200	656
0	0

feet	metres
656	200
3280	1000
6560	2000
13120	4000
19690	6000
26250	8000

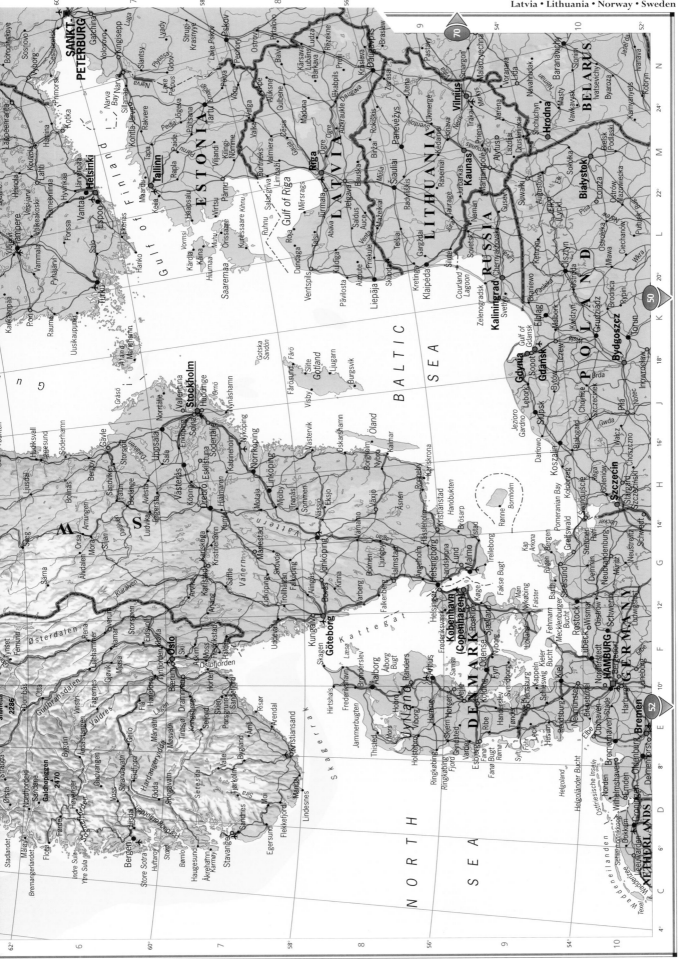

■ over 3 million

■ 1 – 3 million

● 250 000 – 1 million

● 100 000 – 250 000

○ 25 000 – 100 000

· under 25 000

country capital underline

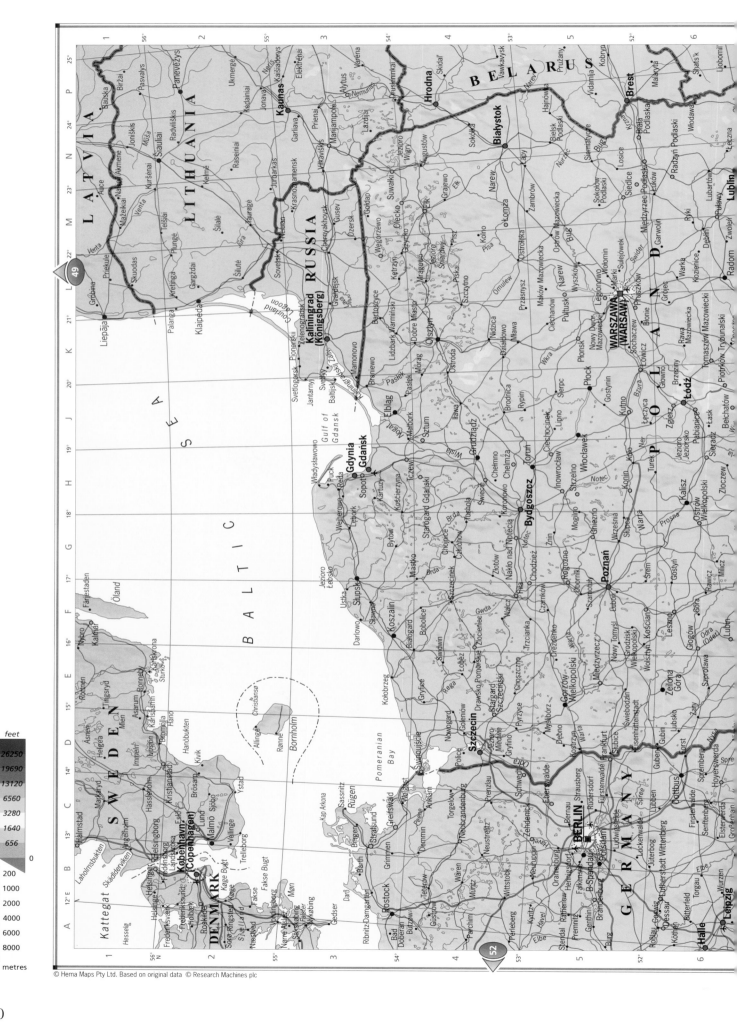

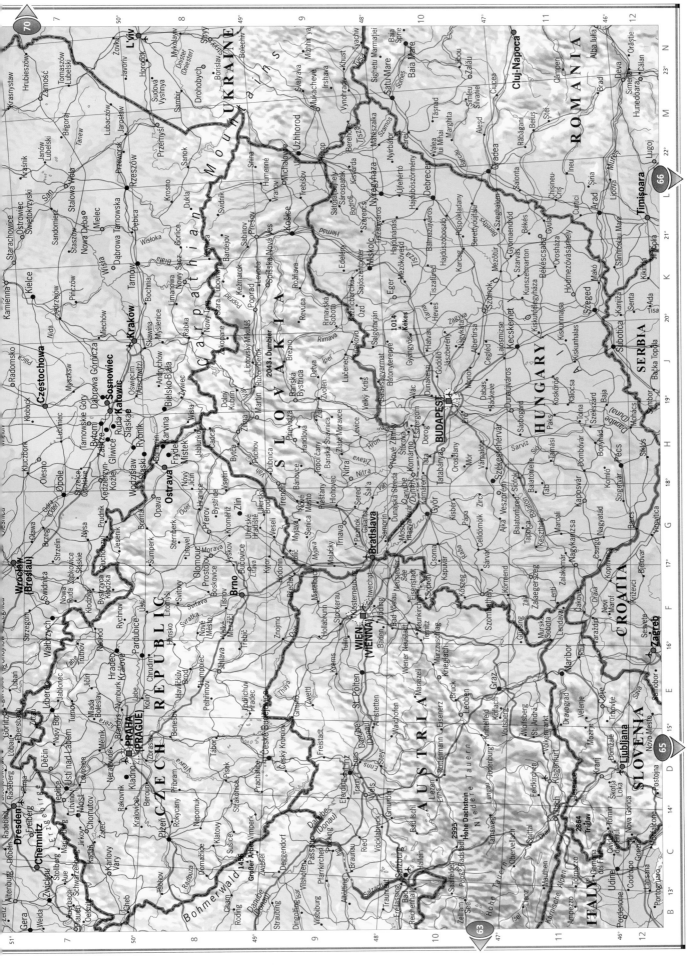

■	over 3 million	●	100 000 – 250 000	—	country capital underline
■	1 – 3 million	○	25 000 – 100 000	⬭	urban area
●	250 000 – 1 million	•	under 25 000		

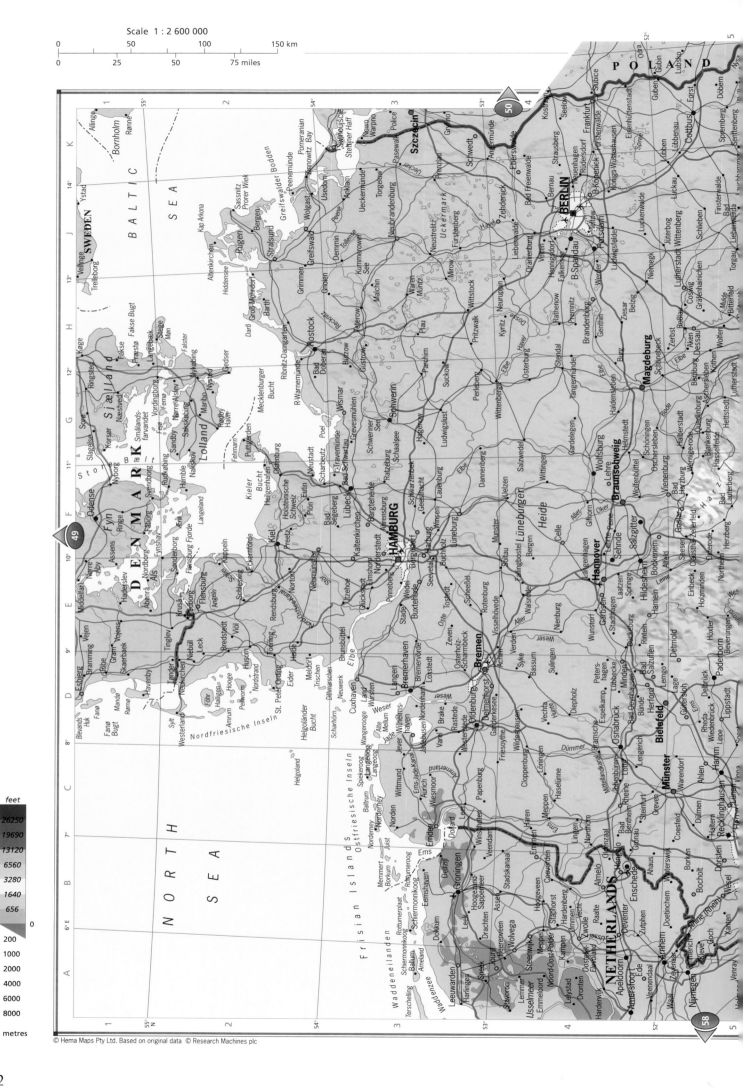

POLAND

BALTIC SEA

SWEDEN

DENMARK

NORTH SEA

NETHERLANDS

BERLIN

Szczecin

HAMBURG

Bremen

Hannover

Braunschweig

Magdeburg

Münster

Bielefeld

Friesian Islands

Ostfriesische Inseln

Nordfriesische Inseln

metres	feet
8000	26250
6000	19690
4000	13120
2000	6560
1000	3280
500	1640
200	656
0	0
656	200
3280	1000
6560	2000
13120	4000
19690	6000
26250	8000

feet   metres

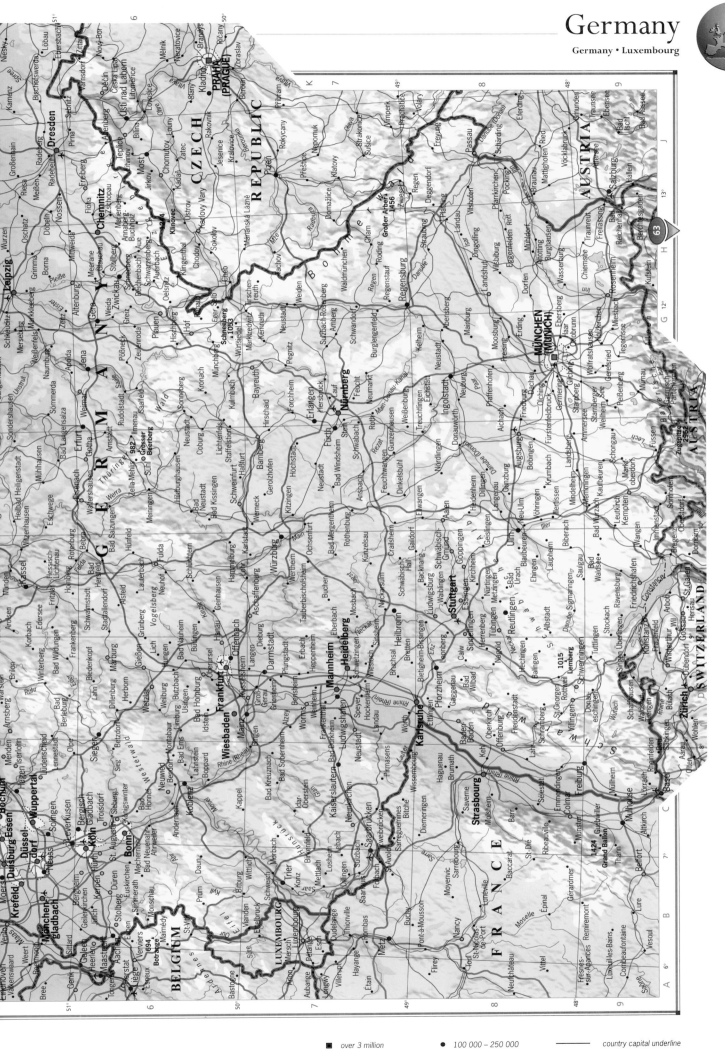

■ over 3 million
■ 1 – 3 million
● 250 000 – 1 million
● 100 000 – 250 000
○ 25 000 – 100 000
• under 25 000
— country capital underline
urban area

A   B   C   D   E   3°

2° W   1°   0°   1°   2°   E

UNITED KINGDOM

NORTH SEA

Buxton · Worksop · East Retford · Louth · Mablethorpe
Chesterfield · Bolsover · Lincoln · Horncastle
Leek · Matlock · Mansfield
Alfreton · Newark-on-Trent
Derby · **Nottingham** · Grantham · Boston · The Wash · Hunstanton · Cromer
Long Eaton · Sleaford
Burton-upon-Trent · Loughborough · King's Lynn · East Dereham · Norwich · The Broads · Great Yarmouth
Cannock · Melton Mowbray · Oakham · Spalding · Wisbech · Lowestoft
Leicester · Stamford · Peterborough · March · The Fens · Thetford · Diss · Southwold
Walsall · Tamworth · Nuneaton · Corby · Huntingdon · Ely · Bury St Edmunds · Stowmarket · Aldeburgh
BIRMINGHAM · Bedworth · Market Harborough · Kettering · Little Ouse · Woodbridge · Orford Ness
Coventry · Rugby · Wellingborough · Cambridge · Newmarket · Ipswich
Redditch · Warwick · Royal Leamington Spa · Northampton · Bedford · Sudbury · Felixstowe · Harwich · The Naze
Stratford-upon-Avon · Daventry · Letchworth · Royston · Stevenage · Bishop's Stortford · Braintree · Colchester
Evesham · Banbury · Towcester · Clacton-on-Sea
ENGLAND · Milton Keynes · Luton · Welwyn Garden City · Harlow · Chelmsford
Chipping Norton · Bicester · Leighton Buzzard · St Albans · Cheshunt · Brentwood · Foulness
Woodstock · Aylesbury · Hemel Hempstead · Watford · Enfield · Basildon · Southend-on-Sea
Witney · Oxford · High Wycombe · Slough · LONDON · Grays · Thames · Walcheren
Thames · Abingdon · Didcot · Maidenhead · Windsor · Kingston upon Thames · Gravesend · Rochester · Margate · Knokke-Heist
Swindon · Reading · Bracknell · Staines · Epsom · Gillingham · North Foreland · Zeebrugge · Blankenberge
Hungerford · Newbury · Camberley · Woking · Whitstable · Ramsgate · Oostende · Brugge
Basingstoke · Farnborough · Guildford · Sevenoaks · Maidstone · Faversham · Canterbury · Deal · Middelkerke
Andover · Aldershot · Reigate · Ashford · Dover · Nieuwpoort · De Panne · Veurne
Salisbury · Alton · Haslemere · Crawley · Royal Tunbridge Wells · Folkestone · Calais · Gravelines · Diksmuide · Roeselare · Izegem
Winchester · Petersfield · Horsham · East Grinstead · Rye · Dungeness · Boulogne-sur-Mer · Poperinge · Ieper · Menen · Kortrijk · Waregem
Romsey · The Weald · Uckfield · Cap Gris-Nez · Desvres · Armentières · Lille · Tourcoing · Roubaix
Southampton · Eastleigh · South Downs · Worthing · Lewes · Bexhill · Hastings · Étaples · Hesdin · Béthune · Lens · Tournai
Fareham · Havant · Brighton · Newhaven · Eastbourne · Berck · Montreul · Hénin-Beaumont · Avion · Denain
Portsmouth · Gosport · Chichester · Shoreham-by-Sea · Beachy Head · St-Pol-sur-Ternoise · Arras · Douai
Lymington · Cowes · Bognor Regis · Rue · Cambrai
Newport · Ryde · The Solent · Isle of Wight · Baie de la Somme · Doullens · Bapaume · Caudr...
Le Crotoy · St-Valéry-sur-Somme · Abbeville · Albert · Péronne
English Channel · Le Tréport · Blangy-sur-Bresle · Amiens · St-Quentin
Fauville-en-Caux · Dieppe · Roye · Tergnier · Chauny
Cherbourg · Fécamp · Tôtes · Neufchâtel-en-Bray · Forges-les-Eaux · Breteuil · Montdidier · Noyon
Valognes · Cap d'Antifer · Étretat · Marseille-en-Beauvaisis · Gournay-en-Bray · Beauvais · Compiègne · Soissons
Baie de la Seine · Bolbec · Yvetôt · Barentin · Clermont · Creil · Crépy-en-Valois · Villers-Cotterêts
Carentan · Gonfreville-l'Orcher · Lillebonne · Rouen · Méru · Chantilly
La Haye-du-Puits · Isigny-sur-Mer · Le Havre · St-Étienne-du-Rouvray · Chambly · Senlis
Périers · Bayeux · Honfleur · Elbeuf · Louviers · Château-Thierry
St-Lô · Ouistreham · Hérouville-St-Clair · Les Andelys · Mantes-la-Jolie · Pontoise · Coulommiers
Coutances · Caen · Lisieux · Vernon · St-Germain-en-Laye · **PARIS** · St-Denis · Meaux · Marne-la-Vallée
Granville · Villers-Bocage · Orbec · Bernay · Évreux · Versailles · Bobigny · Créteil
Jullouville · Villedieu-les-Poêles · Vire · Condé-sur-Noireau · Vimoutiers · Conches-en-Ouche · Dreux · Trappes · Orly · Courtacon
Tinchebray · Flers · Gacé · L'Aigle · Verneuil · Houdan
Avranches · Mortain · Rânes · Argentan · Orsay
Pontorson · Falaise

The Naze · The Weald · South Downs · Isle of Wight · Strait of Dover · Cap Gris-Nez

© Hema Maps Pty Ltd. Based on original data © Research Machines plc

metres / feet

metres	feet
8000	26250
6000	19690
4000	13120
2000	6560
1000	3280
500	1640
200	656
0	0

feet	metres
656	200
3280	1000
6560	2000
13120	4000
19690	6000
26250	8000

feet / metres

■ over 3 million
■ 1 – 3 million
● 250 000 – 1 million
● 100 000 – 250 000
○ 25 000 – 100 000
• under 25 000
—— country capital underline
⬭ urban area

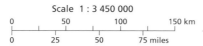

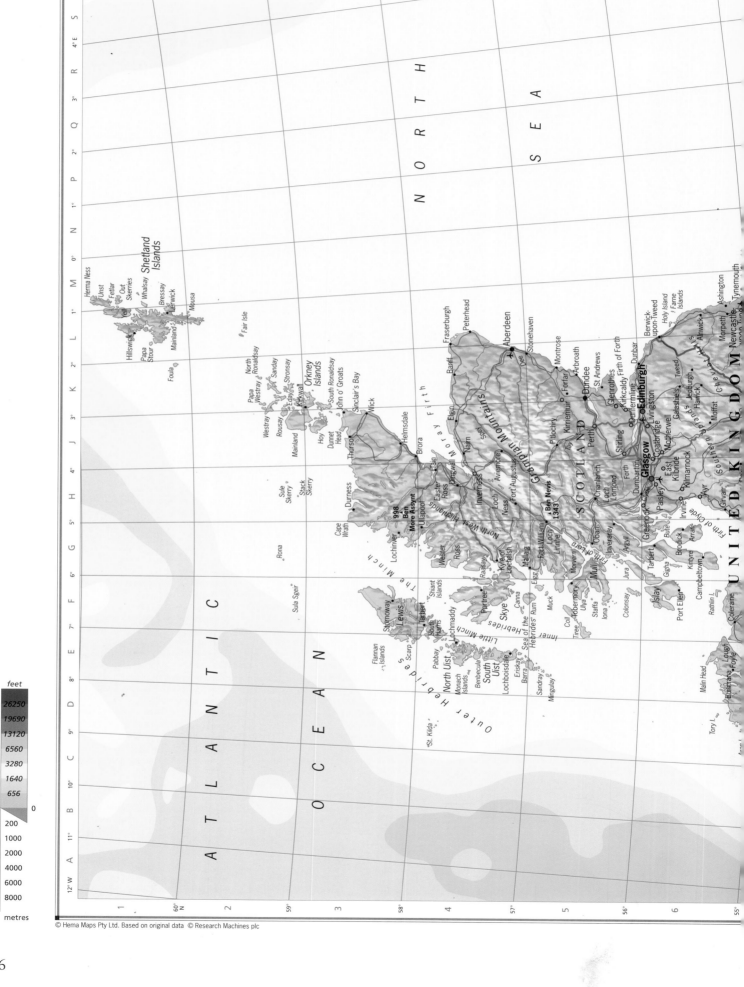

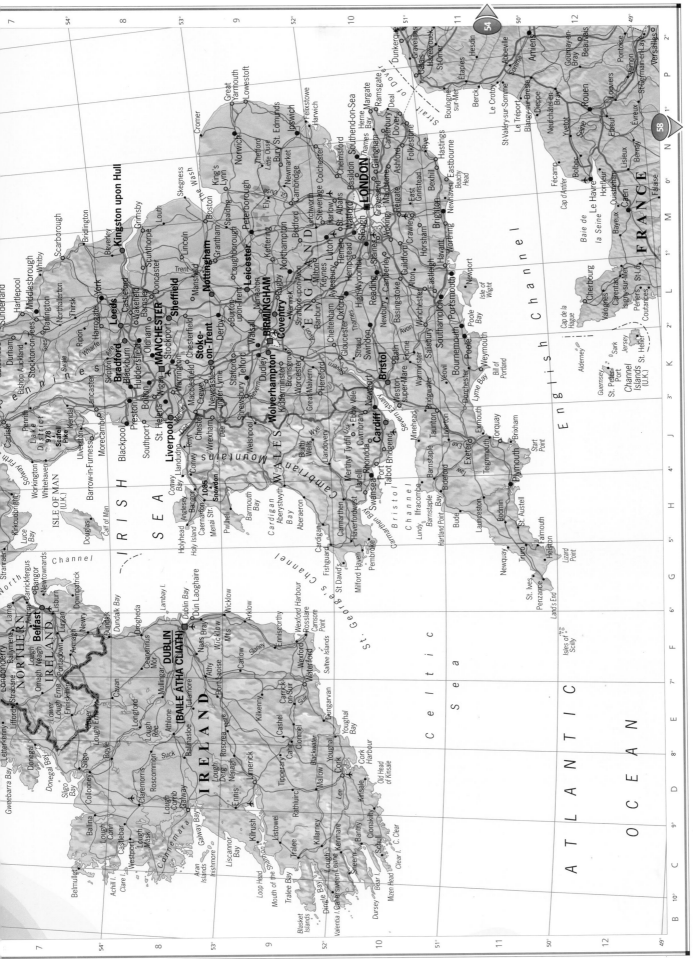

■	over 3 million	
■	1 – 3 million	
●	250 000 – 1 million	
●	100 000 – 250 000	
●	25 000 – 100 000	
•	under 25 000	
	country capital underline	
	state or province capital underline	
	urban area	

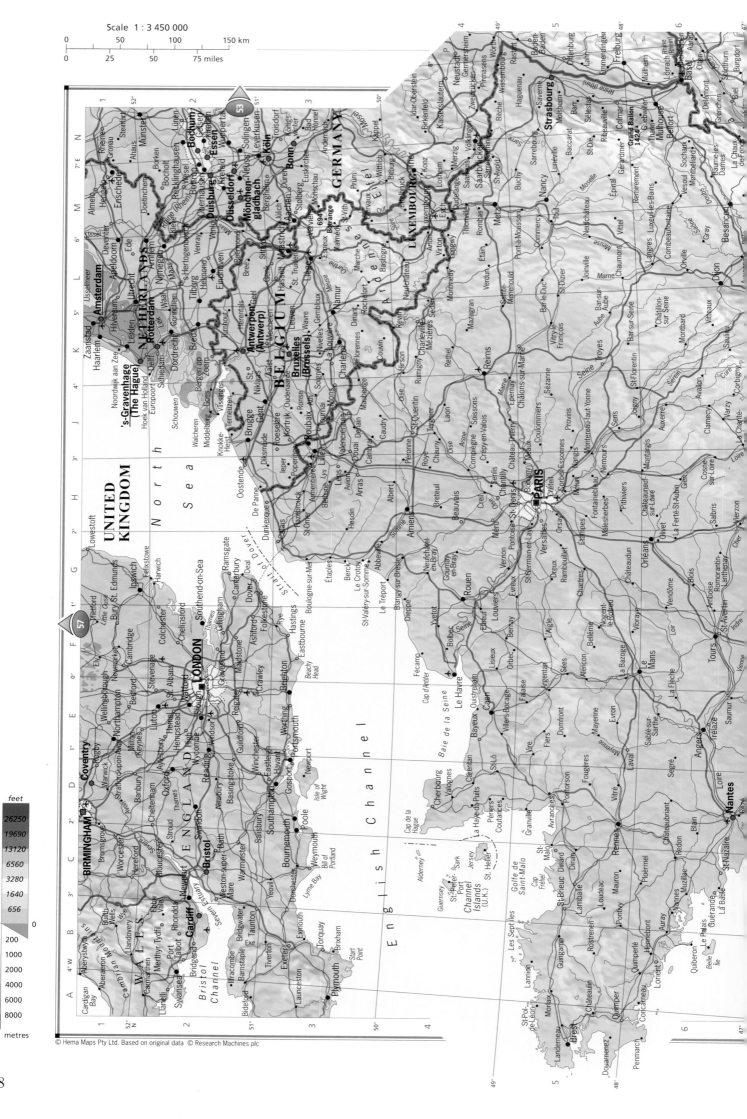

Scale 1 : 3 450 000

0   50   100   150 km
0   25   50   75 miles

57

metres feet
8000   26250
6000   19690
4000   13120
2000   6560
1000   3280
500   1640
200   656
0   0
656   200
3280   1000
6560   2000
13120 4000
19690 6000
26250 8000
feet   metres

© Hema Maps Pty Ltd. Based on original data © Research Machines plc

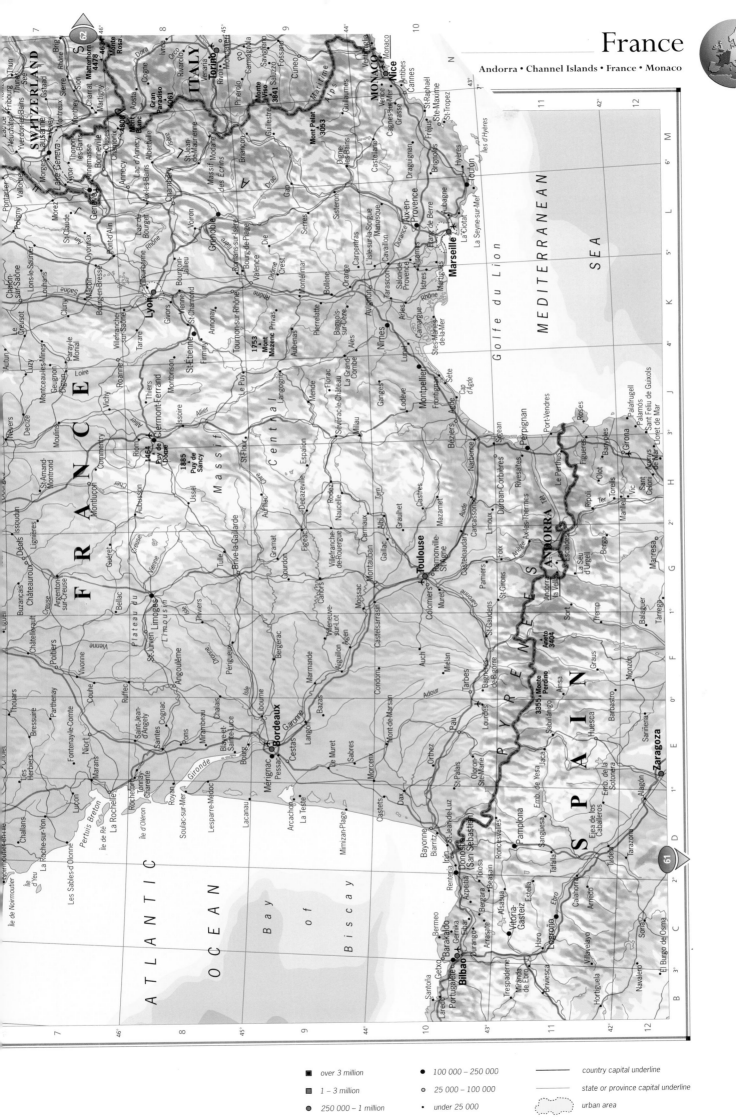

SWITZERLAND

ITALY

Matterhorn 4478
Monte Rosa 4634
Mont Blanc 4808
Gran Paradiso 4061
Monte Viso 3841
Torino

MONACO
Nice
Cannes

Monte Pelat 3053

Îles d'Hyères

MEDITERRANEAN SEA

Golfe du Lion

F R A N C E

Genève
Annecy
Grenoble
Valence
Lyon
St-Étienne
Clermont-Ferrand
1464 Puy de Dôme
1885 Puy de Sancy
1753 Mont Mézenc
Privas
Nîmes
Montpellier
Sète
Arles
Marseille
Aix-en-Provence
Toulon
Hyères

Nevers
Limoges
St-Junien

M a s s i f   C e n t r a l

P l a t e a u   d u   L i m o u s i n

Bordeaux
Mérignac
Pessac

Toulouse

A N D O R R A
Aneto 3404
Monte Perdido 3355

P Y R É N É E S

S P A I N

Zaragoza

Bayonne
Biarritz
Donostia (San Sebastián)
Pamplona

Bilbao

A T L A N T I C   O C E A N

B a y   o f   B i s c a y

Legend:

- ■ over 3 million
- ■ 1 – 3 million
- ● 250 000 – 1 million
- ● 100 000 – 250 000
- ◦ 25 000 – 100 000
- • under 25 000
- —— country capital underline
- —— state or province capital underline
- ⌣ urban area

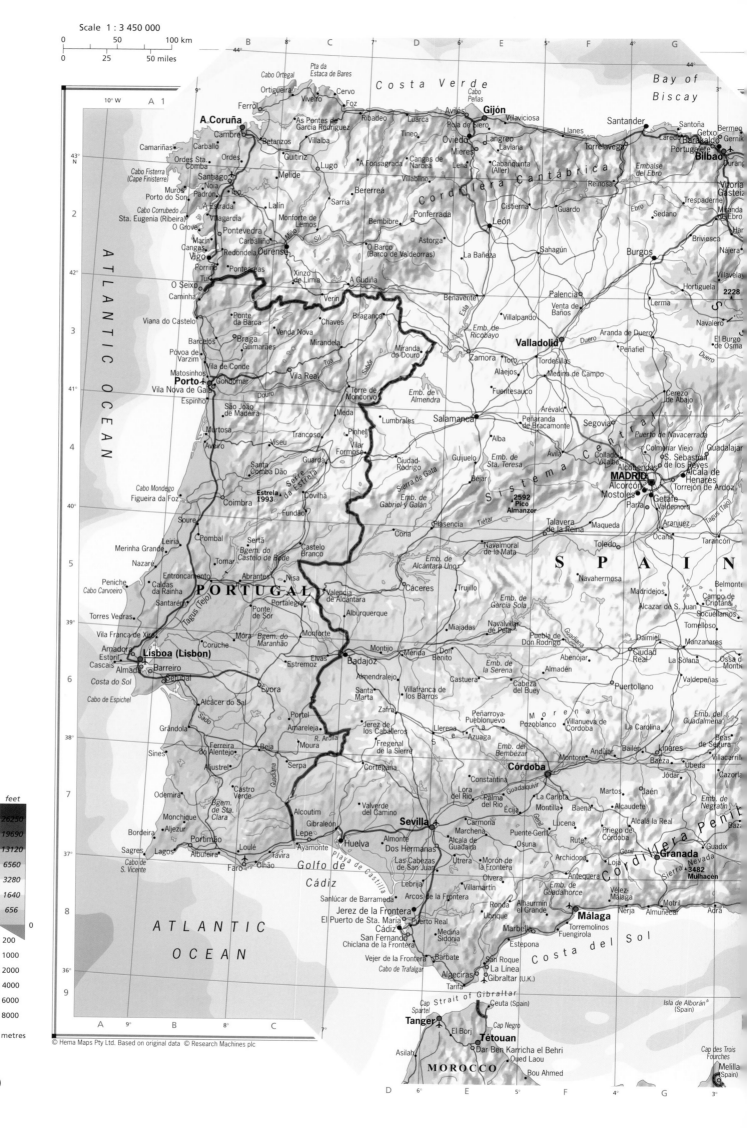

Scale 1 : 3 450 000

© Hema Maps Pty Ltd. Based on original data © Research Machines plc

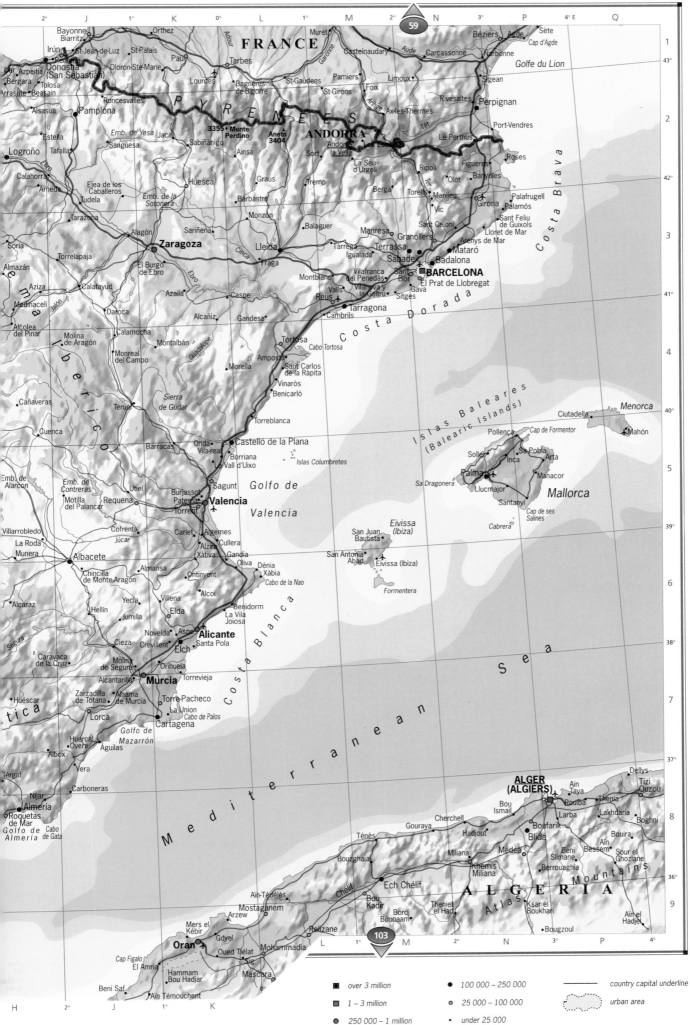

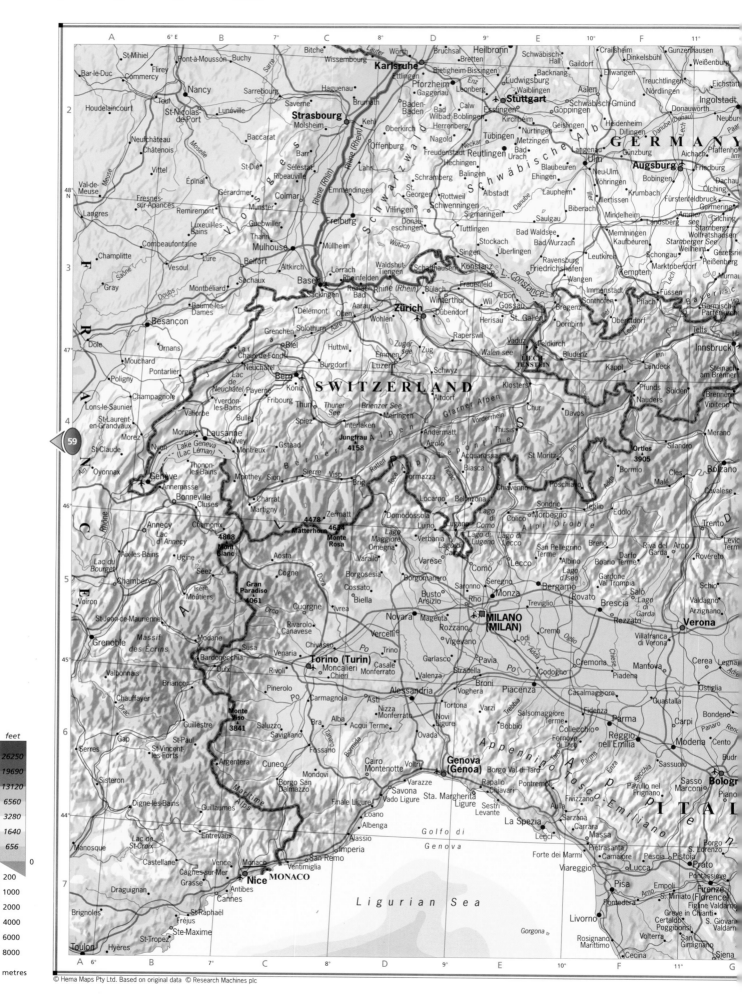

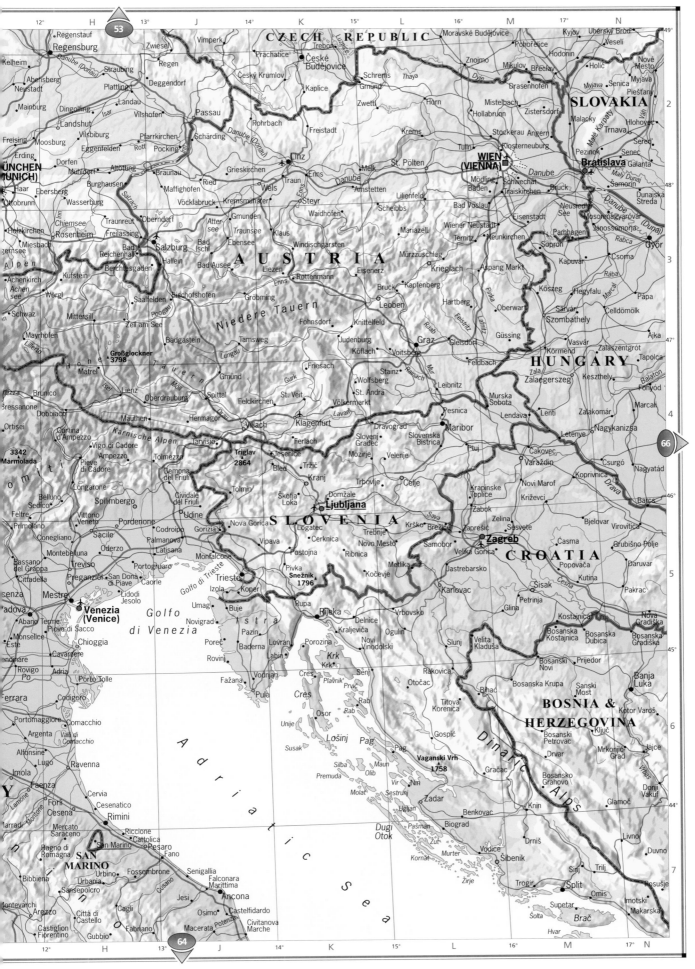

■ over 3 million ● 100 000 – 250 000 ——— country capital underline
■ 1 – 3 million ◦ 25 000 – 100 000 urban area
● 250 000 – 1 million • under 25 000

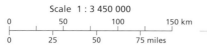

0   50   100   150 km

0   25   50   75 miles

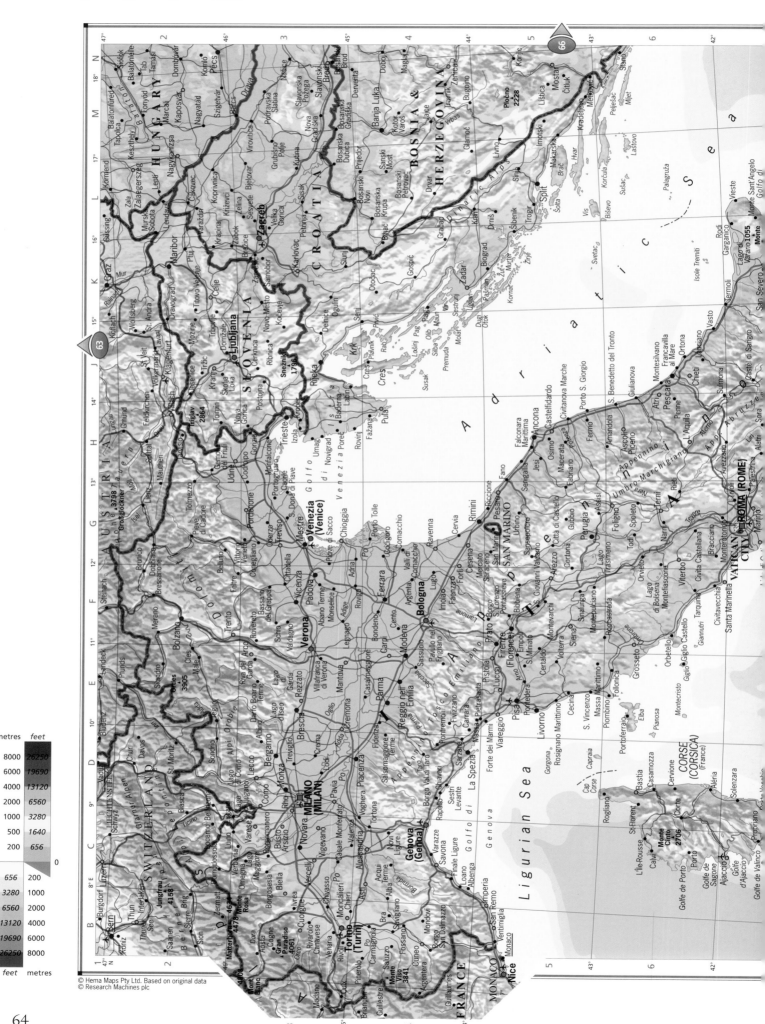

metres	feet
8000	26250
6000	19690
4000	13120
2000	6560
1000	3280
500	1640
200	656
0	0
656	200
3280	1000
6560	2000
13120	4000
19690	6000
26250	8000
feet	metres

© Hema Maps Pty Ltd. Based on original data
© Research Machines plc

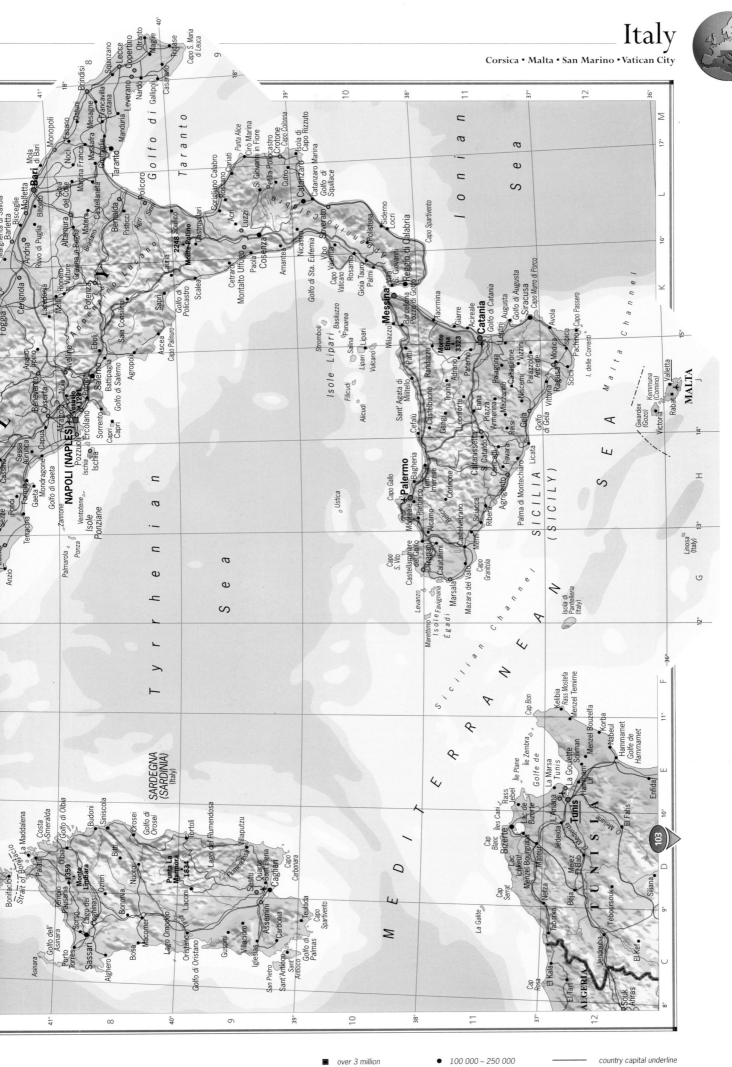

■	over 3 million	●	100 000 – 250 000	——— country capital underline
▪	1 – 3 million	◦	25 000 – 100 000	urban area
●	250 000 – 1 million	•	under 25 000	

K   23°   L   24°   M   25°   N   26°   P   27°   Q

Jzhhorod
Svalyava
Mizhhir"ya
Mukacheve
Berehove
Irshava
Vynohradiv
Khust
Rakhiv
Bila Tisa 2061
UKRAINE
Nadvirna
Kolomyya
Horodenka
Dniester
Borshchiv
Kam"yanets'-Podil's'kyy
Havrylivtsi
Sokyryany
Mohyliv-Podil's'kyy
28°
1 R
29°
S
30°
T

Sáárosnamen y
Mátészalka
Szatmár
Carei
lui
Marghita
arcău
lesd
Simleu
Silvaniei
Zalău

Tyachiv
Bila Tisa
Sighetu
Marmatiei
Viseu
de Sus
Borsa
Chernivtsi
Storozhynets'
Verkhovyna
Siret
Hlyboka
Darăbani
Briceni
Edineţ
Lipcani
Drochia
Yampil'
Soroca
Floreşti
Balta
Kodyma
Kryve
Ozero
Kotovs'k
Anan'yiv
Novoselivka
48°

Mcăsároshamen y
Satu
Mare
Somes
Baia Mare
Baia
Sprie
Rădăuţi
Dorohoi
Botoşani
Hârlău
Fălticeni
Bălţi
Sîngerei
Răut
Rîbniţa
Rezina
Orhei
Dubăsari
Grigoriopol
2

Tăşnad
Baia Mare
Gherla
Dej
Beclean
Bistriţa
Borşa
Vatra
Dornei
Câmpulung
Moldovenesc
Gura
Humorului
Suceava
Paşcani
Târgu
Frumos
Iaşi
Ungheni
Străşeni
Nisporeni
Hânceşti
Chişinău
Tiraspol
Căuşeni
Onestrovsc
Rozdil'na

Carei
lui
Gherla
Reghin
Mureş
Topliţa
Gheorgheni
Bălan
Piatra-Neamţ
Roman
Vaslui
Huşi
Cimişlia
Leova
Comrat
Tighina
Slobozia
ODESA
(ODESSA)
Illichivs'k
3

Cluj-Napoca
Turda
Câmpia
Turzii
Luduş
Târnăveni
Sovata
Miercurea-Ciuc
Comăneşti
Dărmăneşti
Târgu Ocna
Bacău
Adjud
Bârlad
Cahul
Ciadîr-Lunga
Taraclia
Serpneve
Tarutyne
Bilhorod
Dnistrovs'kyy
Ovidiopol'
Sărata
Artsyz
UKRAINE
46°

Gil u
Beiuş
Stei
Abrud
Câmpeni
furile
Aiud
Blaj
Mediaş
Odorheiu
Secuiesc
Baraolt
Oneşti
Târgu
Secuiesc
Putna
Panciu
Tecuci
Mărăşeşti
Tatarbunary
T
4

Brad
Deva
Orăştie
Alba Iulia
Sebeş
Sighişoara
Agnita
ROMANIA
Fagaraş
Sfântu
Gheorghe
Covasna
Mărăşeşti
Focşani
Vulcăneşti
Lacul
Brates
Reni
Bolhrad
Ozero
Yalpug
Kiliya
Izmayil
Vylkove

Hunedoara
Hateg
Călan
Petrila
Sibiu
Avrig
Victoria
2544
Vârful
Moldoveanu
Codlea
Zărneşti
Braşov
Săcele
Râmnicu
Sărat
Nehoiu
Galaţi
Brăila
Măcin
Danube
(Dunărea)
Tulcea
Mouths of
the Danube
Sulina

aransebes
Lupeni
Petroşani
Bumbeşti Jiu
Tălmaciu
Sinaia
Comarnic
Câmpulung
Boldu
Mizil
Buzău
Ianca
Făurei
Brațul
Lacul
Razim
Jurilovca
Sfântu
Gheorghe
45°

Târgu Jiu
Rovinari
Motru
Râmnicu Vâlcea
Curtea de Argeş
Fieni
Câmpina
Văleni de Munte
Ploieşti
Urlaţi
Târgovişte
Urziceni
Slobozia
Hârşova
Babadag
Baia
Lacul Sinoie
5

Orşova
Strehaia
Filiaşi
Ioneşti
Pucioasa
Titu
Buftea
Ialomiţa
Ţăndărei
Corbu

Drobeta-
Turnu Severin
Gratiovica
Pitesti
Colibaşi
Găeşti
BUCUREŞTI
(BUCHAREST)
Fetesti
Cernavodă
Medgidia
Constanţa

egotin
Vidin
Cetate
Bals
Drăgăneşti-
Olt
Slatina
Videle
Bolintin-
Vale
Oltenita
Silistra
Călăraşi
Basarabi
44°

Kula
Calafat
Rast
Daneti
Caracal
Corabia
Turnu
Măgurele
Zimnicea
Vedea
Giurgiu
Danube
(Dunărea)
Tutrakan
Dulovo
Rosita
Băneasa
Negru
Vodă
Mangalia
Durankurak
Nos Shabla

njaževac
Belogradchik
Byala Slatina
Knezha
Iskăr
Svishtov
Byala
Razgrad
Novi
Pazar
Dobrich
Shabla
Kavarna
Balchik
Nos
Kaliakra
6

Midzor
2169
Montana
Berkovitsa
Vratsa
Mezdra
Cherven
Bryag
Pleven
Lukovit
Levski
Pavlikeni
Rosica
Popovo
Türgovishte
Shumen
Provadiya
Devnya
Varna
BLACK

Pirot
Dimitrovgrad
Stara
Botevgrad
Lovech
Osăm
Veliko Türnovo
Gorna
Oryakhovitsa
Preslav
Staro
Oryakhovo
Byala
7

Konstinbrod
Novi Iskür
SOFIYA
(SOFIA)
Teteven
Troyan
Sevlievo
Gabrovo
Dryanovo
Tryavna
Planina
Sliven
Aytos
Karnobat
Nesebür
Pomorie
Burgas
Burgaski Zaliv
Sozopol
Nos Emine
SEA

ulica
Radomir
Pernik
Stanke
Dimitrov
Samokov
Kostenets
Srednogorie
Karlovo
Panagyurishte
Kazanlük
Shipka
Shyama
Yambol
Nova
Zagora
Stara Zagora
BULGARIA
Grudovo
Michurin
42°

Kyustendil
Musala
2925
Ikhtiman
Kostenets
Pazardzhik
Rakovski
Radnevo
Elkhovo
Malko
Türnovo
Rezovo
Igneada
kriva
alanka
amenica
Stanke
Dimitrov
Velingrad
Peshtera
Krichim
Plovdiv
Dimitrovgrad
Chirpan
Gülübovo
Simeonovgrad
Yıldız Dağları

Blagoevgrad
Batak
Asenovgrad
Kharmanli
Kırklareli
Kıyıköy
Razlog
Bansko
Rodopi Planina
Khaskovo
Edirne
Pınarhisar
Vize
Saray
Karacaköy
İstanbul
Boğazı
(Bosporus)
8

IA
Berovo
Gotse
Delchev
Sandanski
Kürdzhali
Ardas
Svilengrad
Babaeski
Lüleburgaz
Çerkezköy
Çorlu
Sariyer
Beykoz
Strumica
Petrich
Pirin
Smolyan
Madan
Momchilgrad
Orestiada
Didymoteicho
TURKEY
Kıyıköy
İSTANBUL
Kartal
41°

Lake
Dojran
K. Nevrokopi
Sidirokastro
Drama
Nea Zichni
Xanthi
Komotini
Soufli
Uzunköprü
Inecik
Tekirdağ
Silivri
Büyükçekmece
Yeşilköy
Büyükada
Pendik
9

vgelija
Kerkinitis
Iraklea
Strimonas
Strumica
Serres
Kavala
Chrysoupoli
Alexandroupoli
Feres
Ipsala
Malkara
Kumbağ
Marmara Denizi
(Sea of Marmara)

polykastro
Kilkis
GREECE
Thrakiko Pelagos
Keşan

K   23°   L   24°   M   25°   N   26°   P   27°   Q   28°   R   29°   S

67

© Hema Maps Pty Ltd. Based on original data © Research Machines plc

Scale 1 : 3 450 000

```
0        50       100        150 km
0    25       50      75 miles
```

metres	feet
8000	26250
6000	19690
4000	13120
2000	6560
1000	3280
500	1640
200	656
0	0
656	200
3280	1000
6560	2000
13120	4000
19690	6000
26250	8000
feet	metres

BLACK SEA

Varna

Provadiya
Devnya
Staro
Oryakhovo
Byala
Aytos
Nos Emine
Nesebŭr
Karnobat
Pomorie
Burgas
Burgaski Zaliv
Sozopol
Grudovo
Michurin
Malko
Tŭrnovo
Resovo
Igneada
Kırklareli
Kıyıköy
Pınarhisar
Vize
Babaeski
Saray
Karacaköy
Lüleburgaz
Çerkezköy
İstanbul
Boğazı
(Bosporus)
Sile
Ağva
Kandıra
Karasu
Akçakoca

Kerempe
Burnu
İnebolu
Cide
Azdavay
Taşköprü
Kastamonu
Bartın
Karrabük
Safranbolu
Zonguldak
Kozlu
Çaycuma
Ereğli
Tosya

İSTANBUL
Sarıyer
Beykoz
Hayrabolu
Muratlı
Çorlu
Silivri
Yeşilköy
Büyükçekmece
Kartal
Pendik
Gebze
İzmit
Hendek
Düzce
Kursunlu
Tekirdağ
Büyükada
Sapanca
Sakarya
Bolu
Gerede
Çerkes
Dağları
Çankırı
Kumbağ
Marmara
Adası
Yalova
Karamürsel
İznik
Gölü
İznik
Geyve
Mudurnu
Köroğlu
Tepesi
2400
Kızılcahamam
Kızılırmak
Şarköy
Türkeli Adası
Kapıdağı
Yarımadası
İmralı Adası
Gemlik Körfezi
Gemlik
Nallıhan
Beypazarı
Çubuk
Çerikli
Erdek
Bandırma
Mudanya
Bursa
Bilecik
Sakarya
ANKARA
Elmadağ
Kırıkkale
Biga
Gönen
Karacabey
İnegöl
Bozüyük
Mustafakemalpaşa
Balâ
92
Susurluk
Eskişehir
Kaymaz
Polatlı
Kaman
Kırşehir
Balıkesir
Dursunbey
Tavşanlı
Kütahya
Sivrihisar
Sakarya
Kulu
Mucur
Gülşehir
Burhaniye
Savaştepe
Bigadiç
Gediz
Yunak
Şereflikoçhisar
Nevşehir
Ayvalık
Demirci
Simav
Emirdağ
Cihanbeyli
Tuz
Gölü
Bergama
Soma
Uşak
Afyon
Bolvadin
Dikili
Kınık
Kırkağaç
Banaz
Çay
Sultanhanı
Aksaray
Akhisar
Gediz
Sandıklı
Akşehir
Ilgın
Kadınhanı
Sarayönü
Niğde
Manisa
Saruhanlı
Gölmarmara
Uşak
Eğridir
Gölü
Dinar
Keçiborlu
Sarıkaraağaç
Bor
Karşıyaka
Menemen
Salihli
Kula
İZMİR
Turgutlu
Alaşehir
Sarıköy
Ağrı
Gölü
Isparta
Eğridir
Beyşehir
Gölü
Konya
Karapınar
Ereğli
Urla
Kemalpaşa
Bayındır
Nazilli
Keçiborlu
Burdur
Burdur
Gölü
Cumra
Seferihisar
Torbalı
Ödemiş
Tire
Germencik
Aydın
İncirliova
Köçarlı
2528
Esler
Dağ
Bucak
Beyşehir
Seydişehir
Kuşadası
Ortaklar
Söke
Cine
Denizli
Kızılkaya
Cevizli
Bozkır
Karaman
Çamiçigölü
Kale
Boz Dağ
2419
Korkuteli
Akseki
Yatağan
Muğla
Serik
**İçel
(Mersin)**
Milas
Köyceğiz
Gölhisar
Geyik Dağ
2877
Kızılalan
Erdemli
Bodrum
Ören
Marmaris
Dalaman
3073
Manavgat
Mut
Datça
Fethiye
Elmalı
Kemer
Antalya
Alanya
Ermenek
Gazipaşa
Silifke
Kalkan
Finike
Kumluca
Antalya Körfezi
Karacal T.
2339
Ovacık
Aydıncık
Rodos
(Rhodes)
Yardımcı
Burnu
Anamur
Megisti
(Greece)
Lindos
Kattavia

MEDITERRANEAN SEA

Aigialousa
Keryneia
Ammochostos
(Famagusta)
Morfou
**Lefkosia
(Nicosia)**
Polis
CYPRUS
C. Arnaoutis
Troodos
Olympus
1952
Larnaka
Pafos
Episkopi
Cape
Greko
Lemesos
(Limassol)

TURKEY
ANATOLIA
Marmara Denizi
(Sea of Marmara)

over 3 million
1 – 3 million
250 000 – 1 million
100 000 – 250 000
25 000 – 100 000
under 25 000
country capital underline
state or province capital underline
urban area

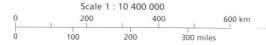
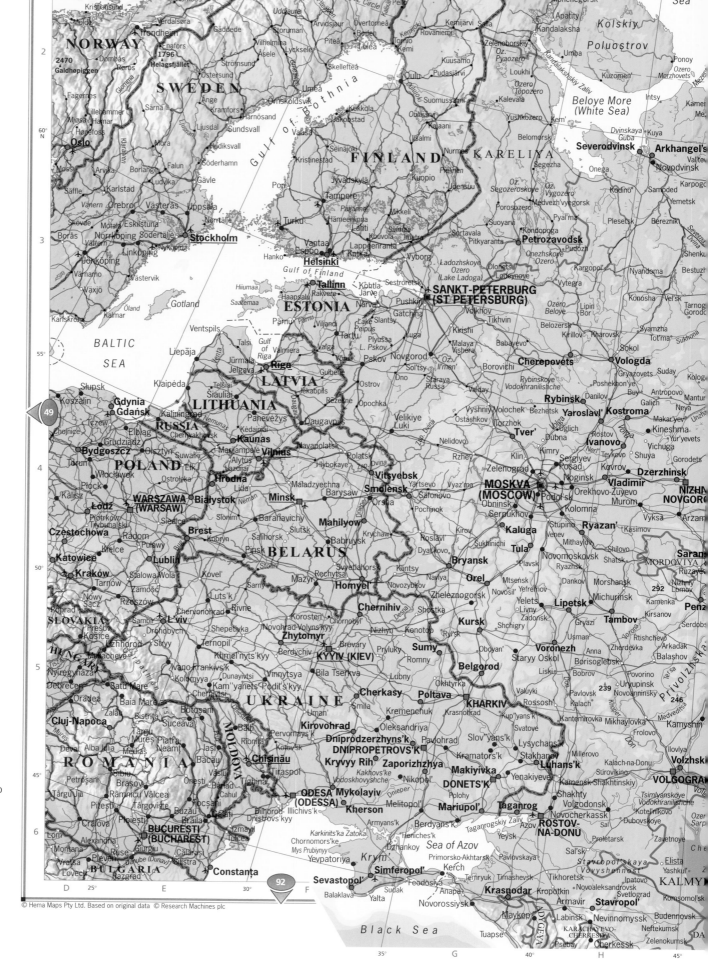

metres / feet

metres	feet
8000	26250
6000	19690
4000	13120
2000	6560
1000	3280
500	1640
200	656
0	0
656	200
3280	1000
6560	2000
13120	4000
19690	6000
26250	8000

feet / metres

© Hema Maps Pty Ltd. Based on original data © Research Machines plc

70

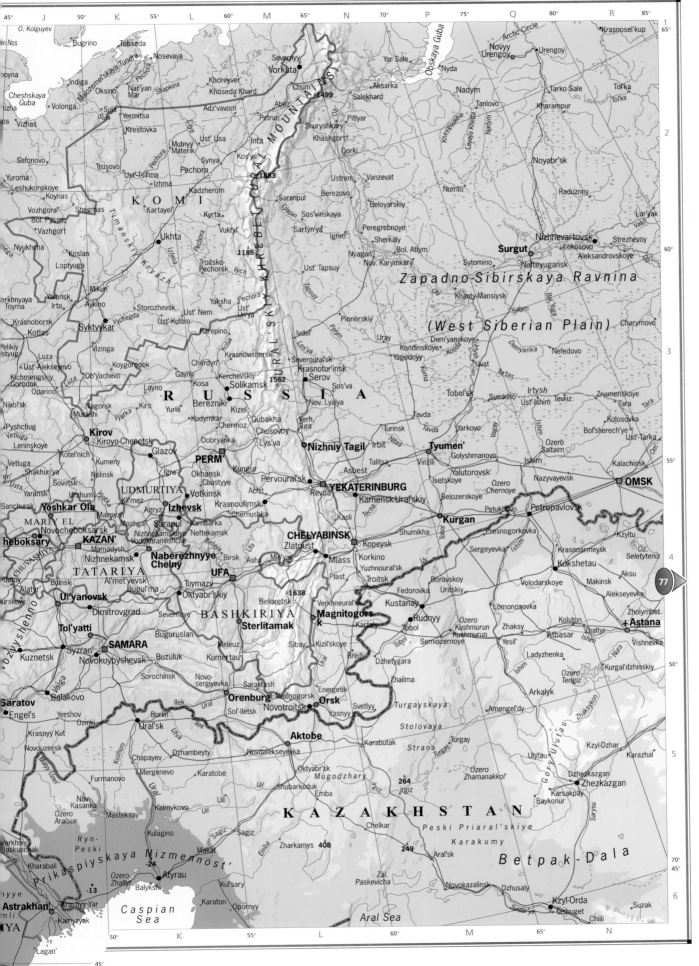

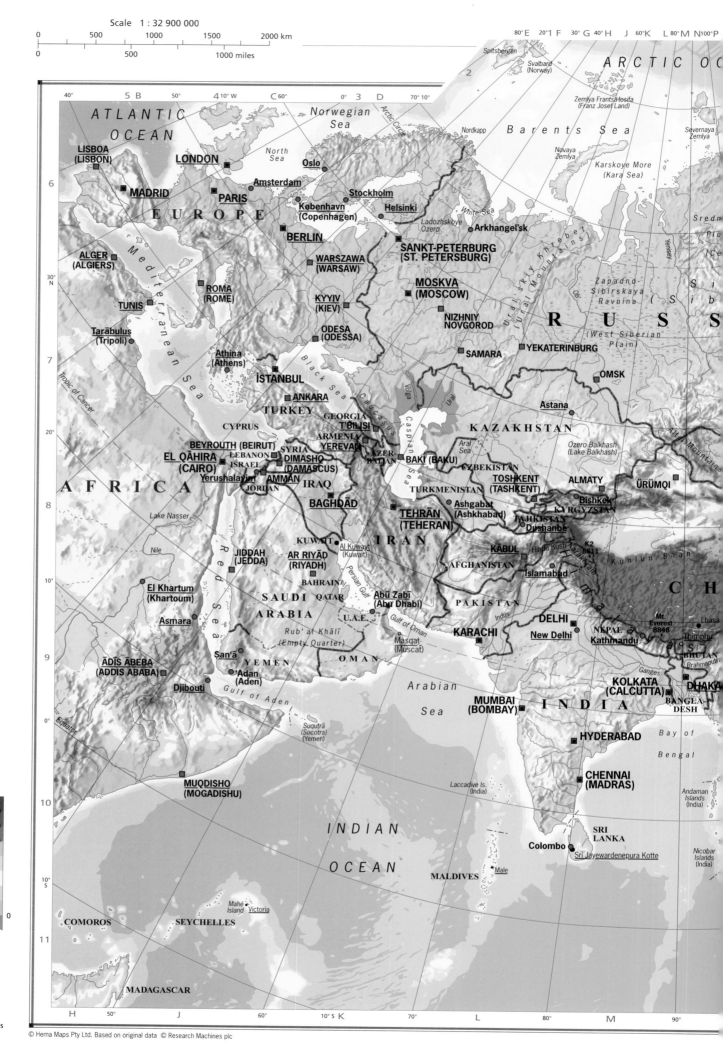

0   500   1000   1500   2000 km

0   500   1000 miles

80°E   20°1 F   30°G 40°H   J   60°K   L 80°M   N100°P

ARCTIC OC

Spitsbergen

Svalbard
(Norway)

Zemlya Frantsa-Iosifa
(Franz Josef Land)

ATLANTIC
OCEAN

Norwegian
Sea

Arctic Circle

Barents Sea

Severnaya
Zemlya

40°   5 B   50°   4 10° W   C 60°   0° 3   D   70° 10°

2

LISBOA
(LISBON)

LONDON

North
Sea

Nordkapp

Novaya
Zemlya

Karskoye More
(Kara Sea)

MADRID

PARIS

Amsterdam

Oslo

Stockholm

København
(Copenhagen)

Helsinki

White Sea

Sredn

Pio

EUROPE

BERLIN

WARSZAWA
(WARSAW)

Ladozhskoye
Ozero

Arkhangel'sk

SANKT-PETERBURG
(ST. PETERSBURG)

RUSS

Ural'skiy Khrebet
(Ural Mountains)

Yenisey

(Ce

ALGER
(ALGIERS)

ROMA
(ROME)

KYYIV
(KIEV)

MOSKVA
(MOSCOW)

Ob'

Zapadno-
Sibirskaya
Ravnina (Sib

(West Siberian
Plain)

R U S S

TUNIS

NIZHNIY
NOVGOROD

Si

Tarābulus
(Tripoli)

ODESA
(ODESSA)

SAMARA

YEKATERINBURG

Tropic of Cancer

Athina
(Athens)

Black Sea

Caucasus

Volga

Ural

OMSK

İSTANBUL

ANKARA

Caspian Sea

Astana

Altai Mountains

TURKEY

GEORGIA

T'BILISI

KAZAKHSTAN

CYPRUS

ARMENIA

YEREVAN

AZER-
BAIJAN

BAKI (BAKU)

Aral
Sea

Ozero Balkhash
(Lake Balkhash)

BEYROUTH (BEIRUT)

SYRIA

LEBANON

DIMASHQ

UZBEKISTAN

TOSHKENT
(TASHKENT)

ALMATY

ÜRÜMQI

EL QÂHIRA
(CAIRO)

ISRAEL

(DAMASCUS)

TURKMENISTAN

Bishkek

KYRGYZSTAN

Yerushalayim

AMMAN

IRAQ

Ashgabat
(Ashkhabad)

TAJIKISTAN

Dushanbe

AFRICA

JORDAN

BAGHDĀD

TEHRĀN
(TEHERAN)

IRAN

KĀBUL

Hindu Kush

K2
8611

Kunlun Shan

C H

Lake Nasser

KUWAIT

Al Kuwayt
(Kuwait)

AFGHANISTAN

Islamabad

Himalaya

Lhasa

Nile

JIDDAH
(JEDDA)

AR RIYĀD
(RIYADH)

PAKISTAN

Indus

Mt.
Everest
8848

Thimphu

El Khartum
(Khartoum)

BAHRAIN

QATAR

Persian Gulf

DELHI

NEPAL

Kathmandu

S

BHUTAN

Asmara

SAUDI

ARABIA

Abū Zabī
(Abu Dhabi)

U.A.E.

Gulf of Oman

KARACHI

New Delhi

Brahmaputra

Rub' al Khālī
(Empty Quarter)

Masqat
(Muscat)

Ganges

KOLKATA
(CALCUTTA)

DHAKA

ĀDĪS ĀBEBA
(ADDIS ABABA)

San'ā

YEMEN

OMAN

BANGLA-
DESH

'Adan
(Aden)

Djibouti

Gulf of Aden

Arabian
Sea

MUMBAI
(BOMBAY)

INDIA

Suqutrā
(Socotra)
(Yemen)

Equator

HYDERABAD

Bay of

Bengal

MUQDISHO
(MOGADISHU)

Laccadive Is.
(India)

CHENNAI
(MADRAS)

Andaman
Islands
(India)

INDIAN

SRI
LANKA

Colombo

Nicobar
Islands
(India)

OCEAN

Sri Jayewardenepura Kotte

MALDIVES

Male

COMOROS

SEYCHELLES

Mahé
Island

Victoria

Mahé
Island

MADAGASCAR

H   50°   J   60°   10° S K   70°   L   80°   90°

metres	feet
8000	26250
6000	19690
4000	13120
2000	6560
1000	3280
500	1640
200	656
0	0
656	200
3280	1000
6560	2000
13120	4000
19690	6000
26250	8000
feet	metres

72

Mt. Everest, China/Nepal : 8,848 m or 29,029 ft

Dead Sea, Israel/Jordan : 400 m or 1312 ft

Aden, Yemen : 4.6 cm or 1.8 in

Mawsynram, India : 1187.2 cm 467.4 in

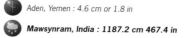

Yangtze, China : 5,980 km or 3,720 mi

Aral Sea, Kazakhstan : 62,000 km² or 23,940 sq mi

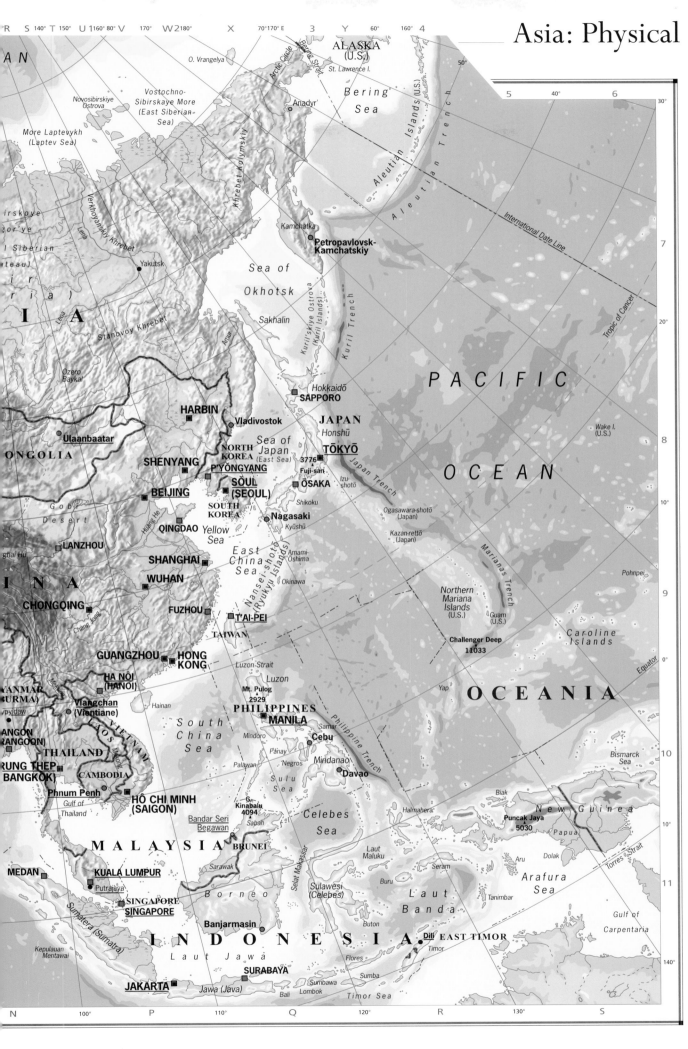

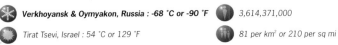

Verkhoyansk & Oymyakon, Russia : -68 ˚C or -90 ˚F

Tirat Tsevi, Israel : 54 ˚C or 129 ˚F

3,614,371,000

81 per km² or 210 per sq mi

44,493,000 km² or 17,179,000 sq mi

48

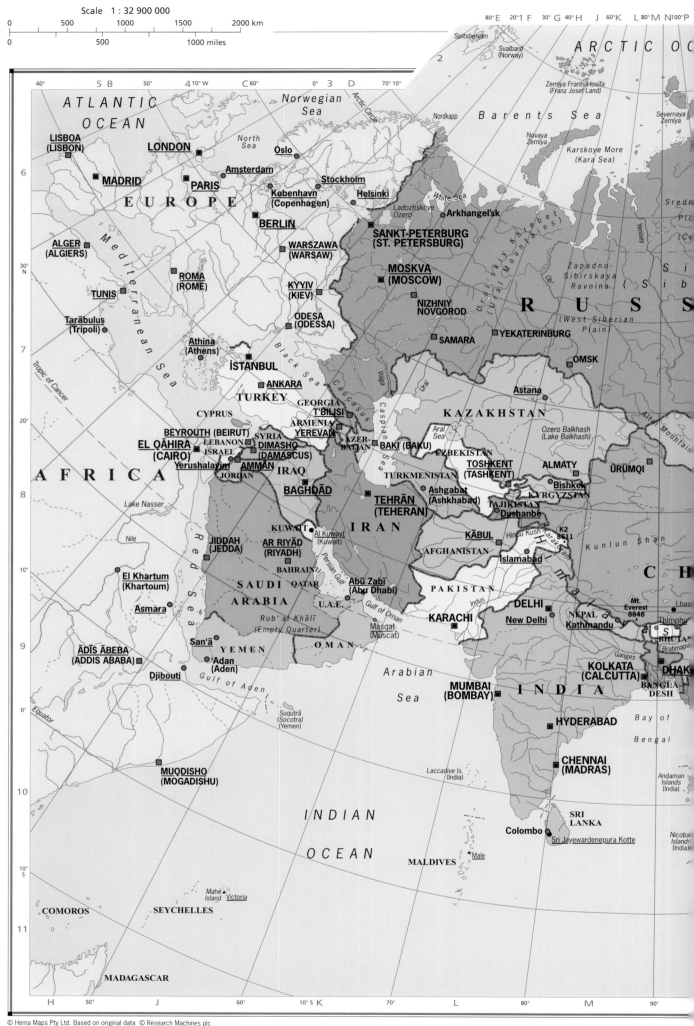

0   500   1000   1500   2000 km

0   500   1000 miles

80°E 20°1 F 30° G 40° H J 60° K L 80° M N 100° P

2

Spitsbergen

ARCTIC OC

Svalbard
(Norway)

Zemlya Frantsa-Iosifa
(Franz Josef Land)

40°   5 B   50°   4 10° W   C 60°   0° 3   D   70° 10°

Severnaya
Zemlya

ATLANTIC
OCEAN

Norwegian
Sea

Arctic Circle

Barents Sea

Nordkapp

Zemlya
Novaya

Sredn
Pl

ATLANTIC
OCEAN

North
Sea

Oslo

Karskoye More
(Kara Sea)

Sr

LISBOA
(LISBON)

LONDON

Amsterdam

Stockholm

White Sea

Arkhangel'sk

Yeni

MADRID

PARIS

København
(Copenhagen)

Helsinki

Ladozhskoye
Ozero

SANKT-PETERBURG
(ST. PETERSBURG)

6

EUROPE

BERLIN

WARSZAWA
(WARSAW)

MOSKVA
(MOSCOW)

Ural'skiy Khrebet
(Ural Mountains)

Zapadno-
Sibirskaya
Ravnina

R U S S

Si
ib

ALGER
(ALGIERS)

30°
N

NIZHNIY
NOVGOROD

YEKATERINBURG

(West Siberian
Plain)

ROMA
(ROME)

KYYIV
(KIEV)

ODESA
(ODESSA)

SAMARA

Ural

OMSK

TUNIS

Athina
(Athens)

Black Sea

Volga

Astana

7

Tarābulus
(Tripoli)

Tropic of Cancer

İSTANBUL

ANKARA

Caucasus

Caspian Sea

KAZAKHSTAN

Ozero Balkhash
(Lake Balkhash)

Altai Mountain

TURKEY

GEORGIA
T'BILISI

Aral
Sea

20°

CYPRUS

BEYROUTH (BEIRUT)
LEBANON
EL QĀHIRA   DIMASHQ
(CAIRO)   (DAMASCUS)
Yerushalayim AMMAN
ISRAEL   JORDAN   IRAQ

SYRIA

ARMENIA
YEREVAN

AZER-
BAIJAN

BAKI (BAKU)

UZBEKISTAN

TOSHKENT
(TASHKENT)

ALMATY

ÜRÜMQI

AFRICA

TURKMENISTAN

Ashgabat
(Ashkhabad)

Bishkek

KYRGYZSTAN

8

Lake Nasser

BAGHDĀD

TEHRĀN
(TEHERAN)

TAJIKISTAN
Dushanbe

Nile

KUWAIT

Al Kuwayt
(Kuwait)

I R A N

KĀBUL

Hindu Kush   Karakoram

K2
8611

Kunlun Shan

C H

JIDDAH
(JEDDA)

AR RIYĀD
(RIYADH)

AFGHANISTAN

Islamabad

BAHRAIN

QATAR

Abū Zabī
(Abu Dhabi)

PAKISTAN

DELHI

Mt.
Everest
8848

Lhas

El Khartum
(Khartoum)

10°

SAUDI

ARABIA

U.A.E.

Gulf of Oman

Indus

KARACHI

New Delhi

NEPAL
Kathmandu

Thimphu

Asmara

Red Sea

Persian Gulf

Masqat
(Muscat)

BHU

Ṣan'ā

Rub' al Khālī
(Empty Quarter)

OMAN

Ganges

Brahmaputra

9

ĀDĪS ĀBEBA
(ADDIS ABABA)

YEMEN

'Adan
(Aden)

Arabian

KOLKATA
(CALCUTTA)

DHAK

Djibouti

Gulf of Aden

Sea

MUMBAI
(BOMBAY)

I N D I A

BANGLA-
DESH

Suqutra
(Socotra)
(Yemen)

HYDERABAD

Bay of

Equator

0°

Bengal

MUQDISHO
(MOGADISHU)

Laccadive Is.
(India)

CHENNAI
(MADRAS)

Andaman
Islands
(India)

10°
S

INDIAN

SRI
LANKA

Nicoba
Islands
(India)

OCEAN

Colombo

Sri Jayewardenepura Kotte

MALDIVES

Male

Mahé
Island

Victoria

10°
S

COMOROS

SEYCHELLES

11

H   50°   J   60°   10° S K   70°   L   80°   M   90°

MADAGASCAR

Mt. Everest, China/Nepal : 8,848 m or 29,029 ft

Aden, Yemen : 4.6 cm or 1.8 in

Yangtze, China : 5,980 km or 3,720 mi

Dead Sea, Israel/Jordan : 400 m or 1312 ft

Mawsynram, India : 1187.2 cm 467.4 in

Aral Sea, Kazakhstan : 62,000 km² or 23,940 sq mi

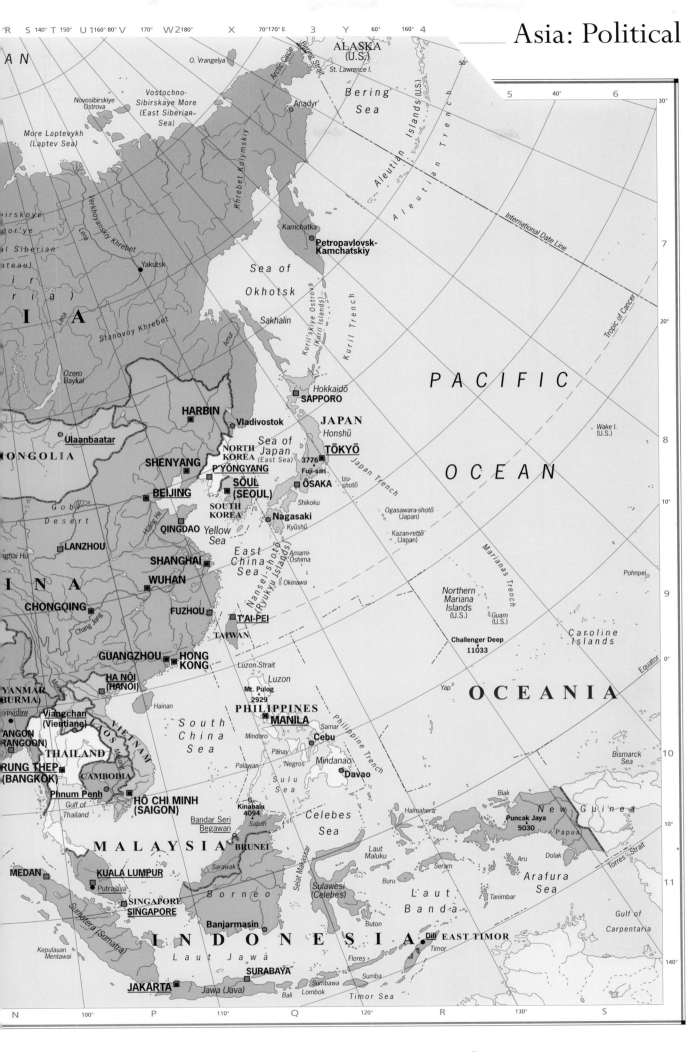

Scale 1 : 13 800 000

```
0        200       400       600 km
0     100     200     300 miles
```

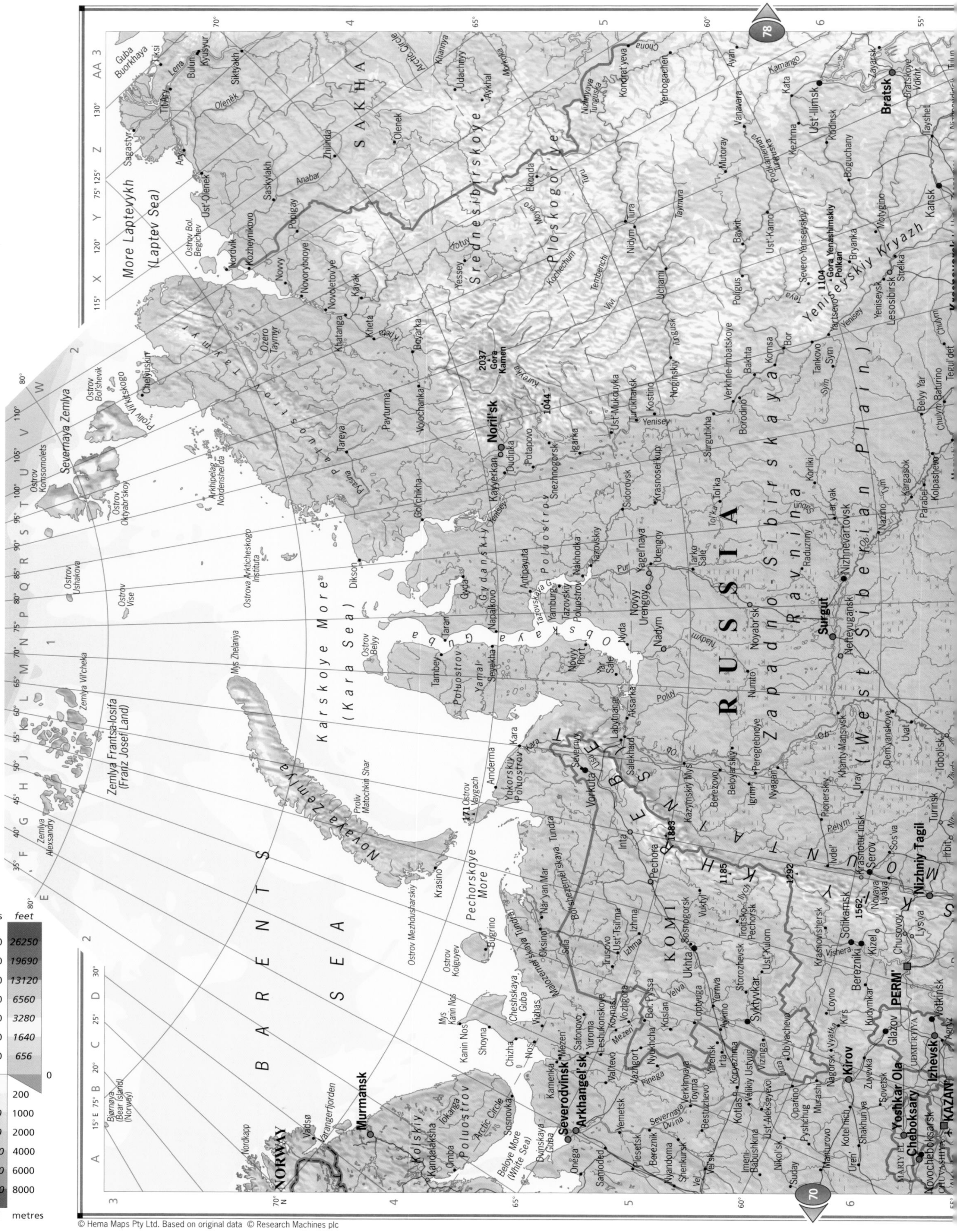

© Hema Maps Pty Ltd. Based on original data © Research Machines plc

metres	feet
8000	26250
6000	19690
4000	13120
2000	6560
1000	3280
500	1640
200	656
0	0

feet	metres
656	200
3280	1000
6560	2000
13120	4000
19690	6000
26250	8000

■ over 3 million
■ 1 – 3 million
● 250 000 – 1 million
● 100 000 – 250 000
◉ 25 000 – 100 000
• under 25 000

——— country capital underline
——— state or province capital underline

Map labels:

More Laptevykh (Laptev Sea)
Severnaya Zemlya
Barents Sea
Karskoye More (Kara Sea)
Pechorskoye More
Beloye More (White Sea)
Zemlya Frantsa-Iosifa (Franz Josef Land)
Novaya Zemlya
Ostrov Kolguyev
Ostrov Vaygach
NORWAY
RUSSIA
SAKHA
KOMI
Zapadno-Sibirskaya Ravnina (West Siberian Plain)
Srednesibirskoye Ploskogo'ye
Yeniseyskiy Kryazh
Taymyr Poluostrov
Yamal Poluostrov
Gydanskiy Poluostrov
Obskaya Guba
Tazovskaya Guba

Cities and towns:
Murmansk, Severodvinsk, Arkhangel'sk, Noril'sk, Dudinka, Surgut, Bratsk, Ust'-Ilimsk, Nizhniy Tagil, PERM', Izhevsk, KAZAN', Kirov, Cheboksary, Yoshkar-Ola, Novocheboksarsk, Vorkuta, Syktyvkar, Ukhta, Pechora, Solikamsk, Berezniki, Kizel, Glazov, Kudymkar, Tiksi, Bulun, Kyusyur, Siktyakh, Olenek, Anabar, Khatanga, Dikson, Igarka, Turukhansk, Yeniseysk, Lesosibirsk, Kansk, Nizhnevartovsk, Nefteyugansk, Khanty-Mansiysk, Tobol'sk, Nar'yan-Mar, Mezen', Onega, Kotlas

2037 Gora Kamen
1104 Gora Yenashimskiy Polkan

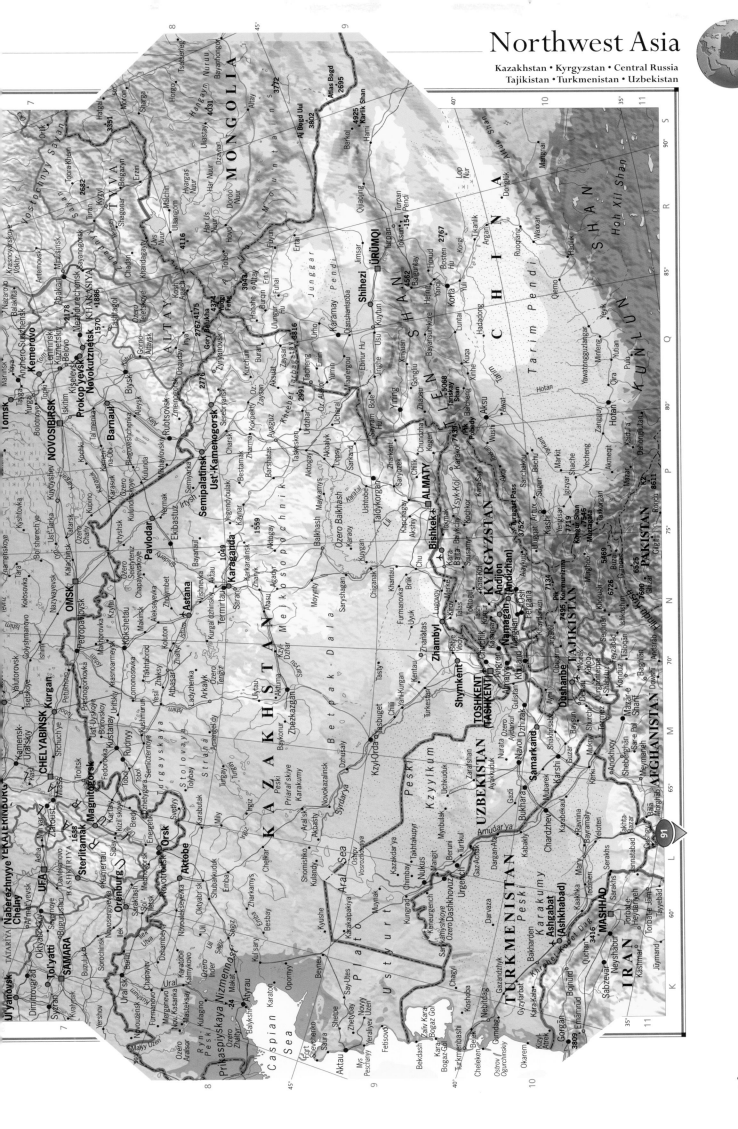

Scale 1 : 13 800 000

0	200 400 600 km
0	100 200 300 miles

More
Laptevykh
(Laptev Sea)

Ostrov Bol'shoy
Begichev

Olenëkskiy
Zaliv

Mys Buorkhaya
Guba

Tiksi Buorkhaya

Vlasc
Yano

SAK

RUSSIA

TYVA
2682

BURYATIYA

Stanovoye
Nagor'ye

Khrebet

MONGOLIA

Gobi Desert

Ulaanbaatar

NEI MONGOL
(INNER MONGOLIA)

CHINA

QIQIHAR
Daqing

HARBIN

CHANGCHUN

JILIN

SHENYANG

KOREA

Sea of
(East

metres	feet
8000	26250
6000	19690
4000	13120
2000	6560
1000	3280
500	1640
200	656
0	0
656	200
3280	1000
6560	2000
13120	4000
19690	6000
26250	8000
feet	metres

© Hema Maps Pty Ltd. Based on original data © Research Machines plc

78

Mongolia • Eastern Russia

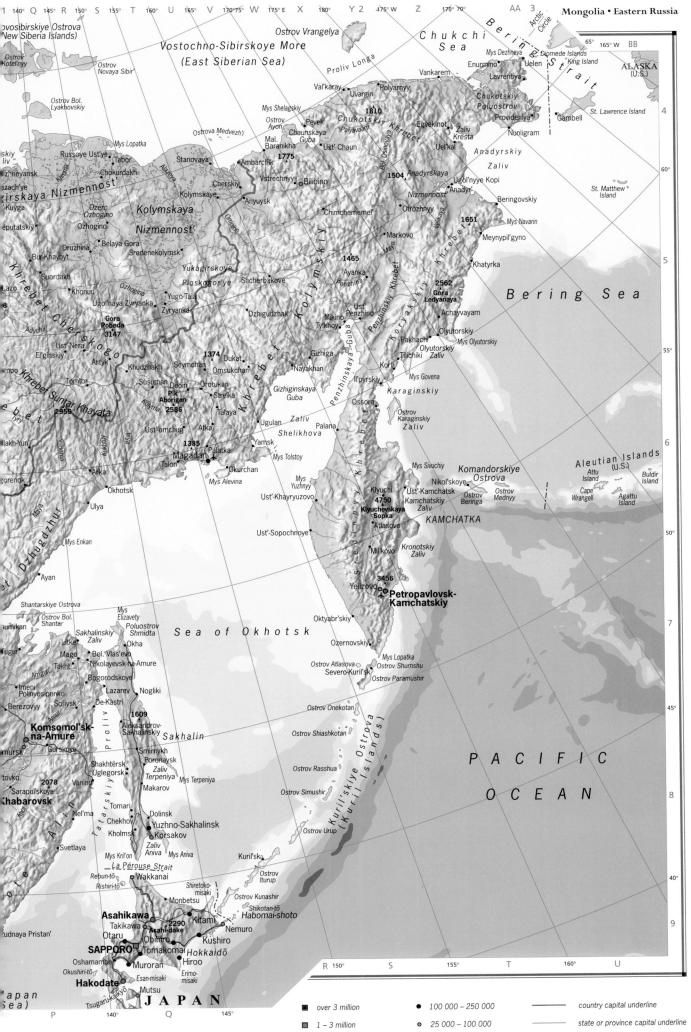

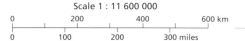
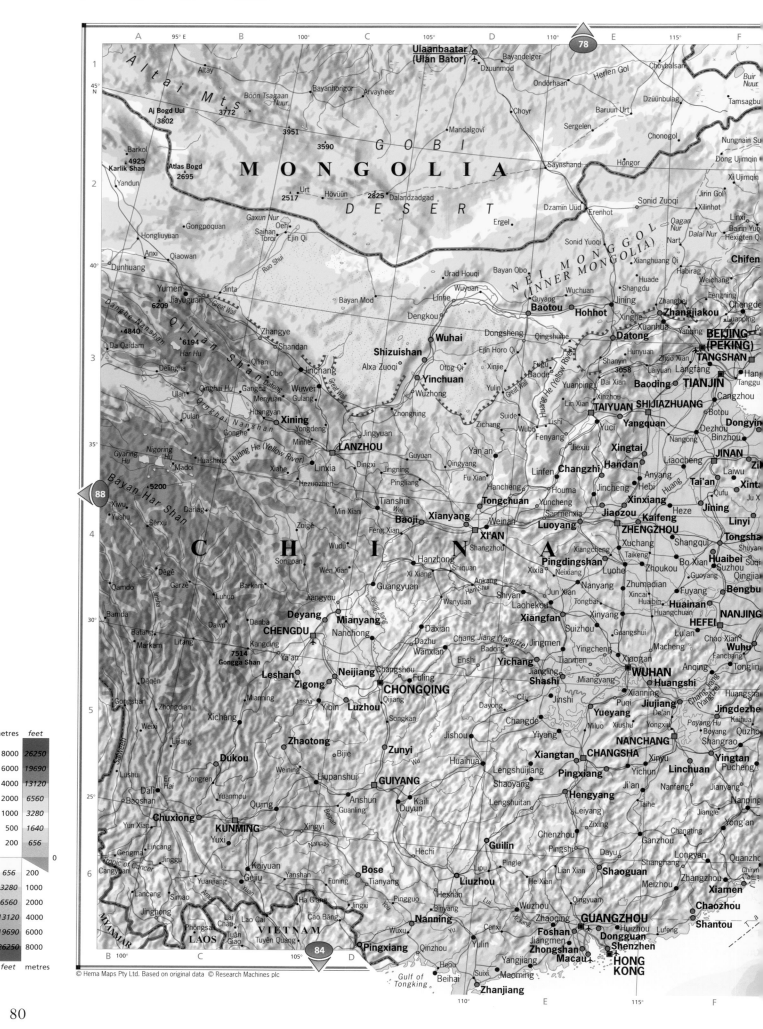

80

■ over 3 million
■ 1 – 3 million
● 250 000 – 1 million
● 100 000 – 250 000
○ 25 000 – 100 000
• under 25 000
—— country capital underline

81

J 138° K 140° L 142° M 144° N 146° P 148° Q 150° R

Wakkanai
Sōya-misaki
Rebun-tō
Rishiri-tō
Teshio
Hamatonbetsu
Esashi
Otoineppu
Ōmū
Okoppe
Haboro
Nayoro
Monbetsu
Tomamae
Shibetsu
Rumoi
Rubeshibe
Bihoro
Kitami
Asahikawa
Takikawa
Asahi-dake
2290
Teshikaga
Kussharo-ko
Shakotan-misaki
Ishikari-wan
Turano
Ashoro
Shakotan-misaki
Otaru
Iwamizawa
Ikeda
Obihiro
Kushiro
Kamoenai
□ **SAPPORO**
Tomakomai
Kutchan
Shikotsu-ko
Date
Oshamambe
Noboribetsu
Monbetsu
Setana
Uchiura-
wan
Muroran
Yakumo
Mori
Urakawa
Okushiri-tō
Erimo
Erimo-misaki

Sea of
Okhotsk

Shiretoko-misaki
1819
Rausu
Ostrov
Iturup
Ostrov
Kunashir
Yuzhno
Kuril'sk
Abashiri
Shibetsu
Shikotan-tō
Nemuro
Shibotsu-jima
Bekkai
Akkeshi

HOKKAIDŌ

Esashi
Kamiiso
Esan-misaki
Kikonai
Hakodate
Ōma
Shiriya-zaki
Ō-shima
Matsumae
Mutsu
Kodomari-misaki
Mutsu-
wan
Yokohama
Noheji
Aomori
Hirosaki
Hachinohe
Ajigasawa
Henashi-zaki
Ōdate
Ninohe
Noshiro
Kazuno
Kuji
Fudai
Morioka
Miyako
Akita
Kawabe
Honjō
Yokote
Hanamaki
Kamaishi
2230
Yuzawa
Kitakami
Sakata
Ichinoseki
Kesennuma
Shinjō
Tsuruoka
Furukawa
Yamagata
Tendo
Ishinomaki
Kinka-san
Ryōtsu
Shibata
Sendai
Natori
Sadoga-shima
Yonezawa
Sōma
Niigata
2105
Sanjō
Haramachi
Suzu-misaki
Nagaoka
Fukushima
...gura-jima
Kashiwazaki
Aizu-
wakamatsu
...ima
Jōetsu
Ojiya
Tajima
Kōriyama
Nanao
Shirakawa
Himi
Nagano
Numata
Kuroiso
Iwaki
...aoka
Mikuni-sammyaku
Utsunomiya
Hitachi
Kanazawa
Maebashi
Kiryū
Katsuta
Komatsu
3180
Ueda
Takasaki
Oyama
Mito
...ga
Matsumoto
Okaya
Chino
Tsuchiura
Kawagoe
TOKYO
Chōshi
...no
Takayama
3192
Kōfu
Hachiōji
Funabashi
Inubō-zaki
Gifu
Iida
3776
YOKOHAMA
Chiba
...aki
NAGOYA
3120
Fuji-san
KAWASAKI
Numazu
Yokosuka
Toyota
Shizuoka
Sagami-
nada
Katsuura
...izuka
Toyohashi
Fujieda
Tateyama
Matsusaka
Hamamatsu
Shimoda
Nojima-zaki
Ise
Ōmae-saki
Izu-
shotō
Kōzu-shima
Miyake-jima
Mikura-jima

HONSHŪ

JAPAN

PACIFIC

OCEAN

Hachijō-jima

Aoga-shima

Sumisu-jima

Tori-shima

J 138° K 140° L 142° M 144° N 146° P 148° Q

0   200   400   600 km
0   100   200   300 miles

95° E   B   100°   C   105°   D   110°

BHUTAN
Tashigang   Hāpoli   Dibrugarh   Tazungdam
Itanagar   Tinsukia   Putao   Zayu   Dêqên
Barpeta   Brahmaputra   Jorhat   Gongshan   Zhongdian   Xichang   **Zunyi**
Goalpara   Nagaon   Golaghat   Maingkwan   Weixi   Lijiang   **Dukou**   Bijie   Huaihua   Jishou
Guwahati   **I N D I A**   Kohima   Myitkyina   Lushui   Dali   Yuanmou   Weining   Liupanshui   **GUIYANG**   Kaili   Duyun
Shillong   Dimapur   Tabong   Yongren   Anshun
Silchar   Imphal   Mogaung   Baoshan   **KUNMING**   Qujing   Xingyi   Guanling   **C H I**
Sylhet   Hopin   Chuxiong   Yuanjiang
Bhairab   Chindwin   Wandingzhen   Yun Xian   Gejiu   Kaiyuan   Yanshan   Funing   **Bose**   Hechi   **Guilin**
Bazar   Agartala   Aizawl   Bhamo   Mong Yu   Lincang   Jinggu   Simao   Lancang   Yangshuo   Pin
Comilla   Katha   Hsweni   Gengma   Lai   Lao Cai   Cao Bằng   Pingguo   Binyang   **Liuzho**
Tropic of Cancer   Karnafuli   Lashio   Châu   Tuyên Quang   Jingxi   **Nanning**   Heshan
Rangamati   Reservoir   Mabein   Muang   Muang   Thai Nguyên   You   Wuxu   Qinzhou
CHITTAGONG   Haka   Mong Yai   Mongkung   Kunhing   Sing   Namtha   Khoua   Viêt Tri   **HA NÔI**   Hôn Gai   **Zhanjiang**   Beihai
BANGLADESH   Monywa   **MANDALAY**   Muang Xai   Son La   **(HANOI)**   **Pingxiang**
Cox's   Myingyan   Amarapura   Kengtung   Phôngsali   Tuân Giao   Tien Yen
Bazar   Kyaukse   Louang   Xam Nua   Mộc Châu   **HAI PHONG**
Teknaf   Paletwa   **3053**   Pakokku   Taung-gyi   Louangphrabang   Ninh Bình   Nam Dinh   Gulf of
Sittwe   **Mt. Victoria**   Chauk   Meiktila   Wan Hsa-la   Salween   Ban   Ban   Thanh Hoa   **Haikou**   Tongking
Magwe   Minbu   **MYANMAR**   Chiang Rai   Mekong   Xiangkhoang   Vinh   Dan Xian   Wencha
Kyaukpyu   Sinbaungwe   **(BURMA)**   Taungdwingyi   Loikaw   Salween   **L A O S**   Ha Tinh   Dongfang   Qionghai   **Hainan**   Tongshi
Ramree Island   Lewe   Mae Hong Son   **Viangchan**   Muang Pakxan   Dông Hôi   Sanya   Lings
Cheduba Island   Taungup   Toungoo   **Naypyidaw**   Chiang   **(Vientiane)**   Khamkkeut   Quang Tri   **Huê**
Sandoway   Pyè   Pasawng   Mai   Nong Khai   Muang   Muang
Bay of   Zigon   Mae Sariang   Loei   Khammouan   Phin   **Da Nǎng**   Hôi An
Kyeintali   Henzada   Papun   Uttaradit   Chiang   Udon Thani   Muang
Bengal   Pathein   Pegu   Thaton   Khan   Sakhon Nakhon   Savannakhét   **V I E T N A M**
Myaungmya   Insein   Moulmein   Phitsanulok   Chum   Mukdahan   Quang Ngai
Cape   Bogale   **YANGON**   Kawkareik   Phichit   Phae   Khon Kaen   Ban   M. Khôngxédôn
Negrais   Labutta   **(RANGOON)**   Tak   Nam Ping   Lam Chi   Khemmarat   Pakxé   Kon
Mouths of   Gulf of   Yel   Chaiyaphum   Roi Et   Ubon   Attapu   Tum
the Irrawaddy   Martaban   **Nakhon**   Nakhon   Suwannaphum   **Ratchathani**   Plây Cu
Preparis North Channel   **Sawan**   Chainat   Mae Nam Mun   Det Udom   Qui Nhon
Preparis South Channel   Sangkhla   **Nakhon**   Surin
Preparis Island   Buri   **Ratchasima**   Sisôphôn   Stœng Trêng   Virôchey   **Buôn Mê**   Tuy Hoa
Coco Channel   Ayutthaya   Sara Buri   Phumĭ Sâmraông   M. Không   **Thuôt**   Ninh Hoa
Coco Island   **T H A I L A N D**   **KRUNG THEP**   Bătdâmbâng   Da Lat   **Nha Tran**
North Andaman   Tavoy   Rat Buri   **(BANGKOK)**   Aranyaprathet   Cam Ranh
Andaman Islands   Phet   Samut Songkhram   Pattaya   **C A M B O D I A**   Kampong Cham   Bao Lôc   Phan Rang
(India)   Buri   Bight   Rayong   Tônlé Sap   Chon Thanh
Middle Andaman   Ritchie's   of   Kâmpóng Chhnǎng   Kampong Cham   Bién Hoa
Archipelago   South Andaman   Bangkok   Ban Hua Hin   Chânthaburi   Krông Kaôh Kông   Tay Ninh   Phan Thiêt
Port Blair   Ko Chang   **Phnum Penh**   Ta Khmau   **HÔ CHI MINH**   Vung Tau
Duncan Passage   Prachuap Khiri Khan   Kâmpôt   **(SAIGON)**
Little Andaman   **A n d a m a n**   Sihanoukville   Lông Xuyên   My Tho
Ten Degree Channel   Bang Saphan Yai   Gulf   Dao Phu Quoc   Rach Gia   Mouths of
Car Nicobar   **S e a**   Chumphon   of   **Cân Tho**   the Mekong
Ranong   Thailand   Ca Mau   Bac Liêu   Côn Son
Takua Pa   Surat Thani   Ko Samui   Nam Can
Katchall   Nicobar Islands   Krabi   **Nakhon Si Thammarat**
Little   (India)   **Phuket**   Thung Song   Phatthalung
Nicobar   Great   Trang   Thale   Songkhla
Nicobar   Luang   **Ban Hat Yai**
Pattani
Satun   Kangar   Yala   Narathiwat
Sabang   Langkawi   Alor Setar   Ban Betong   Kota Bharu
Banda Aceh   Sungei Petan   Kuala Kerai   **M A L A Y**
Bireun   George Town   **G. Korbu**   Kuala Terengganu
Lhokseumawe   Pinang   **2182**   Gerik   Dungun
Takengon   Taiping   **Ipoh**   Kuala Lipis   Kemasik   **Malay**   Laut
I N D I A N   Meulaboh   Langsa   Bentong   Temerloh   Kuantan   **Peninsula**   Natuna Besar   Panarik
SUMATERA   **3145**   **MEDAN**   Bagun Datuk   **Kepulauan**
O C E A N   (SUMATRA)   Gunung Leuser   Tebingtinggi   Temerloh   **Natuna**
Sibigo   Danau Toba   **KUALA LUMPUR**   Seremban   Subi Besar
Simeulue   Sinabang   Pematangsiantar   Putrajaya   Melaka   Segamat   Kepulauan   Tanjung
Singkilbaru   Prapat   Segamat   Mersing   Jemaja   **Anambas**   Datu
Barus   Balige   Bagansiapiapi   Muar   Keluang   (Indonesia)   Siluas
Sibolga   Kotapinang   Dumai
Gunungsitoli   **SINGAPORE**
Nias   **INDONESIA**   Duri   Johor Bahru   **SINGAPORE**   Pemangkat   **Kuchi**

100°   C   105°   D   110°

metres   feet
8000   26250
6000   19690
4000   13120
2000   6560
1000   3280
500   1640
200   656
0   0
656   200
3280   1000
6560   2000
13120   4000
19690   6000
26250   8000
feet   metres

80

E   115°   F   120°   G   125°   H   130°   J

CHINA

Xiangtan
Lianyuan
Lengshuijiang   **CHANGSHA**   Xinyu   Shangrao
oyang   **Hengyang**   Yichun   Pucheng   Wenzhou
Lengshuitang   **Pingxiang**   Ji'an   Fuding
Leiyang   Zixing   Changting   Nanping   Ningde   1
Chenzhou   Taihe   Yong'an   Matsu
Ganzhou   Jiangle   (Taiwan)
Shaoguan   Longyan   Putian   FUZHOU   25°
He Xian   Qingyuan   Quanzhou   T'ao-   Chi-lung
Meizhou   Zhangzhou   yuan   T'AI-PEI
Wuzhou   **Chaozhou**   **Xiamen**   Hsin-chu   3884
GUANGZHOU   Huizhou   **Shantou**   Chinmen   Hsueh-Shan   Tropic of Cancer
Zhaoqing   Dongguan   (Taiwan)   Chang-hua   T'ai-chung
nxi   Jiangmen   **Foshan**   Shenzhen   Chia-i   3950   **TAIWAN**   2
Zhongshan   Shanwei   Yu Shan
Macau   **HONG KONG**   T'ai-nan
Yangjiang   **KAO-HSIUNG**   P'ing-tung
oming   Oluan-pi   T'ai-tung

EAST CHINA
SEA   Nago   Okinawa
Okinawa
Naha
JAPAN
Sakishima-shotō

Nansei-shotō (Ryukyu Islands)

PACIFIC

Luzon
Strait   Batan Islands   20°
Basco

Dongsha Qundao
(Pratas)
(China)   Balintang Channel

Babuyan Islands

Bangui   Claveria   San Vicente   3
Laoag   Aparri
Paracel Islands   Vigan   Kabugao   Lal-lo
Bangued   Tuguegarao
Santa Cruz   Luzon   Palanan
San Fernando   Bontoc   Ilagan
Baguio   Mt. Pulog   Santiago
2929   Casiguran
Alaminos   Dagupan
Lingayen   San Carlos   Baler
Tarlac   Cabanatuan   15°
Angeles   Gapan

SOUTH

CHINA
Olongapo   Polillo Is.
MANILA   **QUEZON CITY**
SEA   **Pasig**   San Pablo   Calauag
Nasugbu   Daet   Pandan
San Pablo   Cantanduanes
Batangas   Lucena   Lopez   Naga
Mamburao   Calapan   Boac   Virac   **Legaspi**
Mindoro   2488   Pinamalayan   Sorsogon
Mount Baco   Masbate   Bulan   Catarman   OCEAN
San Pedro   Masbate   Allen   Samar
Calamian   Coron   Nabas   Placer   Calbayog
Group   El Nido   Kalibo   Roxas   Catbalogan   4
Panay   Borongan
Iloilo   Leyte
Roxas   San Jose de   Bago   **Bacolod**   Ormoc   Tacloban
Buenavista   Cebu   Bogo
Palawan   Bago   **Cebu**   Sogod   Libjo
Puerto Princesa   Carcar   Maasin   Dinagat
Quezon   Cauayan   Bohol   Tagbilaran   Dapa
Negros   Bais   Surigao   Madrid
Brooke's Point   Dumaguete   Butuan   Tandag
Sulu   Sea   Dipolog   **PHILIPPINES**   Prosperidad   10°
Manukan   **Cagayan de Oro**
Bugsuk   2560   Iligan   Bislig
Balabac   Loy   Malaybalay
Balabac   Sibuco   Pagadian   Mindanao   Tagum
Balabac   Strait   Cotabato   **Davao**
Strait   **Zamboanga**   Moro   2954   Mati
Kudat   Isabela   Gulf   Tacurong   Mt. Apo
Langkon   Jolo   Polomoloc   Cape San Agustin
Kota Belud   4094   Palimbang   **General Santos**
G. Kinabalu   Ranau   Pangutaran   Glan   5°
Kota Kinabalu   Sandakan   Group   Sarangani Is.
Beaufort   Tungku   Tawitawi   Kepulauan
SABAH   Lahad Datu   Bongao   Karkaralong   Nanusa
SIA   Semporna   Sulu   Beo
Bandar Seri Begawan   Kalabakan   Archipelago   Kepulauan Talaud
BRUNEI   Seria   Gurung Mulu   Tawau   Celebes   Tahuna   Sangir
2371   Bareo   Sea   **INDONESIA**   6
Bintulu   Belaga   Kepulauan   Morotai
Tarakan   Sangir
SARAWAK   2499   Tanjungselor   Laut Maluku   Daruba
Sibu   Kapit   Tanjungredeb
Sarikei   2988   **INDONESIA**
imangang   **KALIMANTAN**   Sepinang
Muarawahau   Sangkulirang

E   115°   F   120°   G   87   125°   H

■ over 3 million	● 100 000 – 250 000	——— country capital underline
▪ 1 – 3 million	○ 25 000 – 100 000	
● 250 000 – 1 million	• under 25 000	

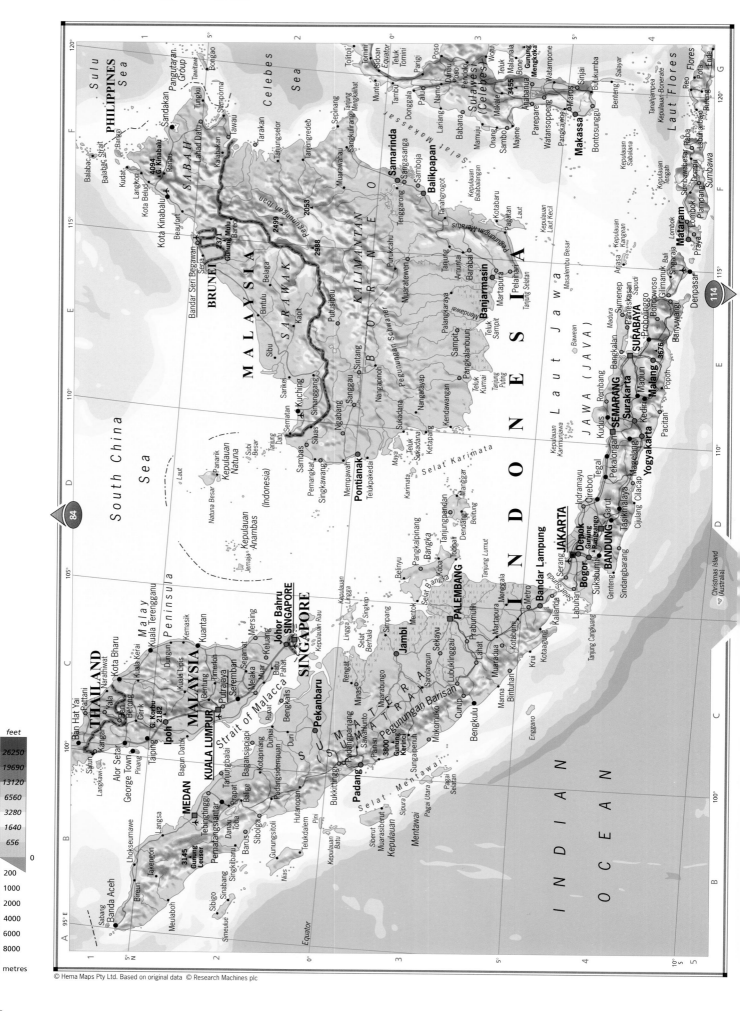

Scale 1 : 11 600 000

metres	feet
8000	26250
6000	19690
4000	13120
2000	6560
1000	3280
500	1640
200	656
0	0
656	200
3280	1000
6560	2000
13120	4000
19690	6000
26250	8000

feet   metres

© Hema Maps Pty Ltd. Based on original data © Research Machines plc

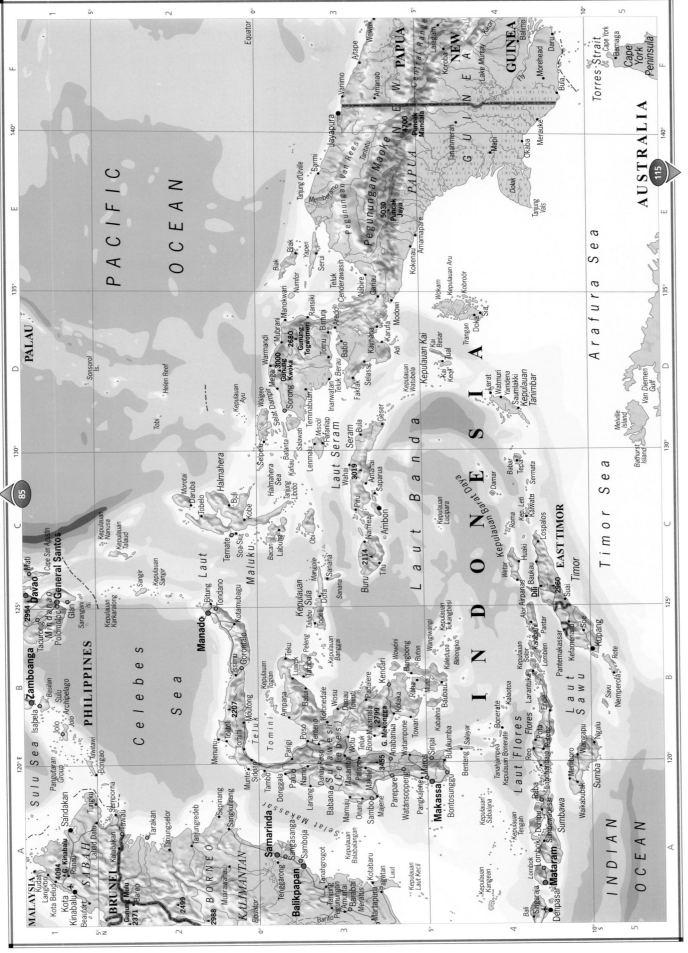

Symbol	Population	Symbol	Population	
■	over 3 million	●	100 000 – 250 000	country capital underline
▪	1 – 3 million	◦	25 000 – 100 000	
●	250 000 – 1 million	•	under 25 000	

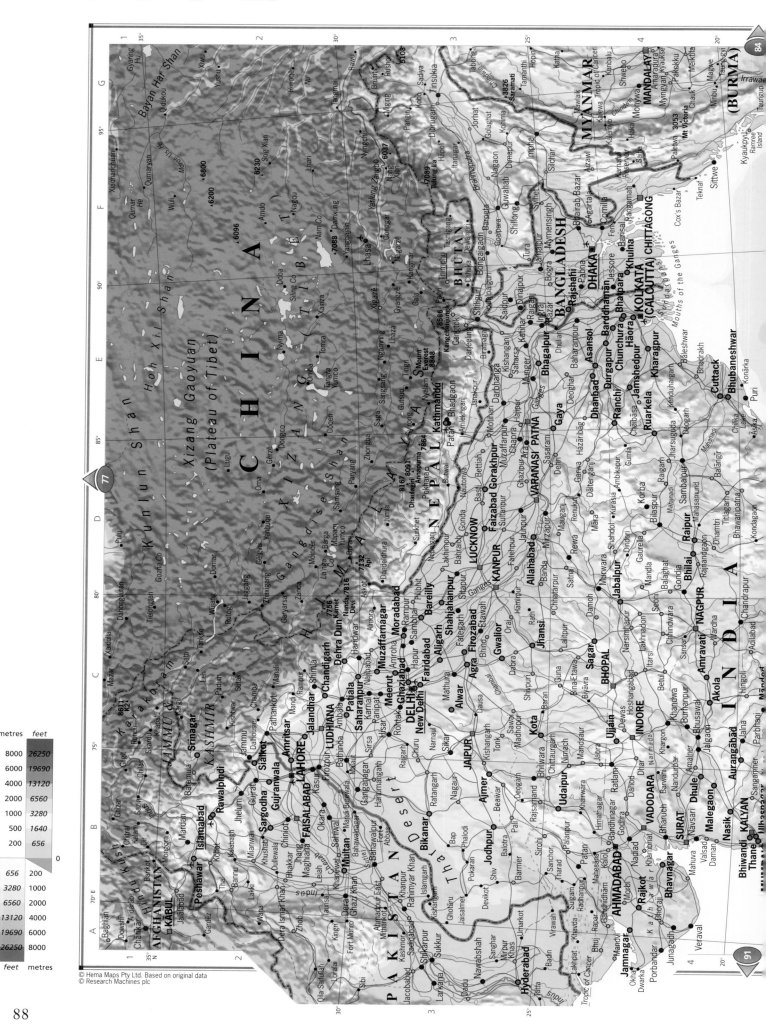

metres feet
8000   26250
6000   19690
4000   13120
2000   6560
1000   3280
500   1640
200   656
0   0
656   200
3280   1000
6560   2000
13120   4000
19690   6000
26250   8000
feet   metres

© Hema Maps Pty Ltd. Based on original data
© Research Machines plc

88

AFGHANISTAN PAKISTAN INDIA NEPAL BHUTAN BANGLADESH MYANMAR (BURMA) CHINA

Bayan Har Shan
Kunlun Shan
Hoh Xil Shan
Xizang Gaoyuan
(Plateau of Tibet)
XIZANG
Gangdise Shan
HIMALAYA
KARAKORAM
JAMMU & KASHMIR
Hindu Kush
Thar Desert

KABUL Peshawar Islamabad Rawalpindi Srinagar LAHORE Amritsar LUDHIANA Jalandhar Chandigarh DELHI New Delhi Meerut JAIPUR Jodhpur Bikaner Ajmer Kota Udaipur AHMADABAD VADODARA SURAT Rajkot Jamnagar Bhavnagar Nasik KALYAN Thane Bhiwandi Aurangabad NAGPUR Amravati Akola INDORE BHOPAL Ujjain Gwalior Agra Firozabad Aligarh Bareilly Moradabad Saharanpur LUCKNOW KANPUR Allahabad VARANASI PATNA Gaya Gorakhpur Faizabad Jhansi Sagar Jabalpur Raipur Bhilai Durgapur Asansol Dhanbad Ranchi Jamshedpur Ruarkela KOLKATA (CALCUTTA) Haora Kharagpur Cuttack Bhubaneshwar DHAKA Khulna CHITTAGONG Rajshahi Barddhaman Bhatpara Chinchura MANDALAY Mt Victoria 3053 Kathmandu Pokhara Thimphu Mount Everest 8848 Kangchenjunga 8586 Annapurna 8091 Dhaulagiri 8167 Nanda Devi 7816 Kamet 7756 Api 7132

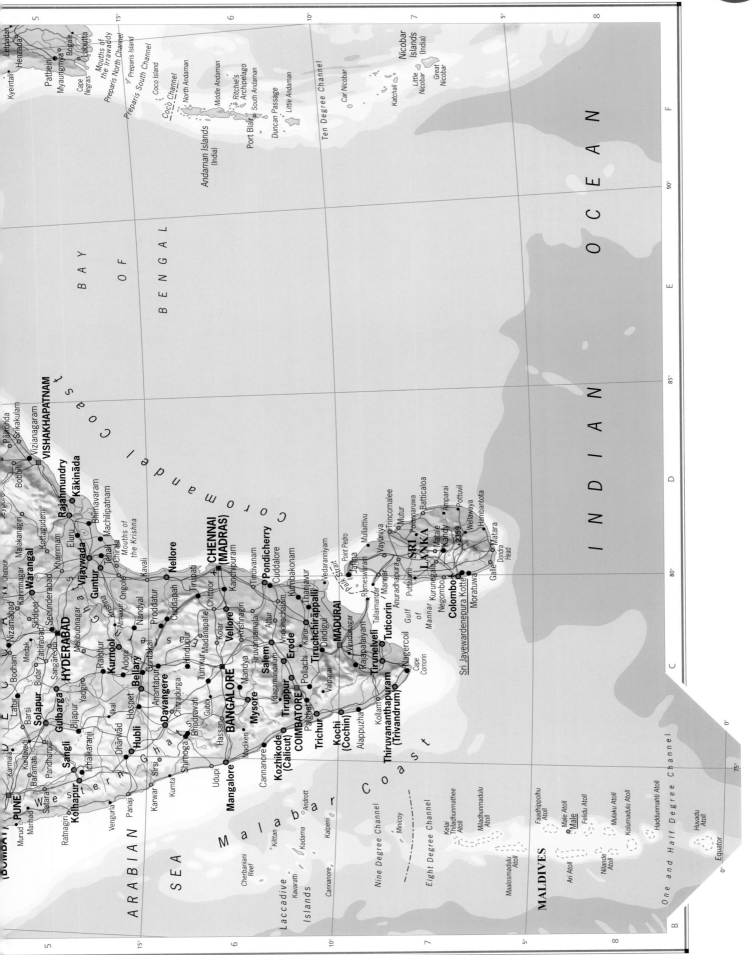

■ over 3 million

■ 1 – 3 million

● 250 000 – 1 million

● 100 000 – 250 000

○ 25 000 – 100 000

• under 25 000

――――― country capital underline

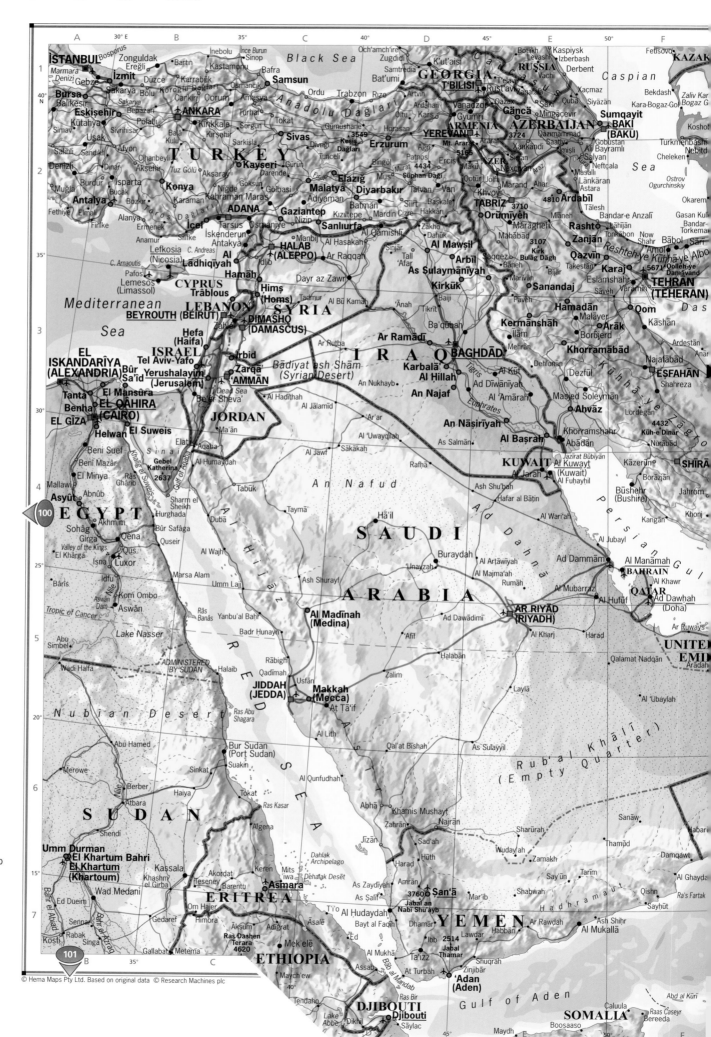

Scale 1 : 12 700 000

| 0 | 200 | 400 | 600 km |
| 0 | 100 | 200 | 300 miles |

metres / feet

metres	feet
8000	26250
6000	19690
4000	13120
2000	6560
1000	3280
500	1640
200	656
0	0

feet	metres
656	200
3280	1000
6560	2000
13120	4000
19690	6000
26250	8000

feet / metres

100

101

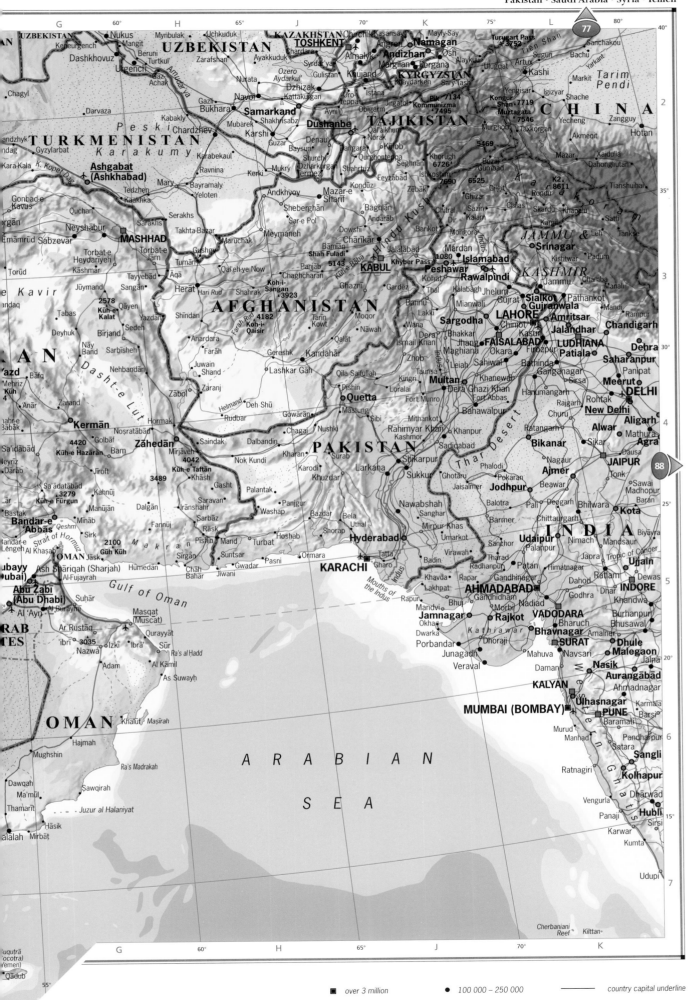

over 3 million

1 – 3 million

250 000 – 1 million

● 100 000 – 250 000

◦ 25 000 – 100 000

• under 25 000

— country capital underline

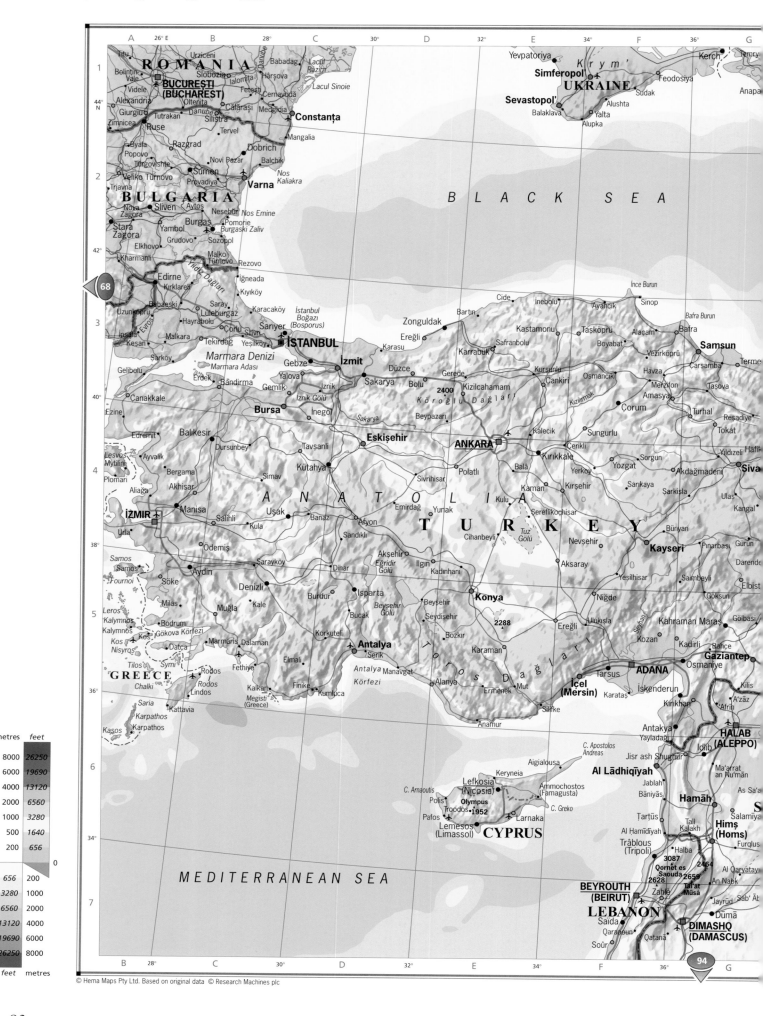

0   100   200   300 km

0   50   100   150 km

A   26° E   B   28°   C   30°   D   32°   E   34°   F   36°   G

ROMANIA

Titu
Bolintin Vale
Videle
BUCUREȘTI (BUCHAREST)
Alexandria
Giurgiu
Zimnicea
Ruse
Tutrakan
Byala
Popovo
Târgovishte
Razgrad
Veliko Târnovo
Șumen
Provadiya
Triavna

Urziceni
Sloboziา
Ialomița
Babadag
Harșova
Cernavodă
Fetești
Medgidia
Călărași
Silistra
Novi Pazar
Dobrich
Balchik
Mangalia

Lacul Razim
Lacul Sinoie

Constanța

BULGARIA

Nova Zagora
Sliven
Stara Zagora
Elkhovo
Kharmanli
Edirne
Kırklareli
Babaeski
Uzunköprü
İpsala
Keșan
Malkara
Șarköy

Aytos
Yambol
Grudovo
Sozopol
Pomorie
Burgas
Burgaski Zaliv
Nesebûr
Nos Emine

Varna
Nos Kaliakra

BLACK SEA

Yevpatoriya
Simferopol
Krym'
Kerch
Temryu

UKRAINE
Sevastopol'
Balaklava
Sudak
Alushta
Yalta
Alupka
Feodosiya
Anapa

İnce Burun
Cide
İnebolu
Ayancik
Sinop
Bafra Burun

Zonguldak
Ereğli
Bartın
Kastamonu
Taşköprü
Alaçam
Bafra
Samsun
Terme

Malko Tûrnovo
Rezovo
İğneada
Kıyıköy
Saray
Lüleburgaz
Hayrabolu
Çorlu
Silivri
Yeşilköy
Karacaköy
İstanbul Boğazı (Bosporus)
Sarıyer
İSTANBUL

Karasu
Karabük
Safranbolu
Boyabat
Vezirköprü
Havza
Merzifon
Çarşamba
Taşova

Tekirdağ
Marmara Denizi
Marmara Adası
Gebze
İzmit
Düzce
Gerede
Kurşunlu
Çankırı
Osmancık
Amasya

Gelibolu
Çanakkale
Ezine
Erdek
Bandırma
Gemlik
Yalova
İznik
İznik Gölü
Sakarya
Bolu
Kızılcahamam
Beypazarı
Kızılırmak
Çorum
Turhal
Reşadiye
Tokat

Bursa
İnegöl
Sakarya
Köroğlu Dağları
2400

Edremit
Balıkesir
Dursunbey
Tavşanlı
Eskişehir
ANKARA
Kalecik
Sungurlu
Yıldızeli
Hafi

Lesvos
Mytilini
Ayvalık
Bergama
Akhisar
Aliağa
Simav
Kütahya
Sivrihisar
Polatlı
Balâ
Kırıkkale
Çerikli
Yozgat
Sorgun
Akdağmadeni
Siva

Plomari
Manisa
Uşak
Banaz
Emirdağ
Yunak
Kırşehir
Kaman
Sarıkaya
Şarkışla
Ulaş
Kangal

İZMİR
Ura
Salihli
Kula
Afyon
Sandıklı
Cihanbeyli
Tuz Gölü
Kulu
Şereflikoçhisar
Nevşehir
Büriyan
Pınarbaşı
Gürün
Darende

Ödemiş
ANATOLIA
TURKEY
Kayseri
Elbist

Samos
Samos
Fournoi
Aydın
Sarayköy
Dinar
Eğridir Gölü
Ilgın
Kadınhanı
Aksaray
Yeşilhisar
Saimbeyli
Goksun

Leros
Kalymnos
Kalymnos
Kos
Gökova Körfezi
Datça
Söke
Milas
Denizli
Burdur
Isparta
Beyşehir Gölü
Beyşehir
Seydişehir
Konya
2288
Niğde
Ereğli
Ulukışla
Kahraman Maraş
Gölbaşı
Kadirli
Kozan

Nisyros
Bodrum
Muğla
Kale
Bucak
Bozkır
Karaman
Ereğli
Şeyhan
Bahçe
Gaziantep
Osmaniye

Tilos
Marmaris
Dalaman
Korkuteli
Antalya
Serik
Manavgat
Alanya
Ermenek
Mut
Tarsus
ADANA

GREECE
Rodos
Fethiye
Elmalı
Antalya Körfezi
Toros Dağları
Karataş
İçel (Mersin)
İskenderun
Kilis
A'zaz

Chalki
Kalkan
Finike
Kumluca
Silifke
Anamur
Antakya
Kırıkhan
Afrin

Saria
Kattavia
Lindos
Megisti (Greece)
HALAB (ALEPPO)
Idlib
Ma'arrat an Nu'man

Karpathos
Karpathos
Kasos

MEDITERRANEAN SEA

C. Apostolos Andreas
Aigialousa
Jisr ash Shughûr
Al Lādhiqīyah
Jablah
Bāniyās
As Sa'a

Keryneia
Ammochostos (Famagusta)
Hamāh

C. Arnaoutis
Lefkosia (Nicosia)
Polis
Olympus
Troodos
1952
Larnaka
C. Greko
Tartūs
Tall Kalakh
Salamīya
Hims (Homs)

Pafos
Lemesos (Limassol)
CYPRUS
Al Hamīdīyah
Trâblous (Tripoli)
Furqlus

3087
Qornet es Saouda
2628
2464
2659
Tal'at Mūsá
Al Qaryatay

BEYROUTH (BEIRUT)
Zablé
Jayrūd
Sab'

LEBANON
Saïda
Halba
Duma

Soûr
Qaraaoun
Qatana
DIMASHQ (DAMASCUS)

metres | feet
8000 | 26250
6000 | 19690
4000 | 13120
2000 | 6560
1000 | 3280
500 | 1640
200 | 656

0 | 0

656 | 200
3280 | 1000
6560 | 2000
13120 | 4000
19690 | 6000
26250 | 8000

feet | metres

■ over 3 million
■ 1 – 3 million
■ 250 000 – 1 million

● 100 000 – 250 000
○ 25 000 – 100 000
• under 25 000

– – – country capital underline
——— state or province capital underline

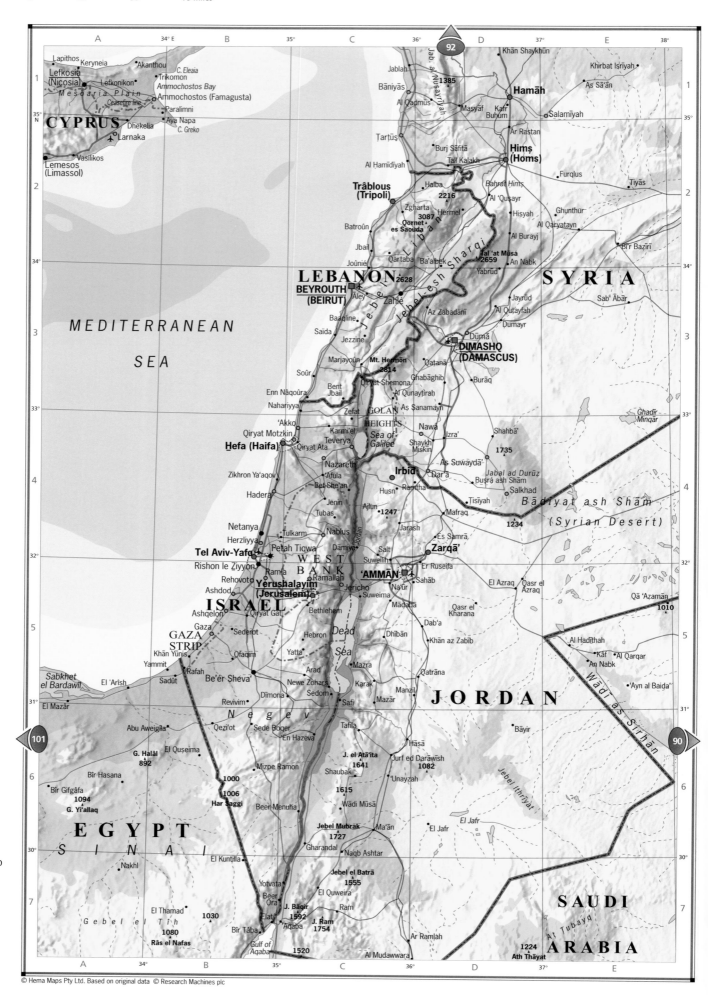

Scale 1 : 2 850 000

| 0 | 50 | 100 | 150 km |

| 0 | 25 | 50 | 75 miles |

CYPRUS

Lapithos Keryneia Akanthou C. Eleaia
Lefkosía Lefkonikon Trikomon Ammochostos Bay
(Nicosia) Mesaoria Plain Ammochostos (Famagusta)
Ceasefire line Paralimni
Dhekelia Aya Napa C. Greko
Larnaka
Lemesos Vasilikos
(Limassol)

MEDITERRANEAN

SEA

Khān Shaykhūn
Jablah
Bāniyās 1385
Al Qadmūs Masyāf Kafr **Hamāh** Khirbat Isrīyah
Buhūm As Sā'ān
Salamīyah
Ṭarṭūs Ār Rastan
Burj Sāfītā Tall Kalakh **Ḥimṣ** Furqlus Tiyās
Al Ḥamīdīyah Halba Baḥrat Ḥimṣ **(Homs)**
Al Quṣayr
Trâblous 2216 Hisyah Ghunthūr
(Tripoli) Zgharta Hermel Al Qaryatayn
Batroûn 3087 Bi'r Bazīrī
Qornet
es Saouda
Jbail Qartaba Ba'albek **Tal 'at Mūsá** An Nabk
Joûnié 2659
LEBANON 2628 Yabrūd Sab' Ābar
BEYROUTH Aley Zahlé Jayrūd
(BEIRUT) Az Zabadānī Al Quṭayfah
Baadline Dūmā Dumayr
Saïda Jezzine **DIMASHQ**
(DAMASCUS)
Marjayoûn Qaṭanā
Soûr **Mt. Hermôn** Ghabāghib Burāq
Bent 2814
Enn Nâqoûra Jbail Al Qunayṭirah
Nahariyya Zefat As Ṣanamayn
'Akko **GOLAN** Nawa Shahbā'
Qiryat Motzkin Teverya **HEIGHTS** Izra' 1735
Ḥefa (Haifa) Qiryat Ata Sea of Shaykh
Karmi'el Galilee Miskin As Suwaydā'
Nazareth Dar'a Jabal ad Durūz
Zikhron Ya'aqov 'Afula Busrá ash Shām
Bet-She'an **Irbid** Ṣalkhad
Hadera Ḥusn Ramtha Tisīyah
Jenin Ajlun 1247 Mafraq **Bādiyat ash Shām**
Netanya Tubas 1234 **(Syrian Desert)**
Herzliyya Nablus Jarash
Tulkarm Jordan Es Samrā'
Petaḥ Tiqwa Dāmiya Salt **Zarqā'**
Tel Aviv-Yafo Ramla Suweilih Er Ruseifa
Rishon le Ziyyon **WEST** Ramallah **'AMMĀN** El Azraq Qaṣr el
Rama **BANK** Jericho Na'ūr Azraq
Rehovot Sahab Qā 'Azamān
Ashdod **Yerushalayim** 1010
(Jerusalem) Mādaba
Ashqelon **ISRAEL** Bethlehem Dab'a Qaṣr el
Qiryat Gat Kharana
Gaza Hebron **Dead** Dhībān Khān az Zabīb
Sederot **Sea**
GAZA Yatta Mazra Qaṭrāna
STRIP Ofaqim Arad
Khān Yûnis Newe Zohars Karak Manzil Al Hadīthah
Yammit Rafah Sedom Kāf Al Qarqar
Be'ér Sheva' Safi Mazār An Nabk
Sabkhet El 'Arîsh Sadūt Dîmona **JORDAN** 'Ayn al Baida
el Bardawîl Revivim Negev Tafila
El Mazâr Qezi'ot Sede Boqer Bāyir
Abu Aweigîla En Hazeva
G. Ḥalâl **EGYPT** J. el Atā'ita Jurf ed Darāwîsh
892 Mizpe Ramon 1641 1082
Bîr Hasana Shaubak
Bîr Gifgâfa 1000 1615 'Unayzah Jebel Ithrīyat
1094 1006 Wādi Mūsá
G. Yi'allaq **Har Saggi** Beer Menuha El Jafr
SINAI Jebel Mubrak Ma'ān El Jafr
1727
El Kuntilla Gharandal Naqb Ashtar
Nakhl Jebel el Batrā
Gebel el Tih 1555
Yotvata El Quweira **SAUDI**
El Thamad Beer Ram
1030 Ora J. Bāgir J. Ram
1080 1592 1754 At Tubayq
Rās el Nafas Bîr Tâba Elat **ARABIA**
Gulf of **Aqaba** 1224
Aqaba 1520 Ar Ramlah Ath Thāyat
Al Mudawwara

SYRIA

92

101

90

metres	feet
8000	26250
6000	19690
4000	13120
2000	6560
1000	3280
500	1640
200	656
0	0

feet	metres
656	200
3280	1000
6560	2000
13120	4000
19690	6000
26250	8000

© Hema Maps Pty Ltd. Based on original data © Research Machines plc

94

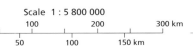

Scale 1 : 5 800 000

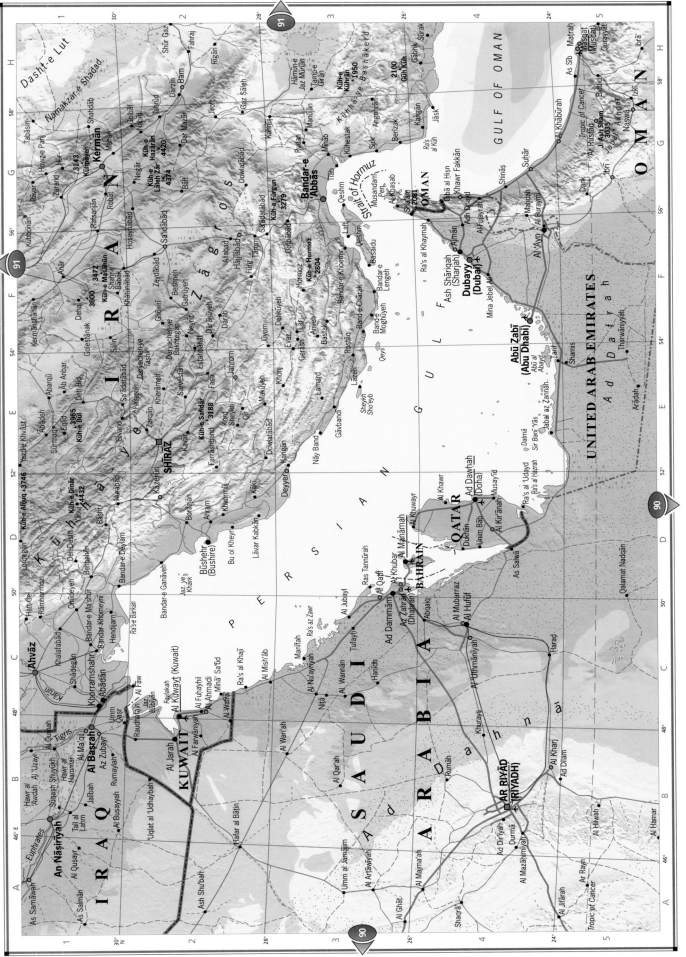

■ over 3 million	● 100 000 – 250 000	—— country capital underline
▪ 1 – 3 million	◦ 25 000 – 100 000	urban area
● 250 000 – 1 million	• under 25 000	

95

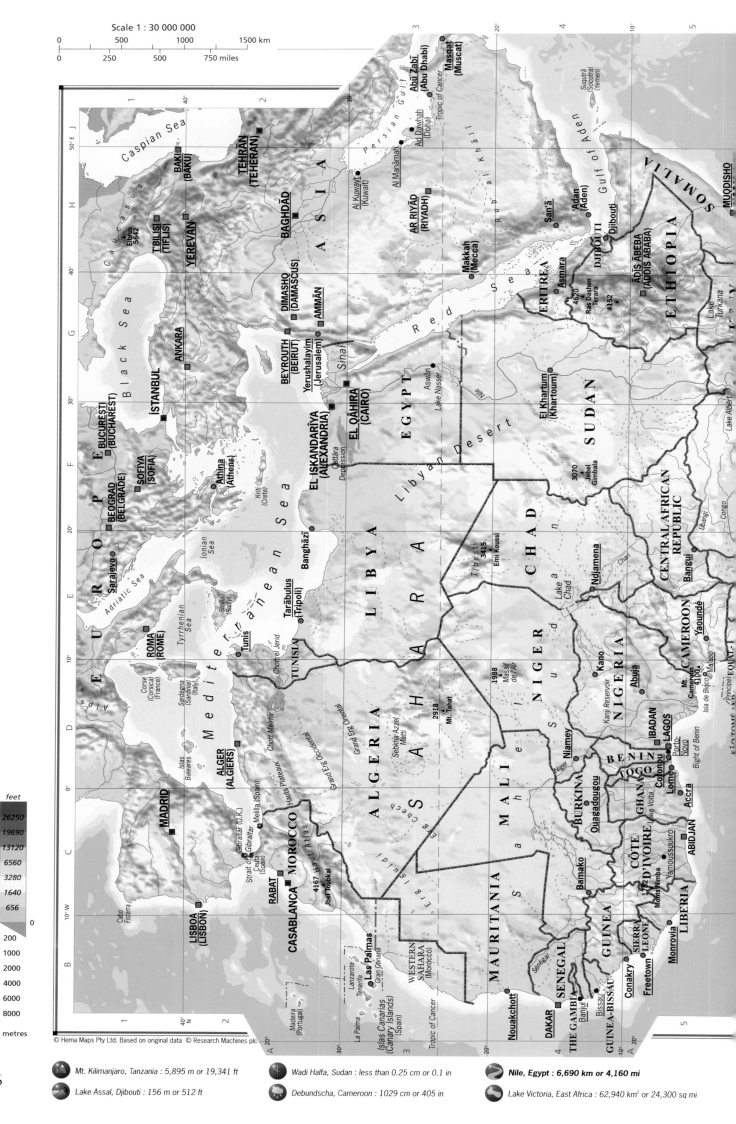

Scale 1 : 30 000 000

| 0 | 500 | 1000 | 1500 km |

| 0 | 250 | 500 | 750 miles |

© Hema Maps Pty Ltd. Based on original data © Research Machines plc

96

metres	feet
8000	26250
6000	19690
4000	13120
2000	6560
1000	3280
500	1640
200	656
0	0

feet	metres
656	200
3280	1000
6560	2000
13120	4000
19690	6000
26250	8000

Mt. Kilimanjaro, Tanzania : 5,895 m or 19,341 ft

Lake Assal, Djibouti : 156 m or 512 ft

Wadi Halfa, Sudan : less than 0.25 cm or 0.1 in

Debundscha, Cameroon : 1029 cm or 405 in

Nile, Egypt : 6,690 km or 4,160 mi

Lake Victoria, East Africa : 62,940 km² or 24,300 sq mi

Ifrane, Morocco : -24 ˚C or -11 ˚F

Al Aziziyah, Libya : 58 ˚C or 136 ˚F

748,927,000

25 per km² or 64 per sq mi

30,293,000 km² or 11,696,000 sq mi

53

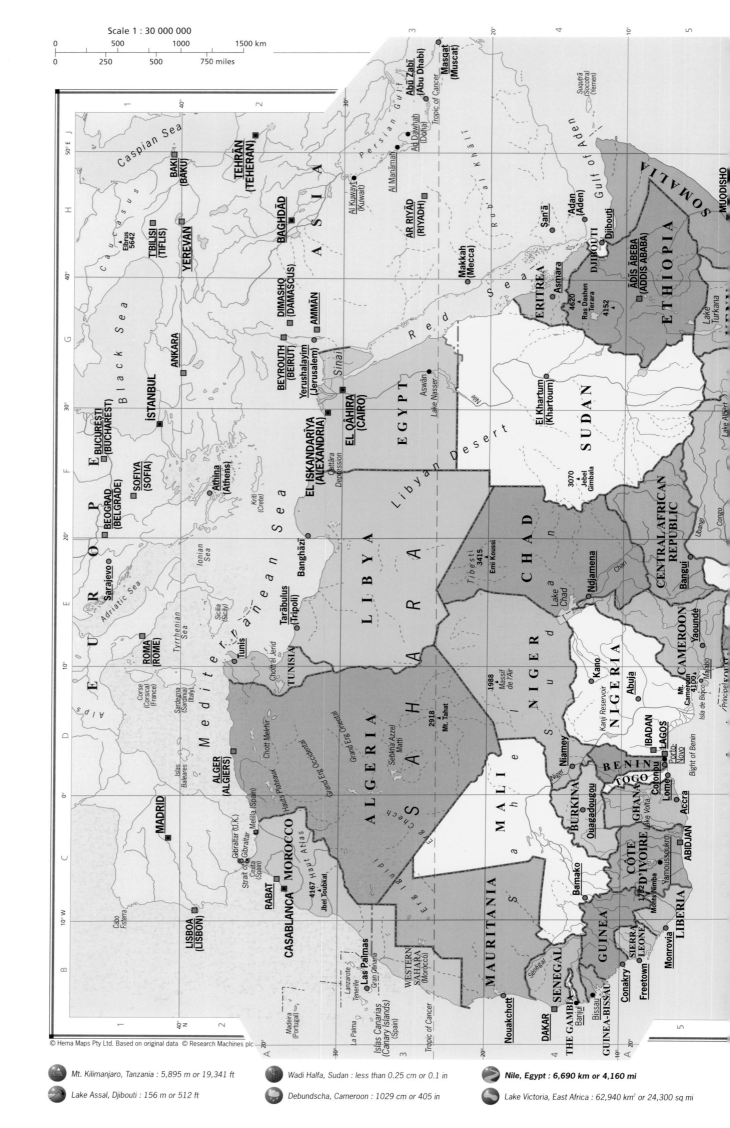

Scale 1 : 30 000 000

| 0 | 500 | 1000 | 1500 km |
| 0 | 250 | 500 | 750 miles |

© Hema Maps Pty Ltd. Based on original data © Research Machines plc

98

Mt. Kilimanjaro, Tanzania : 5,895 m or 19,341 ft

Lake Assal, Djibouti : 156 m or 512 ft

Wadi Halfa, Sudan : less than 0.25 cm or 0.1 in

Debundscha, Cameroon : 1029 cm or 405 in

Nile, Egypt : 6,690 km or 4,160 mi

Lake Victoria, East Africa : 62,940 km² or 24,300 sq mi

INDIAN OCEAN

Seychelles Is.
Coëtivy I.
Amirante Is.
Agalega Is. (Mauritius)
SEYCHELLES
Cosmoledo Group
Glorieuses (France)
Tanjona Bobaomby
COMOROS
Nazidja
Mayotte (France)
Juan de Nova (France)
ANTANANARIVO
MADAGASCAR
Tanjona Vohimena
Tropic of Capricorn

Mombasa
Pemba I.
Zanzibar I.
DAR ES SALAAM
NAIROBI 5199
5895
Mt. Kilimanjaro
Dodoma
TANZANIA
Lake Victoria
Lake Nyasa
Beira
Mozambique Channel
MOZAMBIQUE
Mozambique

Kigali
RWANDA
Bujumbura
BURUNDI
Lake Kivu
Lake Tanganyika
Lake Mweru
MALAWI
3002
Lilongwe
Mt. Mulanje
Lago de Cahora Bassa
HARARE
ZIMBABWE
Bulawayo
Limpopo

REPUBLIC OF THE CONGO
KINSHASA
Kananga
Lomami
Kasai
Lake Mweru
Ndola
Lubumbashi
ZAMBIA
Lusaka
Zambezi
Lake Kariba

MAPUTO
SWAZILAND
Mbabane
Lobamba
DURBAN
Drakensberg
3482
Port Elizabeth
Gaborone
Pretoria (Tshwane)
Johannesburg
Vaal
LESOTHO
Maseru
SOUTH AFRICA
2430
Cape Agulhas
Cape of Good Hope
St. Helena Bay
CAPE TOWN

BOTSWANA
Kalahari Desert
Makgadikgadi
Okavango Delta

ANGOLA
GABON
Brazzaville
CABINDA (Angola)
LUANDA
Cuanza
Kwango
Kwilu
Congo
Annobón I. (Pagalu) (Equatorial Guinea)
São Tomé
Gulf of Guinea

NAMIBIA
Windhoek
Brandberg 2574
Etosha Pan
Cunene
Orange
Namib Desert
Walvis Bay

ATLANTIC OCEAN

St. Helena (U.K.)
Ascension (U.K.)
Tristan da Cunha (U.K.)
Gough I. (U.K.)
Tropic of Capricorn
Equator

Prince Edward Island (South Africa)
Îles Crozet (France)

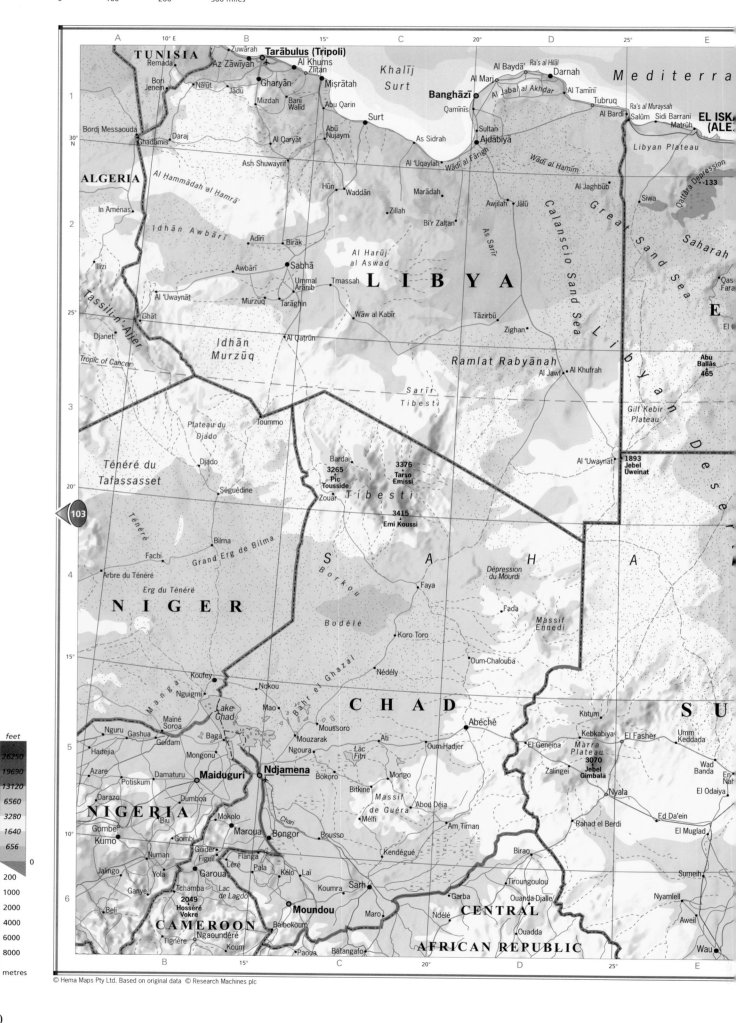

TUNISIA
Remada
Bordj Messaouda
Ghadamis
Daraj
ALGERIA
In Aménas
Idhān Awbārī
Illīzī
Tassili-n-Ajjer
Djanet
Ghāt
Al 'Uwaynāt
Awbārī
Sabhā
Ummal Arānib
Murzūq
Tarāghin
Tropic of Cancer
Idhān Murzūq
Al Qaţrūn

Zuwārah
Az Zāwiyah
Tarābulus (Tripoli)
Al Khums
Zlītan
Gharyān
Mizdah
Bani Walid
Misrātah
Abu Qarin
Al Qaryāt
Abū Nujaym
Surt
Ash Shuwayrif
Hūn
Waddān
Zillah
Adīrī
Birāk
Tmassah
Al Harūj al Aswad
Wāw al Kabīr

LIBYA

Bori Jenein
Jādū
Nālūt

Khalīj Surt
As Sidrah
Al 'Uqaylah
Wādī al Farigh
Marādah
Bi'r Zalţan
Awjilah
Jālū
As Sarīr
Tāzirbū
Zighan
Ramlat Rabyānah
Sarīr Tibesti

Al Bayda'
Ra's al Hilāl
Darnah
Al Marj
Al Jabal al Akhdar
Al Tamīnī
Tubruq
Banghāzī
Qamīnis
Sultan
Ajdābiyā
Wādī al Hamīm
Al Jaghbūb
Al Jawf
Al Khufrah
Al 'Uwaynāt

Mediterra
Ra's al Muraysah
Salūm
Sidi Barrani
Matrūh
Al Bardī
EL ISK.
(ALE
Libyan Plateau
Qattāra Depression
-133
Siwa
Saharah
Great Sand Sea
Qas
Fara
E
El
Abu Ballās
465
Gilf Kebir Plateau
Libyan Dese

Plateau du Djado
Toummo
Ténéré du Tafassasset
Djado
Séguédine
Ténéré
Bilma
Fachi
Grand Erg de Bilma
Arbre du Ténéré
Erg du Ténéré

Bardai
3265 Pic Tousside
Zouar
Tibesti
3415 Emi Koussi

3376 Tarso Emissi

1893 Jebel Uweinat

NIGER

S
A
H
A
R
A
Borkou
Faya
Bodélé
Koro Toro
Depression du Mourdi
Fada
Massif Ennedi
Oum-Chalouba
Nédély

Koufey
Nokou
Nguigmi
Manga
Maïné Soroa
Lake Chad
Mao
Bahr el Ghazal
Moussoro
Kutum

CHAD
Abéché
Kebkabiya
El Geneina
Marra Plateau
3070 Jebel Gimbala
Zalingei
Nyala

SU
El Fasher
Umm Keddada
Wad Banda
En Nah

Nguru
Gashua
Geldam
Baga
Hadejia
Mongonu
Ngoura
Azare
Damaturu
Maiduguri
Dumboa
Ndjamena
Bokoro
Ati
Lác Fitri
Oum-Hadjer
Mongo
Bitkine
Massif de Guéra
Mélfi
Abou Déïa
Am Tīman
Kendégué
Rahad el Berdi
Ed Da'ein
El Muglad
El Odaiya

Darazo
Potiskum
NIGERIA
Gombe
Kumo
Mokolo
Guider
Figuil
Numan
Yola
Jalingo
Ganye
Maroua
Bongor
Bousso
Flanga
Léré
Pala
Kélo
Laï
Tchamba
Garoua
Lac de Lagdo
2049 Hosséré Vokre
Ngaoundéré
Koum
Baïbokoum
Tignère
Beli
Chari
Bogor
Koumra
Sarh
Maro
Moundou
Garba
Tiroungoulou
Ouanda-Djallé
Birao
Ndélé
CENTRAL
AFRICAN REPUBLIC
Paoua
Bātangafo
Ouadda
Sumeih
Nyamlell
Aweil
Wau

CAMEROON

© Hema Maps Pty Ltd. Based on original data © Research Machines plc

metres | feet
8000 | 26250
6000 | 19690
4000 | 13120
2000 | 6560
1000 | 3280
500 | 1640
200 | 656
0 | 0
656 | 200
3280 | 1000
6560 | 2000
13120 | 4000
19690 | 6000
26250 | 8000
feet | metres

103

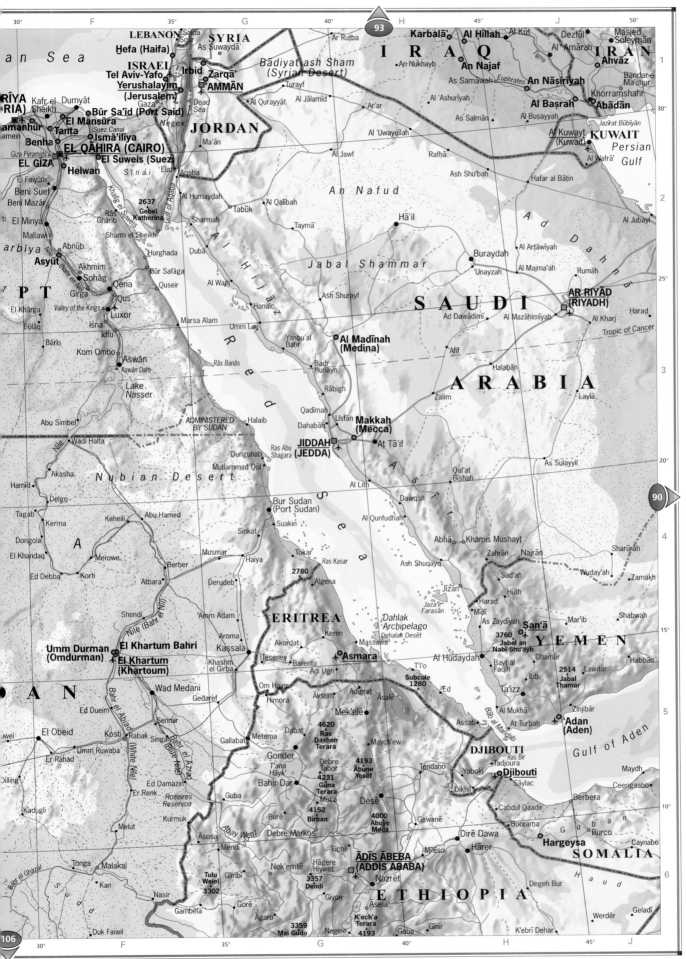

an Sea

LEBANON
Ḥefa (Haifa)
Saïda
Sour
SYRIA
As Suwaydā'
Ar Rutba
Karbalā'
Al Hillah
Al Kūt
Dezfūl
Masjed
Soleymān
I R A Q
Badiyat ash Sham
(Syrian Desert)
An Nukhayb
An Najaf
Al 'Amārah
I R A N

ISRAEL
Tel Aviv-Yafo
Irbid
Zarqā'
AMMĀN
Turayf
As Samāwah
Euphrates
An Nāşirīyah
Ahvāz

RÎYA
RIA)
Yerushalayim
(Jerusalem)
Gaza
Al Qurayyāt
Al Jālamīd
'Ar'ar
Al 'Ashurīyah
Al Başrah
Abādān

Kafr el
Sheikh
Dumyât
Bûr Sa'îd (Port Said)
Dead
Sea
Ma'ān
Al 'Uwayqīlah
Rafḥā
As Busayyah
Al Kuwayt
(Kuwait)
KUWAIT
Bandar-e
Ma'shur
Khorramshahr

amanhûr
amein
El Mansûra
Tanta
Ismâ'ilîya
JORDAN
Negev
'Aqaba
Al Jawf
As Salmān
Al Wafrā'
Persian
Gulf

Benha
EL QÂHIRA (CAIRO)
Suez Canal
Elat
Ma'ān
Ash Shu'bah
Hafar al Bāţin

EL GIZA
Giza Pyramids
Helwan
El Suweis (Suez)
Al Humaydah
Ar'ar

El Faiyûm
Beni Suef
Sinai
2637
Gebel
Katherina
Sharmah
Tabūk
Al Qalībah
Hā'il
Al Artāwīyah
Al Jubayl

Beni Mazâr
Râs
Ghârib
Sharm el Sheikh
An Nafud
Al Majma'ah
Al Jubayl

ti
El Miniya
Mallawi
Abnûb
Hurghada
Dubā
Taymā'
Buraydah
'Unayzah
Rumāḥ
Ad Dahnā

arbîya
PT
Asyût
Akhmîm
Sohâg
Bûr Safâga
Al Wajh
Jabal Shammar
S A U D I
AR RIYĀD
(RIYADH)
Harad

Girga
Qena
Qus
Quseir
Ash Shurayf
Ad Dawādimī
Al Mazāḥimīyah
Al Kharj

El Khârga
Valley of the Kings
Luxor
Isna
Idfu
Marsa Alam
Hanalc
Marsa Alam
'Afif
Halabān
Tropic of Cancer

Bâris
Kom Ombo
Aswân
Umm Lajj
Yanbu'al
Bahr
Al Madīnah
(Medina)
A R A B I A

Aswân Dam
Lake
Nasser
Râs Banâs
Badr
Ḥunayn
Rābigh
Zalim
Layla

Abu Simbel
Wâdi Halfa
Halaib
Ras Abu
Shagara
Muḥammad Qōl
Qadīmah
Usfān
Dahabān
Makkah
(Mecca)
JIDDAH
(JEDDA)
At Ṭā'if
As Sulayyil
Qal'at
Bishah

Hamîd
Akasha
ADMINISTERED
BY SUDAN
Dungunab
Al Lith
Dawqah

Delgo
Nubian Desert
Bur Sudan
(Port Sudan)
Al Qunfudḥah
Abḥā
Khamis Mushayt

Tagab
Kerma
Keheili
Abu Hamed
Suakin
Sinkat
Zahrān
Najrān
Sharūrah

Dongola
El Khandaq
Merowe
Musmar
Tokar
Ras Kasar
Ash Shuqayq
Jīzān
Sad'ah
Ḥūth
Wuday'ah
Zamakh

Ed Debba
Korti
Berber
Haiya
2780
Algena
Jaza'ir
Farasān
Harad
Midi
Mar'ib
Shabwah

Atbara
Ʉerudeb
'Amm Adam
Aroma
ERITREA
Dahlak
Archipelago
Dehalak Deset
As Zaydīyah
San'ā
3760
YEMEN
Habbān

Shendi
Kassala
Akordat
Keren
Massawa
Al Hudaydah
Bayt al
Faqīh
Jabal an
Nabī Shu'ayb
Dhamār
Lawdār

Umm Durman
(Omdurman)
El Khartum Bahri
El Khartum
(Khartoum)
Khashm
el Girba
Teseney
Barentu
Asmara
Adi Ugri
T'i'o
Subcale
1280
Ed
Ta'izz
2514
Jabal
Thamar

Wad Medani
Om Hajer
Himora
Āksum
Adigrat
Aşalē
Al Mukhā
Zinjibār

Ed Dueim
Gedaref
Metema
Dabat
Mek'elē
Maych'ew
Assab
Bāb al Mandab
At Turbah
Adan
(Aden)
Gulf of Aden

El Obeid
Kosti
Rabak
Sennar
Singa
Gallabat
4620
Ras
Dashen
Terara
DJIBOUTI
Ras Bir
Tadjoura
Maydh

Er Rahad
Umm Ruwaba
Gonder
Debre
Tabor
4193
Abune
Yosēf
Tendaho
Yoboki
Djibouti
Ceerigaabo

Dilling
Ed Damazin
Er-Renk
T'ana
Hāyk'
4231
Gŭna
Terara
Dikhil
Şaylac
Berbera

Kadugli
Roseires
Reservoir
Bahir Dar
Mot'a
Desē
Gewanē
Cabdul Qaadir
Boorama
G
u
b
a
n
Burco

Melut
Kurmuk
Guba
4152
Birhan
4000
Abuye
Meda
Directe Dawa
Harēr
Hargeysa
Caynabo

Tonga
Malakal
Āsosa
Mendi
Debre Markos
Fiche
Hāgere
Hiywet
M'eso
Härer
SOMALIA
Degeh Bur

Kan
Tulu
Wejel
3302
Gĭmbī
Nek'emte
ĀDĪS ĀBEBA
(ADDIS ABABA)
Nazrēt
Geladī

Duk Faiwil
Gambēla
Gorē
Āgaro
Giyon
Asela
E T H I O P I A
Goba
K'ebrī Dehar
Werdēr

3359
Mai Gudo
Dendi
Negele
K'ech'a
Terara
4193
Goba

Scale 1 : 11 600 000

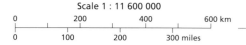

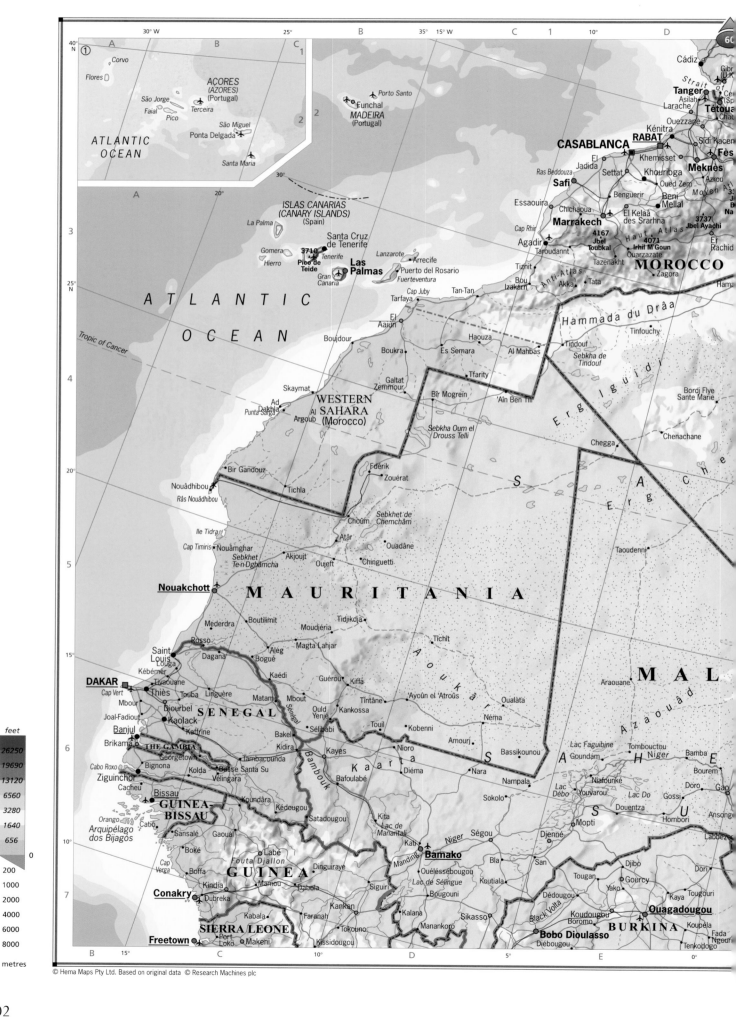

ATLANTIC OCEAN

AÇORES
(AZORES)
(Portugal)

Corvo
Flores
São Jorge
Faial
Pico
Terceira
São Miguel
Ponta Delgada
Santa Maria

Porto Santo
Funchal
MADEIRA
(Portugal)

ISLAS CANARIAS
(CANARY ISLANDS)
(Spain)
La Palma
Gomera
Hierro
Pico de Teide
3710
Tenerife
Santa Cruz
de Tenerife
Gran Canaria
Las Palmas
Lanzarote
Arrecife
Fuerteventura
Puerto del Rosario

ATLANTIC

OCEAN

Tropic of Cancer

Cádiz
Gibr
(U.K.
Strait
of
Gib
Tanger
Asilah
Larache
Ouezzane
Kénitra
RABAT
Tétoua
Chat
Sidi Kacen
Fès
Meknès
Azrou
Moye
CASABLANCA
El Jadida
Khemisset
Settat
Khouribga
Safi
Ras Beddouza
Oued Zem
Beni Mellal
Benguerir
El Kelaâ
des Srarhna
Essaouira
Chichaoua
Marrakech
4167
Jbel
Toubkal
4071
Irhil M'Goun
3737
Jbel Ayachi
El Rachid
Hama
Cap Rhir
Agadir
Taroudannt
Tazenakht
Ouarzazate
Zagora
MOROCCO
Tiznit
Bou Izakarn
Akka
Tata
Anti-Atlas
Haut Atlas
Hammada du Drâa
Tinfouchy
Tan-Tan
Tarfaya
Cap Juby
El Aaiún
Haouza
Es Semara
Al Mahbâs
Tindouf
Sebkha de
Tindouf
Boujdour
Boukra
Skaymat
Galtat Zemmour
Tfarity
WESTERN
SAHARA
(Morocco)
Bîr Mogrein
'Aïn Ben Tili
Bordj Flye
Sante Marie
Ad Dakhla
Punta Sarga
Argoub
Fderik
Zouérat
Sebkha Oum el
Drouss Telli
Chegga
Chenachane
Bir Gandouz
Tichla
Nouâdhibou
Râs Nouâdhibou
Choûm
Sebkhet de
Chemchâm
Atâr
Ouadâne
Taoudenni
Erg Iguidi
Erg Ache
Erg Ag
S A
H A
R A
Ile Tidra
Cap Timiris
Nouâmghar
Sebkhet
Te-n-Dghâmcha
Akjoujt
Oujeft
Chinguetti
MAURITANIA
Nouakchott
Mederdra
Boutilimit
Moudjéria
Tidjikdja
Tichît
Aoukar
Araouane
MAL
Saint Louis
Rosso
Dagana
Aleg
Bogué
Magta Lahjar
Guérou
Kiffa
'Ayoûn el 'Atroûs
Oualâta
Néma
Tombouctou
Lac Faguibine
Goundam
Bamba
Niger
Louga
Kébémer
DAKAR
Cap Vert
Thiès
Tivaouane
Touba
Linguère
Matam
Mbout
Kaédi
Ould Yenjé
Kankossa
Tintâne
Touil
Kobenni
Amourj
Bassikounou
Nampala
Nara
Lac
Débo
Niafunké
Doro
Gao
Mbour
Diourbel
SENEGAL
Joal-Fadiout
Kaolack
Kaffrine
Fatick
Bakel
Sélibâbi
Kayes
Nioro
Diéma
Kaarta
Sokolo
Youvarou
Lac Do
Gossi
Hombori
Ansong
Banjul
Brikama
THE GAMBIA
Georgetown
Kidira
Bambouk
Kita
Lac de
Manantali
Kati
Bla
San
Djenné
Mopti
Douentza
Labbez
Cabo Roxo
Bignona
Ziguinchor
Cacheu
Kolda
Vélingara
Basse Santa Su
Tambacounda
Bafoulabé
BURKINA
Bissau
GUINEA-
BISSAU
Koundâra
Kédougou
Satadougou
Lac de
Manantali
Bamako
Ségou
Koutiala
Tougan
Dédougou
Djibo
Dori
Orango
Arquipélago
dos Bijagós
Sansalé
Gaoual
Boké
Labé
Fouta Djallon
Dinguiraye
Siguiri
Ouéléssébougou
Lac de Sélingue
Bougouni
Koudougou
Yako
Boromo
Kaya
Tougouri
Ouagadougou
Cap Verga
Boffa
GUINEA
Mamou
Dabola
Kankan
Kalana
Sikasso
Black Volta
Gourcy
Fada
Ngou
Tenkodogo
Koupéla
Conakry
Dubreka
Kindia
Kabala
Faranah
Kissidougou
Makeni
SIERRA LEONE
Freetown
Port Loko
Tokouno
Mananko ro
Diébougou
Bobo Dioulasso

metres	feet
8000	26250
6000	19690
4000	13120
2000	6560
1000	3280
500	1640
200	656

0	0
656	200
3280	1000
6560	2000
13120	4000
19690	6000
26250	8000

feet | metres

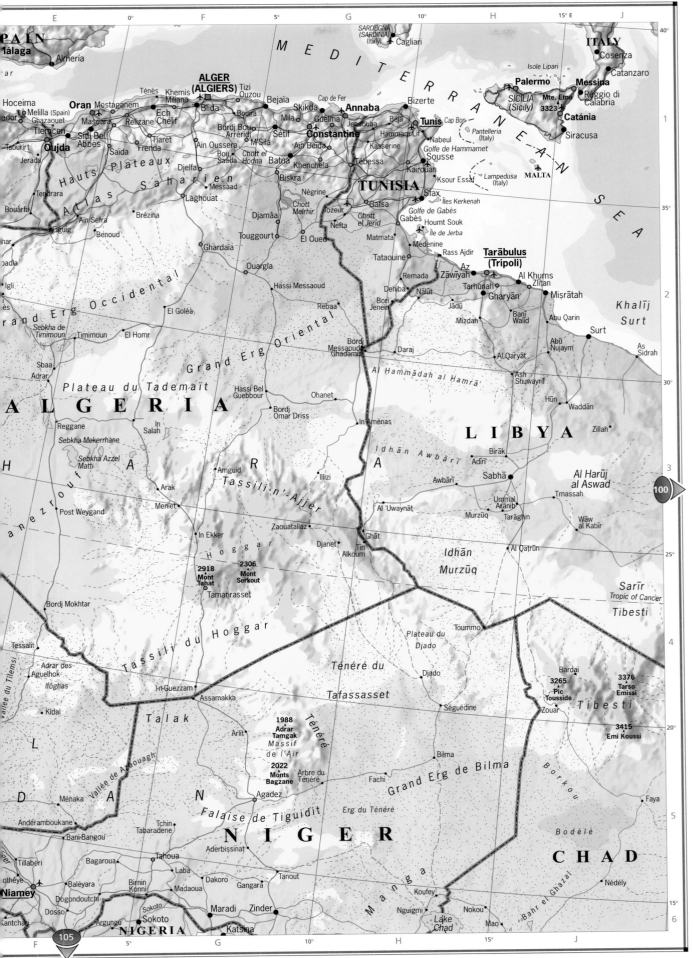

- ■ over 3 million
- ■ 1 – 3 million
- ● 250 000 – 1 million
- ● 100 000 – 250 000
- ● 25 000 – 100 000
- • under 25 000
- —— country capital underline

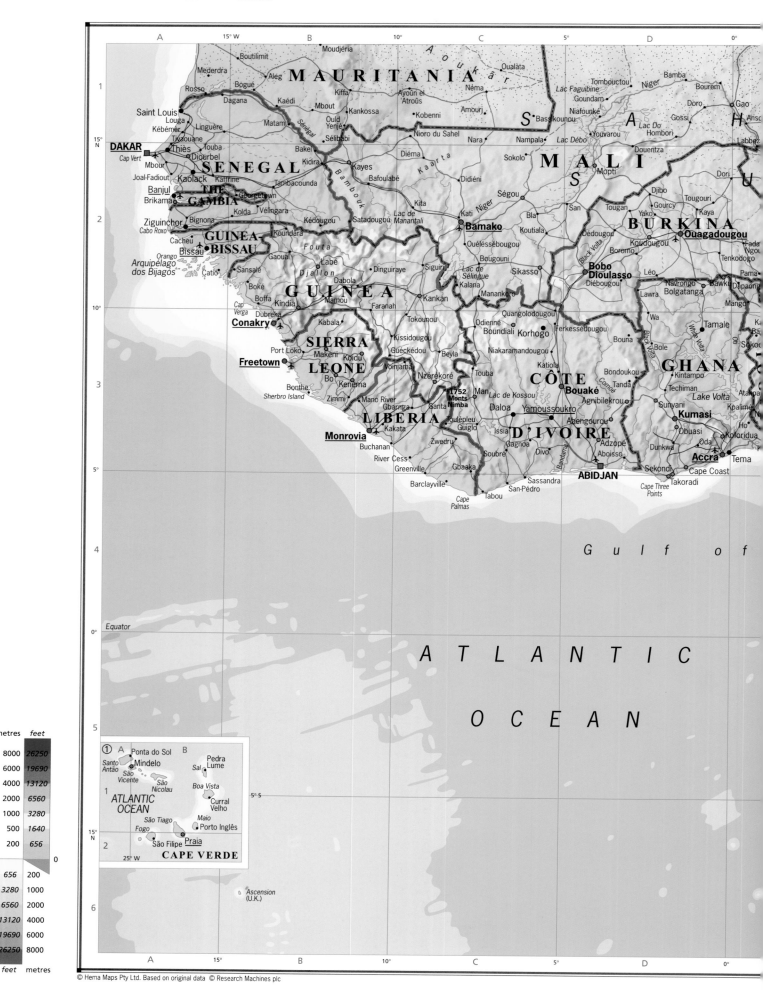

Scale 1 : 11 600 000

0   200   400   600 km
0 100   200   300 miles

Boutilimit
Moudjéria
MAURITANIA
Mederdra   Aleg
Aouker
Rosso   Bogué   Oualàta
Kaédi   Néma   Tombouctou   Niger   Bamba
Dagana   Kiffa   Ayoûn el   Niafounké   Lac Faguibine   Bourem
Saint Louis   Louga   Mbout   'Atroûs   Kobenni   Amourj   Goundam   Doro   Gossi   Gao
Kébémèr   Linguère   Matam   Ould   Nara   Bassikounou   Youvarou   Lac Dô   Hombori   Labbez   Anso
15°N   DAKAR   Thiès   Touba   Yenjé   Nioro du Sahel   Nampala   Lac Débo   Douentza
Cap Vert   Diourbel   Sélibabi   Diéma   Sokolo   Mopti   Dori
Joal-Fadiout   Kaolack   Kaffrine   Tambacounda   Kayes   Bafoulabé   Didiéni   Ségou   Bla   Djibo   Gourcy   Kaya   MALI
Banjul   Kaolack   Georgetown   Kidira   Kita   Kati   Niger   San   Koutiala   Tougan   Yako   BURKINA
Brikama   THE GAMBIA   Vélingara   Kédougou   Satadougou   Lac de   Ouéléssébougou   Dédougou   Koudougou   Ouagadougou
Ziguinchor   Bignona   Kolda   Manantali   Bougouni   Sikasso   Boromo   Léo   Navrongo   Fada Ngou
Cabo Roxo   GUINEA-   Koundâra   Fouta   Lac de   Manankoro   Bóbo   Diébougou   Lawra   Bolgatanga   Pama
Arquipélago   Cacheu   BISSAU   Gaoual   Labé   Séliguê   Dioulasso   Bawku
dos Bijagós   Orango   Catió   Dinguiraye   Siguiri   Kalana   Quangolodougou   Black Volta   Wa   Mango
Bissau   Sansalé   Djallon   Dabola   Odienné   Boundiali   Korhogo   Ferkessédougou   Tamale
Boké   Kindia   Mamou   GUINEA   Kankan   Niakaramandougou   Bouna   Bole   Soko
Cap Verga   Boffa   Faranah   Tokounou   White Volta   GHANA
Dubreka   Kabala   Kissidougou   Beyla   Touba   Katiola   Bondoukou   Kintampo   Techiman
Conakry   Port Loko   Makeni   Guéckédou   Man   Lac de Kossou   Bouaké   Tandà   Sunyani   Kumasi
Freetown   SIERRA   Koidu   Voinjama   Nzérékoré   1752   Daloa   Yamoussoukro   Agnibilekrou   Obuasi   Ho
LEONE   Bo   Kenema   Gbarnga   Monts   CÔTE   Abengourou   Dunkwa   Oda   Koforidua
Bonthe   Zimmi   Mano River   Santa   Nimba   Toulépleu   D'IVOIRE   Adzopé   Sekondi   Accra   Tema
Sherbro Island   LIBERIA   Kakata   Guiglo   Issia   Soubré   Aboisso   Cape Coast
Monrovia   Zwedru   Gagnoa   Divo   ABIDJAN   Cape Three   Takoradi
Buchanan   River Cess   Gbaaka   Sassandra   Points
Greenville   Barclayville   San-Pédro
Cape Palmas   Tabou

Gulf of

Equator

ATLANTIC
OCEAN

metres   feet
8000   26250
6000   19690
4000   13120
2000   6560
1000   3280
500   1640
200   656
0   0
656   200
3280   1000
6560   2000
13120   4000
19690   6000
26250   8000
feet   metres

① A   Ponta do Sol   B
Santo   Mindelo   Pedra
Antão   São   Sal   Lume
Vicente   São   Boa Vista
1   Nicolau
ATLANTIC   Curral
OCEAN   Velho
São Tiago   Maio
15°N   Fogo   Porto Inglês
2   São Filipe   Praia
25° W   CAPE VERDE

5° S

Ascension
(U.K.)

© Hema Maps Pty Ltd. Based on original data © Research Machines plc

104

Benin • Burkina • Cameroon • Cape Verde • Congo • Côte d'Ivoire • Equatorial Guinea • Gabon • The Gambia
• Ghana • Guinea • Guinea-Bissau • Liberia • Nigeria • São Tomé & Príncipe • Senegal • Sierra Leone • Togo

■ over 3 million	● 100 000 – 250 000	――――― country capital underline
■ 1 – 3 million	◉ 25 000 – 100 000	――――― state or province capital underline
● 250 000 – 1 million	• under 25 000	

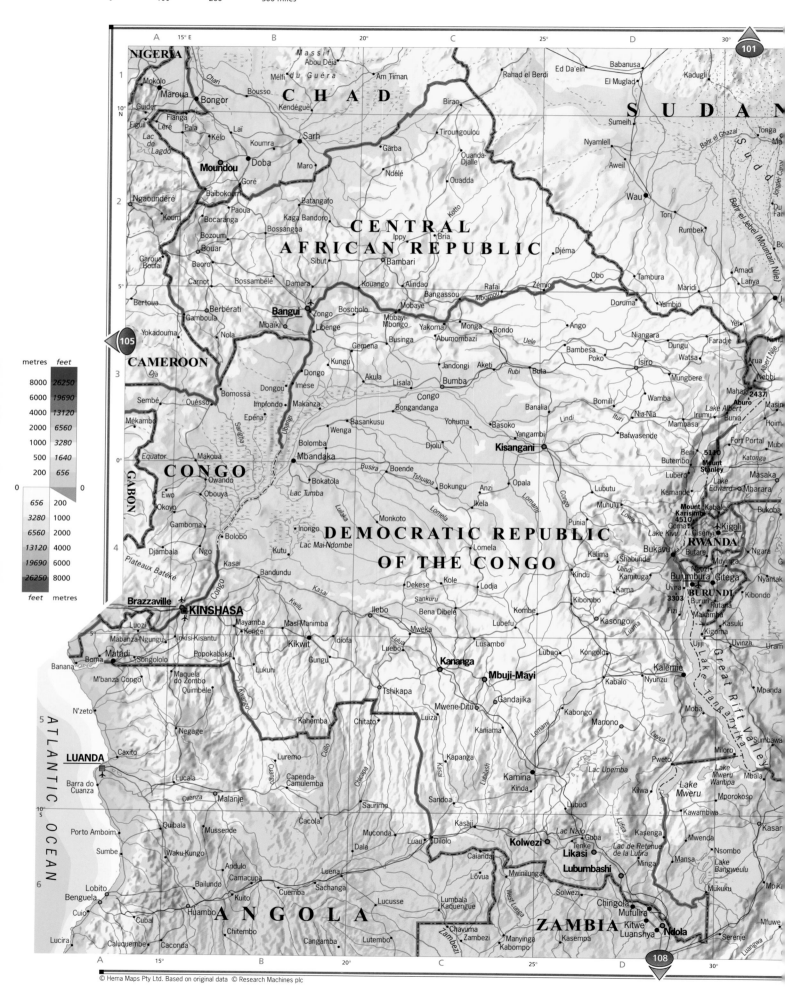

Scale 1 : 11 600 000

```
0        200        400        600 km
0    100        200        300 miles
```

NIGERIA

A 15° E   B   20°   C   25°   D   30°

1

CHAD

Mokolo
Maroua
Guider
Bongor
Fianga
Léré Pala
Figuil Kélo Laï
Lac de Lagdo
Koumra
Sarh
Moundou Doba
Baibokoum Gore
Maro

Massif d u G u é r a
Abou Déïa
Mélfi
Bousso
Kendéguè
Am Timan

Garba
Ndélé

Rahad el Berdi
Birao
Tiroungoulou
Ouanda-Djallé
Ouadda

Ed Da'ein
Babanusa
El Muglad
Kadugli

SUDAN

Tonga

2

Ngaoundéré
Koum
Bocaranga
Paoua
Bozoum
Bouar
Garoua Boulaï
Baoro
Bertoua
Carnot
Bossambélé
Berbérati
Gamboula
Yokadouma
Nola

Batangafo
Kaga Bandoro
Bossangoa

CENTRAL

Sibut
Damara
Bangui
Zongo

AFRICAN REPUBLIC

Ippy Bria
Bambari
Kouango Alindao
Bangassou
Rafaï Zémio
Mobaye
Mbaïki Bosobolo
Libenge
Mobayi-Mbongo
Yakoma Monga
Yakoma

Djéma

Obo
Tambura
Maridi
Zémio

Ed Da'ein

Nyamlell
Aweil
Wau
Tonj
Rumbek

Bahr el Ghazal
Sumeih

Bahr el Jebel (Mountain Nile)
Jonglei Canal

Du Faï

CAMEROON

105

Dja
Sembé
Mékambo
Quésso
Impfondo
Makoua
Equator
Makoua
Owando

GABON

CONGO

Ewo
Okoyo
Gamboma
Djambala
Ngo
Plateaux Batéké
Bolobo

Dongou
Imése
Bomossa
Epéna
Bolomba
Mbandaka
Bokatola
Obouya
Lac Tumba

Kungu
Gemena
Businga
Akula Lisala
Bumba
Congo
Bongandanga
Basankusu
Wenga
Busira
Boende
Tshuapa
Bokungu
Anzi
Djolu
Opala
Ikela
Monkoto
Inongo
Lac Mai-Ndombe
Kutu
Lomela
Lomami

Abumombazi
Jandongi Aketi
Rubi Buta
Banalia
Yohuma
Yangambi
Basoko
Kisangani

Bondo
Uele
Ango
Bambesa
Poko
Bomili
Lindi
Ituri
Nia-Nia
Bafwasende
Lubutu
Punia

Niangara
Dungu
Watsa
Isiro
Wamba
Mungbere
Mambasa
Beni
Butembo
Lubero
Kamande
Muhulu

Faradje
Nebbi
Mahagi
Aburo 2437
Lake Albert
Irumu Bunia
Fort Portal
Mount Stanley 5110
Lake Edward

Arua
Masin
Hoin
Mube
Masaka
Mbarara

3

DEMOCRATIC REPUBLIC

OF THE CONGO

Bandundu
Kasai
Dekese Kole
Lodja
Ilebo
Sankuru
Bena Dibele
Mweka
Lusambo
Lubefu
Kananga
Lubao
Mbuji-Mayi
Mwene-Ditu
Gandajika
Luiza
Kaniama
Kapanga
Kabongo
Kamina
Kinda
Sandoa
Lubudi

Lomela
Kibombo
Kama
Kasongo
Kongolo
Kabalo
Nyunzu
Manono
Manono
Kilwa
Pweto

Kalima
Shabunda
Ulindi
Kamituga
Kindu
Kasongo
Bukavu

Kabambare
Fizi
Uvira
Kabale
Goma
Lake Kivu
Mount Karisimbi 4510

RWANDA
Butare
Kigali
Gisenyi
Ngozi
BURUNDI
Bujumbura Gitega
3303
Bururi Rutana
Makamba
Kigoma
Ujiji
Uvinza

Bukoba
Ngara
Muyinga
Kibondo
Kasulu
Uram
Mpanda

Lake Tanganyika
Great Rift Valley

4

Brazzaville
KINSHASA
Luozi
Mabanza-Ngungu
Boma
Matadi
Songololo
Banana
N'zeto
M'banza Congo

Inkisi-Kisantu
Popokabaka
Mayamba
Kenge
Kikwit
Idiofa
Luebo
Gungu
Lukuni
Kahemba
Negage
Maquela do Zombo
Quimbele

Masi-Manimba
Tshikapa
Chitato
Luremo
Lucala
Malanje

Kalemie
Moba
Miloro
Lake Mweru Wantipa
Lake Mweru
Kasenga
Lac de Retenue de la Lufira
Lac Nzilo
Guba
Likasi
Lubumbashi
Minga
Mansa
Lake Bangweulu

Mpanda
Sumbawa
Mbala
Mporokoso
Kawambwa
Nsombo
Mwenda
Kasar
Mukuku

5

ATLANTIC OCEAN

LUANDA
Barra do Cuanza
Caxito
Porto Amboim

ANGOLA

Quibala
Sumbe
Mussende
Waku-Kungo
Andulo
Camacupa
Cuemba
Sachanga
Lobito
Benguela
Cuio
Cubal
Huambo
Kuito
Bailundo
Lucira
Caluquembe
Caconda
Chitembo
Cangamba
Lutembo

Saurimo
Cacola
Muconda
Dala
Luau
Lóvua
Luena
Lucusse
Lumbala Kaquengue
Caiândà
Dilolo

Kolwezi
Kinda
Kamina
Kasaji
Mwinilunga
Solwezi
West Lunga

Tenke
Chingola
Mufulira
Kitwe Ndola
Luanshya
Kasempa
Kabompo
Manyinga
Kasenga
Zambezi

ZAMBIA

Serenje
Mfuwe
Mpika
Luangwa

6

Zambezi
Chavuma

A 15°   B   20°   C   25°   D   30°

106

Symbol	Population
■ over 3 million	● 100 000 – 250 000
■ 1 – 3 million	○ 25 000 – 100 000
● 250 000 – 1 million	• under 25 000

country capital underline

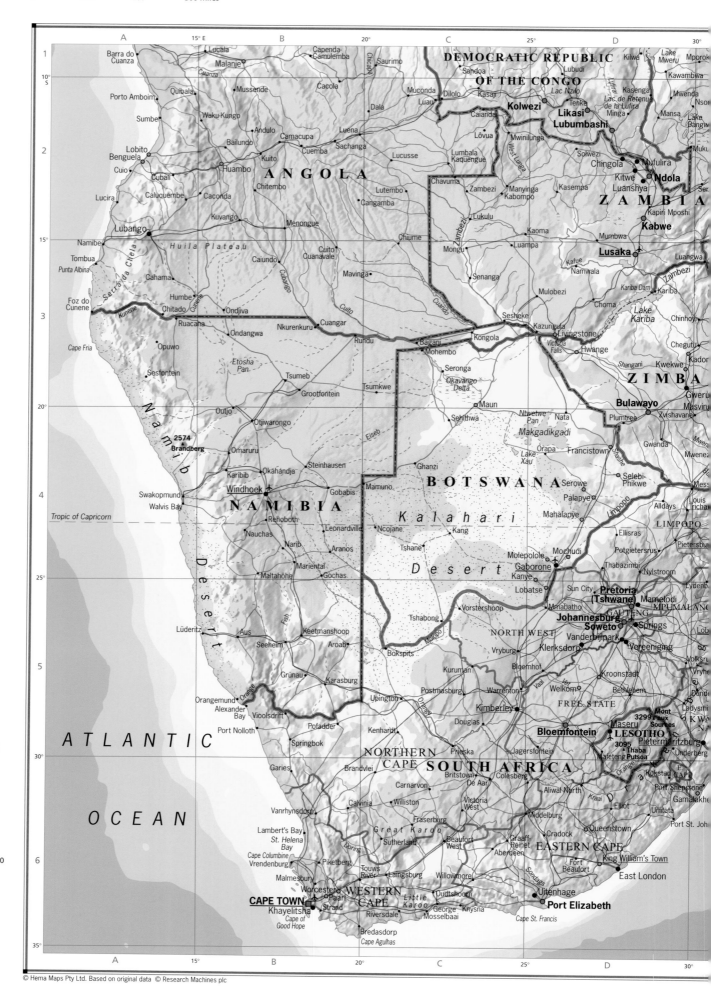

200   400   600 km

0   100   200   300 miles

A   15° E   **B**   20°   **C**   25°   **D**   30°

1

Barra do
Cuanza
Lucala
Malanje
Capenda-
Camulemba
Saurimo
Chicapa
DEMOCRATIC REPUBLIC
Kilwa
Lake
Mweru
Mporoko

Porto Amboim
Quibala
Mussende
Cacola
Cuanza
Muconda
Sandoa
Lubudi
OF THE CONGO
Kawambwa
Kawambwa

Sumbe
Waku-Kungo
Camacupa
Dala
Luau
Dilolo
Kasaji
Lufira
Kasenga
Mwenda
Nsor

Andulo
Bailundo
Camacupa
Sachanga
Luena
Caianda
Kolwezi
Tenke
Lac Nzilo
Lac de Retenue
de la Lufira
Minga
Mansa
Bangw

2
Lobito
Benguela
Huambo
Kuito
Cuemba
Lucusse
Lumbala
Kaquengue
Lôvua
Likasi
Lubumbashi
Solwezi
Mwinilunga
West Lunga
Chingola
Mufulira

Cuio
Cubali
Chitembo
Lutembo
Chavuma
Zambezi
Manyinga
Kabompo
Kasempa
Kitwe
Luanshya
Ndola

Lucira
Caluquembe
Caconda
Cangamba
ANGOLA
Zambezi
ZAMBIA
Kapiri Mposhi
Ser

Kuvango
Lukulu
Kabwe

15°
Lubango
Namibe
Menongue
Chiume
Mongu
Luampa
Kaoma
Mumbwa
Lusaka
Luangwa

Tombua
Punta Albina
Huila Plateau
Cuito
Cuanavale
Senanga
Kafue
Namwala
Zambezi

Cahama
Mavinga
Cuando
Mulobezi
Kariba Dam
Kariba

Foz do
Cunene
Humbe
Chitado
Cuito
Cuangar
Mohembo
Bagani
Sesheke
Kazungula
Choma
Lake
Kariba
Chinhoyi

Cape Fria
Opuwo
Ondangwa
Nkurenkuru
Rundu
Kongola
Livingstone
Victoria
Falls
Hwange
Shangani
Kwekwe
Kador

Sesfontein
*Etosha
Pan*
Tsumeb
Seronga
Okavango
Delta
Maun
ZIMBA

20°
Outjo
Grootfontein
Tsumkwe
Sehithwa
Ntwetwe
Pan
Nata
Orapa
Francistown
Gweru
Masvin

2574
Brandberg
Otjiwarongo
Eiseb
Makgadikgadi
Plumtree
Zvishavane
Gwanda
Mwene

Omaruru
Steinhausen
Ghanzi
Lake
Xau
Selebi-
Phikwe
Mwene

Karibib
Okahandja
Gobabis
Mamuno
BOTSWANA
Serowe
Palapye
Alldays
Louis
Tricha

4
Swakopmund
Walvis Bay
Windhoek
NAMIBIA
Rehoboth
Kalahari
Mahalapye
Limpopo
LIMPOPO

Tropic of Capricorn
Nauchas
Leonardville
Ncojane
Kang
Molepolole
Mochudi
Potgietersrus
Pietersbu

Narib
Aranos
Desert
Tshane
Gaborone
Kanye
Thabazimbi
Nylstroom

25°
Mariental
Gochas
Tshabong
Lobatse
Sun City
Pretoria
(Tshwane)
Mamelodi
Lyden

Maltahöhe
Vorstershoop
Mmabatho
Johannesburg
MPUMALANG

Lüderitz
Aus
Fish
Keetmanshoop
Aroab
Bokspits
Tshabong
Vryburg
NORTH WEST
Vanderbijlpark
Klerksdorp
Soweto
Springs
Vereeniging
Lob

5
Seeheim
Grünau
Karasburg
Kuruman
Bloemhof
Vet
Kroonstad
Volksr
Vryhe

Orange
Postmasburg
Warrenton
Vaal
Welkom
Bethlehem
FREE STATE
Ladysmith
Dund

Orangemund
Alexander
Bay
Vioolsdrift
Upington
Orange
Douglas
Kimberley
Maseru
3299
Mont
aux
Sources
KWA

Port Nolloth
Pofadder
Kenhardt
Prieska
Jagersfontein
Bloemfontein
LESOTHO
Thaba
Putsoa
3095
Pietermaritzburg
Underberg

30°
Springbok
Garies
Brandvlei
NORTHERN
CAPE
SOUTH AFRICA
Colesberg
Aliwal North
Mafeteng
Kraai
Kokstad
CAPE
Port Shepstone
Gamalakhe

Carnarvon
De Aar
Britstown
Victoria
West
Middelburg
Queenstown
Elliot
Umtata
Port St. Joh

Vanrhynsdorp
Calvinia
Williston
Fraserburg
Graaff-
Reinet
Cradock
Sondags
King William's Town

Lambert's Bay
St. Helena
Bay
Great Karoo
Sutherland
Beaufort
West
Aberdeen
Fort
Beaufort
East London

Cape Columbine
Doring
EASTERN CAPE

6
Vrendenburg
Piketberg
Touws
River
Laingsburg
Willowmore
Uitenhage

Malmesbury
*Little
Karoo*
Oudtshoorn
George
Knysna
Cape St. Francis
Port Elizabeth

CAPE TOWN
Worcester
Paarl
Strand
WESTERN
CAPE
Riversdale
Mosselbaai

Khayelitsha
Cape of
Good Hope
Bredasdorp

Cape Agulhas

35°

A   15°   **B**   20°   **C**   25°   **D**   30°

ATLANTIC

OCEAN

Namib

Desert

metres   feet
8000   26250
6000   19690
4000   13120
2000   6560
1000   3280
500   1640
200   656
0   0
656   200
3280   1000
6560   2000
13120   4000
19690   6000
26250   8000
feet   metres

Botswana • Comoros • Lesotho • Madagascar • Malawi • Mauritius
Mozambique • Namibia • Seychelles • South Africa • Swaziland • Zambia • Zimbabwe

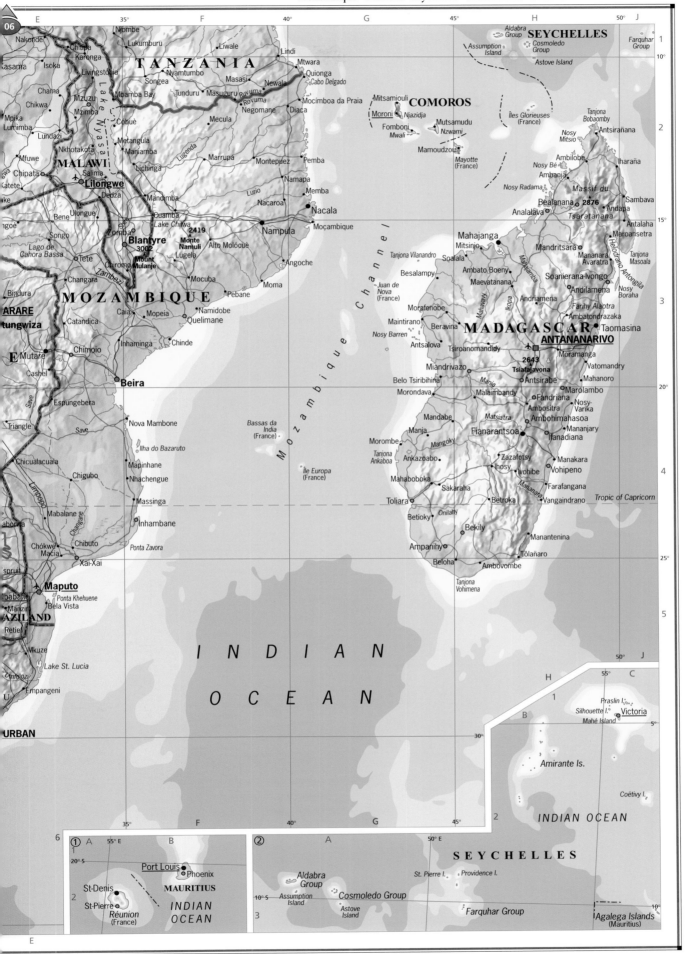

■	over 3 million	●	100 000 – 250 000	▬▬▬	country capital underline
■	1 – 3 million	◉	25 000 – 100 000	▬▬▬	state or province capital underline
●	250 000 – 1 million	•	under 25 000		

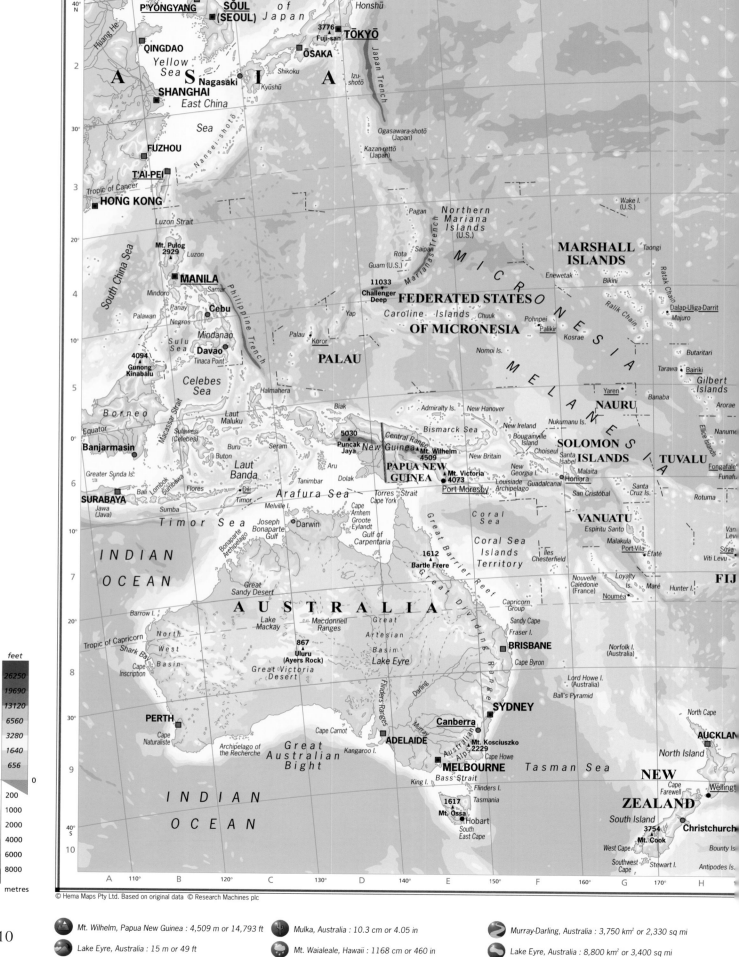

Scale 1 : 40 500 000

0   500   1000   1500   2000 km
0   250   500   750   1000 miles

metres	feet
8000	26250
6000	19690
4000	13120
2000	6560
1000	3280
500	1640
200	656
0	0
656	200
3280	1000
6560	2000
13120	4000
19690	6000
26250	8000

feet   metres

© Hema Maps Pty Ltd. Based on original data © Research Machines plc

110

Mt. Wilhelm, Papua New Guinea : 4,509 m or 14,793 ft

Lake Eyre, Australia : 15 m or 49 ft

Mulka, Australia : 10.3 cm or 4.05 in

Mt. Waialeale, Hawaii : 1168 cm or 460 in

Murray-Darling, Australia : 3,750 km² or 2,330 sq mi

Lake Eyre, Australia : 8,800 km² or 3,400 sq mi

J 170° K 160° L 150° M 140° N 130° P 120° W Q

NORTH AMERICA

LOS ANGELES ■

SAN DIEGO ■

P A C I F I C

Guadalupe (Mexico)

Tropic of Cancer

ore I.

ay Is.

Laysan I.

Necker I.

Hawaiian Islands

HAWAII (U.S.)

Kauai

Oahu

Honolulu ● Maui

Hawaii

Johnston I. (U.S.)

N. W. Christmas Island Ridge

Is. Revillagigedo (Mexico)

O C E A N

Palmyra I. (U.S.)

Tabuaeran

Kiritimati

Line Islands

Howland (U.S.)

Baker (U.S.)

Jarvis (U.S.)

Phoenix Islands

Birnie

Rawaki

KIRIBATI

Orona

Manra

Malden I.

Starbuck I.

Equator

P O L Y N E S I A

Atafu

Nukunonu

Tokelau (New Zealand)

Tongareva

Vostok I.

Caroline I.

Nuku Hiva

Hiva Oa

Marquesas Islands

is et

una

nce)

Swains I.

Danger Is.

Nassau

Manihiki

Flint I.

Îles Désappointement

SAMOA

Savaii

American Samoa

Suvorov I.

Archipel des Tuamotu

Pukapuka

Raroia

doorn Is (France)

Apia

Upolu

Tutuila

Rose I.

Cook Islands

Motu One

Îles Palliser

Tafahi

(New Zealand)

Arch. de la Société

Tahiti

Hao

Îles Duc de Gloucester

Lau Group Islands

Niue (New Zealand)

Palmerston I.

Aitutaki

F r e n c h

P o l y n e s i a

TONGA

Rarotonga

Mangaia

Îles Maria

Rururu

Tubuai

Mururoa

Groupe Actéon

Morane

Gambier Is.

uka'alofa

Ata

Raevavae

Mangareva

erva

Horizon Depth 10882

Tubuai Islands

Oeno

Henderson I.

Tropic of Capricorn

eefs

Rapa

Marotiri

Pitcairn Is. (U.K.)

Ducie I.

Tonga Trench

Kermadec Trench

Easter I. (Chile)

ermadec Islands (New Zealand)

S o u t h   W e s t

P a c i f i c

B a s i n

tham Is.

w Zealand)

J 170° K 160° L 150° M 140° N 130° P 120° Q 110° R

Charlotte Pass, Australia : -23 °C or -9.4 °F

Cloncurry, Australia : 53 °C or 128 °F

29,642,000

3.3 per km² or 8.6 per sq mi

8,945,000 km² or 3,454,000 sq mi

14

111

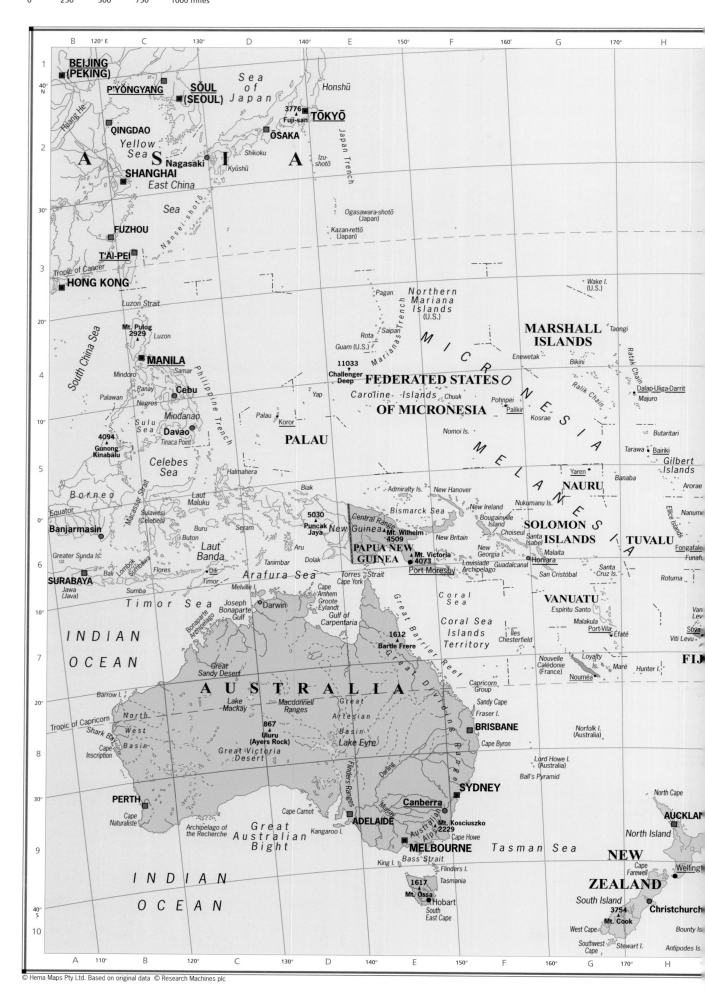

Scale 1 : 40 500 000

| 0 | 500 | 1000 | 1500 | 2000 km |

| 0 | 250 | 500 | 750 | 1000 miles |

BEIJING (PEKING)

P'YŎNGYANG

SŎUL (SEOUL)

Sea of Japan

Honshū

3776 Fuji-san

TŌKYŌ

QINGDAO

ŌSAKA

Yellow Sea

A S I A

Shikoku

Nagasaki

Kyūshū

SHANGHAI

East China Sea

Izu-shotō

Japan Trench

FŪZHOU

Nansei-shotō

Ogasawara-shotō (Japan)

Kazan-rettō (Japan)

T'AI-PEI

Tropic of Cancer

HONG KONG

Luzon Strait

Wake I. (U.S.)

South China Sea

Mt. Pulog 2929

Luzon

Pagan

Northern Mariana Islands (U.S.)

Rota

Saipan

Marianas Trench

MARSHALL ISLANDS

Taongi

Ratak Chain

MANILA

Mindoro

Samar

Guam (U.S.)

Enewetak

Bikini

Dalap-Uliga-Darrit

Majuro

11033 Challenger Deep

FEDERATED STATES

M

Ralik Chain

Cebu

Panay

Negros

Palawan

Yap

Caroline Islands

Chuuk

Pohnpei

Palikir

I

O

C

Butaritari

PALAU

Koror

Kosrae

R

Tarawa

Bairiki

4094 Gunong Kinabalu

Davao

Mindanao

Tinaca Point

Palau

Nomoi Is.

N

Gilbert Islands

Sulu Sea

Celebes Sea

Halmahera

E

Yaren

Banaba

Arorae

Borneo

Laut Maluku

Biak

Admiralty Is.

New Hanover

S

Nukumanu Is.

NAURU

A

Ellice Islands

Nanume

Macassar Strait

Sulawesi (Celebes)

Buru

Seram

Bismarck Sea

New Ireland

Bougainville Island

New Britain

SOLOMON ISLANDS

Choiseul

Santa Isabel

Malaita

Honiara

TUVALU

Fongafale

Equator

Banjarmasin

5030 Puncak Jaya

New Guinea

Central Range

Mt. Wilhelm 4509

M

New Georgia I.

Guadalcanal

San Cristóbal

Santa Cruz Is.

Funafuti

Rotuma

Greater Sunda Is.

Bali

Lombok

Sumbawa

Flores

Buton

Tanimbar

PAPUA NEW GUINEA

Mt. Victoria 4073

Dolak

Louisiade Archipelago

E

L

A

N

E

SURABAYA

Jawa (Java)

Sumba

Dili

Timor

Aru

Arafura Sea

Port Moresby

Torres Strait

Cape York

S

Van Lev

I

A

Timor Sea

Melville I.

Cape Arnhem

Groote Eylandt

Coral Sea

VANUATU

Espiritu Santo

Malakula

Port-Vila

Éfaté

Viti Levu

Súva

INDIAN OCEAN

Joseph Bonaparte Gulf

Darwin

Gulf of Carpentaria

Coral Sea Islands Territory

Îles Chesterfield

Bonaparte Archipelago

1612 Bartle Frere

Great Barrier Reef

Nouvelle Calédonie (France)

Loyalty Is.

Maré

FIJ

Great Sandy Desert

A U S T R A L I A

Capricorn Group

Nouméa

Hunter I.

Barrow I.

Lake Mackay

Macdonnell Ranges

Great Artesian Basin

Sandy Cape

Fraser I.

Great Dividing Range

Tropic of Capricorn

North West Basin

867 Uluru (Ayers Rock)

Lake Eyre

BRISBANE

Cape Byron

Norfolk I. (Australia)

Shark Bay

Great Victoria Desert

Lord Howe I. (Australia)

Cape Inscription

Ball's Pyramid

PERTH

Cape Naturaliste

Darling

Murray

Flinders Ranges

SYDNEY

North Cape

AUCKLAN

Archipelago of the Recherche

Cape Carnot

Canberra

Australian Alps

Mt. Kosciuszko 2229

Cape Howe

North Island

ADELAIDE

Kangaroo I.

Great Australian Bight

MELBOURNE

Tasman Sea

NEW

Cape Farewell

Welling

INDIAN OCEAN

King I.

Bass Strait

Flinders I.

ZEALAND

South Island

Christchurch

1617 Mt. Ossa

Tasmania

Hobart

South East Cape

3754 Mt. Cook

West Cape

Bounty Is

Southwest Cape

Stewart I.

Antipodes Is.

112

Mt. Wilhelm, Papua New Guinea : 4,509 m or 14,793 ft

Mulka, Australia : 10.3 cm or 4.05 in

Murray-Darling, Australia : 3,750 km² or 2,330 sq mi

Lake Eyre, Australia : 15 m or 49 ft

Mt. Waialeale, Hawaii : 1168 cm or 460 in

Lake Eyre, Australia : 8,800 km² or 3,400 sq mi

NORTH AMERICA

■ LOS ANGELES

■ SAN DIEGO

P A C I F I C

Guadalupe (Mexico)

re I.
ray Is.

H*awaiian*

Laysan I.

Necker I.

HAWAII (U.S.)

Is. Revillagigedo (Mexico)

I s l a n d s

Kauai
Oahu
Honolulu ●
Maui

Hawaii

Tropic of Cancer

30°

20°

Johnston I. (U.S.)

N. W. Christmas Island Ridge

O C E A N

10°

Palmyra I. (U.S.)

Tabuaeran

Kiritimati

L i n e   I s l a n d s

Howland (U.S.)
Baker (U.S.)

Jarvis (U.S.)

Phoenix Islands

Rawaki
Birnie
KIRIBATI
Orona
Manra

Malden I.

Starbuck I.

Equator   0°

O   L   Y   N   E   S   I   A

Tokelau (New Zealand)
Atafu
Nukunonu

Tongareva

Vostok I.

Caroline I.

Nuku Hiva

Marquesas Islands

Hiva Oa

s et
na
nce)

Swains I.

Danger Is.
Nassau

Manihiki

Flint I.

Îles Désappointement

SAMOA American Samoa

Savaii
Apia Tutuila
Upolu

Suvorov I.

Pukapuka

Raroia

orn Is.
France)

Tafahi

Rose I.

Cook Islands

Motu One

Îles Palliser

Archipel des Tuamotu

Rose I.

(New Zealand)

TONGA

Niue
(New Zealand)

Palmerston I.

Aitutaki

Arch. de la Société

Tahiti

Hao

Îles Duc de Gloucester

ku'alofa

Rarotonga

F r e n c h
P o l y n e s i a

Ata

Mangaia

Îles Maria

Rurutu

Mururoa

Groupe Actéon

Gambier Is.

rva ▼ **Horizon Depth 10882**
fs

Tubuai

Raevavae

Morane

Mangareva

Oeno

Henderson I.

Tropic of Capricorn   20°

Tubuai Islands

Rapa

Marotiri

Pitcairn Is. (U.K.) Ducie I.

rmadec Islands
New Zealand)

S o u t h   W e s t

Easter I. (Chile)

30°

Kermadec Trench

P a c i f i c

B a s i n

ham Is.
Zealand)

40°

* Charlotte Pass, Australia : -23 ˚C or -9.4 ˚F
* Cloncurry, Australia : 53 ˚C or 128 ˚F
* 29,642,000
* 3.3 per km² or 8.6 per sq mi
* 8,945,000 km² or 3,454,000 sq mi
* 14

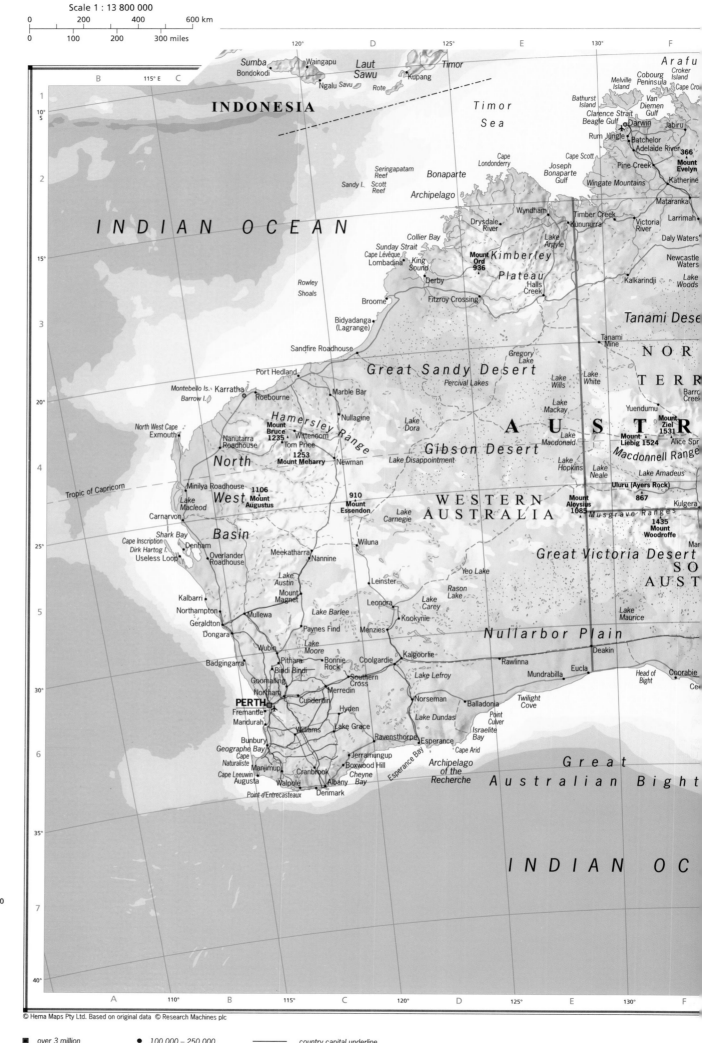

0   200   400   600 km
0   100   200   300 miles

120°   D   125°   E   130°   F

Sumba Waingapu   *Laut*   Timor   Arafu
Bondokodi   *Sawu*   Melville Cobourg Croker
         Ngalu *Savu*   Rote   Kupang   Island Peninsula Island
                                                              Bathurst Van Cape Cro
INDONESIA   *Timor*   Island Clarence Strait Diemen
                            Sea   Beagle Gulf Darwin Jabiru
10°   Rum Jungle Batchelor
S   Adelaide River   366
                              Cape   Pine Creek   **Mount**
                         Londonderry   **Evelyn**
           Seringapatam   Cape   Wingate Mountains Katherine
              Reef   Bonaparte   Joseph
         Sandy I. Scott   Bonaparte   Mataranka
2   Reef Archipelago   Gulf   Daly Waters
                                                          Newcastle
                          Wyndham   Waters
INDIAN OCEAN   Drysdale Timber Creek Victoria Larrimah
                         River   Kununurra   River
                   Collier Bay   Lake   Kalkarindji Lake
             Sunday Strait King Argyle   Woods
15°   Cape Lévêque **Mount** *Kimberley*
       Lombadina Sound **Ord** *Plateau*
             Derby   **936** Halls   *Tanami Dese*
       Rowley   Creek
       Shoals   Broome Fitzroy Crossing   **NOR**
                                                           TERR
       Bidyadanga   Tanami
       (Lagrange)   Mine   Barr
3   Gregory   Creek
       Sandfire Roadhouse   Lake   Yuendumu
                        Great Sandy Desert Lake Lake   **Mount** **Mount**
       Port Hedland   Percival Lakes Wills White   **Liebig 1524** **Ziel**
                                                              Alice Spr **1531**
       Montebello Is. Karratha Marble Bar Lake   Lake
20°   Barrow I. Roebourne   Nullagine Dora Mackay   **AUSTR**
       North West Cape **Mount**   Lake   **Mount**
       Exmouth **Bruce** Wittenoom *Gibson Desert* Macdonald Lake *Macdonnell Range*
             Nanutarra **1235** Tom Price   Hopkins Neale Lake Amadeus
             Roadhouse **1253**   Lake   Uluru (Ayers Rock)
       North **Mount Meharry** Newman Lake Disappointment 867
4   Neale Kulgera
       Tropic of Capricorn
       Minilya Roadhouse **1106**   **WESTERN** Mount **1435**
       Lake *West* **Mount**   **910** **AUSTRALIA** Aloysius **Mount**
       Macleod   **Augustus** **Mount** Lake   **1085** **Woodroffe**
       Carnarvon   **Essendon** Carnegie   *Musgrave Ranges*
                   Basin   *Great Victoria Desert*
25°   Shark Bay Wiluna   Yeo Lake   *SO*
       Cape Inscription   *AUST*
       Dirk Hartog I. Denham Meekatharra Nannine   Lake
       Useless Loop Overlander   Rason
              Roadhouse   Leinster Lake Lake Maurice
       Kalbarri   Lake   Leonora Carey
       Northampton   Austin Mount   Lake
       Geraldton Mullewa Magnet Lake Barlee Kookynie Maurice
       Dongara   Paynes Find Menzies
                                          Nullarbor Plain Deakin
       Badgingarra Wubin Lake Bonnie Coolgardie Kalgoorlie
              Pithara Moore Rock Southern Rawlinna Eucla
       Goomalling Bindi Bindi Cross Lake Lefroy Mundrabilla Head of
30°   Northam   Merredin   Balladonia Point Bight Coorabie
       PERTH Cunderdin Hyden Norseman Culver Twilight Ce
       Fremantle   Lake Dundas Israelite Cove
       Mandurah Williams Lake Grace   Bay
       Bunbury   Ravensthorpe Esperance Cape Arid
       Geographe Bay Jerramungup Esperance Bay *Great*
       Cape Naturaliste Boxwood Hill Archipelago *Australian Bight*
       Manjimup Cranbrook Cheyne of the
       Cape Leeuwin Walpole Albany Bay Recherche
       Augusta   Denmark   *INDIAN OC*
       Point d'Entrecasteaux

metres	feet
8000	*26250*
6000	*19690*
4000	*13120*
2000	*6560*
1000	*3280*
500	*1640*
200	*656*
0	0
656	200
3280	1000
6560	2000
13120	4000
19690	6000
26250	8000
feet	metres

■ over 3 million   ● 100 000 – 250 000   —— country capital underline
◻ 1 – 3 million   ○ 25 000 – 100 000   —— state or province capital underline
◉ 250 000 – 1 million   • under 25 000

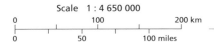

Scale 1 : 4 650 000

0   100   200 km

0   50   100 miles

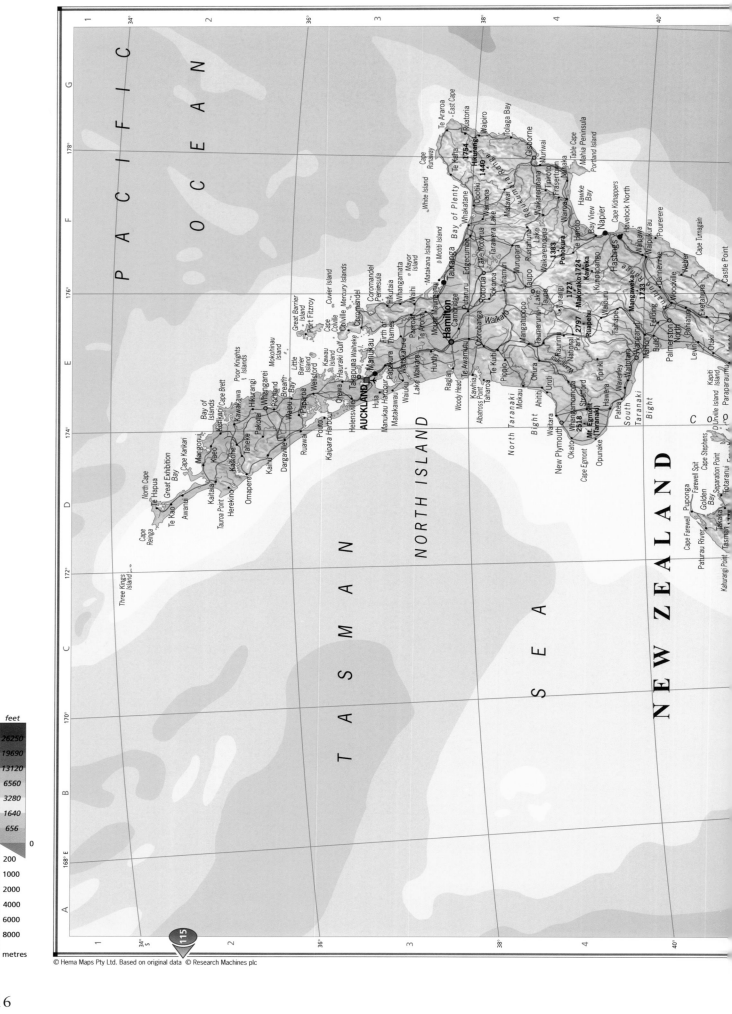

metres	feet
8000	26250
6000	19690
4000	13120
2000	6560
1000	3280
500	1640
200	656
0	0
656	200
3280	1000
6560	2000
13120	4000
19690	6000
26250	8000
feet	metres

PACIFIC OCEAN

TASMAN SEA

NORTH ISLAND

NEW ZEALAND

115

© Hema Maps Pty Ltd. Based on original data © Research Machines plc

116

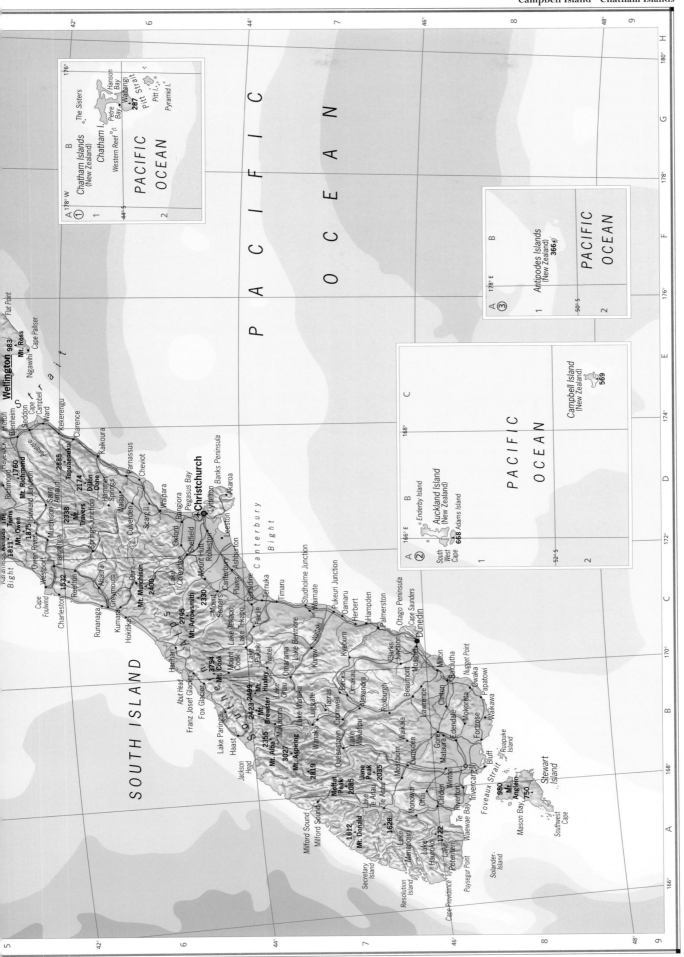

Chatham Islands (New Zealand)

The Sisters
Hanson Bay
Waitangi
Chatham I.
Western Reef
Petre Bay
287
Pitt Strait
Pitt I.
Pyramid I.

PACIFIC OCEAN

Antipodes Islands (New Zealand)
366
PACIFIC OCEAN

Auckland Island (New Zealand)
Enderby Island
Adams Island
668
South West Cape

Campbell Island (New Zealand)
569

PACIFIC OCEAN

PACIFIC OCEAN

Flat Point
Mt. Ross 983
Ngawihi
Cape Palliser
Wellington
Seddon
Cape Campbell
Ward
Blenheim
Kekerengu
Clarence
Picton
Havelock
Kaikoura
Richmond
Mt. Richmond 1760
Mt. Owen 1875
Howard Junction
Murchison
Saint Arnaud
Mt. Travers 2338
Tapuaenuku 2885
Dillon Cone 2174
Hanmer Springs
Parnassus
Cheviot
Waipara
Springs Junction
Otira
Culverden
Scargill
Motueka
Nelson
Mt. Owen 1811
Inangahua
Reefton
Mt. Murchison 2400
Lake Coleridge
Oxford
Rangiora
Waiau
Amberley
The Twins
Westport
Charleston 1532
Cape Foulwind
Runanaga
Greymouth
Kumara
Hokitika
Hari Hari
Mt. Arrowsmith 2795
Mount Somers 2330
Sheffield
Darfield
Christchurch
Lyttelton
Leeston
Rolleston
Akaroa
Banks Peninsula
Pegasus Bay
Geraldine
Fairlie
Temuka
Timaru
Canterbury Plains
Canterbury Bight
Abut Head
Franz Josef Glacier
Fox Glacier
Mt. Cook 3754
Mount Cook
Lake Tekapo
Lake Tekapo
Studholme Junction
Waimate
Pukeuri Junction
Oamaru
Herbert
Hampden
Palmerston
Lake Paringa
Haast
Jackson Head
Lake Ohau
Mt. Brewster 2424
Mt. Huxley 2499
Lake Hawea
Lake Wanaka
Omarama
Kurow
Waitaki
Becks
Kyeburn
Otago Peninsula
Cape Saunders
Dunedin
Mosgiel
Milford Sound
Milford Sound
Mt. Aspiring 3027
Mt. Alba 2355
Wanaka
Cromwell
Tarras
Omakau
Alexandra
Ranfurly
Clarks Junction
Milton
Balclutha
Moffat Peak 2085
June Peak
Te Anau 2035
Te Anau
Queenstown
Lake Wakatipu
Lake Wanaka
Luggate
Roxburgh
Lawrence
Beaumont
Clinton
Mokoreta
Owaka
Nugget Point
Papatowai
Mt. Donald 1612
Mt. Aspiring
Lake Te Anau
Lake Manapouri
1628
Lake Hauroko
1732
Lake Monowai
Ohai
Mossburn
Lumsden
Gore
Mataura
Edendale
Fortrose
Waikawa
Secretary Island
Resolution Island
Lake Poteriteri
Clifden
Winton
Riverton
Invercargill
Bluff
Te Waewae Bay
Mt. Anglem 980
750
Ruapuke Island
Stewart Island
Cape Providence
Puysegur Point
Foveaux Strait
Mason Bay
Southwest Cape
Solander Island

SOUTH ISLAND

Legend
- ■ over 3 million
- ■ 1 – 3 million
- ● 250 000 – 1 million
- ● 100 000 – 250 000
- ◎ 25 000 – 100 000
- · under 25 000
- —— country capital underline

Scale 1 : 34 700 000

© Hema Maps Pty Ltd. Based on original data © Research Machines plc

Mt. McKinley, Alaska : 6,194 m or 20,322 ft

Death Valley, USA : 86 m or 282 ft

Bateques, Mexico : 3.0 cm or 1.2 in

Henderson Lake, Canada : 650 cm or 256 in

Mississippi-Missouri, USA : 6,020 km or 3,740 mi

Lake Superior, USA/Canada : 82,260 km² or 31,760 sq mi

ATLANTIC OCEAN

Bermuda (U.K.)

Tropic of Cancer

NEW YORK
Long Island
PHILADELPHIA
Baltimore
Washington D.C.
Virginia Beach
Cape Hatteras
Raleigh
Charlotte
Cleveland
Lake Erie
Lake Ontario
Columbus
Cincinnati
Knoxville
DETROIT
Milwaukee
CHICAGO
Indianapolis
St. Louis
Nashville
Memphis
Atlanta
Savannah
Jacksonville
Cape Canaveral
THE BAHAMAS
Grand Bahama
Great Abaco
Nassau
Andros
Great Inagua
Turks and Caicos Is. (U.K.)
Virgin Is. (U.K.)
Virgin Is. (U.S.)
San Juan
Puerto Rico (U.S.)
Puerto Rico Trench
Lesser Antilles
Netherlands Antilles
Aruba (Neth.)
CARACAS
Orinoco
Meta
Punta Gallinas
BOGOTÁ
SOUTH AMERICA
Equator
Iquitos
Amazonas

DOMINICAN REPUBLIC
HAITI
SANTO DOMINGO
Duarte 3175
Cabo Beata
PORT-AU-PRINCE
CUBA
Santiago de Cuba
LA HABANA (HAVANA)
Isla de la Juventud
Cayman Is. (U.K.)
JAMAICA
Kingston
Greater Antilles
Caribbean Sea
Cristóbal Colón 5775
BARRANQUILLA
Golfo del Darién
MEDELLÍN
Cordillera Occidental
Cordillera Central
Cordillera Oriental
CALI 5750
QUITO 6310
GUAYAQUIL
Golfo de Guayaquil
Chiclayo

Cabo Camarón
Cabo Gracias á Dios
Swan Is. (Honduras)
HONDURAS
Tegucigalpa
NICARAGUA
Lago de Nicaragua
Managua
San José
COSTA RICA
PANAMA
Golfo de Panamá
Canal de Panamá (Panama Canal)
Punta Mariato
Isla Coiba
I. de Coco (Costa Rica)
Isla de Malpelo (Columbia)

Tampa
Miami
Florida Keys
Straits of Florida
Yucatán Channel
G. de Cozumel
Cozumel
Yucatán
Mérida
Bahía de Campeche
BELIZE
Belmopan
GUATEMALA 4210
GUATEMALA
EL SALVADOR
San Salvador
Cabo

New Orleans
Mobile
Mississippi River Delta
Gulf of Mexico
Houston
Corpus Christi
Matamoros
Ciudad Madero
Veracruz
Vol. Citlaltépetl 5610
Sierra Madre del Sur
Acapulco
Middle America Trench

UNITED STATES
Sioux Falls
Missouri
Kansas City
St. Louis
Little Rock
DALLAS
Fort Worth
Austin
SAN ANTONIO
Oklahoma City
Abilene
Edwards Plateau
Great Plains
Denver
Arkansas
Red
Rio Grande
El Paso
Ciudad Juárez
MONTERREY
Saltillo
Sierra Madre Oriental
León
GUADALAJARA
MÉXICO
MEXICO
Islas Marías
Islas Revillagigedo (Mexico)
I. Clarión
Clipperton Island (France)

4011
Albuquerque
PHOENIX 3951
Tucson
Sierra Madre Occidental
Grand Canyon
Colorado
Hermosillo
Ciudad Obregón
La Paz
Cabo San Lucas
Baja California
Golfo de California

Great Salt Lake
Salt Lake City 4123
Great Salt Desert
Las Vegas
Mojave Desert
Great Basin
Reno
Sierra Nevada
Death Valley
LOS ANGELES
Channel Is.
SAN DIEGO
Mexicali
Ensenada
Guadalupe (Mexico)
Cedros
Sacramento
San Francisco
San Jose
Fresno

PACIFIC OCEAN

Islas Galápagos (Galápagos Is.) (Ecuador)
Isla Isabela

Tropic of Cancer

Northice, Greenland : -66 °C or -87 °F

Death Valley, USA : 57 °C or 134 °F

475,525,000

19 per km² or 50 per sq mi

24,454,000 km² or 9,442,000 sq mi

23

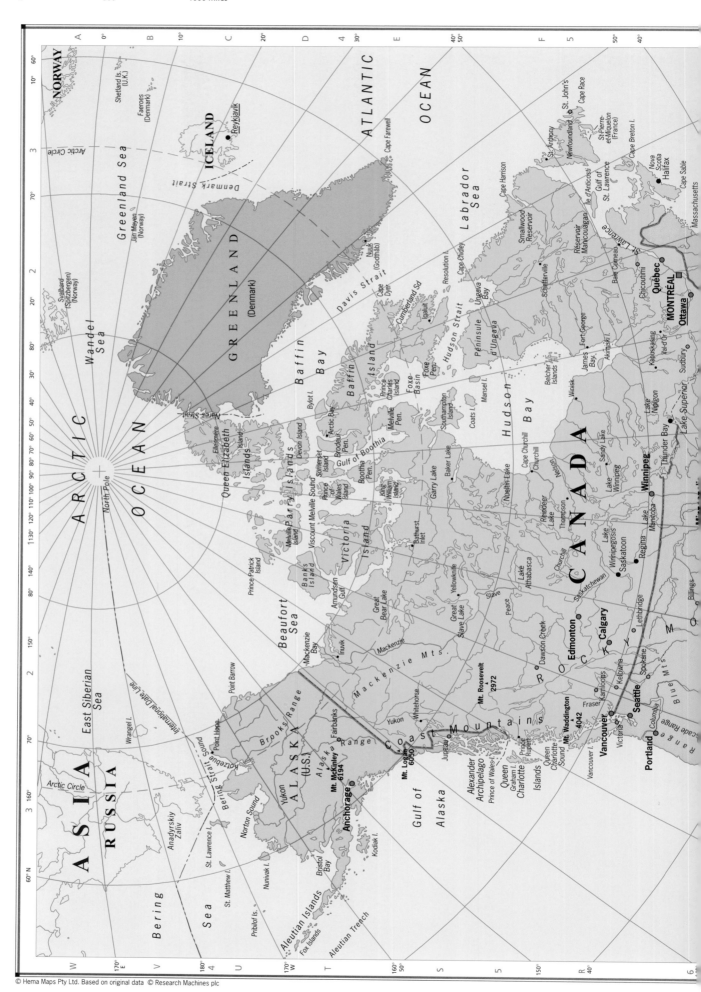

Scale 1 : 34 700 000

0   500   1000   1500   2000 km

0   500   1000 miles

© Hema Maps Pty Ltd. Based on original data   © Research Machines plc

120

Mt. McKinley, Alaska : 6,194 m or 20,322 ft

Death Valley, USA : 86 m or 282 ft

Bateques, Mexico : 3.0 cm or 1.2 in

Henderson Lake, Canada : 650 cm or 256 in

Mississippi-Missouri, USA : 6,020 km or 3,740 mi

Lake Superior, USA/Canada : 82,260 km² or 31,760 sq mi

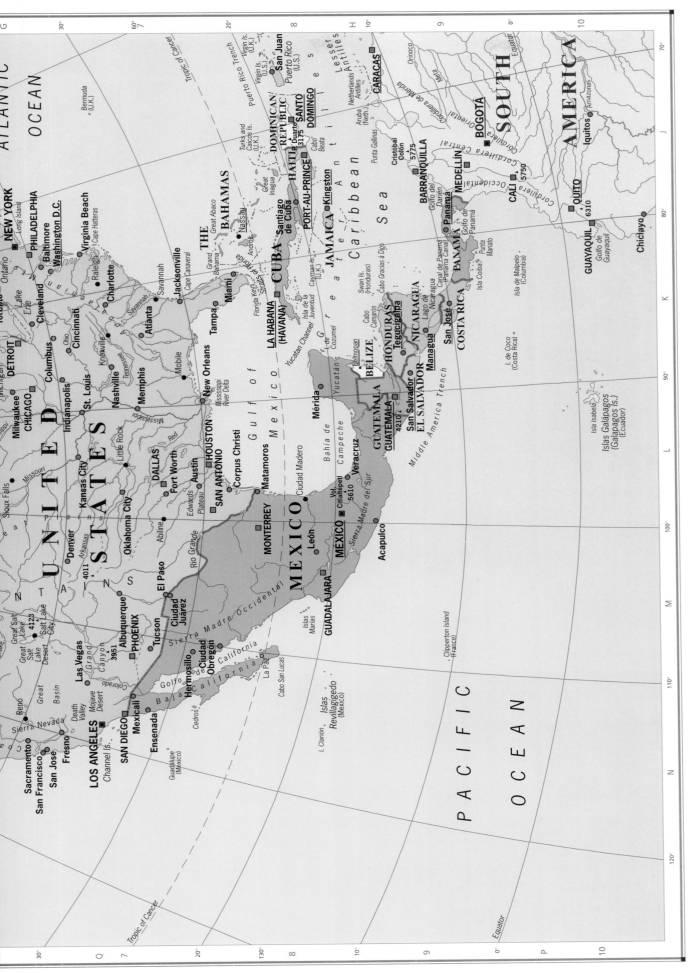

Northice, Greenland : -66 °C or -87 °F

Death Valley, USA : 57 °C or 134 °F

475,525,000

19 per km² or 50 per sq mi

24,454,000 km² or 9,442,000 sq mi

23

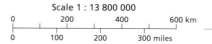
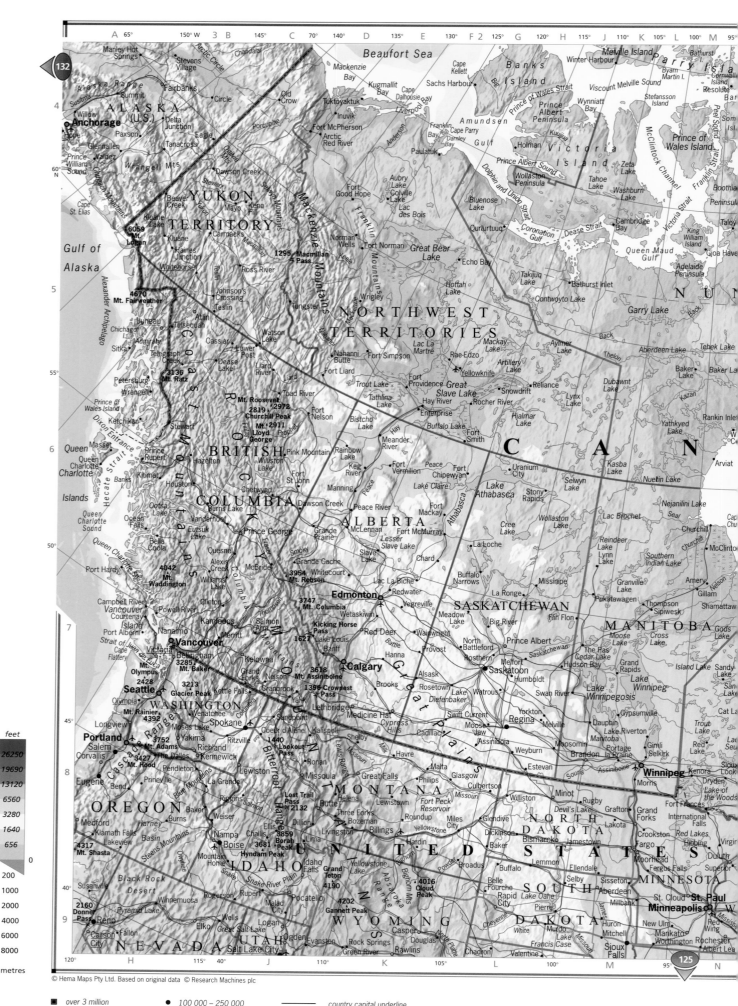

■ over 3 million
■ 1 – 3 million
● 250 000 – 1 million
● 100 000 – 250 000
● 25 000 – 100 000
• under 25 000

country capital underline
state or province capital underline

metres	feet
8000	26250
6000	19690
4000	13120
2000	6560
1000	3280
500	1640
200	656
0	0
656	200
3280	1000
6560	2000
13120	4000
19690	6000
26250	8000

feet | metres

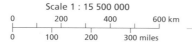

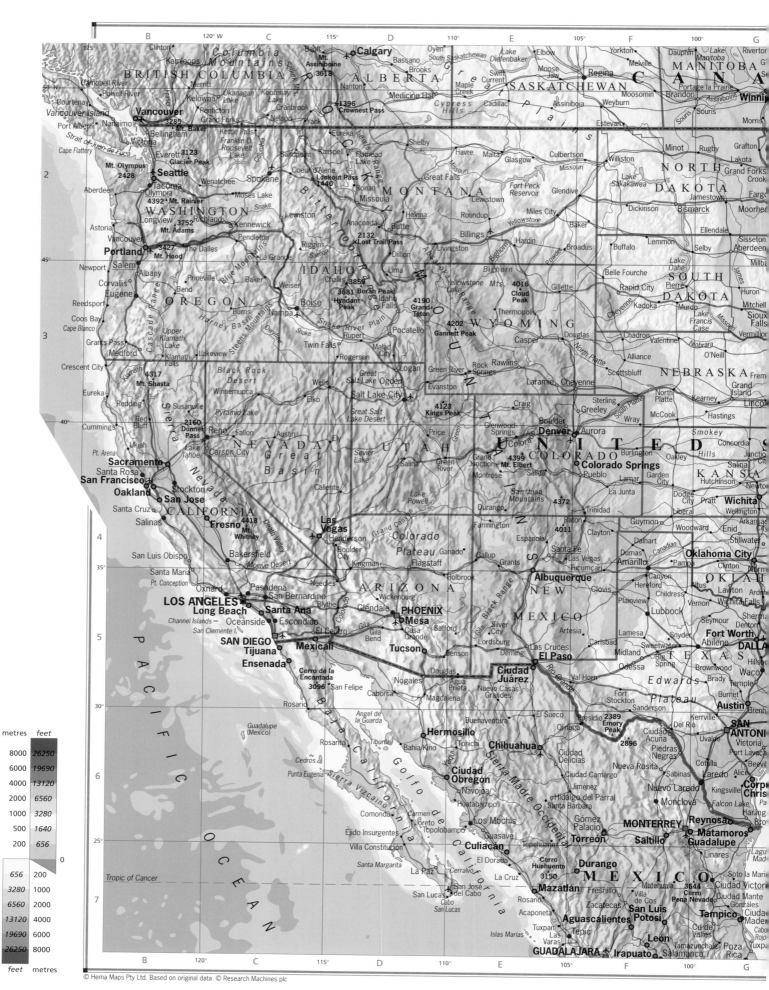

95° H 90° J 85° K 80° L 75° M 70° N

C A N A D A

ake Winnipeg

Trout Lake
Red Lake
Kenora
Dryden
Lake of the Woods
Fort Frances
International Falls
Red Lakes

Lac St. Joseph
Sioux Lookout
Lac Seul
Upsala
Nipigon

O N T A R I O

Nakina
Longlac
Geraldton
Hearst
Kapuskasing
Cochrane
Timmins
Foleyet
Chapleau
Wawa

Missanabi
Coral

Lake Abitibi
Rouyn
Amos
Val-d'Or
Senneterre

Lac Evans
Chibougamau
Miquelon
Réservoir Gouin

Baie du Poste
Mistassini
Chute des Passes
Réservoir Pipmuacan

Q U É B E C

50°

1

Silver Bay
Virginia
Hibbing
Duluth
Superior

Apostle Is.
Ironwood
Marquette
Iron Mountain

Thunder Bay
Isle Royale
Copper Harbor
Keweenaw Pen.

Lake Superior

Sault Ste. Marie
Ste. Marie
Blind River
Manitoulin I.
Sudbury
North Bay

Pembroke
Parry Sound
Orillia

Ottawa
Mont-Laurier
La Tuque

Trois Rivières
Sherbrooke
Granby

Québec
Lévis
St-Jean
Jonquière
Chicoutimi

Rivière-du-Loup
Edmundson

Presque Isle
Houlton
Fredericton
St. Stephen

2

M I N N E S O T A

Fergus Falls
St. Cloud
Benson
New Ulm

St. Paul
Minneapolis

W I S C O N S I N

Eau Claire
Wausau
Rhinelander
Escanaba
Marinette

M I C H I G A N

Mackinaw City
Alpena

Tobermory
Owen Sound

Georgian Bay
Barrie
Oshawa
Peterborough
Kingston

Toronto
Hamilton
London

Smiths Falls
Cornwall
Plattsburgh
Burlington

Ottawa
MONTRÉAL

Drummondville
Jackman

MAINE

Augusta
Lewiston
Portland

45°

Mankato
Rochester
Albert Lea

Appleton
Oshkosh
Sheboygan
Portage
La Crosse

Green Bay
Ludington
Mount Pleasant

Bay City
Saginaw
Flint
Lansing

Traverse City
Muskegon
Grand Rapids

Kalamazoo

Sarnia
Kitchener
St. Catharines
Buffalo

Watertown

Montpelier
VERMONT
NEW HAMPSHIRE
Concord
Nashua
Lowell

Worthington
Mason City
Cedar Falls
Waterloo
Dubuque

Madison
Rockford
Racine
Milwaukee

Lake Michigan

DETROIT
Ann Arbor
Windsor
Chatham

1629

NEW YORK
Rochester
Syracuse
Utica
Albany
Springfield

1295
Catskill Mts.
Hartford

Boston
MASS.
Providence
Worcester

3

Sioux City
omaha
Atlantic
Des Moines

I O W A

Iowa City
Davenport

CHICAGO
Aurora
Joliet
Gary
South Bend

Fort Wayne
Lima

Toledo
Cleveland
Akron
Youngstown
Meadville
Jamestown
Binghamton
Scranton

Bridgeport
New Haven
C. Cod
New Bedford
R.I.
CONN.

Council Bluffs
Creston
Ottumwa
Burlington

Springfield
Decatur
Bloomington
Lafayette
Kokomo

Indianapolis

Peoria

I L L I N O I S

I N D I A N A

Columbus
Muncie
Marion

Columbus
Canton
Dayton

O H I O

Altoona

Pittsburgh
Wheeling

Harrisburg
Allentown
PENNSYLVANIA

NEW YORK
Paterson
Newark

NEW JERSEY
Trenton

40°

St. Joseph
Macon
Hannibal

Kansas City
Jefferson City
St. Louis
East St. Louis

Terre Haute
Bloomington
Vincennes

Effingham

Cincinnati
Covington

Hamilton
Dayton
Portsmouth

Parkersburg
Clarksburg
Clarksville

Washington D.C.
Baltimore
Annapolis
MARYLAND
Cambridge
DELAWARE
Salisbury

T A T E S

Topeka
Ottawa
Emporia
Chanute

Nevada
Rolla

M I S S O U R I

Cape Girardeau
Marion
Mt. Vernon

Louisville
Frankfort
Lexington

Ashland

Owensboro

Charleston
Beckley

WEST VIRGINIA

VIRGINIA
Charlottesville
Lynchburg
Petersburg
Bluefield

Richmond

Alexandria

Norfolk
Virginia Beach
Chesapeake

4

artlesville
Tulsa

Springfield
Joplin

Poplar Bluff
Sikeston
Paducah

K E N T U C K Y

Bowling Green
Kingsport

Winston-Salem
Durham
Raleigh

Greenville
Pamlico Sound
Cape Hatteras

Eufaula Lake
Fayetteville
Jonesboro
Russellville

Nashville
Morristown
Oak Ridge
Knoxville
Jackson

Clarksville

T E N N E S S E E

Chattanooga
Murphy

Greensboro
Charlotte
Fayetteville

NORTH CAROLINA
Goldsboro

Wilmington

35°

Fort Smith
Hot Springs
Little Rock

Memphis
Corinth

Tupelo
Huntsville
Gadsden
Rome

Dalton
Gainesville
Spartanburg
Rock Hill

SOUTH CAROLINA
Columbia
Florence

Myrtle Beach

Cape Fear

A R K A N S A S

Arkadelphia
Hope
Pine Bluff

Clarksdale
Greenwood

Decatur
Anniston

Birmingham
Bessemer
Auburn

Atlanta
La Grange

Macon

Columbia
Summerville
Charleston

Sulphur Springs
Texarkana
Dumas
El Dorado

Monroe
Winnfield
Natchez

Jackson
Brookhaven

Meridian

Demopolis

Montgomery
Troy

ALABAMA

Columbus

Albany
Cordele
Tifton

G E O R G I A

Vidalia
Jesup

Brunswick

Savannah
Hilton Head Island

A T L A N T I C

5

Longview
Tyler
Palestine

Shreveport

Alexandria
Natchitoches

L O U I S I A N A

Laurel
Hattiesburg

Mobile

Evergreen
Dothan

Waycross

Crestview
Marianna
Tallahassee
Bainbridge

Jacksonville

Bryan
Beaumont
Lufkin

HOUSTON
Port Arthur

New Orleans
Lafayette
Baton Rouge
Houma
Biloxi
Panama City

Gainesville
Ocala
Leesburg

St. Augustine
Daytona Beach

O C E A N

30°

Galveston Bay

Freeport

Marsh I.

Mississippi River Delta

Venice
Cape San Blas

Apalachee Bay

Orlando
Cape Canaveral
Melbourne

Tampa
St. Petersburg

FLORIDA
Fort Pierce

atagorda Island

and
ville

G u l f   o f

M e x i c o

Port Charlotte
Fort Myers
Naples

West Palm Beach
Fort Lauderdale
Hollywood

Freeport
Grand Bahama

Little Abaco
Great Abaco

6

THE BAHAMAS

25°

Key Largo
Miami
Key West

Bimini Is.
Nassau
New Providence

Eleuthera

Exuma Sound
Cat I.
San Salvador
Rum Cay

Tropic of Cancer

La Habana (Havana)
Matanzas
Pinar del Río
Güines
Guane

Santa Clara
Santa la Grande
Cienfuegos

Golfo de Batabanó
Isla de la Juventud

1156
Sancti Spíritus
San Juan
Ciego de Ávila
Camagüey
Holguín

Straits of Florida

Andros

Great Bahama Bank

Great Exuma
Long I.
Crooked I.

Acklins I.
Mayaguana
Turks and Caicos Is. (U.K)

Little Inagua
Great Inagua

Caicos Is.
Turks Is.

7

Río Lagartos
Progreso
Cabo Catoche
Cancún

Yucatan Channel

Mérida

CUBA
Victoria de las Tunas

95° H 90° J 85° K 80° L 75° M 70° N

■ over 3 million	● 100 000 – 250 000	——— country capital underline
▣ 1 – 3 million	◦ 25 000 – 100 000	—— state or province capital underline
◉ 250 000 – 1 million	• under 25 000	

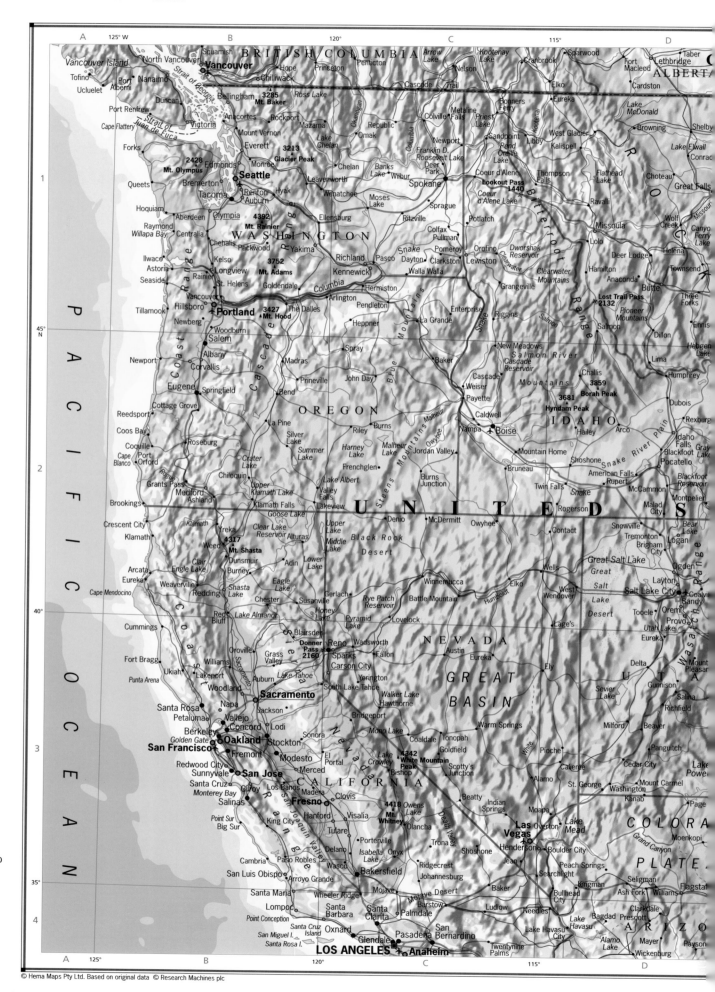

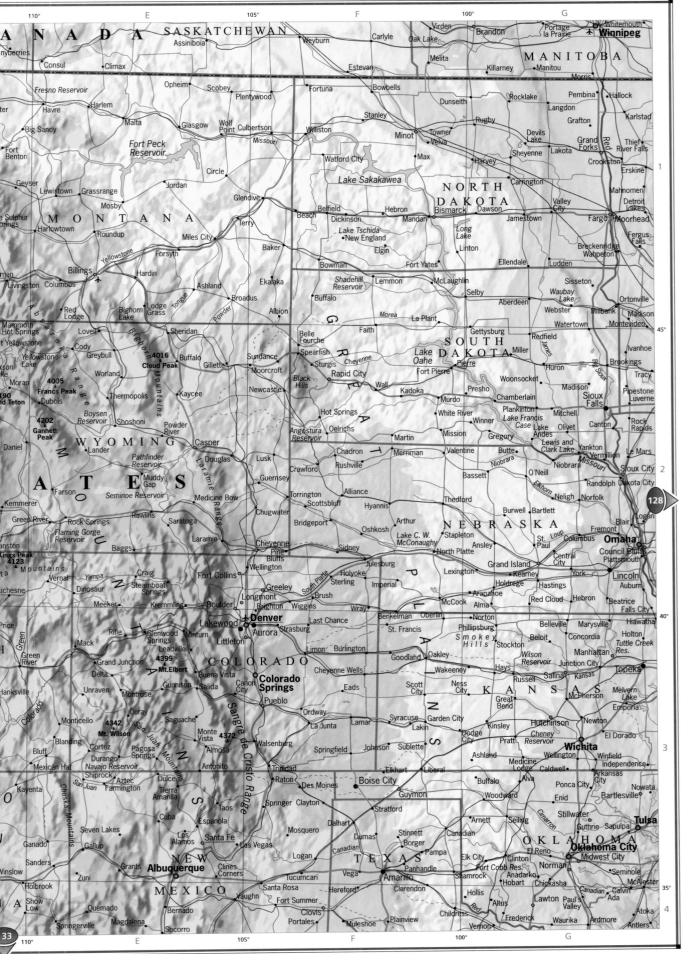

■	over 3 million
▣	1 – 3 million
◉	250 000 – 1 million
●	100 000 – 250 000
◦	25 000 – 100 000
•	under 25 000

────	country capital underline
────	state or province capital underline

Scale 1 : 7 200 000

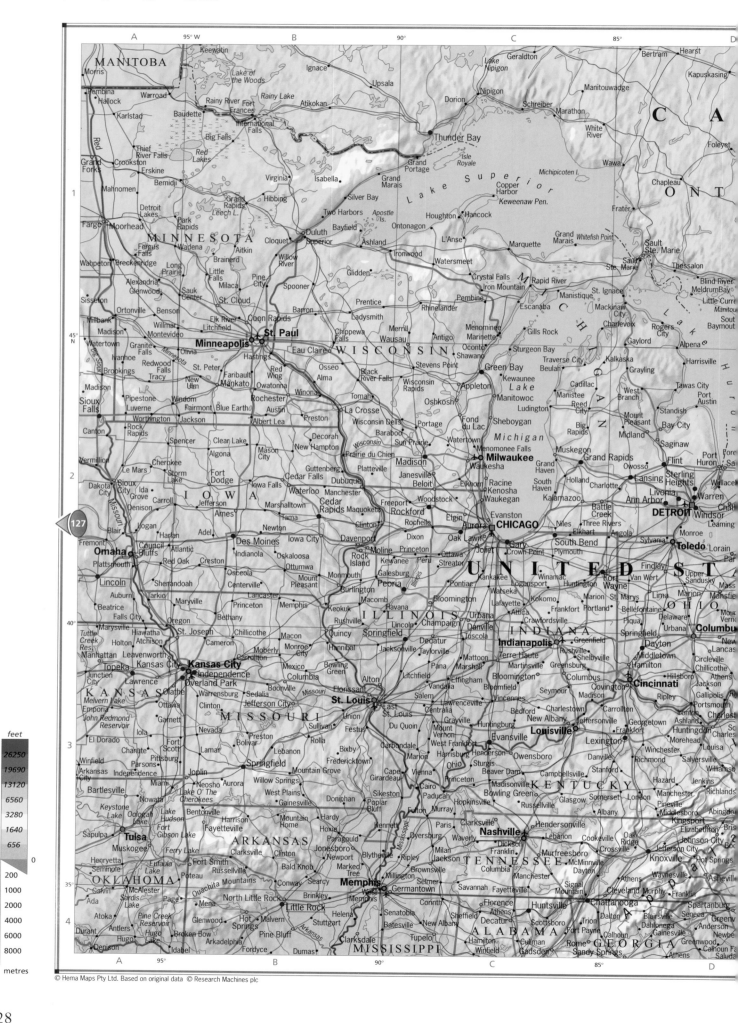

Northeast United States

Connecticut • Delaware • District of Columbia • Illinois • Indiana • Iowa • Maine • Maryland • Massachusetts • Michigan
Minnesota • New Hampshire • New Jersey • New York • Ohio • Pennsylvania • Rhode Island • Vermont • West Virginia • Wisconsin

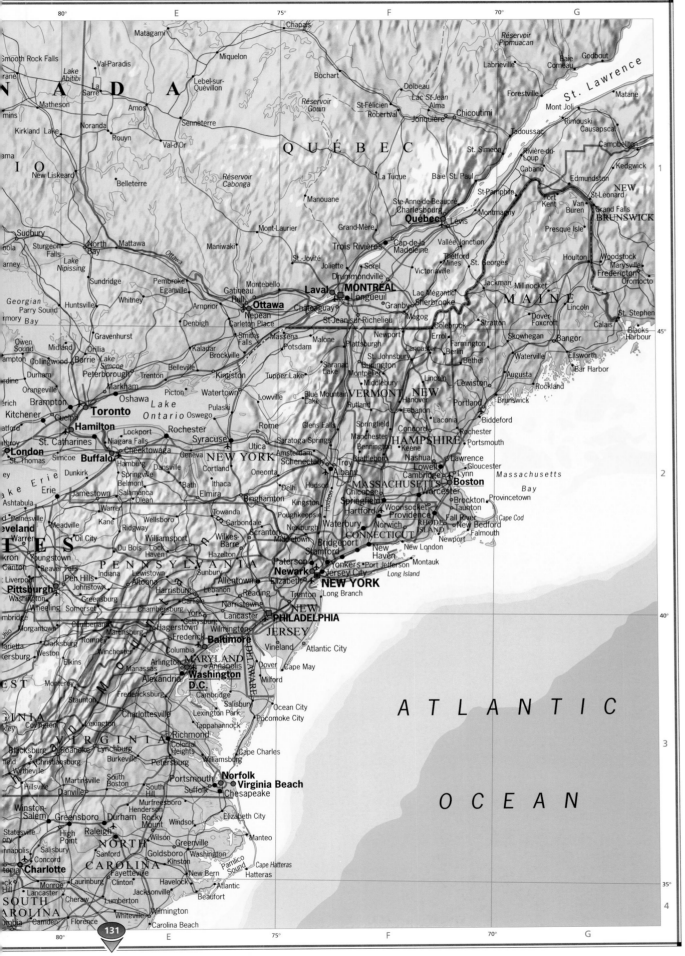

■ over 3 million	● 100 000 – 250 000	——— country capital underline
■ 1 – 3 million	○ 25 000 – 100 000	——— state or province capital underline
● 250 000 – 1 million	• under 25 000	

129

Scale 1 : 7 200 000

© Hema Maps Pty Ltd. Based on original data © Research Machines plc

Southeast United States

Alabama • Arkansas • The Bahamas • Florida • Georgia • Kentucky • Louisiana
Mississippi • Missouri • North Carolina • South Carolina • Tennessee • Texas • Virginia

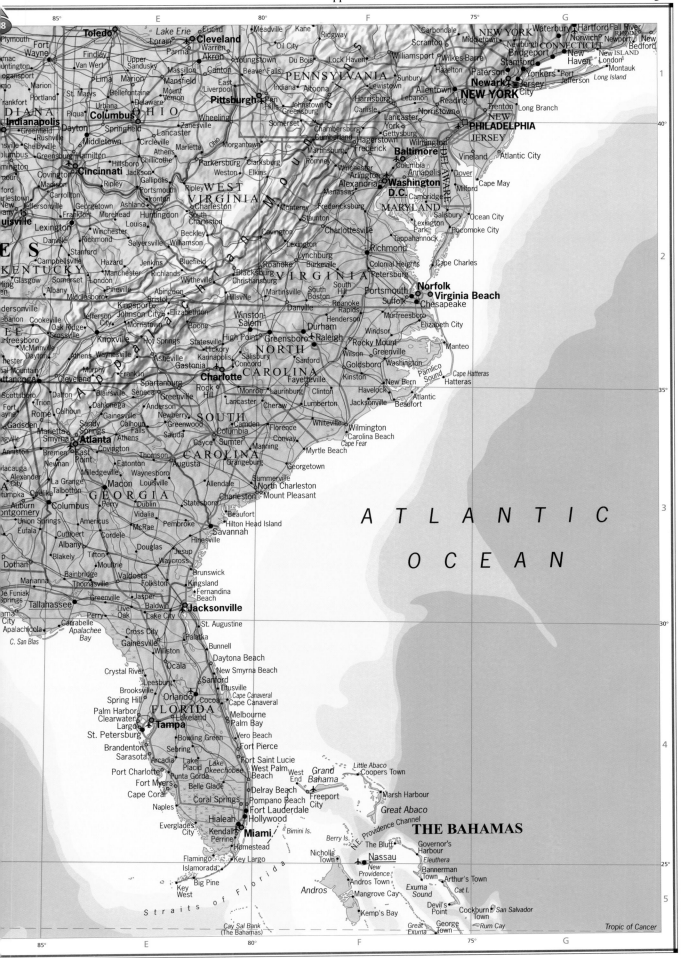

■ over 3 million	● 100 000 – 250 000	country capital underline
■ 1 – 3 million	○ 25 000 – 100 000	state or province capital underline
● 250 000 – 1 million	• under 25 000	

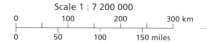
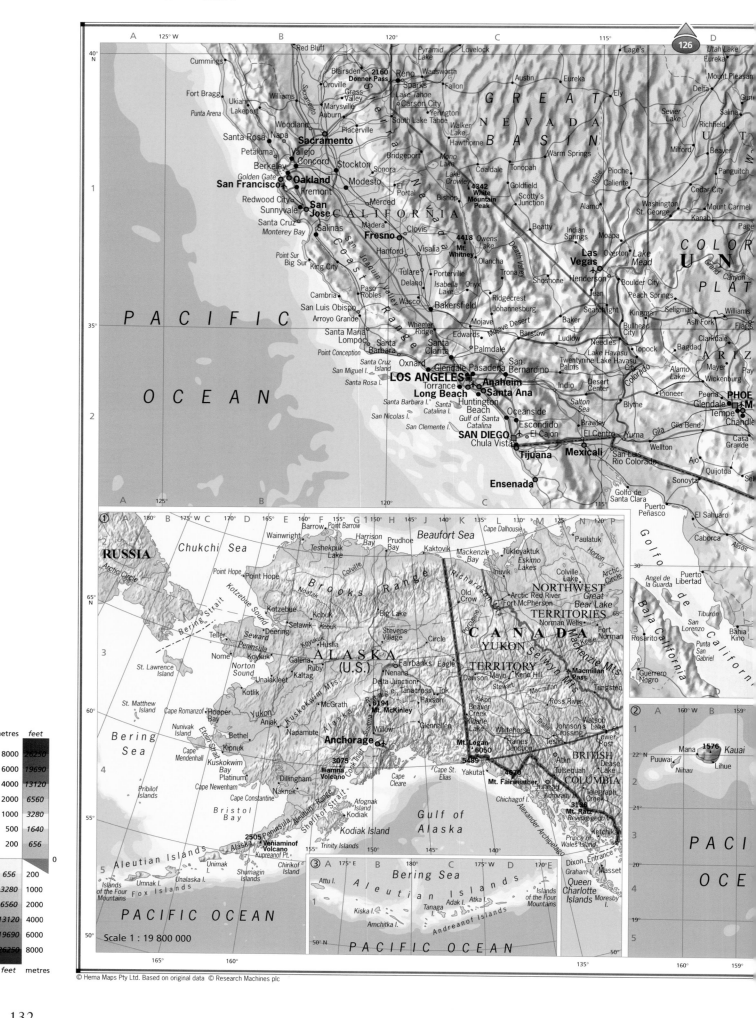

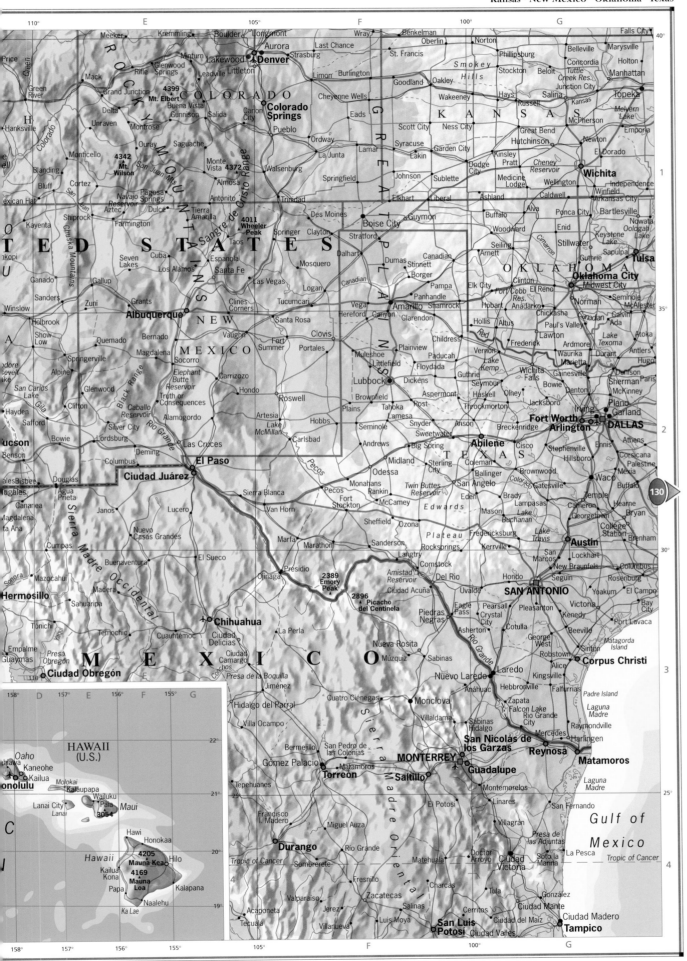

■ over 3 million	● 100 000 – 250 000	—— country capital underline
■ 1 – 3 million	◎ 25 000 – 100 000	—— state or province capital underline
● 250 000 – 1 million	• under 25 000	

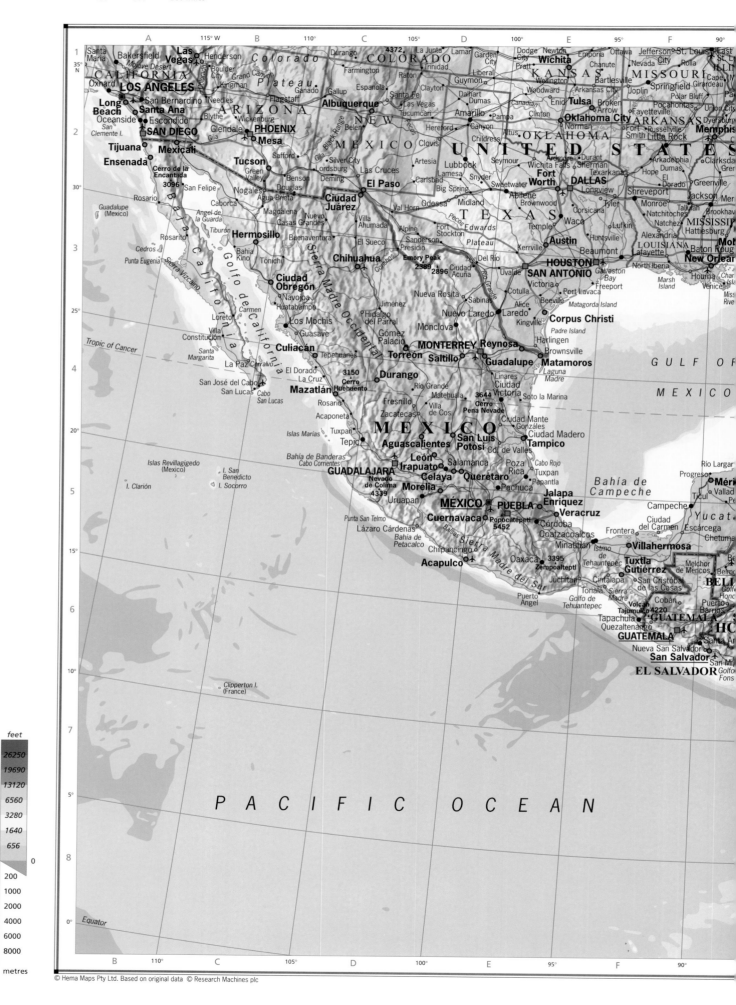

Scale 1 : 16 100 000

metres	feet
8000	26250
6000	19690
4000	13120
2000	6560
1000	3280
500	1640
200	656
0	0
656	200
3280	1000
6560	2000
13120	4000
19690	6000
26250	8000
feet	metres

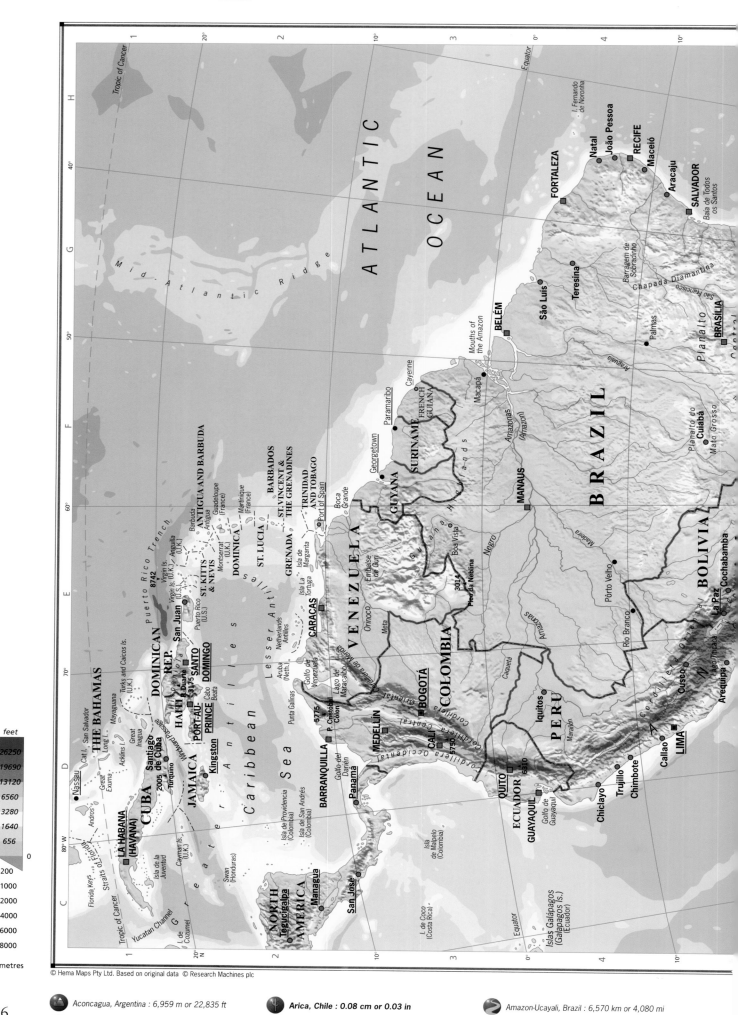

Scale 1 : 28 000 000

0   500   1000   1500 km
0   250   500   750 miles

metres   feet
8000   26250
6000   19690
4000   13120
2000   6560
1000   3280
500   1640
200   656
0   0
656   200
3280   1000
6560   2000
13120   4000
19690   6000
26250   8000
feet   metres

ATLANTIC

OCEAN

Mid-Atlantic Ridge

Puerto Rico Trench
8742

THE BAHAMAS

CUBA
LA HABANA (HAVANA)
Santiago de Cuba
Turquino 2005

JAMAICA
Kingston

HAITI
PORT-AU-PRINCE
DOMINICAN REP.
SANTO DOMINGO
Duarte 3175

Caribbean Sea

ANTIGUA AND BARBUDA
ST KITTS & NEVIS
DOMINICA
ST. LUCIA
BARBADOS
ST VINCENT & THE GRENADINES
GRENADA
TRINIDAD AND TOBAGO
Port of Spain

NORTH AMERICA
Tegucigalpa
Managua
San José
Panamá
BARRANQUILLA

CARACAS
VENEZUELA
COLOMBIA
BOGOTÁ
MEDELLÍN
CALI
QUITO
ECUADOR
GUAYAQUIL

GUYANA
Georgetown
SURINAME
Paramaribo
FRENCH GUIANA
Cayenne

Orinoco

BRAZIL

Mouths of the Amazon
BELÉM
MANAUS
Amazonas (Amazon)
Negro

São Luís
Teresina
FORTALEZA
Natal
João Pessoa
RECIFE
Maceió
Aracaju
SALVADOR
Bahia de Todos os Santos
Palmas
BRASÍLIA
Planalto Central
Cuiabá
Mato Grosso

PERU
Iquitos
LIMA
Callao
Trujillo
Chimbote
Chiclayo

BOLIVIA
La Paz
Cochabamba
Arequipa
Cuzco
Lago Titicaca

Porto Velho
Rio Branco

Islas Galápagos (Galápagos Is.) (Ecuador)

Equator

© Hema Maps Pty Ltd. Based on original data © Research Machines plc

136

Aconcagua, Argentina : 6,959 m or 22,835 ft

Península Valdés, Argentina : 40 m or 131 ft

Arica, Chile : 0.08 cm or 0.03 in

Quibdo, Colombia : 899 cm or 354 in

Amazon-Ucayali, Brazil : 6,570 km or 4,080 mi

Lake Maracaibo, Venezuela : 13,010 km² or 5,020 sq mi

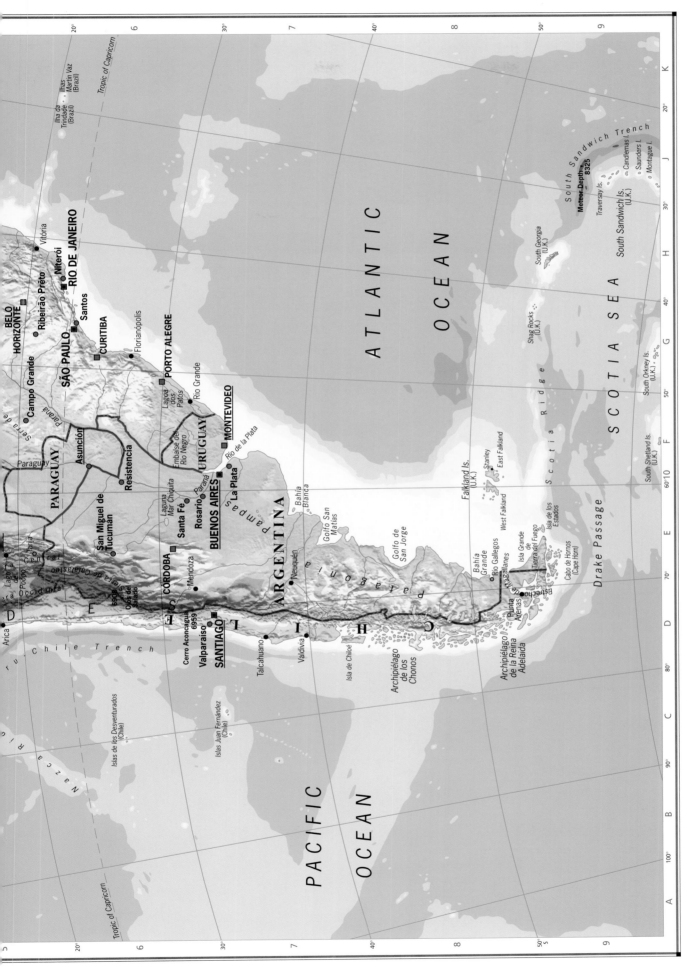

 Sarmiento, Argentina : -33 °C or -27 °F

Rivadavia, Argentina : 49 °C or 120 °F

 335,716,000

19 per km² or 49 per sq mi

 17,838,000 km² or 6,887,000 sq mi

12

ATLANTIC

OCEAN

Mid-Atlantic Ridge

Tropic of Cancer

NORTH AMERICA

THE BAHAMAS

CUBA

LA HABANA (HAVANA)

JAMAICA

Kingston

HAITI

DOMINICAN REP.

PORT-AU-PRINCE

SANTO DOMINGO

San Juan

Puerto Rico (U.S.)

Caribbean Sea

Lesser Antilles

Greater Antilles

Netherlands Antilles

ANTIGUA AND BARBUDA

ST. KITTS & NEVIS

DOMINICA

ST. LUCIA

BARBADOS

ST. VINCENT & THE GRENADINES

GRENADA

TRINIDAD AND TOBAGO

Port of Spain

Isla de Margarita

CARACAS

VENEZUELA

COLOMBIA

BOGOTÁ

MEDELLÍN

CALI

BARRANQUILLA

Panamá

Managua

Tegucigalpa

San José

QUITO

ECUADOR

GUAYAQUIL

PERU

Iquitos

LIMA

Callao

Trujillo

Chimbote

Chiclayo

BOLIVIA

La Paz

Cochabamba

Cusco

Arequipa

Lago Titicaca

Cordillera Oriental

BRAZIL

BRASÍLIA

MANAUS

BELÉM

São Luis

Teresina

FORTALEZA

Natal

João Pessoa

RECIFE

Maceió

Aracaju

SALVADOR

Palmas

Cuiabá

GUYANA

Georgetown

SURINAME

Paramaribo

FRENCH GUIANA

Cayenne

Boa Vista

Pôrto Velho

Rio Branco

Amazonas (Amazon)

Negro

Madeira

Mouths of the Amazon

Macapá

Equator

© Hema Maps Pty Ltd. Based on original data © Research Machines plc

138

Aconcagua, Argentina : 6,959 m or 22,835 ft

Península Valdés, Argentina : 40 m or 131 ft

Arica, Chile : 0.08 cm or 0.03 in

Quibdo, Colombia : 899 cm or 354 in

Amazon-Ucayali, Brazil : 6,570 km or 4,080 mi

Lake Maracaibo, Venezuela : 13,010 km² or 5,020 sq mi

ATLANTIC OCEAN

PACIFIC OCEAN

SCOTIA SEA

Drake Passage

Tropic of Capricorn

ARGENTINA

PARAGUAY

URUGUAY

BUENOS AIRES

SANTIAGO

MONTEVIDEO

ASunción

Falkland Is. (U.K.)

South Georgia (U.K.)

South Sandwich Is. (U.K.)

Meteor Depth 8325

South Sandwich Trench

Chile Trench

BELO HORIZONTE

SÃO PAULO

RIO DE JANEIRO

CURITIBA

PORTO ALEGRE

CÓRDOBA

Cerro Aconcagua 6959

Ojos del Salado 6908

Valparaíso

Tierra del Fuego

Cabo de Hornos (Cape Horn)

Sarmiento, Argentina : -33 °C or -27 °F
Rivadavia, Argentina : 49 °C or 120 °F

335,716,000
19 per km² or 49 per sq mi

17,838,000 km² or 6,887,000 sq mi
12

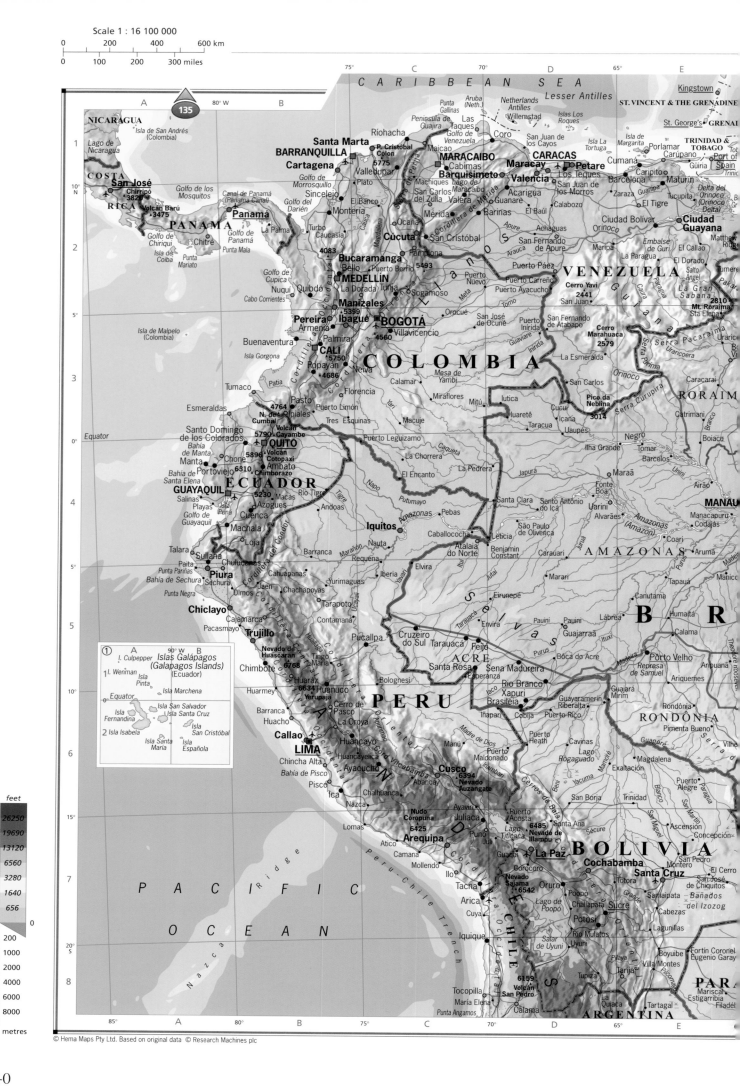

Scale 1 : 16 100 000

| 0 | 200 | 400 | 600 km |
| 0 | 100 | 200 | 300 miles |

CARIBBEAN SEA
Lesser Antilles

NICARAGUA

Lago de Nicaragua

Isla de San Andrés (Colombia)

COSTA
San José
Chirripó
3820
Volcán Barú
3475
RICA

PANAMÁ

Golfo de los Mosquitos

Canal de Panamá (Panama Canal)

Golfo de Chiriquí

Isla de Coiba

Punta Mariato

Chitré

Golfo de Panamá

Punta Mala

Golfo del Darién

La Palma

Golfo de Cupica

Nuquí

Cabo Corrientes

Isla de Malpelo (Colombia)

Buenaventura

Isla Gorgona

Tumaco

Esmeraldas

Santo Domingo de los Colorados

Bahía de Manta

Manta

Portoviejo

Bahía de Santa Elena

GUAYAQUIL

Salinas

Isla Puná

Playas

Golfo de Guayaquil

Machala

Talara

Paita

Punta Pariñas

Bahía de Sechura

Punta Negra

Chiclayo

Pacasmayo

Trujillo

Chimbote

Huarmey

Barranca

Huacho

Callao

LIMA

Chincha Alta

Bahía de Pisco

Pisco

Ica

Nazca

Lomas

PACIFIC

OCEAN

Nazca Ridge

Peru-Chile Trench

NICARAGUA

Ríohacha

Santa Marta
BARRANQUILLA
Cartagena

Golfo de Morrosquillo

Sincelejo

Monteria

Turbo

Caucasia

Bello
MEDELLÍN
La Dorada

Manizales
5399
Pereira
Armenia
Ibagué
CALI
5750
Popayán
4686

Pasto
4764
N. del Cumbal
Volcán 5790 Cayambe
5896 Volcán Cotopaxi
6310 Chimborazo
ECUADOR
5230
Azogues
Cuenca
Loja
Chone
Ambato

Quibdó

Peninsula de Guajira
Punta Gallinas
Las Taques
Golfo de Venezuela
Maicao
P. Cristóbal Colón 5775
Valledupar
Plato
El Banco
Ocaña
Machiques
San Carlos del Zulia
Mérida

Cúcuta
Pamplona
San Cristóbal

Bucaramanga
4083
Puerto Berrío
5493
Tunja
Sogamoso

BOGOTÁ
Villavicencio
4560

Neiva

Florencia

Puerto Limón

Tres Esquinas

Puerto Leguízamo

La Chorrera

El Encanto

Macuje

Mitú

Macoa

Miraflores

Yari

Caquetá

Putumayo

Napo

Río Tigre

Tigre

Macas

Andoas

Iquitos

Nauta

Requena

Barranca

Marañón

Caballococha

Leticia

Atalaia do Norte

Benjamin Constant

Pebas

Santa Clara

Uarini

Ilha Grande

Maraã

Fonte Boa

Santo Antônio do Içá

São Paulo de Olivença

CARACAS
Maracay Petare

MARACAIBO
Cabimas
Barquisimeto
Valencia Los Teques
Valera Acarigua San Juan de los Morros
Barinas Guanare El Baúl Calabozo
El Tigre

San Juan de los Cayos
Coro

Punta Gallinas
Aruba (Neth.)
Netherlands Antilles
Willemstad
Islas Los Roques

Isla La Tortuga

Isla de Margarita
Porlamar

Cumaná
Carúpano
Güiria

VENEZUELA

Maripa

Ciudad Bolívar

Ciudad Guayana

El Callao
El Dorado

Embalse de Guri
La Paragua

Cerro Yaví
2441
San Juan

Cerro Marahuaca
2579

La Esmeralda

San Carlos

Pico da Neblina
3014

Cucuí

Içana

Uaupés

Negro

Tomar

Barcelos

Airão

Carauari

Marari

AMAZONAS

B R

Arumã

Tapauá

Canutama

Coari

Codajás

Manacapuru

Alvarães

Amazonas (Amazon)

MANAU

Pucallpa

Cruzeiro do Sul Tarauacá
Feijó

ACRE
Santa Rosa Sena Madureira
Esperanza Rio Branco
Xapuri
Brasiléia
Iñapari Cobija Puerto Rico

Eirunepé

Envira

Tarauacá

Purus

Boca do Acre

Lábrea

Humaitá

Calama

Porto Velho

Represa de Samuel

Ariquemes

Aripuaná

Theodore Roosevelt

RONDÔNIA

Pimenta Bueno

Vilhe

Nevado de Huascarán
6768

Chimbote

Huaraz
6634 Yerupajá

PERU

Huánuco

Cerro de Pasco

La Oroya

Huancayo

Huancavelica

Ayacucho

Abancay
Cusco
6394
Nevado Auzangate

Nudo Coropuna
6425

Arequipa

Chalhuanca

Puquio

Camana

Atico

Mollendo

Ilo

Tacna

Arica

Iquique

Tocopilla

María Elena

Punta Angamos

Calama

CHILE

Tingo María

Bolognesi

Pucallpa

Rio Branco

Puerto Maldonado

Manu

Madre de Dios

Inambari

Ayaviri

Juliaca

Puno

Lago Titicaca

Guaqui

La Paz
Corocoro

Oruro

Lago de Poopó

Challapata

Potosí

Salar de Uyuni

Uyuni

Río Mulatos

Tupiza

Volcán San Pedro
6159

Riberalta

Guayaramerín

Puerto Heath

Cavinas

Lago Rogaguado

Exaltación

San Borja

Trinidad

Cerros de Paria

Beni

Yacuma

Mamoré

Magdalena

Puerto Alegre

BOLIVIA
Cochabamba
Santa Cruz
Montero
Samaipata

Sucre

Cabezas

Lagunillas

Boyuibe

Fortín Coronel Eugenio Garay

Villa Montes

Tarija

Mariscal Estigarribia

PAR

Pilaya

Pilcomayo

Tartagal

Filadel

La Quiaca

ARGENTINA

metres	feet
8000	26250
6000	19690
4000	13120
2000	6560
1000	3280
500	1640
200	656
0	0
656	200
3280	1000
6560	2000
13120	4000
19690	6000
26250	8000
feet	metres

① A 90° W B
I. Culpepper Islas Galápagos
1 I. Wenman (Galapagos Islands)
Isla Pinta (Ecuador)
Isla Marchena
Isla Fernandina
Equator
Isla San Salvador
Isla Santa Cruz
Isla Santa María
Isla San Cristóbal
Isla Española
2 Isla Isabela

ATLANTIC

OCEAN

Equator

ARBADOS
dgetown

rawhanna
aruma

Georgetown
New Amsterdam
Corriverton
Nieuw Paramaribo
YANA
Ituni
Nickerie
Albina
Nieuw Amsterdam
Iracoubo
Apoerã
St. Laurent
Kourou
Parika
Brokopondo
W. J. van
Embalse
Blommestein-
Cayenne
Oronoque
Toekomstig
meer
FRENCH
Cabo Orange
Apoteri
1230
GUIANA
Oiapoque
them
Juliana Top
Vila Velha
Highlands
Camopi
Regina
Ovapock
Calçoene
Serra Acari
Meriruma
Amapá
Cabo Norte
Serra Tumucumaque
AMAPÁ
Trombetas
Azauri
Pôrto
Grande
Mouths of
the Amazon
Maloca
Pôrto Santana
Mazagão
Macapá
Mapuera
Arere
Chaves
Baía de
Faro
Ilha Grande
Marajó
Salinópolis
de Gurupá
Jatapu
Obidos Monte
Prainha
Afuá
repésa de
Alegre
BELÉM
Bragança
Balbina
Amazonas
Vigia
Ibina
(Amazon)
Breves
Castanhal
Viseu
Urucurituba
Portel
Pará
Acará
Camiranga
Parintins
Santarém
Cametá
Badajós
Ilha de
Itacoatiara
Belo
São Luís
São Luís
Monte
Baião
Canumã
Altamira
Pindaré
Rosário
Camocim
Tucuruí
Mirim
Itaituba
Porto Alegre
Represa
Itapicuru
Sobral
Itapipoca
Tucuruí
Mirim
Codó
Luzilândia
Caucaia FORTALEZA
Lua
Paga Conta
Jacunda
Bacabal
Piripiri
Canindé
Aracati
AZIL
Nova
PARÁ
Pedreiras
MARANHÃO
Caxias
Campo
CEARÁ
Areia Branca
Jacareacanga
Araras
Maraba
Imperatriz
Timon
Maior
Mossoró
Macau
Barra do
São Manuel
São Félix
Araguatins
Barra do Corda
Teresina
Taua
Iguatu
RIO GRANDE
DO NORTE
Barracão do
Manuelzinho
Araguaína
Pôrto Franco
Grajaú
Amarante
Juázeiro
do Norte
Currais Novos
Natal
Barreto
Conceição do
Carolina
Balsas
Uruçuí
Floriano
Picos
Crato
Sousa
João Pessoa
Araguaia
Santa Maria
das Barreiras
TOCANTINS
Pedro
Afonso
Canto do Buriti
Alto
Parnaíba
São Raimundo
Nonato
PIAUÍ
Oeiras
PERNAMBUCO
Ouricuri
Petrolina
Serra dos Dois Irmãos
Campina Grande
Jaboatão
Olinda
RECIFE
Caruaru
Macaúba
Palmas
São Francisco
Juázeiro
Paulo Afonso
Garanhuns
Palmares
Gilbués
Barragem
ALAGOAS
Maceió
Campo de
Diauarum
Pôrto
Nacional
de Sobradinho
Senhor do
Bonfim
Jeremoabo
Arápiraca
São Félix
Dianópolis
Barra
Xique Xique
Tucano
SERGIPE
Aracaju
MATO GROSSO
Peixe
Paranã
Irecê
Mundo
Novo
Serrinha
Estância
Lucas
Porangatu
Barreiras
Ibotirama
BAHIA
Feira de Santana
Esplanada
Alagoinhas
Camaçari
Diamantino
Niquelândia
Posse
Bom Jesus
da Lapa
1850
Santo Antônio
de Jesus
SALVADOR
Baía de Todos
os Santos
Barra do
Bugres
Nova Xavantina
Planalto
Uruaçu
GOIÁS
Guanambi
Jequié
Gandu
Rosário
Oeste
Ceres
Formosa
Manga
Vitória da
Conquista
Itabuna
Ubaitaba
Ilhéus
Cuiabá
do
Barra do
Garças
Goiás
BRASÍLIA
DISTRITO
Januária
Monte
Azul
Itapetinga
Itiquira
Mato Grosso
Aragarças
FEDERAL
Janaúba
Pardo
Cáceres
Rondonópolis
Anápolis
Central
Salinas
Pedra Azul
Itapebi
Belmonte
Ipora
Goiânia
Cristalina
Montes Claros
Bocaiúva
Pantanal
Alto Garças
Serra do Caiapó
Piers do Rio
Paracatu
MINAS
Minas Novas
Teófilo Otoni
Prado
Pôrto Seguro
Taquari
Jataí
Itumbiara
Rio Verde
Ipameri
Patos de
GERAIS
Diamantina
Itambacuri
Caravelas
Corumbá
Claro
Rio Verde de Mato Grosso
Araguari
Minas
Corinto
2033
Nahuque
MATO GROSSO
Uberlândia
Curvelo
Pico de
Itambé
Governador Valadares
DO SUL
Paranaiba
Rep. de Sao
Simao
Ituiutaba
Araxá
Sete Lagoas
Itabira
ESPÍRITO SANTO
Ipatinga
Linhares
Miranda
Campo
Rep. Ilha
Solteira
São José do
Fernandópolis
Rio Preto
Uberaba
Pará de Minas
Divinópolis
BELO HORIZONTE
Cariacica
Grande
Aquidauana
Ribas do
Rio Pardo
Formiga
Manhuaçu
Pico da
Bandeira
Vitória
Jardim
Andradina
Barretos
Passos
Muriaé
Lavras
2890
Cachoeiro de
Itapemirim
UAY
Pôrto Murtinho
Presidente
Prudente
Araçatuba
SÃO
Franca
Três Corações
Juiz de Fora
Campos
Pedro Juan
Caballero
Pontá Porã
Marília
PAULO
Lins
São Carlos
Ribeirão Prêto
Volta
RIO DE JANEIRO
Bauru
Limeira
Agulhas Negras
Redonda
RIO DE JANEIRO
Paranaval
Assis
2797
Nova Iguaçu
Niterói
Piracicaba

Legend

- ■ over 3 million
- ■ 1 – 3 million
- ● 250 000 – 1 million
- ● 100 000 – 250 000
- ◦ 25 000 – 100 000
- • under 25 000
- country capital underline
- state or province capital underline

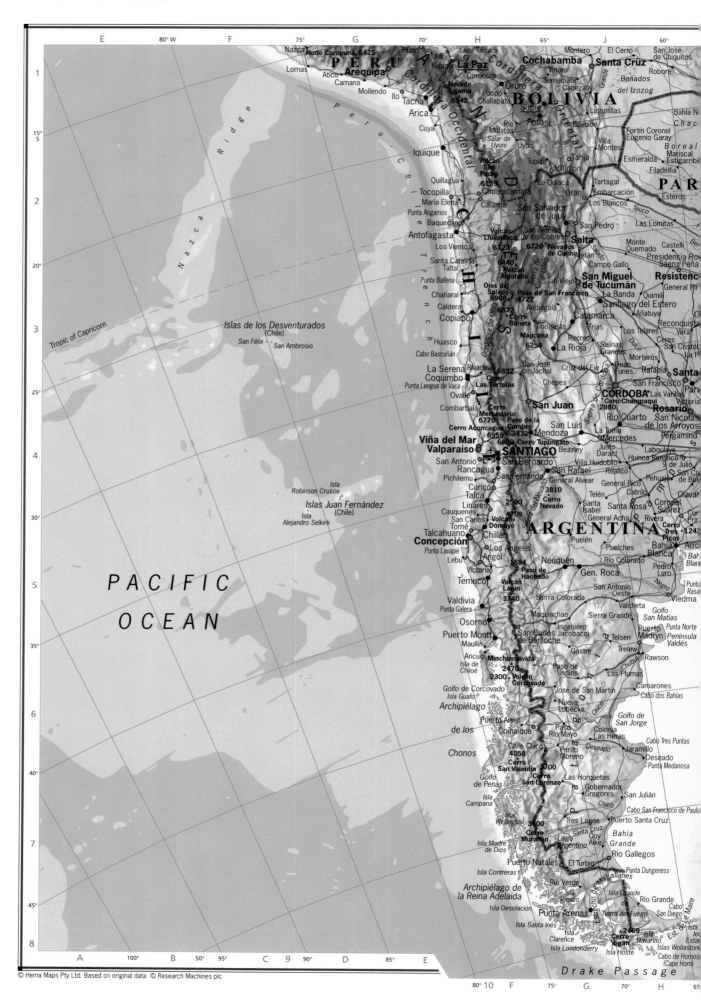

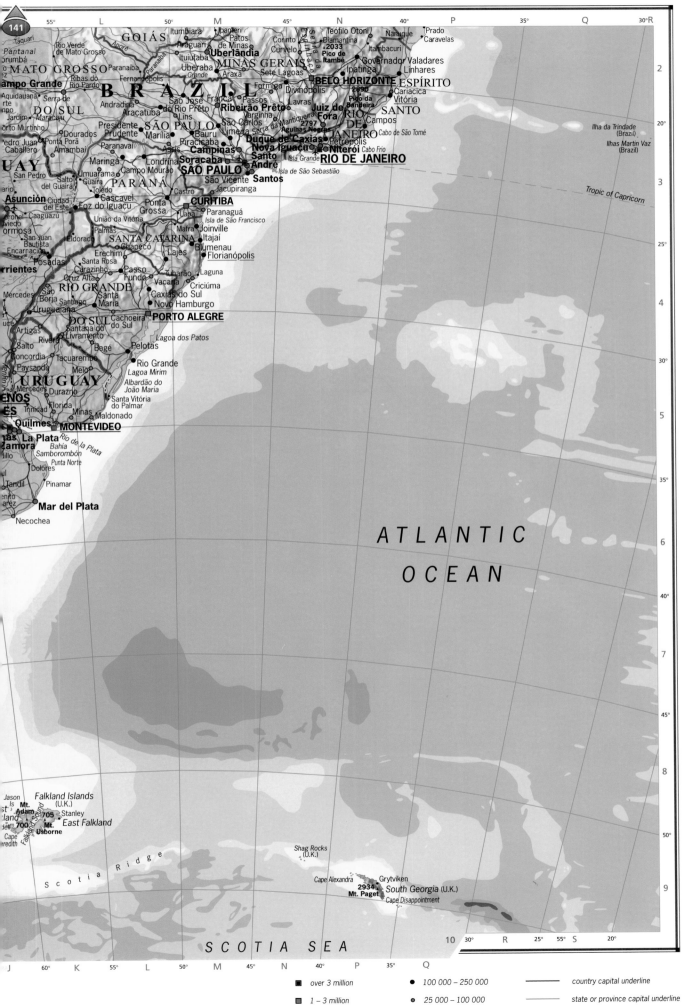

141

GOIÁS
Itumbiara
Araguari
Ituiutaba
Uberlândia
Uberaba
MINAS GERAIS
Araxá
Paranaíba
Fernandópolis
MATO GROSSO
Campo Grande
DO SUL
Aquidauana
Jardim
Dourados
Ponta Porã
Amambaí
Presidente
Prudente
Marília
Andradina
São José
do Rio Prêto
Ribeirão Prêto
São Carlos
Limeira
SÃO PAULO
Bauru
Piracicaba
Campinas
Duque de Caxias
Nova Iguaçu
Santo
André
Teófilo Otoni
2033
Pico de
Itambé
Diamantina
Governador Valadares
Ipatinga
Linhares
BELO HORIZONTE
ESPÍRITO
2890
Divinópolis
Sete Lagoas
Lavras
Varginha
Agulhas Negras
2797
Juiz de
Fora
Petrópolis
Niterói
RIO DE JANEIRO
SANTO
RIO
DE
JANEIRO
Campos
Cariacica
Vitória
Nanuque
Prado
Caravelas

Asunción
Ciudad
del Este
Foz do Iguaçu
PARANÁ
Cascavel
Ponta
Grossa
CURITIBA
Paranaguá
Isla de São Francisco
Joinville
Itajaí
SANTA CATARINA
Blumenau
Florianópolis
Lajes
Tubarão
Laguna
Criciúma
Caxias do Sul
Novo Hamburgo
PORTO ALEGRE
Lagoa dos Patos
Pelotas
Rio Grande
Lagoa Mirim
URUGUAY
MONTEVIDEO
La Plata
Mar del Plata

ATLANTIC
OCEAN

Ilha da Trindade
(Brazil)

Ilhas Martin Vaz
(Brazil)

Tropic of Capricorn

Falkland Islands
(U.K.)
Mt.
Adam
705
Stanley
East Falkland
700
Mt.
Usborne

Shag Rocks
(U.K.)

Cape Alexandra
2934
Mt. Paget
Grytviken
South Georgia (U.K.)
Cape Disappointment

Scotia Ridge

SCOTIA SEA

■ over 3 million
■ 1 – 3 million
● 250 000 – 1 million
● 100 000 – 250 000
● 25 000 – 100 000
• under 25 000
country capital underline
state or province capital underline

Scale 1 : 50 700 000

0	500	1000	1500	2000 km

0	250	500	750	1000 miles

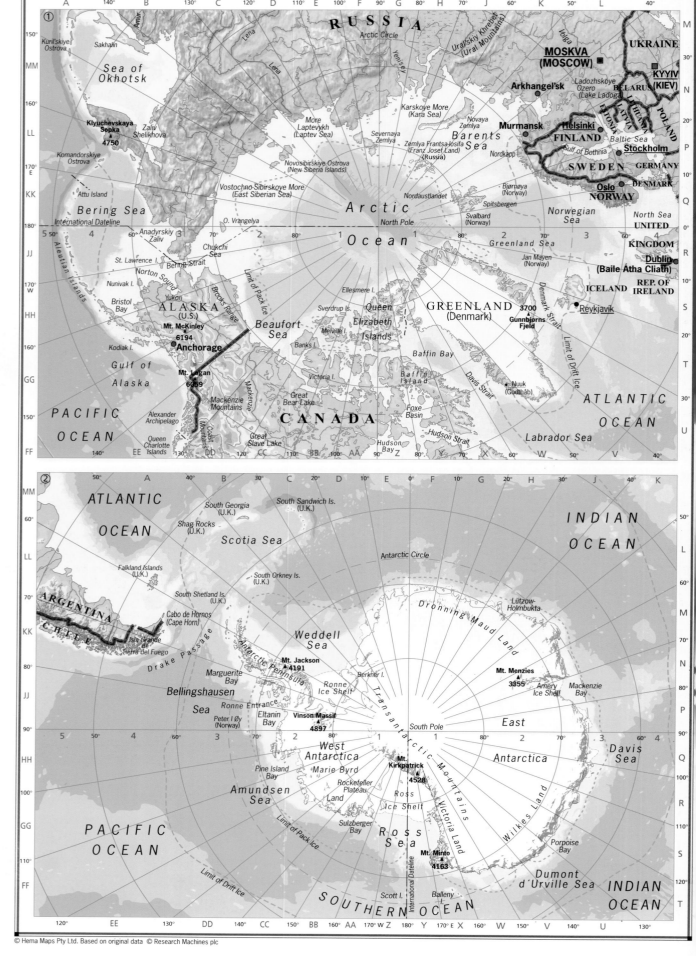

metres	feet
8000	26250
6000	19690
4000	13120
2000	6560
1000	3280
500	1640
200	656
0	0
656	200
3280	1000
6560	2000
13120	4000
19690	6000
26250	8000

feet   metres

© Hema Maps Pty Ltd. Based on original data © Research Machines plc

■ over 3 million
■ 1 – 3 million
● 250 000 – 1 million
● 100 000 – 250 000
○ 25 000 – 100 000
• under 25 000

——— country capital underline

INDEX TO COUNTRY MAPS

GLOSSARY

This is an alphabetically arranged glossary of the geographical terms used on the maps and in this index. The first column shows the map form, the second the language of origin and the third the English translation.

A

açude	Portuguese	reservoir
adası	Turkish	island
akra	Greek	peninsula
alpen	German	mountains
alpes	French	mountains
alpi	Italian	mountains
älven	Swedish	river
archipiélago	Spanish	archipelago
arquipélago	Portuguese	archipelago

B

bab	Arabic	strait
bahía	Spanish	bay
bahir, bahr	Arabic	bay, lake, river
baía	Portuguese	bay
baie	French	bay
baja	Spanish	lower
bandar	Arabic, Somalian, Malay, Persian	harbour, port
baraji	Turkish	dam
barragem	Portuguese	reservoir
ben	Gaelic	mountain
Berg(e)	German	mountain(s)
boğazı	Turkish	strait
Bucht	German	bay
buèayrat	Arabic	lake
burnu, burun	Turkish	cape

C

cabo	Spanish	cape
canal	French, Spanish	canal, channel
canale	Italian	canal, channel
cerro	Spanish	mountain
chott	Arabic	marsh, salt lake
co	Tibetan	lake
collines	French	hills
cordillera	Spanish	range

D

dağ(ı)	Turkish	mountain
dağlar(ı)	Turkish	mountains
danau	Indonesian	lake
daryacheh	Persian	lake
dasht	Persian	desert
djebel	Arabic	mountain(s)
-do	Korean	island

E

embalse	Spanish	reservoir
erg	Arabic	sandy desert
estrecho	Spanish	strait

F

feng	Chinese	mountain
-fjördur	Icelandic	fjord
-flói	Icelandic	bay

G

Gebirge	German	range
golfe	French	bay, gulf
golfo	Italian, Portuguese, Spanish	bay, gulf
göl, gölü	Turkish	lake
gora	Russian	mountain
gory	Russian	mountains
gunong	Malay	mountain
gunung	Indonesian	mountain

H

hai	Chinese	lake, sea
hāmūn	Persian	lake, marsh
hawr	Arabic	lake
hu	Chinese	lake, reservoir

I

île(s)	French	island(s)
ilha(s)	Portuguese	island(s)
isla(s)	Spanish	island(s)

J

jabal	Arabic	mountain(s)
-järvi	Finnish	lake
jazaïr	Arabic	islands
jazīrat	Arabic	island
jbel	Arabic	mountain
jebel	Arabic	mountain
jezero	Serbo-Croatian	lake
jezioro	Polish	lake
jiang	Chinese	river
-jima	Japanese	island
-joki	Finnish	river
-jökull	Icelandic	glacier

K

kepulauan	Indonesian	islands
khrebet	Russian	mountain range
-ko	Japanese	lake
kolpos	Greek	bay, gulf
körfezi	Turkish	bay, gulf
kryazh	Russian	ridge
küh(ha)	Persian	mountain(s)

L

lac	French	lake
lacul	Romanian	lake
lago	Italian, Portuguese, Spanish	lake
lagoa	Portuguese	lagoon
laguna	Spanish	lagoon, lake
limni	Greek	lake
ling	Chinese	mountain(s), peak
liqeni	Albanian	lake
loch, lough	Gaelic	lake

M

massif	French	mountains
-meer	Dutch	lake, sea
mont	French	mount
monte	Italian, Portuguese, Spanish	mount
montes	Portuguese, Spanish	mountains
monts	French	mountains
muntii	Romanian	mountains
mys	Russian	cape

N

nafud	Arabic	desert
nevado	Spanish	snow-capped mountain
nuruu	Mongolian	mountains
nuur	Mongolian	lake

O

ostrov(a)	Russian	island(s)
ozero	Russian	lake

P

pegunungan	Indonesian	mountains
pelagos	Greek	sea
pendi	Chinese	basin
pesky	Russian	sandy desert
pic	French	peak
pico	Portuguese, Spanish	peak
planalto	Portuguese	plateau
planina	Bulgarian	mountains
poluostrov	Russian	peninsula
puerto	Spanish	harbour, port
puncak	Indonesian	peak
punta	Italian, Spanish	point
puy	French	peak

Q

qundao	Chinese	archipelago

R

ras, râs, ra's	Arabic	cape
represa	Portuguese	dam, reservoir
-rettō	Japanese	archipelago
rio	Portuguese	river
río	Spanish	river

S

sahra	Arabic	desert
salar	Spanish	salt flat
-san	Japanese, Korean	mountain
-sanmaek	Korean	mountains
sebkha	Arabic	salt flat
sebkhet	Arabic	salt marsh
See	German	lake
serra	Portuguese	range
severnaya, severo-	Russian	northern
shan	Chinese	mountain(s)
-shima	Japanese	island
-shotō	Japanese	islands
sierra	Spanish	range

T

tanjona	Malagasy	cape
tanjung	Indonesian	cape
teluk	Indonesian	bay, gulf
ténéré	Berber	desert
-tō	Japanese	island

V

vârful	Romanian	mountain
-vesi	Finnish	lake
vodokhranilishche	Russian	reservoir
volcán	Spanish	volcano

W

wādī	Arabic	watercourse
Wald	German	forest

Z

-zaki	Japanese	cape
zaliv	Russian	bay, gulf

Abbreviations

Ak.	Alaska
Al.	Alabama
Ariz.	Arizona
Ark.	Arkansas
B.C.	British Columbia
Calif.	California
Colo.	Colorado
Conn.	Connecticut
Del.	Delaware
Dem. Rep. of the Congo	Democratic Republic of the Congo
Eng.	England
Fla.	Florida
Ga.	Georgia
Ia.	Iowa
Id.	Idaho
Ill.	Illinois
Ind.	Indiana
Kans.	Kansas
Ky.	Kentucky
La.	Louisiana
Man.	Manitoba
Mass.	Massachusetts
Md.	Maryland
Me.	Maine
M.G.	Mato Grosso
Mich.	Michigan
Minn.	Minnesota
Miss.	Mississippi
Mo.	Missouri
Mont.	Montana
N.B.	New Brunswick
N.C.	North Carolina
N.D.	North Dakota
Nebr.	Nebraska
Nev.	Nevada
Nfld.	Newfoundland
N.H.	New Hampshire
N. Ire.	Northern Ireland
N.J.	New Jersey
N. Mex.	New Mexico
N.W.T.	Northwest Territories
N.Y.	New York
Oh.	Ohio
Okla.	Oklahoma
Ont.	Ontario
Oreg.	Oregon
Orkney Is.	Orkney Islands
Pa.	Pennsylvania
R.G.S.	Rio Grande do Sul
R.I.	Rhode Island
S.C.	South Carolina
Scot.	Scotland
S.D.	South Dakota
Shetland Is.	Shetland Islands
Tenn.	Tennessee
Tex.	Texas
UK	United Kingdom
US	United States
Ut.	Utah
Va.	Virginia
Vt.	Vermont
Wash.	Washington
Wis.	Wisconsin
W. Va.	West Virginia
Wyo.	Wyoming
Y.T.	Yukon Territory

How to use the index

This is an alphabetically arranged index of the places and features that can be found on the maps in this atlas. Each name is generally indexed to the largest scale map on which it appears. If that map covers a double page, the name will always be indexed by the left-hand page number.

Names composed of two or more words are alphabetised as if they were one word.

All names appear in full in the index, except for 'St.' and 'Ste.', which although abbreviated, are indexed as though spelled in full.

Where two or more places have the same name, they can be distinguished from each other by the country or province name which immediately follows the entry. These names are indexed in the alphabetical order of the country or province.

Alternative names, such as English translations, can also be found in the index and are cross-referenced to the map form by the '=' sign. In these cases the names also appear in brackets on the maps.

Settlements are indexed to the position of the symbol, all other features are indexed to the position of the name on the map.

Finding a name on the map

Each index entry contains the name, followed by a symbol indicating the feature type (for example, settlement, river), a page reference and a grid reference:

Name	Owosso	●	126	D2
	Owyhee	●	124	C2
	Owyhee	✓	124	C2
Symbol	Oxford, *New Zealand*	●	112	D6
	Oxford, *United Kingdom*	●	40	A3
	Oxnard	●	130	C2
Page reference	Oyama	●	**72**	K5
	Oyapock	✓	140	G3
	Oyem	●	98	G4
Grid reference	Oyen	●	122	D1

The grid reference locates a place or feature within a rectangle formed by the network of lines of longitude and latitude. A name can be found by referring to the red letters and numbers placed around the maps. First find the letter, which appears along the top and bottom of the map, and then the number, down the sides. The name will be found within the rectangle uniquely defined by that letter and number. A number in brackets preceding the grid reference indicates that the name is to be found within an inset map.

Symbols

X	Continent name	●	Settlement
A	Country name	▲	Mountain, volcano, peak
a	State or province name	▲▲	Mountain range
■	Country capital	◫	Physical region or feature
▣	State or province capital	✓	River, canal

✔	Lake, salt lake	◰	Island or island group, rocky or coral reef
◣	Gulf, strait, bay		
◿	Sea, ocean	✳	Place of interest
◿	Cape, point	ℋ	Historical or cultural region

A

Aachen	●	54	J4
Aalborg	●	48	E8
Aalen	●	52	F8
Aalst	●	54	G4
Aarau	●	62	D3
Aare	✓	62	C3
Aarschot	●	54	G4
Aba	●	104	F3
Abādān	●	95	C1
Ābādeh	●	95	E1
Abadla	●	102	E2
Abaji	●	104	F3
Abakaliki	●	104	F3
Abakan	▣	76	S7
Āb Anbār	●	95	E1
Abancay	●	140	C6
Abano Terme	●	62	G5
Abarqū	●	95	E1
Abashiri	●	82	N1
Abava	✓	48	M8
Ābaya Hāyk'	✔	106	F2
Abay Wenz	✓	100	G5
Abbeville, *France*	●	54	D4
Abbeville, *US*	●	130	C4
Abd al Kūrī	◰	90	F7
Abéché	●	100	D5
Abengourou	●	104	D3
Abenójar	●	60	F6
Ābenrå	●	52	E1
Abensberg	●	52	G8
Abeokuta	●	104	E3
Aberaeron	●	56	H9
Aberdeen, *South Africa*	●	108	C6
Aberdeen, *UK*	●	56	K4
Aberdeen, *Miss., US*	●	130	D3
Aberdeen, *S.D., US*	●	126	G1
Aberdeen, *Wash., US*	●	126	B1
Aberdeen Lake	✔	122	M4
Aberystwyth	●	56	H9
Abez'	●	70	M1
Abhā	●	100	H4
Abhar	●	92	N5
Abidjan	■	104	D3
Abilene	●	132	G2
Abilene	●	120	M6
Abingdon, *UK*	●	54	A3
Abingdon, *US*	●	130	E2
Abnūb	●	100	F2
Aboisso	●	104	D3
Abomey	●	104	E3
Abong Mbang	●	104	G4
Abou Déia	●	100	C5
Abqaiq	●	95	C4
Abrantes	●	60	B5

Abrud	●	66	L3
Absaroka Range	▲▲	126	E1
Abū al Abayd	◰	95	E4
Abu Aweigîla	●	94	B6
Abu Ballâs	▲	100	E3
Abu Dhabi = Abū Zabī	●	95	F4
Abu Hamed	●	100	F4
Abuja	■	104	F3
Abumombazi	●	106	C3
Ābune Yosēf	▲	100	G5
Abū Nujaym	●	100	C1
Abu Qarin	●	100	C1
Aburo	▲	106	E3
Abu Simbel	●	100	F3
Abut Head	◿	116	B6
Abuye Meda	▲	106	F1
Abū Zabī	●	95	F4
Abv Nujaym	●	102	J2
Acaponeta	●	124	C7
Acapulco	●	134	E5
Acará	●	140	H4
Acarigua	●	140	D2
Accra	■	104	D3
Achaguas	●	134	L7
Achayvayam	●	78	W4
Acheng	●	80	H1
Achenkirch	●	62	G3
Achen See	✔	62	G3
Achill Island	◰	56	B8
Achim	●	52	E3
Achinsk	●	76	S6
Achit	●	70	L3
Aci Göl	✔	68	M7
A Cihanbeyli	●	68	Q6
Acireale	●	64	K11
Acklins Island	◰	134	K4
Aconcagua	▲	138	D7
Açores	◰	102	(1)B2
A Coruña	●	60	B1
Acquarossa	●	62	D4
Acqui Terme	●	62	D6
Acre	a	140	C5
Acri	●	64	L9
Ada	●	130	K12
Ada	●	130	B3
Adak Island	◰	132	(3)C1
Adam	●	90	G5
Adamas	●	68	G8
Adams Island	◰	116	(2)B1
'Adan	●	90	E7
Adana	●	92	F5
Adda	✓	62	E5
Ad Dafrah	◫	95	E5
Ad Dahnā	◫	95	B3
Ad Dakhla	●	102	B4
Ad Dammām	●	95	D3
Ad Dawādimī	●	90	D5

Ad Dawhah	■	95	D4
Ad Dilam	●	95	B5
Ad Dir'īyah	●	95	B4
Addis Ababa = Ādīs Ābeba	■	106	F2
Ad Dīwānīyah	●	90	D3
Adel	●	128	B2
Adelaide	▣	114	G6
Adelaide Peninsula	◫	122	M3
Adelaide River	●	114	F2
Aden = Adan	●	90	E7
Aderbissinat	●	104	F1
Adh Dhayd	●	95	F4
Adi	◰	87	D3
Adige	✓	62	G5
Adigrat	●	100	G5
Adilabad	●	88	C5
Adin	●	126	B2
Adīrī	●	100	B2
Ādīs Ābeba	■	106	F2
Adi Ugri	●	100	G5
Adiyaman	●	90	C2
Adjud	●	66	Q3
Adler	●	92	H2
Admiralty Island	◰	122	E5
Admiralty Islands	◰	112	E6
Adoni	●	88	C5
Adour	✓	58	F10
Adra	●	60	H8
Adrano	●	64	J11
Adrar	●	102	E3
Adrar des Ifôghas	◫	102	F5
Adrar Tamgak	▲	102	G5
Adria	●	62	H5
Adriatic Sea	◿	64	H4
Adycha	✓	78	P3
Adygeya	a	92	J1
Adygeysk	●	92	H1
Adzopé	●	104	D3
Adz'vavom	●	70	L1
Aegean Sea	◿	68	H5
A Estrada	●	60	B2
Afghanistan	A	90	H3
Afgooye	●	106	H3
'Afif	●	100	H3
Afikpo	●	104	F3
Afmadow	●	106	G3
Afognak Island	◰	132	(1)G4
A Fonsagrada	●	60	C1
Afragola	●	64	J8
'Afrīn	●	92	G5
Afuá	●	140	G4
'Afula	●	94	C4
Afyon	●	68	N6
Agadez	●	102	G5
Agadir	●	102	D2
Agadyr'	●	76	N8
Agalega Islands	◰	98	J7

Agan	✓	78	B4
Āgaro	●	106	F2
Agartala	●	88	F4
Agathonisi	◰	68	J7
Agattu Island	◰	78	W6
Ağcabädi	●	92	M3
Agde	●	58	J10
Agen	●	58	F9
Agia Triada	●	68	D7
Ağin	●	92	H4
Aginskoye	●	76	S6
Agiokampos	●	68	E5
Agios Efstratios	◰	68	H5
Agios Georgios	◰	68	F7
Agios Nikolaos	●	68	H9
Agnibilekrou	●	104	D3
Agnita	●	66	M4
Agra	●	88	C3
Agrakhanskiy Poluostrov	◫	92	M2
Agri	✓	64	L8
Ağri	●	92	K4
Agrigento	●	64	H11
Agrinio	●	68	D6
Agropoli	●	64	K8
Agryz	●	70	K3
Ağsu	●	92	N3
Agua Prieta	●	132	E2
Aguascalientes	●	134	D4
A Gudiña	●	60	C2
Aguelhok	●	102	F5
Águilas	●	60	J7
Agulhas Negras	▲	140	H8
Ağva	●	68	M3
Ahar	●	92	M4
Ahaura	●	116	C6
Ahaus	●	54	K2
Ahititi	●	116	E4
Ahlen	●	54	K3
Ahmadabad	●	88	B4
Ahmadnagar	●	88	B5
Ahmdpur East	●	88	B3
Ahr	✓	52	B6
Ahram	●	95	D2
Ahrensburg	●	52	F3
Ahvāz	●	90	E3
Aichach	●	52	G8
Aigialousa	●	92	F6
Aigina	●	68	F7
Aigina	◰	68	F7
Aigio	●	68	E6
Aigosthena	●	68	F6
Aiguillon	●	58	F9
Aihui	●	78	M6
Aim	●	78	N5
Ain	✓	58	L7
Ain Beida	●	102	G1
'Aïn Ben Tili	●	102	D3

147

Name	Page	Grid
Aïn Bessem	60	P8
Aïn el Hadjel	60	P9
Aïn Oussera	102	F1
Ainsa	60	L2
Aïn Sefra	102	E2
Aïn Taya	60	P8
Aïn-Tédélès	60	L8
Aïn Témouchent	60	J9
Airão	140	E4
Aire	56	L8
Air Force Island	122	S3
Airolo	62	D4
Airpanas	87	C4
Aisne	54	F5
Aitape	87	F3
Aitkin	128	B1
Aitutaki	112	K7
Aiud	66	L3
Aix-en-Provence	58	L10
Aix-les-Bains	58	L8
Aizawl	88	F4
Aizkraukle	48	N8
Aizpute	48	L8
Aizu-wakamatsu	82	K5
Ajaccio	64	C7
Aj Bogd Uul	80	B2
Ajdābiyā	100	D1
Ajigasawa	82	L3
Ajka	50	G10
Ajlun	94	C4
Ajmān	95	F4
Ajmer	88	B3
Ajo	132	D2
Akanthou	94	A1
Akaroa	116	D6
Akasha	100	F3
Akashi	82	H6
Akbalyk	76	P8
Akbasty	76	L8
Akçakale	92	H5
Akçakoca	68	P3
Akdağmadeni	92	F4
Aken	52	H5
Aketi	106	C3
Akhalk'alak'i	92	K3
Akhisar	68	K6
Akhmīm	100	F2
Akhty	92	M3
Akimiski Island	122	Q6
Akita	82	L4
Akjoujt	102	C5
Akka	102	D3
Akkajaure	48	J3
Akkeshi	82	N2
'Akko	94	C4
Akmeqit	90	L2
Aknanes	48	(1)B2
Akobo	106	E2
Akola	88	C4
Akonolinga	104	G4
Akordat	100	G4
Akpatok Island	122	T4
Akqi	76	P9
Akra Drepano	68	G5
Akra Sounio	68	F7
Akra Spatha	68	F9
Akra Trypiti	68	G9
Åkrehamn	48	C7
Akron	128	D2
Aksaray	92	E4
Aksarka	76	M4
Aksehir	68	P6
Akseki	68	P7
Aksha	78	J6
Akshiy	76	P9
Aksu	76	Q9
Aksuat	76	Q8
Āksum	100	G5
Aktau, Kazakhstan	46	K3
Aktau, Kazakhstan	76	N7
Aktobe	70	L4
Aktogay, Kazakhstan	76	N8
Aktogay, Kazakhstan	76	P8
Aktuma	76	M8
Akula	106	C3
Akulivik	122	R4
Akune	82	F8
Akure	104	F3
Akureyri	48	(1)E2
Akwanga	104	F3
Alabama	130	D3
Alaçam	92	F3
Alaejos	60	E3
Alagoas	140	K5
Alagoinhas	140	K6
Alagón	60	J3
Al Ahmadi	95	C2
Al 'Amārah	90	E3
Alaminos	84	F3
Alamo	126	C3
Alamogordo	132	E2
Alamo Lake	132	D2
Åland	48	K6
Alanya	92	E5
Alappuzha	88	C7
Al Argoub	102	B4
Al Arṭāwīyah	90	E4
Alaşehir	68	L6
Al 'Ashurīyah	100	H1
Alaska	132	(1)F2
Alaska Peninsula	132	(1)E4
Alaska Range	132	(1)G3
Alassio	62	D6
Alatri	64	H7
Alatyr'	70	J4
Alaverdi	92	L3
Alavus	48	M5
Alaykuu	76	N9
Al 'Ayn	95	F4
Alazeya	78	S2
Alba, Italy	62	D6
Alba, Spain	60	E4
Albacete	60	J5
Alba Iulia	66	L3
Albania	68	B3
Albany	122	Q6
Albany, Australia	114	C6
Albany, Ga., US	130	E3
Albany, Ky., US	130	E2
Albany, N.Y., US	128	F2
Albany, Oreg., US	126	B2
Albardão do João Maria	142	L4
Al Bardī	100	D1
Al Baṣrah	90	E3
Albatross Bay	114	H2
Albatross Point	116	E4
Al Baydā'	100	D1
Albenga	62	D6
Albert	54	E4
Alberta	122	H6
Albertirsa	50	J10
Albert Kanaal	54	G3
Albert Lea	128	B2
Albert Nile	106	E3
Albertville	58	M8
Albi	58	H10
Albina	140	G2
Albino	62	E5
Albion	126	F1
Ålborg Bugt	48	F8
Albox	60	H7
Albstadt	52	E8
Albufeira	60	B7
Āl Bū Kamāl	92	J6
Albuquerque	132	E1
Al Burayj	94	D2
Al Buraymī	90	G5
Alburquerque	60	D5
Albury	114	J7
Al Buşayyah	95	B1
Alcácer do Sal	60	B6
Alcala de Guadaira	60	E7
Alcala de Henares	60	G4
Alcalá la Real	60	G7
Alcamo	64	G11
Alcañiz	60	K3
Alcantarilla	60	J7
Alcaraz	60	H6
Alcaudete	60	F7
Alcazar de San Juan	60	G5
Alcobendas	60	G4
Alcoi	60	K6
Alcolea del Pinar	60	H3
Alcorcón	60	G4
Alcoutim	60	C7
Aldabra Group	108	(2)A2
Aldan	78	M5
Aldan	78	N5
Aldeburgh	54	D2
Alderney	58	C4
Aldershot	54	B3
Aleg	102	C5
Aleksandrov-Sakhalinskiy	78	Q6
Aleksandrovskiy Zavod	78	K6
Aleksandrovskoye	70	Q2
Alekseyevka	76	N7
Aleksinac	66	J6
Alençon	58	F5
Aleppo = Halab	92	G5
Aléria	64	D6
Alès	58	K9
Aleşd	50	M10
Alessandria	62	D5
Ålesund	48	D5
Aleutian Islands	132	(3)B1
Aleutian Range	132	(1)F4
Aleutian Trench	74	W5
Alexander Archipelago	132	(1)K4
Alexander Bay	108	B5
Alexander City	130	D3
Alexandra	116	B7
Alexandreia	68	E4
Alexandria = El Iskandarîya, Egypt	100	E1
Alexandria, Romania	66	N6
Alexandria, La., US	130	C3
Alexandria, Minn., US	128	A1
Alexandria, Va., US	128	E3
Alexandroupoli	68	H4
Alexis Creek	122	G6
Aley	76	Q7
'Āley	94	C3
Aleysk	76	Q7
Al Farwānīyah	95	B2
Al Fāw	95	C2
Alfeld	52	E5
Alföld	66	H2
Alfonsine	62	H6
Alfreton	54	A1
Al Fuhayhil	95	C2
Al-Fujayrah	95	G4
Algeciras	60	E8
Algemesi	60	K5
Algena	100	G4
Alger	102	F1
Algeria	102	E3
Al Ghaydah	90	F6
Al Ghāt	95	A3
Alghero	64	C8
Algiers = Alger	102	F1
Algona	128	B2
Al Hadīthah	94	E5
Alhama de Murcia	60	J7
Al Hamar	95	B5
Al Hamīdīyah	94	C2
Al Hammādah al Hamrā'	102	G3
Al Harūj al Aswad	100	C2
Al Hasakah	92	J5
Alhaurmin el Grande	60	F8
Al Hijāz	100	G2
Al Hillah	90	D3
Al Hilwah	95	B5
Al Hoceima	102	E1
Al Hudaydah	100	H5
Al Hufūf	95	C4
Al Humaydah	90	C4
Aliabad	95	F2
Aliağa	68	E4
Aliakmonas	68	E4
Āli Bayramlı	92	N4
Alicante	60	K6
Alice	130	B4
Alice Springs	114	F4
Alicudi	64	J10
Aligarh	88	C3
Alindao	106	C2
Alingås	48	G8
Alisos	132	D2
Aliwal North	108	D6
Al Jabal al Akhḍar	100	D1
Al Jaghbūb	100	D2
Al Jarah	95	B2
Al Jawf, Libya	100	D3
Al Jawf, Saudi Arabia	100	D3
Aljezur	60	B7
Al Jifārah	95	A5
Al Jubayl	95	C3
Aljustrel	60	B7
Al Kāmil	90	G5
Al Khābūrah	95	G5
Al Khālis	92	L7
Al Kharj	95	B4
Al Khaşab	95	G3
Al Khawr	95	D4
Al Khubar	95	D3
Al Khufrah	100	D3
Al Khums	102	H2
Al Khuwayr	95	C2
Al Kir'ānah	95	D4
Alkmaar	54	G2
Al Kūt	90	E3
Al Kuwayt	95	C2
Al Lādhiqīyah	92	F6
Allahabad	88	D3
Allakh-Yun'	78	P4
Alldays	108	D4
Allen	84	G4
Allendale	130	E3
Allentown	128	E2
Aller	52	E4
Aller = Cabañaquinta	60	E1
Alliance	126	F2
Allier	58	J8
Allinge	50	D2
Al Lith	100	H3
Alma, Canada	128	F1
Alma, Nebr., US	126	G2
Alma, Wis., US	128	B2
Almada	60	A6
Almadén	60	F6
Al Madīnah	100	G3
Al Mahbas	102	D3
Al Majma'ah	90	E4
Almalyk	76	M9
Al Manāmah	95	D3
Almansa	60	J6
Al Ma'qil	95	B1
Al Marj	100	D1
Almaty	76	P9
Al Mawşil	92	K5
Al Mazāhimīyah	95	B4
Almazán	60	H3
Almeirim	140	G4
Almelo	54	J2
Almendralejo	60	D6
Almería	60	H8
Al'met'yevsk	76	J7
Almiros	68	E5
Al Mish'āb	95	C2
Almonte	60	D7
Almora	88	C3
Almosa	126	E3
Al Mubarraz	95	C4
Al Mudawwara	94	D7
Al Mukallā	90	E7
Al Mukhā	100	H5
Almuñécar	60	G8
Al Muqdādīyah	92	L7
Al Nu'ayrīyah	95	C3
Alnwick	56	L6
Alonnisos	68	F5
Alor	87	B4
Alor Setar	84	C5
Alotau	114	K2
Alpena	128	D1
Alphen	54	G2
Alpi Lepontine	62	D4
Alpine	132	E2
Alpi Orobie	62	E4
Alps	62	B5
Al Qadmūs	94	D1
Al Qalībah	100	G2
Al Qāmishlī	92	J5
Al Qar'ah	95	B3
Al Qarqar	94	E5
Al Qaryāt	100	B1
Al Qaryatayn	94	E2
Al Qaţif	95	C3
Al Qaţrūn	100	B3
Al Qunayţirah	94	C3
Al Qunfudhah	100	H4
Al Qurnah	95	B1
Al 'Quşayr, Iraq	95	A1
Al 'Quşayr, Syria	94	D2
Al Quţayfah	94	D3
Als	52	E1
Alsask	122	K6
Alsasua	60	H2
Alsfeld	52	E6
Alta	48	M2
Altai Mountains	80	A1
Altamira	140	G4
Altamura	64	L8
Altanbulag	78	H6
Altay	76	R7
Altay, China	76	R8
Altay, Mongolia	80	B1
Altdorf	62	D4
Alte Mellum	52	D3
Altenberg	52	J6
Altenburg	52	H6
Altenkirchen	52	J2
Altkirch	62	C3
Alto Garças	140	G7
Alto Molócuè	108	F3
Alton, UK	54	B3
Alton, US	128	B3
Altoona	128	E2
Alto Parnaíba	140	H5
Altötting	62	H2
Altun Shan	76	S10
Alturas	126	B2
Altus	130	B3
Al 'Ubaylah	90	F5
Alūksne	48	P8
Alupka	92	E1
Al 'Uqaylah	100	C1
Alushta	92	F1
Al 'Uthmānīyah	95	C4
Al 'Uwaynāt, Libya	100	B2
Al 'Uwaynāt, Libya	100	D3
Al 'Uwayqīlah	100	H1
Al 'Uzayr	95	B1
Alva	130	B2
Alvarães	140	E4
Älvdalen	48	H6
Älvsbyn	48	L4
Al Wafrā'	95	B2
Al Wajh	100	G2
Al Wannān	95	C3
Alwar	88	C3
Al Wari'ah	95	B3
Alxa Zouqi	80	D3
Alytus	50	P3
Alzey	52	D7
Alzira	60	K5
Amadi	106	E2
Amādīyah	92	K5
Amadjuak Lake	122	S4
Amadora	60	A6
Amahai	87	C3
Amakusa-Shimo-shima	82	E7
Amaliada	68	D7
Amalner	88	C4
Amamapare	87	E3
Amambaí	142	K3
Amami-Ōshima	74	S7
Amanab	87	F3
Amandola	64	H6
Amantea	64	L9
Amapá	140	G3
Amapá	140	G3
Amarante	140	J5
Amarapura	84	B2
Amareleja	60	C6
Amarillo	132	F1
Amasya	92	F3
Amay	54	H4
Amazar	78	L6
Amazon = Amazonas	138	F4
Amazonas	140	D4
Amazonas	140	E4
Ambala	88	C2
Ambanjā	108	H2
Ambarchik	78	U3
Ambato	140	B4
Ambato Boeny	108	H3
Ambatondrazaka	108	H3
Amberg	52	G7
Ambikapur	88	D4
Ambilobe	108	H2
Ambohimahasoa	108	H4
Amboise	58	G6
Ambon	87	C3
Ambositra	108	H4
Ambovombe	108	H5
Amchitka Island	132	(3)B1
Amderma	76	L4
Amdo	88	F2
Ameland	54	H1
Amengel'dy	76	M7
American Falls	126	D2
American Samoa	112	J7
Americus	130	E3
Amersfoort	54	H2
Amery	122	N6
Amery Ice Shelf	144	(2)M2
Ames	128	B2
Amfilochia	68	D6
Amfissa	68	E6
Amga	78	L5
Amga	78	N4
Amguid	102	G3
Amgun'	78	P6
Amherst	122	U7
Amiens	54	E5
Amirante Islands	108	(2)B2
Amistad Reservoir	132	F3
Amlekhganj	88	D3
Åmli	48	E7
'Amm Adam	100	G4
'Ammān	94	C5
Ammerland	54	K1
Ammersee	62	F2
Ammochostós	92	E6
Ammochostos Bay	94	A1
Amo	84	C2
Amol	90	F2
Amorgos	68	H8
Amos	128	E1
Amourj	102	D5
Ampana	87	B3
Ampanihy	108	G4
Amparai	88	D7

Name	Page	Grid
Ampezzo	62	H4
Amposta	60	L4
Amrān	90	D6
Amravati	88	C4
Amritsar	88	B2
Amroha	88	C3
Amrum	52	D2
Amsterdam, *Netherlands*	54	G2
Amsterdam, *US*	128	F2
Amstetten	62	K2
Am Timan	100	D5
Amudar'ya	76	L9
Amundsen Gulf	122	G2
Amundsen Sea	144	(2)GG3
Amungen	48	H6
Amuntai	86	F3
Amur	78	P6
Amursk	78	P6
Amvrakikos Kolpos	68	C6
Anabanua	87	B3
Anabar	78	J2
Anaconda	126	D1
Anacortes	126	B1
Anadarko	126	G3
Anadolu Dağlari	92	H3
Anadyr'	78	X4
Anadyrskaya Nizmennost'	78	X3
Anadyrskiy Zaliv	78	Y3
Anafi	68	H8
'Ānah	92	J6
Anaheim	132	C2
Anáhuac	132	F5
Analalava	108	H2
Anamur	92	E5
Anan	82	H7
Anantapur	88	C6
Anan'yiv	66	T2
Anapa	92	G1
Anápolis	140	H7
Anār	95	F1
Anārak	90	F3
Anardara	90	H3
Anatolia	68	M6
Añatuya	142	J4
Anchorage	132	(1)H3
Ancona	64	H5
Ancud	142	G7
Anda	80	H1
Andalgalá	142	H4
Åndalsnes	48	D5
Andalusia	130	D3
Andaman Islands	84	A4
Andaman Sea	84	A4
Andapa	108	H2
Andarāb	90	J2
Andenne	54	H4
Andéramboukane	104	E1
Andermatt	62	D4
Andernach	54	K4
Anderson	122	F3
Anderson	130	E3
Andes	138	G3
Andfjorden	48	J2
Andijan	76	N9
Andilamena	108	H3
Andipsara	68	H6
Andkhvoy	90	J2
Andoas	140	B4
Andong	82	E5
Andorra	60	L2
Andorra la Vella	60	M2
Andover	54	A3
Andøya	48	H2
Andradina	142	L3
Andreanof Islands	132	(3)C1
Andrews	132	F2
Andria	64	L7
Andriamena	108	H3
Andros	68	G7
Andros, *Greece*	68	G7
Andros, *The Bahamas*	130	F5
Andros Town	130	F5
Andrott	88	B6
Andrychów	50	J8
Andújar	60	F6
Andulo	108	B2
Aneto	60	L2
Angara	78	G5
Angarsk	78	G6
Ånge	48	H5
Angel de la Guarda	132	D3
Ángeles	84	G3
Ängelholm	48	G8
Angeln	52	E2
Angermünde	52	K4
Angern	62	M2
Angers	58	E6
Anglesey	56	H8
Angmagssalik = Tasiilaq	122	Z3
Ango	106	D3
Angoche	108	F3
Angohrān	95	G3
Angol	142	G6
Angola	98	E7
Angola	128	D2
Angostura Reservoir	126	F2
Angoulême	58	F4
Angren	76	M9
Anguilla	134	M5
Aniak	132	(1)F3
Anina	66	J4
Aniyaman	92	H5
Ankang	80	D4
Ankara	92	E4
Ankazoabo	108	G4
Anklam	52	J3
Ankpa	104	F3
Ånn	48	G5
Anna	70	H4
Annaba	102	G1
Annaberg-Buchholz	52	H6
An Nabk, *Saudi Arabia*	94	E5
An Nabk, *Syria*	94	D2
An Nafud	100	G2
An Nāiriyah	90	E3
An Najaf	90	D3
Annapolis	128	E3
Annapurna	88	D3
Ann Arbor	128	D2
An Nāsiriyah	100	J1
Annecy	62	B5
Annemasse	62	B4
Anniston	130	D3
Annobón	104	F5
Annonay	58	K8
An Nukhayb	90	D3
Anqing	80	F4
Ansbach	52	F7
Anshan	82	B3
Anshun	80	D5
Ansley	126	G2
Anson	130	B3
Ansongo	102	F5
Antakya	92	G5
Antalaha	108	J2
Antalya	68	N8
Antalya Körfezi	68	N8
Antananarivo	108	H3
Antarctic Peninsula	144	(2)LL3
Antequera	60	F7
Anti-Atlas	102	D3
Antibes	62	C7
Antigo	128	C1
Antigua	134	M5
Antigua and Barbuda	134	M5
Antikythira	68	F9
Antiparos	68	G7
Antipaxoi	68	C5
Antipayuta	76	P4
Antipodes Islands	116	(3)A1
Antlers	130	B3
Antofagasta	142	G3
Antonito	126	E3
Antrim	56	F7
Antropovo	70	H3
Antsalova	108	G3
Antsirabe	108	H3
Antsirañana	108	H2
Antu	82	E2
Antwerp = Antwerpen	54	G3
Antwerpen	54	G3
Anuradhapura	88	D7
Anveh	95	F3
Anxi	80	B2
Anyang, *China*	80	E3
Anyang, *South Korea*	82	D5
Anyuysk	78	U3
Anzhero-Sudzhensk	76	R6
Anzi	106	C4
Anzio	64	G7
Aoga-shima	82	K7
Aomori	82	L3
Aoraki (Mount Cook)	116	C6
Aosta	62	C5
Aoukâr	102	C5
Aoukoukar	104	C1
Apalachee Bay	130	E4
Apalachicola	130	D4
Aparri	84	G3
Apatin	66	F4
Apatity	70	F1
Ape	48	P8
Apeldoorn	54	H2
Api	88	D2
Apia	112	J7
Apoera	140	F2
Apolda	52	G5
Apollo Bay	114	H7
Aporé	140	G7
Apostle Islands	128	B1
Apoteri	140	F3
Appalachian Mountains	130	E3
Appennino	64	G5
Appennino Abruzzese	64	H6
Appennino Calabro	64	K10
Appennino Lucano	64	K8
Appennino Tosco-Emiliano	62	E6
Appennino Umbro-Marchigiano	64	H6
Appleton	128	C2
Aprilia	64	G7
Apure	140	D2
Apurimac	140	C6
Āqā	90	H3
'Aqaba	94	C7
Aquidauana	140	F8
Ara	88	D3
Arabian Sea	90	H6
Aracaju	140	K6
Aracati	140	K4
Araçatuba	140	G8
Aracuca	134	L7
Arad	66	J3
Arādah	90	F5
Arafura Sea	87	D5
Aragarças	140	G7
Araguaia	138	F4
Araguaína	140	H5
Araguari	140	H7
Araguatins	140	H5
Arāk	90	E3
Arak	102	F3
Aral Sea	76	K8
Aral'sk	70	M5
Aranda de Duero	60	G3
Aranđjelovac	66	H5
Aran Island	56	D6
Aran Islands	56	B8
Aranjuez	60	G4
Aranos	108	B4
Aranyaprathet	84	C4
Araouane	102	E5
Arapahoe	126	G2
Arapiraca	140	K5
'Ar'ar	90	D3
Araras	140	G5
Ararat	92	L4
Arauca	140	D2
Araxá	140	H7
Araz	92	L4
Arbīl	92	K5
Arbon	62	E3
Arbre du Ténéré	102	G5
Arbroath	56	K5
Arcachon	58	D9
Arcadia	130	E4
Arcata	126	B2
Archidona	60	F7
Archipelago of the Recherche	114	D6
Archipel de la Société	112	L7
Archipel des Tuamotu	112	M7
Archipiélago de Camagüey	134	J4
Archipiélago de la Reina Adelaida	142	F9
Archipiélago de los Chonos	142	F7
Arco, *Italy*	62	F5
Arco, *US*	126	D2
Arcos de la Frontera	60	E8
Arctic Bay	122	P2
Arctic Ocean	144	(1)A1
Arctic Red River	122	E3
Arda	68	H3
Ardabīl	92	N4
Ardahan	92	K3
Ardalstangen	48	D6
Ardas	68	J3
Ardatov	70	J4
Ardennes	54	G4
Ardestān	90	F3
Ardila	60	C6
Ardmore	124	G5
Aredo	87	D3
Areia Branca	140	K5
Arendal	48	E7
Arenys de Mar	60	N3
Areopoli	68	E8
Arequipa	140	C7
Arere	140	G4
Arévalo	60	F3
Arezzo	64	F5
Argan	76	R9
Argenta	62	G6
Argentan	54	B6
Argentera	62	B6
Argentina	142	H6
Argenton-sur-Creuse	58	G7
Argeş	66	N5
Argolikos Kolpos	68	E7
Argos	68	E7
Argos Orestiko	68	D4
Argostoli	68	C6
Argun'	78	K6
Argungu	104	E2
Argunsk	78	L6
Argyll	56	G5
Ar Horqin Qi	80	G2
Ariano Irpino	64	K7
Ari Atoll	88	B8
Arica	140	C7
Ariège	58	G11
Arihge	60	M2
Arinos	140	F6
Aripuanã	140	E5
Aripuanã	140	E5
Ariquemes	140	E5
Arizona	132	D2
Arjäng	48	G7
Arjasa	86	F4
Arka	78	Q5
Arkadak	70	H4
Arkadelphia	130	C3
Arkalyk	76	M7
Arkansas	130	C3
Arkansas	130	C3
Arkansas City	130	B2
Arkhalts'ikhe	92	K3
Arkhangel'sk	70	H2
Arkhipelag Nordenshel'da	76	R2
Arklow	56	F9
Arkoudi	68	C6
Arles	58	K10
Arlington, *Oreg., US*	126	B1
Arlington, *Tex., US*	130	B3
Arlington, *Va., US*	128	E3
Arlit	102	G5
Arlon	54	H4
Armagh	56	F7
Armavir	92	J1
Armenia	92	K3
Armenia	140	B3
Armentières	54	E4
Armidale	114	K6
Armstrong	122	P6
Armyans'k	70	F5
Arnedo	60	H2
Arnett	130	B2
Arnhem	54	H3
Arnhem Land	114	F2
Arno	62	F7
Arnøy	48	G3
Arnøya	48	L1
Arnprior	128	E1
Arnsberg	54	L3
Arnstadt	52	F6
Aroab	108	B5
Arolsen	52	E5
Aroma	100	G4
Arorae	112	H6
Arquipélago dos Bijagós	104	A2
Ar Ramādī	90	D3
Ar Ramlah	94	C7
Arran	56	G6
Ar Raqqah	92	H6
Arras	54	E4
Arrasate	60	H1
Ar Rastan	94	D2
Ar Rawdah	90	E7
Ar Rayn	95	A5
Arrecife	102	C3
Ar Riyād	90	E5
Arrow Lake	126	C1
Arroyo Grande	132	B1
Ar Rusāfah	92	H6
Ar Rustāq	90	G5
Ar Rutbah	90	D3
Ar Ruways	90	F5
Årsandøy	48	G4
Arta, *Greece*	68	C5
Arta, *Mallorca*	60	P5
Artem	82	G2
Artemovsk	76	S7
Artemovskiy	78	K5
Artesia	132	F2
Arthur	126	F2
Arthur's Town	130	F5
Artigas	142	K5
Artillery Lake	122	J4
Artsyz	66	S4
Artux	76	P10
Artvin	92	J3
Artyk	78	Q4
Aru	112	D6
Arua	106	E3
Aruba	134	K6
Arumã	140	E4
Arusha	106	F4
Arvayheer	80	C1
Arviat	122	N4
Arvidsjaur	48	K4
Arvika	48	G7
Ary	76	Y3
Aryta	78	M4
Arzamas	70	H3
Arzew	60	K9
Arzignano	62	G5
Asahi-dake	82	M2
Asahikawa	82	M2
Åsalē	100	G5
Asansol	88	E4
Asarum	50	D1
Asbest	70	M3
Ascea	64	K8
Ascension	98	B6
Ascensión	140	E7
Aschaffenburg	52	E7
Aschersleben	52	G5
Ascoli Piceno	64	H6
Åsela	106	F2
Asele	48	J4
Asenovgrad	68	G3
Asha	70	L3
Ashburton	116	C6
Ashdod	94	B5
Asherton	130	B4
Asheville	128	D3
Ashford	54	C3
Ash Fork	132	D1
Ashgabat	90	G2
Ashington	56	L6
Ashizuri-misaki	82	G7
Ashkhabad = Ashgabat	90	G2
Ashland, *Kans., US*	126	G3
Ashland, *Ky., US*	128	D3
Ashland, *Mont., US*	126	E1
Ashland, *Oreg., US*	126	B2
Ashland, *Wis., US*	128	B1
Ashoro	82	M2
Ashqelon	94	B5
Ash Shadādah	92	J5
Ash Shāriqah	95	F4
Ash Sharqāt	92	K6
Ash Shihr	90	E7
Ash Shu'bah	95	A2
Ash Shuqayq	100	H4
Ash Shurayf	100	G2
Ash Shuwayrif	102	H3
Ashtabula	128	D2
Ashuanipi	122	T6
Ashuanipi Lake	122	T6
Asia	112	B2
Āsika	88	D5
Asilah	102	D1
Asinara	64	C7
Asino	76	R6
Asīr	100	H3
Aşkale	92	J4
Askim	48	F7
Askot	88	D3
Asmara	100	G4
Åsnen	48	H8
Āsosa	106	E1
Aspang Markt	62	M3
Aspe	60	K6
Aspermont	132	F2
As Pontes de Garcia Rodriguez	60	C1
As Sa'an	94	E1
Assab	100	H5
Aş Şāliḩ	90	D6
As Salmān	90	E3
As Salwā	95	D4
Assamakka	102	G5
As Samāwah	100	J1
Aş Şanamayn	94	D3
As Sarīr	100	D2
Asse	54	G4
Assemini	64	C9
Assen	54	J2
Assens	52	E1
As Sīb	95	H5
As Sidrah	100	C1
Assiniboia	122	K7
Assiniboine	122	M7
Assis	142	L3
Assisi	64	G5
As Sukhnah	92	H6
As Sulaymānīyah	92	L6

Name		Page	Grid
As Sulayyil	●	90	E5
Assumption Island	●	106	H5
As Suwaydā'	●	94	D4
As Suwayh	●	90	G5
Astakida	🏝	68	J9
Astana	■	76	N7
Astara	●	90	E2
Asti	●	62	D6
Astorga	●	60	D2
Astoria	●	126	B1
Astove Island	🏝	106	H6
Astrakhan'	●	70	J5
Astypalaia	🏝	68	J8
Asunción	■	142	K4
Aswân	●	100	F3
Aswân Dam	⊘	100	F3
Asyût	●	100	F2
As Zaydīyah	●	100	H4
Ata	●	112	J8
Atafu	🏝	112	J6
Atakpamé	●	104	E3
Atalaia do Norte	●	140	C4
Atâr	●	102	C4
Atasu	●	76	N8
Atbara	●	100	F4
Atbasar	●	70	N4
Atchison	●	130	B2
Aterno	↗	64	H6
Ath	●	54	F4
Athabasca	↗	122	J5
Athens = Athina	■	68	F7
Athens, Al., US	●	130	D3
Athens, Ga., US	●	130	E3
Athens, Oh., US	●	130	E2
Athens, Tenn., US	●	130	E2
Athens, Tex., US	●	130	B3
Athina	■	68	F7
Athlone	●	56	E8
Ath Thāyat	▲	94	D7
Athy	●	56	F8
Ati	●	100	C5
Atiamuri	●	116	F4
Atico	●	140	C7
Atikokan	●	128	B1
Atka	●	78	S4
Atka Island	🏝	132	(3)C1
Atlanta	◻	130	E3
Atlantic, Ia., US	●	130	B1
Atlantic, N.C., US	●	130	F3
Atlantic City	●	128	F3
Atlantic Ocean	⌣	46	C3
Atlas Bogd	▲	80	B2
Atlas Mountains	▲	60	N9
Atlasovo	●	78	T5
Atlas Saharien	⊘	102	E2
Atlin	●	122	E5
Atmakur	●	88	C5
Atmore	●	130	D3
Atoka	●	130	B3
Atokos	🏝	68	C6
Atol das Rocas	🏝	140	L4
Atri	●	64	H6
At Tā'if	●	90	D5
Attapu	●	84	D4
Attawapiskat	●	122	Q6
Attersee	↗	62	J3
Attica	●	128	C2
Attu Island	🏝	132	(3)A1
Attu Island	🏝	144	(1)KK4
Attur	●	88	C6
At Turbah	●	100	H5
Atyrau	●	70	K5
Aubagne	●	58	L10
Aubange	●	54	H5
Aube	↗	58	K5
Aubenas	●	58	K9
Aubry Lake	↗	122	F3
Auburn, Al., US	●	130	D3
Auburn, Calif., US	●	126	B3
Auburn, Nebr., US	●	126	G2
Auburn, Wash., US	●	126	B1
Aubusson	●	58	H8
Auce	●	50	M1
Auch	●	58	F10
Auchi	●	104	F3
Auckland	●	116	E3
Auckland Island	🏝	116	(2)B1
Aude	↗	58	H10
Aue	●	52	H6
Auerbach	●	52	H6
Augathella	●	114	J5
Augsburg	●	62	F2
Augusta, Australia	●	114	C6
Augusta, Italy	●	64	K11
Augusta, Ga., US	●	130	E3
Augusta, Me., US	◻	128	G2
Augustów	●	50	M4
Aulla	●	62	E6
Aurangābād	●	88	C5
Auray	●	58	C6
Aurich	●	54	K1
Aurillac	●	58	H9
Aurora, Colo., US	●	126	F3
Aurora, Ill., US	●	128	C2
Aurora, Mo., US	●	130	C2
Aurukun	●	114	H2
Aus	●	108	B5
Auschwitz = Oświęcim	●	50	J7
Austin, Minn., US	●	128	B2
Austin, Nev., US	●	126	C3
Austin, Tex., US	◻	130	B3
Australia	🄰	114	E4
Australian Alps	▲	112	E9
Australian Capital Territory	🄰	114	J7
Austria	🄰	62	J3
Autun	●	58	K7
Auxerre	●	58	J6
Auxonne	●	58	L6
Avallon	●	58	J6
Avam	↗	78	E2
Ävärsin	●	92	M4
Aveiro	●	60	B4

Name		Page	Grid
Avellino	●	64	J8
Averøya	🏝	48	D5
Avesnes-sur-Helpe	●	54	F4
Avesta	●	48	J6
Avezzano	●	64	H6
Aviemore	●	56	J4
Avignon	●	58	K10
Ávila	●	60	F4
Avilés	●	60	E1
Avion	●	54	E4
Avola	●	64	K12
Avon, UK	↗	54	A2
Avon, UK	↗	54	A3
Avranches	●	58	D5
Avrig	●	66	M4
Awaji-shima	🏝	82	H6
Awanui	●	116	E2
Awat	●	76	Q9
Awatere	↗	116	D5
Awbārī	●	100	B2
Aweil	●	106	D2
Awjilah	●	100	D2
Awka	●	104	F3
Ax-les-Thermes	●	58	G11
Ayacucho	●	140	C6
Ayaguz	●	76	Q8
Ayakkuduk	●	76	M9
Ayamonte	●	60	C7
Ayan	↗	78	E3
Ayan	●	78	P5
Aya Napa	●	94	A2
Ayancık	●	92	F3
Ayanka	●	78	V4
Ayaviri	●	140	C6
Aydin	●	92	B5
Aydıncık	●	68	R8
Ayers Rock = Uluru	▲	114	F5
Aykhal	●	78	J3
Aykino	●	76	H5
Aylesbury	●	54	B3
Aylmer Lake	↗	122	K4
'Ayn al Baida'	●	94	D5
Ayni	●	76	M10
Ayni	●	90	J2
Ayn 'Īsā	●	92	H5
Ayoûn el 'Atroûs	●	102	D5
Ayr, Australia	●	114	J3
Ayr, UK	●	56	H6
Aytos	●	66	Q7
Ayutthaya	●	84	C4
Ayvalık	●	68	J5
Azaila	●	60	K3
Azaouâd	⊘	102	E5
Āzarān	●	92	M5
Azare	●	104	G2
Azauri	●	140	G3
A'zāz	●	92	G5
Azdavay	●	68	R3
Azerbaijan	🄰	92	M3
Aziza	●	60	H3
Azogues	●	140	B4
Azov	●	70	G5
Azpeitia	●	60	H1
Azrou	●	102	D2
Aztec	●	126	E3
Azuaga	●	60	E6
Azul	●	142	K6
Az Zabadānī	●	94	D3
Az Zahrān	●	95	D3
Az Zāwīyah	●	100	B1
Az Zubayr	●	95	B1

B

Name		Page	Grid
Ba'albek	●	94	D2
Baaqline	●	94	C3
Baardheere	●	106	G3
Babadag	●	66	R5
Babaeski	●	68	K3
Bāb al Mandab	⊷	90	D7
Babana	●	87	A3
Babanusa	●	106	D1
Babar	🏝	87	C4
Babayevo	●	70	G3
Babayurt	●	92	M2
Babo	●	87	D3
Bābol	●	90	F2
Babruysk	●	70	E4
Babura	●	104	F2
Babushkin	●	78	H6
Babuyan Islands	🏝	84	G3
Bacaadweyn	●	106	H2
Bacabal	●	140	J4
Bacan	🏝	87	C3
Bacău	●	66	P3
Baccarat	●	62	B2
Bachu	●	90	L2
Back	↗	122	M3
Bačka Palanka	●	66	G4
Bačka Topola	●	66	G4
Backnang	●	62	E2
Bac Liêu	●	84	D5
Bacolod	●	84	G4
Badajoz	●	140	H4
Badajós	●	60	D6
Bad al Milh	↗	92	K7
Badalona	●	60	N3
Bad Ausee	●	62	J3
Bad Bentheim	●	54	K2
Bad Berleburg	●	52	D5
Bad Doberan	●	52	G2
Bad Dürkheim	●	52	D7
Bad Ems	●	54	K4
Baden	●	50	F9
Baden-Baden	●	62	D2
Baderna	●	64	H3
Bad Freienwalde	●	52	K4
Badgastein	●	62	J3
Badgingarra	●	114	C6
Bad Harzburg	●	52	F5
Bad Hersfeld	●	52	E6

Name		Page	Grid
Bad Homburg	●	52	D6
Bad Honnef	●	54	K4
Badin	●	88	A4
Bad Ischl	●	62	J3
Bādiyat ash Shām	⊘	94	D4
Bad Kissingen	●	52	F6
Bad Kreuznach	●	54	K5
Bad Langensalza	●	52	F5
Bad Lauterberg	●	52	F5
Bad Liebenwerda	●	52	J5
Bad Mergentheim	●	52	E7
Bad Nauheim	●	52	D6
Bad Neuenahr-Ahrweiler	●	54	K4
Bad Neustadt	●	52	F6
Bad Oeynhausen	●	52	D4
Bad Reichenhall	●	62	H3
Badr Hunayn	●	100	G3
Bad Säckingen	●	52	C9
Bad Salzuflen	●	52	D4
Bad Salzungen	●	52	F6
Bad Schwartau	●	52	F3
Bad Segeberg	●	52	F3
Bad Soberheim	●	54	K5
Bad Urach	●	62	E2
Bad Vöslau	●	66	D2
Bad Waldsee	●	62	E3
Bad Wilbad	●	62	D2
Bad Wildungen	●	52	E5
Bad Windsheim	●	52	F7
Bad Wurzach	●	62	E3
Baena	●	60	F7
Bærum	●	48	F7
Baeza	●	60	G6
Baffin Bay	⊷	120	J2
Baffin Island	🏝	122	R2
Bafia	●	104	G4
Bafoulabé	●	104	B2
Bafoussam	●	104	G3
Bāfq	●	90	G3
Bafra	●	92	F3
Bafra Burun	⊡	92	G3
Bāft	●	95	G2
Bafwasende	●	106	D3
Baga	●	100	B5
Bagani	●	108	C3
Bagansiapiapi	●	86	C2
Bagaroua	●	104	E2
Bagdad	●	132	D2
Bagdarin	●	78	J6
Bagé	●	142	L5
Baggs	●	126	E2
Baghdād	■	90	D3
Bagheria	●	64	H10
Baghlān	●	90	J2
Bagnères-de-Bigorre	●	58	F10
Bagno di Romagna	●	62	G7
Bagnols-sur-Cèze	●	58	K9
Bago	●	84	G4
Baguio	●	84	G3
Bagun Datuk	●	86	C2
Baharampur	●	88	E4
Bahawalnagar	●	88	B3
Bahawalpur	●	88	B3
Bahçe	●	92	G5
Bahia	🄰	140	J6
Bahía Blanca	●	142	J6
Bahía Blanca	⊷	142	J6
Bahía de Banderas	⊷	134	C4
Bahía de Campeche	⊷	134	F4
Bahía de Manta	⊷	140	A4
Bahía de Petacalco	⊘	134	D5
Bahía de Pisco	⊷	140	B6
Bahía de Santa Elena	⊷	140	A4
Bahía de Sechura	⊷	140	A5
Bahía Grande	⊷	142	H9
Bahía Kino	●	124	D6
Bahía Negra	●	142	K3
Bahía Samborombón	⊷	142	K6
Bahir Dar	●	100	G5
Bahraich	●	88	D3
Bahrain	🄰	95	D4
Bahrat Ḩimş	●	94	D2
Bahr el Abiad	↗	100	F5
Bahr el Azraq	↗	100	F5
Bahr el Ghazal	⊘	100	C5
Bahr el Ghazal	↗	106	D2
Bahr el Jebe	↗	106	E2
Bahr el Nîl = Nile	↗	100	F4
Baia	●	66	R5
Baía de Marajó	⊷	140	H4
Baía de Todos os Santos	⊷	140	K6
Baía do Bengo	●	104	G6
Baia Mare	●	66	L2
Baia Sprie	●	66	L2
Baïbokoum	●	106	B2
Baicheng, China	●	76	Q9
Baicheng, China	●	80	G1
Baie Comeau	●	128	G1
Baie de la Seine	⊷	54	B5
Baie de la Somme	⊷	54	D4
Baie du Poste	●	122	S6
Baie St. Paul	●	128	F1
Baiji	●	92	K6
Baile Átha Cliath = Dublin	●	56	F8
Bailén	●	60	G6
Bailleul	●	54	E4
Bailundo	●	108	B2
Bainbridge	●	130	E3
Bairiki	■	112	H5
Bairin Yuoqi	●	80	F2
Bairin Zuoqi	●	80	F2
Bairnsdale	●	114	J7
Baja	●	84	G5
Baja California	●	124	C5
Bajram Curri	●	68	B2
Bakchar	●	76	Q6
Bakel	●	104	B2
Baker	●	112	J5
Baker, Calif., US	●	126	C3

Name		Page	Grid
Baker, Mont., US	●	126	F1
Baker, Oreg., US	●	126	C2
Baker Lake	●	122	M4
Baker Lake	●	122	N4
Bakersfield	●	132	C1
Bakharden	●	76	K10
Bakhta	●	78	D4
Baki	●	90	E1
Bakkafjörður	●	48	(1)F1
Bakkaflói	⊷	48	(1)F1
Baku = Baki	■	90	E1
Balā	●	92	E4
Balabac	●	84	F5
Balabac	🏝	84	F5
Balabac Strait	⊷	84	F5
Balagansk	●	78	G6
Balaghat	●	88	D4
Balaguer	●	60	L3
Balakhta	●	76	S6
Balaklava	●	92	E1
Balakovo	●	70	J4
Bālā Morghāb	●	76	L10
Bālan	●	66	N3
Balāngīr	●	88	D4
Balashov	●	70	H4
Balassagyarmat	●	66	G1
Balaton	↗	66	E3
Balatonfüred	●	66	E3
Balatonlelle	●	66	E3
Balbina	●	140	F4
Balchik	●	92	C2
Balclutha	●	116	B8
Bald Knob	●	128	B3
Baldwin	●	130	E3
Balearic Islands =Islas Baleares	🏝	60	N5
Baler	●	84	G3
Bāleshwar	●	88	E4
Baley	●	78	K6
Baléyara	●	104	E2
Balguntay	●	76	R9
Bali	🏝	86	F4
Balige	●	86	B2
Balikesir	●	68	K5
Balikpapan	●	86	F3
Balimo	●	87	F4
Balingen	●	62	D2
Balintang Channel	⊷	84	G3
Balkhash	●	76	N8
Balladonia	●	114	D6
Ballarat	●	114	H7
Balleny Island	🏝	144	(2)Y3
Ballina, Australia	●	114	K5
Ballina, Ireland	●	56	C7
Ballinasloe	●	56	D8
Ballinger	●	132	G2
Ball's Pyramid	🏝	114	L6
Ballum	●	54	H1
Ballymena	●	56	F7
Balmazújváros	●	66	J2
Balotra	●	88	B3
Balranald	●	114	H6
Balş	●	66	M5
Balsas	↗	134	D5
Balsas	●	140	H5
Balta	●	66	S2
Bālţi	●	66	Q2
Baltic Sea	⌣	48	J8
Baltijsk	●	50	J3
Baltimore	●	128	E3
Baltrum	●	52	C3
Balvi	●	48	P8
Balykchy	●	76	P9
Balykshi	●	70	K5
Bam	●	90	G4
Bamaga	●	114	H2
Bamako	■	104	C2
Bamba	●	102	E5
Bambari	●	106	C2
Bamberg	●	52	F7
Bambesa	●	106	D3
Bambouk	⊘	102	C6
Bambouk Kaarta	⊘	104	B2
Bamda	●	80	B4
Bamenda	●	104	G3
Bāmīān	●	90	J3
Banaba	🏝	112	G6
Bañados del Izozog	⊘	140	E7
Banalia	●	106	D3
Banana, Australia	●	114	K4
Banana, Dem. Rep. of the Congo	●	106	A5
Banaz	●	68	M6
Ban Ban	●	84	C3
Ban Betong	●	86	C1
Banbury	●	56	L9
Banda	●	88	D3
Banda Aceh	●	84	B5
Bandar Lampung	●	86	D4
Bandama	↗	104	C3
Bandar-e 'Abbās	●	95	G3
Bandar-e Anzalī	●	90	E2
Bandar-e Deylam	●	95	D1
Bandar-e Ganāveh	●	95	D2
Bandar-e Khoemir	●	95	F3
Bandar-e Lengeh	●	95	F3
Bandar-e Ma'shur	●	95	C1
Bandar-e Torkeman	●	90	F2
Bandar Khomeynī	●	95	C1
Bandar Seri Begawan	■	86	E2
Band-e Chārak	●	95	F3
Band-e Moghūyeh	●	95	F3
Bandirma	●	68	K4
Bandundu	●	106	B4
Bandung	●	86	D4
Băneasa	●	66	Q5
Bāneh	●	92	L6
Banff, Canada	●	122	H6
Banff, UK	●	56	K4
Bangalore	●	88	C6
Bangangté	●	104	G3
Bangassou	●	106	C3
Bangbong	●	87	B3
Banggi	🏝	86	F1

Banghāzī	**100**	D1
Bangka	**86**	D3
Bangkalan	**86**	E4
Bangkok = Krung Thep	**84**	C4
Bangladesh	**88**	E4
Bangor, *N. Ire., UK*	**56**	G7
Bangor, *Wales, UK*	**56**	H8
Bangor, *US*	**128**	G2
Bang Saphan Yai	**84**	B4
Bangued	**84**	G3
Bangui, *Central African Republic*	**106**	B3
Bangui, *Philippines*	**84**	G3
Ban Hat Yai	**84**	C5
Ban Hua Hin	**84**	B4
Bani-Bangou	**104**	E1
Banī Walīd	**102**	H2
Bāniyās	**92**	F6
Banja Luka	**66**	E5
Banjarmasin	**86**	E3
Banjul	**104**	A2
Ban Khemmarat	**84**	D3
Banks Island = Moa, *Australia*	**114**	H2
Banks Island, *B.C., Canada*	**122**	E6
Banks Island, *N.W.T., Canada*	**122**	G2
Banks Lake	**126**	C1
Banks Peninsula	**116**	D6
Banks Strait	**114**	J8
Bannerman Town	**130**	F5
Bannu	**88**	B2
Bánovce	**50**	H9
Banská	**50**	J9
Banská Štiavnica	**50**	H9
Bansko	**68**	F3
Bantry	**56**	C10
Banyo	**104**	G3
Banyoles	**60**	N2
Banyuwangi	**86**	E4
Baode	**80**	E3
Baoding	**80**	F3
Baoji	**80**	D4
Bao Lôc	**84**	D4
Baoro	**106**	B2
Baoshan	**84**	B1
Baotou	**80**	E2
Baoying	**80**	F4
Bap	**88**	B3
Bapaume	**54**	E4
Ba'qūbah	**90**	D3
Baquedano	**142**	H3
Bar	**66**	G7
Barabai	**86**	F3
Baraboo	**128**	C2
Barakaldo	**60**	H1
Baramati	**88**	B5
Baramula	**88**	B2
Baran	**88**	C3
Baranavichy	**70**	E4
Baraolt	**66**	N3
Barbados	**140**	F1
Barbastro	**60**	L2
Barbate	**60**	E8
Barbuda	**134**	M5
Barcaldine	**114**	J4
Barcău	**66**	K2
Barcellona Pozzo di Gotto	**64**	K10
Barcelona, *Spain*	**60**	N3
Barcelona, *Venezuela*	**134**	M6
Barcelos, *Brazil*	**140**	E4
Barcelos, *Spain*	**60**	B3
Barclayville	**104**	C4
Barco de Valdeorras = O Barco	**60**	D2
Barcs	**66**	E4
Bärdä	**92**	M3
Bardai	**100**	C3
Barddhamān	**88**	E4
Bardejov	**50**	L8
Bardonecchia	**62**	B5
Bareilly	**88**	C3
Barentin	**54**	C5
Barents Sea	**76**	E3
Barentu	**100**	G4
Bareo	**86**	F2
Barga	**88**	D2
Bargaal	**106**	J1
Bargteheide	**52**	F3
Barguzin	**78**	H6
Bar Harbor	**128**	G2
Bari	**64**	L7
Barikot	**88**	B1
Barinas	**140**	C2
Bârîs	**100**	F3
Barisal	**88**	F4
Barito	**87**	A3
Barkam	**80**	C4
Barkava	**48**	P8
Barkly Tableland	**114**	F3
Barkol	**76**	S9
Bârlad	**66**	Q3
Bârlad	**66**	Q3
Bar-le-Duc	**54**	H6
Barletta	**64**	L7
Barmer	**88**	B3
Barmouth Bay	**56**	H9
Barnaul	**76**	Q7
Barnsley	**56**	L8
Barnstaple	**56**	H10
Barnstaple Bay	**56**	H10
Barpeta	**88**	F3
Barquisimeto	**140**	D1
Barr	**62**	C2
Barra, *Brazil*	**140**	J6
Barra, *UK*	**56**	E4
Barracão do Barreto	**140**	F5
Barracas	**60**	K5
Barra do Bugres	**140**	F7
Barra do Corda	**140**	H5
Barra do Cuanza	**106**	A5
Barra do Garças	**140**	G7
Barra do São Manuel	**140**	F5
Barragem de Santa Clara	**60**	B7
Barragem de Sobradinho	**140**	J5
Barragem do Castelo de Bode	**60**	B5
Barragem do Maranhão	**60**	C6
Barranca, *Peru*	**140**	B4
Barranca, *Peru*	**140**	B6
Barranquilla	**134**	K6
Barreiras	**140**	H6
Barreiro	**60**	A6
Barretos	**140**	H8
Barrie	**128**	E2
Barron	**128**	B1
Barrow	**132**	(1)F1
Barrow Creek	**114**	F4
Barrow-in-Furness	**56**	J7
Barrow Island	**114**	B4
Barrow Strait	**122**	N2
Barshatas	**76**	P8
Barsi	**88**	C5
Barstow	**132**	C2
Bar-sur-Aube	**58**	K5
Bar-sur-Seine	**58**	K5
Barth	**52**	H2
Bartın	**92**	E3
Bartle Frere	**112**	E7
Bartlesville	**130**	B2
Bartlett	**126**	G2
Bartoszyce	**50**	K3
Barus	**86**	B2
Baruun Urt	**80**	E1
Barwani	**88**	B4
Barysaw	**70**	E4
Basaidu	**95**	F3
Basankusu	**106**	B3
Basarabeasca	**66**	R3
Basarabi	**66**	R5
Basca	**64**	C2
Basco	**84**	G2
Basel	**62**	C3
Bashkiriya	**70**	K4
Bāsht	**95**	D1
Basilan	**87**	B1
Basildon	**54**	C3
Basiluzzo	**64**	K10
Basingstoke	**56**	L10
Başkale	**92**	K4
Basoko	**106**	C3
Bassano	**124**	D1
Bassano del Grappa	**62**	G5
Bassar	**104**	E3
Bassas da India	**108**	F4
Basse Santa Su	**102**	C6
Basse Terre	**134**	M5
Bassett	**126**	G2
Bassikounou	**102**	D5
Bass Strait	**114**	H7
Bassum	**52**	D4
Bastak	**95**	F3
Bastānābād	**92**	M5
Basti	**88**	D3
Bastia	**64**	D6
Bastogne	**54**	H4
Bastrop, *La., US*	**130**	C3
Bastrop, *Tex., US*	**130**	B3
Bata	**104**	F4
Batagay	**78**	N3
Batagay-Alyta	**78**	N3
Batak	**68**	G3
Batamay	**78**	M4
Batang	**80**	B5
Batangas	**84**	G4
Batan Islands	**84**	G2
Batanta	**87**	C3
Batchelor	**114**	F2
Batemans Bay	**114**	K7
Batesville	**130**	D3
Bath, *UK*	**56**	K10
Bath, *US*	**128**	E2
Bathinda	**88**	B2
Bathurst, *Australia*	**114**	J6
Bathurst, *Canada*	**122**	T7
Bathurst Inlet	**122**	K3
Bathurst Island, *Australia*	**114**	E2
Bathurst Island, *Canada*	**122**	M1
Batman	**90**	D2
Batna	**102**	G1
Baton Rouge	**130**	C3
Bátonyterenye	**66**	G2
Batouri	**104**	G4
Batroûn	**94**	C2
Batticaloa	**88**	D7
Battipaglia	**64**	J8
Battle	**122**	J6
Battle Creek	**128**	C2
Battle Harbour	**122**	V6
Battle Mountain	**126**	C2
Batu	**106**	F2
Batui	**87**	B3
Bat'umi	**92**	J3
Batu Pahat	**86**	C2
Baturino	**76**	R6
Baubau	**87**	B4
Bauchi	**104**	F2
Baudette	**128**	B1
Baukau	**87**	C4
Baume-les-Dames	**58**	M6
Bauru	**142**	M3
Bauska	**48**	N8
Bautzen	**50**	D6
Bawean	**86**	E4
Bawiti	**100**	E2
Bawku	**104**	D2
Bayamo	**134**	J4
Bayanaul	**76**	P7
Bayandelger	**78**	H7
Bayan Har Shan	**80**	B4
Bayanhongor	**80**	C1
Bayan Mod	**80**	C2
Bayan Obo	**80**	D2
Bayansumküre	**76**	Q9
Bayburt	**92**	J3
Bay City, *Mich., US*	**128**	D2
Bay City, *Tex., US*	**130**	B4
Baydhabo	**106**	G3
Bayerische Alpen	**62**	G3
Bayeux	**54**	B5
Bayfield	**128**	B1
Bayindir	**68**	K6
Bāyir	**94**	D6
Baykit	**76**	T5
Baykonur	**76**	M8
Bay Minette	**130**	D3
Bay of Bengal	**88**	E5
Bay of Biscay	**58**	C9
Bay of Fundy	**122**	T8
Bay of Islands	**116**	E2
Bay of Plenty	**116**	F3
Bayonne	**58**	D10
Bayramaly	**90**	H2
Bayramiç	**68**	J5
Bayreuth	**52**	G7
Baysun	**90**	J2
Bayt al Faqīh	**100**	H5
Bay View	**116**	F4
Baza	**60**	H7
Bazas	**58**	E9
Bazdar	**90**	J4
Beach	**126**	F1
Beachy Head	**54**	C4
Beagle Gulf	**114**	E2
Bealanana	**108**	H2
Bear Island = Bjørnøya, *Norway*	**76**	B3
Bear Island, *Republic of Ireland*	**56**	B10
Bear Lake	**126**	D2
Beasain	**60**	H1
Beas de Segura	**60**	H6
Beatrice	**130**	B1
Beatty	**132**	C1
Beaufort, *Malaysia*	**86**	F1
Beaufort, *N.C., US*	**130**	F3
Beaufort, *S.C., US*	**130**	E3
Beaufort Sea	**120**	Q2
Beaufort West	**108**	C6
Beaumont, *New Zealand*	**116**	B7
Beaumont, *US*	**130**	C3
Beaune	**58**	K6
Beauvais	**54**	E5
Beaver	**126**	D3
Beaver Creek	**132**	(1)J3
Beaver Dam	**128**	C3
Beaver Falls	**128**	D2
Beawar	**88**	B3
Beazley	**142**	H5
Bebra	**52**	E6
Bečej	**66**	H4
Béchar	**102**	E2
Beckley	**130**	E2
Becks	**116**	B7
Beckum	**54**	L3
Beclean	**66**	M2
Bedelē	**106**	F2
Bedford, *UK*	**56**	M9
Bedford, *US*	**130**	D2
Bedworth	**54**	A2
Beenleigh	**114**	K5
Beer Menuha	**94**	C6
Beer Ora	**94**	C7
Be'ér Sheva'	**94**	B5
Beeville	**130**	B4
Behbehān	**95**	D1
Bei'an	**78**	M7
Beihai	**84**	D2
Beijing	**80**	F3
Beipan	**80**	D5
Beipiao	**80**	G2
Beira	**108**	E3
Beirut = Beyrouth	**94**	C3
Beiuş	**66**	K3
Beizhen	**82**	A3
Béja	**102**	G1
Bejaïa	**102**	G1
Béjar	**60**	E4
Bekdash	**90**	F1
Békés	**50**	L11
Békéscsaba	**66**	J3
Bekily	**108**	H4
Bekkai	**82**	N2
Bela	**90**	J4
Bela Crkva	**66**	J5
Belaga	**86**	E2
Belarus	**46**	G2
Bela Vista	**108**	E5
Belaya	**70**	K3
Belaya Gora	**78**	R3
Bełchatów	**50**	J6
Belcher Islands	**122**	Q5
Beledweyne	**106**	H3
Belek	**76**	J10
Belém	**140**	H4
Belen	**134**	C2
Belfast	**56**	G7
Belfield	**126**	F1
Belfort	**62**	B3
Belgazyn	**76**	T7
Belgium	**54**	G4
Belgorod	**70**	G4
Belgrade = Beograd	**66**	H5
Beli	**104**	G3
Belice	**64**	H11
Beli Manastir	**66**	F4
Belinyu	**86**	D3
Belitung	**86**	D3
Belize	**134**	G5
Belize	**134**	G5
Bellac	**58**	G7
Bella Coola	**122**	F6
Bellary	**88**	C5
Bellefontaine	**128**	D2
Belle Fourche	**126**	F2
Belle Glade	**130**	E4
Belle Île	**58**	B6
Belle Isle	**122**	V6
Bellême	**58**	F5
Belleterre	**128**	E1
Belleville, *Canada*	**128**	E2
Belleville, *US*	**130**	B2
Bellingham	**126**	B1
Bellingshausen Sea	**144**	(2)JJ4
Bellinzona	**62**	E4
Bello	**140**	B2
Belluno	**62**	H4
Bellyk	**78**	E6
Belmont	**128**	E2
Belmonte, *Brazil*	**140**	K7
Belmonte, *Spain*	**60**	H5
Belmopan	**134**	G5
Belmullet	**56**	B7
Belogorsk	**78**	M6
Belogradchik	**66**	K6
Beloha	**108**	H5
Belo Horizonte	**140**	J7
Beloit, *Kans., US*	**130**	B2
Beloit, *Wis., US*	**128**	C2
Belo Monte	**140**	G4
Belomorsk	**70**	F2
Belorechensk	**92**	H1
Beloretsk	**70**	L4
Belo Tsiribihina	**108**	G3
Belovo	**76**	R7
Beloyarskiy	**76**	M5
Beloye More	**70**	G1
Belozersk	**70**	G2
Belozerskoye	**70**	N3
Belye Vody	**76**	M9
Belyy Yar	**76**	Q6
Belzig	**52**	H4
Bembibre	**60**	D2
Bemidji	**128**	A1
Bena Dibele	**106**	C4
Benavente	**60**	E3
Benbecula	**56**	E4
Bend	**126**	B2
Bender-Bayla	**106**	J2
Bendigo	**114**	H7
Bendorf	**54**	K4
Bene	**108**	E3
Benešov	**50**	D8
Benevento	**64**	J7
Bengbu	**80**	F4
Bengkalis	**86**	C2
Bengkulu	**86**	C3
Benguela	**108**	A2
Benguerir	**102**	D2
Benha	**100**	F1
Beni	**106**	D3
Beni	**140**	D6
Beni Abbès	**102**	E2
Benicarló	**60**	L4
Benidorm	**60**	K6
Benî Mazâr	**100**	F2
Beni Mellal	**102**	D2
Benin	**104**	E2
Benin City	**104**	F3
Beni Saf	**60**	J9
Beni Slimane	**60**	P8
Beni Suef	**100**	F2
Benito Juaréz	**142**	K6
Benjamin Constant	**140**	D4
Benkelman	**126**	F2
Benkovac	**62**	L6
Ben More Assynt	**56**	H3
Ben Nevis	**56**	H5
Bennington	**128**	F2
Benoud	**102**	F2
Bensheim	**52**	D7
Benson, *Ariz., US*	**132**	D2
Benson, *Minn., US*	**124**	G2
Benteng	**87**	B4
Bentinck Island	**114**	G3
Bent Jbail	**94**	C3
Bentonville	**130**	C2
Bentung	**86**	C2
Benue	**104**	G3
Benxi	**80**	G2
Beo	**84**	H6
Beograd	**66**	H5
Bepazarı	**92**	D3
Berat	**68**	B4
Beravina	**108**	H3
Berber	**100**	F4
Berbera	**100**	H5
Berbérati	**106**	B3
Berchtesgaden	**62**	J3
Berck	**54**	D4
Berdigestyakh	**78**	M4
Berdyans'k	**70**	G5
Berdychiv	**70**	E5
Bereeda	**106**	J1
Berehove	**66**	K1
Bererreá	**60**	C2
Berettyóújfalu	**66**	J2
Berettys	**50**	L10
Bereznik	**70**	H2
Berezniki	**70**	L3
Berezovo	**70**	N2
Berezovyy	**78**	P6
Berga	**60**	M2
Bergama	**68**	K5
Bergamo	**62**	E5
Bergara	**60**	H1
Bergby	**48**	J6
Bergedorf	**52**	F3
Bergen, *Germany*	**52**	J2
Bergen, *Germany*	**52**	E4
Bergen, *Netherlands*	**54**	G2
Bergen, *Norway*	**48**	C6
Bergen op Zoom	**54**	G3
Bergerac	**58**	F9
Bergheim	**54**	J4
Bergisch Gladbach	**52**	C6
Bergsfjordhalvøya	**48**	L1
Beringen	**54**	H3
Beringovskiy	**78**	X4
Bering Sea	**132**	(1)C4
Bering Strait	**132**	(1)C2
Berīzak	**95**	G3

Bosa 64 C8
Bosanska Dubica 66 D4
Bosanska Gradiška 66 E4
Bosanska Kostajnica 62 M5
Bosanska Krupa 66 D5
Bosanski Brod 66 F4
Bosanski Novi 66 D4
Bosanski Petrovac 66 D5
Bosansko Grahovo 62 M6
Boşca 66 J4
Bose 84 D2
Bosilegrad 66 K7
Boskovice 50 F8
Bosna 66 F5
Bosnia and Herzegovina 66 E5
Bosobolo 106 B3
Bosporus = İstanbul Boğazı 68 M3
Bosporus 90 A1
Bossambélé 106 B2
Bossangoa 106 B2
Bossier City 130 C3
Bosten Hu 76 R9
Boston, *UK* 56 M9
Boston, *US* 128 F2
Botevgrad 66 L7
Botlikh 90 E1
Botna 66 R3
Botoşani 66 P2
Botou 80 F3
Botrange 54 J4
Botswana 108 C4
Bottrop 54 J3
Bou Ahmed 60 F9
Bouaké 104 C3
Bouar 106 B2
Bouârfa 102 E2
Boufarik 60 N8
Bougainville Island 112 F6
Bougainville Reef 114 J3
Bougouni 104 C2
Bougzoul 60 N9
Bouira 102 F1
Bou Ismail 60 N8
Bou Izakarn 102 D3
Boujdour 102 C3
Bou Kadir 60 M8
Boukra 102 C3
Boulder 126 E2
Boulder City 132 D1
Boulia 114 G4
Boulogne-sur-Mer 54 D4
Bouna 104 D3
Boundiali 104 C3
Bounty Islands 112 H10
Bourem 102 E5
Bourg 58 E8
Bourg-de-Piage 58 L9
Bourg-en-Bresse 58 L7
Bourges 58 H6
Bourgoin-Jallieu 58 L8
Bourke 114 J6
Bournemouth 56 L11
Bou Saâda 102 F1
Bousso 100 C5
Boussu 54 F4
Boutilimit 102 C5
Bouzghaïa 60 M8
Bowbells 126 F1
Bowen 114 J4
Bowie, *Ariz., US* 132 E2
Bowie, *Tex., US* 132 G2
Bowkan 92 M5
Bowling Green, *Fla., US* 130 E4
Bowling Green, *Ky., US* 130 D2
Bowling Green, *Mo., US* 130 C2
Bowman 126 F1
Bowman Bay 122 R3
Bo Xian 80 F4
Boxwood Hill 114 C6
Boyabat 92 F3
Boyang 80 F5
Boyarka 78 F2
Boyle 56 D8
Boysen Reservoir 126 E2
Boyuibe 142 J3
Bozcaada 68 H5
Boz Dağ 68 M7
Bozeman 126 D1
Bozkır 68 Q7
Bozoum 106 B2
Bozova 92 H5
Bozüyük 68 N5
Bra 62 C6
Brač 66 D6
Bracciano 64 G6
Bräcke 48 H5
Bracknell 54 B3
Brad 66 K3
Bradano 64 L8
Bradford 56 L8
Brady 130 B3
Braga 60 B3
Bragança, *Brazil* 140 H4
Bragança, *Portugal* 60 C3
Brahmapur 88 D5
Brahmaputra 88 F3
Brăila 66 Q4
Brainerd 128 B1
Braintree 54 C3
Brake 52 D3
Bramming 52 D1
Brampton 128 E2
Bramsche 52 D4
Branco 140 E3
Brandberg 108 A4
Brandenburg 52 H4
Brandenton 130 E4
Brandon 122 M7
Brandvlei 108 C5
Brandýs 50 D7
Braniewo 50 J3
Brasileia 140 D6
Brasilia 140 H7
Braslaw 48 P9
Braşov 66 N4
Bratislava 50 G9
Bratsk 78 G5
Bratskoye Vodokhranilishche 78 G5
Brattleboro 128 F2
Braţul 66 R4
Bratunac 66 G5
Braunau 62 J2
Braunschweig 52 F4
Brawley 132 C2
Bray 56 F8
Brazil 138 F4
Brazzaville 106 B4
Brčko 66 F5
Brda 50 G4
Bream Bay 116 E2
Breckenridge 132 G2
Břeclav 50 F9
Breda 54 G3
Bredasdorp 108 C6
Bredstedt 52 E2
Bredy 70 M4
Bree 54 H3
Bree 58 L2
Bregenz 62 E3
Breiðafjörður 48 (1)A2
Bremangerlandet 48 B6
Bremen, *Germany* 52 D3
Bremen, *US* 130 D3
Bremerhaven 52 D3
Bremerton 126 B1
Bremervörde 52 E3
Brenham 130 B3
Brennero 62 G4
Breno 62 F5
Brentwood 54 C3
Brescia 62 F5
Breslau = Wrocław 50 G6
Bressanone 62 G4
Bressay 56 M1
Bressuire 58 E7
Brest, *Belarus* 70 D4
Brest, *France* 58 A5
Breteuil 54 E5
Bretten 52 D7
Breves 140 G4
Brewarrina 114 J5
Brewton 130 D3
Brežice 66 C4
Brézina 102 F2
Brezno 50 J9
Bria 106 C2
Briançon 62 B6
Briceni 66 Q1
Bridgend 56 J10
Bridgeport, *Calif., US* 132 C1
Bridgeport, *Conn., US* 128 F2
Bridgeport, *Nebr., US* 126 F2
Bridgetown 140 F1
Bridgewater 122 U8
Bridgwater 56 J10
Bridlington 56 M7
Brienzer See 62 D4
Brig 62 C4
Brigham City 126 D2
Brighton, *UK* 54 B4
Brighton, *US* 126 F3
Brignoles 62 B7
Brikama 104 A2
Brilon 52 D5
Brindisi 64 M8
Brinkley 130 C3
Brisbane 114 K5
Bristol, *UK* 56 K10
Bristol, *US* 130 E2
Bristol Bay 132 (1)E4
Bristol Channel 56 H10
British Columbia 122 F5
Britstown 108 C6
Brive-la-Gaillarde 58 G8
Briviesca 60 G2
Brixham 56 J11
Brlik 76 N9
Brno 50 F8
Broad Sound 114 J4
Broadus 126 E1
Brockton 128 F2
Brockville 128 E2
Brod 66 J9
Brodeur Peninsula 122 P2
Brodick 56 G6
Brodnica 50 J4
Broken Arrow 134 E1
Broken Bow 130 C3
Broken Hill 114 H6
Brokopondo 140 F2
Bromölla 50 D1
Bromsgrove 56 K9
Brønderslev 48 E8
Broni 62 E5
Brooke's Point 84 F5
Brookhaven 124 H5
Brookhaven 130 C3
Brookhaven 134 F2
Brookings, *Oreg., US* 126 B2
Brookings, *S.D., US* 126 G2
Brooks 122 J6
Brooks Range 132 (1)F2
Brooksville 130 E4
Broome 114 D3
Brora 56 J3
Brösarp 48 H9
Broughton Island 122 U3
Brovary 70 F4
Brownfield 132 F2
Browning 126 D1
Brownsville, *Tenn., US* 130 D2
Brownsville, *Tex., US* 130 B4
Brownwood 130 B3
Bruchsal 52 D7
Bruck, *Austria* 62 L3
Bruck, *Austria* 62 M2
Bruck an der Mur 66 C2
Brugge 54 F3
Brühl 54 J4
Bruint 88 G3
Brumado 140 J6
Brumath 62 C2
Bruneau 126 C2
Brunei 86 E2
Brunflo 48 H5
Brunico 64 F2
Brunsbüttel 52 E3
Brunswick, *Ga., US* 130 E3
Brunswick, *Me., US* 128 G2
Bruntal 50 G8
Brush 126 F2
Brussels = Bruxelles 54 G4
Bruxelles 54 G4
Bryan 130 B3
Bryanka 76 S6
Bryansk 70 F4
Brzeg 50 G7
Brzeg Dolny 50 F6
Brzeziny 50 J6
B-Spandau 50 C5
Bubi 108 E4
Bucak 92 D5
Bucaramanga 140 C2
Buchanan 104 B3
Buchan Gulf 122 S2
Bucharest = Bucureşti 66 P5
Buchen 52 E7
Buchholz 52 E3
Buchy 58 M5
Bückeburg 52 E4
Bučovice 50 F8
Bucureşti 66 P5
Budapest 66 G2
Bude 56 H11
Budennovsk 92 L1
Büdingen 52 E6
Budoni 64 D8
Budrio 62 G6
Budva 66 F7
Buenaventura, *Colombia* 140 B3
Buenaventura, *Mexico* 132 E3
Buena Vista 126 E3
Buenos Aires 142 K5
Buffalo, *Okla., US* 130 B2
Buffalo, *N.Y., US* 128 E2
Buffalo, *S.D., US* 126 F1
Buffalo, *Tex., US* 130 B3
Buffalo, *Wyo., US* 126 E2
Buffalo Lake 122 J4
Buffalo Narrows 122 K5
Buftea 66 N5
Bug 50 L5
Bugojno 66 E5
Bugrino 76 H4
Bugsuk 84 F5
Bugul'ma 70 K4
Buguruslan 70 K4
Buḩayrat al Asad 92 H5
Buḩayrat ath Tharthār 92 K6
Buhuşi 66 P3
Builth Wells 56 J9
Buinsk 70 J3
Buir Nuur 80 F1
Bujanovac 66 J7
Buje 62 J5
Bujumbura 106 D4
Bukachacha 78 K6
Bukavu 106 D4
Bukhara 90 H2
Bukkittinggi 86 C3
Bukoba 106 E4
Bula, *Indonesia* 87 D3
Bula, *Papua New Guinea* 87 F4
Bülach 62 D3
Bulan 84 G4
Būlāq 100 F2
Bulawayo 108 D4
Buldir Island 78 X6
Bulgan 78 G7
Bulgaria 66 M7
Buli 87 C2
Bulle 62 C4
Bullhead City 132 D1
Bulls 116 E5
Bulukumba 87 B4
Bulun 78 M2
Bumba 106 C3
Bumbeşti Jiu 66 L4
Buna 106 F3
Bunbury 114 C6
Buncrana 56 E6
Bunda 106 E4
Bundaberg 114 K4
Bünde 52 D4
Bungunya 114 J5
Bunia 106 E3
Bunkie 130 C3
Bunnell 130 E4
Bünyan 92 F4
Bu ol Kheyr 95 D2
Buôn Mê Thuôt 84 D4
Buotama 78 M4
Bura 106 F4
Buran 76 R8
Buranj 88 D2
Burao 106 H2
Burāq 94 D3
Buraydah 90 D4
Burco 100 J6
Burdur 92 D5
Burdur Gölü 68 N7
Burē 100 G5
Büren 54 L3
Burg 52 G4
Burgas 66 Q7
Burgaski Zaliv 66 Q7
Burgdorf 62 C3
Burghausen 62 H2
Burglengenfeld 52 H7
Burgos 60 G2
Burgsvik 48 K8
Burhaniye 68 K5
Burhanpur 88 C4
Burjassot 60 K5
Burj Şāfitā 94 D2
Burketown 114 G3
Burkeville 128 E3
Bur-Khaybyt 78 P3
Burkina 104 D2
Burlin 70 K4
Burlington, *Colo., US* 132 F1
Burlington, *Ia., US* 128 B2
Burlington, *Vt., US* 128 F2
Burma = Myanmar 84 B2
Burnet 130 B3
Burney 126 B2
Burnie 114 J8
Burns 126 C2
Burns Junction 126 C2
Burns Lake 122 F6
Burqin 76 R8
Burra 114 G6
Burrel 68 C3
Bursa 68 M4
Bûr Safâga 100 F2
Bûr Sa'îd 100 F1
Bur Sudan 100 G4
Burtnieks 48 N8
Burton-upon-Trent 56 L9
Buru 87 C3
Burundi 106 D4
Bururi 106 D4
Burwell 126 G2
Buryatiya 78 J6
Bury St. Edmunds 54 C2
Būshehr 95 D2
Bushire = Būshehr 95 D2
Businga 106 C3
Busira 106 C4
Buşrá ash Shām 94 D4
Bussum 54 H2
Busto Arsizio 62 D5
Buta 106 C3
Butare 106 D4
Butaritari 112 H5
Bute 56 G6
Butembo 106 D3
Buðardalur 48 (1)C2
Buton 87 B3
Butte, *Mont., US* 126 D1
Butte, *Nebr., US* 126 G2
Butuan 84 H5
Butwal 88 D3
Butzbach 52 D6
Bützow 52 G3
Buulobarde 106 H3
Buur Gaabo 106 G4
Buurhabaka 106 G3
Buxtehude 52 E3
Buxton 54 A1
Buy 70 H3
Buynaksk 92 M2
Büyükada 68 L4
Büyükçekmece 68 L4
Buzai Gumbad 90 K2
Buzançais 58 G7
Buzău 66 P4
Buzău 66 Q4
Buzuluk 70 K4
Byala, *Bulgaria* 66 N6
Byala, *Bulgaria* 66 Q7
Byala Slatina 66 L6
Byam Martin Island 122 L2
Byaroza 48 N10
Bydgoszcz 50 H4
Bygdin 48 D6
Bygland 48 D7
Bykovskiy 78 M2
Bylot Island 122 R2
Byskeälven 48 L4
Bystřice 50 G8
Bystrzyca Kłodzka 50 F7
Bytatay 78 N3
Bytča 50 H8
Bytom 50 H7
Bytów 50 G3
Bzura 50 J5

C

Caaguazú 142 K4
Caballococha 140 C5
Caballo Reservoir 132 E2
Cabañaquinta 60 E1
Cabanatuan 84 G3
Cabano 128 G1
Cabdul Qaadir 100 H5
Cabeza del Buey 60 E6
Cabezas 140 E7
Cabimas 140 C1
Cabinda 104 G6
Cabinda 104 G6
Cabo Bascuñán 142 G4
Cabo Beata 134 K5
Cabo Camarón 134 G5
Cabo Carvoeiro 60 A5
Cabo Catoche 134 G4
Cabo Corrientes, *Colombia* 140 B2
Cabo Corrientes, *Mexico* 134 C4
Cabo Corrubedo 60 A2
Cabo Cruz 134 J5
Cabo de Espichel 60 A6
Cabo de Gata 60 H8
Cabo de Hornos 142 H10
Cabo de la Nao 60 L6
Cabo Delgado 108 G2
Cabo de Palos 60 K7

Churchill, *Man., Canada* 122 M5
Churchill, *Nfld., Canada* 122 U6
Churchill Falls 122 U6
Churchill Peak 122 F5
Churu 88 B3
Chuska Mountains 132 E1
Chusovoy 70 L3
Chute des Passes 122 S7
Chuuk 112 F5
Chuvashiya 70 J3
Chuxiong 84 C2
Chuya 78 J5
Ciadîr-Lunga 66 R3
Cide 92 E3
Ciechanów 50 K5
Ciechocinek 50 H5
Ciego de Avila 134 J4
Cienfuegos 134 H4
Cieza 60 J6
Cihanbeyli 92 E4
Cijulang 86 D4
Cilacap 86 D4
Cili 80 E5
Cimarron 130 B2
Cimişlia 66 R3
Cîmpeni 50 N11
Cinca 60 L3
Cincinnati 128 D3
Çine 68 L7
Ciney 54 H4
Cintalapa 134 F5
Circle, *Ak., US* 132 (1)J2
Circle, *Mont., US* 126 E1
Circleville 128 D3
Cirebon 86 D4
Cirò Marina 64 M9
Cisco 130 B3
Cistierna 60 E2
Čitluk 66 E6
Citronelle 130 D3
Cittadella 62 G5
Città di Castello 62 H7
Ciucea 66 K3
Ciudad Acuña 132 F3
Ciudad Bolívar 140 E2
Ciudad Camargo 132 E3
Ciudad del Carmen 134 F5
Ciudad del Este 142 L4
Ciudad Delicias 132 E3
Ciudad del Maíz 132 G4
Ciudad de Valles 134 E4
Ciudad Guayana 140 E2
Ciudad Juárez 132 E2
Ciudad Madero 132 G4
Ciudad Mante 134 E4
Ciudad Obregón 134 C3
Ciudad Real 60 G6
Ciudad-Rodrigo 60 D4
Ciudad Valles 132 G4
Ciudad Victoria 124 G7
Ciutadella 60 P4
Cividale del Friuli 62 J4
Civita Castellana 64 G6
Civitanova Marche 64 H5
Civitavecchia 64 F6
Cizre 92 K5
Clacton-on-Sea 54 D3
Clair Engle Lake 126 B2
Clairview 114 J4
Clamecy 58 J6
Clare Island 56 B8
Claremorris 56 D8
Clarence 116 D6
Clarence Strait 114 E2
Clarendon 132 F2
Clarkdale 132 D2
Clarksburg 130 E2
Clarksdale 130 C3
Clarks Junction 116 C7
Clarkston 126 C1
Clarksville, *Ark., US* 130 C2
Clarksville, *Tenn., US* 130 D2
Claro 140 G7
Clausthal-Zellerfeld 52 F5
Claveria 84 G3
Clayton 132 F1
Clear Island 56 C10
Clear Lake 128 B2
Clear Lake Reservoir 126 B2
Clearwater 126 C1
Clearwater 130 E4
Clearwater Mountains 126 C1
Cleburne 130 B3
Clermont, *Australia* 114 J4
Clermont, *France* 54 E5
Clermont-Ferrand 58 J8
Clervaux 54 J4
Cles 62 F4
Cleveland, *Oh., US* 128 D2
Cleveland, *Tenn., US* 130 E2
Cleveland, *Tex., US* 130 B3
Clifden 116 A7
Clifton 132 E2
Climax 126 E1
Clines Corners 132 E2
Clinton, *Canada* 122 G6
Clinton, *New Zealand* 116 B8
Clinton, *Ark., US* 128 B3
Clinton, *Ia., US* 124 H3
Clinton, *Miss., US* 130 C3
Clinton, *Mo., US* 128 B3
Clinton, *N.C., US* 130 F3
Clinton, *Okla., US* 130 B2
Clipperton Island 134 C6
Clonakilty 56 D10
Cloncurry 114 H4
Clonmel 56 E9
Cloppenburg 52 D4
Cloquet 128 B1
Cloud Peak 126 E2
Clovis, *Calif., US* 126 C3
Clovis, *N. Mex., US* 132 F2
Cluj-Napoca 66 L3
Cluny 58 K7
Cluses 62 B4
Clyde 56 H6
Clyde River 122 T2
Coaldale 126 C3
Coalville 126 C2
Coari 140 E4
Coast Mountains 122 E5
Coast Range 126 B3
Coatbridge 56 J6
Coats Island 122 Q4
Coatzacoalcos 134 F5
Cobalt 122 R7
Cobán 134 F5
Cobija 140 D6
Cobourg 124 L3
Cobourg Peninsula 114 F2
Cóbuè 108 E2
Coburg 52 F6
Cochabamba 140 D7
Cochin = Kochi 88 C7
Cochrane 128 D1
Cockburn Town 130 G5
Coco 134 H6
Cocoa 130 E4
Cocobeach 104 F4
Coco Channel 84 A4
Coco Island 84 A4
Codajás 140 E4
Codigoro 62 H6
Cod Island 122 U5
Codlea 66 N4
Codó 140 J4
Codogno 62 E5
Codroipo 62 J5
Cody 126 E2
Coen 114 H2
Coesfeld 52 C5
Coëtivy Island 98 J6
Coeur d'Alene 126 C1
Coeur d'Alene Lake 126 C1
Coevorden 54 J2
Coffs Harbour 114 K6
Cofrents 60 J5
Cognac 58 E8
Cogne 62 C5
Coiba 138 C3
Coihaique 142 G8
Coimbatore 88 C6
Coimbra 60 B4
Colchester 54 C3
Colebrook 128 F1
Coleman 130 B3
Coleraine 56 F6
Colesberg 108 D6
Colfax 126 C1
Colibaşi 66 M5
Colico 62 E4
Coll 56 F5
Collado-Villalba 60 F4
Collecchio 62 F6
College Station 130 B3
Collier Bay 114 D3
Collingwood 128 E2
Collins 130 D3
Collooney 56 D7
Colmar 62 C2
Colmenar Viejo 60 G4
Colombia 140 C3
Colombo 88 C7
Colomiers 58 G10
Colonia Las Heras 142 H8
Colonial Heights 128 E3
Colonsay 56 F5
Colorado 126 E3
Colorado, *Colo., US* 132 E1
Colorado, *Tex., US* 132 G2
Colorado Plateau 132 D1
Colorado Springs 126 F3
Columbia 126 C1
Columbia, *La., US* 130 C3
Columbia, *Md., US* 130 F2
Columbia, *Mo., US* 130 C2
Columbia, *S.C., US* 130 E3
Columbia, *Tenn., US* 130 D2
Columbia Mountains 122 G6
Columbus, *Ga., US* 130 E3
Columbus, *Ind., US* 130 D2
Columbus, *Miss., US* 130 D3
Columbus, *Mont., US* 126 E1
Columbus, *Nebr., US* 126 G2
Columbus, *N. Mex., US* 132 E2
Columbus, *Oh., US* 130 E1
Columbus, *Tex., US* 130 B4
Colville 116 E3
Colville 132 (1)G2
Colville Lake 132 (1)M2
Comacchio 62 H6
Comănești 66 P3
Comarnic 66 N4
Combarbalá 142 G5
Combeaufontaine 58 M6
Comilla 84 A2
Comino = Kemmuna 64 J12
Commentry 58 H7
Commercy 54 H6
Como 62 E5
Comoé 104 D3
Comondú 124 D6
Comoros 108 G2
Compiègne 54 E5
Comrat 66 R3
Comstock 132 F3
Conakry 104 B3
Concarneau 58 B6
Conceição do Araguaia 140 H5
Concepción, *Bolivia* 140 E7
Concepción, *Chile* 142 G6
Conches-en-Ouche 54 C6
Conchos 134 C3
Concord, *Calif., US* 132 B1
Concord, *N.H., US* 128 F2
Concord, *N.C., US* 130 E2
Concordia, *Argentina* 142 K5
Concordia, *US* 130 B2
Condé-sur-Noireau 54 B6
Condobolin 114 J6
Condom 58 F10
Conegliano 62 H5
Conggar 88 F3
Congo 98 E6
Congo 104 G5
Connecticut 128 F2
Connemara 56 C8
Conrad 126 D1
Côn Son 84 D5
Constanța 92 C1
Constantina 60 E7
Constantine 102 G1
Consul 126 E1
Contact 126 D2
Contamana 140 B5
Contwoyto Lake 122 J3
Convay 130 F3
Conway 130 C2
Conwy 56 J8
Conwy Bay 56 H8
Coober Pedy 114 F5
Cookeville 128 C3
Cook Inlet 132 (1)G4
Cook Islands 112 K7
Cook Strait 116 E5
Cooktown 114 J3
Coolabah 114 J6
Coolgardie 114 D6
Cooma 114 J7
Coonabarabran 114 J6
Coon Rapids 128 B1
Coopers Town 130 F4
Coorabie 114 F6
Coos Bay 126 B2
Cootamundra 114 J6
Copenhagen = København 48 G9
Copertino 64 N8
Copiapó 142 G4
Copper Harbor 128 C1
Çôqen 88 E2
Coquille 126 B2
Coquimbo 142 G4
Corabia 66 M6
Coral 124 K1
Coral Harbour 122 Q4
Coral Sea 114 K2
Coral Sea Islands Territory 112 F7
Coral Sea Islands Territory 114 J2
Coral Springs 130 E4
Corantijn 140 F3
Corbeil-Essonnes 58 H5
Corbigny 58 J6
Corbu 66 R5
Corby 54 B2
Cordele 130 E3
Cordillera Cantábrica 60 D2
Cordillera Central 138 E5
Cordillera del Condor 140 B5
Cordillera de Mérida 138 D3
Cordillera de Oliva 142 G4
Cordillera Isabella 134 G6
Cordillera Occidental 138 E5
Cordillera Oriental 138 D5
Cordillera Penibética 60 F8
Cordillera Vilcabamba 140 C6
Córdoba, *Argentina* 142 J5
Córdoba, *Spain* 60 F7
Corfu = Kerkyra 68 B5
Coria 60 D5
Corinth 130 D3
Corinto 140 H7
Cork 56 D10
Cork Harbour 56 D10
Corleone 64 H11
Corlu 68 K3
Corn Islands 138 C2
Cornwall 124 M2
Cornwallis Island 122 M2
Coro 140 D1
Corocoro 140 D7
Coromandel 116 E3
Coromandel Coast 88 D6
Coromandel Peninsula 116 E3
Coron 84 G4
Coronation Gulf 122 J3
Coronel Oviedo 142 K4
Coronel Pringles 142 J6
Coronel Suárez 142 J6
Corpus Christi 130 B4
Corrientes 142 K4
Corrigan 130 C3
Corriverton 140 F2
Corse 64 D6
Corsica = Corse 64 D6
Corsicana 130 B3
Corte 64 D6
Cortegana 60 D7
Cortez 132 E1
Cortina d'Ampezzo 62 H4
Cortland 128 E2
Cortona 64 F5
Coruche 60 B6
Çorum 92 F3
Corumbá 140 F7
Corvallis 126 B2
Corvo 102 (1)A2
Cosenza 64 L9
Cosmoledo Group 108 (2)A2
Cosne-sur-Loire 58 H6
Cossato 62 D5
Costa Blanca 60 K7
Costa Brava 60 P3
Costa del Sol 60 F8
Costa de Mosquitos 134 H6
Costa Dorada 60 M4
Costa do Sol 60 A6
Costa Rica 134 G7
Costa Smeralda 64 D7
Costa Verde 60 D1
Costești 66 M5
Coswig 52 H5
Cotabato 84 G5
Côte d'Ivoire 104 C3
Cotonou 104 E3
Cottage Grove 126 B2
Cottbus 50 D6
Cotulla 130 B4
Couhe 58 F7
Coulommiers 54 F6
Council Bluffs 126 F2
Courland Lagoon 50 L2
Courtacon 54 F6
Courtenay 124 B2
Coushatta 130 C3
Coutances 58 D4
Couvin 54 G4
Covasna 66 P4
Coventry 56 L9
Covilhã 60 C4
Covington, *Ga., US* 130 E3
Covington, *Ky., US* 130 E2
Covington, *Va., US* 128 D3
Cowell 114 G6
Cowes 54 A4
Cowra 114 J6
Cox's Bazar 88 F4
Coy Aike 142 H9
Cradock 108 D6
Craig 126 E2
Crailsheim 52 F7
Craiova 66 L5
Cranbrook, *Australia* 114 C6
Cranbrook, *US* 124 C2
Crater Lake 126 B2
Crato 140 K5
Crawford 126 F2
Crawfordsville 128 C2
Crawley 54 B3
Cree Lake 122 K5
Creil 54 E5
Crema 62 E5
Cremona 62 F5
Crépy-en-Valois 54 E5
Cres 62 K6
Cres 62 K6
Crescent City 126 B2
Crest 58 L9
Creston 128 B2
Crestview 124 J5
Crestview 134 G2
Crete = Kriti 68 H10
Créteil 54 E6
Creuse 58 G7
Crevillent 60 K6
Crewe 56 K8
Crianlarich 56 H5
Criciúma 142 M4
Cristalina 140 H7
Cristóbal Colón 120 J8
Crna Gora 66 F7
Croatia 66 C4
Crockett 130 B3
Croker Island 114 F2
Cromer 56 P9
Cromwell 116 B7
Crooked Island 134 K4
Crookston 124 G2
Cross City 130 E3
Cross Lake 122 M6
Crossville 128 C3
Crotone 64 M9
Crowley 130 C3
Crownest Pass 124 D2
Crown Point 128 C2
Croydon 114 H3
Cruz Alta 142 L4
Cruz del Eje 142 J5
Cruzeiro do Sul 140 C5
Crvenka 66 G4
Crystal City 130 B4
Crystal Falls 128 C1
Crystal River 130 E4
Crystal Springs 130 C3
Csorna 66 E2
Csurgó 62 N4
Cuamba 108 F2
Cuando 108 C3
Cuangar 108 B3
Cuango 106 B5
Cuanza 106 B5
Cuatro Ciénegas 132 F3
Cuauhtémoc 132 E3
Cuba 126 E3
Cuba 134 H4
Cubal 106 A6
Cubali 108 A2
Cubango 108 B3
Çubuk 68 R4
Cucuí 140 D3
Cúcuta 140 C2
Cuddalore 88 C6
Cuddapah 88 C6
Cuemba 108 B2
Cuenca, *Ecuador* 140 B4
Cuenca, *Spain* 60 H4
Cuernavaca 134 E5
Cuero 130 B4
Cuiabá 140 F7
Cuilo 106 B5
Cuio 106 A6
Cuito 108 B3
Cuito Cuanavale 108 B3
Culbertson 126 E1
Culfa 92 L4
Culiacán 134 C4
Cullera 60 K5
Cullman 130 D3
Culpepper 140 (1)A1

Name	Page	Grid
Culuene	140	G6
Culverden	116	D6
Cumaná	140	E1
Cumberland	128	E3
Cumberland Peninsula	122	T3
Cumberland Sound	122	T3
Cummings	126	B3
Cumpas	132	E2
Çumra	68	Q7
Cunderdin	114	C6
Cunene	108	A3
Cuneo	62	C6
Cunnamulla	114	J5
Cuorgne	62	C5
Čuprija	66	J6
Cure	58	J6
Curicó	142	C5
Curitiba	142	M4
Currais Novos	140	K5
Curral Velho	104	(1)B1
Currie	114	H7
Curtea de Argeş	66	M4
Curtici	66	J3
Curtis Island	114	K4
Curuá	140	G5
Curup	86	C3
Curuzú Cuatiá	142	K4
Curvelo	140	J7
Cusco	140	C6
Cuthbert	130	E3
Cutro	64	L9
Cuttack	88	E4
Cuvier Island	116	E3
Cuxhaven	52	D3
Cuya	140	C7
Cuyuni	140	F2
Cwmbran	56	J10
Cyclades = Kyklades	68	G7
Cypress Hills	124	D2
Cyprus	92	E6
Czarnków	50	F5
Czech Republic	50	C8
Częstochowa	50	J7
Człuchów	50	G4

D

Name	Page	Grid
Da'an	80	G1
Daaquam	128	F1
Dab'a	94	D5
Dabas	66	G2
Dabat	100	G5
Dabola	104	B2
Dabra	88	C3
Dąbrowa Górnicza	50	J7
Dąbrowa Tarnowska	50	K7
Dăbuleni	66	M6
Dachau	62	G2
Dadu	88	A3
Daet	84	G4
Dagana	102	B5
Dagestan	92	M2
Dagupan	84	G3
Dahabān	100	G3
Da Hinggan Ling	80	G1
Dahlak Archipelago	100	H4
Dahlonega	130	E3
Dahn	54	K5
Dahod	88	B4
Dahongliutan	90	L2
Dahük	92	K5
Daimiel	60	G5
Dai Xian	80	E3
Dakar	104	A2
Dakoro	104	F2
Dakota City	126	G2
Dakovica	66	H7
Dakovo	66	F4
Dala	106	C6
Dalai Nur	80	F2
Dalälven	48	H6
Dalaman	92	C5
Dalandzadgad	80	C2
Dalap-Uliga-Darrit	112	H5
Da Lat	84	D4
Dalbandin	90	H4
Dalby	114	K5
Dalgān	90	G4
Dalhart	132	F1
Dalhousie	88	C2
Dali	84	C1
Dalian	80	G3
Dalizi	82	D3
Dallas	130	B3
Dalmā	95	E4
Daloa	104	C3
Dalry	56	H6
Dalrymple Lake	114	J4
Dāltenganj	88	D4
Dalton	130	E3
Dalvík	48	(1)D2
Daly Waters	114	F3
Daman	88	B4
Damanhûr	100	F1
Damar	87	C4
Damara	104	H3
Damasak	104	G2
Damascus = Dimashq	94	D3
Damaturu	104	G2
Dāmiya	94	C4
Damoh	88	C4
Damqawt	90	F6
Damxung	88	F2
Danau Poso	87	A3
Danau Toba	86	B2
Danau Towuti	87	B3
Danba	80	C4
Dandeldhura	88	D3
Dandong	82	C3
Da Nẵng	84	D3
Daneți	66	M6
Dangara	90	J2
Danger Islands	112	K7
Danghe Nanshan	80	B3
Daniel	126	D1
Danilov	70	H3
Dank	95	G5
Dankov	70	G4
Dannenberg	52	G3
Dannevirke	116	F5
Dansville	128	E2
Danube	46	F3
Danville, Ill., US	130	D1
Danville, Ky., US	130	E2
Danville, Va., US	130	F2
Dan Xian	84	D3
Dao Phu Quôc	84	C4
Dapa	84	H5
Dapaong	104	E2
Da Qaidam	80	B3
Daqing	78	M7
Dar'ā	94	D4
Dārāb	95	F2
Darabani	66	P1
Daraj	100	B1
Dārākūyeh	95	F2
Darazo	104	G2
Dar Ben Karricha el Behri	60	E9
Darbhanga	88	E3
Dardanelles = Çanakkale Boğazı	68	J4
Darende	92	G4
Dar es Salaam	106	F5
Darfo Boario Terme	62	F5
Dargan-Ata	76	L9
Dargaville	116	D2
Darham	78	H7
Darjeeling	88	E3
Darling	114	H6
Darlington	56	L7
Darłowo	48	J9
Dărmăneşti	66	P3
Dar Mazār	95	G2
Darmstadt	52	D7
Darnah	100	D1
Darnley Bay	122	G3
Daroca	60	J3
Darß	52	H2
Dartmouth	122	U8
Daru	87	F4
Daruba	87	C2
Daruvar	62	N5
Darvaza	76	K9
Darwin	114	F2
Daryacheh-ye Bakhtegan	95	E2
Daryācheh-ye Orūmīyeh	92	L5
Daryācheh-ye Tashk	95	E2
Dārzīn	95	H2
Dashizhai	80	G1
Dashkhovuz	76	K9
Dasht-e Kavir	90	F3
Dasht-e Lut	95	H1
Datça	68	K8
Datça	92	B5
Date	82	L2
Datong	80	C3
Datong	80	E2
Daugava	70	E3
Daugavpils	70	E3
Daun	54	J4
Dauphin	122	M6
Daura	104	F2
Dausa	88	C3
Dāvāci	92	N3
Davangere	88	C6
Davao	84	H5
Davenport	128	B2
Daventry	54	A2
David	134	H7
Davis Sea	144	(2)Q3
Davis Strait	122	V3
Davlekanovo	76	J7
Davos	62	E4
Dawa	80	G2
Dawqah, Oman	90	F6
Dawqah, Saudi Arabia	100	H4
Dawson	132	(1)K3
Dawson Creek, B.C., Canada	122	G5
Dawson Creek, Y.T., Canada	122	D4
Dawu	80	C4
Dax	58	D10
Daxian	80	D4
Dayong	80	E5
Dayr az Zawr	92	J6
Dayton, Oh., US	128	D3
Dayton, Tenn., US	128	C3
Dayton, Tex., US	130	C4
Dayton, Wash., US	126	C1
Daytona Beach	130	E4
Dayu	80	E5
Dazhu	80	D4
De Aar	108	C6
Dead Sea	94	C5
Deakin	114	E6
Deal	54	D3
De'an	80	F5
Deán Funes	142	J5
Dease Lake	132	(1)M4
Dease Strait	122	J3
Death Valley	126	C3
Deba Habe	104	G2
Debar	68	C3
Dębica	50	L7
Debin	78	S4
Deblin	50	L6
Dębno	50	D5
Debre Birhan	106	F2
Debrecen	66	J2
Debre Markos	100	G5
Debreşte	68	D3
Debre Tabor	100	G5
Decatur, Al., US	128	C4
Decatur, Ill., US	128	C3
Decazeville	58	H9
Deccan	88	C5
Děčín	50	D7
Decize	58	J7
De Cocksdorp	54	G1
Decorah	128	B2
Dedoplis	92	M3
Dédougou	104	D2
Dedza	108	E2
Dee, Scot., UK	56	K4
Dee, Wales, UK	56	J9
Deering	132	(1)E2
Deer Lake	122	V7
Deer Lodge	126	D1
Deer Park	126	C1
De Funiak Springs	130	D3
Dêgê	80	B4
Degeh Bur	106	G2
Degema	104	F4
Deggendorf	62	J2
Dehaj	95	F1
Dehalak Desēt	90	D6
Deh Bid	95	E1
Deh-Dasht	95	D1
Dehiba	102	H2
Dehküyeh	95	F3
Dehlonān	90	E3
Dehra	90	L3
Dehra Dun	88	C2
Dehri	88	D4
Deh Shū	90	H3
Deinze	54	F4
Dej	66	L2
De Kalb	130	C3
De-Kastri	78	Q6
Dekese	106	C4
Delano	132	C1
Delaware	128	D2
Delaware	130	F2
Delbrück	52	D5
Delémont	62	C3
Delfoi	68	E6
Delft	54	G2
Delfzijl	54	J1
Delgo	100	F3
Delhi, India	88	C3
Delhi, US	128	F2
Delingha	80	B3
Delitzsch	52	H5
Dellys	60	P8
Delmenhorst	52	D3
Delnice	62	K5
Del Rio	132	F3
Delta, Colo., US	126	E3
Delta, Ut., US	126	D3
Delta del Orinoco	140	E2
Delta Junction	132	(1)H3
Deming	132	E2
Demirci	68	L5
Demmin	52	J3
Dem. Rep. of the Congo	106	C4
Demopolis	130	D3
Demyanka	70	P3
Demyanskoye	70	N3
Denain	54	F4
Denau	90	J2
Denbigh	128	E1
Den Burg	54	G1
Dendang	86	D3
Dender	54	F4
Dendi	106	F2
Dengkou	80	D2
Denham	114	B5
Den Helder	54	G2
Dénia	60	L6
Deniliquin	114	H7
Denio	126	C2
Denison, Ia., US	128	A2
Denison, Tex., US	130	B3
Denizli	92	C5
Denmark	46	E2
Denmark	114	C6
Denmark Strait	120	D3
Denpasar	86	E4
Denton	132	G2
D'Entrecasteaux Islands	114	K1
Denver	126	F3
Deogarh, India	88	B3
Deogarh, India	88	D4
Deoghar	88	E4
Déols	58	G7
De Panne	54	E3
Depok	86	D4
Dépression du Mourdi	100	D4
Deputatskiy	78	P3
Dera Ghazi Khan	90	K3
Dera Ismail Khan	90	K3
Derbent	92	E1
Derby, Australia	114	D3
Derby, UK	56	L9
De Ridder	130	C3
Dermott	130	C3
Derudeb	100	G4
Derventa	66	E5
Desē	100	G5
Deseado	142	H8
Desert Center	132	C2
Des Moines, Ia., US	124	H3
Des Moines, N. Mex., US	132	F1
Desna	70	F4
Dessau	52	H5
Desvres	54	D4
Deta	66	J4
Detmold	52	D5
Detroit	124	K3
Detroit Lakes	128	A1
Det Udom	84	C4
Detva	50	J9
Deurne	54	H3
Deva	66	K4
Deventer	54	J2
Devikot	88	B3
Devil's Lake	122	L7
Devils Lake	126	G1
Devil's Point	130	F5
Devnya	66	Q6
Devon Island	122	P1
Devonport	114	J8
Dewangiri	88	F3
Dewas	88	C4
Deyang	80	C4
Deyhuk	90	G3
Deyyer	95	E3
Dezfūl	90	E3
Dezhou	80	F3
Dhahran = Az Zahrān	95	D3
Dhaka	88	F4
Dhamār	100	H5
Dhamtri	88	D4
Dhanbad	88	E4
Dhar	88	C4
Dhārwād	88	B5
Dhaulagiri	88	D3
Dhekelia	94	A2
Dhībān	94	C5
Dhoraji	88	B4
Dhule	88	B4
Dhulian	88	E4
Dhuudo	106	J2
Dhuusa Mareeb	106	H2
Dia	68	H9
Diaca	106	G6
Diamantina	140	H7
Diamantino	140	F6
Diamond Islets	114	K3
Diane Bank	114	J3
Dianópolis	140	H6
Dibā al Hiṣn	95	G4
Dibbiena	64	F5
Dibrugarh	88	F3
Dickens	132	F2
Dickinson	126	F1
Dickson	130	D2
Didcot	54	A3
Didiéni	104	C2
Didymoteicho	68	J3
Die	58	L9
Diébougou	104	D2
Dieburg	52	D7
Diéma	104	C2
Diemel	52	E5
Diemeringen	52	C8
Diepholz	52	D4
Dieppe	54	D5
Diest	54	H4
Diffa	104	G2
Digne-les-Bains	62	B6
Digoin	58	J7
Dijon	58	L6
Dikhil	100	H5
Dikili	68	J5
Diklosmta	92	L2
Diksmuide	54	E3
Dikson	76	Q3
Dikwa	104	G2
Dīla	106	F2
Dili	87	C4
Dilijan	92	L3
Dillenburg	52	D6
Dilling	100	E5
Dillingen, Germany	52	F8
Dillingen, Germany	52	B7
Dillingham	132	(1)F4
Dillion	124	D2
Dillon	126	D1
Dillon Cone	116	D6
Dilolo	108	C2
Dimapur	88	F3
Dimashq	94	D3
Dimitrovgrad, Bulgaria	66	N7
Dimitrovgrad, Russia	70	J4
Dimitrovgrad, Serbia	66	K7
Dīmona	94	C5
Dinagat	84	H4
Dinajpur	88	E3
Dinan	58	C5
Dinant	54	G4
Dinar	92	D4
Dinard	58	C5
Dinaric Alps	62	L6
Dindigul	88	C6
Dindori	88	D4
Dingle Bay	56	B9
Dingolfing	62	H2
Dinguiraye	104	B2
Dingwall	56	H4
Dingxi	80	C3
Dinkelsbühl	52	F7
Dinosaur	126	E2
Diomede Islands	78	AA3
Dioriga Kointhou	68	F7
Diourbel	102	B6
Dipolog	84	G5
Dir	88	B1
Dirē Dawa	106	G2
Dirk Hartog Island	114	B5
Dirranbandi	114	J5
Disko Bugt = Qeqertarsuup Tunua	122	V3
Diss	54	D2
Distrito Federal	140	H7
Dithmarschen	52	D2
Dīvāndarreh	92	M6
Divinópolis	142	N3
Divo	104	C3
Divriği	92	H4
Dixon	128	C2
Dixon Entrance	132	(1)L5
Diyarbakır	92	J5
Dja	104	G4

Name	Page	Grid
Djado	102	H4
Djamâa	102	G2
Djambala	104	G5
Djanet	102	G4
Djelfa	102	F2
Djéma	106	D2
Djenné	102	E6
Djibo	104	D2
Djibouti [A]	100	H5
Djibouti	100	H5
Djolu	106	C3
Djougou	104	E3
Djúpivogur	48	(1)F2
Dnestrovsc	66	S3
Dnieper	70	F5
Dniester	66	Q1
Dnipro	46	H3
Dniprodzerzhyns'k	70	F5
Dnipropetrovs'k	70	F5
Dnister	46	G3
Dno	70	E3
Doba, Chad	106	B2
Doba, China	88	E2
Dobbiaco	62	H4
Döbeln	52	J5
Döbern	52	K5
Doboj	66	F5
Dobre Miasto	50	K4
Dobrich	66	Q6
Dobryanka	70	L3
Doctor Arroyo	132	F4
Dodecanese = Dodekanisos	68	J8
Dodge City	126	F3
Dodoma [■]	106	F5
Doetinchem	54	J3
Dofa	87	C3
Doğanşehir	92	G4
Dōgo	82	G5
Dogondoutchi	104	E2
Dogubeyazit	92	L4
Doha = Ad Dawḩah [■]	95	D4
Doka	87	D4
Dokkum	52	B3
Dolak	87	E4
Dolbeau	128	F1
Dole	62	A3
Dolgany	78	E2
Dolinsk	78	Q7
Dollard	52	C3
Dolný Kubín	50	J8
Dolomiti	62	G4
Dolo Odo	106	G3
Dolores	142	K6
Dolphin and Union Strait	122	H3
Domar	88	D2
Domažlice	52	H7
Dombås	48	E5
Dombóvár	66	F3
Domfront	58	E5
Dominica [A]	138	E2
Dominican Republic [A]	138	D1
Domodossola	62	D4
Domokos	68	E5
Dompu	87	A4
Domžale	62	K4
Don	46	H2
Donau = Danube	62	H2
Donaueschingen	62	D3
Donauwörth	52	F8
Don Benito	60	E6
Doncaster	56	L8
Dondra Head	88	D7
Donegal	56	D7
Donegal Bay	56	D7
Donets	46	H3
Donets'k	70	G5
Dongara	114	B5
Dongco	88	D2
Dongfang	84	D3
Donggala	87	A3
Donggou	82	C4
Dongguan	84	E2
Dông Hôi	84	D3
Dongjingcheng	82	E1
Donglük	76	R10
Dongning	82	F2
Dongo	104	H4
Dongola	100	F4
Dongou	104	H4
Dongsha Qundao	84	F2
Dongsheng	80	E3
Dong Ujimqin Qi	80	F1
Dongying	80	F3
Doniphan	130	C2
Donji Vakuf	62	N6
Donner Pass	126	B3
Donostia	60	J1
Donousa	68	H7
Dora	62	C5
Dorchester	56	K11
Dordrecht	54	G3
Dorfen	62	H2
Dori	104	D2
Doring	108	B6
Dorion	128	C1
Dormagen	54	J3
Dornbirn	62	E3
Doro	104	D1
Dorog	50	H10
Dorohoi	66	P2
Döröö Nuur	76	S8
Dorotea	48	J4
Dorsten	54	J3
Dortmund	52	C5
Doruma	106	D3
Dos Hermanas	60	E7
Dosse	52	H4
Dosso	104	E2
Dothan	130	D3
Douai	54	F4
Douala	104	F4
Douarnenez	58	A5
Doubs	62	B3
Douentza	104	C2
Douglas, South Africa	108	C5
Douglas, UK	56	H7
Douglas, Ariz., US	132	E2
Douglas, Ga., US	130	E3
Douglas, Wyo., US	126	E2
Doullens	54	E4
Dourados	142	L3
Douro	60	B3
Dover, UK	54	D3
Dover, US	130	F2
Dover, Australia	114	J8
Dover-Foxcroft	128	G1
Dowlatābād, Iran	95	E2
Dowlatābād, Iran	95	G2
Downpatrick	56	G7
Dowshī	90	J2
Drac	62	B6
Drachten	54	J1
Dragan	48	H4
Drăgăneşti-Olt	66	M5
Drăgăşani	66	M5
Draguignan	62	B7
Drakensberg	108	D6
Drake Passage	142	G10
Drama	68	G3
Drammen	48	F7
Drasenhofen	62	M2
Drau	62	J4
Drava	66	E4
Dravograd	64	K2
Drawsko Pomorskie	50	E4
Dresden	52	J5
Dreux	54	D6
Drezdenko	50	E5
Drina	66	G5
Driva	48	E5
Drniš	66	D6
Drobeta-Turnu Severin	66	K5
Drochia	66	Q1
Drogheda	56	F8
Drohobych	50	N8
Drôme	58	K9
Dronne	58	F8
Dronning Maud Land	144	(2)F2
Dronten	54	H2
Drummondville	128	F1
Druskininkai	48	M9
Druzhina	78	Q3
Drvar	66	D5
Dryanovo	66	N7
Dryden	124	H2
Drysdale River	114	E3
Dschang	104	G3
Dubã	100	G2
Dubai = Dubayy	95	F4
Dubăsari	66	S2
Dubawnt Lake	122	L4
Dubayy	95	F4
Dubbo	114	J6
Dübendorf	62	D3
Dublin, Ireland	56	F8
Dublin, US	130	E3
Dublin Bay	56	F8
Dubna	70	G3
Dubnica	50	H9
Du Bois	128	E2
Dubois, Id., US	126	D2
Dubois, Wyo., US	126	E2
Dubovskoye	70	H5
Dubreka	104	B3
Dubrovnik	66	F7
Dubuque	128	B2
Duchesne	126	D2
Ducie Island	112	P8
Dudelange	54	J5
Duderstadt	52	F5
Dudinka	76	R4
Dudley	56	K9
Duero	60	F3
Dugi Otok	66	B6
Duifken Point	114	H2
Duisburg	54	J3
Duiveland	54	F3
Dukat	78	T4
Duk Faiwil	106	E2
Dukhān	95	D4
Dukla	50	L8
Dukou	80	C5
Dulan	80	B3
Dulce	132	E1
Dulce	142	J4
Dul'Durga	78	J6
Dullewala	88	B2
Dülmen	52	C5
Dulovo	66	Q6
Duluth	128	B1
Dūmā	94	D3
Dumaguete	84	G5
Dumai	86	C2
Dumas, Ark., US	130	C3
Dumas, Tex., US	126	F3
Dumayr	94	D3
Dumbarton	56	H5
Ďumbier	50	J9
Dumboa	104	G2
Dumfries	56	J6
Dümmer	52	D4
Dumont d'Urville Sea	144	(2)U3
Dumyât	100	F1
Duna = Danube	66	E2
Dunaj = Danube	50	G10
Dunajská Streda	66	E2
Dunakeszi	66	G2
Dunărea = Danube	66	K5
Dunaújváros	66	F3
Dunav = Danube	66	J5
Dunayivtsi	70	L5
Dunbar, UK	56	K6
Duncan	126	B1
Duncan Passage	84	A4
Dundaga	48	M8
Dundalk	56	F7
Dundalk Bay	56	F8
Dundee, South Africa	108	E5
Dundee, UK	56	K5
Dunedin	116	C7
Dunfermline	56	J5
Dungarvan	56	E9
Dungeness	54	C4
Dungu	106	D3
Dungun	84	C6
Dunhua	82	E2
Dunhuang	80	A2
Dunkerque	54	E3
Dunkirk	128	E2
Dunkwa	104	D3
Dun Laoghaire	56	F8
Dunnet Head	56	J3
Dunseith	126	G1
Dunsmuir	126	B2
Duque de Caxias	142	N3
Du Quoin	130	D2
Durance	58	L10
Durango, Mexico	132	F4
Durango, Spain	60	H1
Durango, US	126	E3
Durankurak	66	R6
Durant	130	B3
Durazno	142	K5
Durban	108	E5
Durban-Corbières	58	H10
Düren	54	J4
Durgapur	88	E4
Durham, Canada	128	D2
Durham, UK	56	L7
Durham, US	130	F2
Duri	86	C2
Durmã	95	B4
Durmanec	66	C3
Durmitor	66	G6
Durness	56	H3
Durrës	68	B3
Dursey	56	B10
Dursunbey	68	L5
D'Urville Island	116	D5
Dushanbe [■]	90	J2
Düsseldorf	54	J3
Duvno	62	N7
Duyun	80	D5
Düzce	92	P4
Dvina	46	H2
Dvinskaya Guba	70	G1
Dwarka	88	A4
Dworshak Reservoir	126	C1
Dyat'kovo	70	F4
Dyersburg	130	D2
Dyje	62	M2
Dzamin Uüd	78	J8
Dzavhan	76	S8
Dzerzhinsk	70	H3
Dzhalinda	78	L6
Dzhambeyty	70	K4
Dzhankoy	70	F5
Dzhardzhan	78	L3
Dzharkurgan	90	J2
Dzhetygara	70	M4
Dzhezkazgan	70	N5
Dzhigudzhak	78	T4
Dzhizak	76	M9
Dzhusaly	70	M5
Działdowo	50	K4
Dziúnbulag	80	F1
Dzüünmod	80	D1

E

Name	Page	Grid
Eads	126	F3
Eagle	132	(1)J3
Eagle Lake	126	B2
Eagle Pass	132	F3
East Antarctica	144	(2)P2
Eastbourne	54	C4
East Cape	116	G3
East China Sea	80	H4
East Dereham	54	C2
Easter Island	112	Q8
Eastern Cape [a]	108	D6
Eastern Ghats	88	C6
Easter Ross	56	H4
East Falkland	142	K9
East Grinstead	54	C3
East Kilbride	56	H6
Eastleigh	54	A4
East Liverpool	130	E1
East London	108	D6
Eastmain	122	R6
Eastmain	122	S6
East Point	130	E3
East Retford	54	B1
East St. Louis	128	B3
East Sea = Sea of Japan	82	G3
East Siberian Sea = Vostochno-Sibirskoye More	78	U2
East Timor [A]	87	C4
Eatonton	130	E3
Eau Claire	128	B2
Ebbw Vale	56	J10
Ebensee	62	J3
Eberbach	52	D7
Ebersbach	50	D6
Ebersberg	62	G2
Eberswalde	52	J4
Ebinur Hu	76	Q9
Eboli	64	K8
Ebolowa	104	G4
Ebro	60	K3
Eceabat	68	J4
Ech Chélif	102	F1
Echinos	68	G3
Echo Bay	122	H3
Écija	60	E7
Eckernförde	52	E2
Ecuador [A]	140	B4
Ed	100	H5
Edam	54	H2
Eday	56	K2
Ed Da'ein	100	E5
Ed Damazin	100	F5
Ed Debba	100	F4
Ed Dueim	100	F5
Ede, Netherlands	54	H2
Ede, Nigeria	104	E3
Edéa	104	G4
Edelény	50	K9
Eden, Australia	114	J7
Eden, US	132	G2
Edendale	116	B8
Eder	52	D5
Edersee	52	E5
Edessa	68	E4
Edgecumbe	116	F3
Edinburgh	56	J6
Edineţ	66	Q1
Edirne	68	J3
Edmonds	126	B1
Edmonton	122	J6
Edmundson	124	N2
Edmundston	128	G1
Edolo	62	F4
Edremit	68	J5
Edremit Körfezi	68	H5
Edwards	132	C2
Edwards Plateau	132	F2
Eeklo	54	F3
Eemshaven	54	J1
Éfaté	112	G7
Eferding	50	D9
Effingham	130	D2
Eganville	128	E1
Eger	52	G6
Eger	66	H2
Egersund	48	D7
Eggenfelden	62	H2
Egilsstaðir	48	(1)F2
Eğridir	68	N7
Eğridir Gölü	68	N6
Egvekinot	78	Y3
Egypt [A]	100	E2
Ehingen	62	E2
Eibar	60	H1
Eichstätt	62	G2
Eider	52	D2
Eidfjord	48	D6
Eidsvold	114	K5
Eidsvoll	48	F6
Eifel	54	J4
Eigg	56	F5
Eight Degree Channel	88	B7
Eilenburg	52	H5
Einbeck	52	E5
Eindhoven	54	H3
Eirunepé	140	D5
Eiseb	108	C4
Eisenach	52	F6
Eisenerz	62	K3
Eisenhüttenstadt	50	D5
Eisenstadt	62	M3
Eisleben	52	G5
Eivissa	60	M5
Eivissa	60	M6
Ejea de los Caballeros	60	J2
Ejido Insurgentes	124	D6
Ejin Horo Qi	80	D3
Ejin Qi	80	C2
Ejmiadzin	92	L3
Ekalaka	126	F1
Ekenäs	48	M7
Eketahuna	116	E5
Ekibastuz	76	P7
Ekimchan	78	N6
Ekonda	76	V4
Eksjo	48	H8
Ekwan	122	Q6
El Aaiún	102	C3
Elafonisos	68	E8
El 'Alamein	100	E1
El Amria	60	J9
El 'Arîsh	94	A5
Elat	94	B7
Elazığ	92	H4
El Azraq	94	D5
Elba	64	E6
El Banco	140	C2
Elbasan	68	C3
El Baúl	140	D2
Elbe	52	F3
Elbeuf	54	D5
Elbistan	92	G4
Elblag	50	J3
El Borj	60	E9
Elbow	124	E1
Elbrus	92	K2
El Burgo de Ebro	60	K3
El Burgo de Osma	60	G3
El Cajon	132	C2
El Callao	140	E2
El Campo	130	B4
El Centro	132	C2
El Cerro	140	E7
Elch	60	K6
Elda	60	K6
El'dikan	78	P4
Eldorado	142	L4
El Dorado, Mexico	124	E7
El Dorado, Ark., US	130	C3
El Dorado, Kans., US	130	B2
El Dorado, Venezuela	140	E2
Eldoret	106	F3
Elefsína	68	F6
Elektrénai	50	P3
El Encanto	140	C4
Elephant Butte Reservoir	132	E2

Eleuthera 124 L6
El Fahs 64 D12
El Faiyûm 100 F2
El Fasher 100 E5
El Geneina 100 D5
Elgin, *UK* 56 J4
Elgin, *Ill., US* 128 C2
Elgin, *N.D., US* 126 F1
El'ginskiy 78 Q4
El Gîza 100 F1
El Goléa 102 F2
El Homr 102 F3
El Iskandarîya 100 E1
Elista 70 H5
Elizabeth 128 F2
Elizabeth City 130 F2
Elizabethton 130 E2
El Jadida 102 D2
El Jafr 94 D6
El Jafr 94 D6
Ełk 50 M4
Ełk 50 M4
El Kala 64 C12
Elk City 132 G1
El Kef 64 C12
El Kelaâ des Srarhna 102 D2
El Khandaq 100 F4
El Khârga 100 F2
Elkhart, *Ind., US* 128 C2
Elkhart, *Kans., US* 130 A2
El Khartum 100 F4
El Khartum Bahri 100 F4
Elkhorn 126 G2
Elkhorn 128 C2
Elkhovo 68 J2
Elkins 128 E3
Elko, *Canada* 126 C1
Elko, *US* 126 C2
Elk River 128 B1
El Kuntilla 94 B7
Ellendale 124 G2
Ellensburg 126 B1
Ellesmere Island 120 K1
Ellice Islands 112 H6
Elliot 108 D6
Ellis 122 J8
Ellisras 108 D4
Elliston 114 F6
Ellsworth 128 G2
Ellwangen 62 F2
Elmadağ 68 R5
Elmali 68 M8
El Mansûra 100 F1
El Mazâr 94 A5
El Minya 100 F2
Elmira 128 E2
Elmshorn 52 E3
El Muglad 100 E5
El Nido 84 F4
El Obeid 100 F5
El Odaiya 100 E5
El Oued 102 G2
El Paso 132 E2
El Portal 132 C1
El Potosi 132 F4
El Prat de Llobregat 60 N3
El Puerto de Santa Maria 60 D8
El Qâhira 100 F1
El Qasr 100 E2
El Quseima 94 B6
El Quweira 94 C7
El Reno 130 B2
El Sahuaro 132 D2
El Salvador 134 F6
Elster 52 H5
Elsterwerda 52 J5
El Sueco 132 E3
El Suweis 100 F2
Eltanin Bay 144 (2)JJ2
El Tarf 64 C12
El Thamad 94 B7
El Tigre 140 E2
El Turbio 142 G9
Eluru 88 D5
Elvas 60 C6
Elverum 48 F6
Elvira 140 C5
El Wak 106 G3
Ely, *UK* 56 N9
Ely, *US* 126 D3
Emajõgi 48 P7
Emāmrūd 90 F2
Emba 70 L5
Emba 70 L5
Embalse de Alarcon 60 H5
Embalse de Alcántara Uno 60 D5
Embalse de Almendra 60 D3
Embalse de Contreras 60 J5
Embalse de Gabriel y Galán 60 D4
Embalse de Garcia Sola 60 E5
Embalse de Guadalhorce 60 F8
Embalse de Guadalmena 60 G6
Embalse de Guri 140 E2
Embalse de la Serena 60 E6
Embalse de la Sotonera 60 K2
Embalse del Bembézar 60 E6
Embalse del Ebro 60 G1
Embalse del Rio Negro 138 F7
Embalse de Negratín 60 G7
Embalse de Ricobayo 60 E3
Embalse de Santa Teresa 60 E4
Embalse de Yesa 60 J2
Embalse Toekomstig 140 F3
Embarcación 142 J3
Emden 52 C3
Emerald 114 J4
Emi Koussi 100 C4
Emin 76 Q8
Emirdağ 68 P5
Emmeloord 54 H2
Emmen 54 J2
Emmendingen 62 C2
Emmerich 54 J3
Emory Peak 132 F3
Empalme 132 D3
Empangeni 108 E5
Empoli 62 F7
Emporia 130 B2
Empty Quarter = Rub' al Khālī 90 E6
Ems 54 J1
Ems-Jade-Kanal 52 C3
Enafors 70 B2
Encarnación 142 K4
Encs 66 J1
Ende 87 B4
Enderby Island 116 (2)B1
Energetik 70 L4
Enewetak 112 F4
Enez 68 J4
Enfida 64 E12
Enfield 54 B3
Engel's 70 J4
Enggano 86 C4
Enghien 54 G4
England 56 L9
English Channel 56 J12
Engozero 48 S4
'En Hazeva 94 C6
Enid 130 B2
Enkhuizen 54 H2
Enköping 48 J7
Enna 64 J11
En Nahud 100 E5
Enngonia 114 J5
Ennis, *Ireland* 56 D9
Ennis, *US* 126 D1
Enniscorthy 56 F9
Enniskillen 56 E7
Enn Nâqoûra 94 C3
Enns 62 K2
Enns 62 K3
Enschede 54 J2
Ensenada 132 C2
Enshi 80 D4
Entebbe 106 E3
Enterprise 126 C1
Entrevaux 62 B7
Entroncamento 60 B5
Enugu 104 F3
Enurmino 78 Z3
Envira 140 C5
Enz 62 D2
Enza 62 F6
Epanomi 68 E4
Epéna 106 B3
Épernay 58 J4
Épinal 62 B2
Episkopi 68 Q10
Epsom 54 B3
Eqlīd 95 E1
Equatorial Guinea 104 F4
Erbach 52 D7
Erçek 92 K4
Erciş 92 K4
Ercolano 64 J8
Érd 66 F2
Erdek 68 K4
Erdemli 68 S8
Erdenet 78 G7
Erding 62 G2
Erechim 142 L4
Ereğli, *Turkey* 92 D3
Ereğli, *Turkey* 92 F5
Ereikoussa 68 B5
Erenhot 80 E2
Erfurt 52 G6
Ergani 92 H4
Erg Chech 102 D4
Erg du Ténéré 102 H5
Ergel 80 D2
Erg Iguidi 102 D3
Er Hai 80 C5
Erie 128 D2
Erimo 82 M2
Erimo-misaki 82 M3
Eriskay 56 E4
Eritrea 100 G4
Erlangen 52 G7
Ermenek 92 E5
Ermoupoli 68 G7
Erode 88 C6
Er Rachidia 102 E2
Er Rahad 100 F5
Er Renk 106 E1
Errol 128 F2
Er Ruseifa 94 D4
Ersekë 68 C4
Erskine 128 A1
Ertai 76 S8
Ertix 76 R8
Erzgebirge 52 H6
Erzin 76 S7
Erzincan 92 H4
Erzurum 92 J4
Esan-misaki 82 L3
Esashi, *Japan* 82 L3
Esashi, *Japan* 82 M1
Esbjerg 48 E9
Escanaba 128 C1
Escárcega 134 F5
Esch 54 J5
Eschwege 52 F5
Eschweiler 54 J4
Escondido 132 C2
Eséka 104 G4
Eşfahān 90 F3
Eskifjöður 48 (1)G2
Eskilstuna 48 J7
Eskimo Lakes 132 (1)L2
Eskişehir 92 D4
Esla 60 E3
Eslāmābād e Gharb 92 M6
Eslamshahr 90 F2
Esler Dağ 68 M7
Eslö 50 C2
Esmeraldas 140 B3
Esneux 54 H4
Espalion 58 H9
Espanola, *Canada* 128 D1
Espanola, *US* 126 E3
Espelkamp 52 D4
Esperance 114 D6
Esperance Bay 114 D6
Esperanza 140 C5
Espinho 60 B4
Espírito Santo 140 J7
Espíritu Santo 112 G7
Esplanada 140 K6
Espoo 48 N6
Espungebera 108 E4
Es Samrā 94 D4
Essaouira 102 D2
Es Semara 102 C3
Essen, *Belgium* 54 G3
Essen, *Germany* 54 K3
Essequibo 140 F2
Esslingen 62 E2
Eşṭahbānāt 95 F2
Este 62 G5
Estella 60 H2
Estepona 60 E8
Esteros 142 J3
Estevan 124 F2
Estonia 48 M7
Estoril 60 A6
Estrecho de Le Maire 142 H10
Estrecho de Magallanes 142 G9
Estrela 60 C4
Estremoz 60 C6
Estuário do Rio Amazonaz 140 H3
Esztergom 66 F2
Étain 54 H5
Étampes 58 H5
Étang de Berre 58 L10
Étaples 54 D4
Etawah 88 C3
Ethiopia 98 G5
Etolin Strait 132 (1)D3
Etosha Pan 108 B3
Étretat 54 C5
Ettelbruck 54 B7
Ettlingen 52 D8
Eucla 114 E6
Euclid 128 D2
Eufala 130 D3
Eufaula Lake 130 B2
Eugene 126 B2
Eupen 52 B6
Euphrates = Firat 92 H4
Eure 54 D6
Eureka, *Calif., US* 126 B2
Eureka, *Mont., US* 126 C1
Eureka, *Nev., US* 132 C1
Eureka, *Ut., US* 126 D3
Europoort 54 F3
Euskirchen 52 B6
Eutin 52 F2
Eutsuk Lake 122 F6
Evans Strait 122 Q4
Evanston, *Ill., US* 128 C2
Evanston, *Wyo., US* 126 D2
Evansville 130 D2
Evaz 95 F3
Everett 126 B1
Everglades City 130 E4
Evergreen 130 D3
Evesham 54 A2
Évora 60 C6
Évreux 54 D5
Evron 58 E5
Evros 68 J3
Evvoia 68 F6
Ewo 104 G5
Exaltación 140 D6
Exe 56 J11
Exeter 56 J11
Exmouth, *Australia* 114 B4
Exmouth, *UK* 56 J11
Exuma Sound 124 L7
Eyl 106 H2
Eyre Peninsula 114 G2
Ezine 68 J5

F

Faadippolu Atoll 88 B8
Fåborg 52 F1
Fabriano 62 H7
Fachi 102 H5
Fada 100 D4
Fada Ngourma 104 E2
Faenza 62 G6
Færingehavn = Kangerluarsoruseq 122 W4
Faeroes 46 D1
Fafanlap 87 D3
Făgăraş 66 M4
Fagernes 48 E6
Fagersta 48 H6
Făget 66 K4
Fagurhólsmýri 48 (1)E3
Fahraj 95 H2
Faial 102 (1)B2
Fairbanks 132 (1)H3
Fair Isle 56 L2
Fairlie 116 C7
Fairmont 128 B2
Faisalabad 88 B2
Faith 126 F1
Faizabad 88 D3
Fakfak 87 D3
Fakse 52 H1
Fakse Bugt 48 G9
Faku 80 G2
Falaise 54 B6
Falaise de Tiguidit 102 G5
Falconara Marittima 62 J7
Falcon Lake 130 B4
Fălești 66 Q2
Falfurrias 130 B4
Falkenberg 48 G8
Falkensee 52 J4
Falkland Islands 142 K9
Falkland Sound 142 J9
Falköping 48 G7
Fallingbostel 52 E4
Fallon 126 C3
Fall River 128 F2
Falls City 124 G3
Falmouth, *UK* 56 G11
Falmouth, *US* 128 F2
Falster 52 H2
Fălticeni 66 P2
Falun 48 H6
Famagusta = Ammochostos 94 A1
Fanchang 80 F4
Fandriana 108 H4
Fangzheng 80 H1
Fannūj 90 G4
Fanø 52 D1
Fano 62 J7
Fanø Bugt 52 D1
Faradje 106 D3
Farafangana 108 H4
Farāh 90 H3
Farah Rud 90 H3
Faranah 104 B2
Fareham 54 A4
Farewell Spit 116 D5
Fargo 124 G2
Faribault 128 B2
Faridabad 88 C3
Farihy Alaotra 108 H3
Färjestaden 50 F1
Farmington, *Me., US* 128 F2
Farmington, *N. Mex., US* 132 E1
Farnborough 54 B3
Farne Islands 56 L6
Fårö 48 K8
Faro, *Brazil* 140 F4
Faro, *Portugal* 60 C7
Fårösund 48 K8
Farquhar Group 108 (2)B3
Farrāshband 95 E2
Farson 126 E2
Fasā 95 E2
Fasano 64 M8
Fategarh 88 C3
Fatehpur 88 D3
Făurei 66 Q4
Fauske 48 H3
Fauville-en-Caux 54 C5
Favara 64 H11
Faversham 54 C3
Favignana 64 G11
Faxaflói 48 (1)B2
Faya 100 C4
Fayette 130 D3
Fayetteville, *Ark., US* 130 C2
Fayetteville, *N.C., US* 128 E3
Fayetteville, *Tenn., US* 130 D2
Faylakah 95 C2
Fažana 64 H4
Fdérik 102 C4
Featherston 116 E5
Fécamp 54 C5
Federated States of Micronesia 112 E5
Fedorovka 70 M4
Fehmarn 52 G2
Feijó 140 C5
Feilding 116 E5
Feira de Santana 140 K6
Feistritz 62 L3
Fejø 52 G2
Feldbach 62 L4
Feldkirch 62 E3
Feldkirchen 62 K4
Felidu Atoll 88 B8
Felixstowe 54 D3
Feltre 62 G4
Femø 52 G2
Femund 48 F5
Fengcheng 82 C3
Fenghua 80 G5
Fengning 80 F2
Feng Xian 80 D4
Feni 88 F4
Fenyang 80 E3
Feodosiya 92 F1
Feres 68 J4
Fergana 90 K1
Fergus Falls 124 G2
Ferkessédougou 104 C3
Ferlach 62 K4
Fermo 64 H5
Fernandina Beach 130 E3
Fernandópolis 142 L3
Ferrara 62 G6
Ferreira do Alentejo 60 B7
Ferrol 60 B1
Ferry Lake 130 C2
Fès 102 E2
Festus 128 B3
Fetești 66 Q5
Fethiye 68 M8
Fetisovo 90 F1
Fetlar 56 M1
Feucht 52 G7
Feuchtwangen 52 F7
Feyzābād 90 K2
Fianarantsoa 108 H4
Fianga 106 B2
Fichē 106 F2
Fidenza 62 F6
Fieni 66 N4
Fier 68 B4

Gbaaka	**104**	C3
Gbarnga	**104**	C3
Gdańsk	**50**	H3
Gdov	**48**	P7
Gdyel	**60**	K9
Gdynia	**50**	H3
Gebel el Tîh	**94**	A7
Gebel Halâl	**94**	A6
Gebel Katherina	**100**	F2
Gebel Yi'allaq	**94**	A6
Gebze	**68**	M4
Gedaref	**100**	G5
Gediz	**68**	K6
Gediz	**68**	M6
Gedser	**52**	G2
Geel	**54**	H3
Geelong	**114**	H7
Geesthacht	**52**	F3
Gê'gvai	**88**	D2
Geidam	**104**	G2
Geilenkirchen	**54**	J4
Geilo	**48**	E6
Geinhausen	**52**	E6
Geislingen	**62**	E2
Geita	**106**	E4
Gejiu	**84**	C2
Gela	**64**	J11
Geladī	**106**	H2
Geldern	**54**	J3
Geleen	**54**	H4
Gelendzhik	**92**	H1
Gelibolu	**68**	J4
Gelibolu Yarimadasi	**68**	J4
Gelsenkirchen	**54**	K3
Gembloux	**54**	G4
Gembu	**104**	G3
Gemena	**106**	B3
Gemlik	**68**	M4
Gemlik Körfezi	**68**	L4
Gemona del Friuli	**62**	J4
Genalē Wenz	**106**	G2
General Acha	**142**	J6
General Alvear	**142**	H6
General Pico	**142**	J6
General Pinedo	**142**	J4
General Roca	**142**	H6
General Santos	**84**	H5
Geneva	**128**	E2
Genève	**62**	B4
Gengma	**84**	B2
Genil	**60**	F7
Genk	**54**	H4
Genoa = Genova	**62**	D6
Genova	**62**	D6
Gent	**54**	F3
Genteng	**86**	D4
Genthin	**52**	H4
Geographe Bay	**114**	B6
George	**108**	C6
George	**122**	T5
George Town, *Australia*	**114**	J8
George Town, *Malaysia*	**86**	C1
George Town, *US*	**130**	F5
Georgetown, *Australia*	**114**	H3
Georgetown, *Gambia*	**104**	B2
Georgetown, *Guyana*	**140**	F2
Georgetown, *Ky., US*	**130**	E2
Georgetown, *S.C., US*	**130**	F3
Georgetown, *Tex., US*	**130**	B3
George West	**130**	B4
Georgia	**92**	K2
Georgia	**130**	E3
Georgian Bay	**128**	D1
Gera	**52**	H6
Geraldine	**116**	C7
Geraldton, *Australia*	**114**	B5
Geraldton, *Canada*	**124**	J2
Gérardmer	**62**	B2
Gerāsh	**95**	F3
Gerede	**92**	E3
Gerefsried	**62**	G3
Gereshk	**90**	H3
Gérgal	**60**	H7
Gerik	**84**	C5
Gerlach	**126**	C2
Germantown	**128**	C3
Germany	**52**	E6
Germencik	**68**	K7
Germering	**62**	G2
Germersheim	**54**	L5
Gernika	**60**	H1
Gerolzhofen	**52**	F7
Gêrzê	**88**	D2
Geser	**87**	D3
Getafe	**60**	G4
Gettysburg	**126**	F2
Getxo	**60**	H1
Geugnon	**58**	K7
Gevaş	**92**	K4
Gevgelija	**68**	E3
Gewanē	**100**	H5
Geyik Dağ	**68**	Q8
Geyser	**126**	D1
Geyve	**68**	N4
Ghabāghib	**94**	D3
Ghadāmis	**102**	G2
Ghadīr Minqār	**94**	E3
Ghana	**104**	D3
Ghanzi	**108**	C4
Gharandal	**94**	C6
Ghardaïa	**102**	F2
Gharo	**90**	J5
Gharyān	**102**	H2
Ghāt	**100**	B2
Ghazaouet	**102**	E1
Ghaziabad	**88**	C3
Ghazipur	**88**	D3
Ghazn	**90**	J3
Gheorgheni	**66**	N3
Gherla	**66**	L2
Ghizar	**88**	B1
Ghotāru	**88**	B3
Ghōwrī	**95**	F2
Ghunthur	**94**	E2
Giannitsa	**68**	E4
Giannutri	**64**	F6
Giarre	**64**	K11
Gibraleón	**60**	D7
Gibraltar	**60**	E8
Gibson Desert	**114**	D4
Gideån	**48**	K5
Gien	**58**	H6
Gießen	**52**	D6
Gifhorn	**52**	F4
Gifu	**82**	J6
Gigha	**56**	G6
Giglio	**64**	E6
Giglio Castello	**64**	E6
Gijón	**60**	E1
Gila	**132**	E2
Gila Bend	**132**	D2
Gilan Garb	**92**	L6
Gilău	**66**	L3
Gilazi	**92**	N3
Gilbert Islands	**112**	H5
Gilbués	**140**	H5
Gilching	**62**	G2
Gilf Kebir Plateau	**100**	E3
Gilgandra	**114**	J6
Gilgit	**88**	B1
Gilgit	**90**	K2
Gilimanuk	**86**	E4
Gillam	**122**	N5
Gillette	**126**	E2
Gillingham	**54**	C3
Gills Rock	**128**	C1
Gilroy	**126**	B3
Gīmbī	**106**	F2
Gimli	**122**	M6
Gimol'skoe Ozero	**48**	R5
Gīnīr	**106**	G2
Gioia del Colle	**64**	L8
Gioia Tauro	**64**	K10
Gioura	**68**	F5
Giresun	**92**	H3
Girga	**100**	F2
Girona	**60**	N3
Gironde	**58**	E8
Girvan	**56**	H6
Gisborne	**116**	G4
Gisenyi	**106**	D4
Gitega	**106**	D4
Giurgiu	**66**	N6
Givet	**54**	G4
Givors	**58**	K8
Giyon	**106**	F2
Gizhiga	**78**	U4
Gizhiginskaya Guba	**78**	T4
Giżycko	**50**	L3
Gjiri i Vlorës	**68**	B4
Gjirokaster	**68**	C4
Gjoa Haven	**122**	M3
Gjøvik	**48**	F6
Glacier Peak	**126**	B1
Gladstone	**114**	K4
Glamoč	**66**	D5
Glan	**52**	C7
Glan	**87**	C1
Glarner Alpen	**62**	D4
Glasgow, *UK*	**56**	H6
Glasgow, *Ky., US*	**128**	C3
Glasgow, *Mont., US*	**126**	E1
Glauchau	**52**	H6
Glazov	**76**	J6
Gleisdorf	**62**	L3
Glendale, *Ariz., US*	**132**	D2
Glendale, *Calif., US*	**132**	C2
Glendambo	**114**	G6
Glendive	**126**	F1
Glenmorgan	**114**	J5
Glennallen	**132**	(1)H3
Glenn Innes	**114**	K5
Glenrothes	**56**	J5
Glens Falls	**128**	F2
Glenwood, *Ark., US*	**128**	B4
Glenwood, *Minn., US*	**128**	A1
Glenwood, *N. Mex., US*	**132**	E2
Glenwood Springs	**126**	E3
Glidden	**128**	B1
Glina	**62**	M5
Gliwice	**50**	H7
Glodeni	**66**	Q2
Głogów	**50**	F6
Glomfjord	**48**	H3
Glomma	**48**	F5
Glorieuses	**98**	H7
Gloucester, *UK*	**56**	K10
Gloucester, *US*	**128**	F2
Głowno	**50**	J6
Głuchołazy	**50**	G7
Glückstadt	**52**	E3
Gmünd, *Austria*	**62**	J4
Gmünd, *Austria*	**62**	L2
Gmunden	**62**	J3
Gniezno	**50**	G5
Gnjilane	**68**	D2
Gnoien	**52**	H3
Goalpara	**88**	F3
Goba	**106**	F2
Gobabis	**108**	B4
Gobernador Gregores	**142**	G8
Gobi Desert	**80**	C2
Gobo	**82**	H7
Gobustan	**90**	E1
Goch	**54**	J3
Gochas	**108**	B4
Godbout	**128**	G1
Godé	**106**	G2
Goderich	**128**	D2
Godhra	**88**	B4
Gödöllő	**66**	G2
Gods Lake	**122**	N6
Godthåb = Nuuk	**122**	W4
Goeree	**54**	F3
Goes	**54**	F3
Gogama	**128**	D1
Goiânia	**140**	H7
Goiás	**140**	G6
Goiás	**140**	G7
Gökçeada	**68**	H4
Gökova Körfezi	**68**	K8
Göksun	**92**	G5
Golaghat	**88**	F3
Golan Heights	**94**	C3
Golbāf	**95**	G2
Gölbasi	**92**	G5
Gol'chikha	**76**	Q3
Gölcük	**68**	K5
Gołdap	**50**	M3
Gold Coast	**114**	K5
Golden Bay	**116**	D5
Goldendale	**126**	B1
Golden Gate	**132**	B1
Goldfield	**126**	C3
Goldsboro	**128**	E3
Göle	**92**	K3
Goleniów	**50**	D4
Golestānak	**95**	F1
Golfe d'Ajaccio	**64**	C7
Golfe de Gabès	**102**	H2
Golfe de Hammamet	**102**	H1
Golfe de Porto	**64**	C6
Golfe de Sagone	**64**	C6
Golfe de Saint-Malo	**58**	C5
Golfe de Tunis	**64**	E11
Golfe de Valinco	**64**	C7
Golfe du Lion	**58**	J10
Golfo de Almería	**60**	H8
Golfo de Batabanó	**134**	H4
Golfo de Cádiz	**60**	C7
Golfo de California	**134**	B3
Golfo de Chiriquí	**134**	H7
Golfo de Corcovado	**142**	F7
Golfo de Cupica	**140**	B2
Golfo de Fonseca	**134**	G6
Golfo de Guayaquil	**140**	A4
Golfo de Honduras	**134**	G5
Golfo del Darién	**140**	B2
Golfo dell' Asinara	**64**	C7
Golfo de los Mosquitos	**140**	A2
Golfo de Mazarrón	**60**	J7
Golfo de Morrosquillo	**140**	B1
Golfo de Panamá	**134**	J7
Golfo de Penas	**142**	F8
Golfo de San Jorge	**142**	H8
Golfo de Santa Clara	**132**	D2
Golfo de Tehuantepec	**134**	E5
Golfo de València	**60**	L5
Golfo de Venezuela	**140**	C1
Golfo di Augusta	**64**	K11
Golfo di Catania	**64**	K11
Golfo di Gaeta	**64**	H7
Golfo di Gela	**64**	J11
Golfo di Genova	**64**	C4
Golfo di Manfredonia	**64**	L7
Golfo di Olbia	**64**	D8
Golfo di Oristano	**64**	C9
Golfo di Orosei	**64**	D8
Golfo di Palmas	**64**	C10
Golfo di Policastro	**64**	K9
Golfo di Salerno	**64**	J8
Golfo di Santa Eufemia	**64**	K10
Golfo di Squillace	**64**	L10
Golfo di Taranto	**64**	L8
Golfo di Trieste	**62**	J5
Golfo di Venezia	**62**	H5
Golfo San Matías	**142**	J6
Gölhisar	**68**	M8
Golin Baixing	**82**	A1
Gölköy	**92**	G3
Gölmarmara	**68**	K6
Golyshmanovo	**76**	M6
Goma	**106**	D4
Gombe	**104**	G2
Gombi	**104**	G2
Gomera	**102**	B3
Gómez Palacio	**132**	F3
Gonam	**78**	M5
Gonbad-e Kavus	**90**	G2
Gonda	**88**	D3
Gonder	**100**	G5
Gondia	**88**	D4
Gondomar	**60**	B3
Gönen	**68**	K4
Gonfreville-Orcher	**54**	C5
Gongga Shan	**80**	C5
Gonghe	**80**	C3
Gongliu	**76**	Q9
Gongpoquan	**80**	B2
Gongshan	**84**	B1
Gonzáles	**124**	G7
Gonzales	**130**	B4
González	**132**	G4
Goodland	**126**	F3
Goolgowi	**114**	J6
Goomalling	**114**	C6
Goondiwindi	**114**	K5
Goose Lake	**126**	B2
Göppingen	**62**	E2
Góra	**50**	F6
Gora Bazardyuzi	**92**	M3
Gora Kamen	**76**	S4
Gorakhpur	**88**	D3
Gora Ledyanaya	**78**	W4
Gora Pobeda	**78**	R4
Gora Yenashimskiy Polkan	**76**	S6
Goražde	**66**	F6
Gorbitsa	**78**	K6
Goré	**104**	H3
Gorē	**106**	F2
Gore	**116**	B8
Gorgān	**90**	F2
Gorgona	**62**	E7
Gori	**92**	L2
Gorinchem	**54**	H3
Goris	**92**	M4
Gorizia	**62**	J5
Gorki	**70**	N1
Gorlice	**50**	L8
Görlitz	**50**	D6
Gorna Oryakhovitsa	**66**	N6
Gornji Milanovac	**66**	H5
Gorno-Altaysk	**76**	R7
Gorno Oryakhovitsa	**68**	H1
Gorodets	**70**	H3
Gorontalo	**87**	B2
Goryachiy Klyuch	**92**	H1
Gory Belukha	**76**	R8
Gory Ulutau	**70**	N5
Gorzów Wielkopolski	**50**	E5
Goslar	**52**	F5
Gospić	**64**	K4
Gosport	**58**	D3
Gossau	**62**	E3
Gossi	**104**	D1
Gostivar	**68**	C3
Gostyń	**50**	G6
Gostynin	**50**	J5
Göteborg	**48**	F8
Gotha	**52**	F6
Gothèye	**104**	E2
Gotland	**48**	K8
Gotō-rettō	**82**	E7
Gotse Delchev	**68**	F3
Gotska Sandön	**48**	K7
Göttingen	**52**	E5
Gouda	**54**	G2
Gough Island	**98**	B10
Goundam	**102**	E5
Gouraya	**60**	M8
Gourcy	**104**	D2
Gourdon	**58**	G9
Gournay-en-Bray	**54**	D5
Governador Valadares	**140**	J7
Governor's Harbour	**130**	F4
Govorovo	**78**	M3
Gowārān	**90**	J4
Goya	**142**	K4
Gozha Co	**88**	D1
Gozo = Gwardex	**64**	J12
Graaff-Reinet	**108**	C6
Grabovica	**66**	K5
Gračac	**62**	L6
Gračanica	**66**	F5
Gradačac	**66**	F5
Gräfenhainichen	**52**	H5
Grafton, *Australia*	**114**	K5
Grafton, *US*	**126**	G1
Graham Island	**132**	(1)L5
Grajaú	**140**	H5
Grajewo	**50**	M4
Gram	**52**	E1
Gramat	**58**	G9
Grampian Mountains	**56**	H5
Granada, *Nicaragua*	**134**	G6
Granada, *Spain*	**60**	G7
Granby	**128**	F1
Gran Canaria	**102**	B3
Grand Bahama	**130**	F4
Grand Ballon	**58**	N6
Grand Bank	**122**	V7
Grand Canyon	**126**	D3
Grande, *Bolivia*	**140**	E7
Grande, *Brazil*	**140**	J6
Grande Cache	**122**	H6
Grande Prairie	**122**	H5
Grand Erg de Bilma	**102**	H5
Grand Erg Occidental	**102**	E3
Grand Erg Oriental	**102**	F3
Grand Falls, *N.B., Canada*	**128**	G1
Grand Falls, *Nfld., Canada*	**122**	V7
Grand Forks, *Canada*	**124**	C2
Grand Forks, *US*	**126**	G1
Grand Haven	**128**	C2
Grand Island	**126**	G2
Grand Junction	**126**	E3
Grand Marais, *Mich., US*	**128**	C1
Grand Marais, *Minn., US*	**128**	B1
Grand-Mère	**128**	F1
Grândola	**60**	B6
Grand Portage	**128**	C1
Grand Rapids, *Canada*	**122**	M6
Grand Rapids, *Mich., US*	**128**	C2
Grand Rapids, *Minn., US*	**128**	B1
Grand Teton	**126**	D2
Grangeville	**126**	C1
Granite Falls	**128**	A2
Granollers	**60**	N3
Gran Paradiso	**62**	C5
Grantham	**56**	M9
Grants	**132**	E1
Grants Pass	**126**	B2
Granville	**58**	D5
Granville Lake	**122**	M5
Gräsö	**48**	K6
Grasse	**62**	B7
Grassrange	**126**	E1
Grass Valley	**126**	B3
Graulhet	**58**	G10
Graus	**60**	L2
Gravelines	**54**	E3
Gravenhurst	**128**	E2
Gravesend	**54**	C3
Gravina in Puglia	**64**	L8
Gray	**58**	L6
Grayling	**128**	D2
Grays	**54**	C3
Grays Lake	**126**	D2
Grayville	**128**	C3
Graz	**62**	L3
Great Abaco	**130**	F4
Great Artesian Basin	**114**	H4
Great Australian Bight	**114**	E6
Great Bahama Bank	**134**	J4
Great Barrier Island	**116**	E3
Great Barrier Reef	**114**	J2
Great Basin	**126**	C3
Great Bear Lake	**132**	(1)M2

Harrison Bay 132 (1)G1
Harrisville 128 D2
Harrogate 56 L8
Har Saggi 94 B6
Harsin 92 M6
Hârşova 66 Q5
Harstad 48 J2
Hartberg 62 L3
Hartford 128 F2
Hartland Point 56 H10
Hartlepool 56 L7
Har Us Nuur 76 S8
Harvey 126 G1
Harwich 54 D3
Harz 52 F5
Hāsā 94 C6
Haselünne 52 C4
Hashtpar 92 N5
Hāsik 90 G6
Haskell 130 B3
Haslemere 54 B3
Hassan 88 C6
Hasselfelde 52 F5
Hasselt 54 H4
Haßfurt 52 F6
Hassi Bel Guebbour 102 G3
Hassi Messaoud 102 G2
Hässleholm 48 G8
Hastings, New Zealand 116 F4
Hastings, UK 54 C4
Hastings, Minn., US 128 B2
Hastings, Nebr., US 126 G2
Haţeg 66 K4
Hatgal 78 G6
Ha Tinh 84 D3
Hatteras 130 F2
Hattiesburg 130 D3
Hatvan 66 G2
Haud 100 H6
Haud Ogadēn 106 G2/H2
Haugesund 48 C7
Hauraki Gulf 116 E3
Haut Atlas 102 D2
Hauts Plateaux 102 E2
Havana 130 C1
Havana = La Habana 134 H4
Havant 56 M11
Havel 50 C5
Havelock, New Zealand 116 D5
Havelock, US 130 F3
Havelock North 116 F4
Havenby 52 D1
Haverfordwest 56 H10
Havlíčkův Brod 50 E8
Havre 126 E1
Havre-St-Pierre 122 U6
Havrylivtsi 66 P1
Havza 92 F3
Hawaii 132 (2)E2
Hawaii 132 (2)E4
Hawaiian Islands 112 J3
Hawera 116 E4
Hawi 132 (2)F3
Hawick 56 K6
Hawke Bay 116 F4
Hawker 114 G6
Hawr al'Awdah 95 B1
Hawr al Ḩammar 95 B1
Hawthorne 126 C3
Hay 114 H6
Hay 122 H5
Hayange 54 J5
Haydarābad 92 L5
Hayden 132 D2
Hayrabolu 68 K3
Hay River 122 H4
Hays 130 B2
Hazard 128 D3
Hazāribāg 88 E4
Hazebrouck 54 E4
Hazelton, Canada 122 F5
Hazelton, US 128 E2
Head of Bight 114 F6
Hearne 130 B3
Hearst 128 D1
Hebbronville 132 G3
Hebgen Lake 126 D2
Hebi 80 E3
Hebron, Canada 122 U5
Hebron, Israel 94 C5
Hebron, Nebr., US 126 G2
Hebron, N.D., US 126 F1
Hecate Strait 122 E6
Hechi 84 D2
Hechingen 62 D2
Hede 48 G5
Heerenveen 54 H2
Heerlen 54 J4
Ḩefa 94 B4
Hefei 80 F4
Hegang 80 J1
Hegura-jima 82 J5
Hegyfalu 62 M3
Heide 52 E2
Heidelberg 52 D7
Heidenheim 62 F2
Heilbad Heiligenstadt 52 F5
Heilbronn 52 E7
Heilgenhafen 52 F2
Heimaey 48 (1)C3
Heinola 48 N6
Hejing 76 R9
Hekla 48 (1)D3
Helagsfjället 48 G5
Helena, Ark., US 130 C3
Helena, Mont., US 126 D1
Helen Reef 87 D2
Helensville 116 E3
Helgea 50 D1
Helgoland 52 C2
Helgoländer Bucht 52 D2
Hellin 60 J6
Helmand 90 H3
Helmond 54 H3
Helmsdale 56 J3
Helmstedt 52 G4
Helodrano Antongila 108 H3
Helong 82 E2
Helsingborg 48 G8
Helsinge 50 B1
Helsingør 48 G8
Helsinki 48 N6
Helston 56 G11
Helwan 100 F2
Hemel Hempstead 56 M10
Henashi-zaki 82 K3
Hendek 68 N4
Henderson, Ky., US 128 C3
Henderson, Nev., US 126 D3
Henderson, N.C. US 130 F2
Henderson Island 112 P8
Hendersonville 128 C3
Hendijarn 95 C1
Hengelo 54 J2
Hengyang 80 E5
Henichesk 70 F5
Hénin-Beaumont 54 E4
Hennebont 58 B6
Hennigsdorf 52 J4
Henryetta 128 A3
Henzada 84 B3
Heppenheim 52 D7
Heppner 126 C1
Hepu 84 D2
Héradsflói 48 (1)F2
Herald Cays 114 J3
Herāt 90 H3
Herbert 116 C7
Herborn 52 D6
Herceg-Novi 66 F7
Hereford, UK 56 K9
Hereford, US 134 D2
Herekino 116 D2
Herentals 54 G3
Herford 52 D4
Herisau 62 E3
Herlen Gol 80 E1
Hermagor 62 J4
Herma Ness 56 M1
Hermel 94 D2
Hermiston 126 C1
Hermosillo 124 D6
Hernád 50 L9
Herne 52 C5
Herne Bay 54 D3
Herning 48 E8
Hérouville-St-Clair 54 B5
Herrenberg 62 D2
Hersbruck 52 G7
Herstat 54 H4
Hertlay 54 E6
Hervey Bay 114 K5
Herzberg 52 F5
Herzliyya 94 B4
Hesdin 54 E4
Heshan 84 D2
Hesselø 50 A1
Hessisch-Lichtenau 52 E5
Hettstedt Lutherstadt 52 G5
Heves 50 K10
He Xian 84 E2
Hexigten Qi 80 F2
Heze 80 F3
Hezuozhen 80 C3
Hialeah 130 E4
Hiawatha 130 B2
Hibbing 128 B1
Hickory 128 D3
Hidaka-sammyaku 82 M2
Hidalgo del Parral 134 C3
Hiddensee 52 H2
Hierro 102 B3
Higashi-suidō 82 E7
High Point 128 E3
High Wycombe 54 B3
Hiiumaa 48 M7
Hikurangi 116 E2
Hikurangi 116 G3
Hikutaia 116 E3
Hildburghausen 52 F6
Hildesheim 52 E4
Hillsboro, Oh., US 130 E2
Hillsboro, Oreg., US 126 B1
Hillsboro, Tex., US 132 G2
Hillsville 128 D3
Hillswick 56 L1
Hilo 132 (2)F4
Hilton Head Island 130 E3
Hilva 92 H5
Hilversum 54 H2
Himalayas 74 L6
Himarë 68 B4
Himatnagar 88 B4
Himeji 82 H6
Himi 82 J5
Himora 100 G5
Himş 94 D2
Hindu Kush 88 A1
Hindupur 88 C6
Hinesville 130 E3
Hingoli 88 C5
Hinnøya 48 H2
Hiroo 82 M2
Hirosaki 82 L3
Hiroshima 82 G6
Hirschaid 52 F7
Hirson 54 G5
Hirtshals 48 E8
Hisar 88 C3
Hischberg 52 G6
Hisdal 48 C6
Hispaniola 138 D2
Hisyah 94 D2
Hīt 92 K7
Hitachi 82 L5
Hitoyoshi 82 F7
Hitra 48 D5
Hiuchi-nada 82 G6
Hiva Oa 112 M6
Hjälmaren 48 H7
Hjalmar Lake 122 K4
Hjelmsøya 48 M1
Hlinsko 50 E8
Hlohovec 62 N2
Hlyboka 66 N1
Hlybokaye 70 E3
Ho 104 E3
Hobart, Australia 114 J8
Hobart, US 132 G1
Hobbs 132 F2
Hobro 48 E8
Hobyo 106 H3
Hô Chi Minh 84 D4
Höchstadt 52 F7
Hockenheim 52 D7
Hódmezővásárhely 66 H3
Hodonin 50 G9
Hoek van Holland 54 G3
Hoeryŏng 82 E2
Hoeyang 82 D4
Hof 52 G6
Hofgeismar 52 E5
Höfn 48 (1)F2
Hofsjökull 48 (1)D2
Hofsos 48 (1)D2
Hōfu 82 F6
Hohe 62 H3
Hohe Dachstein 50 C10
Hohe Tauern 64 G1
Hohhot 80 E2
Hoh Xil Shan 88 E1
Hôi An 84 D3
Hoima 106 E3
Hokitika 116 C6
Hokkaidō 82 N2
Holbæk 50 A2
Holbrook 132 D2
Holdrege 126 G2
Holguín 134 J4
Holič 62 N2
Hollabrunn 62 M2
Holland 128 C2
Hollis 132 G2
Hollywood 130 E4
Holman 122 H2
Hólmavik 48 (1)C2
Holmes Reefs 114 J3
Holstebro 48 E8
Holsteinische Schweiz 52 F2
Holsteinsborg = Sisimiut 122 W3
Holton 130 B2
Holyhead 56 H8
Holy Island, Eng., UK 56 L6
Holy Island, Wales, UK 56 H8
Holyoke 126 F2
Holzkirchen 62 G3
Holzminden 52 E5
Homa Bay 106 E4
Homberg 52 E5
Hombori 102 E5
Home Bay 122 T3
Homestead 130 E4
Homewood 130 D3
Homs = Himş 94 D2
Homyel' 70 F4
Hondo, N. Mex., US 132 E2
Hondo, Tex., US 132 G3
Honduras 134 G6
Hønefoss 48 F6
Honey Lake 126 B2
Honfleur 54 C5
Hon Gai 84 D2
Hong Kong 84 E2
Hongliuyuan 80 B2
Hongor 80 E1
Honiara 112 F6
Honjō 82 K4
Honokaa 132 (2)F3
Honolulu 132 (2)D2
Honshū 82 L5
Hooge 52 D2
Hoogeveen 54 J2
Hoogezand-Sappemeer 54 J1
Hooper Bay 132 (1)D3
Hoorn 54 H2
Hoorn Islands 112 H7
Hopa 92 J3
Hope, Canada 126 B1
Hope, Ak., US 122 B4
Hope, Ark., US 130 C3
Hopedale 122 U5
Hopetoun 114 H7
Hopin 88 G4
Hopkinsville 128 C3
Hoquiam 126 B1
Horadiz 92 M4
Horasan 92 K3
Horgo 78 F7
Horizon Depth 112 D8
Hormak 90 H4
Hormoz 95 F3
Horn 62 L2
Hornavan 48 J3
Horncastle 54 B1
Horodenka 66 N1
Horodok 50 N8
Horqin Youyi Qianqi 78 L7
Horsens 48 E9
Horsham, Australia 114 H7
Horsham, UK 54 B3
Horten 48 F7
Hortiguela 60 G2
Horton 132 (1)N2
Ḩoseynābād 95 G2
Hoshab 90 H4
Hoshangabad 88 C4
Hospet 88 C5
Hosséré Vokre 104 G3
Hotan 76 Q10
Hotan 76 Q10
Hot Springs, Ark., US 128 B4
Hot Springs, N.C., US 128 D3
Hottah Lake 122 H3
Houdan 54 D6
Houdelaincourt 62 A2
Houghton 128 C1
Houlton 128 G1
Houma, China 80 E3
Houma, US 124 H6
Houmt Souk 102 H2
Houston 124 G6
Hovd 76 S8
Hövsgöl Nuur 78 F6
Hövüün 80 C2
Howard Junction 116 D5
Howland 112 J5
Ḩowz-e Panj 95 G1
Hoxie 130 C2
Höxter 52 E5
Hoxud 76 R9
Hoy 56 J3
Høyanger 48 D6
Hoyerswerda 52 K5
Hradeç Králové 50 E7
Hranice 50 G8
Hrazdan 92 L3
Hrodna 50 N4
Hron 50 H9
Hrubieszów 50 N7
Hsin-chu 84 G2
Hsueh-Shan 84 G2
Hsweni 84 B2
Huacho 140 B6
Huade 80 E2
Huadian 82 D2
Huaibei 80 F4
Huaibin 80 F4
Huaihua 80 D5
Huainan 80 F4
Huaiyin 80 F4
Huaki 87 C4
Huallaga 140 B5
Huambo 108 B2
Huancayelica 140 B6
Huancayo 140 B6
Huang 80 F3
Huangchuan 80 F4
Huangshan 80 F5
Huangshi 80 F4
Huang Xian 80 G3
Huangyan, China 80 C3
Huangyan, China 80 G5
Huanren 82 C3
Huanuco 140 B5
Huaráz 140 B5
Huarmey 140 B6
Huasco 142 G4
Huashixia 80 B3
Huatabampo 124 E6
Hubli 88 C5
Huch'ang 82 D3
Huddersfield 56 L8
Huddinge 48 K7
Hudiksvall 48 J6
Hudson 128 F2
Hudson 128 F2
Hudson Bay 122 L6
Hudson Bay 122 P5
Hudson Strait 122 S4
Huê 84 D3
Huelva 60 D7
Huercal Overa 60 J7
Huesca 60 K2
Huéscar 60 H7
Huftaroy 48 C6
Hughenden 114 H4
Hugo 130 B3
Hugo Lake 130 B3
Huia 116 E3
Huich'ŏn 82 D3
Huila Plateau 108 A3
Huinan 82 C2
Huinca Renancó 142 J5
Huizhou 84 E2
Hulin 78 N7
Hull 128 E1
Hulst 54 G3
Hulun Nur 78 K7
Huma 78 M6
Huma 78 M6
Humaitá 140 E5
Humbe 108 A3
Humble 52 F2
Humboldt 122 L6
Humboldt 126 C2
Hūmedān 90 G4
Humenné 50 L9
Humphrey 126 D2
Humpolec 50 E8
Hūn 100 C2
Húnaflói 48 (1)C2
Hunchun 82 F2
Hunedoara 66 K4
Hünfeld 52 E6
Hungary 66 F3
Hungen 52 D6
Hungerford, Australia 114 H5
Hungerford, UK 54 A3
Hŭngnam 82 D4
Hunjiang 82 D3
Hunsrück 52 B7
Hunstanton 54 C2
Hunte 52 D4
Hunter Island 112 H8
Huntingburg 130 D2
Huntingdon, UK 54 B2
Huntingdon, US 130 E2
Huntington 130 D1

Name	Page	Grid
Izegern	54	F4
Izhevsk	70	K3
Izhma	70	K1
Izhma	70	K2
Izk	90	G5
Izkī	95	G5
Izmayil	66	R4
İzmir	92	B4
İzmir Körfezi	68	J6
İzmit	92	C3
İznik	92	C3
İznik Gölü	92	C3
Izola	62	J5
Izra'	94	D4
Izuhara	82	E6
Izumo	82	G6
Izu-shotō	82	K6

J

Name	Page	Grid
Jabal ad Durūz	94	D4
Jabal Akhḍar	95	G5
Jabal al Nuşayrīyah	94	D1
Jabal an Nabī Shu'ayb	100	H4
Jabal Ash Sham	95	G5
Jabal aẓ Ẓannah	95	E4
Jabalpur	88	C4
Jabal Shammar	100	G2
Jabal Thamar	100	J5
Jabiru	114	F2
Jablah	94	C1
Jablonec	50	E7
Jablunkov	50	H8
Jaboatão	140	K5
Jaca	60	K2
Jacareacanga	140	F5
Jackman	128	F1
Jacksboro	130	B3
Jackson, Calif., US	126	B3
Jackson, Minn., US	128	B2
Jackson, Miss., US	130	C3
Jackson, Oh., US	130	E2
Jackson, Tenn., US	130	D2
Jackson Head	116	B6
Jackson Lake	126	D2
Jacksonville, Fla., US	130	E3
Jacksonville, Ill., US	128	B3
Jacksonville, N.C., US	130	F3
Jacksonville, Tex., US	130	B3
Jacmel	134	K5
Jacobabad	88	A3
Jacobina	140	J6
Jacunda	140	H4
Jacupiranga	142	M3
Jade	52	D3
Jadebusen	52	D3
Jādū	102	H2
Jaén	60	G7
Jaen	140	B5
Jaffna	88	D7
Jagdalpur	88	D5
Jagersfontein	108	D5
Jaggang	88	C2
Jagst	52	E7
Jahrom	95	E2
Jaipur	88	C3
Jaisalmer	88	B3
Jajce	66	E5
Jakarta	86	D4
Jäkkvik	48	J3
Jakobshavn = Iiulissat	122	W3
Jakobstad	48	M5
Jalālābād	88	B2
Jalandhar	88	C2
Jalapa Enriquez	134	E5
Jalgaon	88	C4
Jalībah	95	B1
Jalingo	104	G3
Jalna	88	C5
Jalón	60	J3
Jalpaiguri	88	E3
Jālū	100	D2
Jalūlā	92	L6
Jamaica	134	H5
Jamalpur	88	E3
Jambi	86	C3
James	126	G2
James Bay	122	Q6
Jamestown, N.Y., US	128	E2
Jamestown, N.D., US	126	G1
Jammerbugten	48	E8
Jammu	88	B2
Jammu and Kashmir	88	C2
Jamnagar	88	B4
Jämsä	48	N6
Jamshedpur	88	E4
Janakpur	88	E3
Janaúba	140	J7
Jandaq	90	F3
Jandongi	106	C3
Jane Peak	116	B7
Janesville	128	C2
Jan Mayen	120	C2
Jannatabad	76	L10
Janos	132	E2
Jánossomorja	62	N3
Janów Lubelski	50	M7
Jantarnyj	50	J3
Januária	140	J7
Jaora	88	C4
Japan	82	L5
Japan Trench	112	E2
Japurá	140	D4
Jarābulus	92	H5
Jaramillo	142	H8
Jarash	94	C4
Jardim	142	K3
Jarosław	50	M7
Järpen	48	G5
Jarud Qi	80	G2
Järvenpää	48	N6
Jarvis	112	K6
Jasel'da	48	N10
Jäsk	95	G4
Jason Islands	142	J9
Jasper, Al., US	130	D3
Jasper, Fla., US	130	E3
Jasper, Tex., US	130	C3
Jastrebarsko	62	L5
Jászberény	66	G2
Jataí	140	G7
Jatapu	140	F4
Jaunpur	88	D3
Java = Jawa	86	E4
Javarthushuu	78	J4
Javoriv	50	N8
Jawa	86	E4
Jawhar	106	H3
Jayapura	87	F3
Jayrūd	94	D3
Jaza'ir Farasān	100	H4
Jazīrat Būbīyan	95	C2
Jazīrat-ye Khārk	95	D2
Jbail	94	C2
Jbel Ayachi	102	E2
Jbel Bou Naceur	102	E2
Jbel Toubkal	102	D2
Jean	126	C3
Jebba	104	E3
Jebel Bāqir	94	C7
Jebel el Atā'ita	94	C6
Jebel el Batrā	94	C7
Jebel-esh Sharqi	94	C3
Jebel Gimbala	100	D5
Jebel Ithrīyat	94	D6
Jebel Liban	94	C3
Jebel Mubrak	94	C6
Jebel Ram	94	C7
Jebel Uweinat	100	E3
Jedburgh	56	K6
Jedda = Jiddah	90	C5
Jedeida	64	D12
Jędrzejów	50	K7
Jefferson	128	B2
Jefferson City, Mo., US	128	B3
Jefferson City, Tenn., US	130	E2
Jeffersonville	128	C3
Jega	104	E2
Jēkabpils	48	N8
Jelgava	48	M8
Jemaja	86	D2
Jena	52	G6
Jendouba	102	G1
Jenin	94	C4
Jenkins	128	D3
Jequié	140	J6
Jequitinhonha	140	J7
Jerada	102	E2
Jeremoabo	140	K6
Jerez	132	F4
Jerez de la Frontera	60	D8
Jerez de los Caballeros	60	D6
Jericho, Australia	114	J4
Jericho, Israel	94	C5
Jerramungup	114	C6
Jersey	58	C4
Jersey City	130	G1
Jerusalem = Yerushalayim	94	C5
Jesenice	66	B3
Jesenik	50	G7
Jesi	62	J7
Jessore	88	E4
Jesup	130	E3
Jeumont	54	G4
Jever	52	C3
Jeypore	88	D5
Jezioro	50	K3
Jezioro Gardno	48	J9
Jezioro Jeziorsko	50	H6
Jezioro Łebsko	50	F3
Jezioro Śniardwy	50	L4
Jezioro Wigry	50	N2
Jezzine	94	C3
Jhang Maghiana	88	B2
Jhansi	88	C3
Jharsuguda	88	D4
Jhelum	88	B2
Jialing Jiang	80	D4
Jiamusi	80	J1
Ji'an	80	E5
Jiangle	80	F5
Jiangling	80	E4
Jiangmen	80	E6
Jiangyou	80	C4
Jianyang	80	F5
Jiaonan	80	F3
Jiaozuo	80	E3
Jiaxing	80	G4
Jiayuguan	80	B3
Jibou	66	L2
Jičín	50	E7
Jiddah	90	C5
Jiesjavrre	48	N2
Jiexiu	80	E3
Jihlava	50	E8
Jijia	66	Q2
Jijiga	106	G2
Jilib	106	G3
Jilin	82	D2
Jima	106	F2
Jimbolia	66	H4
Jiménez	132	F3
Jimsar	76	R9
Jinan	80	F3
Jinapo Hu	82	E2
Jinchang	80	C3
Jincheng	80	E3
Jindřichův Hradec	50	E8
Jingdezhen	80	F5
Jinggu	80	C6
Jinghe	76	Q9
Jinghong	80	C6
Jingmen	80	E4
Jingning	80	D3
Jingxi	80	D6
Jingyuan	80	C3
Jinhua	80	F5
Jining, China	80	E2
Jining, China	80	F3
Jinja	106	E3
Jinka	106	F2
Jinsha	80	C5
Jinshi	80	E5
Jinta	80	B2
Jinxi	80	G2
Jinzhou	80	G2
Jirgatol	90	K2
Jirin Gol	80	F2
Jirkov	52	J6
Jiroft	95	G2
Jirriiban	106	H2
Jishou	80	D5
Jisr ash Shughūr	92	G6
Jiu	66	L4
Jiujiang	80	F5
Jiwani	90	H4
Jixi	82	F1
Jīzān	100	H4
Jizera	50	D7
J. J. Castelli	140	D4
Joal-Fadiout	102	B6
João Pessoa	140	L5
Jódar	60	G7
Jodhpur	88	B3
Joensuu	70	E2
Jōetsu	82	K5
Jõgeva	48	P7
Johannesburg, South Africa	108	D5
Johannesburg, US	132	C1
John Day	126	C2
John o' Groats	56	J3
John Redmond Reservoir	130	B2
Johnson	130	A2
Johnson City	128	D3
Johnson's Crossing	132	(1)L3
Johnston Island	112	J4
Johnstown	128	E2
Johor Bahru	86	C2
Joigny	58	J5
Joinville, Brazil	142	M4
Joinville, France	58	L5
Jokkmokk	48	K3
Jökulsá á Fjöllum	48	(1)E1
Jolfa	92	L4
Joliet	124	J3
Joliette	128	F1
Jolo	87	B1
Jolo	87	B1
Jonava	50	P2
Jonesboro	128	B3
Jones Sound	122	P1
Jonesville	130	C3
Jonglei Canal	106	E2
Jongunjärvi	48	P4
Joniškis	50	N1
Jönköping	48	H8
Jonquière	128	F1
Joplin	130	C2
Jordan	126	E1
Jordan	126	E1
Jordan Valley	126	C2
Jorhat	88	F3
Jörn	48	L4
Jos	104	F3
José de San Martin	142	G7
Joseph Bonaparte Gulf	114	E2
Joûnié	94	C2
Joure	54	H2
Juan de Nova	108	G3
Juàzeiro	140	J5
Juàzeiro do Norte	140	K5
Juba	106	E3
Jubba	106	G3
Júcar	60	J5
Juchitán	134	F5
Judenburg	62	K3
Juhre	78	L8
Juist	52	B3
Juiz de Fora	142	N3
Julesburg	126	F2
Juli	140	C7
Juliaca	140	C7
Juliana Top	140	F3
Jülich	54	J4
Jullouville	54	A6
Jumilla	60	J6
Jumla	88	D3
Junagadh	88	B4
Junction	130	B3
Junction City	130	B2
Jundah	114	H4
Juneau	132	(1)L4
Jungfrau	62	C4
Junggar Pendi	76	R8
Junsele	48	J5
Jun Xian	80	E4
Jūra	50	M2
Jura	56	G5
Jura	62	B4
Jurbarkas	50	M2
Jurf ad Darāwīsh	94	C6
Jurhe	80	G2
Jurilovca	66	R5
Jūrmala	48	M8
Jūrmala	70	D3
Juruá	140	D4
Juruena	140	F5
Juruena	140	F6
Justo Daract	142	H5
Jutaí	140	D5
Jüterbog	52	J5
Juwain	90	H3
Ju Xian	80	F3
Jūymand	90	G3
Jūyom	95	F2
Juzur al Halaniyat	90	G6
Jylland	48	E8
Jyvädskylä	70	E2
Jyväskylä	48	N5

K

Name	Page	Grid
K2	88	C1
Kaakhka	90	G2
Kaamanen	48	P2
Kaaresuvanto	48	M2
Kaarta	102	C6
Kabaena	87	B4
Kabakly	90	H2
Kabala	104	B3
Kabale	106	E4
Kabalo	106	D5
Kabardino-Balkariya	92	K2
Kabompo	108	C2
Kabongo	106	D5
Kabugao	84	G3
Kābul	90	J3
Kabwe	108	D2
Kachikattsy	78	M4
Kachug	78	H6
Kadama	88	B6
Kadañ	50	C7
Kadinhanı	68	Q6
Kadirli	92	G5
Kadoka	126	F2
Kadoma	108	D3
Kadugli	100	E5
Kaduna	104	F2
Kadzherom	70	L2
Kaédi	102	C5
Kaeo	116	D2
Kaesŏng	82	D5
Kāf	94	E5
Kafanchan	104	F3
Kaffrine	104	A2
Kafiau	87	C3
Kåfjord	48	N1
Kafr Buhum	94	D1
Kafr el Sheikh	100	F1
Kafue	108	D3
Kaga	82	J5
Kaga Bandoro	106	B2
Kagoshima	82	F8
Kahemba	106	B5
Kahnūj	95	G3
Kahraman Maraş	92	G5
Kahta	92	H5
Kahurangi Point	116	C5
Kai Besar	87	D4
Kaifeng	80	E4
Kaihu	116	D2
Kaihua	80	F5
Kai Kecil	87	D4
Kaikohe	116	D2
Kaikoura	116	D6
Kaili	80	D5
Kailua	132	(2)D2
Kailua Kona	132	(2)E4
Kaimana	87	D3
Käina	48	M7
Kainji Reservoir	104	E2
Kaipara Harbour	116	D3
Kairouan	102	H1
Kaiserslautern	52	C7
Kaišiadorys	50	P3
Kaitaia	116	D2
Kaiwatu	87	C4
Kaiyuan	84	C4
Kajaani	48	P4
Kakamega	106	E3
Kakata	104	B3
Kakhovs'ke Vodoskhovyshche	70	F5
Kākī	95	D2
Kākināda	88	D5
Kaktovik	132	(1)J1
Kalabagh	88	B2
Kalabahi	87	B4
Kalabakan	86	F2
Kalach	70	H4
Kalachinsk	70	P3
Kalach-na-Donu	70	H5
Kaladar	128	E2
Ka Lae	132	(2)F5
Kalahari Desert	108	C4
Kalajoki	48	M4
Kalakan	78	K5
Kalam	88	B1
Kalamata	68	E7
Kalamazoo	128	C2
Kalampaka	68	D5
Kalana	104	C2
Kalaotoa	87	B4
Kalapana	132	(2)G4
Kalaupapa	132	(2)E2
Kalavryta	68	E6
Kalbarri	114	B5
Kale	68	L7
Kalecik	92	E3
Kaledupa	87	B4
Kalemie	106	D5
Kalemyo	84	F4
Kalevala	48	R4
Kalewa	84	F4
Kalgoorlie	114	D6
Kalianda	86	D4
Kalibo	84	G4
Kalima	106	D4
Kalimantan	86	E3
Kaliningrad	50	K3
Kaliningradskij Zaliv	50	J3
Kalispell	126	D1
Kalisz	50	H6
Kalixälven	48	M3

Name	Page	Grid
Kalkan	68	M8
Kalkarindji	114	F3
Kalkaska	128	C2
Kallavesi	48	P5
Kallsjön	48	G5
Kalmar	48	J8
Kalmykiya	92	M1
Kalmykovo	70	K5
Kalocsa	66	F3
Kalol	88	B4
Kalpakio	68	C5
Kalpeni	88	B6
Kaltag	132	(1)F3
Kaltenkirchen	52	E3
Kaluga	70	G4
Kalyan	88	B5
Kalymnos	68	J7
Kalymnos	68	J8
Kama	46	K1
Kama	106	D4
Kamaishi	82	L4
Kaman	92	E4
Kamande	106	D4
Kamango	76	U6
Kamares	68	G8
Kambarka	70	K3
Kambo Ho	82	E3
Kamchatka	78	U6
Kamchatskiy Zaliv	78	U5
Kamenica	68	E2
Kamenka, Russia	70	H1
Kamenka, Russia	70	H4
Kamen'-na-Obi	76	Q7
Kamen'-Rybolov	82	F1
Kamensk-Shakhtinskiy	70	H5
Kamensk-Ural'skiy	70	M3
Kamenz	50	D6
Kamet	88	C2
Kamiiso	82	L3
Kamina	106	C5
Kamitsushima	82	E6
Kamituga	106	D4
Kamiyaku	82	F8
Kamloops	122	G6
Kamoenai	82	L2
Kampala	106	E3
Kampen	54	H2
Kampong Cham	84	D4
Kâmpóng Chhnăng	84	C4
Kâmpôt	84	C4
Kamsuuma	106	G3
Kam"yanets-Podil's'kyy	70	E5
Kamyanyets	48	M10
Kämyärän	92	M6
Kamyshin	70	J4
Kamyzyak	70	J5
Kan	100	F6
Kanab	132	D1
Kananga	106	C5
Kanazawa	82	J5
Kanbalu	88	G4
Kanchipuram	88	C6
Kandahär	90	J3
Kandalaksha	48	S3
Kandalakshskiy Zaliv	70	F1
Kandi	104	E2
Kandira	68	N3
Kandy	88	D7
Kane	128	E2
Kaneohe	132	(2)D2
Kang	108	C4
Kangaatsiaq	122	W3
Kangal	92	G4
Kangân, Iran	95	E3
Kangân, Iran	95	G4
Kangar	86	C1
Kangaroo Island	114	G7
Kangchenjunga	88	E3
Kangding	80	C4
Kangeq	122	Y4
Kangerluarsoruseq	122	W4
Kangersuatsiaq	122	W2
Kangetet	106	F3
Kanggye	82	D3
Kangiqsualujjuaq	122	T5
Kangiqsujuaq	122	S4
Kangirsuk	122	S4
Kangmar	88	E3
Kangnüng	82	E5
Kango	104	G4
Kangping	80	G2
Kaniama	106	C5
Kanin Nos	76	G4
Kanji Reservoir	98	D4
Kanjiža	66	H3
Kankaanpää	48	M6
Kankakee	128	C2
Kankan	104	C2
Kankossa	102	C5
Kannapolis	130	E2
Kano	104	F2
Kanoya	82	F8
Kanpur	88	D3
Kansas	130	A2
Kansas	130	B2
Kansas City, Kans., US	130	C2
Kansas City, Mo., US	130	C2
Kansk	76	T6
Kanta	106	F2
Kantchari	104	E2
Kantemirovka	70	G5
Kanye	108	C4
Kao-Hsiung	80	G6
Kaolack	102	B6
Kaoma	108	C2
Kapanga	106	C5
Kap Arkona	50	C3
Kapchagay	76	P9
Kap Cort Adelaer = Kangeq	122	Y4
Kap Farvel = Uummannarsuaq	122	Y5
Kapfenberg	62	L3
Kapıdağı Yarimadası	68	K4
Kapiri Mposhi	108	D2
Kapit	86	E2
Kapiti Island	116	E5
Kaplice	62	K2
Kapoeta	106	E3
Kaposvár	66	E3
Kappel	52	C6
Kappeln	52	E2
Kappl	62	F3
Kapsan	82	E3
Kapuskasing	124	K2
Kapuvár	66	E2
Kara	76	M4
Kara, Russia	76	M4
Kara, Togo	104	E3
Kara Ada	68	K8
Kara-Balta	76	N9
Karabekaul	90	H2
Kara-Bogaz-Gol	90	F1
Karabutak	70	M5
Karacabey	68	L4
Karacaköy	68	L3
Karacal Tepe	68	Q8
Karachayevo-Cherkesiya	92	J2
Karachayevsk	92	J2
Karachi	90	J5
Karaganda	76	N8
Karaginskiy Zaliv	78	V5
Karaj	90	F2
Karak	94	C5
Kara-Kala	90	G2
Karakalpakiya	76	K9
Karakoçan	92	J4
Kara-Köl	76	N9
Karakol	76	P9
Karakoram	74	L6
Karaksar	78	K6
Karam	78	H5
Karaman	92	E5
Karamay	76	R8
Karamea	116	D5
Karamea Bight	116	C5
Karamürsel	68	M4
Karand	92	M6
Karaoy	76	N8
Karapınar	68	R7
Kara-Say	76	P9
Karasburg	108	B5
Karasu	92	D3
Karasuk	76	P7
Karasuk	76	P7
Karatal	76	P8
Karataş	92	F5
Karatobe	70	K5
Karaton	70	K5
Karatsu	82	E7
Karazhal	70	P5
Karbalā'	90	D3
Karcag	66	H2
Karditsa	68	D5
Kärdla	48	M7
Kareliya	48	R4
Karepino	70	L2
Karesuando	48	M2
Kargalinskaya	92	M2
Kargasok	76	Q6
Kargat	76	P6
Kargil	88	C2
Kargopol'	70	G2
Kariba	108	D3
Kariba Dam	108	D3
Karibib	108	B4
Karimata	86	D3
Karimnagar	88	C5
Karkaralinsk	76	P8
Karkinits'ka Zatoka	70	F5
Karlik Shan	80	A2
Karlovac	66	C4
Karlovasi	68	J7
Karlovo	68	G2
Karlovy Vary	52	H6
Karlshamn	50	D1
Karlskoga	48	H7
Karlskrona	48	H8
Karlsruhe	52	D8
Karlstad, Norway	48	G7
Karlstad, US	128	A1
Karlstadt	52	E7
Karmala	88	C5
Karmi'el	94	C4
Karmøy	48	C7
Karnafuli Reservoir	88	F4
Karnal	88	C3
Karnische Alpen	62	H4
Karnobat	68	J2
Karodi	90	J4
Karonga	106	E5
Karpathos	68	K9
Karpathos	68	K9
Karpenisi	68	D6
Karpogory	70	H2
Karratha	114	C4
Kars	92	K3
Karsakpay	70	N5
Kārsava	48	P8
Karshi	90	J2
Karskoye More	76	L3
Karslyaka	68	K6
Karstula	48	N5
Kartal	68	M4
Kartaly	70	M4
Kartayel'	70	K2
Kartuzy	50	H3
Karufa	87	D3
Karur	88	C6
Karvina	50	H8
Karwar	88	B6
Karystos	68	G6
Kasai	106	B4
Kasaji	108	C2
Kasama	108	E2
Kasansay	76	N9
Kasba Lake	122	L4
Kasempa	108	D2
Kasenga	108	D2
Kāshān	90	F3
Kashi	90	L2
Kashima	80	L3
Kashiwazaki	82	K5
Kāshmar	90	G2
Kashmor	90	J4
Kasimov	70	H4
Kasli	70	M3
Kasongo	106	D4
Kasos	68	K9
Kaspi	92	L3
Kaspiysk	92	M2
Kassala	100	G4
Kassandreia	68	F4
Kassel	52	E5
Kasserine	102	G1
Kastamonu	92	E3
Kastelli	68	F9
Kastoria	68	D4
Kasulu	106	E4
Kasumkent	92	N3
Kasur	88	B2
Kata	78	G5
Katchall	88	F7
Katerini	68	E4
Katete	108	E2
Katha	88	G4
Katherine	114	F2
Kathiawar	90	K5
Kathmandu	88	E3
Kati	104	C2
Katihar	88	E3
Katiola	104	C3
Kato Nevrokopi	68	F3
Katonga	106	E3
Katoomba	114	K6
Katowice	50	J7
Katrineholm	48	J7
Katsina	104	F2
Katsina-Ala	104	F3
Katsuta	82	L5
Katsuura	82	L6
Kattakurgan	90	J2
Kattavia	68	K9
Kattegat	48	F8
Katun'	76	R7
Katwijkaan Zee	54	G2
Kauai	132	(2)B1
Kaufbeuren	62	F3
Kauhajoki	48	M5
Kaunas	50	N3
Kaunus	46	G2
Kaura Namoda	104	F2
Kavadarci	68	D3
Kavajë	68	B3
Kavala	68	G4
Kavali	88	C5
Kavār	95	E2
Kavaratti	88	B6
Kavarna	66	R6
Kawabe	82	L4
Kawagoe	82	K6
Kawakawa	116	E2
Kawambwa	106	D5
Kawasaki	82	K6
Kawau Island	116	E3
Kaweka	116	F4
Kawhia	116	E4
Kawkareik	84	B3
Kawthaung	84	B4
Kaya	104	D2
Kayak	76	U3
Kaycee	126	E2
Kayenta	132	D1
Kayes	104	B2
Kaymaz	68	P5
Kaynar	76	P8
Kayseri	92	F4
Kayyerkan	76	R4
Kazachinskoye	78	E5
Kazach'ye	78	P2
Kazakdar'ya	76	K9
Kazakhstan	76	L8
Kazan'	70	J3
Kazan	122	M4
Kazanlŭk	68	H2
Kazan-rettō	112	E3
Kazbek	92	L2
Kāzerūn	95	D2
Kazincbarcika	66	H1
Kazungula	108	D3
Kazuno	82	L3
Kazymskiy Mys	76	M5
Kea	68	G7
Kea	68	G7
Kearney	124	G3
Keban Barajı	92	H4
Kébémèr	102	B5
Kebkabiya	100	D5
Kebnekajse	48	K3
K'ebrī Dehar	106	G2
K'ech'a Terara	106	F2
Keçiborlu	68	N7
Kecskemet	66	G3
Kėdainiai	50	N2
Kedgwick	128	G1
Kediri	86	E4
Kédougou	104	B2
Kędzierzyn-Koźle	50	H7
Keele	132	(1)M3
Keene	128	F2
Keetmanshoop	108	B5
Keewatin	128	B1
Kefallonia	68	C6
Kefamenanu	87	B4
Keflavik	48	(1)B2
Kegen'	76	P9
Keg River	122	H5
Keheili	100	F4
Kehl	62	C2
Keila	48	N7
Keitele	48	N5
Kekerengu	116	D5
Kékes	66	H2
Kelai Thiladhunmathee Atoll	88	B7
Kelheim	62	G2
Kelibia	64	F12
Kelkit	92	G3
Kelmė	50	M2
Kélo	104	H3
Kelowna	122	H7
Kelso	126	B1
Keluang	86	C2
Kem'	70	F2
Kemah	92	H4
Kemalpaşa	68	K6
Kemasik	86	C2
Kemer, Turkey	68	M8
Kemer, Turkey	68	N8
Kemerovo	76	R6
Kemi	48	N4
Kemijärvi	48	P3
Kemijärvi	48	P3
Kemijoki	48	P3
Kemmerer	126	D3
Kemmuna	64	J12
Kemnath	52	G7
Kemp's Bay	130	F5
Kempten	62	F3
Kendal	56	K7
Kendall	130	E4
Kendari	87	B3
Kendawangan	86	E3
Kendégué	104	H2
Kendujhargarh	88	E4
Kenedy	130	B4
Kenema	104	B3
Keneurgench	90	G1
Kenge	106	B4
Kengtung	84	B2
Kenhardt	108	C5
Kénitra	102	D2
Kenmare	56	C10
Kennett	130	D2
Kennewick	126	C1
Keno Hill	132	(1)K3
Kenora	124	H2
Kenosha	128	C2
Kentau	76	M9
Kentucky	124	J4
Kentwood	130	C3
Kenya	98	G5
Keokuk	128	B2
Kępno	50	H6
Kepulauan Anambas	86	D2
Kepulauan Aru	87	E4
Kepulauan Ayu	87	D2
Kepulauan Balabalangan	86	F3
Kepulauan Banggai	87	B3
Kepulauan Barat Daya	87	C4
Kepulauan Batu	86	B3
Kepulauan Bonerate	87	A4
Kepulauan Kai	87	D4
Kepulauan Kangean	86	F4
Kepulauan Karimunjawa	86	D4
Kepulauan Karkaralong	87	B2
Kepulauan Laut Kecil	86	F3
Kepulauan Leti	87	C4
Kepulauan Lingga	86	C2
Kepulauan Lucipara	87	C4
Kepulauan Mentawai	86	B3
Kepulauan Nanusa	87	C2
Kepulauan Natuna	86	D2
Kepulauan Riau	86	C2
Kepulauan Sabalana	86	F4
Kepulauan Sangir	87	C2
Kepulauan Solor	87	B4
Kepulauan Sula	87	B3
Kepulauan Talaud	87	C2
Kepulauan Tanimbar	87	D4
Kepulauan Tengah	86	F4
Kepulauan Togian	87	B3
Kepulauan Tukangbesi	87	B4
Kepulauan Watubela	87	D3
Kerch	92	G1
Kerchevskiy	70	L3
Kerempe Burnu	68	R2
Keren	100	G4
Kericho	106	F4
Kerikeri	116	D2
Kerio	106	F3
Kerki	90	J2
Kerkrade	54	J4
Kerkyra	68	B5
Kerkyra	68	B5
Kerma	100	F4
Kermadec Islands	112	H8
Kermadec Trench	112	J9
Kermān	95	G1
Kermānshāh	90	E3
Kermānshāhān	95	F1
Keros	68	H8
Kerpen	54	B3
Kerrville	130	B3
Kerulen	78	J7
Keryneia	92	E6
Keşan	68	J4
Kesennuma	82	L4
Keşiş Dağları	90	E4
Keszthely	66	E3
Keta	104	E3
Ketapang	86	D3
Ketchikan	132	(1)L4
Kêtou	104	E3
Kętrzyn	50	L3
Kettering	56	M9

Name	Page	Grid
Kettle Falls	124	C2
Kewanee	128	C2
Keweenaw Peninsula	128	C1
Key Largo	130	E5
Keystone Lake	130	B2
Key West	130	E5
Kezhma	78	G5
Kežmarok	50	K8
Khabarovsk	78	P7
Khadyzhensk	92	H1
Khakasiya	76	R7
Khairwāra	88	B4
Khalafābād	95	C1
Khalīg el Suweis	100	F2
Khalīj Surt	100	C1
Khalūf	90	G5
Khambhat	88	B4
Khamis Mushay	90	D6
Khamis Mushayt	100	H4
Khamkkeut	84	C3
Khampa	78	L4
Khamrà	78	J4
Khān al Baghdād	92	K7
Khān az Zabīb	94	C3
Khandagayty	76	S7
Khandwa	88	C4
Khanewal	88	B2
Khannya	76	X4
Khanpur	88	B3
Khān Shaykhūn	94	D1
Khantau	76	N9
Khantayka	78	D3
Khanty-Mansiysk	70	N2
Khān Yūnis	94	B5
Khapalu	88	C1
Kharabali	70	J5
Kharagpur	88	E4
Kharampur	78	B4
Kharan	90	J4
Khargon	88	C4
Kharkiv	70	G5
Kharlu	48	R6
Kharmanli	68	H3
Kharnmam	88	D5
Kharovsk	70	H3
Khartoum = El Khartum	100	F4
Khasavyurt	92	M2
Khāsh	90	H4
Khashgort	70	N1
Khashm el Girba	100	G4
Khashuri	92	K3
Khaskovo	68	H3
Khatanga	78	G2
Khātūnābād	95	F1
Khatyrka	78	X4
Khavda	90	J5
Khawr Fakkān	95	G4
Khaydarken	90	K2
Khayelitsha	108	B6
Khemis Miliana	102	F1
Khemisset	102	D2
Khenchela	102	E1
Kherāmeh	95	E2
Kherson	70	F5
Kheta	76	T3
Kheta	76	T3
Kheygiyakha	70	P2
Khilok	78	J6
Khirbat Isrīyah	94	E1
Khīyāv	92	M4
Khmel'nyts'kyy	70	E5
Khodā Afarīn	92	M4
Kholmsk	78	Q7
Khonj	95	E3
Khon Kaen	84	C3
Khonuu	78	Q3
Khoper	70	H4
Khor	78	P7
Khor	78	P7
Khoreyver	70	L1
Khorinsk	78	H6
Khorramābād	90	E3
Khorramshahr	95	C1
Khorugh	90	K2
Khoseda Khard	70	L1
Khouribga	102	D2
Khrebet Cherskogo	78	P3
Khrebet Dzhagdy	78	N6
Khrebet Dzhugdzhur	78	N5
Khrebet Khamar Daban	78	G6
Khrebet Kolymskiy	74	U3
Khrebet Kopet Dag.	90	G2
Khrebet Suntar Khayata	78	P4
Khrebet Tarbagatay	76	Q8
Khroma	78	Q2
Khudoseya	78	C3
Khudzhakh	78	R4
Khujand	90	J1
Khulna	88	E4
Khurays	95	B4
Khushab	88	B2
Khust	66	L1
Khuwei	100	E5
Khuzdar	90	J4
Khvormūj.	95	D2
Khvoy	92	L4
Khyber Pass	90	K3
Kibaya	106	F4
Kibombo	106	D4
Kibondo	106	E4
Kibre Mengist	106	F2
Kičevo	68	C3
Kichmengskiy Gorodok	70	J3
Kicking Horse Pass	122	H6
Kidal	102	F5
Kidderminster	56	K9
Kidira	104	B2
Kiel	52	F2
Kielce	50	K7
Kieler Bucht.	52	F2
Kiev = Kyyiv	70	F4
Kiffa	102	C5
Kigali	106	E4
Kigoma	106	D4
Kihnu	48	M7
Kıkıköy	68	L3
Kikinda	66	H4
Kikonai	82	L3
Kikori	87	F4
Kikwit	106	B5
Kilchu	82	E3
Kilifi	106	F4
Kilindoni	106	F5
Kilingi-Nõmme	48	N7
Kilis	92	G5
Kiliya	66	S4
Kilkenny	56	E9
Kilkis	68	E4
Killarney, Canada	128	D1
Killarney, Ireland	56	C9
Kilmarnock	56	H6
Kil'mez	70	K3
Kilosa	106	F5
Kilrush	56	C9
Kilttan	88	B6
Kilwa	106	D5
Kilwa Masoko	106	F5
Kimberley	108	C5
Kimberley Plateau	114	E3
Kimch'aek	82	E3
Kimolos.	68	G8
Kimongo	104	G5
Kimry	70	G3
Kinango	106	F4
Kincardine	128	D2
Kinda	106	C5
Kinder	130	C3
Kindia	104	B2
Kindu	106	D4
Kineshma	70	H3
Kingaroy	114	K5
King City	126	B3
King George Islands	122	R5
Kingisepp	48	Q7
King Island, Australia	114	H7
King Island, Canada	78	AA3
Kingman	132	D1
Kingri	90	J3
Kingscote	114	G7
Kingsland	130	E3
King's Lynn	56	N9
King Sound	114	D3
Kings Peak	126	D2
Kingsport	130	E2
Kingston, Canada.	128	E2
Kingston, Jamaica	134	J5
Kingston, US	128	F2
Kingston-upon-Hull	56	M8
Kingston upon Thames	54	B3
Kingstown	140	E1
Kingsville.	130	B4
Kingville	134	E3
King William Island	122	M3
King William's Town	108	D6
Kinik	68	K5
Kinka-san	82	L4
Kinna	48	G8
Kinsale	56	D10
Kinshasa	106	B4
Kinsley	130	B2
Kinston	128	E3
Kintampo	104	D3
Kintyre	56	G6
Kinyeti	106	E3
Kinzig	52	E6
Kipini	106	G4
Kipnuk	132	(1)E3
Kirchheim	62	E2
Kirchheimbolanden	54	L5
Kirenga	78	H5
Kirensk	78	H5
Kiribati	112	J6
Kırıkhan	92	G5
Kırıkkale	92	E4
Kirillov	70	G3
Kirinyaga	106	F4
Kirishi	70	F3
Kiritimati	112	L5
Kırkağaç	68	K5
Kirk Bulāg Dāgh	90	E2
Kirkcaldy	56	J5
Kirkcudbright.	56	H7
Kirkjubæjarklaustur.	48	(1)E3
Kirkland Lake	128	D1
Kırklareli	68	K3
Kirkūk	92	L6
Kirkwall	56	K3
Kirov, Kyrgyzstan	76	N9
Kirov, Russia	70	J3
Kirov, Russia	70	J3
Kirovohrad.	70	F5
Kiroyo-Chepetsk.	70	K3
Kirriemuir.	56	K5
Kirs	70	K3
Kirsanov	70	H4
Kırşehir	92	F4
Kiruna	48	L3
Kiryū	82	K5
Kisangani	106	D3
Kisbér	66	E2
Kiselevsk.	76	R7
Kishanganj.	88	E3
Kishangarh, India	88	B3
Kishangarh, India	88	B3
Kishi	104	E3
Kishiwada	82	H6
Kishtwar	88	C2
Kisii	106	E4
Kiska Island	132	(3)B1
Kiskőrös	66	G3
Kiskunfélegyháza	66	G3
Kiskunhalas	66	G3
Kiskunmajsa	66	G3
Kislovodsk.	92	K2
Kismaayo	106	G4
Kissidougou.	104	B3
Kisumu	106	E4
Kisvárda	66	K1
Kita	104	C2
Kitakami	82	L4
Kita-Kyūshū	80	H4
Kita-Kyūshū	82	F7
Kitami	82	M2
Kitchener	128	D2
Kitgum	106	E3
Kitimat	122	F6
Kittilä	48	N3
Kitunda	106	E5
Kitwe	108	D2
Kitzingen	52	F7
Kiuruvesi	48	P5
Kivijärvi	48	N5
Kivik	50	D2
Kiya	78	D5
Kıyıköy	92	C3
Kizel	70	L3
Kizilalan	68	R8
Kızılcahamam	92	E3
Kızılırmak	92	F3
Kızılkaya	68	N7
Kizil'skoye	70	L4
Kızıltepe	92	J5
Kizlyar	92	M2
Kizlyarskiy Zaliv	92	M1
Kizyl-Atrek	76	J10
Kladanj	66	F5
Kladno	50	D7
Klagenfurt	62	K4
Klaipėda	48	L9
Klamath	126	B2
Klamath	126	B2
Klamath Falls	126	B2
Klarälven	48	G6
Klatovy	52	J7
Klaus	62	K3
Klerksdorp	108	D5
Kleve	52	B5
Klin.	70	G3
Klingenthal	52	H6
Klínovec	52	H6
Klintsy	70	F4
Ključ	62	M6
Klobuck	50	H7
Kłodzko	50	F7
Kløfta	48	F6
Klosterneuburg	62	M2
Klosters	62	E4
Kluane	122	D4
Kluane Lake.	132	(1)J3
Kluczbork	50	H7
Klyuchevskaya Sopka	78	U5
Klyuchi	78	U5
Knezha	66	M6
Knin	66	D5
Knittelfeld	66	B2
Knjaževac	66	K6
Knokke-Heist	54	F3
Knoxville	128	D3
Knysna	108	C6
Koba.	86	D3
Kōbe.	82	H6
Kobe	87	C2
København	48	G9
Kobenni	102	D5
Koblenz	52	C6
Kobo	88	G3
Kobroör	87	E4
Kobryn	50	P5
Kobuk	132	(1)F2
Kobuk	132	(1)F2
Kočani	68	E3
Koçarli	68	K7
Kočevje.	66	B4
Koch'ang	82	E6
Ko Chang	84	C4
Kochechum	78	F3
Kōchi	82	G7
Kochi	88	C7
Kochkor	76	P9
Kochki	76	Q7
Kochubey	92	M1
Kodiak	132	(1)G4
Kodiak Island	132	(1)G4
Kodino	70	G2
Kodinsk.	78	F5
Kodomari-misaki	82	L3
Kodyma	66	S1
Köflach	66	C2
Kōfu	82	K6
Køge	50	B2
Køge Bugt.	50	B2
Kohat	88	B2
Kohima	88	F3
Koh-i-Qaisir	90	H3
Koh-i-Sangan	90	J3
Kohtla-Järve	48	P7
Koidu	104	B3
Koi Sanjaq.	92	L6
Koitere	48	R5
Kokenau	87	E3
Kokkola	48	M5
Kokomo	130	D1
Kokpekty	76	Q8
Kokshetau	70	N4
Kokstad	108	D6
Kolaka	87	B3
Kolar	88	C6
Kolari	48	M3
Kolašin	66	G7
Kolda	104	B2
Kolding	48	E9
Kole	106	C4
Kolhapur	88	B5
Kolin	50	E7
Kolkata	88	E4
Kollam	88	C7
Köln	52	B6
Kolno	50	L4
Koło	50	H5
Kołobrzeg	50	E3
Kologriv	70	H3
Kolomna	70	G3
Kolomyya	66	N1
Kolonedale	87	B3
Kolosovka	70	P3
Kolpashevo	76	Q6
Kolpos Agiou Orous	68	F4
Kolpos Kassandras	68	F4
Kolpos Murampelou	68	H9
Kolskijzaliv	48	S2
Kolskiy Poluostrov	70	G1
Kolumadulu Atoll	88	B8
Koluton	70	N4
Kolva	70	L2
Kolwezi	108	D2
Kolyma	78	R4
Kolymskaya Nizmennost'.	78	S3
Kolymskaye	78	T3
Komandorskiye Ostrova	78	V5
Komárno	66	F2
Komárom	66	F2
Komatsu	82	J5
Kombe	106	D4
Komi.	70	K2
Komló	66	F3
Kom Ombo	100	F3
Komotini	68	H3
Komsa	76	R5
Komsomol'skiy.	70	J5
Komsomol'sk-na-Amure	78	P6
Konārka	88	E5
Konda	70	N3
Kondagaon	88	D5
Kondinskoye	70	N3
Kondoa	106	F4
Kondopoga	70	F2
Kondrat'yeva	76	V5
Kondūz	90	J2
Kong Frederik VI Kyst	122	Y4
Kongi	76	R9
Kongola	108	C3
Kongolo	106	D5
Kongsberg	48	E7
Kongur Shan	76	N10
Königsberg = Kaliningrad	50	K3
Königswinter	52	C6
Königs-Wusterhausen	52	J4
Konin	50	H5
Konispol	68	C5
Konitsa	68	C4
Köniz	62	C4
Konjic	66	E6
Konosha	70	H2
Konotop	70	F4
Konstanz	62	E3
Konstinbrod.	66	L7
Kontagora	104	F2
Kon Tum	84	D4
Konya	92	E5
Konz	52	B7
Kookynie	114	D5
Kootenai	126	C1
Kootenay Lake	124	C2
Kópasker	48	(1)E1
Kópavogur.	48	(1)C2
Koper	62	J5
Kopeysk	70	M3
Köping	48	J7
Koplik	66	G7
Koprivnica	66	D3
Korba, India	88	D4
Korba, Tunisia	64	E12
Korbach	52	D5
Korçë	68	C4
Korčula	66	D7
Kord Sheykh	95	E2
Korea Bay	82	B4
Korea Strait	82	E6
Korf	78	V4
Korhogo	104	C3
Korinthiakos Kolpos	68	E6
Korinthos	68	E7
Kōriyama	82	L5
Korkino	70	M4
Korkuteli	92	D5
Korla	76	R9
Korliki	78	C4
Körmend	66	D2
Kornat	66	C6
Koroba	87	F4
Köroğlu Dağları	68	Q4
Köroğlu Tepesi.	68	P4
Korogwe	106	F5
Koronowo	50	G4
Koror	112	D5
Koro Toro	100	C4
Korsakov.	78	Q7
Korsør	52	G1
Korti	100	F4
Kortrijk	54	F4
Korumburra	114	J7
Koryakskiy Khrebet	78	V4
Koryazhma	76	H5
Kos	68	K8
Kos	68	K8
Kosa.	70	L3
Ko Samui	84	C5
Kościan	50	F5
Kościerzyna	50	H3
Kosciusko	130	D3
Kosh Agach	76	R8
Koshoba	90	F1
Koslan	70	J2
Košöng	82	E4
Kosovo	68	C2
Kosovska Mitrovica	68	C2

Name	Page	Grid
Le Perthus	58	H11
Lepoura	68	G6
Lepsy	76	P8
Le Puy	58	J8
Léré	104	G3
Lerici	62	E6
Lerik	92	N4
Lerma	60	G2
Leros	68	J7
Lerwick	56	L1
Lešak	66	H6
Les Andelys	54	D5
Lesatima	106	F4
Lesbos = Lesvos	68	H5
Les Escaldes	58	G11
Les Escoumins	122	T7
Leshan	80	C5
Les Herbiers	58	D7
Leshukonskoye	70	J2
Leskovac	66	J7
Lesosibirsk	76	S6
Lesotho	108	D5
Lesozavodsk	82	G1
Lesparre-Médoc	58	E8
Les Sables-d'Olonne	58	D7
Les Sept Îles	58	B5
Lesser Antilles	134	L6
Lesser Slave Lake	122	J5
Lesvos	68	H5
Leszno	50	F6
Letaba	108	E4
Letchworth	54	B3
Letenye	62	M4
Lethbridge	126	D1
Lethem	140	F3
Leticia	140	D4
Letpadan	84	B3
Le Tréport	54	D4
Letterkenny	56	E7
Leutkirch	62	F3
Leuven	54	G4
Leuze	54	F4
Levadeia	68	E6
Levanzo	64	G10
Levashi	92	M2
Levaya Khetta	70	P2
Leverano	64	N8
Leverkusen	54	J3
Levice	50	H9
Levico Terme	62	G4
Levin	116	E5
Lévis	128	F1
Levitha	68	J7
Levoča	50	K9
Levski	66	N6
Lewe	84	B3
Lewes	54	C4
Lewis	56	F3
Lewis and Clark Lake	126	G2
Lewis Range	122	J7
Lewiston, Id., US	126	C1
Lewiston, Me., US	128	F2
Lewistown, Mont., US	126	E1
Lewistown, Pa., US	128	E2
Lexington, Ky., US	128	D3
Lexington, Nebr., US	126	G2
Lexington, Va., US	128	E3
Lexington Park	130	F2
Leyte	84	G4
Lezhë	66	G8
Lhari	88	F2
Lhasa	88	F3
Lhazà	88	E3
Lhokseumawe	84	B5
Lian Xian	84	E2
Lianyuan	84	E1
Lianyungang	80	F4
Liaocheng	80	F3
Liao He	82	B3
Liaoyang	82	B3
Liaoyuan	82	C2
Liard	122	F5
Liard River	122	F5
Libby	126	C1
Libenge	106	B3
Liberal	130	A2
Liberec	50	E7
Liberia	104	B3
Liberia	134	G6
Liberty	130	C1
Libjo	84	H4
Libourne	58	E9
Libreville	104	F4
Libya	100	C2
Libyan Desert	100	D2
Libyan Plateau	100	E1
Licata	64	H11
Lich	52	D6
Lichinga	108	F2
Lichtenfels	52	G6
Lida	48	N10
Lidköping	48	G7
Lidodi Jesolo	62	H5
Lido di Ostia	64	G7
Lidzbark Warmiński	50	K3
Liebenwalde	52	J4
Liechtenstein	62	E3
Liège	54	H4
Lieksa	48	R5
Lienz	62	H4
Liepāja	50	L1
Lier	54	G3
Liezen	62	K3
Lifford	56	E7
Lignières	58	H7
Ligueil	58	F6
Ligurian Sea	62	D7
Lihue	132	B2
Lijiang	84	C1
Likasi	106	D6
Lilienfeld	62	L2
Lille	54	F4
Lillebonne	54	C5
Lillehammer	48	F6
Lillerto	62	G3
Lilongwe	108	G2
Liloy	84	G5
Lima, Peru	140	B6
Lima, Mont., US	126	D2
Lima, Oh., US	128	D2
Limanowa	50	K8
Limassol = Lemesos	68	Q10
Limbaži	48	N8
Limburg	54	L4
Limeira	142	M3
Limerick	56	D9
Limingen	48	G4
Limni Kastorias	68	C4
Limni Kerkinitis	68	E3
Limni Koronia	68	F4
Limni Trichonida	68	D6
Limni Vegoritis	68	D4
Limni Volvi	68	F4
Limnos	68	H5
Limoges	58	G8
Limon	126	F3
Limón	134	H7
Limoux	58	H10
Limpopo	108	D4
Limpopo	108	D4
Linares, Chile	142	G6
Linares, Mexico	132	G4
Linares, Spain	60	G6
Linaria	68	G6
Lincang	84	C2
Linchuan	80	F5
Lincoln, UK	54	B1
Lincoln, Ill., US	128	C2
Lincoln, Me., US	128	G1
Lincoln, Nebr., US	126	G2
Lincoln, N.H., US	128	F2
Lindenow Fjord	122	Y4
Lindesnes	48	D8
Lindi	106	D3
Lindi	106	F6
Lindos	68	L8
Line Islands	112	L5
Linfen	80	E3
Lingayen	84	G3
Lingen	54	K2
Lingga	86	C3
Lingshui	84	D3
Linguère	104	A1
Lingyuan	80	F2
Linhal	80	G5
Linhares	140	J7
Linhe	80	D2
Linjiang	82	D3
Linköping	48	H7
Linkou	82	F1
Linosa	64	G13
Lins	142	M3
Linton	126	F1
Linxi	80	F2
Linxia	80	C3
Lin Xian	80	E3
Linyi	80	F3
Linz	62	K2
Liobomil'	50	P6
Lipari	64	J10
Lipari	64	J10
Lipcani	66	P1
Lipetsk	70	G4
Lipin Bor	70	G2
Lipno	50	J5
Lipova	66	J3
Lippe	54	L3
Lippstadt	54	L3
Lipsoi	68	J7
Liptovský-Mikuláš	50	J8
Lipu	84	E2
Liqeni i Fierzës	66	H7
Liqeni Komanit	66	G7
Lira	106	E3
Liri	64	H7
Lisala	106	C3
Lisboa	60	A6
Lisbon = Lisboa	60	A6
Lisburn	56	G7
Liscannor Bay	56	C9
Lishi	80	E3
Lishui	80	F5
Lisieux	54	C5
Liski	70	G4
L'Isle-sur-la-Sorgue	58	L10
Lisse	54	G2
Lištica	64	M5
Listowel	56	C9
Listvyanka	78	H6
Litang	80	C5
Litani	140	G3
Litava	50	F8
Litchfield, Ill., US	128	C3
Litchfield, Minn., US	128	B1
Lithgow	114	K6
Lithuania	48	L9
Litke	78	Q6
Litomerice	52	K6
Litomyši	50	F8
Litovel	50	G8
Litovko	78	P7
Little Abaco	130	F4
Little Andaman	88	F6
Little Barrier Island	116	E3
Little Current	128	D1
Little Desert	114	H7
Little Falls	128	B1
Littlefield	132	F2
Little Inagua	134	K4
Little Karoo	108	C6
Little Minch	56	E4
Little Nicobar	88	F7
Little Ouse	54	C2
Little Rock	130	C3
Littleton	126	E3
Litvinov	52	J6
Liupanshui	80	C5
Liuzhou	80	D6
Live Oak	130	E3
Liverpool, Canada	122	U8
Liverpool, UK	56	K8
Liverpool Bay	122	F2
Livingston, UK	56	J6
Livingston, US	126	D1
Livingstone	108	D3
Livingstonia	108	E2
Livno	66	E6
Livny	70	G4
Livonia	128	D2
Livorno	62	F7
Liwale	106	F5
Lizard Point	56	G12
Ljubljana	62	K4
Ljugarn	48	K8
Ljungan	48	J5
Ljungby	48	G8
Ljusdal	48	J6
Ljusnan	70	C2
Llandovery	56	J9
Llandudno	56	J8
Llanelli	56	H10
Llanes	60	F1
Llanos	140	C2
Lleida	60	L3
Llerena	60	E6
Lli	76	P9
Lloret de Mar	60	N3
Llucmajor	60	N5
Loano	62	D6
Lobamba	108	E5
Lobatse	108	D5
Löbau	52	K5
Łobez	50	E4
Lobito	108	A2
Locarno	62	D4
Lochboisdale	56	E4
Lochem	54	J2
Lochinver	56	G3
Loch Linnhe	56	G5
Loch Lomond	56	H5
Lochmaddy	56	E4
Loch Ness	56	H4
Lockhart	130	B4
Lock Haven	128	E2
Lockport	128	E2
Locri	64	K10
Lodève	58	J10
Lodeynoye	70	F2
Lodge Grass	126	E1
Lodi, Italy	62	E5
Lodi, US	126	B3
Lodja	106	C4
Lodwar	106	F3
Łódź	50	J6
Loei	84	C3
Lofoten	48	G3
Logan, Ia., US	128	A2
Logan, N. Mex., US	132	F1
Logan, Ut., US	126	D2
Logansport	128	C2
Logatec	62	K5
Logroño	60	H2
Lohiniva	48	N3
Lohr	52	E7
Loikaw	84	B3
Loir	58	F6
Loire	58	D6
Loja, Ecuador	140	B4
Loja, Spain	60	F7
Lokan tekojärvi	48	P3
Lokeren	54	F3
Lokichar	106	F3
Lokichokio	106	E3
Lokoja	104	F3
Lokosovo	70	P2
Loks Land	122	U4
Lolland	52	G2
Lollondo	106	F4
Lolo	126	D1
Lom	66	L6
Lomami	106	C4
Lomas	140	C7
Lomas de Zamora	142	K5
Lombadina	114	D3
Lomblen	87	B4
Lombok	86	F4
Lombok	86	F4
Lomé	104	E3
Lomela	106	C4
Lomela	106	C4
Lommel	54	H3
Lomonosovka	70	N4
Lompoc	132	B2
Łomża	50	M4
London, Canada	128	D2
London, UK	54	B3
London, US	130	E2
Londonderry	56	E6
Londrina	142	L3
Longarone	62	H4
Long Bay	134	J2
Long Beach	132	C2
Long Branch	128	F2
Long Eaton	54	A2
Longford	56	E8
Long Island, Canada	122	Q5
Long Island, US	128	F2
Longlac	122	P7
Long Lake	126	F1
Longmont	126	E2
Long Prairie	128	B1
Long Range Mountains	122	V6
Longreach	114	H4
Longueuil	128	F1
Longview, Tex., US	130	C3
Longview, Wash., US	126	B1
Longwy	54	H5
Long Xuyên	84	D4
Longyan	84	F1
Löningen	54	K2
Lönsdalen	48	H3
Lons-le-Saunier	62	A4
Lookout Pass	126	C1
Loop Head	56	B9
Lopez	84	G4
Lop Nur	76	S9
Lopphavet	48	L1
Loptyuga	70	J2
Lora del Rio	60	E7
Lorain	128	D2
Loralai	88	A2
Lorca	60	J7
Lordegān	95	D1
Lord Howe Island	114	L6
Lordsburg	132	E2
Loreto	134	B3
Lorient	58	B6
Lörrach	62	C3
Los Alamos	132	E1
Los Angeles, Chile	142	G6
Los Angeles, US	132	C2
Los Banos	126	B3
Los Blancos	142	J3
Losheim	54	J5
Losice	50	M5
Lošinj	62	K6
Los Mochis	134	C3
Lospalos	87	C4
Los Telares	142	J4
Los Teques	140	D1
Lost Trail Pass	126	D1
Los'va	70	M2
Los Vientos	142	H3
Lotta	48	Q2
Lotte	54	K2
Louang Namtha	84	C2
Louangphrabang	84	C3
Loubomo	104	G5
Loudéac	58	C5
Louga	104	A1
Loughborough	54	A2
Lough Conn	56	C7
Lough Corrib	56	C8
Lough Derg	56	D8
Lough Foyle	56	E6
Lough Leane	56	C9
Lough Mask	56	C8
Lough Neagh	56	F7
Lough Ree	56	E8
Louhans	58	L7
Louisa	128	D3
Louisiade Archipelago	114	K2
Louisiana	130	C3
Louis Trichardt	108	D4
Louisville, Ga., US	130	E3
Louisville, Ky., US	130	D2
Louisville, Miss., US	130	D3
Loukhi	48	S3
Loulé	60	C7
Louny	52	J6
Loup	126	G2
Lourdes	58	E10
Louros	68	C5
Louth, Australia	114	J6
Louth, UK	54	C1
Loutra Aidipsou	68	F6
Louviers	54	D5
Lovech	66	M6
Lovell	126	E2
Lovelock	126	C2
Lovosice	52	K6
Lovran	62	K5
Lõvua	108	C2
Lowa	106	D4
Lowell	128	F2
Lower Hutt	116	E5
Lower Lake	126	B2
Lower Lough Erne	56	E7
Lower Post	122	F5
Lowestoft	54	D2
Lowicz	50	J5
Lowville	128	F2
Loxstedt	52	D3
Loyalty Islands	112	G8
Loyno	70	K3
Loznica	66	G5
L-Travemünde	52	F3
Luama	106	D4
Luampa	108	C3
Lu'an	80	F4
Luanda	106	A5
Luangwa	108	E3
Lua Nova	140	F5
Luanping	80	F2
Luanshya	108	D2
Luarca	60	D1
Luau	108	C2
Lubaczów	50	N7
Lubań	50	E6
Lubango	108	A2
Lubāns	48	P8
Lubao	106	D5
Lubartów	50	M6
Lübbecke	54	L2
Lübben	52	J5
Lübbenau	52	J5
Lubbock	132	F2
Lübeck	52	F3
Lubefu	106	C4
Lubero	106	D4
Lubilash	106	C5
Lubin	50	F5
Lublin	50	M6
Lubliniec	50	H7
Lubny	70	F4
Luboń	50	F5
Lubsko	50	D6

Merced	**126**	B3
Mercedes, *Argentina*	**142**	H5
Mercedes, *Argentina*	**142**	K4
Mercedes, *US*	**130**	B4
Mercedes, *Uruguay*	**142**	K5
Mercury Islands	**116**	E3
Mere	**54**	F4
Mergenevo	**70**	K5
Mergui	**84**	B4
Mergui Archipelago	**84**	B4
Merichas	**68**	G7
Mérida, *Mexico*	**134**	G4
Mérida, *Spain*	**60**	D6
Mérida, *Venezuela*	**134**	K7
Meridian	**130**	D3
Mérignac	**58**	E9
Merinha Grande	**60**	B5
Meriruma	**140**	G3
Merke	**76**	N9
Merkys	**48**	N9
Merowe	**100**	F4
Merredin	**114**	C6
Merrill	**128**	C1
Merriman	**126**	F2
Merritt	**122**	G6
Mersch	**54**	J5
Merseburg	**52**	H5
Mers el Kébir	**60**	K9
Mersey	**56**	J8
Mersin = İcel	**68**	S8
Mersing	**86**	C2
Mērsrags	**48**	M8
Merthyr Tydfil	**56**	J10
Méru	**54**	E5
Meru	**106**	F3
Merzifon	**92**	F3
Merzig	**54**	J5
Mesa	**132**	D2
Mesa de Yambi	**140**	C3
Mesagne	**64**	M8
Meschede	**54**	L3
Mesöaria Plain	**94**	A1
Mesolongi	**68**	D6
Mesopotamia	**92**	K6
Messaad	**102**	F2
Messina, *Italy*	**64**	K10
Messina, *South Africa*	**108**	D4
Messini	**68**	E7
Messiniakos Kolpos	**68**	D8
Mestre	**62**	H5
Meta	**140**	C2
Metairie	**130**	C4
Metaline Falls	**126**	C1
Metán	**142**	J4
Metangula	**108**	E2
Metema	**100**	G5
Meteor Depth	**138**	J9
Metković	**66**	E6
Metlika	**62**	L5
Metro	**86**	D4
Metsovo	**68**	D5
Mettet	**54**	G4
Mettlach	**54**	J5
Metz	**54**	J5
Metzingen	**62**	E2
Meulaboh	**84**	B6
Meuse	**54**	G4
Mexia	**130**	B3
Mexicali	**132**	C2
Mexican Hat	**132**	E1
Mexico	**128**	B3
Mexico	**134**	D4
México	**134**	E5
Meymaneh	**90**	H2
Meynypil'gyno	**78**	X4
Mezdra	**66**	L6
Mezen'	**70**	H1
Mezenskaya Guba	**70**	H1
Mezhdurechensk	**76**	R7
Mezőberény	**66**	J3
Mezőkövesd	**66**	H2
Mezőtúr	**66**	H2
Mfuwe	**108**	E2
Miajadas	**60**	E5
Miami, *Fla., US*	**130**	E4
Miami, *Okla., US*	**130**	C2
Miandowāb	**92**	M5
Miandrivazo	**108**	H3
Mīāneh	**92**	M5
Miangyang	**80**	E4
Mianning	**80**	C5
Mianwali	**88**	B2
Mianyang	**80**	C4
Miaodao Qundao	**80**	G3
Miao'ergou	**76**	Q8
Miass	**70**	M4
Miastko	**50**	G4
Michalovce	**50**	L9
Michigan	**128**	C1
Michipicoten Island	**128**	C1
Michurin	**66**	Q7
Michurinsk	**70**	H4
Micronesia	**112**	F4
Mid-Atlantic Ridge	**138**	G1
Middelburg, *Netherlands*	**54**	F3
Middelburg, *South Africa*	**108**	D6
Middelfart	**52**	E1
Middelkerke	**54**	E3
Middle America Trench	**120**	L8
Middle Andaman	**84**	A4
Middlebury	**128**	F2
Middle Lake	**126**	C2
Middlesboro	**128**	D3
Middlesbrough	**56**	L7
Middletown, *N.Y., US*	**128**	F2
Middletown, *Oh., US*	**128**	D3
Mīdī	**100**	H4
Midland, *Canada*	**128**	E2
Midland, *Mich., US*	**128**	D2
Midland, *Tex., US*	**132**	F2
Midway Islands	**112**	J3
Midwest City	**130**	B2
Midzor	**66**	K6
Miechów	**50**	K7
Międzyrzec Podlaski	**50**	M5
Miedzyrzecz	**50**	E5
Mielan	**58**	F10
Mielec	**50**	L7
Miembwe	**106**	F5
Mien	**50**	D1
Miercurea-Ciuc	**66**	N3
Mieres	**60**	E1
Miesbach	**62**	G3
Mī'ēso	**106**	G2
Miging	**88**	F3
Miguel Auza	**132**	F4
Mikhaylovka	**70**	H4
Mikhaylovskiy	**76**	P7
Mikino	**78**	U4
Mikkeli	**48**	P6
Mikulov	**62**	M2
Mikun'	**70**	K2
Mikuni-sammyaku	**82**	K5
Mikura-jima	**82**	K7
Mila	**102**	G1
Milaca	**128**	B1
Miladhunmadulu Atoll	**88**	B7
Milan = Milano, *Italy*	**62**	E5
Milan, *US*	**130**	D2
Milano	**62**	E5
Milas	**68**	K7
Milazzo	**64**	K10
Mildura	**114**	H6
Miles	**114**	K5
Miles City	**126**	E1
Milford, *Del., US*	**128**	E3
Milford, *Ut., US*	**126**	D3
Milford Haven	**56**	G10
Milford Sound	**116**	A7
Milford Sound	**116**	A7
Miliana	**60**	N8
Milicz	**50**	G6
Milk	**122**	J7
Mil'kovo	**78**	T6
Millau	**58**	J9
Millbank	**126**	G1
Milledgeville	**130**	E3
Miller	**126**	G2
Millerovo	**70**	H5
Millington	**128**	C3
Millinocket	**128**	G1
Miloro	**106**	E5
Milos	**68**	G8
Milton, *New Zealand*	**116**	B8
Milton, *US*	**130**	D3
Milton Keynes	**54**	B2
Miluo	**80**	E5
Milwaukee	**128**	C2
Mily	**76**	L8
Mimizan-Plage	**58**	D9
Mīnāb	**95**	G3
Mina Jebel Ali	**95**	F4
Minas, *Indonesia*	**86**	C3
Minas, *Uruguay*	**142**	K5
Mīnā' Sa'ūd	**95**	C2
Minas Gerais	**140**	H7
Minas Novas	**140**	J7
Minatitián	**134**	F5
Minbu	**84**	A2
Minchinmávida	**142**	G7
Mincivan	**92**	M4
Mindanao	**84**	G5
Mindelheim	**62**	F2
Mindelo	**104**	(1)B1
Minden	**54**	L2
Mindoro	**84**	G4
Mindoro Strait	**84**	G4
Minehead	**56**	J10
Mineola	**130**	B3
Mineral'nyye Vody	**92**	K1
Minerva Reefs	**112**	J8
Minfeng	**76**	Q10
Minga	**106**	D6
Mingäçevir	**92**	M3
Mingäçevir Su Anbarı	**92**	M3
Mingulay	**56**	D5
Minhe	**80**	C3
Minicoy	**88**	B7
Minilya Roadhouse	**114**	B4
Minna	**104**	F3
Minneapolis	**128**	B2
Minnesota	**128**	A1
Minnesota	**128**	A2
Miño	**60**	C2
Minot	**126**	F1
Minsk	**70**	E4
Minturn	**126**	E3
Minusinsk	**76**	S7
Min Xian	**80**	C4
Min'yar	**70**	L3
Miquelon	**128**	E1
Miraflores	**140**	C3
Miramas	**58**	K10
Mirambeau	**58**	E8
Miranda	**140**	F8
Miranda de Ebro	**60**	H2
Miranda do Douro	**60**	D3
Mirandela	**60**	C3
Mirbāt	**90**	F6
Mīrjāveh	**90**	H4
Mirnyy	**78**	J4
Mirow	**52**	H3
Mirpur Khas	**88**	A3
Mirtoö Pelagos	**68**	F7
Mirzapur	**88**	D3
Miskolc	**66**	H1
Misoöl	**87**	D3
Miṣrātah	**100**	C1
Missinaibi	**122**	Q6
Missinipe	**122**	L5
Mission	**126**	F2
Mississippi	**130**	C3
Mississippi	**130**	D2
Mississippi River Delta	**130**	D4
Missoula	**126**	D1
Missouri	**126**	F1
Missouri	**128**	B3
Missouri City	**130**	B4
Mistassibi	**122**	S7
Mistelbach	**62**	M2
Mitchell	**126**	G2
Mithankot	**90**	K4
Mithaylov	**70**	G4
Mithymna	**68**	J5
Mito	**82**	L5
Mitsamiouli	**108**	G2
Mitsinjo	**108**	H3
Mits'iwa	**90**	C6
Mittellandkanal	**54**	K2
Mittersill	**62**	H3
Mittweida	**52**	H6
Mitú	**140**	C3
Mitzic	**104**	G4
Miyake-jima	**82**	K6
Miyako	**82**	L4
Miyakonojō	**82**	F8
Miyazaki	**82**	F8
Miyoshi	**82**	G6
Mīzan Teferī	**106**	F2
Mizdah	**102**	H2
Mizen Head	**56**	B10
Mizhhir"ya	**66**	L1
Mizil	**66**	P4
Mizpe Ramon	**94**	B6
Mjölby	**48**	H7
Mjøsa	**48**	F6
Mkuze	**108**	E5
Mladá Boleslav	**50**	D7
Mladenovac	**66**	H5
Mława	**50**	K4
Mljet	**66**	E7
Mmabatho	**108**	D5
Moa	**114**	H2
Moanda	**104**	G5
Moapa	**126**	D3
Moba	**106**	D5
Mobaye	**106**	C3
Mobayi-Mbongo	**106**	C3
Moberly	**128**	B3
Mobile	**130**	D3
Moçambique	**108**	G3
Môc Châu	**84**	C2
Mochudi	**108**	D4
Mocimboa da Praia	**108**	G2
Mocuba	**108**	F3
Modane	**62**	B5
Modena	**62**	F6
Modesto	**126**	B3
Modica	**64**	J12
Mödling	**62**	M2
Modowi	**87**	D3
Modriča	**66**	F5
Moenkopi	**132**	D1
Moers	**54**	J3
Moffat	**56**	J6
Moffat Peak	**116**	B7
Mogadishu = Muqdisho	**106**	H3
Mogaung	**84**	B1
Mogilno	**50**	G5
Mogocha	**78**	K6
Mogochin	**76**	Q6
Mogok	**84**	B2
Mohács	**66**	F4
Mohammadia	**60**	L9
Mohe	**78**	L6
Mohembo	**108**	C3
Mohoro	**106**	F5
Mohyliv-Podil's'kyy	**66**	Q1
Moi	**48**	D7
Moincêr	**88**	D2
Moinești	**66**	P3
Mo i Rana	**48**	H3
Moissac	**58**	G9
Mojave	**132**	C1
Mojave Desert	**132**	C2
Mokau	**116**	E4
Mokohinau Island	**116**	E2
Mokolo	**104**	G2
Mokoreta	**116**	B8
Mokp'o	**82**	D6
Mol	**54**	H3
Mola di Bari	**64**	M7
Molat	**62**	K6
Molde	**48**	D5
Moldova	**66**	P2
Moldova	**66**	R2
Moldova Nouă	**66**	J5
Molepolole	**108**	C4
Molfetta	**64**	L7
Molina de Aragón	**60**	J4
Molina de Segura	**60**	J6
Moline	**128**	B2
Möll	**62**	J4
Mollendo	**140**	C7
Molokai	**132**	(2)D2
Molopo	**108**	C5
Molsheim	**62**	C2
Moma	**108**	F3
Mombasa	**106**	G4
Momchilgrad	**66**	N8
Møn	**52**	H2
Monach Islands	**56**	E4
Monaco	**62**	C7
Monaco	**62**	C7
Monahans	**132**	F2
Mona Passage	**134**	L5
Monbetsu, *Japan*	**82**	M1
Monbetsu, *Japan*	**82**	M2
Moncalieri	**62**	C5
Monchegorsk	**48**	S3
Mönchengladbach	**54**	J3
Monchique	**60**	B7
Monclova	**132**	F3
Moncton	**122**	U7
Mondovi	**62**	C6
Mondragone	**64**	H7
Mondy	**78**	G6
Monemvasia	**68**	F8
Monfalcone	**62**	J5
Monforte	**60**	C5
Monforte de Lemos	**60**	C2
Monfredónia	**64**	K7
Monga	**106**	C3
Mongkung	**84**	B2
Mongo	**100**	C5
Mongolia	**80**	B2
Mongonu	**104**	G2
Mongora	**88**	B2
Mongu	**108**	C3
Mong Yai	**84**	B2
Mong Yu	**84**	B2
Monkoto	**106**	C4
Monmouth	**128**	B2
Mono	**104**	E3
Mono Lake	**126**	C3
Monopoli	**64**	M8
Monor	**50**	J10
Monowai	**116**	A7
Monreal del Campo	**60**	J4
Monreale	**64**	H10
Monroe, *La., US*	**130**	C3
Monroe, *Mich., US*	**128**	D2
Monroe, *N.C., US*	**130**	E3
Monroe, *Wash., US*	**126**	B1
Monroe City	**130**	C2
Monrovia	**104**	B3
Mons	**54**	F4
Monschau	**54**	J4
Monselice	**62**	G5
Montabaur	**54**	K4
Montague Island	**138**	J9
Montalbán	**60**	K4
Montalto Uffugo	**64**	L9
Montana	**66**	L6
Montana	**126**	E1
Montargis	**58**	H6
Montauban	**58**	G10
Montauk	**128**	F2
Mont aux Sources	**108**	D5
Montbard	**58**	K6
Montbéliard	**62**	B3
Montblanc	**60**	M3
Mont Blanc	**62**	B5
Montbrison	**58**	K8
Mont Cameroun	**104**	F4
Montceau-les-Mines	**58**	K7
Mont-de-Marsan	**58**	E10
Montdidier	**54**	E5
Monte Alegre	**140**	G4
Monte Azul	**140**	J7
Montebello	**128**	F1
Montebello Islands	**114**	B4
Montebelluna	**62**	H5
Monte Calvo	**64**	K7
Monte Cinto	**64**	C6
Montecristo	**64**	E6
Monte Etna	**64**	J11
Montefiascone	**64**	G6
Montego Bay	**134**	J5
Montélimar	**58**	K9
Monte Limbara	**64**	D8
Monte Lindo	**142**	K4
Montemorelos	**130**	B4
Monte Namuli	**108**	F3
Monte Perdino	**60**	L2
Monte Pollino	**64**	L9
Montepuez	**108**	F2
Montepulciano	**64**	F5
Monte Quemado	**142**	J4
Montereau-faut-Yonne	**58**	H5
Monterey	**128**	E3
Monterey Bay	**126**	B3
Montería	**140**	B2
Montero	**140**	E7
Monte Rosa	**62**	C5
Monterotondo	**64**	G6
Monterrey	**132**	F3
Monte Sant'Angelo	**64**	K7
Montes Claros	**140**	J7
Montesilvano	**64**	J6
Montevarchi	**62**	G7
Montevideo, *US*	**128**	A1
Montevideo, *Uruguay*	**142**	K5
Monte Viso	**62**	C6
Monte Vista	**132**	E1
Montgomery	**130**	D3
Monthey	**62**	B4
Monticello	**126**	E3
Montijo	**60**	D6
Montilla	**60**	F7
Mont Joli	**128**	G1
Mont-Laurier	**128**	E1
Montluçon	**58**	H7
Montmagny	**128**	F1
Montmedy	**54**	H5
Mont Mézenc	**58**	K9
Montone	**62**	G6
Montoro	**60**	F6
Mont Pelat	**58**	M9
Montpelier, *Id., US*	**126**	D2
Montpelier, *Vt., US*	**128**	F2
Montpellier	**58**	J10
Montréal	**128**	F1
Montreul	**54**	D4
Montreux	**62**	B4
Montrose, *UK*	**56**	K5
Montrose, *US*	**126**	E3
Monts Bagzane	**102**	G5
Mont Serkout	**102**	G4
Montserrat	**134**	M5
Monts Nimba	**104**	C3
Monts Otish	**122**	S6
Mont Tahat	**102**	G4
Monywa	**84**	A2
Monza	**62**	E5
Monzón	**60**	L3
Moonie	**114**	K5
Moorcroft	**126**	F2

Moorhead	▣	**128**	A1
Moosburg	▣	**62**	G1
Moose Jaw	▣	**122**	K6
Moose Lake	◩	**122**	M6
Moosomin	▣	**122**	L6
Moosonee	▣	**122**	Q6
Mopeia	▣	**108**	F3
Mopti	▣	**102**	E6
Moqor	▣	**90**	J3
Mór	▣	**66**	F2
Mora	▣	**48**	H6
Móra	▣	**60**	B6
Moradabad	▣	**88**	C3
Morafenobe	▣	**108**	G3
Morag	▣	**50**	J4
Moramanga	▣	**108**	H3
Moran	▣	**126**	D2
Morane	⊡	**112**	N8
Moratuwa	▣	**88**	D7
Morava	⧄	**50**	G8
Moravské Budějovice	▣	**62**	L1
Morawhanna	▣	**140**	F2
Moray Firth	⚑	**56**	J4
Morbach	▣	**54**	K5
Morbegno	▣	**62**	E4
Morbi	▣	**88**	B4
Morcenx	▣	**58**	E9
Mordaga	▣	**78**	L6
Mordoviya	ⓐ	**70**	H4
Moreau	⧄	**126**	F1
Morecambe	▣	**56**	K7
Moree	▣	**114**	J5
Morehead, *Papua New Guinea*	▣	**87**	F4
Morehead, *US*	▣	**128**	D3
More Laptevykh	≋	**78**	L1
Morelia	▣	**134**	D5
Morella	▣	**60**	K4
Moresby Island	⊡	**132**	(1)L5
Moreton Island	⊡	**114**	K5
Morez	▣	**58**	M7
Morfou	▣	**68**	Q9
Morgan	▣	**114**	G6
Morgan City	▣	**130**	C4
Morgantown	▣	**128**	D3
Morges	▣	**62**	B4
Mori	▣	**82**	L2
Morioka	▣	**82**	L4
Morkoka	⧄	**78**	J4
Morlaix	▣	**58**	B5
Mornington Island	⊡	**114**	G3
Morocco	Ⓐ	**98**	C2
Morogoro	▣	**106**	F5
Moro Gulf	⚑	**84**	G5
Morombe	▣	**108**	G4
Mörön	▣	**78**	G7
Morondava	▣	**108**	G4
Morón de la Frontera	▣	**60**	E7
Moroni	■	**108**	G2
Moron Us He	⧄	**88**	F2
Morotai	⊡	**87**	C2
Moroto	▣	**106**	E3
Morpeth	▣	**56**	L6
Morris	▣	**126**	G1
Morristown	▣	**130**	E2
Mors	⊡	**48**	E8
Morshansk	▣	**70**	H4
Mortain	▣	**54**	B6
Morteros	▣	**142**	J5
Morvern	⊡	**56**	G5
Morwell	▣	**114**	J7
Mosbach	▣	**52**	E7
Mosby	▣	**126**	D1
Moscow = Moskva	■	**70**	G3
Mosel	⧄	**54**	K4
Moselle	⧄	**54**	G6
Moses Lake	▣	**126**	C1
Mosgiel	▣	**116**	C7
Moshi	▣	**106**	F4
Mosjøen	▣	**48**	G4
Moskenesøy	⊡	**48**	F3
Moskva	■	**70**	G3
Mosonmagyaróvár	▣	**62**	N3
Mosquero	▣	**132**	F1
Moss	▣	**48**	F7
Mossburn	▣	**116**	B7
Mosselbaai	▣	**108**	C6
Mossoró	▣	**140**	K5
Most	▣	**52**	J6
Mostaganem	▣	**60**	L9
Mostar	▣	**66**	E6
Mostoles	▣	**60**	G4
Møsvatn	◩	**48**	E7
Mot'a	▣	**100**	G5
Motala	▣	**48**	H7
Motherwell	▣	**56**	J6
Motihari	▣	**88**	D3
Motilla del Palancar	▣	**60**	J5
Motiti Island	⊡	**116**	F3
Motril	▣	**60**	G8
Motru	▣	**66**	K5
Motu One	⊡	**112**	L7
Motygino	▣	**76**	S6
Mouchard	▣	**62**	A4
Moudjéria	▣	**102**	C5
Moudros	▣	**68**	H5
Mouila	▣	**104**	G5
Moulins	▣	**58**	J7
Moulmein	▣	**84**	B3
Moultrie	▣	**130**	E3
Moundou	▣	**100**	C6
Mount Adam	▲	**142**	J9
Mount Adams	▲	**126**	B1
Mountain Grove	▣	**128**	B3
Mountain Home	▣	**128**	B3
Mountain Nile = Bahr el Jebel	⧄	**106**	E2
Mount Alba	▲	**116**	B7
Mount Aloysius	▲	**114**	E5
Mount Anglem	▲	**116**	A8
Mount Apo	▲	**84**	H5
Mount Ararat	▲	**92**	L4
Mount Arrowsmith	▲	**116**	C6
Mount Aspiring	▲	**116**	B7
Mount Assiniboine	▲	**122**	H6
Mount Augustus	▲	**114**	C4
Mount Baco	▲	**84**	G3
Mount Baker	▲	**126**	B1
Mount Bartle Frere	▲	**114**	J3
Mount Bogong	▲	**114**	J7
Mount Brewster	▲	**116**	B7
Mount Bruce	▲	**114**	C4
Mount Cameroun	▲	**98**	D5
Mount Carmel	▣	**126**	D3
Mount Columbia	▲	**122**	H6
Mount Cook = Aoraki	▲	**116**	C6
Mount Cook	▣	**116**	C6
Mount Donald	▲	**116**	A7
Mount Douglas	▲	**114**	J4
Mount Egmont	▲	**116**	E4
Mount Elbert	▲	**126**	E3
Mount Elgon	▲	**106**	E3
Mount Essendon	▲	**114**	D4
Mount Evelyn	▲	**114**	F2
Mount Everest	▲	**88**	E3
Mount Fairweather	▲	**122**	D5
Mount Gambier	▣	**114**	H7
Mount Garnet	▣	**114**	J3
Mount Hermōn	▲	**94**	C3
Mount Hood	▲	**126**	B1
Mount Hutt	▣	**116**	C6
Mount Huxley	▲	**116**	B7
Mount Isa	▣	**114**	G4
Mount Jackson	▲	**144**	(2)MM2
Mount Karisimbi	▲	**106**	D4
Mount Kendall	▲	**116**	D5
Mount Kenya = Kirinyaga	▲	**106**	F4
Mount Kilimanjaro	▲	**106**	F4
Mount Kirkpatrick	▲	**144**	(2)AA1
Mount Kosciuszko	▲	**114**	J7
Mount Liebig	▲	**114**	F4
Mount Lloyd George	▲	**122**	G5
Mount Logan	▲	**122**	C4
Mount Magnet	▣	**114**	C5
Mount Maunganui	▣	**116**	F3
Mount McKinley	▲	**132**	(1)G3
Mount Meharry	▲	**114**	C4
Mount Menzies	▲	**144**	(2)L2
Mount Minto	▲	**144**	(2)Y2
Mount Mulanje	▲	**108**	F3
Mount Murchison	▲	**116**	C6
Mount Nyiru	▲	**106**	F3
Mount Olympus	▲	**126**	B1
Mount Ord	▲	**114**	E3
Mount Ossa	▲	**114**	J8
Mount Owen	▲	**116**	D5
Mount Paget	▲	**142**	P9
Mount Pleasant, *Ia., US*	▣	**128**	B2
Mount Pleasant, *Mich., US*	▣	**128**	D2
Mount Pleasant, *S.C., US*	▣	**130**	F3
Mount Pleasant, *Tex., US*	▣	**130**	B3
Mount Pleasant, *Ut., US*	▣	**126**	D3
Mount Pulog	▲	**84**	G3
Mount Rainier	▲	**126**	B1
Mount Ratz	▲	**122**	E5
Mount Richmond	▲	**116**	D5
Mount Roberts	▲	**114**	K5
Mount Robson	◎	**122**	H6
Mount Roosevelt	▲	**122**	F5
Mount Roraima	▲	**140**	E2
Mount Ross	▲	**116**	E5
Mount Shasta	▲	**126**	B2
Mount Somers	▣	**116**	C6
Mount Stanley	▲	**106**	D3
Mount Tahat	▲	**98**	D3
Mount Travers	▲	**116**	D6
Mount Tuun	▣	**82**	D3
Mount Usborne	▲	**142**	K9
Mount Vernon, *Al., US*	▣	**130**	D3
Mount Vernon, *Ill., US*	▣	**128**	C3
Mount Vernon, *Oh., US*	▣	**128**	D2
Mount Vernon, *Wash., US*	▣	**126**	B1
Mount Victoria, *Myanmar*	▲	**84**	A2
Mount Victoria, *Papua New Guinea*	▲	**112**	E6
Mount Waddington	▲	**122**	F6
Mount Washington	▲	**122**	S8
Mount Whitney	▲	**126**	C3
Mount Wilson	▲	**126**	E3
Mount Woodroffe	▲	**114**	F5
Mount Ziel	▲	**114**	F4
Moura	▣	**60**	C6
Mousa	⊡	**56**	L2
Moussoro	▣	**100**	C5
Moutamba	▣	**104**	G5
Mouth of the Shannon	⚑	**56**	B9
Mouths of the Amazon	⚑	**138**	G3
Mouths of the Danube	⧄	**66**	S4
Mouths of the Ganges	⚑	**88**	E4
Mouths of the Indus	⚑	**90**	J5
Mouths of the Irrawaddy	⚑	**84**	A3
Mouths of the Krishna	⚑	**88**	D5
Mouths of the Mekong	⚑	**84**	D5
Mouths of the Niger	⚑	**104**	F4
Moûtiers	▣	**62**	B5
Moutong	▣	**87**	B2
Mouzarak	▣	**104**	H2
Moyale	▣	**106**	F3
Moyen Atlas	⛰	**102**	D2
Moyenvic	▣	**54**	J6
Moyeroo	⧄	**76**	U4
Moyynty	▣	**76**	N8
Mozambique	Ⓐ	**108**	E3
Mozambique Channel	⚑	**108**	F4
Mozdok	▣	**92**	L2
Mozhga	▣	**70**	K3
Mozirje	▣	**62**	K4
Mpanda	▣	**106**	E5
Mpika	▣	**108**	E2
Mporokoso	▣	**106**	E5
Mpumalanga	ⓐ	**108**	D5
Mrągowo	▣	**50**	L4
Mrkonjić-Grad	▣	**62**	N6
M'Sila	▣	**102**	F1
Mtsensk	▣	**70**	G4
Mtwara	▣	**106**	G6
Muang Khammouan	▣	**84**	C3
Muang Không	▣	**84**	D4
Muang Khôngxédôn	▣	**84**	D3
Muang Khoua	▣	**84**	C2
Muang Pakxan	▣	**84**	C3
Muang Phin	▣	**84**	D3
Muang Sing	▣	**84**	C2
Muang Xai	▣	**84**	C2
Muar	▣	**86**	C2
Muarabungo	▣	**86**	C3
Muaradua	▣	**86**	C3
Muarasiberut	▣	**86**	B3
Muaratewen	▣	**86**	E3
Muarawahau	▣	**86**	F2
Mubarek	▣	**76**	M10
Mubende	▣	**106**	E3
Mubrani	▣	**87**	D3
Muck	⊡	**56**	F5
Muckadilla	▣	**114**	J5
Muconda	▣	**106**	C6
Mucur	▣	**68**	S5
Mudanjiang	▣	**82**	E1
Mudanya	▣	**68**	L4
Muddy Gap	▣	**126**	E2
Mudurnu	▣	**68**	P4
Mufulira	▣	**108**	D2
Mughshin	▣	**90**	F6
Muğla	▣	**68**	L7
Mugodzhary	◎	**70**	L5
Muhammad Qol	▣	**100**	G3
Mühldorf	▣	**62**	H2
Mühlhausen	▣	**52**	F5
Muhos	▣	**48**	N4
Muhu	⊡	**48**	M7
Muhulu	▣	**106**	D4
Mukacheve	▣	**50**	M9
Mukdahan	▣	**84**	C3
Mukomuko	▣	**86**	C3
Mukry	▣	**90**	J2
Mukuku	▣	**108**	D2
Mulaku Atoll	⊡	**88**	B8
Mulde	⧄	**52**	H5
Muleshoe	▣	**132**	F2
Mulgrave Island	⊡	**114**	H2
Mulhacén	▲	**60**	G7
Mülheim	▣	**54**	J3
Mulhouse	▣	**62**	C3
Muling	⧄	**82**	G1
Mull	⊡	**56**	G5
Mullaittivu	▣	**88**	D7
Mullewa	▣	**114**	C5
Müllheim	▣	**62**	C3
Mullingar	▣	**56**	E8
Mulobezi	▣	**108**	D3
Multan	▣	**90**	K3
Mumbai	▣	**88**	B5
Mumbwa	▣	**108**	D2
Muna	⊡	**87**	B4
Münchberg	▣	**52**	G6
München	▣	**62**	G2
Münden	▣	**52**	E5
Mundo Novo	▣	**140**	J6
Mundrabilla	▣	**114**	E6
Muneðarnes	▣	**48**	(1)C1
Munera	▣	**60**	H5
Mungbere	▣	**106**	D3
Munger	▣	**88**	E3
Munich = München	▣	**62**	G2
Munster, *France*	▣	**62**	C2
Munster, *Germany*	▣	**52**	F4
Münster, *Germany*	▣	**54**	K3
Munte	▣	**87**	A2
Muojärvi	◩	**48**	Q4
Muonio	▣	**48**	M3
Muqdisho	■	**106**	H3
Mur	⧄	**62**	L4
Muradiye	▣	**92**	K4
Murang'a	▣	**106**	F4
Murashi	▣	**70**	J3
Murat	⧄	**92**	K4
Muratlı	▣	**68**	K3
Murchison	▣	**116**	D5
Murcia	▣	**60**	J7
Murdo	▣	**126**	F2
Mureș	⧄	**66**	J3
Muret	▣	**58**	G10
Murfreesboro, *N.C., US*	▣	**130**	F2
Murfreesboro, *Tenn., US*	▣	**130**	D2
Murghob	▣	**90**	K2
Muriaé	▣	**140**	J8
Müritz	◩	**52**	H3
Muriwai	▣	**116**	F4
Murmansk	▣	**48**	S2
Murnau	▣	**62**	G3
Murom	▣	**70**	H3
Muroran	▣	**82**	L2
Muros	▣	**60**	A2
Muroto	▣	**82**	H7
Murphy	▣	**130**	E2
Murray	⧄	**114**	H6
Murray	▣	**128**	C3
Murray Bridge	▣	**114**	G7
Murray River Basin	◎	**114**	H6
Murska Sobota	▣	**62**	M4
Murter	⊡	**62**	L7
Murtosa	▣	**60**	B4
Murud	▣	**88**	B5
Murupara	▣	**116**	F4
Mururoa	⊡	**112**	M8
Murwara	▣	**88**	D4
Murzūq	▣	**102**	H3
Mürzzuschlag	▣	**62**	L3
Muş	▣	**92**	J4
Mūša	⧄	**50**	N1
Musala	▲	**68**	F2
Musandam Peninsula	◎	**95**	G3
Musayʿīd	▣	**95**	D4
Muscat = Masqaț	■	**95**	H5
Musgrave Ranges	⛰	**114**	E5
Mushin	▣	**104**	E3
Muskegon	▣	**128**	C2
Muskogee	▣	**130**	B2
Musmar	▣	**100**	G4
Musoma	▣	**106**	E4
Mussende	▣	**106**	B6
Mustafakemalpaşa	▣	**68**	L4
Mut, *Egypt*	▣	**100**	E2
Mut, *Turkey*	▣	**68**	R8
Mutare	▣	**108**	E3
Mutarnee	▣	**114**	J3
Mutnyy Materik	▣	**70**	L1
Mutoray	▣	**76**	U5
Mutsamudu	▣	**108**	G2
Mutsu	▣	**82**	L3
Mutsu-wan	⚑	**82**	L3
Muttaburra	▣	**114**	H4
Mutur	▣	**88**	D7
Muyezerskiy	▣	**48**	R5
Muyinga	▣	**106**	E4
Muynak	▣	**76**	K9
Muzaffarnagar	▣	**88**	C3
Muzaffarpur	▣	**88**	E3
Muzillac	▣	**58**	C6
Múzquiz	▣	**132**	F3
Muztagata	▲	**76**	N10
Mwali	⊡	**108**	G2
Mwanza	▣	**106**	E4
Mweka	▣	**106**	C4
Mwenda	▣	**106**	D6
Mwene-Ditu	▣	**106**	C5
Mwenezi	▣	**108**	E4
Mwenezi	⧄	**108**	E4
Mwinilunga	▣	**108**	C2
Myanmar	Ⓐ	**84**	B2
Myaungmya	▣	**84**	A3
Myingyan	▣	**84**	B2
Myitkyina	▣	**84**	B1
Myjava	▣	**62**	N2
Myjava	⧄	**62**	N2
Mykolayiv	▣	**50**	N8
Mykonos	⊡	**68**	H7
Mymensingh	▣	**88**	F4
Mynbulak	▣	**76**	L9
Myndagayy	▣	**78**	N4
Myōjin	⊡	**80**	K4
Myonggan	▣	**82**	E3
Myrdalsjökull	◎	**48**	(1)D3
Myrina	▣	**68**	H5
Myrtle Beach	▣	**130**	F3
Mys Alevina	▷	**78**	S5
Mys Aniva	▷	**80**	L1
Mys Buorkhaya	▷	**78**	N2
Mys Dezhneva	▷	**78**	Z3
Mys Elizavety	▷	**78**	Q6
Mys Enkan	▷	**78**	P5
Mys Govena	▷	**78**	V5
Mys Kanin Nos	▷	**70**	H1
Mys Kekurskij	▷	**48**	S2
Mys Kril'on	▷	**80**	L1
Myślenice	▣	**50**	J8
Myślibórz	▣	**50**	D5
Mys Lopatka, *Russia*	▷	**78**	T6
Mys Lopatka, *Russia*	▷	**78**	S2
Mys Navarin	▷	**78**	X4
Mys Olyutorskiy	▷	**78**	W5
Mysore	▣	**88**	C6
Mys Peschanyy	▷	**76**	J9
Mys Povorotnyy	▷	**82**	G2
Mys Prubiynyy	▷	**70**	F5
Mys Shelagskiy	▷	**78**	V2
Mys Sivuchiy	▷	**78**	U5
Mys Terpeniya	▷	**78**	Q7
Mys Tolstoy	▷	**78**	T5
Mys Yuzhnyy	▷	**78**	T5
Mys Zhelaniya	▷	**76**	M2
Myszksw	▣	**50**	J7
My Tho	▣	**84**	D4
Mytilini	▣	**68**	J5
Mývatn	◩	**48**	(1)E2
Mže	⧄	**52**	H7
Mzimba	▣	**108**	E2
Mzuzu	▣	**108**	E2

N

Naalehu	▣	**132**	(2)F4
Naas	▣	**56**	F8
Nabas	▣	**84**	G4
Naberezhnyye Chelny	▣	**70**	K3
Nabeul	▣	**64**	E12
Nabīd	▣	**95**	G2
Nabire	▣	**87**	E3
Nablus	▣	**94**	C4
Nacala	▣	**108**	G2
Nacaroa	▣	**108**	F2
Náchod	▣	**50**	F7
Nacogdoches	▣	**130**	C3
Nadiad	▣	**88**	B4
Nador	▣	**102**	E2
Nadvirna	▣	**66**	M1
Nadym	▣	**70**	P1
Nadym	⧄	**70**	P2
Næstved	▣	**52**	G1
Nafpaktos	▣	**68**	D6
Nafplio	▣	**68**	E7
Naga	▣	**84**	G4
Nagano	▣	**82**	K5
Nagaoka	▣	**82**	K5
Nagaon	▣	**88**	F3
Nagarzê	▣	**88**	F3
Nagasaki	▣	**82**	E7
Nagaur	▣	**88**	B3
Nagercoil	▣	**88**	C7
Nago	▣	**80**	H5
Nagold	▣	**52**	D8
Nagorsk	▣	**70**	K3
Nagoya	▣	**82**	J6
Nagpur	▣	**88**	C4
Nagqu	▣	**88**	F2
Nagyatád	▣	**62**	N4
Nagykálló	▣	**66**	J2
Nagykanizsa	▣	**62**	N4
Nagykáta	▣	**50**	J10
Nagykőrös	▣	**66**	G2

Name	Page	Grid
Naha	80	H5
Nahanni	122	G4
Nahanni Butte	122	G4
Nahr en Nile = Nile	100	F2
Naiman Qi	80	G2
Nain	122	U5
Nairn	56	J4
Nairobi	106	F4
Naivasha	106	F4
Naizishan	82	D2
Najafābād	90	F3
Nájera	60	H2
Najibabad	88	C3
Najin	82	F2
Najrān	100	H4
Naju	82	D6
Nakamura	82	G7
Nakatsu	82	F7
Nakhl	94	A7
Nakhodka, *Russia*	76	P4
Nakhodka, *Russia*	82	G2
Nakhon Ratchasima	84	C3
Nakhon Sawan	84	B3
Nakhon Si Thammarat	84	B5
Nakina	122	P6
Nakło nad Notecią	50	G4
Naknek	132	(1)F4
Nakonde	106	E5
Nakskov	52	F2
Nakten	48	H5
Nakuru	106	F4
Nal'chik	92	K2
Nallihan	68	P4
Nālūt	102	H2
Namagan	76	N9
Namakzar-e Shadad	95	G1
Namanga	106	F4
Namapa	108	F2
Namasagali	106	E3
Nam Can	84	C5
Nam Co	88	F2
Namdalen	48	G4
Nam Dinh	84	D2
Namib Desert	108	A4
Namibe	108	A3
Namibia	108	B4
Namidobe	108	F3
Namlea	87	C3
Namo	87	A3
Nampa	126	C2
Nampala	104	C1
Nam Ping	84	B3
Namp'o	82	C4
Nampula	108	F3
Namsos	48	F4
Namtsy	78	M4
Namur	54	G4
Namwala	108	D3
Namwŏn	82	D6
Nan	84	C3
Nanaimo	126	B1
Nanao	82	J5
Nanchang	80	F5
Nanchong	80	D4
Nancy	62	B2
Nanda Devi	88	C2
Nānded	88	C5
Nandurbar	88	B4
Nandyal	88	C5
Nanfeng	80	F5
Nangalala	114	G2
Nangapinoh	86	E3
Nangatayap	86	E3
Nangis	58	J5
Nangong	80	F3
Nang Xian	88	F3
Nanjing	80	F4
Nankoku	82	G7
Nannine	114	C5
Nanning	84	D2
Nanortalik	122	X4
Nanpan	84	D2
Nanping	80	F5
Nansei-shotō	80	H5
Nantes	58	D6
Nanton	124	D1
Nantong	80	G4
Nanumea	112	H6
Nanuque	140	J7
Nanutarra Roadhouse	114	C4
Nanyang	80	E4
Napa	126	B3
Napalkovo	76	N3
Napamute	132	(1)F3
Napas	78	C4
Napasoq	122	W3
Napier	116	F4
Naples = Napoli	64	J8
Naples	130	E4
Napo	140	C4
Napoli	64	J8
Naqb Ashtar	94	C6
Nara, *Japan*	82	H6
Nara, *Mali*	102	D5
Narathiwat	84	C5
Narbonne	58	H10
Nardò	64	N8
Nares Strait	120	J2
Narev	50	N5
Narew	50	L5
Narib	108	B4
Narmada	88	C4
Narnaul	88	C3
Narni	64	G6
Narok	106	F4
Närpes	48	L5
Narrabri	114	J6
Narrandera	114	J6
Narsimhapur	88	C4
Nart	80	F2
Narva	48	P7
Narva	48	Q7
Narva Bay	48	P7
Narvik	48	J2
Nar'yan Mar	70	K1
Naryn	78	F6
Năsăud	66	M2
Nashua	128	F2
Nashville	130	D2
Našice	66	F4
Nasik	88	B4
Nasir	106	E2
Nassarawa	104	F3
Nassau	130	F4
Nässjö	48	H8
Nastapoka Islands	122	R5
Nasugbu	84	G4
Naswá	95	G5
Nata	108	D4
Natal	140	K5
Natara	78	L3
Natashquan	122	U6
Natchez	130	C3
Natchitoches	130	C3
National Park	116	E4
Natitingou	104	E2
Natori	82	L4
Natuna Besar	86	D2
Naucelle	58	H9
Nauchas	108	B4
Nauders	62	F4
Naujoji Akmenė	50	M1
Naumburg	52	G5
Na'ūr	94	C5
Nauru	112	G6
Nauta	140	C4
Nautonwa	88	D3
Navahermosa	60	F5
Navahrudak	48	N10
Navajo Reservoir	126	E3
Navalero	60	H3
Navalmoral de la Mata	60	E5
Navalvillar de Pela	60	E5
Navapolatsk	70	E3
Navlya	70	F4
Navoi	76	M9
Navojoa	124	E6
Navrongo	104	D2
Navsari	88	B4
Nawá	94	D4
Nawabshah	90	J4
Nāwah	90	J3
Naxçivan	92	L4
Naxos	68	H7
Naxos	68	H7
Nayakhan	78	T4
Nāy Band, *Iran*	90	G3
Nāy Band, *Iran*	95	E3
Nayoro	82	M1
Naypyidaw	84	B3
Nazaré	60	A5
Nazareth	94	C4
Nazarovo	76	S6
Nazca	140	C6
Nazca Ridge	142	E3
Naze	80	H5
Nazilli	68	L7
Nazino	76	P6
Nazran'	92	L2
Nazrēt	106	F2
Nazwá	90	G5
Nazyvayevsk	70	P3
Ncojane	108	C4
Ndélé	106	C2
Ndjamena	100	B5
Ndjolé	104	G5
Ndola	108	D2
Nea Ionia	68	E5
Neale Junction	114	E5
Neapoli	68	F8
Nea Roda	68	F4
Nea Zichni	68	F3
Nebbi	106	E3
Nebitdag	90	F2
Nebo	114	J4
Nebraska	126	G2
Neckar	52	D7
Neckar	52	D8
Neckarsulm	52	E7
Necker Island	112	K3
Necochea	142	K6
Nédély	100	C4
Nedre Soppero	48	L3
Needles	132	D2
Nefedovo	70	P3
Nefta	102	G2
Neftçala	92	N4
Neftekamsk	70	K3
Neftekumsk	92	L1
Nefteyugansk	70	P2
Nefza	64	D12
Negage	106	B5
Negār	95	G2
Negēlē	106	F2
Negele	106	F2
Negev	94	B6
Negomane	108	F2
Negombo	88	C7
Negotin	66	K5
Negotino	68	E3
Négrine	102	G2
Negro, *Argentina*	142	J7
Negro, *Brazil*	140	E4
Negros	84	G5
Negru Vodă	66	R6
Nehbandān	90	G3
Nehe	78	M7
Nehoiu	66	P4
Neijiang	80	C5
Nei Monggol	80	E2
Neiva	140	B3
Neixiang	80	E4
Nejanilini Lake	122	M5
Nek'emtē	106	F2
Nelidovo	70	F3
Neligh	126	G2
Nellore	88	C6
Nel'ma	78	P7
Nelson	122	N5
Nelson, *Canada*	126	C1
Nelson, *New Zealand*	116	D5
Nelspruit	108	E5
Néma	102	D5
Néman	48	N10
Neman	50	M2
Nemours	58	H5
Nemperola	87	B5
Nemunas	50	P3
Nemuro	82	N2
Nen	78	L7
Nenagh	56	D9
Nenana	132	(1)H3
Nene	54	B2
Nenjiang	78	M7
Neosho	128	B3
Nepa	78	H5
Nepal	88	D3
Nepalganj	88	D3
Nepean	128	E1
Nepomuk	52	J7
Ner	50	H5
Nera	64	G6
Neratovice	52	K6
Neris	50	P2
Nerja	60	G8
Neryungri	78	L5
Nesebŭr	66	Q7
Ness City	130	B2
Netanya	94	B4
Netherlands	54	H2
Netherlands Antilles	134	L6
Nettilling Lake	122	S3
Neubrandenburg	52	J3
Neuburg	52	G8
Neuchâtel	62	B3
Neuenhagen	52	J4
Neufchâteau, *Belgium*	54	H5
Neufchâteau, *France*	58	L5
Neufchâtel-en-Bray	54	D5
Neuhof	52	E6
Neukirchen	52	D2
Neumarkt	52	G7
Neumünster	52	F2
Neunkirchen, *Austria*	62	M3
Neunkirchen, *Germany*	52	C7
Neuquén	142	H6
Neuruppin	52	H4
Neusiedler	50	F10
Neusiedler See	62	M3
Neuss	54	J3
Neustadt, *Germany*	52	F2
Neustadt, *Germany*	52	F7
Neustadt, *Germany*	52	G6
Neustadt, *Germany*	52	G8
Neustadt, *Germany*	52	H7
Neustadt, *Germany*	54	L5
Neustrelitz	52	J3
Neu-Ulm	52	F8
Neuwerk	52	D3
Neuwied	54	K4
Nevada	126	C3
Nevada	128	B3
Nevado Auzangate	140	C6
Nevado de Colima	134	D5
Nevado de Cumbal	140	B3
Nevado de Huascaran	140	B5
Nevado de Illampu	140	D7
Nevado Sajama	140	D7
Nevados de Cachi	142	H4
Never	78	L6
Nevers	58	J7
Nevesinje	66	F6
Nevėžis	48	M9
Nevinnomyssk	92	J1
Nevşehir	68	S6
Newala	106	F6
New Albany, *Ind., US*	128	C3
New Albany, *Miss., US*	130	D3
New Amsterdam	140	F2
Newark, *N.J., US*	128	F2
Newark, *Oh., US*	128	D3
Newark-on-Trent	54	B1
New Bedford	128	F2
Newberg	126	B1
New Bern	130	F2
Newberry	130	E3
New Braunfels	130	B4
New Britain	112	F6
New Brunswick	122	T7
Newburgh	128	F2
Newbury	54	A3
New Bussa	104	E3
Newcastle, *Australia*	114	K6
Newcastle, *US*	126	F2
Newcastle-under-Lyme	56	K8
Newcastle-upon-Tyne	56	L6
Newcastle Waters	114	F3
New Delhi	88	C3
New England	126	F1
Newe Zohars	94	C5
Newfoundland	122	V7
Newfoundland and Labrador	122	V5
New Georgia Island	112	F6
New Glasgow	122	U7
New Guinea	74	S10
New Hampshire	128	F2
New Hampton	128	B2
New Hanover	112	F6
Newhaven	54	C4
New Haven	128	F2
New Iberia	130	C3
New Ireland	112	F6
New Jersey	128	F2
New Liskeard	128	E1
New London	128	F2
Newman	114	C4
Newmarket	54	C2
New Meadows	126	C2
New Mexico	132	E2
Newnan	130	E3
New Orleans	130	D4
New Plymouth	116	E4
Newport, *Eng., UK*	54	A4
Newport, *Wales, UK*	56	K10
Newport, *Ark., US*	130	C2
Newport, *Oreg., US*	126	B2
Newport, *R.I., US*	128	F2
Newport, *Vt., US*	128	F2
Newport, *Wash., US*	126	C1
New Providence	130	F5
Newquay	56	G11
Newry	56	F7
New Siberia Islands = Novosibirskiye Ostrova	78	P1
New Smyrna Beach	130	E4
New South Wales	114	H6
Newton, *Ia., US*	128	B2
Newton, *Kans., US*	130	B2
Newtownards	56	G7
New Ulm	128	B2
New York	128	E2
New York	128	F2
New Zealand	116	B5
Neya	70	H3
Neyrīz	95	F2
Neyshābūr	90	G2
Ngabang	86	D2
Ngalu	87	B5
Ngamring	88	E3
Ngaoundéré	104	G3
Ngara	106	E4
Ngawihi	116	E5
Ngo	104	H5
Ngoura	100	C5
Ngozi	106	D4
Nguigmi	104	G2
Nguru	104	G2
Nhachengue	108	F4
Nha Trang	84	D4
Nhulunbuy	114	G2
Niafounké	102	E5
Niagara Falls	128	E2
Niakaramandougou	104	C3
Niamey	104	E2
Niangara	106	D3
Nia-Nia	106	D3
Nias	86	B2
Nicaragua	134	G6
Nicastro	64	L10
Nice	62	C7
Nicholls Town	130	F4
Nicobar Islands	84	A5
Nicosia = Lefkosia	68	R9
Nida	50	K7
Nidym	78	F4
Nidzica	50	K4
Niebüll	52	D2
Niedere Tauern	62	J3
Niefang	104	G4
Niemegk	52	H4
Nienburg	52	E4
Niesky	52	K5
Nieuw Amsterdam	140	F2
Nieuw Nickerie	140	F2
Nieuwpoort	54	E3
Niğde	68	S7
Niger	102	G5
Niger	104	E2
Nigeria	104	F2
Nigoring Hu	80	B3
Niigata	82	K5
Niihau	132	(2)A2
Nii-jima	82	K6
Nijar	60	H8
Nijmegen	54	H3
Nikel'	48	R2
Nikolayevsk-na-Amure	78	Q6
Nikol'sk	70	J3
Nikol'skoye	78	V5
Nikopol'	70	F5
Nik Pey	92	N5
Nikšić	66	F7
Nilande Atoll	88	B8
Nile	100	F3
Niles	128	C2
Nimach	88	B4
Nîmes	58	K10
Nimule	106	E3
Nin	62	L6
Nine Degree Channel	88	B7
9 de Julio	142	J6
Ning'an	82	E1
Ningbo	80	G5
Ningde	80	F5
Ninghai	80	G5
Ninh Binh	84	D2
Ninh Hoa	84	D4
Ninohoe	82	L3
Niobrara	126	F2
Niobrara	126	G2
Nioro	102	D5
Nioro du Sahel	104	C1
Niort	58	E7
Nipigon	128	C1
Niquelândia	140	H6
Nirmal	88	C5
Niš	66	J6
Nisa	60	C5
Niscemi	64	J11
Nishinoomote	82	F8
Nisporeni	66	R2
Nisyros	68	K8
Nitā	95	C3
Niterói	142	N3
Nitra	50	H9
Nitra	50	H9
Nitsa	70	M3
Niue	112	K7

Name	Page	Grid
Olivet, *France*	58	G6
Olivet, *US*	126	G2
Olivia	128	B2
Olmos	140	B5
Olney	130	B3
Olochi	78	K6
Olonets	70	F2
Olongapo	84	G4
Oloron-Ste-Marie	58	E10
Olot	60	N2
Olovyannaya	78	K6
Olpe	54	K3
Olsztyn	50	K4
Olt	66	M4
Olten	62	C3
Oltenița	66	P5
Oltu	92	K3
Oluan-pi	84	G2
Olvera	60	E8
Olympia	126	B1
Olympos	68	E4
Olympus	68	Q10
Olyutorskiy	78	W4
Olyutorskiy Zaliv	78	V4
Om'	76	N6
Oma	88	D2
Omae-saki	82	K6
Omagh	56	E7
Omaha	126	G2
Omak	126	C1
Omakau	116	B7
Oman	90	G5
Omapere	116	D2
Omarama	116	B7
Omaruru	108	B4
Omba, *China*	88	E2
Omba, *Russia*	76	E4
Omboué	104	F5
Ombrone	64	F6
Omdurman = Umm Durman	100	F4
Omegna	62	D5
Omeo	114	J7
Om Hajer	100	G5
Omīdeyeh	95	C1
Omis	62	M7
Ommen	54	J2
Omolon	78	T3
Omoloy	78	N3
Omo Wenz	106	F2
Omsk	76	N6
Omsukchan	78	S4
Ōmū	82	M1
Omulew	50	L4
Ōmura	82	F7
Ōmuta	82	F7
Onang	87	A3
Onda	60	K5
Ondangwa	108	B3
Ondjiva	108	B3
Ondo	104	E3
Ondörhaan	80	E1
One and a Half Degree Channel	88	B8
Onega	70	G2
O'Neill	126	G2
Oneonta	128	F2
Onești	66	P3
Onezhskoye Ozero	70	F2
Ongjin	82	C5
Ongole	88	D5
Onguday	76	R7
Oni	92	K2
Onilahy	108	G4
Onitsha	104	F3
Ono	82	J6
Onon	78	J7
Onon	78	J7
Onslow Bay	134	J2
Onsong	82	E2
Ontario	122	N6
Ontinyent	60	K6
Ontonagon	128	C1
Onyx	132	C1
Oodnadatta	114	G5
Oologah Lake	130	B2
Oostburg	54	F3
Oostelijk-Flevoland	54	H2
Oostende	54	E3
Oosterhout	54	G3
Oosterschelde	54	F3
Oost-Vlieland	54	H1
Ootsa Lake	122	F6
Opala	106	C4
Oparino	70	J3
Opava	50	G8
Opelika	130	D3
Opelousas	130	C3
Opheim	126	E1
Opochka	70	E3
Opoczno	50	K6
Opole	50	J8
Opornyy	76	J8
Opotiki	116	F4
Opp	130	D3
Opunake	116	D4
Opuwo	108	A3
Oradea	66	J2
Orahovac	66	H7
Orai	88	C3
Oran	60	K9
Orán	142	J3
Orange	108	C5
Orange, *Australia*	114	J6
Orange, *France*	58	K9
Orange, *US*	130	C3
Orangeburg	130	E3
Orangemund	108	B5
Orangeville	128	D2
Orango	104	A2
Oranienburg	52	G3
Orapa	108	D4
Orăștie	66	L4
Oravița	66	J4
Orbec	58	F4
Orbetello	64	F6
Orco	62	C5
Ordes	60	B1
Ordes Santa Comba	60	B1
Ordu	92	G3
Ordway	126	F3
Örealven	48	K4
Örebro	48	H7
Oregon	126	B2
Oregon	128	A3
Orekhovo-Zuyevo	70	G3
Orel	70	G4
Orem	126	D2
Ören	68	K7
Orenburg	70	L4
Orestiada	68	J3
Orewa	116	E3
Orford Ness	54	D2
Orhei	66	R2
Orihuela	60	K6
Orillia	128	E2
Orinoco	140	D2
Orinoco Delta = Delta del Orinoco	140	E2
Orissaare	48	M7
Oristano	64	C9
Orivesi	48	Q5
Orkla	48	F5
Orkney Islands	56	K3
Orlando	130	E4
Orléans	58	G6
Orlik	78	F6
Orly	54	E6
Ormara	90	H4
Ormoc	84	G4
Ormos Almyrou	68	G9
Ormos Mesara	68	G9
Ornans	58	M6
Ornö	48	K7
Örnsköldsvik	48	K5
Orocué	140	C3
Orofino	126	C1
Oromocto	128	G1
Orona	112	J6
Oronoque	140	F3
Oroqen Zizhiqi	78	L6
Orosei	64	D8
Orosháza	66	H3
Oroszlany	50	H10
Orotukan	78	S4
Oroville	126	B3
Ororoo	114	G6
Orsa	48	H6
Orsay	58	H5
Orsha	70	F4
Orsk	70	L4
Orșova	66	K5
Ørsta	48	D5
Ortaklar	68	K7
Orthez	58	E10
Ortigueira	60	C1
Ortisei	62	G4
Ortles	62	F4
Ortona	64	J6
Ortonville	128	A1
Orūmīyeh	92	L5
Oruro	140	D7
Orvieto	64	G6
Orville	58	L6
Ōsaka	82	H6
Osăm	66	M6
Osceola	128	B2
Oschatz	52	J5
Oschersleben	52	G4
O Seixo	60	B3
Osh	76	N9
Oshamambe	82	L2
Oshawa	128	E2
Oshkosh, *Nebr., US*	126	F2
Oshkosh, *Wis., US*	128	C2
Oshogbo	104	E3
Osijek	66	F4
Osimo	62	J7
Oskaloosa	128	B2
Oskarshamn	48	J8
Oslo	48	F7
Oslofjorden	48	F7
Osmancık	92	F3
Osmaniye	92	G5
Osnabrück	54	L2
Osor	62	K6
Osorno	142	G7
Osprey Reef	114	J2
Oss	54	H3
Ossa de Montiel	60	H6
Osseo	128	B2
Ossora	78	U5
Ostashkov	70	F3
Oste	52	E3
Osterburg	52	G4
Österdalen	48	F6
Osterholz-Scharmbeck	52	D3
Osterode	52	F5
Östersund	48	H5
Ostfriesische Inseln	52	C3
Ostiglia	62	G5
Ostrava	50	H8
Ostróda	50	K4
Ostrołęka	50	L4
Ostrov, *Czech Republic*	52	H6
Ostrov, *Russia*	70	E3
Ostrova Arkticheskogo Instituta	76	P2
Ostrov Medvezh'I	78	T2
Ostrov Atlasova	78	S6
Ostrova Vrangelya	120	V4
Ostrov Ayon	78	V2
Ostrov Belyy	76	N3
Ostrov Beringa	78	V6
Ostrov Bol'shevik	76	V2
Ostrov Bol'shoy Begichev	78	J2
Ostrov Bol'shoy Lyakhovskiy	78	Q2
Ostrov Bol'shoy Shantar	78	P6
Ostrov Chechen'	92	M2
Ostrov Iturup	82	P1
Ostrov Karaginskiy	78	U5
Ostrov Kil'din	48	T2
Ostrov Kolguyev	76	H4
Ostrov Komsomolets	76	T1
Ostrov Kotel'nyy	78	P1
Ostrov Kunashir	82	P1
Ostrov Mednyy	78	V6
Ostrov Mezhdusharskiy	76	H3
Ostrov Novaya Sibir'	78	S2
Ostrov Ogurchinskiy	90	F2
Ostrov Oktyabr'skoy	76	S2
Ostrov Onekotan	78	S7
Ostrov Paramushir	78	T6
Ostrov Rasshua	78	S7
Ostrov Shiashkotan	78	S7
Ostrov Shumshu	78	T6
Ostrov Simushir	78	S7
Ostrov Urup	78	S7
Ostrov Ushakova	76	Q1
Ostrov Vaygach	76	K3
Ostrov Vise	76	P2
Ostrov Vosrozhdeniya	76	K9
Ostrov Vrangelya	78	W2
Ostrowiec Świętokrzyski	50	L7
Ostrów Mazowiecka	50	L5
Ostrów Wielkopolski	50	G6
Ostuni	64	M8
Osum	68	C4
Ōsumi-shotō	82	F8
Osuna	60	E7
Oswego	128	E2
Oświęcim	50	J7
Otago Peninsula	116	C7
Otaki	116	E5
Otaru	82	L2
Oțelu Roșu	66	K4
Othonoi	68	B5
Oti	104	E3
Otira	116	C6
Otjiwarongo	108	B4
Otočac	62	L6
Otog Qi	80	D3
Otoineppu	82	M1
Otorohanga	116	E4
Otranto	64	N8
Otrøy	48	D5
Otrozhnyy	78	W3
Ōtsu	82	H6
Otta	48	E6
Ottawa	128	E1
Ottawa, *Canada*	128	E1
Ottawa, *Ill., US*	128	C2
Ottawa, *Kans., US*	130	B2
Ottawa Islands	122	Q5
Otterøy	48	F4
Ottobrunn	62	G2
Ottumwa	128	B2
Otukpo	104	F3
Ouachita Mountains	130	C3
Ouâdâne	102	C4
Ouadda	106	C2
Ouagadougou	104	D2
Oualàta	102	D5
Ouallam	104	E2
Ouanda-Djalle	106	C2
Ouargla	102	G2
Ouarzazate	102	D2
Oudenaarde	54	F4
Oudenbosch	54	G3
Oudtshoorn	108	C6
Oued Laou	60	E9
Oued Medjerda	64	D12
Oued Meliane	64	D12
Oued Tiélat	60	K9
Oued Zem	102	D2
Ouéléssébougou	104	C2
Ouésso	104	H4
Ouezzane	102	D2
Oujda	102	E2
Oujeft	102	C4
Oulainen	48	N4
Ould Yenjé	102	C5
Oulu	48	N4
Oulujärvi	48	P4
Oulujoki	48	P4
Oulx	62	B5
Oum-Chalouba	100	D4
Oum-Hadjer	100	C5
Ounarjoki	48	N3
Our	54	J4
Ouray	126	E3
Ourense	60	C2
Ouricurí	140	J5
Ourthe	54	H4
Oustreham	54	B5
Outer Hebrides	56	D4
Outjo	108	B4
Outokumpu	48	Q5
Out Skerries	56	M1
Ouyen	114	H7
Ovacık	68	R8
Ovada	62	D6
Ovalle	142	G5
Ovareli	92	L3
Overflakkee	54	G3
Overlander Roadhouse	114	B5
Overland Park	130	C2
Overton	126	D3
Övertorneå	48	M3
Ovidiopol'	66	T3
Oviedo	60	E1
Owaka	116	B8
Owando	104	H5
Owase	82	J6
Owatonna	128	B2
Owen River	116	D5
Owensboro	128	C3
Owens Lake	126	C3
Owen Sound	128	D2
Owerri	104	F3
Owo	104	F3
Owosso	128	D2
Owyhee	126	C2
Owyhee	126	C2
Oxford, *New Zealand*	116	D6
Oxford, *UK*	54	A3
Oxnard	132	C2
Oyama	82	K5
Oyapock	140	G3
Oyem	104	G4
Oyen	124	D1
Oyonnax	62	A4
Ózd	50	K9
Ozernovskiy	78	T6
Ozero Alakol'	76	Q8
Ozero Aralsor	70	J5
Ozero Aydarkul'	76	M9
Ozero Balkhash	76	N8
Ozero Baykal	78	H6
Ozero Beloye	70	G2
Ozero Chany	76	P7
Ozero Chernoye	70	N3
Ozero Il'men'	70	F3
Ozero-Imandra	48	R2
Ozero Inder	76	J8
Ozero Janis'jarvi	48	R5
Ozero Kamennoje	48	R4
Ozero Kanozero	48	T3
Ozero Khanka	82	G1
Ozero Kolvitskoye	48	S3
Ozero Kovdozero	48	S3
Ozero Kulundinskoye	76	P7
Ozero Kushmurun	70	N4
Ozero Lama	78	D2
Ozero Leksozero	48	R5
Ozero Lovozero	48	T2
Ozero Morzhovets	70	H1
Ozero Njuk	48	R4
Ozero Ozhogino	78	R3
Ozero Pirenga	48	R3
Ozero Pyaozero	48	R3
Ozero Saltaim	70	P3
Ozero Sarpa	70	J5
Ozero Segozerskoye	70	F2
Ozero Seletyteniz	76	N7
Ozero Sredneye Kuyto	48	R4
Ozero Taymyr	76	U3
Ozero Teletskoye	76	R7
Ozero Tengiz	70	N4
Ozero Topozero	48	R4
Ozero Umbozero	48	T3
Ozero Vygozero	70	G2
Ozero Yalpug	66	R4
Ozero Zaysan	76	Q8
Ozero Zhaltyr	70	K5
Ozero Zhamanakkol'	70	M5
Ozersk	50	M3
Ozhogina	78	R3
Ozhogino	78	R3
Ozieri	64	C8
Ozinki	70	J4
Ozona	132	F2
Ozurget'i	92	J3

P

Name	Page	Grid
Paamiut	122	X4
Paar	52	G8
Paarl	108	B6
Pabbay	56	E4
Pabianice	50	J6
Pabna	88	E4
Pacasmayo	140	B5
Pachino	64	K12
Pachuca	134	E4
Pacific Ocean	112	M3
Pacitan	86	E4
Packwood	126	B1
Padalere	87	B3
Padang	86	C3
Padangpanjang	86	C3
Padangsidempuan	86	B2
Padborg	52	E2
Paderborn	52	D5
Padova	62	G5
Padre Island	130	B4
Padrón	60	B2
Paducah, *Ky., US*	128	C3
Paducah, *Tex., US*	132	F2
Padum	88	C2
Paekdu San	82	D3
Paeroa	116	E3
Pafos	68	Q10
Pag	62	K6
Pag	62	L6
Paga Conta	140	G4
Pagadian	84	G5
Pagai Selatan	86	B3
Pagai Utara	86	B3
Pagalu = Annobón	104	F5
Pagan	112	E4
Pagatan	86	F3
Page, *Ariz., US*	132	D1
Page, *Okla., US*	130	C3
Pagosa Springs	126	E3
Pagri	88	E3
Pahiatua	116	E5
Paia	132	(2)E3
Paide	48	N7
Päijänne	48	N6
Painan	86	C3
Painesville	128	D2
Paisley	56	H6
Paita	140	A5
Pakaraima Mountains	140	E2
Pakch'ŏn	82	C4
Pakhachi	78	V4
Paki	104	F2

Pik Aborigen 78 R4
Piketberg 108 B6
Pik Kommunizma 90 K2
Pik Pobedy 76 P9
Piła 50 F4
Pilaya 142 H3
Pilcomayo 140 E8
Pilibhit 88 C3
Pilica 50 J7
Pimba 114 G6
Pimenta Bueno 140 E6
Pinamalayan 84 G4
Pinamar 142 K6
Pinang 84 B5
Pınarbaşı 92 G4
Pinar del Río 134 H4
Pinarhisar 68 K3
Pińczów 50 K7
Pindaré Mirim 140 H4
Pine Bluff 128 B4
Pine Bluffs 126 F2
Pine City 128 B1
Pine Creek 114 F2
Pine Creek Reservoir 128 A4
Pinega 70 H2
Pineios 68 E5
Pine Island Bay 144 (2)GG3
Pineland 130 C3
Pinerolo 62 C6
Pineville, *Ky., US* 128 D3
Pineville, *La., US* 130 C3
Pingdingshan 80 E4
Pingguo 84 D2
Pingle 84 E2
Pingliang 80 D3
Pingshi 80 E5
P'ing-tung 84 G2
Pingxiang, *China* 84 D2
Pingxiang, *China* 84 E1
Pinhel 60 C4
Pini 86 B2
Pinka 62 M3
Pink Mountain 122 G5
Pinneberg 52 E3
Pinsk 70 E4
Pioche 126 D3
Piombino 64 E6
Pioneer 132 D2
Pioneer Mountains 126 D1
Pionerskii 50 K3
Pionerskiy 70 M2
Piopio 116 E4
Piotrków Trybunalski 50 J6
Piove di Sacco 62 H5
Piperi 68 G5
Pipestone 128 A2
Pipiriki 116 E4
Piqua 128 D2
Piracicaba 142 M3
Pireas 68 F7
Pirin 68 F3
Piripiri 140 J4
Pirmasens 52 C7
Pirna 52 J6
Pirot 66 K6
Piru 87 C3
Pisa 50 L4
Pisa 62 F7
Pisco 140 B6
Písek 50 D8
Pīshīn 90 H4
Pishin 90 J3
Piska 50 L4
Pisticci 64 L8
Pistoia 62 F7
Pisz 50 L4
Pitcairn Islands 112 P8
Piteå 48 L4
Piteälven 70 C1
Pitești 66 M5
Pithara 114 C6
Pithiviers 58 H5
Pitkyaranta 70 F2
Pitlochry 56 J5
Pitlyar 70 N1
Pitt Island 116 (1)B2
Pittsburg 130 C2
Pittsburgh 128 D2
Pitt Strait 116 (1)B2
Piura 140 A5
Pivka 62 K5
Placer 84 G4
Placerville 132 B1
Plaiamonas 68 E5
Plains 132 F2
Plainview 132 F2
Plampang 86 F4
Planalto Central 140 H6
Planalto da Borborema 140 K5
Planalto do Mato Grosso 140 G6
Plankinton 126 G2
Plano 130 B3
Plasencia 60 D5
Plast 70 M4
Plateau du Djado 102 H4
Plateau du Limousin 58 F8
Plateau du Tademaït 102 F3
Plateau of Tibet = Xizang Gaoyuan 88 D2
Plateaux Batéké 104 G5
Platinum 132 (1)E4
Plato 134 K7
Plato Ustyurt 76 J9
Platte 130 B1
Platteville 128 B2
Plattling 52 H8
Plattsburgh 128 F2
Plattsmouth 130 B1
Plau 52 H3
Plauen 52 H6
Plavnik 62 K6
Plavsk 70 G4
Playa de Castilla 60 D7
Playas 140 A4
Plây Cu 84 D4
Pleasanton 132 G3
Pleiße 52 H5
Plentywood 126 F1
Plesetsk 70 H2
Pleven 66 M6
Pljevlja 66 G6
Płock 50 J5
Pločno 66 E6
Ploërmel 58 C6
Ploiești 66 P5
Plomari 68 J6
Plön 52 F2
Płońsk 50 K5
Plovdiv 66 M7
Plumtree 108 D4
Plungė 50 L2
Plymouth, *UK* 56 H11
Plymouth, *US* 128 C2
Plyussa 48 Q7
Plyussa 70 E3
Plzeň 50 C8
Po 62 E5
Pocahontas 134 F1
Pocatello 126 D2
Pochet 78 F5
Pochinok 70 F4
Pocking 62 J2
Pocomoke City 128 E3
Podgorica 66 G7
Podkamennaya Tunguska 78 F4
Podol'sk 70 G3
Podravska Slatina 66 E4
Poel 52 G2
Pofadder 108 B5
Poggibonsi 62 G7
Pogradec 68 C4
P'ohang 82 E5
Pohnpei 112 F5
Pohokura 116 F4
Pohořelice 62 M2
Point Arena 124 B4
Point Barrow 132 (1)F1
Point Conception 132 B2
Point Culver 114 D6
Point d'Entrecasteaux 114 B6
Pointe-Noire 104 G5
Point Hope 132 (1)D2
Point Hope 132 (1)D2
Point Pedro 88 D7
Point Sur 126 B3
Poitiers 58 F7
Pokaran 88 B3
Pokhara 88 D3
Poko 106 D3
Pokrovsk 78 M4
Pola de Siero 60 E1
Poland 50 G6
Polar Bluff 134 F1
Polatlı 68 Q5
Polatsk 70 E3
Police 52 K3
Polichnitos 68 J5
Policoro 64 L8
Poligny 58 L7
Poligus 76 S5
Polillo Islands 84 G4
Poliocastro 64 L9
Polis 68 Q9
Polistena 64 L10
Pollachi 88 C6
Pollença 60 P5
Polohy 70 G5
Polomoloc 84 H5
Polonnaruwa 88 D7
Poltava 70 F5
Poltavka 82 F1
Põltsamaa 48 N7
Poluostrov Shmidta 78 Q6
Poluostrov Taymyr 76 R3
Poluostrov Yamal 76 M3
Poluy 76 M4
Põlva 48 P7
Polyaigos 68 G8
Polyarnye Zori 48 S3
Polyarnyy 78 X3
Polykastro 68 E4
Polynesia 112 J6
Pombal 60 B5
Pomeranian Bay 50 D3
Pomeroy 126 C1
Pomorie 66 Q7
Pompano Beach 130 E4
Pompei 64 J8
Ponca City 130 B2
Ponce 134 L5
Pondicherry 88 C6
Pond Inlet 122 R2
Ponferrada 60 D2
Poniatowa 50 M6
Ponoy 70 H1
Pons 58 E8
Ponta Delgada 102 (1)B2
Ponta do Podrão 104 G6
Ponta do Sol 104 (1)B1
Ponta Grossa 142 L4
Ponta Khehuene 108 E5
Pont-à-Mousson 58 M5
Ponta Porã 142 K3
Pontarlier 58 M7
Pontassieve 62 G7
Ponta Zavora 108 F4
Pont-d'Alin 58 L7
Ponteareas 60 B2
Ponte da Barca 60 B3
Pontedera 62 F7
Ponte de Sor 60 C5
Pontevedra 60 B2
Pontiac 128 C2
Pontianak 86 D3
Pontivy 58 C5
Pontoise 54 E5
Pontorson 58 D5
Pontremoli 62 E6
Ponza 64 G8
Poogau 62 J3
Poole 56 L11
Poole Bay 56 L11
Pooncarie 114 H6
Poopó 140 D7
Poopó Challapata 142 H2
Poor Knights Islands 116 E2
Popayán 134 J8
Poperinge 54 E4
Popigay 76 W3
Poplar Bluff 128 B3
Poplarville 130 D3
Popocatépetl 134 E5
Popoh 86 E4
Popokabaka 104 H6
Popovača 62 M5
Popovo 66 P6
Poprad 50 K8
Poprad 50 K8
Porangatu 140 H6
Porbandar 90 J5
Porcupine 132 (1)K2
Pordenone 62 H5
Poreč 62 J5
Poret 64 H3
Pori 48 L6
Porirua 116 E5
Porlamar 134 M6
Poronaysk 78 Q7
Poros 68 F7
Porosozero 70 F2
Porozina 62 K5
Porpoise Bay 144 (2)T3
Porriño 60 B2
Porsangen 48 N1
Porsgrunn 48 E7
Portadown 56 F7
Portage 128 C2
Portage la Prairie 126 G1
Port Alberni 126 B1
Port Albert 114 J7
Portalegre 60 C5
Portales 132 F2
Port Arthur, *Australia* 114 J8
Port Arthur, *US* 130 C4
Port Augusta 114 G6
Port-au-Prince 134 K5
Port Austin 128 D2
Port Blair 84 A4
Port Burwell 122 U4
Port Charlotte 130 E4
Port Douglas 114 J3
Portel, *Brazil* 140 G4
Portel, *Portugal* 60 C6
Port Elizabeth 108 D6
Port Ellen 56 F6
Porterville 132 C1
Port Fitzroy 116 E3
Port-Gentil 104 F5
Port Harcourt 104 F4
Port Hardy 122 F6
Port Hawkesbury 122 U7
Port Hedland 114 C4
Port Hope Simpson 122 V6
Port Huron 128 D2
Portimão 60 B7
Port Jefferson 128 F2
Portland, *Australia* 114 H7
Portland, *New Zealand* 116 E2
Portland, *Ind., US* 128 D2
Portland, *Me., US* 128 F2
Portland, *Oreg., US* 126 B1
Portland Island 116 F4
Port Laoise 56 E8
Port Lavaca 130 B4
Port Lincoln 114 G6
Port Loko 104 B3
Port Louis 108 (1)B2
Port Macquarie 114 K6
Port-Menier 122 U7
Port Moresby 114 J1
Port Nolloth 108 B5
Porto, *Corsica* 64 C6
Porto, *Portugal* 60 B3
Porto Alegre, *R.G.S., Brazil* 142 L5
Porto Alegre, *Pará, Brazil* 140 G4
Porto Amboim 108 A2
Portocheli 68 F7
Porto do Son 60 A2
Pôrto Esperidião 140 F7
Portoferraio 64 E6
Pôrto Franco 140 H5
Port of Spain 140 E1
Pôrto Grande 140 G3
Portogruaro 62 H5
Porto Inglês 104 (1)B1
Portomaggiore 62 G6
Pôrto Murtinho 142 K3
Pôrto Nacional 140 H6
Porto-Novo 104 E3
Port Orford 126 B2
Porto San Giorgio 64 H5
Pôrto Santana 140 G3
Porto Santo 102 B2
Pôrto Seguro 140 K7
Porto Tolle 62 H6
Porto Torres 64 C8
Porto-Vecchio 64 D7
Pôrto Velho 140 E5
Portoviejo 140 A4
Port Pire 114 G6
Portree 56 F4
Port Renfrew 126 B1
Port Said = Bûr Sa'îd 100 F1
Port St. Johns 108 D6
Port Shepstone 108 E6
Portsmouth, *UK* 54 A4
Portsmouth, *N.H., US* 128 F2
Portsmouth, *Oh., US* 128 D3
Portsmouth, *Va., US* 128 E3
Port Sudan = Bur Sudan 100 G4
Port Sulphur 130 D4
Port Talbot 56 J10
Portugal 60 B5
Portugalete 60 G1
Port-Vendres 58 J11
Port-Vila 112 G7
Posadas 142 K4
Poschiavo 62 F4
Poshekhon'ye 70 G3
Poso 87 B3
Posŏng 82 D6
Posse 140 H6
Pößneck 52 G6
Post 132 F2
Postmasburg 108 C5
Postojna 62 K5
Post Weygand 102 F4
Posušje 66 E6
Pota 86 G4
Potapovo 76 R4
Poteau 130 C2
Potenza 62 J7
Potenza 64 K8
Potgietersrus 108 D4
P'ot'i 92 J2
Potiskum 104 G2
Potlatch 126 C1
Potosí 140 D7
Potsdam, *Germany* 52 J4
Potsdam, *US* 128 F2
Pottuvil 88 D7
Poughkeepsie 128 F2
Pourerere 116 F5
Pouto 116 E3
Póvoa de Varzim 60 B3
Povorino 70 H4
Powder 126 E1
Powder River 126 E2
Powell River 122 G7
Poyang Hu 80 F5
Požarevac 66 J5
Poza Rica 134 E4
Požega 66 H6
Poznań 50 F5
Pozoblanco 60 F6
Pozzuoli 64 J8
Prabumulih 86 C3
Prachatice 50 D8
Prachuap Khiri Khan 84 B4
Prado 140 K7
Præstø 52 H1
Prague = Praha 50 D7
Praha 50 D7
Praia 104 (1)B2
Prainha 140 G4
Prairie du Chien 128 B2
Prapat 86 B2
Praslin Island 108 (2)B1
Pratas = Dongsha Qundao 84 F2
Prato 62 G7
Pratt 126 G3
Prattville 130 D3
Praya 86 F4
Preetz 52 F2
Preganziòl 62 H5
Preiļi 48 P8
Premnitz 52 H4
Premuda 62 K6
Prentice 128 B1
Prenzlau 50 C4
Preobrazhenka 78 H4
Preparis Island 84 A4
Preparis North Channel 84 A3
Preparis South Channel 84 A4
Přerov 50 G8
Presa de la Boquilla 132 E3
Presa de las Adjuntas 132 G4
Presa Obregón 132 E3
Prescott 126 D4
Preševo 66 J7
Presho 126 G2
Presidencia Roque Sáenz Peña 142 J4
Presidente Prudente 142 L3
Presidio 132 F3
Preslav 66 P6
Presnogorkovka 70 N4
Prešov 50 L9
Presque Isle 128 G1
Přeštice 52 J7
Preston, *UK* 56 K8
Preston, *Minn., US* 128 B2
Preston, *Mo., US* 128 B3
Pretoria 108 D5
Preveza 68 C6
Priargunsk 78 K6
Pribilof Islands 132 (1)D4
Priboj 66 G6
Příbram 50 D8
Price 126 D3
Prichard 130 D3
Priego de Córdoba 60 F7
Priekule 48 L8
Prienai 50 N3
Prieska 108 C5
Priest Lake 126 C1
Prievidza 50 H9
Prijedor 66 D5
Prijepolje 66 G6
Prikaspiyskaya Nizmennost' 70 K5
Prilep 68 D3
Primolano 62 G5
Primorsk 48 Q6
Primorsko Akhtarsk 70 G5
Prince Albert 122 K6
Prince Albert Peninsula 122 H2
Prince Albert Sound 122 H2
Prince Charles Island 122 R3
Prince Edward Island 98 G10

Rat Buri	84	B4
Rath	88	C3
Rathenow	52	H4
Rathlin Island	56	F6
Rathluirc	56	D9
Ratlam	88	C4
Ratnagiri	90	K6
Raton	126	F3
Ratta	78	C4
Ratten	62	D4
Ratzeburg	52	F3
Rauđamýri	48	(1)B2
Raudhatain	95	B1
Raukumara Range	116	F4
Rauma	48	L6
Raurimu	116	E4
Rausu	82	N1
Răut	66	R2
Ravalli	126	D1
Ravānsar	92	M6
Rāvar	95	G1
Ravenna	62	H6
Ravensburg	62	E3
Ravensthorpe	114	D6
Ravnina	90	H2
Rāwah	92	J6
Rawaki	112	J6
Rawalpindi	90	K3
Rawa Mazowiecka	50	K6
Rawāndiz	92	L5
Rawicz	50	F6
Rawlinna	114	E6
Rawlins	126	E2
Rawson	142	J7
Rawu	88	G3
Raychikhinsk	78	M7
Raymond	126	B1
Raymondville	132	G3
Rayong	84	C4
Razdol'noye	82	F2
Razgrad	66	P6
Razlog	66	L8
Reading, *UK*	56	M10
Reading, *US*	128	E2
Realicó	142	J6
Rebaa	102	G2
Rebbenesøya	48	J1
Rebun-tō	80	L1
Rechytsa	70	F4
Recife	140	L5
Recklinghausen	54	K3
Recknitz	52	H3
Reconquista	142	K4
Recreo	142	H4
Red, *Canada/US*	126	G1
Red, *US*	130	B3
Reda	50	H3
Red Bluff	132	B1
Red Cloud	130	B1
Red Deer	122	J6
Redding	126	B2
Redditch	54	A2
Redfield	126	G2
Red Lake	122	N6
Red Lakes	124	H2
Red Lodge	126	E1
Red Oak	128	A2
Redon	58	C6
Redondela	60	B2
Red River = Song Hông	84	C2
Red Sea	100	G3
Redwater	122	J6
Red Wing	128	B2
Redwood City	126	B3
Redwood Falls	128	A2
Reed City	128	C2
Reedsport	126	B2
Reefton	116	C6
Rega	50	E4
Regen	52	H7
Regen	52	J8
Regensburg	52	H7
Regenstauf	52	H7
Reggane	102	F3
Reggio di Calabria	64	K10
Reggio nell'Emilia	62	F6
Reghin	66	M3
Regina, *Brazil*	140	G3
Regina, *Canada*	124	F1
Rehau	52	H6
Rehoboth	108	B4
Rehovot	94	B5
Reichenbach	52	H6
Reigate	56	M10
Reims	54	G5
Reinach Bad	62	C3
Reindeer Lake	122	L5
Reinosa	60	F1
Reisi	64	J11
Reliance	122	K4
Relizane	102	F1
Remada	102	H2
Remagen	54	K4
Rembang	86	E4
Remeshk	95	H3
Remiremont	58	M6
Remscheid	54	K3
Rena	48	F6
Rendína	68	F4
Rendsburg	52	E2
Rengat	86	C3
Reni	66	R4
Renmark	114	H6
Rennes	58	D5
Reno	62	G6
Reno	126	C3
Rentería	60	J1
Renton	126	B1
Renukut	88	D4
Reo	87	B4
Replot	48	L5
Reprêsa de Balbina	140	F4
Represa de Samuel	140	E5
Represa de Sao Simao	140	G7
Represa Ilha Solteira	140	G7
Represa Tucuruí	140	H4
Republic	126	C1
Repulse Bay	114	J4
Repulse Bay	122	P3
Requena, *Peru*	140	C5
Requena, *Spain*	60	J5
Reşadiye	92	G3
Resen	66	J8
Réservoir Cabonga	128	E1
Réservoir Caniapiscau	122	T6
Réservoir de La Grande 2	122	R6
Réservoir de La Grande 3	122	R6
Réservoir de La Grande 4	122	S6
Réservoir Gouin	128	F1
Réservoir Manicouagan	122	T6
Réservoir Opinaca	122	R6
Réservoir Pipmuacan	128	G1
Reshteh-ye Kūhhā-ye Alborz	90	F2
Resistencia	142	K4
Reşiţa	66	J4
Resolute	122	N2
Resolution Island, *Canada*	122	U4
Resolution Island, *New Zealand*	116	A7
Resovo	68	K3
Rethel	54	G5
Rethymno	68	G9
Réunion	108	(1)B2
Reus	60	M3
Reutlingen	52	E8
Revda	70	L3
Revillagigedo Island	132	(1)L4
Revin	54	G5
Revivim	94	B5
Revúca	50	K9
Rewa	88	D4
Rexburg	126	D2
Reykjanes	48	(1)B3
Reykjavík	48	(1)C2
Reynosa	130	B4
Rezat	52	F7
Rezé	58	D6
Rēzekne	48	P8
Rezina	66	R2
Rezovo	66	R8
Rezzato	62	F5
Rheda-Wiedenbrück	52	D5
Rhein = Rhine	62	C2
Rheinbach	54	K4
Rheine	54	K2
Rheinfelden	62	C3
Rhin = Rhine	62	C2
Rhine	62	C2
Rhinelander	128	C1
Rho	62	E5
Rhode Island	128	F2
Rhodes = Rodos	68	L8
Rhondda	56	J10
Rhône	58	K9
Rhyl	56	J8
Ribadeo	60	C1
Ribas do Rio Pardo	142	L3
Ribe	48	E9
Ribeauville	58	N5
Ribeirão Prêto	142	M3
Ribeiria = Santa Eugenia	60	A2
Ribera	64	H11
Riberalta	140	D6
Ribnica	64	J3
Rîbniţa	66	S2
Ribnitz-Damgarten	52	H2
Říčany	52	K6
Riccione	62	H7
Richardson Mountains	132	(1)K2
Richfield	126	D3
Richland	126	C1
Richlands	128	D3
Richmond, *Australia*	114	H4
Richmond, *New Zealand*	116	D5
Richmond, *Ky., US*	128	D3
Richmond, *Va., US*	128	E3
Ridgecrest	132	C1
Ridgway	128	E2
Ried	62	J2
Riesa	52	J5
Rieti	64	G6
Rifle	126	E3
Rīga	48	N8
Rīgān	95	H2
Riggins	126	C1
Rigolet	122	V6
Rijeka	62	K5
Riley	126	C2
Rimava	50	J9
Rimavská Sobota	50	K9
Rimini	62	H6
Rimouski	128	G1
Rineia	68	H7
Ringe	52	F1
Ringkøbing	48	E8
Ringkøbing Fjord	48	D9
Ringsted	52	G1
Ringvassøya	48	J1
Rinteln	52	E4
Rio Branco	140	D5
Río Colorado	142	J6
Río Cuarto	142	J5
Rio de Janeiro	142	N3
Rio de Janeiro	142	N3
Río de la Plata	142	K6
Río Gallegos	142	H9
Rio Grande	132	E2
Río Grande, *Argentina*	142	H9
Río Grande, *Mexico*	132	F4
Rio Grande	142	L5
Rio Grande City	130	B4
Rio Grande do Norte	140	K5
Rio Grande do Sul	142	L4
Riohacha	134	K6
Río Largartos	134	G4
Riom	58	J8
Río Mulatos	140	D7
Rionero in Vulture	64	K8
Rio Tigre	140	B4
Rio Verde, *Brazil*	140	G7
Rio Verde, *Chile*	142	G9
Rio Verde de Mato Grosso	140	G7
Ripley, *Oh., US*	128	D3
Ripley, *Tenn., US*	128	C3
Ripley, *W.Va., US*	128	D3
Ripoll	60	N2
Ripon	56	L7
Rishiri-tō	78	Q7
Rishon le Ẕiyyon	94	B5
Risør	48	E7
Ritchie's Archipelago	84	A4
Ritzville	126	C1
Rivadavia	142	G4
Riva del Garda	62	F5
Rivarolo Canavese	62	C5
Rivas	134	G6
Rivera, *Argentina*	142	J6
Rivera, *Uruguay*	142	K5
River Cess	104	C3
Riversdale	108	C6
Riversdale Beach	116	E5
Riverton, *Canada*	122	M6
Riverton, *New Zealand*	116	A8
Rivesaltes	58	H11
Rivière-du-Loup	128	G1
Rivne	70	E4
Rivoli	62	C5
Riwoqê	88	G2
Riyadh = Ar Riyāḍ	95	B4
Rıze	92	J3
Rizhao	80	F3
Roanne	58	K7
Roanoke	128	D3
Roanoke Rapids	130	F2
Robāṭ	95	G1
Robe	114	G7
Robertsfors	48	L4
Robertval	128	F1
Roboré	140	F7
Robstown	130	B4
Roccastrada	64	F6
Rochefort, *Belgium*	54	H4
Rochefort, *France*	58	E8
Rochelle	128	C2
Rocher River	122	J4
Rochester, *UK*	54	C3
Rochester, *Minn., US*	128	B2
Rochester, *N.H., US*	128	F2
Rochester, *N.Y., US*	128	E2
Rockall	46	C2
Rockefeller Plateau	144	(2)EE2
Rockford	128	C2
Rockhampton	114	K4
Rock Hill	128	D4
Rock Island	128	B2
Rocklake	126	G1
Rockport	126	B1
Rock Rapids	128	A2
Rock Springs	126	E2
Rocksprings	132	F3
Rocky Mount	128	E3
Rocky Mountains	122	F5
Rødby Havn	52	G2
Roddickton	122	V6
Roden	54	J1
Rodez	58	H9
Rodi Garganico	64	K7
Roding	52	H7
Rodney	128	D2
Rodopi Planina	66	M7
Rodos	68	L8
Rodos	68	L8
Roebourne	114	C4
Roermond	54	J3
Roeselare	54	F4
Roes Welcome Sound	122	P4
Rogers City	128	D1
Rogerson	126	D2
Rogliano	64	D6
Rogozno	50	G5
Rogue	126	B2
Rohrbach	62	K2
Rohtak	88	C3
Roi Et	84	C3
Roja	48	M8
Rokiškis	48	N9
Rokycany	50	C8
Rolla	128	B3
Rolleston	116	D6
Rolvsøya	48	M1
Roma	87	C4
Roma, *Australia*	114	J5
Roma, *Italy*	64	G7
Roman	66	P3
Romania	66	L4
Romans-sur-Isère	58	L8
Rombas	54	J5
Rome = Roma	64	G7
Rome, *Ga., US*	130	D3
Rome, *N.Y., US*	128	E2
Romney	128	E3
Romny	70	F4
Rømø	52	D1
Romorantin-Lanthenay	58	G6
Romsey	54	A3
Rona	56	G2
Ronan	124	D2
Roncesvalles	60	J2
Ronda	60	E8
Rondônia	140	E6
Rondônia	140	E6
Rondonópolis	140	G7
Rondu	90	L2
Rongcheng	80	G3
Rønne	50	D2
Ronneby	48	H8
Ronne Entrance	144	(2)JJ3
Ronne Ice Shelf	144	(2)MM2
Ronse	54	F4
Roosendaal	54	G3
Roper Bar	114	F2
Roquetas de Mar	60	H8
Roraima	140	E3
Røros	48	F5
Rosário	140	J4
Rosario, *Argentina*	142	J5
Rosario, *Mexico*	124	D6
Rosario, *Mexico*	124	E7
Rosario, *Paraguay*	142	K3
Rosário Oeste	140	F6
Rosarito	124	C6
Rosarno	64	K10
Roscommon	56	D8
Roscrea	56	E9
Roseau	134	M5
Roseburg	126	B2
Roseires Reservoir	100	F5
Rose Island	112	K7
Rosenburg	132	G3
Rosenheim	62	H3
Roses	60	P2
Rosetown	122	K6
Rosica	66	N6
Rosignano Marittimo	62	F7
Roşiori de Vede	66	N5
Rosita	66	Q6
Roskilde	48	G9
Roslavl'	70	F4
Rossano	64	L9
Ross Ice Shelf	144	(2)Z1
Ross Lake	126	B1
Rosslare	56	F9
Roßlau	52	H5
Rosso	102	B5
Rossosh'	70	G4
Ross River	122	E4
Ross Sea	144	(2)AA2
Røssvatnet	48	G4
Røst	48	G3
Rostāq	95	E3
Rosthern	122	K6
Rostock	52	H2
Rostov	70	G3
Rostov-na-Donu	70	G5
Rostrenen	58	B5
Roswell	132	F2
Rota	112	E4
Rote	87	B5
Rotenburg, *Germany*	52	E3
Rotenburg, *Germany*	52	E5
Roth	52	G7
Rothenburg	52	F7
Roto	114	J6
Rotorua	116	F4
Rott	62	H2
Rottenmann	62	K3
Rotterdam	58	K2
Rottnen	50	E1
Rottumeroog	54	J1
Rottumerplaat	54	J1
Rottweil	62	D2
Rotuma	112	H7
Roubaix	54	F4
Rouen	54	D5
Rouiba	60	P8
Round Mountain	114	K6
Round Rock	130	B3
Roundup	126	E1
Rousay	56	J2
Rouyn	128	E1
Rovaniemi	48	N3
Rovato	62	E5
Rovereto	62	G5
Rovigo	62	G5
Rovinari	66	L5
Rovinj	62	J5
Rovuma	106	F6
Rowley Island	122	R3
Rowley Shoals	114	C3
Roxas	84	G4
Roxburgh	116	B7
Royal Leamington Spa	54	A2
Royal Tunbridge Wells	54	C3
Royan	58	D8
Roye	54	E5
Royston	54	C2
Rozdil'na	66	T3
Rožňava	50	K9
Rozzano	62	E5
Rrëshen	68	B3
Rtishchevo	70	H4
Ruacana	108	A3
Ruahine Range	116	E5
Ruapehu	116	E4
Ruapuke Island	116	B8
Ruarkela	88	D4
Ruatahuna	116	F4
Ruatoria	116	G3
Ruawai	116	D3
Rub' al Khālī	90	E6
Rubeshibe	82	M2
Rubi	106	C3
Rubtsovsk	76	Q7
Ruby	132	(1)F3
Rudan	95	G3
Ruda Śląska	50	H7
Rudbar	90	H3
Rüdersdorf	52	J4
Rudkøbing	52	F2
Rudnaya Pristan'	82	H2
Rudnyy	70	M4
Rudolstadt	52	G6
Rue	54	D4
Ruffec	58	F7
Rufiji	106	F5
Rugby, *UK*	54	A2
Rugby, *US*	124	G2
Rügen	50	C3
Ruhnu	48	M8

Sanghar 90 J4
San Gimignano 62 G7
San Giovanni in Fiore 64 L9
San Giovanni Valdarno 62 G7
Sangir 87 C2
Sangkhla Buri 84 B3
Sangkulirang 86 F2
Sangli 88 B5
Sangmélima 104 G4
Sangre de Cristo Range 132 E1
Sangsang 88 E3
Sangue 140 F6
Sangüesa 60 J2
Sanjō 82 K5
San Joaquin Valley 126 B3
San Jose 126 B3
San José 134 H7
San Jose de Buenavista 84 G4
San José de Chiquitos 140 E7
San Jose de Jáchal 142 H5
San José del Cabo 134 C4
San José de Ocuné 140 C3
San Juan 134 H4
San Juan, *Argentina* 142 H5
San Juan, *Costa Rica* 134 H6
San Juan, *Puerto Rico* 134 L5
San Juan, *US* 132 E1
San Juan, *Venezuela* 140 D2
San Juan Bautista, *Paraguay* 142 K4
San Juan Bautista, *Spain* 60 M5
San Juan de los Cayos 140 D1
San Juan de los Morros 140 D2
San Juan Mountains 126 E3
San Julián 142 H8
Sankt-Peterburg 70 F3
Sankuru 106 C4
Sanlıurfa 92 H5
San Lorenzo 132 D3
Sanlúcar de Barrameda 60 D8
San Lucas 134 C4
San Luis 142 H5
San Luis Obispo 132 B1
San Luis Potosí 134 D4
San Luis Rio Colorado 132 D2
San Marcos 130 B4
San Marino 62 H7
San Marino 62 H7
San Martín 140 E6
Sanmenxia 80 E4
San Miguel 134 G6
San Miguel 140 E7
San Miguel de Tucumán 142 H4
San Miguel Island 132 B2
San Miniato 62 F7
San Nicolas de los Arroyos 142 J5
San Nicolás de los Garzas 130 A4
San Nicolas Island 132 C2
Sânnicolau Mare 66 H3
Sanok 50 M8
San Pablo 84 G4
San-Pédro 104 C4
San Pedro, *Argentina* 142 J3
San Pedro, *Bolivia* 140 E7
San Pedro, *Paraguay* 142 K3
San Pedro, *Philippines* 84 G4
San Pedro de las Colonias 132 F3
San Pedro Sula 134 G5
San Pellegrino Terme 62 E5
San Pietro 64 C9
Sanqaçal 92 N3
San Rafael 142 H5
San Remo 62 C7
San Roque 60 E8
Sansalé 104 B2
San Salvador 130 G5
San Salvador 134 G6
San Salvador de Jujuy 142 H3
Sansar 88 C4
San Sebastián = Donostia 60 J1
San Sebastian de los Reyes 60 G4
Sansepolcro 62 H7
San Severo 64 K7
Sanski Most 62 M6
Santa Ana, *Bolivia* 140 D7
Santa Ana, *El Salvador* 134 G6
Santa Ana, *Mexico* 132 D2
Santa Ana, *US* 132 C2
Santa Bárbara 124 E6
Santa Barbara 132 C2
Santa Barbara Island 132 C2
Santa Catalina 142 H4
Santa Catalina Island 132 C2
Santa Catarina 142 L4
Santa Clara, *Columbia* 140 D4
Santa Clara, *Cuba* 124 K7
Santa Clarita 132 C2
Santa Comba Dão 60 B4
Santa Cruz 142 G9
Santa Cruz, *Bolivia* 140 E7
Santa Cruz, *Philippines* 84 G3
Santa Cruz, *US* 132 B1
Santa Cruz de Tenerife 102 B3
Santa Cruz Island 132 B2
Santa Cruz Islands 112 G7
Santa Elena 140 E3
Santa Eugenia 60 A2
Santa Fe 126 E3
Santa Fé 142 J5
Sant'Agata di Militello 64 J10
Santa Isabel 112 F6
Santa Isabel 142 H6
Santa la Grande 124 K7
Santa Margarita 124 D7
Santa Margherita Ligure 62 E6
Santa Maria 102 (1)B2
Santa Maria, *Brazil* 142 L4
Santa Maria, *US* 132 B2
Santa Maria das Barreiras 140 H5
Santa Marinella 64 F6
Santa Marta, *Colombia* 134 K6
Santa Marta, *Spain* 60 D6
Santana do Livramento 142 K5
Santander 60 G1
Sant'Antioco 64 C9
Sant'Antioco 64 C9
Santanyí 60 P5
Santa Pola 60 K6
Santarém, *Brazil* 140 G4
Santarém, *Spain* 60 B5
Santa Rosa, *Argentina* 142 J6
Santa Rosa, *R.G.S., Brazil* 142 L4
Santa Rosa, *Acre, Brazil* 140 C5
Santa Rosa, *Calif., US* 126 B3
Santa Rosa, *N. Mex., US* 132 F2
Santa Rosa Island 132 B2
Santa Vitória do Palmar 142 L5
Sant Boi 60 N3
Sant Carlos de la Ràpita 60 L4
Sant Celoni 60 N3
Sant Feliu de Guixols 60 P3
Santiago 142 G5
Santiago, *Brazil* 142 L4
Santiago, *Dominican Republic* 134 K5
Santiago, *Philippines* 84 G3
Santiago, *Spain* 60 B2
Santiago de Cuba 134 J5
Santiago del Estero 142 J4
Santo André 142 M3
Santo Antão 104 (1)A1
Santo Antônio de Jesus 140 K6
Santo Antônio do Içá 140 D4
Santo Domingo 134 L5
Santo Domingo de los Colorados 140 B4
Santoña 60 G1
Santos 142 M3
San Vicente 84 G3
San Vincenzo 64 E5
Sanya 84 D3
Sao Bernardo do Campo 140 E4
São Borja 142 K4
São Carlos 142 M3
São Félix, *M.G., Brazil* 140 G6
São Félix, *Pará, Brazil* 140 G5
São Filipe 104 (1)B2
São Francisco 140 J6
São João de Madeira 60 B4
São Jorge 102 (1)B2
São José do Rio Prêto 142 L3
São Luís 140 J4
São Miguel 102 (1)B2
Saône 58 K7
São Nicolau 104 (1)B1
São Paulo 142 L3
São Paulo 142 M3
São Paulo de Olivença 140 D4
São Raimundo Nonato 140 J5
São Tiago 104 (1)B1
São Tomé 104 F4
São Tomé 104 F4
São Tomé and Príncipe 104 F4
São Vicente 104 (1)A1
São Vicente 142 M3
Sapanca 68 M4
Saparua 87 C3
Sapele 104 F3
Sapes 68 H4
Sapientza 68 D8
Sa Pobla 60 P5
Sapporo 82 L2
Sapri 64 K8
Sapudi 86 E4
Sapulpa 130 B2
Saqqez 92 M5
Sarāb 92 M5
Sara Buri 84 C4
Sarajevo 66 F6
Sarakhs 90 H2
Saraktash 70 L4
Saramati 88 G3
Saran 76 N8
Saranac Lake 128 F2
Sarandë 68 C5
Sarangani Islands 87 C1
Saranpul 70 M2
Saransk 70 J4
Sarapul 70 K3
Sarapul'skoye 78 P7
Sarasota 130 E4
Sarata 66 S3
Saratoga 126 E2
Saratoga Springs 128 F2
Saratov 70 J4
Saravan 90 H4
Sarawak 86 E2
Saray 68 K3
Sarayköy 68 L7
Sarayönü 68 Q6
Sarbāz 90 H4
Sarbīsheh 90 G3
Sárbogárd 66 F3
Sar Dasht 92 L5
Sardegna 64 E8
Sardinia = Sardegna 64 E8
Sardis Lake 130 B3
Sar-e Pol 90 J2
Sargodha 90 K3
Sarh 104 H3
Sārī 90 F2
Saria 68 K9
Sarıkamış 92 K3
Sarıkaya 92 F4
Sarikei 86 E2
Sarina 114 J4
Sariñena 60 K3
Sarīr Tibesti 100 C3
Sariwŏn 82 C4
Sar?yer 68 M3
Sark 58 C4
Sarkad 66 J3
Sarkand 76 P8
Sarkikaraağaç 68 P6
Şarkişla 92 G4
Şarköy 68 K4
Sarmi 87 E3
Särna 48 G6
Sarnia 128 D2
Sarny 70 E4
Sarolangun 86 C3
Saronno 62 E5
Saros Körfezi 68 J4
Sárospatak 50 L9
Sarre 58 M5
Sarrebourg 58 N5
Sarreguemines 58 N4
Sarria 60 C2
Sartène 64 C7
Sartyn'ya 70 M2
Saruhanli 68 K6
Sārur 92 L4
Sárvár 62 M3
Sarvestān 95 E2
Sarviz 66 F2
Sarykamyshkoye Ozero 76 K9
Saryozek 76 P9
Saryshagan 76 N8
Sarysu 76 M8
Sary-Tash 90 K2
Sarzana 62 E6
Sasaram 88 D4
Sasebo 82 E7
Saskatchewan 122 K6
Saskatchewan 122 L6
Saskatoon 122 K6
Saskylakh 76 W3
Sassandra 104 C4
Sassari 64 C8
Sassnitz 52 J2
Sasso Marconi 62 G6
Sassuolo 62 F6
Satadougou 104 B2
Satara 88 B5
Satna 88 D4
Sátoraljaújhely 50 L9
Satti 88 C2
Sättna 48 J5
Satu Mare 66 K2
Satun 86 B1
Sauce 142 K5
Saudi Arabia 90 D4
Sauk Center 128 B1
Saulgau 62 E2
Saulieu 58 K6
Sault Ste. Marie, *Canada* 128 D1
Sault Ste. Marie, *US* 128 D1
Saumlakki 87 D4
Saumur 58 E6
Saunders Island 138 J9
Saura 76 J9
Saurimo 106 C5
Sauðarkrókur 48 (1)D2
Sava 62 L5
Savaii 112 J7
Savalou 104 E3
Savannah 120 K6
Savannah, *Ga., US* 130 E3
Savannah, *Tenn., US* 130 D2
Savannakhet 84 C3
Savaştepe 68 K5
Savè 104 E3
Save 108 E4
Säveh 90 F2
Saverne 52 C8
Savigliano 62 C6
Savona 62 D6
Savonlinna 48 Q6
Savu 87 B5
Sawahlunto 86 C3
Sawai Madhopur 88 C3
Sawqirah 90 G6
Sayanogorsk 76 S7
Sayansk 78 G6
Sayhūt 90 F6
Saylac 100 H5
Saynshand 80 E2
Sayram Hu 76 Q9
Say'ūn 90 E6
Say-Utes 76 J9
Sazan 68 B4
Sazin 90 K2
Sbaa 102 E3
Scafell Pike 56 J7
Scalea 64 K9
Scarborough 56 M7
Scargill 116 D6
Scarp 56 E3
Schaalsee 52 F3
Schaffhausen 62 D3
Schagen 54 G2
Scharbeutz 52 F2
Schärding 62 J2
Scharhörn 52 D3
Scheeßel 52 E3
Schefferville 122 T6
Scheibbs 62 L3
Schelde 54 F3
Schenectady 128 F2
Scheveningen 54 G2
Schiedam 54 G3
Schiermonnikoog 54 H1
Schiermonnikoog 54 J1
Schio 62 G5
Schiza 68 D8
Schkeuditz 52 H5
Schlei 52 E2
Schleiden 54 J4
Schleswig 52 E2
Schlieben 52 J5
Schlüchtern 52 E6
Schneeberg 52 G6
Schneeberg 52 H6
Schönebeck 52 G4
Schongau 62 F3
Schöningen 52 F4
Schouwen 54 F3
Schramberg 62 D2
Schreiber 128 C1
Schrems 62 L2
Schull 56 C10
Schwabach 52 G7
Schwäbische Alb 62 E2
Schwäbisch-Gmünd 62 E2
Schwäbisch-Hall 52 E7
Schwalmstadt 52 E6
Schwandorf 52 H7
Schwarzenbek 52 F3
Schwarzenberg 52 H6
Schwarzwald 62 D3
Schwaz 62 G3
Schwechat 50 F9
Schwedt 50 D4
Schweich 54 J5
Schweinfurt 52 F6
Schwenningen 62 D2
Schwerin 52 G3
Schweriner See 52 G3
Schwetzingen 52 D7
Schwyz 62 D3
Sciacca 64 H11
Scicli 64 J12
Scobey 126 E1
Scotia Ridge 142 K9
Scotia Sea 144 (2)A4
Scotland 56 H5
Scott City 126 F3
Scott Inlet 122 T2
Scott Island 144 (2)Z3
Scott Reef 114 D2
Scottsbluff 126 F2
Scottsboro 128 C4
Scotty's Junction 132 C1
Scranton 128 E2
Scunthorpe 56 M8
Seal 122 M5
Sea of Azov 70 G5
Sea of Galilee 94 C4
Sea of Japan 82 G3
Sea of Marmara = Marmara Denizi 68 L4
Sea of Okhotsk 78 Q5
Sea of the Hebrides 56 E4
Searchlight 132 D1
Searcy 128 B3
Seaside 126 B1
Seattle 126 B1
Sebeş 66 L4
Sebkha Azzel Matti 102 F3
Sebkha de Timimoun 102 E3
Sebkha de Tindouf 102 D3
Sebkha Mekerrhane 102 F3
Sebkha Oum el Drouss Telli 102 C4
Sebkhet de Chemchâm 102 C4
Sebnitz 52 K6
Sebring 130 E4
Secchia 62 F6
Sechura 140 A5
Secretary Island 116 A7
Secunderabad 88 C5
Sécure 140 D7
Sedalia 128 B3
Sedan 54 G5
Sedano 60 G2
Seddon 116 D5
Sede Boqer 94 B6
Sedeh 90 G3
Sederot 94 B5
Sedico 62 H4
Sedom 94 C5
Seeheim 108 B5
Seelow 52 K4
Sées 58 F5
Seesen 52 F5
Seevetal 52 E3
Séez 62 B5
Seferihisar 68 J6
Segamat 86 C2
Segezha 70 F2
Seghnān 90 K2
Ségou 104 C2
Segovia 60 F4
Segré 58 E6
Séguédine 102 H4
Seguin 130 B4
Segura 60 H6
Sehithwa 108 C4
Sehnde 52 E4
Seiland 48 M1
Seiling 130 B2
Seinäjoki 48 M5
Seine 58 F4
Sekayu 86 C3
Sekondi 104 D3
Selassi 87 D3
Selat Bangka 86 D3
Selat Berhala 86 C3
Selat Dampir 87 D3
Selat Karimata 86 D3
Selat Makassar 86 F3
Selat Mentawai 86 B3
Selat Sunda 86 D4
Selawik 132 (1)F2
Selb 52 H6
Selby 126 G1
Selçuk 68 K7
Selebi-Phikwe 108 D4
Sélestat 62 C2
Selfoss 48 (1)C3
Sélibabi 102 C5
Seligman 132 D1
Seljord 48 E7
Selkirk 124 G1
Selkirk Mountains 124 C1
Sells 132 D2
Selm 54 K3
Selmer 128 C3
Selpele 87 D3
Selvas 140 C5
Selwyn Lake 122 L5

Selwyn Mountains 132 (1)L3
Semanit 68 B4
Semarang 86 E4
Sematan 86 D2
Sembé 104 G4
Seminoe Reservoir 126 E2
Seminole, *Okla., US* 126 G3
Seminole, *Tex., US* 132 F2
Semiozernoye 76 L7
Semipalatinsk 76 Q7
Semiyarka 76 P7
Semois 54 H5
Semporna 86 F2
Sena Madureira 140 D5
Senanga 108 C3
Senatobia 130 D3
Sendai 82 L4
Senec 62 N2
Seneca 130 E3
Senegal 104 A2
Sénégal 104 B1
Senftenberg 52 J5
Sengerema 106 E4
Senhor do Bonfim 140 J6
Senica 50 G9
Senigallia 62 J7
Senj 62 K6
Senja 48 J2
Senlis 54 E5
Sennar 90 B7
Senneterre 128 E1
Sens 58 J5
Senta 66 H4
Seoni 88 C4
Seoul = Sŏul 82 D5
Separation Point 116 D5
Sepinang 86 F2
Sept-Îles 122 T6
Seraing 54 H4
Serakhs 90 H2
Seram 87 D3
Serang 86 D4
Serbia = Srbija 66 H6
Serbia 66 H6
Serdobsk 70 H4
Serebryansk 76 Q8
Sered' 66 E1
Şereflikoçhisar 68 R6
Seregno 62 E5
Serein 58 J6
Seremban 86 C2
Serenje 108 E2
Sergelen 80 E1
Sergeyevka 70 N4
Sergipe 140 K6
Sergiyev Posad 70 G3
Seria 86 E2
Serifos 68 G7
Serifos 68 G7
Serik 68 P8
Seringapatam Reef 114 D2
Sermata 87 C4
Seronga 108 C3
Serov 70 M3
Serowe 108 D4
Serpa 60 C7
Serpneve 66 S3
Serpukhov 70 G4
Serra Acari 140 F3
Serra Curupira 140 E3
Serra da Chela 108 A3
Serra da Espinhaço 140 J7
Serra da Ibiapaba 140 J4
Serra da Mantiqueira 142 M3
Serra de Maracaju 142 K3
Serra do Cachimbo 140 F5
Serra do Caiapó 140 G7
Serra do Roncador 140 G6
Serra dos Carajás 140 G5
Serra dos Dois Irmãos 140 J5
Serra dos Parecis 140 E6
Serra do Tiracambu 140 H4
Serra Estrondo 140 H5
Serra Formosa 140 F6
Serra Geral de Goiás 140 H6
Serra Geral do Paranã 140 H7
Serra Lombarda 140 G3
Serra Pacaraima 140 E3
Serra Parima 140 E3
Serra Tumucumaque 140 F3
Serre da Estrela 60 C4
Serres, *France* 58 L9
Serres, *Greece* 68 F3
Serrinha 140 K6
Sertã 60 B5
Serui 87 E3
Servia 68 D4
Sêrxü 80 B4
Sese Islands 106 E4
Sesfontein 108 A3
Sesheke 108 C3
Sessa Aurunca 64 H7
Sestri Levante 62 E6
Sestroretsk 48 Q6
Sestrunj 62 K6
Sestu 64 D9
Sesvete 62 M5
Setana 82 K2
Sète 58 J10
Sete Lagoas 140 J7
Setesdal 48 D7
Sétif 102 G1
Settat 102 D2
Setúbal 60 B6
Sŏul 112 C2
Seurre 58 L7
Sevana Lich 92 L3
Sevastopol' 92 E1
Seven Lakes 132 E1
Sevenoaks 54 C3
Sévérac-le-Château 58 J9
Severn, *Canada* 122 P5
Severn, *UK* 56 K10
Severnaya Dvina 70 H2
Severnaya Osetiya 92 L2
Severnaya Zemlya 76 U1
Severn Estuary 56 J10
Severnoye 70 K4
Severnyy 76 L4
Severobaykal'sk 78 H5
Severodvinsk 70 G2
Severo-Kuril'sk 78 T6
Severomorsk 48 S2
Severoural'sk 70 M2
Severo-Yeniseyskiy 76 S5
Sevier Lake 126 D3
Sevilla 60 E7
Sevlievo 66 N7
Seward Peninsula 132 (1)E2
Seyakha 76 N3
Seychelles 108 (2)B2
Seychelles Islands 98 J6
Seydişehir 68 P7
Seydisfjöður 48 (1)G2
Seyhan 92 F5
Seymchan 78 S4
Seymour, *Ind., US* 130 D2
Seymour, *Tex., US* 130 B3
Sézanne 58 J5
Sezze 64 H7
Sfakia 68 G9
Sfântu Gheorghe, *Romania* 66 N4
Sfântu Gheorghe, *Romania* 66 S5
Sfax 102 H2
's-Gravenhage 54 G2
Sha'am 95 G3
Shabla 66 R6
Shabunda 106 D4
Shabwah 90 E6
Shache 76 P10
Shādegān 95 C1
Shadehill Reservoir 126 F1
Shagamu 104 E3
Shagonar 76 S7
Shag Rocks 142 N9
Shahbā' 94 D4
Shahdāb 95 G1
Shahdol 88 D4
Shah Fuladi 90 J3
Shahjahanpur 88 C3
Shahrak 90 H3
Shahr-e Bābāk 95 F1
Shahreza 90 F3
Shahrtuz 90 J2
Shakhrisabz 90 J2
Shakhtërsk 78 Q7
Shakhty 70 H5
Shakhun'ya 70 J3
Shaki 104 E3
Shakotan-misaki 82 L2
Shama 106 E5
Shamattawa 122 N5
Shamis 95 E5
Shamrock 132 F1
Shand 90 H3
Shandan 80 C3
Shandong Bandao 80 G3
Shangani 108 D3
Shangdu 80 E2
Shanghai 80 G4
Shanghang 80 F6
Shangqui 80 F4
Shangrao 80 F5
Shangzhi 80 H1
Shangzhou 80 D4
Shantarskiye Ostrova 78 P5
Shantou 80 F6
Shanwei 84 F2
Shanyin 80 E3
Shaoguan 80 E6
Shaoxing 80 G5
Shaoyang 80 E5
Shapkina 70 K1
Shaqrā' 95 A4
Sharga 76 T8
Sharjah = Ash Shāriqah 95 F4
Shark Bay 112 B8
Shark Reef 114 J2
Sharmah 100 G2
Sharm el Sheikh 100 F2
Sharūrah 90 E6
Shashe 108 D4
Shashi 80 E4
Shasta Lake 126 B2
Shats'k 50 N6
Shatsk 70 H4
Shaubak 94 C6
Shawano 128 C2
Shaykh Miskīn 94 D4
Shcherbakove 78 U3
Shchigry 70 G4
Shchuch'ye 76 L6
Shchuchyn 48 N10
Sheberghān 90 J2
Sheboygan 128 C2
Sheffield, *New Zealand* 116 D6
Sheffield, *UK* 56 L8
Sheffield, *Al., US* 128 C4
Sheffield, *Tex., US* 132 F2
Shegmas 70 J2
Shelburne 122 T8
Shelby 126 D1
Shelbyville 128 C3
Shelikof Strait 132 (1)F4
Shenandoah 128 A2
Shendam 104 F3
Shendi 100 F4
Shenkursk 70 H2
Shenyang 82 B3
Shenzhen 80 E6
Shepetivka 70 E4
Shepparton 114 J7
Sherbro Island 104 B3
Sherbrooke 128 F1
Sheridan 126 E2
Sherkaly 70 N2
Sherlovaya Gora 78 K6
Sherman 130 B3
's-Hertogenbosch 54 H3
Shetland Islands 56 M1
Shetpe 76 J9
Sheyenne 126 G1
Sheykh Sho'eyb 95 E3
Shiant Islands 56 F4
Shibata 82 K5
Shibetsu, *Japan* 82 M1
Shibetsu, *Japan* 82 N2
Shibotsu-jima 82 P2
Shiderty 76 N7
Shihezi 76 R9
Shijiazhuang 80 E3
Shikarpur 90 J4
Shikoku 82 G7
Shikoku-sanchi 82 G7
Shikotan-tō 82 P2
Shikotsu-ko 82 L2
Shiliguri 88 E3
Shilka 78 K6
Shilka 78 K6
Shillong 88 F3
Shilovo 70 H4
Shimabara 82 F7
Shimla 88 C2
Shimoda 82 K6
Shimoga 88 C6
Shimo-Koshiki-jima 82 E8
Shimoni 106 F4
Shimonoseki 82 F7
Shināş 95 G4
Shīndan 90 H3
Shingū 82 H7
Shinjō 82 L4
Shinyanga 106 E4
Shiono-misaki 82 H7
Shiprock 126 E3
Shiquan 80 D4
Shirakawa 82 L5
Shīrāz 95 E2
Shire 108 E3
Shiretoko-misaki 82 N1
Shiriya-zaki 82 L3
Shır Kūh 90 F3
Shiv 88 B3
Shivpuri 88 C3
Shiyan 80 E4
Shizuishan 80 D3
Shizuoka 82 K6
Shkodër 66 G7
Shomishko 76 K8
Shorap 90 J4
Shoreham 54 B4
Shoshone, *Calif., US* 126 C3
Shoshone, *Id., US* 126 D2
Shoshoni 126 E2
Shostka 70 F4
Show Low 132 E2
Shoyna 70 H1
Shreveport 130 C3
Shrewsbury 56 K9
Shuangliao 82 B2
Shuangyashan 78 N7
Shubarkuduk 76 K8
Shulan 82 D1
Shumagin Islands 132 (1)E5
Shumen 66 P6
Shumikha 70 M3
Shuqrah 90 E7
Shurchi 90 J2
Shūr Gaz 95 H2
Shurinda 78 J5
Shuryshkary 70 N1
Shuya 70 H3
Shuyang 80 F4
Shwebo 84 B2
Shymkent 76 M9
Sia 87 D4
Sialkot 90 K3
Siatista 68 D4
Šiauliai 50 N2
Sibay 70 L4
Šibenik 66 C6
Siberia = Sibir 74 N3
Siberut 86 B3
Sibi 90 J4
Sibigo 86 B2
Sibir 74 N3
Sibiu 66 M4
Sibolga 86 B2
Sibu 86 E2
Sibuco 84 G5
Sibut 106 B2
Sicilia 64 G11
Sicilian Channel 64 F11
Sicily = Sicilia 64 G11
Šid 66 G4
Siddipet 88 C5
Siderno 64 L10
Sidi Barrani 100 E1
Sidi Bel Abbès 102 E1
Sidi Kacem 102 D2
Sidirokastro 68 F3
Sidney 126 F2
Sidoan 87 B2
Sidorovsk 76 Q4
Sieburg 54 K4
Siedlce 50 M5
Sieg 54 K4
Siegen 54 L4
Siemiatycze 50 M5
Siĕmréab 84 C4
Siena 62 G7
Sieradz 50 H6
Sierpc 50 J5
Sierra Blanca 132 E2
Sierra Colorada 142 H7
Sierra de Calalasteo 142 H4
Sierra de Córdoba 142 H5
Sierra de Gata 60 D4
Sierra de Gúdar 60 K4
Sierra del Nevado 142 H6
Sierra de Perija 134 K7
Sierra Grande 142 H7
Sierra Leone 104 B3
Sierra Madre 134 F5
Sierra Madre del Sur 134 E5
Sierra Madre Occidental 124 E6
Sierra Madre Oriental 132 F3
Sierra Morena 60 E6
Sierra Nevada, *Spain* 60 G7
Sierra Nevada, *US* 132 B1
Sierra Vizcaino 124 D6
Sierre 62 C4
Sifnos 68 G8
Sig 60 K9
Sigean 58 H10
Sighetu Marmaţiei 66 L2
Sighişoara 66 M3
Siglufjörður 48 (1)D1
Sigmaringen 62 E2
Signal Mountain 128 C3
Siguiri 104 C2
Sihanoukville 84 C4
Siilinjärvi 48 P5
Siirt 92 J5
Sikar 88 C3
Sikasso 104 C2
Sikea 68 F4
Sikeston 128 C3
Sikhote Alin 82 H1
Sikinos 68 G8
Siklós 66 F4
Siktyakh 78 L3
Sil 60 C2
Šilalė 50 M2
Silandro 62 F4
Silba 62 K6
Silchar 88 F4
Şile 68 M3
Silhouette Island 108 (2)B1
Siliana 64 D12
Silifke 92 E5
Siling Co 88 E2
Silistra 66 Q5
Silivri 68 L3
Siljan 48 H6
Sillamäe 48 P7
Silsbee 130 C3
Siluas 86 D2
Šilutė 50 L2
Silvan 92 J4
Silver Bay 128 B1
Silver City 132 E2
Silver Lake 126 B2
Silver Plains 114 H2
Simanggang 86 E2
Simao 80 C6
Simav 92 C4
Simcoe 128 D2
Simeonovgrad 66 N7
Simeria 50 N12
Simeuluë 86 A2
Simferopol' 92 F1
Şimleu Silvaniei 66 K2
Simmerath 54 J4
Simojärvi 48 P3
Simpang 86 C3
Simpson Desert 114 G4
Sinabang 86 B2
Sinai 100 F2
Sinaia 66 N4
Şinak 92 K5
Sinalunga 64 F5
Sinanju 82 C4
Sinbaungwe 84 B3
Sincelejo 140 B2
Sinclair's Bay 56 J3
Sindangbarang 86 D4
Sindelfingen 52 E8
Sines 60 B7
Singa 100 F5
Singapore 86 C2
Singapore 86 C2
Singaraja 86 E4
Singen 62 D3
Sîngerei 66 R2
Singida 106 E4
Singkawang 86 D2
Singkep 86 C3
Singkilbaru 86 B2
Singleton 114 K6
Siniscola 64 D8
Sinj 66 D6
Sinjai 87 B4
Sinjār 92 J5
Sinkat 100 G4
Sinni 64 L8
Sinop 92 F2
Sinsheim 52 D7
Sintang 86 E2
Sinton 130 B4
Sinŭiju 82 C3
Sinyaya 78 L4
Sió 66 F3
Siófok 66 F3
Sion 62 C4
Sioux City 128 A2
Sioux Falls 128 A2
Sioux Lookout 124 H2
Siping 82 C2
Sipiwesk 122 M5
Sipura 86 B3
Sira 48 D7
Siracusa 64 K11
Sir Banī 'Yās 95 E4
Sir Edward Pellew Group 114 G3
Siret 66 P2
Siret 66 Q4
Sîrgān 90 H4

Place	Page	Ref.	Place	Page	Ref.	Place	Page	Ref.	Place	Page	Ref.
Şiria	50	L11	Snina	50	M9	Sorrento	64	J8	Springfield, Mo., US	128	B3
Şiri Kit Dam	84	B3	Snøhetta	48	E5	Sorsele	48	J4	Springfield, Oh., US	128	D3
Sirk	95	G3	Snøtinden	48	G3	Sorso	64	C8	Springfield, Oreg., US	126	B2
Sirohi	88	B4	Snowdon	56	H8	Sorsogon	84	G4	Springfield, Vt., US	128	F2
Sirsa	88	C3	Snowdrift	122	J4	Sort	60	M2	Spring Hill	130	E4
Sirsi	88	B6	Snowville	126	D2	Sortavala	48	R6	Springs	108	D5
Sisak	66	D4	Snyder	132	F2	Sørvagen	48	G3	Springs Junction	116	D6
Sisian	92	L4	Soalala	108	H3	Sōsan	82	D5	Springsure	114	J4
Sisimiut	122	W3	Soanierana-Ivongo	108	H3	Sosnogorsk	76	J5	Springville, Al., US	130	D3
Sisöphön	84	C4	Soa-Siu	87	C2	Sosnovka	76	G4	Springville, N.Y., US	128	E2
Sisseton	126	G1	Sobral	140	J4	Sosnovo	48	R6	Spulico	64	L9
Sistema Central	60	E4	Sochaczew	50	K5	Sosnowiec	50	J7	Squamish	126	B1
Sistema Ibérico	60	H3	Sochaux	62	B3	Sos'va	70	M3	Squinzano	64	N8
Sisteron	62	A6	Sochi	92	H2	Sos'vinskaya	70	M2	Srbija	66	H6
Sitapur	88	D3	Socorro	132	E2	Soto la Marina	132	G4	Srbobran	66	G4
Sitasjaure	48	J3	Socotra = Suquṭrā	90	F7	Soubré	104	C3	Srebrenica	66	G5
Siteia	68	J9	Socuéllamos	60	H5	Soufli	68	J3	Sredenekolymsk	78	S3
Sitges	60	M3	Sodankylä	48	P3	Souilly	54	H5	Sredinnyy Khrebet	78	T6
Sithonia	68	F4	Söderhamn	48	J6	Souk Ahras	64	B12	Srednesibirskoye Ploskogor'ye	78	F3
Sitka	122	D5	Södertälje	48	J7	Sŏul	82	D5	Srednogorie	68	G2
Sittard	54	H4	Sodo	106	F2	Soulac-sur-Mer	58	D8	Šrem	50	G5
Sittwe	88	B4	Soe	87	B4	Soumussalmi	48	Q4	Sretensk	78	K6
Sivand	95	E1	Soest	54	L3	Soûr	94	C3	Sri Jayewardenepura-Kotte	88	D7
Sivas	92	G4	Sofia = Sofiya	66	L7	Soure	60	B5	Srikakulam	88	D5
Siverek	92	H5	Sofiya	66	L7	Sour el Ghozlane	60	P8	Sri Lanka	88	D7
Sivrihisar	68	P5	Sofiysk, Russia	78	N6	Souris	124	F2	Srinagar	88	B2
Siwa	100	E1	Sofiysk, Russia	78	P6	Souris	124	G2	Stack Skerry	56	H2
Siyäzän	92	N3	Soforog	48	R4	Sousa	140	K5	Stade	48	E10
Sjælland	48	F9	Sōfu-gan	80	L5	Sousse	102	H1	Stadlandet	48	C5
Sjenica	66	H6	Sogamoso	140	C2	South Africa	108	C6	Stadskanaal	54	J2
Sjenica Jezero	66	G6	Sognefjorden	48	C6	South America	120	J9	Stadtallendorf	52	E6
Sjöbo	50	C2	Sogod	84	G4	Southampton, Canada	128	D2	Stadthagen	52	E4
Skädlderviken	50	B1	Sog Xian	88	F2	Southampton, UK	54	A4	Staffa	56	F5
Skaerbaek	52	D1	Sohâg	100	F2	Southampton Island	122	Q4	Staffelstien	52	F6
Skagen	48	F8	Soignies	54	G4	South Andaman	88	F6	Stafford	56	K9
Skagerrak	48	D8	Soissons	54	F5	South Atlantic Ocean	142	P6	Staines	54	B3
Skala	68	E8	Sokch'o	82	E4	South Australia	114	F5	Stainz	62	L4
Skantzoura	68	G5	Söke	68	K7	South Baymouth	128	D1	Stakhanov	70	G5
Skardu	90	E4	Sokhumi	92	J2	South Bend	128	C2	Stalowa Wola	50	M7
Skarżysko-Kamienna	50	K6	Sokode	104	E3	South Boston	128	E3	Stambolijski	68	G2
Skaulo	48	L3	Sokol	70	H3	South Carolina	130	E3	Stamford, UK	54	B2
Skawina	50	J8	Sokółka	48	M10	South Charleston	130	E2	Stamford, US	128	F2
Skaymat	102	B4	Sokolo	104	C2	South China Sea	84	E4	Standish	128	D2
Skegness	54	C1	Sokolov	52	H6	South Dakota	126	F2	Stanford	128	D3
Skellefteå	48	L4	Sokołów Podlaski	50	M5	South Downs	54	B4	Stanke Dimitrov	68	F2
Ski	48	F7	Sokoto	104	F2	South East Cape	114	J8	Stanley, Australia	114	J8
Skiathos	68	F5	Sokoto	104	F2	South East Point	114	J7	Stanley, Falkland Islands	142	K9
Skibotn	48	L2	Sokyryany	66	Q1	Southend-on-Sea	54	C3	Stanley, US	126	F1
Skidal'	50	P4	Solander Island	116	A8	Southern Alps	116	B6	Stanovaya	78	T3
Skien	48	E7	Solapur	88	C5	Southern Cross	114	C6	Stanovoye Nagor'ye	78	J5
Skikda	102	G1	Sölden	62	F4	Southern Indian Lake	122	M5	Stanovoy Khrebet	78	L5
Skipton	56	L8	Solenzara	64	D7	Southern Uplands	56	H6	Staphorst	54	J2
Skjern	48	E9	Solhan	92	J4	South Georgia	142	P9	Stapleton	126	F2
Škofja Loka	62	K4	Solikamsk	70	L3	South Harris	56	F4	Starachowice	50	L6
Skopelos	68	F5	Sol'-Iletsk	70	L4	South Haven	128	C2	Stara L'ubovňa	50	K8
Skopje	66	J7	Soliman	64	E12	South Hill	128	E3	Stara Pazova	66	H5
Skövde	48	G7	Solingen	54	K3	South Island	116	B6	Stara Planina	70	F3
Skovorodino	78	L6	Sollefteå	48	J5	South Korea	82	D5	Staraya Russa	70	F3
Skowhegan	128	G2	Soller	60	N5	South Lake Tahoe	126	B3	Stara Zagora	66	N7
Skuodas	48	L8	Solna	48	J7	South Orkney Islands	144	(2)A3	Starbuck Island	112	L6
Skye	56	F4	Solomon Islands	112	F6	South Pacific Ocean	142	P6	Stargard Szczeciński	48	H10
Skyros	68	G6	Solothurn	62	C3	South Platte	126	F2	Starkville	130	D3
Skyros	68	G6	Solov'yevsk	78	K6	Southport	56	J8	Starnberg	62	G2
Slagelse	52	G1	Šolta	66	G6	South Ronaldsay	56	K3	Starnberger See	62	G3
Slagnäs	48	K4	Soltau	52	E4	South Sandwich Islands	144	(2)C4	Starogard Gdański	50	H4
Slaney	56	F9	Sol'tsy	70	F3	South Sandwich Trench	138	H9	Staro Oryakhovo	66	Q7
Slano	66	E7	Solway Firth	56	J7	South Saskatchewan	124	D1	Start Point	58	B3
Slantsy	48	Q7	Solwezi	108	D2	South Shetland Islands	144	(2)MM4	Staryy Oskol	70	G4
Slaný	52	K6	Soma	68	K5	South Shields	56	L7	Staszów	50	L7
Slatina	66	M5	Sōma	82	L5	South Taranaki Bight	116	D4	Statesboro	130	E3
Slave	120	N3	Sombor	66	G4	South Uist	56	E4	Statesville	130	E2
Slave Lake	122	J5	Sombrerete	132	F4	South West Cape, Auckland Island	116	(2)A1	Staunton	130	F2
Slavonska Požega	66	E4	Somerset, Australia	114	H2	South West Cape, Australia	114	H8	Stavanger	48	C7
Slavonski Brod	66	F4	Somerset, Ky., US	128	C3	Southwest Cape	116	A8	Stavoron	54	H2
Slavyanka	82	F2	Somerset, Pa., US	128	E2	South West Pacific Basin	112	L9	Stavropol'	92	J1
Slavyansk-na-Kubani	92	H1	Somerset Island	122	N2	Southwold	54	D2	Stavropol'skaya Vovyshennost'	70	H5
Sławno	50	F3	Someș	66	K2	Sovata	66	N3	Steamboat Springs	126	E2
Sleaford	54	B1	Somme	54	E4	Soverato	64	L10	Steens Mountains	126	C2
Sleeper Islands	122	Q5	Sommen	48	H8	Sovetsk, Russia	48	L9	Steenwijk	54	J2
Slidell	130	D3	Sömmerda	52	G5	Sovetsk, Russia	70	J3	Stefansson Island	122	L2
Sligo	56	D7	Sømna	48	F4	Soweto	108	D5	Stege	52	H1
Sligo Bay	56	D7	Sondags	108	D6	Sōya-misaki	82	L1	Ştei	66	K3
Slite	48	K8	Sønderborg Ærø	52	E2	Sozopol	66	Q7	Stein	52	G7
Sliven	66	P7	Sondershausen	52	F5	Spa	54	H4	Steinach am Brenner	62	G3
Slobozia, Moldova	66	S3	Sondrio	62	E4	Spain	60	F5	Steinfurt	54	K2
Slobozia, Romania	66	Q5	Songavatn	48	D7	Spalding	54	B2	Steinhausen	108	B4
Slonim	48	N10	Songea	106	F6	Sparks	132	C1	Steinjker	48	F4
Slough	54	B3	Song Hông	84	C2	Spartanburg	130	E3	Stenay	54	H5
Slovakia	50	H9	Songhua	80	H1	Sparti	68	E7	Stendal	52	G4
Slovenia	62	K4	Songhua Hu	82	D2	Sparwood	126	D1	Steno Antikythiro	68	F9
Slovenj Gradec	62	L4	Songhua Jiang	82	D1	Spassk-Dal'niy	82	G1	Stephenville	130	B3
Slovenska Bistrica	62	L4	Songkan	80	D5	Spearfish	126	F2	Sterling	126	F2
Slov''yans'k	70	G5	Songkhla	84	C5	Spencer	128	A2	Sterling City	132	F2
Słubice	50	D5	Songnam	82	D5	Spencer Gulf	114	G6	Sterling Heights	128	D2
Slunj	62	L5	Songnim	82	C4	Spetses	68	F7	Sterlitamak	70	L4
Słupca	50	G5	Songo	108	E3	Spey	56	J4	Sternberk	50	G8
Słupsk	50	G3	Songololo	104	G6	Speyer	54	L5	Stettiner Haff	48	G10
Slussfors	48	J4	Songpan	80	C4	Spiekeroog	52	C3	Stevenage	54	B3
Slutsk	70	E4	Sonid Yuoqi	80	E2	Spiez	62	C4	Stevens Point	128	C2
Slyudyanka	78	G6	Sonid Zuoqi	80	E2	Spilimbergo	62	H4	Stevens Village	132	(1)H2
Smålandsfarvandet	52	G1	Son La	84	C2	Spišská Nová Ves	50	K9	Stewart	122	F5
Smallwood Reservoir	122	U6	Sonneberg	52	G6	Spitsbergen	144	(1)P2	Stewart	132	(1)K3
Smargon'	48	P9	Sono	140	H6	Spittal	62	J4	Stewart Island	116	A8
Smederevo	66	H5	Sonora	132	B1	Split	66	D6	Steyr	62	K2
Smila	70	F5	Sonora	132	D3	Spokane	126	C1	Stillwater	130	B2
Smirnykh	78	Q7	Sonoyta	132	D2	Spoleto	64	G6	Stinnett	132	F1
Smiths Falls	128	E2	Sonsorol Islands	87	D1	Spooner	128	B1	Ştip	68	E3
Smokey Hills	130	B2	Sonthofen	62	F3	Sprague	126	C1	Stirling	56	J5
Smoky	122	H6	Sopot	48	K9	Spratly Islands	84	E4	Stjørdal	48	F5
Smøla	48	D5	Sopron	62	M3	Spray	126	C2	Stockach	62	E3
Smolensk	70	F4	Sora	64	H7	Spree	52	K4	Stockerau	62	M2
Smolyan	68	G3	Soracaba	142	M3	Spremberg	52	K5	Stockholm	48	K7
Smooth Rock Falls	128	D1	Sorel	128	F1	Sprimont	54	H4	Stockport	56	K8
Smyrna	130	E3	Sorgun	92	F4	Spring	130	B3	Stockton, Calif., US	132	B1
Smyrna	48	(1)F2	Soria	60	H3	Springbok	108	B5	Stockton, Kans., US	132	G1
Snæfell	48	C1	Sørøya	52	G1	Springe	52	E4	Stockton-on-Tees	56	L7
Snake	126	C1	Soroca	66	R1	Springer	132	F1	Stœng Trêng	84	D4
Snake River Plain	126	D2	Sorochinsk	70	K4	Springerville	132	E2	Stoke-on-Trent	56	K8
Snåsavatnet	48	F4	Sorong	87	D3	Springfield, Colo., US	132	F1	Stokksnes	48	(1)F2
Sneek	54	H1	Soroti	106	E3	Springfield, Ill., US	128	C3	Stolac	66	F6
Sneem	56	C10	Sørøya	48	L1	Springfield, Mass., US	128	F2	Stolberg	54	J4
Snezhnogorsk	76	R4									
Snežnik	62	K5									

Name	Page	Grid
Stolin	70	E4
Stollberg	52	H6
Stomio	68	E5
Stonehaven	56	K5
Stony Rapids	122	K5
Stör	52	E2
Stora Lulevatten	48	K3
Stord	48	C7
Store Bælt	52	F1
Støren	48	F5
Store Sotra	48	B6
Storjord	48	H3
Storlien	48	G5
Storm Bay	114	J8
Storm Lake	128	A2
Stornoway	56	F3
Storozhevsk	70	K2
Storozhynets'	66	N1
Storsjøen	48	F6
Storsjön, Sweden	48	G5
Storsjön, Sweden	48	J6
Storuman	48	J4
Storuman	48	J4
Stour	54	C2
Stowmarket	54	D2
Strabane	56	E7
Stradella	62	E5
Strait of Belle Isle	122	V6
Strait of Bonifacio	64	D7
Strait of Dover	54	D4
Strait of Georgia	126	B1
Strait of Gibraltar	60	E9
Strait of Hormuz	95	G3
Strait of Juan de Fuca	126	B1
Strait of Malacca	86	C2
Straits of Florida	130	E5
Strakonice	52	J7
Stralsund	48	G9
Strand	108	B6
Stranda	48	D5
Strandavatn	48	D6
Stranraer	56	H7
Strasbourg	62	C2
Strasburg	132	F1
Strãşeni	66	R2
Stratford, Canada	128	D2
Stratford, New Zealand	116	E4
Stratford, US	126	F3
Stratford-upon-Avon	54	A2
Strathroy	128	D2
Stratoni	68	F4
Stratton	128	F1
Straubing	62	H2
Straumnes	48	(1)B1
Strausberg	52	J4
Streaky Bay	114	F6
Streator	128	C2
Strehaia	66	L5
Strelka, Russia	78	E5
Strelka, Russia	78	S4
Strezhevoy	70	Q2
Strimonas	68	F4
Strofades	68	C7
Stromboli	64	K10
Strömsund	48	H5
Stronsay	56	K2
Stroud	56	K10
Struga	68	C3
Strugi-Krasnyye	48	Q7
Strumica	68	E3
Stryjama	66	M7
Stryy	50	N8
Stryy	50	N8
Strzegom	50	F7
Strzelce Opolskie	50	H7
Strzelin	50	G7
Strzelno	50	H5
Studholme Junction	116	C7
Sturgeon Bay	128	C2
Sturgeon Falls	128	E1
Sturgis, Ky., US	128	C3
Sturgis, S.D., US	126	F2
Sturkö	50	E1
Štúrova	50	H10
Sturt Stony Desert	114	G5
Stuttgart, Germany	62	E2
Stuttgart, US	130	C3
Stykkishólmur	48	(1)B2
Suai	87	C4
Suakin	100	G4
Subcule	100	H5
Subi Besar	86	D2
Sublette	132	F1
Subotica	66	G3
Suceava	66	P2
Suck	56	D8
Suckow	52	G3
Sucre	140	D7
Sudak	92	F1
Sudan	100	E5
Sudan	104	D2
Suday	70	H3
Sudbury, Canada	128	D1
Sudbury, UK	54	C2
Sudd	106	D2
Sudová Vyshnya	50	N8
Suez = El Suweis	100	F2
Suez Canal	100	F1
Suffolk	130	F2
Sugun	90	L2
Suhãr	95	G4
Suhl	52	F6
Suide	80	E3
Suifenhe	82	F1
Suigam	88	B4
Suihua	78	M7
Suippes	54	G5
Suir	56	E9
Suixi	80	E6
Suizhong	80	G2
Suizhou	80	E4
Sukabumi	86	D4
Sukadana	86	D3
Sukhinichi	70	G4
Sukhona	70	H3
Sukkertoppen = Maniitsoq	122	W3
Sukkur	90	J4
Sula	70	K1
Sula	70	K1
Sula Sgeir	56	F2
Sulawesi	87	A3
Sulejówek	50	L5
Sule Skerry	56	H2
Sulgachi	78	N4
Sulina	66	S4
Sulingen	54	L2
Sullana	140	A4
Sullivan	130	C2
Sulmona	64	H6
Sulphur Springs	130	B3
Sultan	100	D1
Sultanhanı	68	R6
Sultanpur	88	D3
Sulu Archipelago	84	G5
Sulu Sea	84	F5
Sulzbach	54	K5
Sulzbach-Rosenberg	52	G7
Sulzberger Bay	144	(2)CC2
Sumatera	86	C2
Sumatra = Sumatera	86	C2
Sumba	87	A5
Sumbawa	87	A4
Sumbawabesar	87	A4
Sumbawanga	106	E5
Sumbe	108	A2
Sumeih	106	D2
Šumen	92	B2
Sumenep	86	E4
Sumisu-jima	82	L8
Sumkino	70	N3
Summer Lake	126	B2
Summerville	130	E3
Summit	122	B4
Šumperk	50	G8
Sumqayıt	92	N3
Sumter	130	E3
Sumy	70	F4
Sunbury	128	E2
Sunch'ŏn	82	D6
Sun City	108	D5
Sundance	126	F2
Sundarbans	88	E4
Sunday Strait	114	D3
Sunderland	56	L7
Sundridge	128	E1
Sundsvall	48	J5
Sundsvallsbukten	48	J5
Sungaipenuh	86	C3
Sungei Petani	84	C5
Sungurlu	92	F3
Sunnyvale	126	B3
Sun Prairie	128	C2
Suntar	78	K4
Suntsar	90	H4
Sunwu	78	M7
Sunyani	104	D3
Suomussalmi	70	E2
Suō-nada	82	F7
Suonenjoki	48	P5
Suordakh	78	P3
Suoyarvi	70	F2
Superior	124	H2
Supetar	66	D6
Süphan Dağı	92	K4
Sūqash Shuyūkh	95	B1
Suqian	80	F4
Suquṭrā	90	F7
Sūr	90	G5
Sura	70	J4
Surab	90	J4
Surabaya	86	E4
Sūrak	95	H4
Surakarta	86	E4
Šurany	66	F1
Surat	88	B4
Surat Thani	84	B5
Surdulica	66	K7
Şūre	54	L2
Surfers Paradise	114	K5
Surgut	76	N5
Surgutikha	76	R5
Surigao	84	H5
Surin	84	C4
Surinam	140	F3
Surkhet	88	D3
Sūrmaq	95	E1
Surovikino	70	H5
Surskoye	70	J4
Surt	102	J2
Surtsey	48	(1)C3
Susa	62	C5
Şuşa	92	M4
Sušac	66	D7
Susak	62	K6
Susanville	126	B2
Suşehri	92	H3
Sušice	52	J7
Susitma	132	(1)G3
Susuman	78	R4
Susurluk	68	L5
Sutak	88	C2
Sutherland	108	C6
Sutlej	88	B3
Suusamyr	76	N9
Suva	112	H7
Suvorov Island	112	K7
Suwałki	50	M3
Suwannaphum	84	C3
Suweilih	94	C4
Suweima	94	C5
Suwŏn	82	D5
Suzak	70	N6
Suzhou, China	80	F4
Suzhou, China	80	G4
Suzuka	82	J6
Suzu-misaki	82	J5
Svalbard	144	(1)Q2
Svalyaya	66	L1
Svappavaara	48	L3
Svartenhuk Halvø	122	V2
Svatove	70	G5
Sveg	48	H5
Svendborg	48	F9
Šventoji	48	N9
Sverdrup Islands	144	(1)DD2
Svetac	66	C6
Sveti Nikole	68	D3
Svetlaya	78	P7
Svetlogorsk	50	K3
Svetlograd	92	K1
Svetlyy, Russia	50	K3
Svetlyy, Russia	76	L7
Svidník	50	L8
Svilengrad	68	J3
Svishtov	66	N6
Svitava	50	F8
Svitovy	50	F8
Svobodnyy	78	M6
Svratka	50	F8
Svyetlahorsk	70	E4
Swain Reefs	114	K4
Swains Island	112	J7
Swakopmund	108	A4
Swale	56	K7
Swan	138	C2
SwanHill	114	H7
Swan Islands	134	H5
Swan River	122	L6
Swansea, Australia	114	J8
Swansea, UK	56	J10
Swaziland	108	E5
Sweden	48	H6
Sweetwater	132	F2
Swider	50	L5
Swidnica	50	F7
Świdnik	50	M6
Świdwin	50	E4
Świebodzin	50	E5
Świecie	50	H4
Swift Current	124	E1
Swindon	54	A3
Świnoujście	48	H10
Switzerland	62	C4
Syalakh	78	L3
Syamzha	70	H2
Syców	50	G6
Sydney, Australia	114	K6
Sydney, Canada	122	U7
Syke	54	L2
Syktyvkar	70	K2
Sylacauga	130	D3
Sylhet	88	F4
Sylt	48	E9
Sylvania	128	D2
Sym	76	R5
Sym	76	R5
Symi	68	K8
Synya	70	L1
Syracuse, Kans., US	132	F1
Syracuse, N.Y., US	128	E2
Syrdar'ya	76	L8
Syrdar'ya	90	J1
Syria	90	C3
Syrian Desert = Bãdiyat ash Shãm	94	D4
Syrna	68	J8
Syros	68	G7
Sytomino	70	P2
Syzran'	70	J4
Szamos	66	K1
Szamotuły	50	F5
Szarvas	50	K11
Szczecin	50	D4
Szczecinek	50	F4
Szczytno	50	K4
Szeged	66	H3
Szeghalom	66	J2
Székesfehérvár	66	F2
Szekszárd	66	F3
Szentendre	66	G2
Szentes	66	H3
Szerencs	50	L9
Szigetvár	66	E3
Szolnok	66	H2
Szombathely	66	D2
Szprotawa	50	E6
Sztum	50	J4
Szydłowiec	50	K6

T

Name	Page	Grid
Tab	66	F3
Tabarka	64	C12
Tabas	90	G3
Tabãsin	95	G1
Taber	126	D1
Table Cape	116	G4
Tabong	88	G3
Tábor	50	D8
Tabor	78	R2
Tabora	106	E5
Tabou	104	C4
Tabrīz	92	M4
Tabuaeran	112	K5
Tabūk	90	C4
Tacheng	76	Q8
Tachov	52	H7
Tacloban	84	H4
Tacna	140	C7
Tacoma	124	B2
Tacuarembó	142	K5
Tacurong	87	B1
Tadjoura	100	H5
Tadmur	92	H6
Tadoussac	128	G1
Taech'ŏn	82	D5
Taegu	82	E3
Taejŏn	80	H3
Tafahi	112	(1)J7
Tafalla	60	J2
Tafila	94	C6
Tafi Viejo	142	H4
Tagab	100	F4
Taganrog	70	G5
Taganrogskiy Zaliv	70	G5
Tagbilaran	84	G5
Tagul	78	F6
Tagum	84	H5
Tagus	60	B5
Taharoa	116	E4
Taheke	116	D2
Tahiti	112	M7
Tahoe Lake	122	K2
Tahoka	132	F2
Tahoua	104	F2
Tahrūd	95	G2
Tahuna	84	H6
Tai'an	80	F3
Taihape	116	E5
Taihe	80	E5
Taikeng	80	E4
Tailem Bend	114	G7
Tain	56	H4
T'ai-nan	80	G6
T'ai-Pei	80	G6
Taiping	86	C1
Taipingchuan	82	B1
T'ai-tung	84	G2
Taivalkoski	48	Q4
Taiwan	84	G2
Taiwan Strait	84	F2
Taiyuan	80	E3
Taizhou	80	F4
Ta'izz	90	D7
Tajikistan	90	J2
Tajima	82	K5
Tajo	46	D3
Tak	84	B3
Takaka	116	D5
Takamatsu	82	H6
Takaoka	82	J5
Takapuna	116	E3
Takasaki	82	K5
Takayama	82	J5
Takefui	82	J6
Takengon	86	B2
Takestān	90	E2
Ta Khmau	84	D4
Takht	78	P6
Takhta-Bazar	90	H2
Takhtabrod	76	M7
Takhtakupyr	76	L9
Takijung Lake	122	J3
Takikawa	82	L2
Takoradi	104	D4
Taksimo	78	J5
Takua Pa	84	B5
Takum	104	G3
Talak	102	F5
Talara	140	A4
Talas	76	N9
Tal'at Mūsá	92	G6
Talavera de la Reina	60	F5
Talaya	78	S4
Talbotton	130	E3
Talca	142	G6
Talcahuano	142	G6
Taldykorgan	76	P9
Tãlesh	90	E2
Taliabu	87	B3
Talibon	84	G4
Talitsa	70	M3
Tall 'Afar	92	K5
Tallahassee	130	E3
Tallaimannar	88	C7
Tall al Lahm	95	B1
Tallinn	48	N7
Tall Kalakh	94	D2
Tallulah	124	H5
Tall 'Uwaynāt	92	K5
Tãlmaciu	66	M4
Tal'menka	76	Q7
Talon	78	R5
Tãloqãn	76	N10
Taloyoak	122	N3
Talsi	48	M8
Taltal	142	G4
Tama	128	B2
Tamale	104	D3
Tamanrasset	102	G4
Tamanthi	88	G3
Tamási	66	F3
Tamazunchale	124	G7
Tambacounda	104	B2
Tambey	76	N3
Tambo	114	J4
Tambov	70	H4
Tambu	87	A3
Tambura	106	D2
Tâmega	130	E4
Tamp-e Gīrãn	95	H3
Tampere	48	M6
Tampico	134	E4
Tamsagbulag	80	F1
Tamsweg	62	J3
Tamworth, Australia	114	K6
Tamworth, UK	54	A2
Tana, Kenya	106	G4
Tana, Norway	48	P2
Tanabe	82	H7
Tana bru	48	P1
Tanacross	132	(1)J3
Tanafjorden	48	Q1
Tanaga Island	132	(3)C1
T'ana Hāyk'	100	G5
Tanahgrogot	86	F3

Name	Page	Grid
Tanahjampea	87	A4
Tanahmerah	87	F4
Tanami Mine	114	E4
Tanami Desert	114	F3
Tanaro	62	C6
Tanch'ŏn	82	E3
Tanda	104	D3
Tandag	84	H5
Tăndărei	66	Q5
Tandil	142	K6
Tanega-shima	82	F8
Tanew	50	M7
Tanezrouft	102	E4
Tanga, *Russia*	78	J6
Tanga, *Tanzania*	106	F5
Tanger	102	D1
Tangermünde	52	G2
Tanggu	80	F3
Tangmai	88	G2
Tangra Yumco	88	E2
Tangshan	80	F3
Tanimbar	112	D6
Tanjona Ankaboa	108	G4
Tanjona Bobaomby	108	H2
Tanjona Masoala	108	J3
Tanjona Vilanandro	108	G3
Tanjona Vohimena	108	H5
Tanjung	86	F3
Tanjungbalai	86	B2
Tanjung Cangkuang	86	C4
Tanjung Datu	86	D2
Tanjung d'Urville	87	E3
Tanjung Libobo	87	C3
Tanjung Lumut	86	D3
Tanjung Mengkalihat	86	F2
Tanjungpandan	86	D3
Tanjung Puting	86	E3
Tanjungredeb	86	F2
Tanjung Selatan	86	E3
Tanjungselor	86	F2
Tanjung Vals	87	E4
Tankovo	76	R5
Tankse	88	C2
Tanlovo	70	P1
Tanney	54	G5
Tanout	104	F2
Tanta	100	F1
Tan-Tan	102	C3
Tanzania	106	E4
Tao'an	80	G1
Taomasina	108	H3
Taongi	112	J4
Taormina	64	K11
Taos	132	E1
Taoudenni	102	E5
Taourirt	102	E2
T'ao-yuan	84	G2
Tapa	48	N7
Tapachula	134	F6
Tapajós	140	F4
Tapauá	140	E5
Tapolca	66	E3
Tappahannock	130	F2
Tapsuy	70	M2
Tapuaenuku	116	D6
Taquarí	140	F7
Tara	70	Q3
Tara	76	N6
Tarābulus	102	H2
Taraclia	66	R4
Taracua	140	D3
Tarāghin	102	H3
Tarakan	84	F6
Taran	76	N3
Taranaki = Mount Egmont	116	E4
Tarancón	60	H5
Taranto	64	M8
Tarapoto	140	B5
Tarare	58	K8
Tarascon	58	K10
Tarauacá	140	C5
Tarauacá	140	C5
Tarawa	112	H5
Tarawera Lake	116	F4
Tarazona	60	J3
Tarbert, *UK*	56	G6
Tarbes	58	F10
Tarbet, *UK*	56	F4
Tarcoola	114	F6
Taree	114	K6
Tareya	76	S3
Tarfaya	102	C3
Târgovişte	66	N5
Târgu Frumos	66	Q2
Târgu Jiu	66	L4
Târgu Lăpuş	66	L2
Târgu Mureş	66	M3
Târgu-Neamţ	66	P2
Târgu Ocna	66	P3
Târgu Secuiesc	66	P3
Tarhunah	102	H2
Tarif	95	E4
Tarifa	60	E8
Tarija	142	J3
Tarim	76	Q9
Tarim	90	E6
Tarim Pendi	76	Q10
Tarīn Kowt	90	J3
Tariskay Shan	76	Q9
Taritatu	87	E3
Tarkio	130	B1
Tarko Sale	76	P5
Tarlac	84	G3
Tarn	58	H10
Tarna	50	K10
Tärnaby	48	H4
Târnăveni	66	M3
Tarnogskiy Gorodok	70	H2
Tărnovo	68	K2
Tarnów	50	K7
Tarnowskie Góry	50	H7
Taro	62	E6
Tārom	95	F2
Taroom	114	J5
Taroudannt	102	D2
Tarquinia	64	F6
Tarragona	60	M3
Tarras	116	B7
Tárrega	60	M3
Tarso Emissi	100	C3
Tarsus	92	F5
Tartagal	142	J3
Tartu	48	P7
Tartūs	94	C2
Tarutyne	66	S3
Tarvisio	62	J4
Tasbuget	76	M9
Tashigang	88	F3
Tashir	92	L3
Tashkent = Toshkent	76	M9
Tash-Kömür	76	N9
Tashtagol	76	R7
Tasiilaq	122	Z3
Tasikmalaya	86	D4
Taskesken	76	Q8
Taşköprü	92	F3
Tasman Bay	116	D5
Tasmania	112	E10
Tasmania	114	H8
Tasman Mountains	116	D5
Tasman Sea	116	B3
Tăşnad	66	K2
Taşova	92	G3
Tassili du Hoggar	102	F4
Tassili-n'-Ajjer	102	G3
Tasty	76	M9
Tasūj	92	L4
Tata, *Hungary*	66	F2
Tata, *Morocco*	102	D3
Tataba	87	B3
Tatabánya	66	F2
Tataouine	102	H2
Tatarbunary	66	S4
Tatariya	70	J3
Tatarsk	76	P6
Tatarskiy Proliv	76	P7
Tateyama	82	K6
Tathlina Lake	122	H4
Tatta	90	J5
Tatvan	92	K4
Tauá	140	J5
Tauberbischofsheim	52	E7
Tauern	62	J4
Taumarunui	116	E4
Taungdwingyi	84	B2
Taung-gyi	88	G4
Taungup	88	F5
Taunsa	88	B2
Taunton, *UK*	56	J10
Taunton, *US*	128	F2
Taunus	54	L4
Taunusstein	54	L4
Taupo	116	E4
Tauragë	50	M2
Tauranga	116	F3
Tauroa Point	116	D2
Tavda	70	N3
Tavda	70	N3
Tavira	60	C7
Tavoy	84	B4
Tavşanli	92	C4
Taw	56	J11
Tawas City	128	D2
Tawau	86	F2
Tawitawi	86	F1
Taxkorgan	76	P10
Tay	56	J5
Tayga	76	R6
Taylorville	130	D2
Taym	90	C4
Taymā'	100	G2
Taymura	78	F4
Taymylyr	78	L2
Tay Ninh	84	D4
Tayshet	78	F5
Tayuan	78	L6
Tayyebād	90	H3
Taza	102	E2
Tazeh Kand	92	M4
Tazenakht	102	D2
Tāzirbū	100	D2
Tazovskaya Guba	76	N4
Tazovskiy	76	P4
Tazovskiy Poluostrov	76	N4
Tazungdam	84	B1
T'bilisi	92	L3
Tchamba	104	G3
Tchibanga	104	G5
Tchin Tabaradene	102	G5
Tczew	50	H3
Te Anau	116	A7
Te Araroa	116	G3
Te Aroha	116	E3
Te Awamutu	116	E4
Teberda	92	J2
Tébessa	102	G1
Tebingtinggi	86	B2
Téboursouk	64	D12
Techa	70	M3
Techiman	104	D3
Tecuala	132	D4
Tecuci	66	Q4
Tedzhen	90	H2
Tees	56	L7
Tegal	86	D4
Tegina	104	G3
Tegernsee	62	F4
Teglio	62	F4
Tegucigalpa	134	G6
Tegul'det	76	R6
Te Hapua	116	D2
Te Haroto	116	F4
Tehek Lake	122	M3
Teheran = Tehrān	90	F2
Tehrān	90	F2
Teignmouth	56	J11
Tejo = Tagus	60	B5
Te Kaha	116	F3
Te Kao	116	D2
Teknaf	88	F4
Teku	87	B3
Te Kuiti	116	E4
T'elavi	92	L3
Tel Aviv-Yafo	94	B4
Telegraph Creek	132	(1)L4
Telén	142	H6
Teles Pires	140	F5
Telford	56	K9
Telfs	62	G3
Teller	132	(1)D2
Telsen	142	H7
Telšiai	50	M2
Teltow	52	J4
Teluk Berau	87	D3
Teluk Bone	87	B3
Teluk Cenderawasih	87	E3
Telukdalem	86	B2
Teluk Kumai	86	E3
Telukpakedai	86	D3
Teluk Sampit	86	E3
Teluk Sukadana	86	D3
Teluk Tomini	87	B2
Tema	104	D3
Tembenchi	76	T4
Temerin	66	G4
Temerloh	84	C6
Teminabuan	87	D3
Temochic	132	E3
Tempe	132	D2
Tempio Pausaria	64	D8
Temple	132	G2
Temryuk	92	G1
Temuco	142	G6
Tenali	88	D5
Tendaho	100	H5
Ten Degree Channel	88	F7
Tendo	82	L4
Tendrara	102	E2
Ténéré	102	G5
Ténéré du Tafassasset	102	G4
Tenerife	102	B3
Ténès	102	F1
Tenggarong	86	F3
Tenke	108	D2
Tenkodogo	104	D2
Tennant Creek	114	F3
Tennessee	120	K6
Tennessee	124	J4
Tenojoki	48	P2
Tenteno	87	B3
Tenterfield	114	K5
Teo	60	B2
Teófilo Otoni	140	J7
Tepa	87	C4
Tepehuanes	124	E6
Tepic	124	F7
Teplice	50	C7
Ter	60	N2
Terceira	102	(1)B2
Terek	92	L2
Teresina	140	J5
Tergnier	54	F5
Terme	92	G3
Termez	90	J2
Termini Imerese	64	H11
Termirtau	76	N7
Termoli	66	C8
Ternate	87	C2
Terneuzen	54	F3
Terni	64	G6
Ternitz	62	M3
Ternopil'	70	E5
Ternuka	116	C7
Terracina	64	H7
Terrassa	60	N3
Terre Haute	130	D2
Terry	126	E1
Tersa	70	H4
Terschelling	54	H1
Teruel	60	J4
Tervel	92	B2
Tervola	48	N3
Teseney	100	G4
Teshekpuk Lake	132	(1)F1
Teshikaga	82	N2
Teshio	82	L1
Teslin	132	(1)L3
Teslin	132	(1)L3
Tessalit	102	F4
Têt	58	H11
Tete	108	E3
Teterow	52	H3
Teteven	68	G2
Tétouan	102	D1
Tetovo	68	H8
Teuco	142	J3
Teulada	64	C10
Tevere	64	G6
Teverya	94	C4
Tevriz	70	C4
Te Waewae Bay	116	A8
Texarkana	130	C3
Texas	124	F5
Texel	54	G1
Teya	76	S5
Teykovo	70	H3
Tfarïti	102	C3
Thaba Putsoa	108	D5
Thabazimbi	108	D4
Thailand	84	C4
Thai Nguyên	84	D2
Thal	88	B2
Thale Luang	84	C5
Thamarit	90	F6
Thames	56	L10
Thamūd	90	E6
Thane	88	B5
Thanh Hoa	84	D3
Thanjavur	88	C6
Thann	62	C3
Tharad	88	B4
Thar Desert	88	B3
Thargomindah	114	H5
Tharwāniyyah	95	E5
Thasos	68	G4
Thasos	68	G4
Thaton	84	B3
Thaya	50	E9
The Bahamas	130	F4
The Bluff	130	F4
The Dalles	126	B1
Thedford	126	F2
The Fens	56	L8
The Gambia	104	A2
The Granites	114	E4
The Hague = 's-Gravenhage	54	G2
Thelon	122	L4
The Minch	56	F3
The Naze	54	D3
Thenia	60	P8
Theniet el Had	60	N9
Theodore Roosevelt	140	E5
Theodore Roosevelt Lake	132	D2
The Pas	122	L6
Thermaikos Kolpos	68	E4
Thermopolis	126	E2
The Sisters	116	(1)B1
The Solent	54	A4
Thessalon	128	D1
Thessaloniki	68	E4
Thetford	56	N9
Thetford Mines	128	F1
The Twins	116	D5
The Wash	56	N9
The Weald	54	B3
The Whitsundays	114	J4
Thief River Falls	128	A1
Thiers	58	J8
Thiès	104	A2
Thika	106	F4
Thimphu	88	E3
Þingvallavatn	48	(1)C2
Thionville	54	J5
Thira	68	H8
Thira	68	H8
Thirasia	68	H8
Thirsk	56	L7
Thiruvananthapuram	88	C7
Thisted	48	E8
Þistilfjöður	48	(1)F1
Thiva	68	F6
Thiviers	58	F8
Þjórsá	48	(1)D2
Tholen	54	G3
Thomasville	130	E3
Thompson	122	H6
Thompson	122	M5
Thompson Falls	126	C1
Thomson	130	E3
Thonon-les-Bains	62	B4
Þórisvatn	48	(1)D2
Þorlákshöfn	48	(1)C3
Þorshöfn	48	(1)F1
Thouars	58	E7
Thrakiko Pelagos	68	H4
Three Forks	126	D1
Three Kings Island	116	C2
Three Rivers	128	C2
Throckmorton	130	B3
Thuin	54	G4
Thun	62	C4
Thunder Bay	128	C1
Thuner See	62	C4
Thung Song	84	B5
Thüringer Wald	52	F6
Thurso	56	J3
Thusis	62	E4
Tiāb	95	G3
Tianjin	80	F3
Tianmen	80	E4
Tianqiaoling	82	E2
Tianshifu	82	C3
Tianshui	80	D4
Tianshuihai	90	L2
Tianyang	80	D6
Tiaret	102	F1
Tibati	104	G3
Tibesti	100	C3
Tibet = Xizang	88	E2
Tibooburra	114	H5
Tiburón	134	B3
Tīchīt	102	D5
Tichla	102	C4
Ticino	62	D4
Ticul	134	G4
Tidjikdja	102	C5
Tieling	82	C1
Tielongtan	88	C1
Tielt	54	G4
Tienen	54	G4
Tien Shan	76	Q9
Tien Yen	84	D2
Tierra Amarilla	126	E3
Tiétar	60	E4
Tiflis = T'bilisi	98	H1
Tifton	130	E3
Tifu	87	C3
Tighina	66	S3
Tignère	104	G3
Tigre	140	B4
Tigris	92	K6
Tijuana	124	C5
Tikanlik	76	R9
Tikhoretsk	70	H5
Tikhvin	70	F3
Tikrīt	92	K6

Name	Page	Ref
Tiksi	78	M2
Tilburg	54	H3
Tilichiki	78	V4
Tillabéri	104	E2
Tillamook	126	B1
Tilos	68	K8
Timanskiy Kryazh	70	K2
Timaru	116	C7
Timashevsk	70	G5
Timber Creek	114	F3
Timerloh	86	C2
Timimoun	102	F3
Timişoara	66	J4
Timmins	128	D1
Timon	140	J5
Timor	87	C4
Timor Sea	114	E2
Tinaca Point	112	C5
Tin Alkoum	102	H4
Tinchebray	54	B6
Tindivanam	88	C6
Tindouf	102	D3
Tineo	60	D1
Tinfouchy	102	D3
Tinglev	52	E2
Tingo Maria	140	B5
Tingri	88	E3
Tingsryd	50	E1
Tiniroto	116	F4
Tinnsjø	48	E7
Tinogasta	142	H4
Tinos	68	H7
Tinos	68	H7
Tinsukia	88	G3
Tintâne	102	C5
Ti'i'o	100	H5
Tipperary	56	D9
Tirana = Tiranë	68	B3
Tiranë	68	B3
Tirari Desert	114	G5
Tiraspol	66	S3
Tire	68	K6
Tiree	56	F5
Tiroungoulou	106	C2
Tirschenreuth	52	H7
Tirso	64	C9
Tiruchchirāppalli	88	C6
Tirunelveli	88	C7
Tirupati	88	C6
Tiruppur	88	C6
Tiruvannamalai	88	C6
Tisa	66	H4
Tisīyah	94	D4
Tišnov	50	F8
Tisza	50	M9
Tiszaföldvár	66	H3
Tiszafüred	66	H2
Tiszaújváros	50	L10
Tit-Ary	76	Z3
Titel	66	H4
Titlagarh	88	D4
Titova Korenica	62	L6
Titovo Velenje	64	K2
Titu	66	N5
Titusville	130	E4
Tivaouane	102	B6
Tiverton	56	J11
Tivoli	64	G7
Tiyās	94	E2
Tizi Ouzou	102	F1
Tiznit	102	D3
Tjeldøya	48	H2
Tjørkolm	48	D7
Tlemcen	102	E2
Tmassah	100	C2
Toad River	122	F5
Tobago	134	M6
Tobelo	87	C2
Tobermory, UK	56	F5
Tobermory, US	128	D1
Tobi	87	D2
Toboali	86	D3
Tobol	70	M4
Tobol	70	M4
Tobol'sk	70	N3
Tobseda	70	K1
Tocantins	140	H5
Tocantins	140	H5
Toce	62	D4
Tocopilla	142	G3
Todeli	87	B3
Todi	64	G6
Tofino	126	A1
Togo	104	E3
Toimin	64	H2
Toi-misaki	82	F8
Tōjō	82	G6
Tok	132	(1)J3
Tokar	100	G4
Tokat, Sudan	90	C6
Tokat, Turkey	90	C1
Tokelau	112	J6
Tokmak	76	P9
Tokoroa	116	E4
Tokounou	104	C3
Toksun	76	R9
Tok-tō	80	J3
Toktogul	76	N9
Tokushima	82	H6
Tokuyama	82	F6
Tōkyō	82	K6
Tolaga Bay	116	G4
Tôlañaro	108	H4
Tolbo	76	S8
Toledo, Brazil	142	L3
Toledo, Spain	60	F5
Toledo, US	128	D2
Toliara	108	G4
Tolitoli	87	B2
Tol'ka	76	Q5
Tol'ka	76	Q5
Tollense	52	J3
Tolmezzo	62	J4
Tolmin	62	J4
Tolna	66	F3
Tolosa	60	H1
Tol'yatti	70	J4
Tolybay	76	L7
Tom'	76	R6
Tomah	128	B2
Tomakomai	82	L2
Tomamae	82	L1
Tomar, Brazil	140	E4
Tomar, Portugal	60	B5
Tomari	78	Q7
Tomaszów Lubelski	50	N7
Tomaszów Mazowiecki	50	K6
Tombouctou	102	E5
Tombua	108	A3
Tomé	142	G6
Tomelloso	60	H5
Tomini	87	B2
Tommot	78	M5
Tomo	140	D2
Tompo	78	P4
Tom Price	114	C4
Tomra	88	E2
Tomsk	76	Q6
Tomtor	78	Q4
Tomu	87	D3
Tonalá	134	F5
Tondano	87	B2
Tønder	52	D2
Tonga	106	E2
Tonga	112	J7
Tonga Islands	112	J8
Tongareva	112	K6
Tonga Trench	112	J8
Tongbai	80	E4
Tongchuan	80	D4
Tongduch'ŏn	82	D5
Tongeren	54	H4
Tonghae	82	E5
Tonghua	82	C3
Tongliao	80	G2
Tongling	80	F4
Tongshan	80	F4
Tongshi	84	D3
Tongue	126	E1
Tongyu	80	G2
Tónichi	124	E6
Tonj	106	D2
Tonk	88	C3
Tonkābon	90	F2
Tônlé Sab	84	C4
Tonnay-Charente	58	E8
Tönning	52	D2
Tonopah	126	C3
Tooele	126	D2
Toora-Khem	76	T7
Toowoomba	114	K5
Topeka	124	G4
Topki	76	R6
Topliţa	66	N3
Topock	132	D2
Topol'čany	50	H9
Topolobampo	124	E6
Torbali	68	K6
Torbat-e Heydarīyeh	90	G2
Torbat-e Jām	90	H2
Tordesillas	60	F3
Töre	48	M4
Torells	60	N2
Torgau	52	H5
Torgelow	50	C4
Torhout	54	F3
Torino	62	C5
Tori-shima	82	L8
Torneälven	48	L3
Torneträsk	48	K2
Tornio	48	N4
Toro	60	E3
Toronto	128	E2
Tororo	106	E3
Toros Dağları	92	E5
Torquay	56	J11
Torrance	132	C2
Torreblanca	60	L4
Torre de Moncorvo	60	C3
Torrejón de Ardoz	60	G4
Torrelapaja	60	J3
Torrelavega	60	F1
Torremolinos	60	F8
Torrent	60	K5
Torreón	132	F3
Torre-Pacheco	60	K7
Torres Strait	114	H2
Torres Vedras	60	A5
Torrevieja	60	K6
Torrington	126	F2
Tortoli	64	D9
Tortona	62	D6
Tortosa	60	L4
Tortum	92	J3
Torüd	90	G2
Toruń	50	H4
Tory Island	56	D6
Torzhok	70	G3
Tosa-wan	82	G7
Toshkent	76	M9
Tostedt	52	E3
Tosya	68	S3
Totaranui	116	D5
Tôtes	54	D5
Tot'ma	70	H3
Totora	140	D7
Tottori	82	H6
Touba, Côte d'Ivoire	104	C3
Touba, Senegal	104	A2
Tougan	104	D2
Touggourt	102	G2
Tougouri	104	D2
Touil	102	C5
Toul	58	L5
Toulépleu	104	C3
Toulon	58	L10
Toulouse	58	G10
Toummo	102	H4
Toungoo	84	B3
Tourcoing	54	F4
Tournai	54	F4
Tournon-sur-Rhône	58	K8
Tours	58	F6
Touws River	108	C6
Tovuz	92	L3
Towanda	128	E2
Towari	87	B3
Towcester	54	B2
Towner	126	F1
Townsend	126	D1
Townshend Island	114	K4
Townsville	114	J3
Toxkan	76	P9
Toyama	82	J5
Toyohashi	82	J6
Toyooka	82	H6
Toyota	82	J6
Tozeur	102	G2
Tqvarch'eli	92	J2
Trâblous	94	C2
Trabzon	92	H3
Tracy	128	A2
Trail	126	C1
Traiskirchen	62	M2
Trakai	48	N9
Tralee	56	C9
Tralee Bay	56	B9
Tramán Tepuí	140	E2
Tranås	48	H7
Trancoso	60	C4
Trang	84	B5
Trangan	87	D4
Transantarctic Mountains	144	(2)B1
Trapani	64	G11
Trappes	54	E6
Traun	62	K2
Traunreut	62	H3
Traunsee	62	J3
Traversay Islands	138	H9
Traverse City	128	C2
Travnik	66	E5
Trbovlje	62	L4
Trebbia	62	E6
Třebíč	50	E8
Trebinje	66	F7
Trebišov	66	J1
Trebnje	62	L5
Trebon	62	K1
Tregosse Islets	114	K3
Trélazé	58	E6
Trelew	142	H7
Trelleborg	48	G9
Tremonton	126	D2
Tremp	60	L2
Trenčín	50	H9
Trent	56	M8
Trento	62	G4
Trenton, Canada	128	E2
Trenton, US	128	F2
Trepassey	122	W7
Tres Arroyos	142	J6
Três Corações	140	H8
Tres Esquinas	140	B3
Tres Lagos	142	G8
Trespaderne	60	G2
Treuchtlingen	62	F2
Treviglio	62	E5
Treviso	62	H5
Triangle	108	E4
Tricase	64	N9
Trichur	88	C6
Trier	54	J5
Trieste	62	J5
Triglav	62	J4
Trikala	68	D5
Trikomon	94	A1
Trilj	62	M7
Trincomalee	88	D7
Trinidad	140	E1
Trinidad, Bolivia	140	E6
Trinidad, US	132	F1
Trinidad, Uruguay	142	K5
Trinidad and Tobago	140	E1
Trinity Islands	132	(1)G4
Trino	62	D5
Trion	130	D3
Tripoli, Greece	68	E7
Tripoli = Trâblous, Lebanon	94	C2
Tripoli = Tarābulus, Libya	102	H2
Tristan da Cunha	98	B9
Trivandrum = Thiruvananthapuram	88	C7
Trjavna	92	A2
Trnava	66	E1
Trogir	66	D6
Troina	64	J11
Troisdorf	52	C6
Trois Rivières	128	F1
Troitsk	70	M4
Troitsko-Pechorsk	70	L2
Trojan	68	G2
Trollhättan	48	G7
Trombetas	140	F4
Tromsø	48	K2
Trona	126	C3
Trondheim	48	F5
Trondheimsfjorden	48	E5
Troodos	92	E6
Trotuş	66	P3
Trout Lake, N.W.T., Canada	122	G4
Trout Lake, Ont ., Canada	122	N6
Troy, Al., US	130	D3
Troy, N.Y., US	128	F2
Troyan	66	M7
Troyes	58	K5
Trstenik	66	J6
Trudovoye	82	G2
Trujillo, Peru	140	B5
Trujillo, Spain	60	E5
Truro, Canada	122	U7
Truro, UK	56	G11
Trusovo	76	J4
Truth or Consequences	132	E2
Trutnov	50	E7
Tryavana	68	H2
Trzcianka	50	F4
Trzebnica	50	G6
Tržič	62	K4
Tsetserleg	78	G2
Tshabong	108	C5
Tshane	108	C4
Tshikapa	106	C5
Tshuapa	106	C4
Tsiafajavona	108	H3
Tsimlyanskoy Vodokhranilishche	70	H5
Tsiroanomandidy	108	H3
Ts'khinvali	92	K2
Tsuchiura	82	L5
Tsugaru-kaikyō	82	L3
Tsumeb	108	B3
Tsumkwe	108	C3
Tsuruga	82	J6
Tsuruoka	82	K4
Tsushima	82	E6
Tsuyama	82	H6
Tua	60	C3
Tual	87	D4
Tuân Giao	84	C2
Tuapse	92	H1
Tubarão	142	M4
Tubas	94	C4
Tübingen	62	E2
Tubize	54	G4
Tubruq	100	D1
Tubuai	112	M8
Tubuai Islands	112	L8
Tucano	140	K6
Tuchola	50	G4
Tucson	132	D2
Tucumcari	132	F1
Tucupita	140	E2
Tucuruí	140	H4
Tudela	60	J2
Tufayh	95	C3
Tuguegarao	84	G3
Tugur	78	P6
Tui	60	B2
Tuktoyaktuk	132	(1)L2
Tula, Mexico	132	G4
Tula, Russia	70	G4
Tulcán	126	C3
Tulcea	66	R4
Tulkarm	94	B4
Tullamore	56	E8
Tulle	58	G8
Tulln	62	M2
Tuloma	48	S2
Tulsa	124	G4
Tulsequah	132	(1)L4
Tulun	78	G6
Tulung La	88	F3
Tulu Weiel	106	E2
Tumaco	140	B3
Tumān	90	H2
Tumen	82	E2
Tumereng	140	E2
Tumkur	88	C6
Tumut	114	J7
Tunca	68	J3
Tunceli	92	H4
Tunduru	108	F2
Tundzha	66	P8
Tungir	78	L5
Tungku	86	F1
Tungsten	132	(1)M3
Tungusk	76	S5
Tunis	102	H1
Tunisia	102	E2
Tunja	140	C2
Tupelo	130	D3
Tupik	78	L6
Tupiza	142	H3
Tupper Lake	128	F2
Tuquan	80	G1
Tura, India	88	F3
Tura, Russia	78	G4
Turan	76	S7
Turangi	116	E4
Turayf	100	G1
Turbat	90	H4
Turbo	140	B2
Turda	66	L3
Turek	50	H5
Turgay	76	L8
Turgay	76	L8
Turgayskaya Stolovaya Strana	76	L7
Türgovishte	66	P6
Turgutlu	68	K6
Turhal	92	G3
Turin = Torino	62	C5
Turinsk	70	M3
Turiy Rog	82	F1
Turka	78	H6
Türkeli Adası	68	K4
Turkestan	76	M9
Turkey	92	D4
Turkmenbashi	90	F1
Turkmenistan	90	G2
Turks and Caicos Islands	134	K4
Turks Islands	134	K4
Turku	48	M6
Turma	78	N6
Turnhout	54	G3
Turnov	50	E7
Turnu Măgurele	66	M6
Turpan	76	R9

Name	Page	Grid
Turpan Pendi	76	S9
Turquino	138	D2
Turtas	70	N3
Turtkul'	90	H1
Turtle Island	114	K3
Turu	76	U5
Turugart Pass	76	P9
Turukhan	78	C3
Turukhansk	76	R4
Turukta	78	K4
Tuscaloosa	130	D3
Tuscola	130	D2
Tuticorin	88	C7
Tutonchany	78	E4
Tutrakan	66	P5
Tuttle Creek Reservoir	130	B2
Tuttlingen	62	D3
Tutuila	112	K7
Tuvalu	112	H6
Tuxpan, Mexico	124	E7
Tuxpan, Mexico	124	G7
Tuxtla Gutiérrez	134	F5
Tuyên Quang	84	D2
Tuy Hoa	84	D4
Tuymazy	70	K4
Tuz Gölü	92	E4
Tuz Khurmātū	92	L6
Tuzla	66	F5
Tver'	70	G3
Tweed	56	K6
Twentynine Palms	132	C2
Twilight Cove	114	E6
Twin Buttes Reservoir	132	F2
Twin Falls	126	D2
Twizel	116	C7
Two Harbors	128	B1
Tyachiv	66	L1
Tygda	78	M6
Tyler	124	G5
Tylkhoy	78	U4
Tym	76	Q6
Tynda	78	L5
Tyne	56	K6
Tynemouth	56	L6
Tynset	48	F5
Tyra	76	S7
Tyrifjorden	48	F6
Tyrnavos	68	E5
Tyrrhenian Sea	64	F8
Tyry	78	P4
Tysa	50	N9
Tyukyan	78	K4
Tyumen'	76	M6
Tyung	78	K3
Tyva	78	F6

U

Name	Page	Grid
Uarini	140	D4
Uaupés	140	D3
Ubá	140	J8
Ubaitaba	140	K6
Ubangi	106	B3
Ube	82	F7
Úbeda	60	G6
Uberaba	140	H7
Uberlândia	140	H7
Überlingen	62	E3
Ubon Ratchathani	84	C3
Ubrique	60	E8
Ucayali	140	B5
Uchami	76	T5
Ucharal	76	Q8
Uchiura-wan	82	L2
Uchkuduk	76	L9
Uckermark	52	J3
Ucluelet	126	A1
Uda, Russia	78	F5
Uda, Russia	78	N6
Udachnyy	78	J3
Udagamandalam	88	C6
Udaipur	88	B4
Uddevalla	48	F7
Uddjaure	70	C1
Uddjaure Storavan	48	K4
Udine	62	J4
Udmurtiya	70	K5
Udon Thani	84	C3
Udupi	88	B4
Uecker	52	J3
Ueckermünde	52	J3
Ueda	82	K5
Uele	106	C3
Uelen	78	AA3
Uel'kal	78	Y3
Uelzen	52	F4
Ufa	70	L3
Ufa	70	L4
Uganda	106	C3
Ugep	104	E3
Ugine	62	B5
Uglegorsk	78	Q7
Uglich	70	G3
Ugljan	62	L6
Ugol'naya Zyryanka	78	R3
Ugol'nyye Kopi	78	X4
Ugulan	78	S4
Uh	66	K1
Uherské Hradiště	50	G8
Uherský Brod	50	G8
Uiju	82	C3
Uil	70	K5
Uil	70	K5
Uinta Mountains	126	D2
Uitenhage	108	D6
Újfehértó	66	J2
Ujiji	106	D4
Ujjain	88	C4
Ukerewe Island	106	E4
Ukhta	76	J5
Ukiah	126	B3
Ukkusissat	122	W2
Ukmergé	50	P2
Ukraine	46	G3
Ulaanbaatar	78	H7
Ulaangom	76	S8
Ulan	80	B3
Ulan Bator = Ulaanbaatar	80	D1
Ulan-Ude	78	H6
Ulaş	92	G4
Ulchin	82	E5
Ulcinj	66	G8
Uldz	78	J7
Ulety	78	J6
Ulhasnagar	88	B5
Uliastay	76	T8
Ulindi	106	D4
Ullapool	56	G4
Ullŭng do	82	F5
Ulm	62	F2
Ulog	66	F6
Ulongue	108	E2
Ulsan	82	E6
Ulu	78	M4
Ulubat Gölü	68	L4
Ulugqat	90	K2
Ulukışla	92	F5
Ulungur Hu	76	R8
Ulunkhan	78	J5
Uluru	114	F5
Ulu-Yul	78	D5
Ulva	56	F5
Ulverston	56	J7
Ulya	78	Q5
Ul'yanovsk	70	J4
Ulytau	76	M8
Umag	64	H3
Uman'	70	F5
Umarkot	90	J4
Umba	70	F1
Umeå	48	L5
Umeälven	48	J4
Umfolozi	108	E5
Ummal Arānib	102	H3
Umm al Jamājim	95	A3
Umm Durman	100	F4
Umm Keddada	100	E5
Umm Lajj	100	G3
Umm Qasr	95	B1
Umm Ruwaba	100	F5
Umnak Island	132	(1)E5
Umtata	108	D6
Umuarama	142	L3
Unalakleet	132	(1)D3
Unalaska Island	132	(1)E5
'Unayzah	94	C6
Underberg	108	D5
Ungava Bay	122	T5
Ungheni	66	Q2
Ungwana Bay	106	G4
União da Vitória	142	L4
Unije	62	K6
Unimak Island	132	(1)D5
Unim Bāb	95	D4
Unini	140	E4
Union	128	B3
Union City	134	G1
Union Springs	130	D3
United Arab Emirates	90	F5
United Kingdom	56	G6
United States	120	M5
Unna	54	K3
Unraven	132	E1
Unst	56	M1
Unstrut	52	G5
Unzha	70	H3
Upernavik	122	W2
Upernavik Kujalleq	122	V2
Upington	108	C5
Upolu	112	J7
Upper Hutt	116	E5
Upper Klamath Lake	126	B2
Upper Lake	126	C2
Upper Lough Erne	56	E7
Upper Sandusky	128	D2
Uppsala	48	J7
Upsala	128	B1
'Uqlat al 'Udhaybah	95	B2
Urad Houqi	80	D2
Urakawa	82	M2
Ural	70	K5
Ural Mountains = Ural'skiy Khrebet	46	L1
Ural'sk	70	K4
Ural'skiy Khrebet	46	L1
Urambo	106	E5
Uranium City	122	K5
Uraricoera	140	E3
Uraricoera	140	E3
Uray	70	M2
Urbana, Ill., US	128	C2
Urbana, Oh., US	128	D2
Urbania	62	H7
Urbino	62	H7
Urdzhar	76	Q8
Uren'	70	J3
Urengoy	76	P4
Urgench	90	H1
Urho	76	R8
Uritskiy	70	N4
Urla	68	J6
Urlaţi	66	P5
Uroševac	66	J7
Uro-teppa	90	J2
Urt	80	C2
Uruaçu	140	H6
Uruapan	134	D5
Urucurituba	140	F4
Uruguaiana	142	K4
Uruguay	142	K5
Uruguay	142	K5
Ürümqi	76	R9
Urus Martan	92	L2
Uruti	116	E4
Uryupino	78	L6
Uryupinsk	70	H4
Urzhum	70	K3
Urziceni	66	P5
Usa	76	L4
Usa	82	F7
Uşak	92	C4
Usedom	52	J3
Useless Loop	114	B5
Usfān	90	C5
Ushtobe	76	P8
Usingen	52	D6
Usk	56	J10
Usman'	70	G4
Usol'ye Sibirskoye	78	G6
Ussel	58	H8
Ussuri	82	G1
Ussuriysk	80	J2
Usta	70	J3
Ust'-Alekseyevo	70	J2
Ust'-Barguzin	78	H6
Ust' Chaun	78	W3
Ústí	50	F8
Ustica	64	H10
Ust'-Ilimsk	78	G5
Ústí nad Labem	50	D7
Ust'-Ishim	76	N6
Ustka	50	F3
Ust'-Kamchatsk	78	U5
Ust'-Kamenogorsk	76	Q8
Ust'-Kamo	76	T5
Ust'-Karenga	78	K6
Ust'-Khayryuzovo	78	T5
Ust'-Kulom	70	K2
Ust'-Kut	78	G5
Ust'-Kuyga	78	P3
Ust'-Labinsk	92	H1
Ust'-Maya	78	N4
Ust'-Mukduyka	76	R4
Ust'-Muya	78	K5
Ust' Nem	70	K2
Ust'-Nera	78	Q4
Ust'-Nyukzha	78	L5
Ust'-Olenek	78	K2
Ust'-Omchug	78	R4
Ust' Ozernoye	78	D5
Ust' Penzhino	78	V4
Ust'-Pit	78	E5
Ustrem	70	N2
Ust'-Sopochnoye	78	T5
Ust' Tapsuy	70	M2
Ust'-Tarka	76	P6
Ust'-Tatta	78	N4
Ust'-Tsil'ma	76	J4
Ust' Un'ya	70	L2
Ust'-Urkima	78	L5
Ust' Usa	70	L1
Ust'-Uyskoye	76	L7
Usu	76	Q9
Usuki	82	F7
Utah	124	D4
Utah Lake	126	D2
Utata	78	G6
Utena	48	N9
Uthal	90	J4
Utica	128	E2
Utiel	60	J5
Utrecht	54	H2
Utrera	60	E7
Utsjoki	48	P2
Utsunomiya	82	K5
Uttaradit	84	C3
Utva	70	K4
Uummannaq Fjord	122	V2
Uummannarsuaq	122	Y5
Uusikaupunki	48	L6
Uvalde	134	E3
Uvarovo	78	X3
Uvat	70	N3
Uvinza	106	E5
Uvira	106	D4
Uvs Nuur	76	S7
Uwajima	82	G7
Uy	70	M4
Uyar	76	S6
Uyuk	76	N9
Uyuni	142	H3
Uzbekistan	76	L9
Uzhhorod	66	K1
Užice	66	G6
Uzunköprü	66	P8

V

Name	Page	Grid
Vaal	108	D5
Vaasa	48	L5
Vác	66	G2
Vacaria	142	M4
Vachi	90	E1
Vadodara	88	B4
Vado Ligure	62	D6
Vadsø	48	Q1
Vaduz	62	E3
Værøy	48	G3
Vaganski Vhr	62	L6
Vagay	70	N3
Váh	50	H8
Vakh	70	Q2
Valbonnais	62	A6
Valcheta	142	H7
Valdagno	62	G5
Valday	62	F3
Val-de-Meuse	62	A2
Valdemoro	60	G4
Valdepeñas	60	G6
Valdez	122	B4
Valdivia	142	G6
Val-d'Or	128	E1
Valdosta	124	K5
Valdres	48	E6
Valea lui Mihai	66	K2
Valence	58	K9
Valencia, Spain	60	K5
Valencia, Venezuela	140	D1
Valencia de Alcántara	60	C5
Valenciennes	54	F4
Vălenii de Munte	66	P4
Valentia Island	56	B10
Valentine	126	F2
Valenza	62	D5
Valera	140	C2
Valga	70	E3
Val Horn	124	F5
Valjevo	66	G5
Valka	48	N8
Val'karay	78	X3
Valkeakoski	48	N6
Valkenswaard	54	H3
Valladolid, Mexico	134	G4
Valladolid, Spain	60	F3
Valle	48	D7
Valledupar	140	C1
Vallée de Azaouagh	102	F5
Vallée du Tîlemsi	102	F5
Vallée-Jonction	128	F1
Vallejo	126	B3
Vallentuna	48	K7
Valletta	64	J13
Valley City	126	G1
Valley Falls	126	B2
Valley of the Kings	100	F2
Valli di Comacchio	62	H6
Vallorbe	62	B4
Valls	60	M3
Valmiera	48	N8
Valognes	54	A5
Val-Paradis	128	E1
Valparai	88	C6
Valparaíso, Chile	142	G5
Valparaíso, Mexico	132	F4
Valsad	88	B4
Val'tevo	70	H2
Valuyki	70	G4
Valverde del Camino	60	D7
Vammala	48	M6
Van	92	K4
Vanadzor	92	L3
Vanavara	78	G4
Van Buren	128	G1
Vancouver, Canada	126	B1
Vancouver, US	126	B1
Vancouver Island	122	F7
Vandalia	130	D2
Vanderbijlpark	108	D5
Vanderhoof	122	G6
Van Diemen Gulf	114	F2
Vänern	48	G7
Vangaindrano	108	H4
Van Gölü	92	K4
Van Horn	132	F2
Vanimo	87	F3
Vanino	78	Q7
Vankarem	78	Y3
Vanna	48	K1
Vännäs	48	K5
Vannes	58	C6
Vanrhynsdorp	108	B6
Vantaa	48	N6
Vanua Levu	112	H7
Vanuatu	112	G7
Van Wert	128	D2
Vanzevat	70	N2
Vanzhil'kynak	78	C4
Varāmīn	90	F2
Varanasi	88	D3
Varangerfjorden	48	R2
Varaždin	66	D3
Varazze	62	D6
Varberg	48	G8
Varda	68	D6
Vardar	68	E3
Varde	48	E9
Vardenis	92	L3
Vardø	48	R1
Varel	52	D3
Varéna	50	P3
Varese	62	D5
Vârful Moldoveanu	66	M4
Vârfurile	66	K3
Varginha	142	M3
Varkaus	48	P5
Varna	92	B2
Värnamo	48	H8
Varnsdorf	52	K6
Várpalota	66	F2
Varto	92	J4
Varzi	62	E6
Varzy	58	J6
Vásárosnamény	66	K1
Vasilikos	94	A2
Vaslui	66	Q3
Västerås	48	J7
Västervik	48	J8
Vasto	64	J6
Vasvár	62	M3
Vatan	58	G6
Vathia	68	E8
Vatican City	64	F7
Vatnajökull	48	(1)E2
Vatomandry	108	H3
Vatra Dornei	66	N2
Vättern	48	H7
Vaughn	132	E2
Vawkavysk	50	P4
Växjö	48	H8
Vayuniyá	88	D7
Vazhgort	70	J2
Vecht	54	J2
Vecsés	66	G2
Vedaranniyam	88	C6

Wangerooge 52 D3
Wangiwangi 87 B4
Wan Hsa-la 84 B2
Wanxian 80 D4
Wanyuan 80 D4
Warangal 88 C5
Warburg 52 D5
Ward 116 E5
Wardha 88 C4
Waregem 54 F4
Waremme 54 H4
Waren 52 H3
Warendorf 54 K3
Warka 50 L6
Warla 50 H6
Warmandi 87 D3
Warminster 56 K10
Warm Springs 126 C3
Warren, *Mich., US* 128 D2
Warren, *Oh., US* 128 D2
Warren, *Pa., US* 128 E2
Warrensburg 128 B3
Warrenton 108 C5
Warri 104 F3
Warrington, *UK* 56 K8
Warrington, *US* 130 D3
Warrnambool 114 H7
Warroad 128 A1
Warsaw = Warszawa 50 K5
Warstein 52 D5
Warszawa 50 K5
Warta 50 F5
Warwick 56 L9
Wasatch Range 132 D1
Wasco 132 C1
Washap 90 H4
Washburn Lake 122 K2
Washington 126 B1
Washington, *N.C., US* 128 E3
Washington, *Pa., US* 128 D2
Washington, *Ut., US* 126 D3
Washington D.C. 120 J6
Wassenaar 54 G2
Wasserburg 62 H2
Watampone 87 B3
Watansoppeng 87 A3
Waterbury 128 F2
Waterford 56 E9
Waterloo, *Belgium* 54 G4
Waterloo, *US* 128 B2
Watersmeet 128 C1
Watertown, *N.Y., US* 128 E2
Watertown, *S.D., US* 126 G1
Watertown, *Wis., US* 128 C2
Waterville 128 G2
Watford 54 B3
Watford City 126 F1
Watmuri 87 D4
Watrous 122 K6
Watsa 106 D3
Watseka 130 D1
Watson Lake 132 (1)M3
Wau 106 D2
Waubay Lake 126 G1
Waukegan 128 C2
Waukesha 128 C2
Waurika 130 B3
Wausau 124 J3
Waverley 116 E4
Waverly 128 C3
Wavre 54 G4
Wawa 128 D1
Wāw al Kabīr 100 C2
Waxxari 76 R10
Waycross 130 E3
Waynesboro, *Ga., US* 130 E3
Waynesboro, *Miss., US* 130 D3
Waynesville 128 D3
Weaverville 126 B2
Weber 116 F5
Webi Shaabeelle 106 G3
Webster 126 G1
Weddell Island 142 J9
Weddell Sea 144 (2)A2
Wedel 52 E3
Weed 126 B2
Weert 54 H3
Węgorzewo 50 L3
Wei 80 D4
Weichang 80 F2
Weida 52 H6
Weiden 52 H7
Weifang 80 F3
Weihai 80 G3
Weilburg 52 D6
Weilheim 62 G3
Weimar 52 G6
Weinan 80 D4
Weinheim 52 D7
Weining 80 C5
Weipa 114 H2
Weiser 126 C2
Weißenburg 52 F7
Weißenfels 52 G5
Weißwasser 52 K5
Weixi 84 B1
Wejherowo 50 H3
Welkom 108 D5
Welland 54 B2
Wellawaya 88 D7
Wellesley Islands 114 G3
Wellingborough 58 E1
Wellington, *New Zealand* 116 E5
Wellington, *Colo., US* 126 F2
Wellington, *Kans., US* 130 B2
Wells 126 C2
Wellsboro 128 E2
Wellsford 116 E3
Wellton 132 D2
Wels 62 K2
Welshpool 56 J9
Welwyn Garden City 54 B3
Wenatchee 126 B1
Wenchang 84 E3
Wenga 106 B3
Wenman 140 (1)A1
Wen Xian 80 C4
Wenzhou 80 G5
Werder 52 H4
Werdēr 106 H2
Werl 54 K3
Werneck 52 F7
Wernigerode 52 F5
Werra 52 F6
Wertheim 52 E7
Wesel 54 J3
Wesel Dorsten 52 B5
Weser 52 E4
Wessel Islands 114 G2
West Antarctica 144 (2)GG2
West Bank 94 C4
West Branch 128 D2
West Cape 112 G10
West End 130 F4
Westerland 52 D2
Western Australia 114 D5
Western Cape 108 B6
Western Ghats 88 B5
Western Reef 116 (1)B1
Western Sahara 102 C4
Wester Ross 56 G4
Westerschelde 54 F3
Westerstede 54 K1
Westervoort 54 J3
Westerwald 54 K4
West Falkland 142 J9
West Frankfort 130 D2
West Glacier 126 D1
West Lunga 108 C2
West Memphis 130 C2
Weston 128 D3
Weston-super-Mare 56 K10
West Palm Beach 130 E4
West Plains 128 B3
Westport, *New Zealand* 116 C5
Westport, *Ireland* 56 C8
Westray 56 J2
West Siberian Plain = Zapadno-Sibirskaya Ravnina 74 L3
West-Terschelling 54 H1
West Virginia 128 D3
West Wendover 126 D2
West Yellowstone 126 D2
Wetar 87 C4
Wetaskiwin 122 J6
Wete 106 F5
Wetumpka 130 D3
Wetzlar 52 D6
Wewak 87 F3
Wexford 56 F9
Wexford Harbour 56 F9
Weyburn 124 F2
Weymouth 56 K11
Whakatane 116 F3
Whale Cove 122 N4
Whalsay 56 M1
Whangamata 116 E3
Whangamomona 116 E4
Whangarei 116 E2
Wharfe 56 L7
Wheeler Peak 132 E1
Wheeler Ridge 132 C2
Wheeling 130 E1
Whitby 56 M7
White, *Nev., US* 126 C3
White, *S.D., US* 122 L8
White Bay 122 V6
White Cliffs 114 H6
Whitecourt 122 H6
Whitefish Point 128 C1
Whitehaven 56 J7
Whitehorse 132 (1)L3
White Island 116 F3
Whitemark 114 J8
White Mountain Peak 126 C3
White Mountains 122 S8
Whitemouth 126 G1
White Nile = Bahr el Abiad 100 F5
White River, *Canada* 128 C1
White River, *US* 126 F2
White Sea = Beloye More 70 G1
White Sulphur Springs 126 D1
Whiteville 130 F3
White Volta 104 D3
Whitney 128 E1
Whitstable 54 D3
Whyalla 114 G6
Wichita 130 B2
Wichita Falls 130 B3
Wick 56 J3
Wickenburg 132 D2
Wicklow 56 F9
Wicklow Mountains 56 F8
Widawka 50 J6
Wieluń 50 H6
Wien 62 M2
Wiener Neustadt 62 M3
Wieringermeer Polder 54 G2
Wiesbaden 52 D6
Wiesloch 52 D7
Wiesmoor 52 C3
Wigan 56 K8
Wiggins 126 F2
Wil 62 E3
Wilbur 126 C1
Wilcannia 114 H6
Wildeshausen 52 D4
Wilhelmshaven 52 D3
Wilkes-Barre 128 E2
Wilkes Land 144 (2)U2
Willapa Bay 126 B1
Willemstad 140 D1
Williams, *Australia* 114 C6
Williams, *Ariz., US* 126 D3
Williams, *Calif., US* 126 B3
Williamsburg 128 E3
Williams Lake 122 G6
Williamson 130 E2
Williamsport 128 E2
Willis Group 114 K3
Williston, *South Africa* 108 C6
Williston, *Fla., US* 130 E4
Williston, *N.D., US* 126 F1
Williston Lake 122 G5
Willmar 128 A1
Willow 132 (1)H3
Willowmore 108 C6
Willow River 128 B1
Willow Springs 128 B3
Wilmington, *Del., US* 128 E3
Wilmington, *N.C., US* 130 F3
Wilson 128 E3
Wilson Reservoir 130 B2
Wilson's Promontory 114 J7
Wiluna 114 D5
Winamac 128 C2
Winchester, *UK* 56 L10
Winchester, *Ky., US* 128 D3
Winchester, *Va., US* 128 E3
Windhoek 108 B4
Windischgarsten 62 K3
Windom 128 A2
Windorah 114 H5
Windsor, *Canada* 128 D2
Windsor, *UK* 54 B3
Windsor, *US* 130 F2
Windward Islands 134 N6
Windward Passage 138 D2
Winfield, *Al., US* 130 D3
Winfield, *Kans., US* 132 G1
Wingate Mountains 114 E2
Winisk 122 P5
Winisk 122 P6
Winisk Lake 122 P6
Winnemucca 126 C2
Winner 126 G2
Winnfield 124 H5
Winnipeg 122 M7
Winona, *Minn., US* 128 B2
Winona, *Miss., US* 130 D3
Winschoten 54 K1
Winsen 52 F3
Winslow 132 D1
Winston-Salem 128 D3
Winterberg 52 D5
Winter Harbour 122 J2
Winterswijk 54 J3
Winterthur 62 D3
Winton, *Australia* 114 H4
Winton, *New Zealand* 116 B8
Wisbech 54 C2
Wisconsin 124 H2
Wisconsin 128 B2
Wisconsin Dells 128 C2
Wisconsin Rapids 128 C2
Wisil Dabarow 106 H2
Wisła 50 H4
Wisła 50 H8
Wisłoka 50 L8
Wismar 52 G3
Wissembourg 52 C7
Witney 54 A3
Witten 54 K3
Wittenberge 52 G3
Wittenoom 114 C4
Wittingen 52 F4
Wittlich 54 J5
Wittmund 52 C3
Wittstock 52 H3
Witzenhausen 52 E5
W. J. van Blommesteinmeer 140 G2
Wkra 50 K5
Władysławowo 50 H3
Włocławek 50 J5
Włodawa 50 N6
Wodzisław Śląski 50 H7
Wohlen 62 D3
Wokam 87 D4
Woking 56 M10
Wolf Creek 126 D1
Wolfen 52 H5
Wolfenbüttel 52 F4
Wolf Point 126 E1
Wolfratshausen 62 G3
Wolfsberg 62 K4
Wolfsburg 52 F4
Wolgast 52 J2
Wollaston Lake 122 K5
Wollaston Peninsula 122 H3
Wollongong 114 K6
Wołomin 50 L5
Wolsztyn 50 F5
Wolvega 54 J2
Wolverhampton 56 K9
Wŏnju 82 D5
Wŏnsan 82 D4
Woodbridge 54 D2
Woodburn 126 B1
Woodland 126 B3
Woodstock, *Canada* 128 G1
Woodstock, *UK* 54 A3
Woodstock, *US* 128 C2
Woodville, *New Zealand* 116 E5
Woodville, *Miss., US* 130 C3
Woodville, *Tex., US* 130 C3
Woodward 126 G3
Woody Head 116 E3
Woonsocket, *R.I., US* 128 F2
Woonsocket, *S.D., US* 126 G2
Worcester, *South Africa* 108 B6
Worcester, *UK* 56 K9
Worcester, *US* 124 M3
Wörgl 62 H3
Workington 56 J7
Worksop 54 A1
Worland 126 E2
Worms 52 D7
Wörth 52 D7
Worthing 56 M11
Worthington 124 G3
Wosu 87 B3
Wotu 87 B3
Wowoni 87 B3
Wrangell 122 E5
Wrangell Mountains 122 C4
Wray 124 F3
Wrexham 56 K8
Wrigley 122 G4
Wrocław 50 G6
Września 50 G5
Wu 80 D5
Wubin 114 C6
Wubu 80 E3
Wuchang 80 H2
Wuchuan 80 E2
Wuday'ah 90 E6
Wudu 80 C4
Wuhai 80 D3
Wuhan 80 E4
Wuhu 80 F4
Wüjang 88 C2
Wukari 104 F3
Wuli 88 F2
Wunsiedel 52 G6
Wunstorf 52 E4
Wuppertal 52 C5
Würzburg 52 E7
Wurzen 52 H5
Wushi 76 P9
Wusuli 80 J1
Wutach 62 D3
Wuwei 80 C3
Wuxi 80 G4
Wuxu 84 D2
Wuyuan 80 D2
Wuzhong 80 D3
Wuzhou 84 E2
Wye 56 J9
Wyndham 114 E3
Wynniatt Bay 122 J2
Wyoming 124 E3
Wyszków 50 L5
Wytheville 130 E2

X

Xaafuun 106 J1
Xàbia 60 L6
Xaçmaz 92 N3
Xaidulla 76 P10
Xainza 88 E2
Xai-Xai 108 E4
Xam Nua 84 C2
Xankändi 92 M4
Xanten 54 J3
Xanthi 68 G3
Xapuri 140 D6
Xar Moron 78 K8
Xàtiva 60 K6
Xiahe 80 C3
Xiamen 84 F2
Xi'an 80 D4
Xiangcheng 80 E4
Xiangfan 80 E4
Xianghoang 84 C3
Xianghuang Qi 80 E2
Xiangtan 80 E5
Xianning 80 E5
Xianyang 80 D4
Xiaogan 80 E4
Xiao Hinggan Ling 78 M7
Xiaonanchuan 88 F1
Xichang 84 C1
Xigazê 88 E3
Xi Jiang 80 E6
Xilinhot 80 F2
Xincai 80 E4
Xingcheng 80 G2
Xinghe 80 E2
Xinghua 80 F4
Xingtai 80 F3
Xingu 140 G5
Xingyi 84 C1
Xinhe 76 Q9
Xining 80 C3
Xinjie 80 D3
Xinjin 80 G3
Xinmin 82 B2
Xintai 80 E3
Xinxiang 80 E3
Xinyang 80 E4
Xinyu 80 F5
Xinyuan 76 Q9
Xinzhou 80 E3
Xinzo de Limia 60 C2
Xique Xique 140 J6
Xi Ujimqin Qi 80 F2
Xiushu 80 E5
Xiwu 88 G2
Xixia 80 E4
Xi Xiang 80 D4
Xizang 88 E2
Xizang Gaoyuan 88 D2
Xuanhua 80 E2
Xuchang 80 E4
Xuddur 106 G3
Xuwen 84 E2

Y

Ya'an 80 D3
Yabassi 104 F4
Yabēlo 106 F3
Yablonovyy Khrebet 78 J6
Yabrūd 94 D3
Yabuli 82 E1

Name	Page	Grid
Yacuma	140	D6
Yadgir	88	D5
Yagel'naya	76	P4
Yagodnyy	70	N3
Yahk	122	H7
Yakima	126	B1
Yako	104	D2
Yakoma	106	C3
Yaksha	70	L2
Yakumo	82	L2
Yaku-shima	82	F8
Yakutat	132	(1)K4
Yakutsk	78	M4
Yala	84	C5
Yalova	68	M4
Yalta	92	F1
Yalu	82	D3
Yalutorovsk	70	N3
Yamagata	82	L4
Yamaguchi	82	F6
Yamarovka	78	J6
Yambio	106	D3
Yambol	66	P7
Yamburg	76	P4
Yamdena	87	D4
Yammit	94	B5
Yamoussoukro	104	C3
Yampa	126	E2
Yampil'	66	R1
Yamsk	78	S5
Yan'an	80	D3
Yanbu'al Baḥr	90	C5
Yancheng	80	G4
Yandun	80	A2
Yangambi	106	C3
Yangbajain	88	F2
Yangdok	82	D4
Yangi Kand	92	N5
Yangjiang	84	E2
Yangon	84	B3
Yangquan	80	E3
Yangshuo	84	E2
Yangtze = Chang Jiang	80	D4
Yangzhou	80	F4
Yanhuqu	88	D2
Yani-Kurgan	76	M9
Yanji	82	E2
Yankton	126	G2
Yano-Indigirskaya Nizmennost'.	78	N2
Yanqi	76	R9
Yanqing	80	F2
Yanshan	84	C2
Yanskiy Zaliv	78	N2
Yantai	80	G3
Yaoundé	104	G4
Yap	112	D5
Yapen	87	E3
Yaqui	124	E6
Yaraka	114	H4
Yaransk	70	J3
Yardımcı Burnu	68	E8
Yare	54	D2
Yaren	112	G6
Yarensk	70	J2
Yari	140	C3
Yarkant	90	L2
Yarkovo	70	N3
Yarlung Zangbo	88	F3
Yarmouth	122	T8
Yaroslavl'	70	G3
Yar Sale	70	P1
Yartsevo	70	F3
Yashkul'	70	J5
Yasnyy	70	L4
Yāsūj	95	D1
Yatağan	68	L7
Yathkyed Lake	122	M4
Yatsushiro	82	F7
Yatta	94	C5
Yavari	140	C5
Yawatongguzlangar	76	Q10
Yaya	76	R6
Yayladağı	92	F6
Yazd	90	F3
Yazdān	90	H3
Yazd-e Khvāst	95	E1
Yazoo City	130	C3
Ydra	68	F7
Ye	84	B3
Yea	114	J7
Yecheng	90	L2
Yecla	60	J6
Yefremov	70	G4
Yegendybulak	76	P8
Yei	106	E3
Yekaterinburg	70	M3
Yelets	70	G4
Yelizovo	78	T6
Yell	56	L1
Yellowknife	122	J4
Yellow River = Huang He	80	C3
Yellow Sea	80	G3
Yellowstone	126	E1
Yellowstone Lake	126	D2
Yeloten	90	H2
Yelva	76	J2
Yelwa	104	E2
Yemen	90	D7
Yemetsk	70	H2
Yenakiyeve	70	G5
Yengisar	90	L2
Yenihisar	68	K7
Yenisey	76	S6
Yeniseysk	76	S6
Yeniseyskiy Kryazh	76	S5
Yeo Lake	114	D5
Yeovil	56	K11
Yeppoon	114	K4
Yeraliyev	76	J9
Yerbogachen	78	H4
Yerevan	92	L3
Yerington	126	C3

Name	Page	Grid
Yerkov	68	S5
Yerkoy	92	F4
Yermak	76	P7
Yermitsa	70	K1
Yernva	76	J5
Yershov	70	J4
Yerupaja	140	B6
Yerushalayim	94	C5
Yesil'	70	N4
Yesilhisar	92	F4
Yesilköy	68	L4
Yessey	76	U4
Yevlax	92	M3
Yevpatoriya	70	F5
Yeyik	76	Q10
Yeysk	70	G5
Yibin	80	C5
Yichang	80	E4
Yichun, China	80	E5
Yichun, China	80	H1
Yilan	80	H1
Yıldız Dağları	68	K2
Yıldızeli	92	G4
Yinchuan	80	D3
Yingcheng	80	E4
Yingkou	80	G2
Yingtan	80	F5
Yining	76	Q9
Yirga Alem	106	F2
Yitomio	48	M3
Yitulihe	78	L6
Yiyang	80	E5
Yli-Kitka	48	Q3
Ylivieska	48	N4
Ylöjärvi	48	M6
Yoakum	130	B4
Yoboki	100	H5
Yogyakarta	86	E4
Yohuma	106	C3
Yokadouma	104	G3
Yoko	104	G3
Yokohama, Japan	82	K6
Yokohama, Japan	82	L3
Yokosuka	82	K6
Yokote	82	L4
Yola	104	G3
Yonago	82	G6
Yonezawa	82	L5
Yong'an	84	F1
Yongdeng	80	C3
Yŏnghŭng	82	D4
Yongren	84	C1
Yongxiu	80	F5
Yonkers	128	F2
York, UK	56	L8
York, Nebr., US	126	G2
York, Pa., US	128	E3
Yorkton	122	L6
Yoshkar Ola	70	J3
Yŏsu	82	D6
Yotvata	94	C7
You	84	D2
Youghal	56	E10
Youghal Bay	56	E10
Youngstown	128	D2
Youvarou	104	D1
Yozgat	92	F4
Yreka	126	B2
Ystad	50	C2
Ysyk-Köl	76	P9
Ytre Sula	48	B6
Ytyk-Kyuyel'	78	N4
Yu	84	D2
Yuan	84	C2
Yuanjiang	84	C2
Yuanmou	84	C1
Yuanping	80	E3
Yucatán	134	F5
Yucatan Channel	134	G4
Yuci	80	E3
Yudoma	78	Q4
Yuendumu	114	F4
Yueyang	80	E5
Yugorenok	78	P5
Yugo-Tala	78	S3
Yukagirskoye Ploskogor'ye	78	S3
Yukon	132	(1)E3
Yukon Territory	132	(1)K2
Yukorskiy Poluostrov	76	L4
Yüksekova	92	L5
Yukta	78	H4
Yuli	76	R9
Yulin, China	80	D3
Yulin, China	84	E2
Yuma	132	C2
Yumen	80	B3
Yumin	76	Q8
Yunak	92	D4
Yuncheng	80	E3
Yun Xian	84	C2
Yuogi Feng	76	R8
Yurga	76	Q6
Yurimaguas	140	B5
Yurla	70	K3
Yuroma	70	J1
Yur'yevets	70	H3
Yu Shan	84	G2
Yushkozero	48	S4
Yushu, China	80	B4
Yushu, China	80	H2
Yusufeli	92	J3
Yutian	76	Q10
Yuxi	84	C6
Yuyao	80	G4
Yuzawa	82	L4
Yuzhno Kuril'sk	82	N1
Yuzhno-Sakhalinsk	78	Q7
Yuzhno-Sukhokumsk	92	L1
Yuzhnoural'sk	70	M4
Yverdon-les-Bains	62	B4
Yvetot	54	C5

Z

Name	Page	Grid
Zaanstad	54	G2
Ząbkowice Śląskie	50	F7
Zabok	62	L4
Zābol	90	H3
Zabrze	50	H7
Zacatecas	132	F4
Zadar	62	L6
Zadonsk	70	G4
Zafora	68	J8
Zafra	60	D6
Zāgheh-ye-Bālā	92	M6
Zagora	102	D2
Zagreb	62	L5
Zagyva	50	K10
Zāhedān	90	H4
Zahirabad	88	C5
Zahlé	94	C3
Zahrān	90	D6
Zaječar	66	K6
Zakamensk	78	G6
Zākhō	92	K5
Zakopane	50	J8
Zakynthos	68	C7
Zakynthos	68	C7
Zala	62	M4
Zalaegerszeg	62	M4
Zalakomár	66	E3
Zalari	78	G6
Zalaszentgrót	62	N4
Zalău	66	L2
Zalim	90	D5
Zalingei	100	D5
Zaliv Aniva	78	Q7
Zaliv Kara-Bogaz Gol	90	F1
Zaliv Kresta	78	Y3
Zaliv Paskevicha	70	L5
Zaliv Shelikhova	78	T5
Zaliv Terpeniya	78	Q7
Zamakh	90	E6
Zambezi	108	C2
Zambezi	108	E3
Zambia	108	D2
Zamboanga	84	G5
Zambrów	50	M5
Zamora	60	E3
Zamość	50	N7
Zanda	88	C2
Zandvoort	54	G2
Zanesville	130	E2
Zangguy	90	L2
Zanjān	92	N5
Zannone	64	H8
Zanzibar	106	F5
Zanzibar Island	106	F5
Zaouatallaz	102	G4
Zaozernyy	76	S6
Zapadnaya Dvina	70	E3
Zapadno-Sibirskaya Ravnina	76	L5
Zapadnyy Sayan	76	S7
Zapata	132	G3
Zapolyarnyy	48	R2
Zaporizhzhya	70	G5
Zaprešić	62	L5
Zaqatala	92	M3
Zara	92	G4
Zarafshan	76	L9
Zaragoza	60	K3
Zarand	95	G1
Zaranj	90	H3
Zarasai	48	P9
Zaraza	140	D2
Zarechensk	48	R3
Zaria	104	F2
Zărneşti	66	N4
Zarqā'	94	D4
Zarqān	95	E2
Žary	50	E6
Zarzadilla de Totana	60	J7
Žatec	50	C7
Zavetnoye	70	H5
Zavidovići	66	F5
Zavitinsk	78	M6
Zayarsk	76	U6
Zaysan	76	Q8
Zayü	84	B1
Zazafotsy	108	H4
Zbraslav	50	D8
Zēbāk	90	K2
Zēbār	92	L5
Zeebrugge	54	F3
Zefat	94	C4
Zehdenick	52	J4
Zeilona Góra	50	E6
Zeist	54	H2
Zeitz	52	H5
Zelenoborskiy	48	S3
Zelenograd	70	G3
Zelenogradsk	50	K3
Zelenokumsk	92	K1
Zelina	66	D4
Zella-Mehlis	52	F6
Zell am See	62	H3
Zémio	106	D2
Zemlya Alexsandry	76	G1
Zemlya Frantsa-Iosifa	76	J2
Zemlya Vil'cheka	76	L1
Zempoalteptl	134	E5
Zenica	66	E5
Zerbst	52	H5
Zermatt	62	C4
Zeta Lake	122	K2
Zeulenroda	52	G6
Zeven	52	E3
Zevenaar	54	J3
Zeya	78	M6
Zeya	78	M6
Zgdābād	95	F2
Zeyskoye Vodokhranilishche	78	M5
Zgharta	94	C2
Zgierz	50	J6

Name	Page	Grid
Zgorzelec	50	E6
Zhailma	70	M4
Zhaksy	70	N4
Zhaksykon	70	N5
Zhaltyr	70	N4
Zhambyl	76	N9
Zhanatas	76	M9
Zhangbei	80	E2
Zhangguangcai Ling	80	H2
Zhangjiakou	80	E2
Zhangling	78	L6
Zhangwu	80	G2
Zhangye	80	B3
Zhangzhou	84	F2
Zhanjiang	84	E2
Zhaodong	78	M7
Zhaoqing	84	E2
Zhaosu	76	Q9
Zhaotong	80	C5
Zhaoyuan	80	H1
Zharkamys	76	K8
Zharkent	76	P9
Zharma	76	Q8
Zharyk	76	N8
Zhaxigang	88	C2
Zhelezonogorsk	70	G4
Zhengzhou	80	E4
Zhenjiang	80	F4
Zherdevka	70	H4
Zhetybay	76	J9
Zhezkazgan	76	M8
Zhigalovo	78	H5
Zhigansk	78	L3
Zhilinda	78	J2
Zhob	90	J3
Zholymbet	76	N7
Zhongba	88	D3
Zhongdian	80	B5
Zhongning	80	D3
Zhongshan	84	E2
Zhongze	80	G5
Zhoukou	80	E4
Zhuanghe	80	G3
Zhucheng	80	F3
Zhumadian	80	E4
Zhuo Xian	80	F3
Zhytomyr	70	E4
Žiar	50	H9
Zibo	80	F3
Zichang	80	D3
Zierikzee	54	F3
Ziesar	52	H4
Zighan	100	D2
Zigon	84	B3
Zigong	80	C5
Ziguinchor	102	B6
Zikhron Ya'aqov	94	B4
Žilina	50	H8
Zillah	100	C2
Zima	78	G6
Zimbabwe	108	D3
Zimmi	104	B3
Zimnicea	66	N6
Zinder	104	F2
Zinjibār	100	J5
Zinnowitz	52	J2
Zirc	50	G10
Žirje	64	K5
Zistersdorf	62	M2
Zitava	50	H9
Zittau	52	K6
Ziway Hāyk'	106	F2
Zixing	84	E1
Zlaté Moravce	50	H9
Zlatoust	70	L3
Zlín	50	G8
Zlītan	102	H2
Zlocieniec	50	F4
Złoczew	50	H6
Złotów	50	G4
Zmeinogorsk	76	Q7
Znamenskoye	76	N6
Znin	50	G5
Znojmo	62	M2
Zoigê	80	C4
Zolotinka	78	M5
Zomba	108	F3
Zongo	106	B3
Zonguldak	68	P3
Zouar	100	C3
Zouérat	102	C4
Žovka	50	N7
Zrenjanin	66	H4
Zschopau	52	J6
Zug	62	D3
Zugdidi	92	J2
Zuger See	62	D3
Zugspitze	52	F9
Zuid-Beveland	54	F3
Zuni	132	E1
Zunyi	80	D5
Županja	66	F4
Zürich	62	D3
Zuru	104	F2
Žut	64	K5
Zutphen	54	J2
Zuwārah	100	B1
Zuyevka	70	J6
Zvishavane	108	E4
Zvolen	50	J9
Zvornik	66	G5
Zwedru	104	C3
Zweibrücken	54	K5
Zwettl	62	L2
Zwickau	52	H6
Zwiesel	52	J7
Zwoleń	50	L6
Zwolle	54	J2
Zyryanka	78	S3
Zyryanovsk	76	Q8
Żywiec	50	J8